T0292820

Programming: Principles and Practice Using C++ Third Edition

Bjarne Stroustrup

Addison-Wesley

Hoboken, New Jersey

Cover photo by Photowood Inc./Corbis.
Author photo courtesy of Bjarne Stroustrup.
Page 294: "Promenade a Skagen" by Peder Severin Kroyer.
Page 308: Photo of NASA's Ingenuity Mars Helicopter, The National Aeronautics and Space Administration (NASA).
Page 354: Photo of Hurricane Rita as seen from space, The National Oceanic and Atmospheric Administration (NOAA).

For information about buying this title in bulk quantities, or for special sales opportunities (which may include electronic versions; custom cover designs; and content particular to your business, training goals, marketing focus, or branding interests), please contact our corporate sales department at corpsales@pearsoned.com or (800) 382-3419.

For government sales inquiries, please contact governmentsales@pearsoned.com.

For questions about sales outside the U.S., please contact intlcs@pearson.com.

Visit us on the Web: informit.com/aw

Library of Congress Control Number: 2024932369

This book was typeset in Times and Helvetica by the author.

ISBN-13: 978-0-13-830868-1
ISBN-10: 0-13-83086-3
First printing, May 2024

1 2024

Contents

Preface ix

0 Notes to the Reader 1

0.1 The structure of this book 2
0.2 A philosophy of teaching and learning 5
0.3 ISO standard C++ 8
0.4 PPP support 11
0.5 Author biography 13
0.6 Bibliography 13

Part I: The Basics

1 Hello, World! 17

1.1 Programs 18
1.2 The classic first program 18
1.3 Compilation 21
1.4 Linking 23
1.5 Programming environments 24

2 Objects, Types, and Values 29

2.1 Input 30
2.2 Variables 32
2.3 Input and type 33
2.4 Operations and operators 34
2.5 Assignment and initialization 36
2.6 Names 40
2.7 Types and objects 42
2.8 Type safety 43
2.9 Conversions 44
2.10 Type deduction: **auto** 46

3 Computation 51

3.1 Computation 52
3.2 Objectives and tools 53
3.3 Expressions 55
3.4 Statements 58
3.5 Functions 68
3.6 **vector** 71
3.7 Language features 77

4 Errors! 83

4.1 Introduction 84
4.2 Sources of errors 85
4.3 Compile-time errors 86
4.4 Link-time errors 88
4.5 Run-time errors 89
4.6 Exceptions 94
4.7 Avoiding and finding errors 99

5 Writing a Program 115

5.1 A problem 116
5.2 Thinking about the problem 116
5.3 Back to the calculator! 119
5.4 Back to the drawing board 126
5.5 Turning a grammar into code 130
5.6 Trying the first version 136
5.7 Trying the second version 140
5.8 Token streams 142
5.9 Program structure 146

6 Completing a Program 151

6.1 Introduction 152
6.2 Input and output 152
6.3 Error handling 154
6.4 Negative numbers 156
6.5 Remainder: % 157
6.6 Cleaning up the code 158
6.7 Recovering from errors 164
6.8 Variables 167

7 Technicalities: Functions, etc. 179

7.1 Technicalities 180
7.2 Declarations and definitions 181
7.3 Scope 186
7.4 Function call and return 190
7.5 Order of evaluation 206
7.6 Namespaces 209
7.7 Modules and headers 211

8 Technicalities: Classes, etc. 221

8.1 User-defined types 222
8.2 Classes and members 223
8.3 Interface and implementation 223
8.4 Evolving a class: Date 225
8.5 Enumerations 233
8.6 Operator overloading 236
8.7 Class interfaces 237

Part II: Input and Output

9 Input and Output Streams 251

9.1 Input and output 252
9.2 The I/O stream model 253
9.3 Files 254
9.4 I/O error handling 258
9.5 Reading a single value 261
9.6 User-defined output operators 266
9.7 User-defined input operators 266
9.8 A standard input loop 267

9.9 Reading a structured file ... 269
9.10 Formatting ... 276
9.11 String streams ... 283

10 A Display Model **289**

10.1 Why graphics? ... 290
10.2 A display model ... 290
10.3 A first example ... 292
10.4 Using a GUI library ... 295
10.5 Coordinates ... 296
10.6 Shapes ... 297
10.7 Using Shape primitives ... 297
10.8 Getting the first example to run ... 309

11 Graphics Classes **315**

11.1 Overview of graphics classes ... 316
11.2 Point and Line ... 317
11.3 Lines ... 320
11.4 Color ... 323
11.5 Line_style ... 325
11.6 Polylines ... 328
11.7 Closed shapes ... 333
11.8 Text ... 346
11.9 Mark ... 348
11.10 Image ... 350

12 Class Design **355**

12.1 Design principles ... 356
12.2 Shape ... 360
12.3 Base and derived classes ... 367
12.4 Other Shape functions ... 375
12.5 Benefits of object-oriented programming ... 376

13 Graphing Functions and Data **381**

13.1 Introduction ... 382
13.2 Graphing simple functions ... 382
13.3 Function ... 386
13.4 Axis ... 390

13.5 Approximation 392
13.6 Graphing data 397

14 Graphical User Interfaces **409**

14.1 User-interface alternatives 410
14.2 The "Next" button 411
14.3 A simple window 412
14.4 **Button** and other **Widgets** 414
14.5 An example: drawing lines 419
14.6 Simple animation 426
14.7 Debugging GUI code 427

Part III: Data and Algorithms

15 Vector and Free Store **435**

15.1 Introduction 436
15.2 **vector** basics 437
15.3 Memory, addresses, and pointers 439
15.4 Free store and pointers 442
15.5 Destructors 447
15.6 Access to elements 451
15.7 An example: lists 452
15.8 The **this** pointer 456

16 Arrays, Pointers, and References **463**

16.1 Arrays 464
16.2 Pointers and references 468
16.3 C-style strings 471
16.4 Alternatives to pointer use 472
16.5 An example: palindromes 475

17 Essential Operations **483**

17.1 Introduction 484
17.2 Access to elements 484
17.3 List initialization 486
17.4 Copying and moving 488
17.5 Essential operations 495

17.6 Other useful operations 500
17.7 Remaining Vector problems 502
17.8 Changing size 504
17.9 Our Vector so far 509

18 Templates and Exceptions **513**

18.1 Templates 514
18.2 Generalizing Vector 522
18.3 Range checking and exceptions 525
18.4 Resources and exceptions 529
18.5 Resource-management pointers 537

19 Containers and Iterators **545**

19.1 Storing and processing data 546
19.2 Sequences and iterators 552
19.3 Linked lists 555
19.4 Generalizing Vector yet again 560
19.5 An example: a simple text editor 566
19.6 vector, list, and string 572

20 Maps and Sets **577**

20.1 Associative containers 578
20.2 map 578
20.3 unordered_map 585
20.4 Timing 586
20.5 set 589
20.6 Container overview 591
20.7 Ranges and iterators 597

21 Algorithms **603**

21.1 Standard-library algorithms 604
21.2 Function objects 610
21.3 Numerical algorithms 614
21.4 Copying 619
21.5 Sorting and searching 620

Index **625**

Preface

Damn the torpedoes!
Full speed ahead.
– Admiral Farragut

Programming is the art of expressing solutions to problems so that a computer can execute those solutions. Much of the effort in programming is spent finding and refining solutions. Often, a problem is only fully understood through the process of programming a solution for it.

This book is for someone who has never programmed before but is willing to work hard to learn. It helps you understand the principles and acquire the practical skills of programming using the C++ programming language. It can also be used by someone with some programming knowledge who wants a more thorough grounding in programming principles and contemporary C++.

Why would you want to program? Our civilization runs on software. Without understanding software, you are reduced to believing in "magic" and will be locked out of many of the most interesting, profitable, and socially useful technical fields of work. When I talk about programming, I think of the whole spectrum of computer programs from personal computer applications with GUIs (graphical user interfaces), through engineering calculations and embedded systems control applications (such as digital cameras, cars, and cell phones), to text manipulation applications as found in many humanities and business applications. Like mathematics, programming – when done well – is a valuable intellectual exercise that sharpens our ability to think. However, thanks to feedback from the computer, programming is more concrete than most forms of math and therefore accessible to more people. It is a way to reach out and change the world – ideally for the better. Finally, programming can be great fun.

There are many kinds of programming. This book aims to serve those who want to write non-trivial programs for the use of others and to do so responsibly, providing a decent level of system quality. That is, I assume that you want to achieve a level of professionalism. Consequently, I chose the topics for this book to cover what is needed to get started with real-world programming, not just what is easy to teach and learn. If you need a technique to get basic work done right, I describe it, demonstrate concepts and language facilities needed to support the technique, and provide exercises for it. If you just want to understand toy programs or write programs that just call code provided by others, you can get along with far less than I present. In such cases, you will probably also be better served by a language that's simpler than C++. On the other hand, I won't waste your time with material of marginal practical importance. If an idea is explained here, it's because you'll almost certainly need it.

Programming is learned by writing programs. In this, programming is similar to other endeavors with a practical component. You cannot learn to swim, to play a musical instrument, or to drive a car just from reading a book – you must practice. Nor can you become a good programmer without reading and writing lots of code. This book focuses on code examples closely tied to explanatory text and diagrams. You need those to understand the ideals, concepts, and principles of programming and to master the language constructs used to express them. That's essential, but by itself, it will not give you the practical skills of programming. For that, you need to do the exercises and get used to the tools for writing, compiling, and running programs. You need to make your own mistakes and learn to correct them. There is no substitute for writing code. Besides, that's where the fun is!

There is more to programming – much more – than following a few rules and reading the manual. This book is not focused on "the syntax of C++." C++ is used to illustrate fundamental concepts. Understanding the fundamental ideals, principles, and techniques is the essence of a good programmer. Also, "the fundamentals" are what last: they will still be essential long after today's programming languages and tools have evolved or been replaced.

Code can be beautiful as well as useful. This book is written to help you to understand what it means for code to be beautiful, to help you to master the principles of creating such code, and to build up the practical skills to create it. Good luck with programming!

Previous Editions

The third edition of *Programming: Principles and Practice Using C++* is about half the size of the second edition. Students having to carry the book will appreciate the lighter weight. The reason for the reduced size is simply that more information about C++ and its standard library is available on the Web. The essence of the book that is generally used in a course in programming is in this third edition ("PPP3"), updated to C++20 plus a bit of C++23. The fourth part of the previous edition ("PPP2") was designed to provide extra information for students to look up when needed and is available on the Web:

- Chapter 1: Computers, People, and Programming
- Chapter 11: Customizing Input and Output
- Chapter 22: Ideas and History
- Chapter 23 Text Manipulation
- Chapter 24: Numerics
- Chapter 25: Embedded Systems Programming
- Chapter 26: Testing
- Chapter 27: The C Programming Language
- Glossary

Where I felt it useful to reference these chapters, the references look like this: PPP2.Ch22 or PPP2.§27.1.

Acknowledgments

Special thanks to the people who reviewed drafts of this book and suggested many improvements: Clovis L. Tondo, Jose Daniel Garcia Sanchez, J.C. van Winkel, and Ville Voutilainen. Also, Ville Voutilainen did the non-trivial mapping of the GUI/Graphics interface library to Qt, making it portable to an amazing range of systems.

Also, thanks to the many people who contributed to the first and second editions of this book. Many of their comments are reflected in this third edition.

0

Notes to the Reader

$e^{i\pi} + 1$
– Leonhard Euler

This chapter is a grab bag of information; it aims to give you an idea of what to expect from the rest of the book. Please skim through it and read what you find interesting. Before writing any code, read "PPP support" (§0.4). A teacher will find most parts immediately useful. If you are reading this book as a novice, please don't try to understand everything. You may want to return and reread this chapter once you feel comfortable writing and executing small programs.

§0.1 The structure of this book
General approach; Drills, exercises, etc.; What comes after this book?
§0.2 A philosophy of teaching and learning
A note to students; A note to teachers
§0.3 ISO standard C++
Portability; Guarantees; A brief history of C++
§0.4 PPP support
Web resources
§0.5 Author biography
§0.6 Bibliography

0.1 The structure of this book

This book consists of three parts:

- Part I (Chapter 1 to Chapter 8) presents the fundamental concepts and techniques of programming together with the C++ language and library facilities needed to get started writing code. This includes the type system, arithmetic operations, control structures, error handling, and the design, implementation, and use of functions and user-defined types.
- Part II (Chapter 9 to Chapter 14) first describes how to get numeric and text data from the keyboard and from files, and how to produce corresponding output to the screen and to files. Then, we show how to present numeric data, text, and geometric shapes as graphical output, and how to get input into a program from a graphical user interface (GUI). As part of that, we introduce the fundamental principles and techniques of object-oriented programming.
- Part III (Chapter 15 to Chapter 21) focuses on the C++ standard library's containers and algorithms framework (often referred to as the STL). We show how containers (such as **vector**, **list**, and **map**) are implemented and used. In doing so, we introduce low-level facilities such as pointers, arrays, and dynamic memory. We also show how to handle errors using exceptions and how to parameterize our classes and functions using templates. As part of that, we introduce the fundamental principles and techniques of generic programming. We also demonstrate the design and use of standard-library algorithms (such as **sort**, **find**, and **inner_product**).

The order of topics is determined by programming techniques, rather than programming language features.

CC To ease review and to help you if you miss a key point during a first reading where you have yet to discover which kind of information is crucial, we place three kinds of "alert markers" in the margin:

- **CC**: concepts and techniques (this paragraph is an example of that)
- **AA**: advice
- **XX**: warning

The use of **CC**, **AA**, and **XX**, rather than a single token in different colors, is to help where colors are not easy to distinguish.

0.1.1 General approach

In this book, we address you directly. That is simpler and clearer than the conventional "professional" indirect form of address, as found in most scientific papers. By "you" we mean "you, the reader," and by "we" we mean "you, the author, and teachers," working together through a problem, as we might have done had we been in the same room. I use "I" when I refer to my own work or personal opinions.

AA This book is designed to be read chapter by chapter from the beginning to the end. Often, you'll want to go back to look at something a second or a third time. In fact, that's the only sensible approach, as you'll always dash past some details that you don't yet see the point in. In such cases, you'll eventually go back again. Despite the index and the cross-references, this is not a book that you can open to any page and start reading with any expectation of success. Each section and each chapter assume understanding of what came before.

Each chapter is a reasonably self-contained unit, meant to be read in "one sitting" (logically, if not always feasible on a student's tight schedule). That's one major criterion for separating the text into chapters. Other criteria include that a chapter is a suitable unit for drills and exercises and that each chapter presents some specific concept, idea, or technique. This plurality of criteria has left a few chapters uncomfortably long, so please don't take "in one sitting" too literally. In particular, once you have thought about the review questions, done the drill, and worked on a few exercises, you'll often find that you have to go back to reread a few sections.

A common praise for a textbook is "It answered all my questions just as I thought of them!" That's an ideal for minor technical questions, and early readers have observed the phenomenon with this book. However, that cannot be the whole ideal. We raise questions that a novice would probably not think of. We aim to ask and answer questions that you need to consider when writing quality software for the use of others. Learning to ask the right (often hard) questions is an essential part of learning to think as a programmer. Asking only the easy and obvious questions would make you feel good, but it wouldn't help make you a programmer.

We try to respect your intelligence and to be considerate about your time. In our presentation, we aim for professionalism rather than cuteness, and we'd rather understate a point than hype it. We try not to exaggerate the importance of a programming technique or a language feature, but please don't underestimate a simple statement like "This is often useful." If we quietly emphasize that something is important, we mean that you'll sooner or later waste days if you don't master it.

Our use of humor is more limited than we would have preferred, but experience shows that people's ideas of what is funny differ dramatically and that a failed attempt at humor can be confusing.

CC

We do not pretend that our ideas or the tools offered are perfect. No tool, library, language, or technique is "the solution" to all of the many challenges facing a programmer. At best, a language can help you to develop and express your solution. We try hard to avoid "white lies"; that is, we refrain from oversimplified explanations that are clear and easy to understand, but not true in the context of real languages and real problems.

0.1.2 Drills, exercises, etc.

AA

Programming is not just an intellectual activity, so writing programs is necessary to master programming skills. We provide three levels of programming practice:

- *Drills*: A drill is a very simple exercise devised to develop practical, almost mechanical skills. A drill usually consists of a sequence of modifications of a single program. You should do every drill. A drill is not asking for deep understanding, cleverness, or initiative. We consider the drills part of the basic fabric of the book. If you haven't done the drills, you have not "done" the book.
- *Exercises*: Some exercises are trivial, and others are very hard, but most are intended to leave some scope for initiative and imagination. If you are serious, you'll do quite a few exercises. At least do enough to know which are difficult for you. Then do a few more of those. That's how you'll learn the most. The exercises are meant to be manageable without exceptional cleverness, rather than to be tricky puzzles. However, we hope that we have provided exercises that are hard enough to challenge anybody and enough exercises to exhaust even the best student's available time. We do not expect you to do them all, but feel free to try.

- *Try this*: Some people like to put the book aside and try some examples before reading to the end of a chapter; others prefer to read ahead to the end before trying to get code to run. To support readers with the former preference, we provide simple suggestions for practical work labeled *Try this* at natural breaks in the text. A *Try this* is generally in the nature of a drill but focused narrowly on the topic that precedes it. If you pass a *Try this* without trying it out – maybe because you are not near a computer or you find the text riveting – do return to it when you do the chapter drill; a *Try this* either complements the chapter drill or is a part of it.

In addition, at the end of each chapter we offer some help to solidify what's learned:

- *Review*: At the end of each chapter, you'll find a set of review questions. They are intended to point you to the key ideas explained in the chapter. One way to look at the review questions is as a complement to the exercises: the exercises focus on the practical aspects of programming, whereas the review questions try to help you articulate the ideas and concepts. In that, they resemble good interview questions.
- *Terms*: A section at the end of each chapter presents the basic vocabulary of programming and of C++. If you want to understand what people say about programming topics and to articulate your own ideas, you should know what each term means.
- *Postscript*: A paragraph intended to provide some perspective for the material presented.

In addition, we recommend that you take part in a small project (and more if time allows for it). A project is intended to produce a complete useful program. Ideally, a project is done by a small group of people (e.g., three people) working together (e.g., while progressing through the later chapters of the book). Most people find such projects the most fun and that they tie everything together.

CC Learning involves repetition. Our ideal is to make every important point at least twice and to reinforce it with exercises.

0.1.3 What comes after this book?

AA At the end of this book, will you be an expert at programming and at C++? Of course not! When done well, programming is a subtle, deep, and highly skilled art building on a variety of technical skills. You should no more expect to become an expert at programming in four months than you should expect to become an expert in biology, in math, in a natural language (such as Chinese, English, or Danish), or at playing the violin in four months – or in half a year, or a year. What you should hope for, and what you can expect if you approach this book seriously, is to have a really good start that allows you to write relatively simple useful programs, to be able to read more complex programs, and to have a good conceptual and practical background for further work.

The best follow-up to this initial course is to work on a project developing code to be used by someone else; preferably guided by an experienced developer. After that, or (even better) in parallel with a project, read either a professional-level general textbook, a more specialized book relating to the needs of your project, or a textbook focusing on a particular aspect of C++ (such as algorithms, graphics, scientific computation, finance, or games); see §0.6.

AA Eventually, you should learn another programming language. We don't consider it possible to be a professional in the realm of software – even if you are not primarily a programmer – without knowing more than one language. Why? No large program is written in a single language. Also, different languages typically differ in the way code is thought about and programs are constructed. Design techniques, availability of libraries, and the way programs are built differ, sometimes dramatically. Even when the syntaxes of two languages are similar, the similarity is typically only skin deep. Performance, detection of errors, and constraints on what can be expressed typically differ. This is similar to the ways natural languages and cultures differ. Knowing only a single language and a single culture implies the danger of thinking that "the way we do things" is the only way or the only good way. That way opportunities are missed, and sub-optimal programs are produced. One of the best ways to avoid such problems is to know several languages (programming languages and natural languages).

0.2 A philosophy of teaching and learning

What are we trying to help you learn? And how are we approaching the process of teaching? We try to present the minimal concepts, techniques, and tools for you to do effective practical programs, including

- Program organization
- Debugging and testing
- Class design
- Computation
- Function and algorithm design
- Graphics (two-dimensional only)
- Graphical user interfaces (GUIs)
- Files and stream input and output (I/O)
- Memory management
- Design and programming ideals
- The C++ standard library
- Software development strategies

To keep the book lighter than the small laptop on which it is written, some supplementary topics from the second edition are placed on the Web (§0.4.1):

- Computers, People, and Programming (PPP2.Ch1)
- Ideals and History (PPP2.Ch22)
- Text manipulation (incl. Regular expression matching) (PPP2.Ch23)
- Numerics (PPP2.Ch24)
- Embedded systems programming (PPP2.Ch25)
- C-language programming techniques (PPP2.Ch27)

Working our way through the chapters, we cover the programming techniques called procedural programming (as with the C programming language), data abstraction, object-oriented programming, and generic programming. The main topic of this book is *programming*, that is, the ideals, techniques, and tools of expressing ideas in code. The C++ programming language is our main tool, so we describe many of C++'s facilities in some detail. But please remember that C++ is just a tool, rather than the main topic of this book. This is "programming using C++," not "C++ with a bit of programming theory."

Each topic we address serves at least two purposes: it presents a technique, concept, or principle and also a practical language or library feature. For example, we use the interface to a two-dimensional graphics system to illustrate the use of classes and inheritance. This allows us to be economical with space (and your time) and also to emphasize that programming is more than simply slinging code together to get a result as quickly as possible. The C++ standard library is a major source of such "double duty" examples – many even do triple duty. For example, we introduce the standard-library **vector**, use it to illustrate widely useful design techniques, and show many of the programming techniques used to implement it. One of our aims is to show you how major library facilities are implemented and how they map to hardware. We insist that craftsmen must understand their tools, not just consider them "magical."

Some topics will be of greater interest to some programmers than to others. However, we encourage you not to prejudge your needs (how would you know what you'll need in the future?) and at least look at every chapter. If you read this book as part of a course, your teacher will guide your selection.

CC We characterize our approach as "depth-first." It is also "concrete-first" and "concept-based." First, we quickly (well, relatively quickly, Chapter 1 to Chapter 9) assemble a set of skills needed for writing small practical programs. In doing so, we present a lot of tools and techniques in minimal detail. We focus on simple concrete code examples because people grasp the concrete faster than the abstract. That's simply the way most humans learn. At this initial stage, you should not expect to understand every little detail. In particular, you'll find that trying something slightly different from what just worked can have "mysterious" effects. Do try, though! Please do the drills and exercises we provide. Just remember that early on you just don't have the concepts and skills to accurately estimate what's simple and what's complicated; expect surprises and learn from them.

AA We move fast in this initial phase – we want to get you to the point where you can write interesting programs as fast as possible. Someone will argue, "We must move slowly and carefully; we must walk before we can run!" But have you ever watched a baby learning to walk? Babies really do run by themselves before they learn the finer skills of slow, controlled walking. Similarly, you will dash ahead, occasionally stumbling, to get a feel of programming before slowing down to gain the necessary finer control and understanding. You must run before you can walk!

XX It is essential that you don't get stuck in an attempt to learn "everything" about some language detail or technique. For example, you could memorize all of C++'s built-in types and all the rules for their use. Of course you could, and doing so might make you feel knowledgeable. However, it would not make you a programmer. Skipping details will get you "burned" occasionally for lack of knowledge, but it is the fastest way to gain the perspective needed to write good programs. Note that our approach is essentially the one used by children learning their native language and also the most effective approach used to learn a foreign language. We encourage you to seek help from teachers, friends, colleagues, Mentors, etc. on the inevitable occasions when you are stuck. Be assured that nothing in these early chapters is fundamentally difficult. However, much will be unfamiliar and might therefore feel difficult at first.

Later, we build on your initial skills to broaden your base of knowledge. We use examples and exercises to solidify your understanding, and to provide a conceptual base for programming.

AA We place a heavy emphasis on ideals and reasons. You need ideals to guide you when you look for practical solutions – to know when a solution is good and principled. You need to understand the reasons behind those ideals to understand why they should be your ideals, why aiming for them will help you and the users of your code. Nobody should be satisfied with "because that's the way it is" as an explanation. More importantly, an understanding of ideals and reasons allows you to generalize from what you know to new situations and to combine ideas and tools in novel ways to address new problems. Knowing "why" is an essential part of acquiring programming skills. Conversely, just memorizing lots of poorly understood rules is limiting, a source of errors, and a massive waste of time. We consider your time precious and try not to waste it.

Many C++ language-technical details are banished to other sources, mostly on the Web (§0.4.1). We assume that you have the initiative to search out information when needed. Use the index and the table of contents. Don't forget the online help facilities of your compiler. Remember, though, to consider every Web resource highly suspect until you have reason to believe better of it. Many an authoritative-looking Web site is put up by a programming novice or someone with something to sell. Others are simply outdated. We provide a collection of links and information on our support Web site: www.stroustrup.com/programming.html.

Please don't be too impatient for "realistic" examples. Our ideal example is the shortest and simplest code that directly illustrates a language facility, a concept, or a technique. Most real-world examples are far messier than ours, yet do not consist of more than a combination of what we demonstrate. Successful commercial programs with hundreds of thousands of lines of code are based on techniques that we illustrate in a dozen 50-line programs. The fastest way to understand real-world code is through a good understanding of the fundamentals.

We do not use "cute examples involving cuddly animals" to illustrate our points. We assume that you aim to write real programs to be used by real people, so every example that is not presented as specifically language-technical is taken from a real-world use. Our basic tone is that of professionals addressing (future) professionals.

C++ rests on two pillars:

- *Efficient direct access to machine resources*: making C++ effective for low-level, machine-near, programming as is essential in many application domains.
- *Powerful (Zero-overhead) abstraction mechanisms*: making it possible to escape the error-prone low-level programming by providing elegant, flexible, and type-and-resource-safe, yet efficient facilities needed for higher-level programming.

This book teaches both levels. We use the implementation of higher-level abstractions as our primary examples to introduce low-level language features and programming techniques. The aim is always to write code at the highest level affordable, but that often requires a foundation built using lower-level facilities and techniques. We aim for you to master both levels.

0.2.1 A note to students

Many thousands of first-year university students taught using the first two editions of this book had never before seen a line of code in their lives. Most succeeded, so you can do it, too. **AA**

You don't have to read this book as part of a course. The book is widely used for self-study. However, whether you work your way through as part of a course or independently, try to work with others. Programming has an – unfair – reputation as a lonely activity. Most people work better and learn faster when they are part of a group with a common aim. Learning together and discussing problems with friends is not cheating! It is the most efficient – as well as most pleasant – way of making progress. If nothing else, working with friends forces you to articulate your ideas, which is just about the most efficient way of testing your understanding and making sure you remember. You don't actually have to personally discover the answer to every obscure language and programming environment problem. However, please don't cheat yourself by not doing the drills and a fair number of exercises (even if no teacher forces you to do them). Remember: programming is (among other things) a practical skill that you must practice to master.

Most students – especially thoughtful good students – face times when they wonder whether their hard work is worthwhile. When (not if) this happens to you, take a break, reread this chapter, look at the "Computers, People, and Programming" and "Ideals and History" chapters posted on the Web (§0.4.1). There, I try to articulate what I find exciting about programming and why I consider it a crucial tool for making a positive contribution to the world.

Please don't be too impatient. Learning any major new and valuable skill takes time.

The primary aim of this book is to help you to express your ideas in code, not to teach you how to get those ideas. Along the way, we give many examples of how we can address a problem, usually through analysis of a problem followed by gradual refinement of a solution. We consider programming itself a form of problem solving: only through complete understanding of a problem and its solution can you express a correct program for it, and only through constructing and testing a program can you be certain that your understanding is complete. Thus, programming is inherently part of an effort to gain understanding. However, we aim to demonstrate this through examples, rather than through "preaching" or presentation of detailed prescriptions for problem solving.

0.2.2 A note to teachers

CC No. This is not a traditional Computer Science 101 course. It is a book about how to construct working software. As such, it leaves out much of what a computer science student is traditionally exposed to (Turing completeness, state machines, discrete math, grammars, etc.). Even hardware is ignored on the assumption that students have used computers in various ways since kindergarten. This book does not even try to mention most important CS topics. It is about programming (or more generally about how to develop software), and as such it goes into more detail about fewer topics than many traditional courses. It tries to do just one thing well, and computer science is not a one-course topic. If this book/course is used as part of a computer science, computer engineering, electrical engineering (many of our first students were EE majors), information science, or whatever program, we expect it to be taught alongside other courses as part of a well-rounded introduction.

Many students like to get an idea why subjects are taught and why they are taught in the way they are. Please try to convey my teaching philosophy, general approach, etc. to your students along the way. Also, to motivate students, please present short examples of areas and applications where C++ is used extensively, such as aerospace, medicine, games, animation, cars, finance, and scientific computation.

0.3 ISO standard C++

C++ is defined by an ISO standard. The first ISO C++ standard was ratified in 1998, so that version of C++ is known as C++98. The code for this edition of the book uses contemporary C++, C++20 (plus a bit of C++23). If your compiler does not support C++20 [C++20], get a new compiler. Good, modern C++ compilers can be downloaded from a variety of suppliers; see www.stroustrup.com/compilers.html. Learning to program using an earlier and less supportive version of the language can be unnecessarily hard.

On the other hand, you may be in an environment where you are able to use only C++14 or C++17. Most of the contents of this book will still apply, but you'll have trouble with features introduced in C++20:

- modules (§7.7.1). Instead of modules use header files (§7.7.2). In particular, use #include "PPPheaders.h" to compile our examples and your exercises, rather than #include "PPP.h" (§0.4).
- ranges (§20.7). Use explicit iterators, rather than ranges. For example, sort(v.begin(),v.end()) rather than ranges::sort(v). If/when that gets tedious, write your own ranges versions of your favorite algorithms (§21.1).
- span (§16.4.1). Fall back on the old "pointer and size" technique. For example, void f(int* p, int n); rather than void f(span<int> s); and do your own range checking as needed.
- concepts (§18.1.3). Use plain template<typename T> and hope for the best. The error messages from that for simple mistakes can be horrendous.

0.3.1 Portability

It is common to write C++ to run on a variety of machines. Major C++ applications run on machines we haven't ever heard of! We consider the use of C++ on a variety of machine architectures and operating systems most important. Essentially every example in this book is not only ISO Standard C++, but also portable. By *portable*, we mean that we make no assumptions about the computer, the operating system, and the compiler beyond that an up-to-date standard-conforming C++ implementation is available. Unless specifically stated, the code we present should work on every C++ implementation and has been tested on several machines and operating systems. CC

The details of how to compile, link, and run a C++ program differ from system to system. Also, most systems offer you a choice of compilers and tools. Explaining the many and often mutating tool sets is beyond the scope of the book. We might add some such information to the PPP support Web site (§0.4).

If you have trouble with one of the popular, but rather elaborate, IDEs (integrated development environments), we suggest you try working from the command line; it's surprisingly simple. For example, here is the full set of commands needed to compile, link, and execute a simple program consisting of two source files, my_file1.cpp and my_file2.cpp, using the GNU C++ compiler on a Linux system:

```
c++ -o my_program my_file1.cpp my_file2.cpp
./my_program
```

Yes, that really is all it takes.

Another way to get started is to use a build system, such as Cmake (§0.4). However, that path is best taken when there are someone experienced who can guide those first steps.

0.3.2 Guarantees

Except when illustrating errors, the code in this book is type-safe (an object is used only according to its definition). We follow the rules of *The C++ Core Guidelines* to simplify programming and eliminate common errors. You can find the Core Guidelines on the Web [CG] and rule checkers are available when you need guaranteed conformance.

We don't recommend that you delve into this while still a novice, but consider it reassuring that the recommended styles and techniques illustrated in this book have industrial backing. Once you are comfortable with C++ and understand the potential errors (say after Chapter 16), we suggest you read the introduction to the CG and try one of the CG checkers to see how they can eliminate errors before they make it into running code.

0.3.3 A brief history of C++

I started the design and implementation of C++ in late 1979 and supported my first user about six months later. The initial features included classes with constructors and destructors (§8.4.2, §15.5), and function-argument declarations (§3.5.2). Initially, the language was called *C with Classes*, but to avoid confusion with C, it was renamed *C++* in 1984.

The basic idea of C++ was to combine C's ability to utilize hardware efficiently (e.g., device drivers, memory managers, and process schedulers) [K&R] with Simula's facilities for organizing code (notably classes and derived classes) [Simula]. I needed that for a project where I wanted to build a distributed Unix. Had I succeeded, it might have become the first Unix cluster, but the development of C++ "distracted" me from that.

In 1985, the first implementation of a C++ compiler and foundation library was shipped commercially. I wrote most of that and most of its documentation. The first book on C++, *The C++ Programming Language* [TC++PL], was published simultaneously. Then, the language supported what was called data abstraction and object-oriented programming (§12.3, §12.5). In addition, it had feeble support for generic programming (§21.1.2).

In the late 1980s, I worked on the design of exceptions (§4.6) and templates (Chapter 18). The templates were aimed to support *generic programming* along the lines of the work of Alex Stepanov [AS,2009].

In 1989, several large corporations decided that we needed an ISO standard for C++. Together with Margaret Ellis, I wrote the book that became the base document for C++'s standardization "The ARM" [ARM]. The first ISO standard was approved by 20 nations in 1998 and is known as C++98. For a decade, C++98 supported a massive growth in C++ use and gave much valuable feedback to its further evolution. In addition to the language, the standard specifies an extensive standard library. In C++98 the most significant standard-library component was the STL providing iterators (§19.3.2), containers (such as `vector` (§3.6) and `map` (§20.2)), and algorithms (§21).

C++11 was a significant upgrade that added improved facilities for compile-time computation (§3.3.1), lambdas (§13.3.3, §21.2.3), and formalized support for concurrency. Concurrency had been used in C++ from the earliest days, but that interesting and important topic is beyond the scope of this book. Eventually, see [AW,2019]. The C++11 standard library added many useful components, notably random number generation (§4.7.5) and resource-management pointers (unique_ptr (§18.5.2) and shared_ptr; §18.5.3)).

C++14 and C++17 added many useful features without adding support for significantly new programming styles.

C++20 [C++20] was a major improvement of C++, about as significant as C++11 and coming close to meeting my ideals for C++ as articulated in *The Design and Evolution of C++* in 1994 [DnE]. Among many extensions, it added modules (§7.7.1), concepts (§18.1.3), coroutines (beyond the scope of this book), and ranges (§20.7).

These changes over decades have been evolutionary with a great concern for backwards compatibility. I have small programs from the 1980s that still run today. Where old code fails to compile or work correctly, the reason is usually changes to the operating systems or third-party libraries. This gives a degree of stability that is considered a major feature by organizations that maintain software that is in use for decades.

For a more thorough discussion of the design and evolution of C++, see *The Design and Evolution of C++* [DnE] and my three *History of Programming* papers [HOPL-2] [HOPL-3] [HOPL-4]. Those were not written for novices, though.

0.4 PPP support

All the code in this book is ISO standard C++. To start compiling and running the examples, add two lines at the start of the code:

```
import std;
using namespace std;
```

This makes the standard library available.

Unfortunately, the standard does not guarantee range checking for containers, such as the standard **vector**, and most implementations do not enforce it by default. Typically, enforcement must be enabled by options that differ between different compilers. We consider range checking essential to simplify learning and minimize frustration. So, we supply a module **PPP_support** that makes a version of the C++ standard library with guaranteed range checking for subscripting available (see **www.stroustrup.com/programming.html**). So instead of directly using module **std** directly, use:

```
#include "PPP.h"
```

We also supply **"PPPheaders.h"** as a similar version to **"PPP.h"** for people who don't have access to a compiler with good module support. This supplies less of the C++ standard library than **"PPP.h"** and will compile slower.

In addition to the range checking, **PPP_support** provides a convenient **error()** function and a simplified interface to the standard random number facilities that many students have found useful in the past. We strongly recommend using **PPP.h** consistently.

Some people have commented about our use of a support header for PPP1 and PPP2 that "using a non-standard header is not real C++." Well, it is because the content of those headers is 100% ISO C++ and doesn't change the meaning of correct programs. We consider it important that our PPP support does a decent job at helping you to avoid non-portable code and surprising behavior. Also, writing libraries that makes it easier to support good and efficient code is one of the main uses of C++. **PPP_support** is just one simple example of that.

AA If you cannot download the files supporting PPP, or have trouble getting them to compile, use the standard library directly, but try to figure out how to enable range checking. All major C++ implementations have an option for that, but it is not always easy to find and enable it. For all startup problems, it is best to take advice from someone experienced.

In addition, when you get to Chapter 10 and need to run Graphics and GUI code, you need to install the Qt graphics/GUI system and an interface library specifically designed for this book. See _display.system_ and **www.stroustrup.com/programming.html**.

0.4.1 Web resources

There is an overwhelming amount of material about C++, both text and videos, on the Web. Unfortunately, it is of varying quality, much is aimed at advanced users, and much is outdated. So use it with care and a healthy dose of skepticism.

AA The support site for this book is **www.stroustrup.com/programming.html**. There, you can find

- The **PPP_support** module source code (§0.4).
- The **PPP.h** and **PPPheaders.h** headers (§0.4).
- Some installation guidance for PPP support.
- Some code examples.
- Errata.
- Chapters from PPP2 (the second edition of *Programming: Principles and Practice using C++*) [PPP2] that were eliminated from the print version to save weight and because alternative sources have become available. These chapters are available at **www.stroustrup.com/programming.html** and referred to in the PPP3 text like this: PPP2.Ch22 or PPP2.§22.1.2.

Other Web resources:

- My Web site **www.stroustrup.com** contains a lot of material related to C++.
- The C++ Foundation's Web site **www.isocpp.org** has various useful and interesting information, much about the standardization but also a stream of articles and news items.
- I recommend **cppreference.com** as an on-line reference. I use it myself daily to look up obscure details of the language and the standard library. I don't recommend using it as a tutorial.
- The major C++ implementers, such as Clang, GCC, and Microsoft, offer free downloads of good versions of their products (**www.stroustrup.com/compilers.html**). All have options enforcing range checking of subscripting.
- There are several Web sites offering (free) on-line C++ compilation, e.g., the *compiler explorer* **https://godbolt.org**. These are easy to use and very useful for testing out small examples and for seeing how different compilers and different versions of compilers handle source code.
- For guidance on how to use contemporary C++, see *The C++ Core Guidelines*: The C++ Core Guidelines (**https://github.com/isocpp/CppCoreGuidelines**) [CG] and its small support library (**https://github.com/microsoft/GSL**). Except when illustrating mistakes, the CG is used in this book.
- For Chapter 10 to Chapter 14, we use Qt as the basis of our graphics and GUI code: **www.qt.io**.

0.5 Author biography

You might reasonably ask: "Who are you to think you can help me to learn how to program?" Here is a canned bio:

> Bjarne Stroustrup is the designer and original implementer of C++ as well as the author of *The C++ Programming Language (4th edition)*, *A Tour of C++ (3rd edition)*, *Programming: Principles and Practice Using C++ (3rd edition)*, and many popular and academic publications. He is a professor of Computer Science at Columbia University in New York City. Dr. Stroustrup is a member of the US National Academy of Engineering, and an IEEE, ACM, and CHM fellow. He received the 2018 Charles Stark Draper Prize, the IEEE Computer Society's 2018 Computer Pioneer Award, and the 2017 IET Faraday Medal. Before joining Columbia University, he was a University Distinguished Professor at Texas A&M University and a Technical Fellow and Managing Director at Morgan Stanley. He did much of his most important work in Bell Labs. His research interests include distributed systems, design, programming techniques, software development tools, and programming languages. To make C++ a stable and up-to-date base for real-world software development, he has been a leading figure with the ISO C++ standards effort for more than 30 years. He holds a master's in mathematics from Aarhus University, where he is an honorary professor in the Computer Science Department, and a PhD in Computer Science from Cambridge University, where he is an honorary fellow of Churchill College. He is an honorary doctor at Universidad Carlos III de Madrid. **www.stroustrup.com**.

In other words, I have serious industrial and academic experience.

I used earlier versions of this book to teach thousands of first-year university students, many of whom had never written a line of code in their lives. Beyond that, I have taught people of all levels from undergraduates to seasoned developers and scientists. I currently teach final-year undergraduates and grad students at Columbia University.

I do have a life outside work. I'm married with two children and five grandchildren. I read a lot, including history, science fiction, crime, and current affairs. I like most kinds of music, including classical, classical rock, blues, and country. Good food with friends is essential and I enjoy visiting interesting places all over the world. To be able to enjoy the good food, I run.

For more biographical information, see **www.stroustrup.com/bio.html**.

0.6 Bibliography

Along with listing the publications mentioned in this chapter, this section also includes publications you might find helpful.

[ARM] M. Ellis and B. Stroustrup: *The Annotated C++ Reference Manual* Addison Wesley. 1990. ISBN 0-201-51459-1.

[AS,2009] Alexander Stepanov and Paul McJones: *Elements of Programming*. Addison-Wesley. 2009. ISBN 978-0-321-63537-2.

[AW,2019] Anthony Williams: *C++ Concurrency in Action: Practical Multithreading (Second edition)*. Manning Publishing. 2019. ISBN 978-1617294693.

[BS,2022] B. Stroustrup: *A Tour of C++ (3rd edition)*. Addison-Wesley, 2022. ISBN 978-0136816485.

[CG] B. Stroustrup and H. Sutter: *C++ Core Guidelines*. https://github.com/isocpp/CppCoreGuidelines/blob/master/CppCoreGuidelines.md.

[C++20] Richard Smith (editor): *The C++ Standard*. ISO/IEC 14882:2020.

[DnE] B. Stroustrup: *The Design and Evolution of C++*. Addison-Wesley, 1994. ISBN 0201543303.

[HOPL-2] B. Stroustrup: *A History of C++: 1979–1991*. Proc. ACM History of Programming Languages Conference (HOPL-2). ACM Sigplan Notices. Vol 28, No 3. 1993.

[HOPL-3] B. Stroustrup: *Evolving a language in and for the real world: C++ 1991-2006*. ACM HOPL-III. June 2007.

[HOPL-4] B. Stroustrup: *Thriving in a crowded and changing world: C++ 2006-2020*. ACM/SIGPLAN History of Programming Languages conference, HOPL-IV. June 2021.

[K&R] Brian W. Kernighan and Dennis M. Ritchie: *The C Programming Language*. Prentice-Hall. 1978. ISBN 978-0131101630.

[Simula] Graham Birtwistle, Ole-Johan Dahl, Bjørn Myhrhaug, and Kristen Nygaard: *SIMULA BEGIN*. Studentlitteratur. 1979. ISBN 91-44-06212-5.

[TC++PL] B. Stroustrup: *The C++ Programming Language (Fourth Edition)*. Addison-Wesley, 2013. ISBN 0321563840.

Postscript

Each chapter provides a short "postscript" that attempts to give some perspective on the information presented in the chapter. We do that with the realization that the information can be – and often is – daunting and will only be fully comprehended after doing exercises, reading further chapters (which apply the ideas of the chapter), and a later review. *Don't panic!* Relax; this is natural and expected. You won't become an expert in a day, but you can become a reasonably competent programmer as you work your way through the book. On the way, you'll encounter much information, many examples, and many techniques that many thousands of programmers have found stimulating and fun.

Part I
The Basics

Part I presents the fundamental concepts and techniques of programming together with the C++ language and library facilities needed to get started writing code. This includes the type system, arithmetic operations, control structures, error handling, and the design, implementation, and use of functions and user-defined types.

Chapter 1: Hello, World!
Chapter 2: Objects, Types, and Values
Chapter 3: Computation
Chapter 4: Errors!
Chapter 5: Writing a Program
Chapter 6: Completing a Program
Chapter 7: Technicalities: Functions, etc.
Chapter 8: Technicalities: Classes, etc.

1

Hello, World!

Programming is learned
by writing programs.
– Brian Kernighan

Here, we present the simplest C++ program that actually does anything. The purpose of writing this program is to

- Let you try your programming environment
- Give you a first feel of how you can get a computer to do things for you

Thus, we present the notion of a program, the idea of translating a program from human-readable form to machine instructions using a compiler, and finally executing those machine instructions.

§1.1 Programs
§1.2 The classic first program
§1.3 Compilation
§1.4 Linking
§1.5 Programming environments

1.1 Programs

To get a computer to do something, you (or someone else) have to tell it exactly – in excruciating detail – what to do. Such a description of "what to do" is called a *program*, and *programming* is the activity of writing and testing such programs.

In a sense, we have all programmed before. After all, we have given descriptions of tasks to be done, such as "how to drive to the nearest cinema," "how to find the upstairs bathroom," and "how to heat a meal in the microwave." The difference between such descriptions and programs is one of degree of precision: humans tend to compensate for poor instructions by using common sense, but computers don't. For example, "turn right in the corridor, up the stairs, it'll be on your left" is probably a fine description of how to get to the upstairs bathroom. However, when you look at those simple instructions, you'll find the grammar sloppy and the instructions incomplete. A human easily compensates. For example, assume that you are sitting at the table and ask for directions to the bathroom. You don't need to be told to get up from your chair to get to the corridor, somehow walk around (and not across or under) the table, not to step on the cat, etc. You'll not have to be told not to bring your knife and fork or to remember to switch on the light so that you can see the stairs. Opening the door to the bathroom before entering is probably also something you don't have to be told.

In contrast, computers are *really* dumb. They have to have everything described precisely and in detail. Consider again "turn right in the corridor, up the stairs, it'll be on your left." Where is the corridor? What's a corridor? What is "turn right"? What stairs? How do I go up stairs? (One step at a time? Two steps? Slide up the banister?) What is on my left? When will it be on my left? To be able to describe "things" precisely for a computer, we need a precisely defined language with a specific grammar (English is far too loosely structured for that) and a well-defined vocabulary for the kinds of actions we want performed. Such a language is called a *programming language*, and C++ is a programming language designed for a wide selection of programming tasks. When a computer can perform a complex task given simple instructions, it is because someone has taught it to do so by providing a program.

If you want greater philosophical detail about computers, programs, and programming, see PPP2.Ch1 and PPP2.Ch22. Here, we start with a very simple program and the tools and techniques you need to get it to run.

1.2 The classic first program

Here is a version of the classic first program. It writes "Hello, World!" on your screen:

```
// This program outputs the message "Hello, World!" to the monitor

import std;          // gain access to the C++ standard library

int main()           // C++ programs start by executing the function main
{
        std::cout << "Hello, World!\n";          // output "Hello, World!"
        return 0;
}
```

Think of this text as a set of instructions that we give to the computer to execute, much as we would give a recipe to a cook to follow, or as a list of assembly instructions for us to follow to get a new toy working. Let's discuss what each line of this program does, starting with the line

```
std::cout << "Hello, World!\n";            // output "Hello, World!"
```

That's the line that actually produces the output. It prints the characters **Hello, World!** followed by a newline; that is, after writing **Hello, World!**, the cursor will be placed at the start of the next line. A *cursor* is a little blinking character or line showing where you can type the next character. **CC**

In C++, string literals are delimited by double quotes ("); that is, **"Hello, World!\n"** is a string of characters. The **\n** is a *special character* indicating a newline. The name **cout** refers to a standard output stream. Characters "put into **cout**" using the output operator << will appear on the screen. The name **cout** is pronounced "see-out" and is an abbreviation of "**c**haracter **out**put stream." You'll find abbreviations rather common in programming. Naturally, an abbreviation can be a bit of a nuisance the first time you see it and have to remember it, but once you start using abbreviations repeatedly, they become second nature, and they are essential for keeping program text short and manageable.

The **std::** in **std::cout** says that the **cout** is to be found in the standard library that we made accessible with **import std;**

The end of that line

```
// output "Hello, World!"
```

is a comment. Anything written after the token // (that's the character /, called "slash," twice) on a line is a comment. Comments are ignored by the compiler and written for the benefit of programmers who read the code. Here, we used the comment to tell you what the beginning of that line actually did.

Comments are written to describe what the program is intended to do and in general to provide information useful for humans that can't be directly expressed in code. The person most likely to benefit from the comments in your code is you – when you come back to that code next week, or next year, and have forgotten exactly why you wrote the code the way you did. So, document your programs well. In §4.7.2.1 and §6.6.4, we'll discuss what makes good comments.

A program is written for two audiences. Naturally, we write code for computers to execute. However, we spend long hours reading and modifying the code. Thus, programmers are another audience for programs. So, writing code is also a form of human-to-human communication. In fact, it makes sense to consider the human readers of our code our primary audience: if they (we) don't find the code reasonably easy to understand, the code is unlikely to ever become correct. So, please don't forget: code is for reading – do all you can to make it readable. **CC**

The first line of the program is a typical comment; it simply tells the human reader what the program is supposed to do:

```
// This program outputs the message "Hello, World!" to the monitor
```

Such comments are useful because the code itself says what the program does, not what we meant it to do. Also, we can usually explain (roughly) what a program should do to a human much more concisely than we can express it (in detail) in code to a computer. Often such a comment is the first part of the program we write. If nothing else, it reminds us what we are trying to do.

The next line

```
import std;
```

is a module import statement. It instructs the computer to make available ("to import") facilities from a module called `std`. This is a standard module making all facilities from the C++ standard library available. We will explain its contents as we go along. For this program, the importance of `std` is that we make the standard C++ stream I/O facilities available. Here, we just use the standard output stream, `cout`, and its output operator, `<<`.

How does a computer know where to start executing a program? It looks for a function called `main` and starts executing the instructions it finds there. Here is the function `main` of our "Hello, World!" program:

```
int main()      // C++ programs start by executing the function main
{
        std::cout << "Hello, World!\n";            // output "Hello, World!"
        return 0;
}
```

CC Every C++ program must have a function called `main` to tell it where to start executing. A function is basically a named sequence of instructions for the computer to execute in the order in which they are written. A function has four parts:

- A *return type*, here `int` (meaning "integer"), which specifies what kind of result, if any, the function will return to whoever asked for it to be executed. The word `int` is a reserved word in C++ (a *keyword*), so `int` cannot be used as the name of anything else.
- A *name*, here `main`.
- A *parameter list* enclosed in parentheses (see §7.2 and §7.4), here `()`; in this case, the parameter list is empty.
- A *function body* enclosed in a set of "curly braces," `{ }`, which lists the actions (called *statements*) that the function is to perform.

It follows that the minimal C++ program is simply

```
int main() { }
```

That's not of much use, though, because it doesn't do anything. The `main()` ("the main function") of our "Hello, World!" program has two statements in its body:

```
std::cout << "Hello, World!\n";                 // output "Hello, World!"
return 0;
```

First it'll write `Hello, World!` to the screen, and then it will return a value `0` (zero) to whoever called it. Since `main()` is called by "the system," we won't use that return value. However, on some systems (notably Unix/Linux) it can be used to check whether the program succeeded. A zero (`0`) returned by `main()` indicates that the program terminated successfully.

A part of a C++ program that specifies an action is called a *statement*.

1.3 Compilation

C++ is a compiled language. That means that to get a program to run, you must first translate it from the human-readable form to something a machine can "understand." That translation is done by a program called a *compiler*. What you read and write is called *source code* or *program text*, and what the computer executes is called *object code* or *machine code*. Typically, C++ source code files are given the suffix **.cpp** (e.g., **hello_world.cpp**) and object code files are given the suffix **.obj** (on Windows) or **.o** (Linux). The plain word *code* is therefore ambiguous and can cause confusion; use it with care only when it is obvious what's meant by it. Unless otherwise specified, we use *code* to mean "source code" or even "the source code except the comments," because comments really are there just for us humans and are not seen by the compiler generating object code. **CC**

The compiler reads your source code and tries to make sense of what you wrote. It looks to see if your program is grammatically correct, if every word has a defined meaning, and if there is anything obviously wrong that can be detected without trying to actually execute the program. You'll find that compilers are rather picky about syntax. Leaving out any detail of our program, such as **importing** a **module** file, a semicolon, or a curly brace, will cause errors. Similarly, the compiler has absolutely zero tolerance for spelling mistakes. Let us illustrate this with a series of examples, each of which has a single small error. Each error is an example of a kind of mistake we often make:

```
int main()
{
        std::cout << "Hello, World!\n";
        return 0;
}
```

We didn't provide the compiler with anything to explain what **std::cout** was, so the compiler complains. To correct that, let's add the **import**:

```
import std;
int main()
{
        cout << "Hello, World!\n";
        return 0;
}
```

The compiler again complains: We made the standard library available but forgot to tell the compiler to look in **std** for **cout**. The compiler also objects to this:

```
import std;
int main()
{
        std::cout << "Hello, World!\n;
        return 0;
}
```

We didn't terminate the string with a ". The compiler also objects to this:

```
import std;
integer main()
{
	std::cout << "Hello, World!\n";
	return 0;
}
```

The abbreviation int is used in C++ rather than the word integer. The compiler doesn't like this:

```
import std;
int main()
{
	std::cout < "Hello, World!\n";
	return 0;
}
```

We used < (the less-than operator) rather than << (the output operator). Another error:

```
import std;
int main()
{
	std::cout << 'Hello, World!\n';
	return 0;
}
```

We used single quotes rather than double quotes to delimit the string. Finally, the compiler gives an error for this:

```
import std;
int main()
{
	std::cout << "Hello, World!\n"
	return 0;
}
```

We forgot to terminate the output statement with a semicolon. Note that many C++ statements are terminated by a semicolon (;). The compiler needs those semicolons to know where one statement ends and the next begins. There is no really short, fully correct, and nontechnical way of summarizing where semicolons are needed. For now, just copy our pattern of use, which can be summarized as: "Put a semicolon after every expression that doesn't end with a right curly brace (})."

Finally, let's try something that surprisingly works:

```
import std;
int main()
{
	std::cout << "Hello, World!\n";
}
```

For historical reasons, we can leave out the return statement in main (and only in main) and it is as if we had written return 0; and the end of main's body to indicate successful completion.

Why do we spend two pages of good space and minutes of your precious time showing you examples of trivial errors in a trivial program? To make the point that you – like all programmers – will spend a lot of time looking for errors in program source text. Most of the time, we look at text with errors in it. After all, if we were convinced that some code was correct, we'd be looking at some other code or taking the time off. It came as a major surprise to the brilliant early computer pioneers that they were making mistakes and had to devote a major portion of their time to finding them. It is still a surprise to most newcomers to programming.

AA

When you program, you'll get quite annoyed with the compiler at times. Sometimes it appears to complain about unimportant details (such as a missing semicolon) or about things you consider "obviously right." However, the compiler is usually right: when it gives an error message and refuses to produce object code from your source code, there is something not quite right with your program; that is, the meaning of what you wrote isn't precisely defined by the C++ standard.

XX

The compiler has no common sense (it isn't human) and is very picky about details. Since it has no common sense, you wouldn't like it to try to guess what you meant by something that "looked OK" but didn't conform to the definition of C++. If it did and its guess was different from yours, you could end up spending a lot of time trying to figure out why the program didn't do what you thought you had told it to do. When all is said and done, the compiler saves us from a lot of self-inflicted problems. It saves us from many more problems than it causes. So, please remember: the compiler is your friend; possibly, the compiler is the best friend you have when you program.

AA

1.4 Linking

CC

A program usually consists of several separate parts, often developed by different people. For example, the "Hello, World!" program consists of the part we wrote plus parts of the C++ standard library. These separate parts (sometimes called *modules* or *translation units*) must be compiled and the resulting object code files must be linked together to form an executable program. The program that links such parts together is (unsurprisingly) called a *linker*:

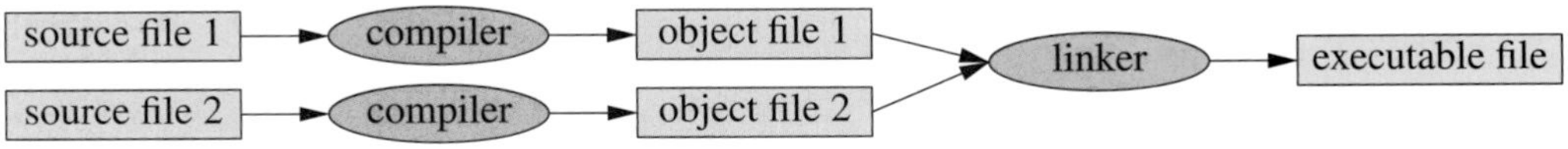

The output from a linker is called an *executable file* and on Windows its name is often given the suffix **.exe**. Please note that object code and executables are *not* portable among systems. For example, when you compile for a Windows machine, you get object code for Windows that will not run on a Linux machine.

A *library* is simply some code – usually written by others – that we access using declarations found in an **imported module**. For example:

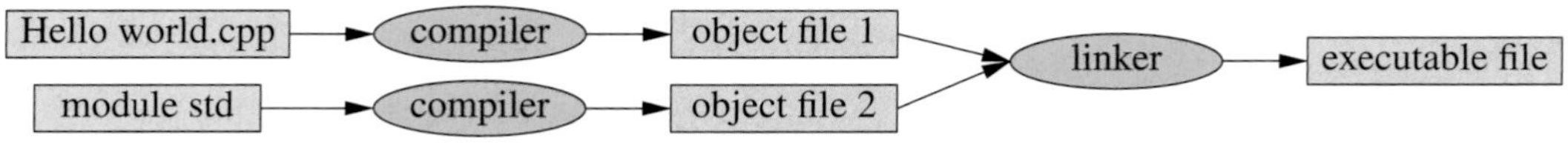

A *declaration* is a program statement specifying how a piece of code can be used; we'll examine declarations in detail later (§3.5.2, §7.2).

Errors found by the compiler are called *compile-time errors*, errors found by the linker are called *link-time errors*, and errors not found until the program is run are called *run-time errors* or *logic errors*. Generally, compile-time errors are easier to understand and fix than link-time errors, and link-time errors are often easier to find and fix than run-time errors. In §4, we discuss errors and the ways of handling them in greater detail.

1.5 Programming environments

To program, we use a programming language. We also use a compiler to translate our source code into object code and a linker to link our object code into an executable program. In addition, we use some program to enter our source code text into the computer and to edit it. These are just the first and most crucial tools that constitute our programmer's tool chest or "program development environment."

If you work from a command-line window, as many professional programmers do, you will have to issue the compile and link commands yourself (§0.3.1). If instead you use an IDE ("interactive development environment" or "integrated development environment"), as many professional programmers also do, a simple click on the correct button will do the job.

IDEs usually include an editor with helpful features like color coding to help distinguish between comments, keywords, and other parts of your program source code, plus other facilities to help you debug your code, compile it, and run it. *Debugging* is the activity of finding errors in a program and removing them; you'll hear a lot about that along the way. An error in a program is often called a *bug*, hence the term "debugging." The reason for calling an error "a bug" is that in a very early system a program failed because an insect had found its way into the computer PPP2.§22.2.2.2.

Working with this book, you can use any system that provides an up-to-date, standards-conforming implementation of C++. Most of what we say will be true for all implementations of C++, and the code will run everywhere. In our work, we use several different implementations.

Drill

So far, we have talked about programming, code, and tools (such as compilers). Now you have to get a program to run. This is a crucial point in this book and an important step in learning to program. This is where you start to develop practical skills and good programming habits. The exercises for this chapter are focused on getting you acquainted with your software development environment. Once you get the "Hello, World!" program to run, you will have passed the first major milestone as a programmer.

The purpose of a drill is to establish or reinforce your practical programming skills and give you experience with programming environment tools. Typically, a drill is a sequence of modifications to a single program, "growing" it from something completely trivial to something that might be a useful part of a real program. A traditional set of exercises is designed to test your initiative, cleverness, or inventiveness. In contrast, a drill requires little invention from you. Typically, sequencing is crucial, and each individual step should be easy (or even trivial). Please don't try to be clever and skip steps; on average that will slow you down or even confuse you. AA

You might think you understand everything you read and everything your Mentor or instructor told you, but repetition and practice are necessary to develop programming skills. In this regard, programming is like athletics, music, dance, or any skill-based craft. Imagine people trying to compete in any of those fields without regular practice. You know how well they would perform. Constant practice – for professionals that means lifelong constant practice – is the only way to develop and maintain a high-level practical skill.

So, never skip the drills, no matter how tempted you are; they are essential to the learning process. Just start with the first step and proceed, testing each step as you go to make sure you are doing it right. XX

Don't be alarmed if you don't understand every detail of the syntax you are using, and don't be afraid to ask for help from instructors or friends. Keep going, do all of the drills and many of the exercises, and all will become clear in due time. AA

So, here is your first drill:

[1] Figure out how to compile and run a program on your machine. This may be a good time to get a bit of help from someone who has done that before.

[2] If you use an IDE, set up an empty console C++ project called **hello_world**. Otherwise, if you plan to use the command line, get a command window, figure out how to use an editor to type in your code, and see §0.3.1.

[3] Type in **hello_world.cpp**, exactly as specified below, save it in your practice directory (folder), and include it in your hello_world project.

```
import std;
int main()          // C++ programs start by executing the function main
{
        std::cout << "Hello, World!\n";        // output "Hello, World!"
}
```

What if you don't have an up-to-date C++ implementation that supports module **std**? Then, use a less elegant and less efficient technique that has worked since the early days of C: **#include** a *header file* as is explained in §7.7.2:

```
#include<iostream>
int main()          // C++ programs start by executing the function main
{
        std::cout << "Hello, World!\n";        // output "Hello, World!"
}
```

[4] Compile and run the "Hello, World!" program. An IDE will have a compile-and-run button. Even something as simple as "Hello, World!" very rarely compiles and runs in a first attempt to use a new programming language or a new programming environment.

Find the problem and fix it! This is a point where asking for help from a more experienced person is sensible, but be sure to understand what you are shown so that you can do it all by yourself before proceeding further.

[5] By now, you have probably encountered some errors and had to correct them. Now is the time to get a bit better acquainted with your compiler's error-detection and error-reporting facilities! Try the eight programs from §1.3 to see how your programming environment reacts. Think of at least five more errors you might have made typing in your program (e.g., leave the Caps Lock key on while typing a word, or type a comma instead of a semicolon) and try each to see what happens when you try to compile and run those versions.

Review

AA The basic idea of these review questions is to give you a chance to see if you have noticed and understood the key points of the chapter. You may have to refer back to the text to answer a question; that's normal and expected. You may have to reread whole sections; that too is normal and expected. However, if you have to reread the whole chapter or have problems with every review question, you should consider whether your style of learning is effective. Are you reading too fast? Did you follow some of the "Try this" suggestions? Should you study with a friend so that you can discuss problems with the explanations in the text?

[1] What is the purpose of the "Hello, World!" program?
[2] Name the four parts of a function.
[3] Name a function that must appear in every C++ program.
[4] In the "Hello, World!" program, what is the purpose of the line `return 0;`?
[5] What is the purpose of the compiler?
[6] What is the purpose of the `import` statement?
[7] What is the purpose of the `#include` directive?
[8] What does a `.cpp` suffix at the end of a file name signify in C++?
[9] What does the linker do for your program?
[10] What is the difference between a source file and an object file?
[11] What is an executable?
[12] What is an IDE and what does it do for you?
[13] How do you get a compiled program to run?
[14] What is a comment?
[15] What is the purpose of a drill?
[16] If you understand everything in the textbook, why is it necessary to practice?

Most review questions have a clear answer in the chapter in which they appear. However, we do occasionally include questions to remind you of relevant information from other chapters and sometimes even relating to the world outside this book. We consider that fair; there is more to writing good software and thinking about the implications of doing so than fits into an individual chapter or book.

Terms

These terms present the basic vocabulary of programming and of C++. If you want to understand what people say about programming topics and to articulate your own ideas, you should know what each means.

//	executable	main()	<<
function	object code	C++	header file
output	comment	IDE	program
compiler	import	source code	compile-time
error	library	statement	cout
linker	module	#include	std
command line	bug	debugging	

You might like to gradually develop a glossary written in your own words. You can do that by repeating exercise 5 below for each chapter.

Exercises

We list drills separately from exercises; always complete the chapter drill before attempting an exercise. Doing so will save you time.

[1] Change the program to output the two lines

```
Hello, programming!
Here we go!
```

[2] Expanding on what you have learned, write a program that lists the instructions for a computer to find the upstairs bathroom, discussed in §1.1. Can you think of any more steps that a person would assume, but that a computer would not? Add them to your list. This is a good start in "thinking like a computer." Warning: For most people, "go to the bathroom" is a perfectly adequate instruction. For someone with no experience with houses or bathrooms (imagine a stone-age person, somehow transported into your dining room) the list of necessary instructions could be *very* long. Please don't use more than a page. For the benefit of the reader, you may add a short description of the layout of the house you are imagining.

[3] Write a description of how to get from the front door of your dorm room, apartment, house, whatever, to the door of your classroom (assuming you are attending some school; if you are not, pick another target). Have a friend try to follow the instructions and annotate them with improvements as he or she goes along. To keep friends, it may be a good idea to "field test" those instructions yourself before giving them to a friend.

[4] Find a good cookbook. Read the instructions for baking blueberry muffins (if you are in a country where "blueberry muffins" is a strange, exotic dish, use a more familiar dish instead). Please note that with a bit of help and instruction, most of the people in the world can bake delicious blueberry muffins. It is not considered advanced or difficult fine cooking. However, for the author, few exercises in this book are as difficult as this one. It is amazing what you can do with a bit of practice.

- Rewrite those instructions so that each individual action is in its own numbered paragraph. Be careful to list all ingredients and all kitchen utensils used at each step. Be careful about crucial details, such as the desired oven temperature, preheating the oven, the preparation of the muffin pan, the way to time the cooking, and the need to protect your hands when removing the muffins from the oven.

- Consider those instructions from the point of view of a cooking novice (if you are not one, get help from a friend who does not know how to cook). Fill in the steps that the book's author (almost certainly an experienced cook) left out for being obvious.
- Build a glossary of terms used. (What's a muffin pan? What does preheating do? What do you mean by "oven"?)
- Now bake some muffins and enjoy your results.

[5] Write a definition for each of the terms from "Terms." First try to see if you can do it without looking at the chapter (not likely), then look through the chapter to find definitions. You might find the difference between your first attempt and the book's version interesting. You might consult some suitable online glossary, such as **www.stroustrup.com/glossary.html**. By writing your own definition before looking it up, you reinforce the learning you achieved through your reading. If you have to reread a section to form a definition, that just helps you to understand. Feel free to use your own words for the definitions and make the definitions as detailed as you think reasonable. Often, an example after the main definition will be helpful. You may like to store the definitions in a file so that you can add to them from the "Terms" sections of later chapters.

Postscript

CC What's so important about the "Hello, World!" program? Its purpose is to get us acquainted with the basic tools of programming. We tend to do an extremely simple example, such as "Hello, World!" whenever we approach a new tool. That way, we separate our learning into two parts: first we learn the basics of our tools with a trivial program, and later we learn about more complicated programs without being distracted by our tools. Learning the tools and the language simultaneously is far harder than doing first one and then the other. This approach to simplifying learning a complex task by breaking it into a series of small (and more manageable) steps is not limited to programming and computers. It is common and useful in most areas of life, especially in those that involve some practical skill.

2

Objects, Types, and Values

Fortune favors the prepared mind.
– Louis Pasteur

This chapter introduces the basics of storing and using data in a program. To do so, we first concentrate on reading in data from the keyboard. After establishing the fundamental notions of objects, types, values, and variables, we introduce several operators and give many examples of use of variables of types **char**, **int**, **double**, and **string**.

§2.1 Input
§2.2 Variables
§2.3 Input and type
§2.4 Operations and operators
§2.5 Assignment and initialization
An example: detect repeated words; Composite assignment operators; An example: find repeated words
§2.6 Names
§2.7 Types and objects
§2.8 Type safety
§2.9 Conversions
§2.10 Type deduction: **auto**

2.1 Input

The "Hello, World!" program just writes to the screen. It produces output. It does not read anything; it does not get input from its user. That's rather a bore. Real programs tend to produce results based on some input we give them, rather than just doing exactly the same thing each time we execute them.

CC To read something, we need somewhere to read into; that is, we need somewhere in the computer's memory to place what we read. We call such a "place" an object. An *object* is a region of memory with a *type* that specifies what kind of information can be placed in it. A named object is called a *variable*. For example, character strings are put into **string** variables and integers are put into **int** variables. You can think of an object as a "box" into which you can put a value of the object's type:

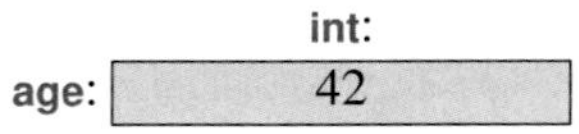

This would represent an object of type **int** named **age** containing the integer value **42**. Using a string variable, we can read a string from input and write it out again like this:

```
// read and write a first name
#include "PPP.h"

int main()
{
        cout << "Please enter your first name (followed by "enter"):\n";
        string first_name;              // first_name is a variable of type string
        cin >> first_name;              // read characters into first_name
        cout << "Hello, " << first_name << "!\n";
}
```

The **#include** and the **main()** are familiar from Chapter 1. Since the **#include** or the equivalent direct use of **import** is needed for all our programs, we'll leave it out of our presentation to avoid distraction. Similarly, we'll sometimes present code that will work only if it is placed in **main()** or some other function, like this:

```
cout << "Please enter your first name (followed by 'enter'):\n";
```

We assume that you can figure out how to put such code into a complete program for testing.

The first line of **main()** simply writes out a message encouraging the user to enter a first name. Such a message is typically called a *prompt* because it prompts the user to take an action. The next lines define a variable of type **string** called **first_name**, read input from the keyboard into that variable and write out a greeting. Let's look at those three lines in turn:

```
string first_name;    // first_name is a variable of type string
```

This sets aside an area of memory for holding a string of characters and gives it the name **first_name**:

A statement that introduces a new name into a program and sets aside memory for a variable is called a *definition*.

The next line reads characters from input (the keyboard) into that variable:

```
cin >> first_name;    // read characters into first_name
```

The name **cin** refers to the standard input stream (pronounced "see-in," for "character input") defined in the standard library. The second operand of the >> operator ("get from") specifies where that input goes. So, if we type some first name, say **Nicholas**, followed by a newline, the string **"Nicholas"** becomes the value of **first_name**:

The newline is necessary to get the machine's attention. Until a newline is entered (the Enter key is hit), the computer simply collects characters. That "delay" gives you the chance to change your mind, erase some characters and replace them with others before hitting Enter. The newline will not be part of the string stored in memory. **AA**

Having gotten the input string into **first_name**, we can use it:

```
cout << "Hello, " << first_name << "!\n";
```

This prints **Hello,** followed by **Nicholas** (the value of **first_name**) followed by **!** and a newline (**'\n'**) on the screen:

```
Hello, Nicholas!
```

If we had liked repetition and extra typing, we could have written three separate statements instead:

```
cout << "Hello, ";
cout << first_name;
cout << "!\n";
```

However, we are indifferent typists, and – more importantly – strongly dislike needless repetition (because repetition provides opportunity for errors), so we combined those three output operations into a single statement.

Note the way we use quotes around the characters in **"Hello, "** but not for **first_name**. We use quotes when we want a literal string. When we don't quote, we refer to the value of something with a name. Consider:

```
cout << "first_name" << " is " << first_name;
```

Here, **"first_name"** gives us the ten characters **first_name** and plain **first_name** gives us the value of the variable **first_name**, in this case, **Nicholas**. So, we get

```
first_name is Nicholas
```

2.2 Variables

CC Basically, we can do nothing of interest with a computer without storing data in memory, the way we did it with the input string in the example above. The "places" in which we store data are called *objects*. To access an object, we need a *name*. A named object is called a *variable* and has a specific *type* (such as **int** or **string**) that determines what can be put into the object (e.g., **123** can go into an **int** and **"Hello, World!\n"** can go into a **string**) and which operations can be applied (e.g., we can multiply **int**s using the * operator and compare **string**s using the **<=** operator). The data items we put into variables are called *values*. A statement that defines a variable is (unsurprisingly) called a *definition*, and a definition can (and usually should) provide an initial value. Consider:

```
string name = "Annemarie";
int number_of_steps = 39;
```

The value after the {=} is called an *initializer*.

You can visualize these variables like this:

You cannot put values of the wrong type into a variable:

```
string name2 = 39;                     // error: 39 isn't a string
int number_of_steps = "Annemarie";     // error: "Annemarie" is not an int
```

The compiler remembers the type of each variable and makes sure that you use it according to its type, as specified in its definition.

C++ provides a rather large number of types. You can find complete lists on the Web (e.g., **cppreference.com**). However, you can write perfectly good programs using only five of those:

```
int number_of_steps = 39;          // int for integers
double flying_time = 3.5;          // double for floating-point numbers
char decimal_point = '.';          // char for individual characters
string name = "Annemarie";         // string for character strings
bool tap_on = true;                // bool for logical variables
```

The reason for the name **double** is historical: **double** is short for "double-precision floating point." Floating point is the computer's approximation to the mathematical concept of a real number.

Note that each of these types has its own characteristic style of literals:

```
39              // int: an integer
3.5             // double: a floating-point number
'.'             // char: an individual character enclosed in single quotes
"Annemarie"     // string: a sequence of characters delimited by double quotes
true            // bool: either true or false
```

That is, a sequence of digits (such as **1234**, **2**, or **976**) denotes an integer, a single character in single quotes (such as **'1'**, **'@'**, or **'x'**) denotes a character, a sequence of digits with a decimal point (such as **1.234**, **0.12**, or **.98**) denotes a floating-point value, and a sequence of characters enclosed in double quotes (such as **"1234"**, **"Howdy!"**, or **"Annemarie"**) denotes a string.

2.3 Input and type

The input operation >> ("get from") is sensitive to type; that is, it reads according to the type of variable you read into. For example: CC

```
int main()        // read name and age
{
	cout << "Please enter your first name and age\n";
	string first_name = "???";      // string variable ("???" indicates "don't know the name")
	int age = -1;                   // integer variable (-1 means "don't know the age")
	cin >> first_name >> age;       // read a string followed by an integer
	cout << "Hello, " << first_name << " (age " << age << ")\n";
}
```

So, if you type in **Carlos 22** the >> operator will read **Carlos** into **first_name**, **22** into **age**, and produce this output:

```
Hello, Carlos (age 22)
```

Why won't it read (all of) **Carlos 22** into **first_name**? Because, by convention, reading of **string**s is terminated by what is called *whitespace*, that is, space, newline, and tab characters. Otherwise, whitespace by default is ignored by >>. For example, you can add as many spaces as you like before a number to be read; >> will just skip past them and read the number.

Just as we can write several values in a single output statement, we can read several values in a single input statement. Note that << is sensitive to type, just as >> is, so we can output the **int** variable **age** as well as the **string** variable **first_name** and the string literals **"Hello, "**, **" (age "**, and **")\n"**.

If you type in **22 Carlos**, you'll see something that might be surprising until you think about it. The (misguided) input **22 Carlos** will output

```
Hello, 22 (age -1)
```

The **22** will be read into **first_name** because, after all, **22** is a sequence of characters, and they are terminated by whitespace. On the other hand, **Carlos** isn't an integer, so it will not be read. The output will be **22** and **age**'s initial value **-1**. Why? You didn't succeed in reading a value into it, so it kept its initial value.

A **string** read using >> is (by default) terminated by whitespace; that is, it reads a single word. But sometimes, we want to read more than one word. There are of course many ways of doing this. For example, we can read a name consisting of two words like this: AA

```
int main()
{
	cout << "Please enter your first and second names\n";
	string first;
	string second;
	cin >> first >> second;                 // read two strings
	cout << "Hello, " << first << " " << second << '\n';
}
```

We simply used >> twice, once for each name. When we want to write the names to output, we must insert a space between them.

Note the absence of initializers for the two **strings** used as targets for input (**first** and **second**). By default, a **string** is initialized to the empty string, that is "".

> TRY THIS
>
> Get the "name and age" example to run. Then, modify it to write out the age in number of months: read the input in years and multiply (using the * operator) by 12. Read the age into a **double** to allow for children who can be very proud of being five and a half years old rather than just five.

2.4 Operations and operators

In addition to specifying what values can be stored in a variable, the type of a variable determines what operations we can apply to it and what they mean. For example:

```
int age = -1;
cin >> age;                    // >> reads an integer into age

string name;
cin >> name;                   // >> reads a string into name

int a2 = age+2;                // + adds integers
string n2 = name + " Jr. ";    // + concatenates strings

int a3 = age-2;                // - subtracts integers
string n3 = name - " Jr. ";    // error: - isn't defined for strings
```

XX By "error" we mean that the compiler will reject a program trying to subtract strings. The compiler knows exactly which operations can be applied to each variable and can therefore prevent many mistakes. However, the compiler doesn't know which operations make sense to you for which values, so it will happily accept legal operations that yield results that may look absurd to you. For example:

```
age = -100;
```

It may be obvious to you that you can't have a negative age (why not?) but nobody told the compiler, so it'll produce code for that definition.

Here is a table of useful operators for some common and useful types:

operation	bool	char	int	double	string
assignment	=	=	=	=	=
addition			+	+	
concatenation					+
subtraction			-	-	
multiplication			*	*	
division			/	/	
remainder (modulo)			%		

operation	bool	char	int	double	string
increment by 1			++	++	
decrement by 1			--	--	
increment by n			+= n	+= n	
add to end					+=
decrement by n			-= n	-= n	
multiply and assign			*=	*=	
divide and assign			/=	/=	
remainder and assign			%=		
read from s into x	s >> x	s >> x	s >> x	s >> x	s >> x
write x to s	s << x	s << x	s << x	s << x	s << x
equals	==	==	==	==	==
not equal	!=	!=	!=	!=	!=
greater than	>	>	>	>	>
greater than or equal	>=	>=	>=	>=	>=
less than	<	<	<	<	<
less than or equal	<=	<=	<=	<=	<=

A blank square indicates that an operation is not directly available for a type (though there may be indirect ways of using that operation; see §2.9).

We'll explain these operations, and more, as we go along. The key points here are that there are a lot of useful operators and that their meaning tends to be the same for similar types.

Let's try an example involving floating-point numbers:

```
int main()      // simple program to exercise operators
{
        cout << "Please enter a floating-point value: ";
        double n = 0;
        cin >> n;
        cout << "n == " << n
                << "\nn+1 == " << n+1
                << "\nthree times n == " << 3*n
                << "\ntwice n == " << n+n
                << "\nn squared == " << n*n
                << "\nhalf of n == " << n/2
                << "\nsquare root of n == " << sqrt(n)
                << '\n';
}
```

Obviously, the usual arithmetic operations have their usual notation and meaning as we know them from primary school. The exception is that the notation for equal is ==, rather than just =. Plain = is used for assignment. Naturally, not everything we might want to do to a floating-point number, such as taking its square root, is available as an operator. Many operations are represented as named functions. In this case, we use sqrt() from the standard library to get the square root of n: sqrt(n). The notation is familiar from math. We'll use functions along the way and discuss them in some detail in §3.5 and §7.4.

TRY THIS

Get this little program to run. Then, modify it to read an **int** rather than a **double**. Also, "exercise" some other operations, such as the modulo operator, **%**. Note that for **ints** **/** is integer division and **%** is remainder (modulo), so that **5/2** is **2** (and not **2.5** or **3**) and **5%2** is **1**. The definitions of integer *****, **/**, and **%** guarantee that for two positive **ints** **a** and **b** we have **a/b * b + a%b == a**.

Strings have fewer operators, but they have plenty of named operations (PPP2.Ch23). However, the operators they do have can be used conventionally. For example:

```
int main()        // read first and second name
{
        cout << "Please enter your first and second names\n";
        string first;
        string second;
        cin >> first >> second;                    // read two strings

        string name = first + ' ' + second;        // concatenate strings
        cout << "Hello, " << name << '\n';
}
```

For strings, **+** means concatenation; that is, when **s1** and **s2** are strings, **s1+s2** is a string where the characters from **s1** are followed by the characters from **s2**. For example, if **s1** has the value **"Hello"** and **s2** the value **"World"**, then **s1+s2** will have the value **"HelloWorld"**. Comparison of **strings** is particularly useful:

```
int main()        // read and compare names
{
        cout << "Please enter two names\n";
        string first;
        string second;
        cin >> first >> second;    // read two strings

        if (first == second)
                cout << "that's the same name twice\n";
        if (first < second)
                cout << first << " is alphabetically before " << second <<'\n';
        if (first > second)
                cout << first << " is alphabetically after " << second <<'\n';
}
```

Here, we used an **if**-statement, which will be explained in detail in §3.4.1.1, to select actions based on conditions.

2.5 Assignment and initialization

CC In many ways, the most interesting operator is assignment, represented as **=**. It gives a variable a new value. For example:

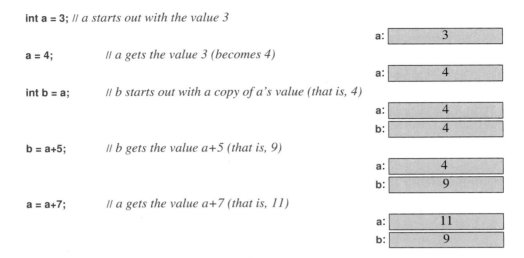

```
int a = 3; // a starts out with the value 3
                                                    a: | 3 |
a = 4;          // a gets the value 3 (becomes 4)
                                                    a: | 4 |
int b = a;      // b starts out with a copy of a's value (that is, 4)
                                                    a: | 4 |
                                                    b: | 4 |
b = a+5;        // b gets the value a+5 (that is, 9)
                                                    a: | 4 |
                                                    b: | 9 |
a = a+7;        // a gets the value a+7 (that is, 11)
                                                    a: | 11 |
                                                    b: | 9 |
```

That last assignment deserves notice. First of all it clearly shows that = does not mean equals – clearly, a doesn't equal a+7. It means assignment, that is, to place a new value in a variable. What is done for a=a+7 is the following: XX

[1] First, get the value of a; that's the integer 4.
[2] Next, add 7 to that 4, yielding the integer 11.
[3] Finally, put that 11 into a.

We can also illustrate assignments using strings:

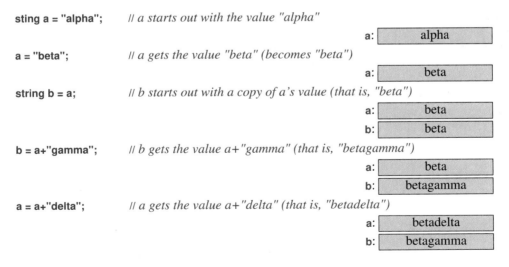

```
sting a = "alpha";      // a starts out with the value "alpha"
                                                    a: | alpha |
a = "beta";             // a gets the value "beta" (becomes "beta")
                                                    a: | beta |
string b = a;           // b starts out with a copy of a's value (that is, "beta")
                                                    a: | beta |
                                                    b: | beta |
b = a+"gamma";          // b gets the value a+"gamma" (that is, "betagamma")
                                                    a: | beta |
                                                    b: | betagamma |
a = a+"delta";          // a gets the value a+"delta" (that is, "betadelta")
                                                    a: | betadelta |
                                                    b: | betagamma |
```

We use "starts out with" and "gets" to distinguish two similar, but logically distinct, operations: CC

- *Initialization*: giving a variable its initial value.
- *Assignment*: giving a variable a new value.

Logically assignment and initialization are different. In principle, an initialization always finds the variable empty. On the other hand, an assignment (in principle) must clear out the old value from the variable before putting in the new value. You can think of the variable as a kind of small box and the value as a concrete thing, such as a coin, that you put into it. Before initialization, the box is empty, but after initialization it always holds a coin so that to put a new coin in, you (i.e., the assignment operator) first have to remove the old one ("destroy the old value"). Things are not quite this literal in the computer's memory, but it's not a bad way of thinking of what's going on.

2.5.1 An example: detect repeated words

Assignment is needed when we want to put a new value into an object. When you think of it, it is obvious that assignment is most useful when you do things many times. We need an assignment when we want to do something again with a different value. Let's have a look at a little program that detects adjacent repeated words in a sequence of words. Such code is part of most grammar checkers:

```
int main()
{
        string previous;                        // previous word; initialized to ""
        string current;                         // current word
        while (cin>>current) {                  // read a stream of words
                if (previous == current)        // check if the word is the same as last
                        cout << "repeated word: " << current << '\n';
                previous = current;
        }
}
```

This program is not the most helpful since it doesn't tell where the repeated word occurred in the text, but it'll do for now. We will look at this program line by line starting with

```
string current;        // current word
```

By default, a **string** is initialized to the empty string, so we don't have to explicitly initialize it. We read a word into **current** using

```
while (cin>>current)
```

AA This construct, called a **while**-statement, is interesting in its own right, and we'll examine it further in §3.4.2.1. The **while** says that the statement after **(cin>>current)** is to be repeated as long as the input operation **cin>>current** succeeds, and **cin>>current** will succeed as long as there are characters to read on the standard input. Remember that for a **string**, **>>** reads whitespace-separated words. You terminate this loop by giving the program an end-of-input character (usually referred to as *end of file*). On a Windows machine, that's Ctrl+Z (Control and Z pressed together) followed by an Enter (return). On a Linux machine, that's Ctrl+D (Control and D pressed together).

So, what we do is to read a word into **current** and then compare it to the previous word (stored in **previous**). If they are the same, we say so:

```
if (previous == current)          // check if the word is the same as last
        cout << "repeated word: " << current << '\n';
```

Then we have to get ready to do this again for the next word. We do that by copying the **current** word into **previous**:

```
previous = current;
```

This handles all cases provided that we can get started. What should we do for the first word where we have no previous word to compare? This problem is dealt with by the definition of **previous**:

```
string previous;          // previous word; initialized to ""
```

The empty string is not a word. Therefore, the first time through the **while**-statement, the test

```
if (previous == current)
```

fails (as we want it to).

One way of understanding program flow is to "play computer," that is, to follow the program line for line, doing what it specifies. Just draw boxes on a piece of paper and write their values into them. Change the values stored as specified by the program. **AA**

> TRY THIS
>
> Execute this program yourself using a piece of paper. Use the input **The cat cat jumped**. Even experienced programmers use this technique to visualize the actions of small sections of code that somehow don't seem completely obvious.

> TRY THIS
>
> Get the "repeated word detection program" to run. Test it with the sentence **She she laughed "he he he!" because what he did did not look very very good good**. How many repeated words were there? Why? What is the definition of *word* used here? What is the definition of *repeated word*? (For example, is **She she** a repetition?)

2.5.2 Composite assignment operators

Incrementing a variable (that is, adding 1 to it) is so common in programs that C++ provides a special syntax for it. For example:

```
++counter
```

means

```
counter = counter + 1
```

There are many other common ways of changing the value of a variable based on its current value. For example, we might like to add 7 to it, to subtract 9, or to multiply it by 2. Such operations are also supported directly by C++. For example:

```
a += 7;     // means a = a+7
b -= 9;     // means b = b-9
c *= 2;     // means c = c*2
```

In general, for any binary operator oper, a oper= b means a = a oper b. For starters, that rule gives us operators +=, −=, *=, /=, and %=. This provides a pleasantly compact notation that directly reflects our ideas. For example, in many application domains *= and /= are referred to as "scaling."

2.5.3 An example: find repeated words

Consider the example of detecting repeated adjacent words above. We could improve that by giving an idea of where the repeated word was in the sequence. A simple variation of that idea simply counts the words and outputs the count for the repeated word:

```
int main()
{
        int number_of_words = 0;
        string previous;                        // previous word; initialized to ""
        string current;
        while (cin>>current) {
                ++number_of_words;              // increase word count
                if (previous == current)
                        cout << "word number " << number_of_words << " repeated: " << current << '\n';
                previous = current;
        }
}
```

We start our word counter at 0. Each time we see a word, we increment that counter:

```
++number_of_words;
```

That way, the first word becomes number 1, the next number 2, and so on. We could have accomplished the same by saying

```
number_of_words += 1;
```

or even

```
number_of_words = number_of_words+1;
```

but ++number_of_words is shorter and expresses the idea of incrementing directly.

AA Note how similar this program is to the one from §2.5.1. Obviously, we just took the program from §2.5.1 and modified it a bit to serve our new purpose. That's a very common technique: when we need to solve a problem, we look for a similar problem and use our solution for that with suitable modification. Don't start from scratch unless you really have to. Using a previous version of a program as a base for modification often saves a lot of time, and we benefit from much of the effort that went into the original program.

2.6 Names

We name our variables so that we can remember them and refer to them from other parts of a program. What can be a name in C++? In a C++ program, a name starts with a letter and contains only letters, digits, and underscores. For example:

```
x
number_of_elements
Fourier_transform
z2
Polygon
```

The following are not names:

```
2x               // a name must start with a letter
time@to@market   // @ is not a letter, digit, or underscore
Start menu       // space is not a letter, digit, or underscore
```

When we say "not names," we mean that a C++ compiler will not accept them as names.

XX

If you read system code or machine-generated code, you might see names starting with underscores, such as _foo. Never write those yourself; such names are reserved for implementation and system entities. By avoiding leading underscores, you will never find your names clashing with some name that the implementation generated.

Names are case sensitive; that is, uppercase and lowercase letters are distinct, so x and X are different names. This little program has at least four errors:

```
import std;

int Main()
{
      STRING s = "Goodbye, cruel world! ";
      cOut << S << '\n';
}
```

It is usually not a good idea to define names that differ only in the case of a character, such as one and One; that will not confuse a compiler, but it can easily confuse a programmer.

> TRY THIS
>
> Compile the "Goodbye, cruel world!" program and examine the error messages. Did the compiler find all the errors? What did it suggest as the problems? Did the compiler get confused and diagnose more than four errors? Remove the errors one by one, starting with the lexically first, and see how the error messages change (and improve).

XX

The C++ language reserves many names as *keywords*, such as if, else, class, int, and module. You can find complete lists on the Web (e.g., cppreference.com). You can't use those to name your variables, types, functions, etc. For example:

```
int if = 7;    // error: if is a keyword
```

You can use names of facilities in the standard library, such as string for your own variables, but you shouldn't. Reuse of such a common name will cause trouble if you should ever want to use the standard library:

```
int string = 7;  // this will lead to trouble
```

AA When you choose names for your variables, functions, types, etc., choose meaningful names; that is, choose names that will help people understand your program. Even you will have problems understanding what your program is supposed to do if you have littered it with variables with "easy to type" names like x1, x2, s3, and p7. Abbreviations and acronyms can confuse people, so use them sparingly. These acronyms were obvious to us when we wrote them, but we expect you'll have trouble with at least one:

```
mtbf    TLA    myw    NBV
```

We expect that in a few months, we'll also have trouble with at least one.

Short names, such as x and i, are meaningful when used conventionally; that is, x should be a local variable or a parameter (see §3.5 and §7.4) and i should be a loop index (§3.4.2.3).

Don't use overly long names; they are hard to type, make lines so long that they don't fit on a screen, and are hard to read quickly. These are probably OK:

```
partial_sum    element_count    stable_partition
```

These are probably too long:

```
the_number_of_elements    remaining_free_slots_in_symbol_table
```

Our "house style" is to use underscores to separate words in an identifier, such as element_count, rather than alternatives, such as elementCount and ElementCount. We never use names with all capital letters, such as ALL_CAPITAL_LETTERS, because that's conventionally reserved for macros (PPP2.§27.8), which we avoid. We use an initial capital letter for types we define, such as Square and Graph. The C++ language and standard library don't use the initial-capital-letter style, so it's int rather than Int and string rather than String. Thus, our convention helps to minimize confusion between our types and the standard ones.

XX Avoid names that are easy to mistype, misread, or confuse. For example:

```
Name    names    nameS    foo    f00    fl    f1    fI    fi
```

The characters 0 (zero), o (lowercase O), O (uppercase o), 1 (one), I (uppercase i), and l (lowercase L) are particularly prone to cause trouble.

2.7 Types and objects

CC The notion of type is central to C++ and most other programming languages. Let's take a closer and slightly more technical look at types:

- A *type* defines a set of possible values and a set of operations (for an object).
- An *object* is some memory that holds a value of a given type.
- A *value* is a set of bits in memory interpreted according to a type.
- A *variable* is a named object.
- A *declaration* is a statement that gives a name and a type to an object.
- A *definition* is a declaration that sets aside memory for an object.

Informally, we think of an object as a box into which we can put values of a given type. An int box can hold integers, such as 7, 42, and -399. A string box can hold character string values, such as

"Interoperability", "operators: +−∗/%", and "Old MacDonald had a farm". Graphically, we can think of it like this:

```
int a = 7;
int b = 9;
char c = 'a';
double x = 1.2;
string s1 = "Hello, World!";
string s2 = "1.2";
```

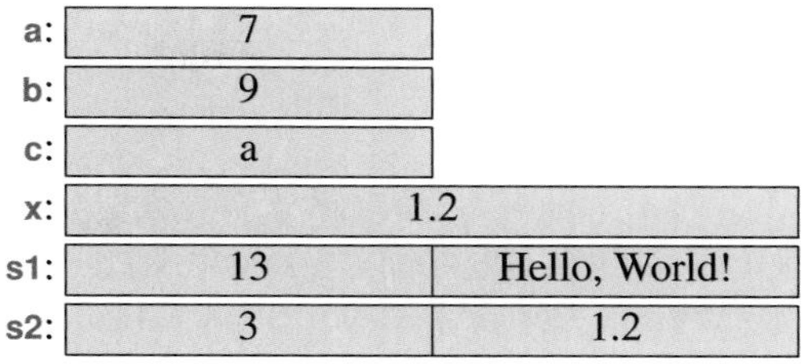

The representation of a string is a bit more complicated than that of an int because a string keeps track of the number of characters it holds. Note that a double stores a number whereas a string stores characters. For example, x stores the number 1.2, whereas s2 stores the three characters '1', '.', and '2'. The quotes for character and string literals are not stored.

Every int is of the same size; that is, the compiler sets aside the same fixed amount of memory for each int. On a typical computer or phone, that amount is 4 bytes (32 bits). Similarly, bools, chars, and doubles are fixed size. You'll typically find that a computer uses a byte (8 bits) for a bool or a char and 8 bytes for a double. Note that different types of objects take up different amounts of space. In particular, a char takes up less space than an int, and string differs from double, int, and char in that different strings can take up different amounts of space.

The meaning of bits in memory is completely dependent on the type used to access it. Think of it this way: computer memory doesn't know about our types; it's just memory. The bits of memory get meaning only when we decide how that memory is to be interpreted. This is similar to what we do every day when we use numbers. What does 12.5 mean? We don't know. It could be $12.5, 12.5cm, or 12.5 gallons. Only when we supply the unit does the notation 12.5 mean anything. **CC**

For example, the very same bits of memory that represent the integer value 120 when looked upon as an int would be the character 'x' when looked upon as a char. If looked at as a string, it wouldn't make sense at all and would become a run-time error if we tried to use it. We can illustrate this graphically like this, using 1 and 0 to indicate the value of bits in memory:

This is the setting of the bits of an area of memory (a word) that could be read as an int (120) or as a char ('x', looking at the rightmost 8 bits only). A *bit* is a unit of computer memory that can hold the value 0 or 1.

2.8 Type safety

Every object is given a type when it is defined, and that type never changes. A program – or a part of a program – is type-safe when all objects are used only according to the rules for their type. Complete type safety is the ideal and the general rule for the language. Unfortunately, a C++ **AA** compiler cannot by itself guarantee complete type safety for arbitrary code, so we must avoid unsafe techniques. That is, we must obey some coding rules to achieve type safety. There are ways of enforcing such rules, but historically such rules have been considered overly restrictive and have not been consistently enforced. Given older versions of C++ (earlier than recent ISO C++ standards) and techniques adopted from the C language, this was unavoidable and therefore not unreasonable. However, when using modern C++ and modern analysis tools, type safety can be verified for most uses of C++. The ideal is never to use language features that cannot be proven type-safe before the program starts executing: *static type safety*. With the obvious exception of code used to illustrate unsafe techniques (e.g., §16.1.1), the code in this book follows the C++ Core Guidelines [CG] and has been verified to be type safe.

XX The ideal of type safety is incredibly important when writing reliable code. That's why we spend time on it this early in the book. Please note the pitfalls and avoid them. If you don't, you will face much frustration and your code will contain many obscure errors.

AA For example, using an uninitialized variable is not type-safe:

```
int main()
{
	double x;			// we "forgot" to initialize: the value of x is undefined
	double y = x;		// the value of y is undefined
	double z = 2.0+x;	// the meaning of + and the value of z are undefined
}
```

AA Always initialize your variables! Implementations can easily enforce this rule, but unfortunately they typically don't do so by default. Except, fortunately, for types such as **string** and **vector** where default initialization is guaranteed (§2.5, §7.2.3, §8.4.2). Figure out how to enable warnings (often a **-Wall** compiler option) and adhere to them. Doing so will save you a lot of grief.

CC Modern C++ implementations also come with significant static-analysis tools that allow us to prevent more subtle problems. Professionals use such tools extensively, and so will you if you become or aim to become a professional, but at this initial stage of learning just follow the rules and styles used in this book.

2.9 Conversions

In §2.4, we saw that we can't directly add **chars** or compare a **double** to an **int**. However, C++ provides indirect ways to do both. When needed in an expression, a **char** is converted to an **int** and an **int** is converted to a **double**. For example:

```
char c = 'x';
int i1 = c;			// i1 gets the integer value of c
int i2 = c+1000;		// i2 gets the integer value of c added to 1000
double d = i2+7.3;	// d gets the floating-point value of i2 plus 7.3
```

Here, **i1** gets the value **120**, which is the integer value of the character **'x'** in the popular 8-bit character set, ASCII. This is a simple way of getting the numeric representation of a character. To get the value of **i2**, the addition is done using integer arithmetic and gives the value **1120**. The **char** is said to be *promoted* to **int** before the addition.

Similarly, when having a mixture of floating-point values and integer values, the integers are promoted to floating point to give unsurprising results. Here, **d** gets the value **1127.3**.

Conversions are of two kinds

- *widening*: Conversions that preserve information, such as **char** to **int**.
- *narrowing*: Conversions that may lose information, such as **int** to **char**.

A widening conversion converts a value to an equal value or to the best approximation of an equal value. Widening conversions are usually a boon to the programmer and simplify writing code.

Unfortunately, C++ also allows for implicit narrowing conversions. By narrowing, we mean XX
that a value is turned into a value of another type that does not equal the original value.

Consider **int** and **char**. Conversions from **char** to **int** don't have problems with narrowing. However, a **char** can hold only very small integer values. Often, a **char** is an 8-bit byte whereas an **int** is 4 bytes:

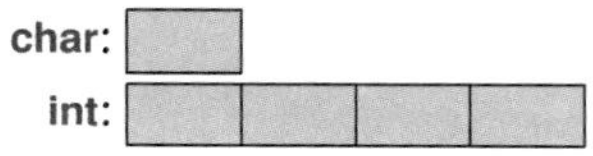

We can't put a large number, such as **1000**, into a **char**. Such conversions are called *narrowing* XX
because they put a value into an object that may be too small ("narrow") to hold all of it. Unfortunately, conversions such as **double** to **int** and **int** to **char** are by default accepted by most compilers even though they are narrowing. Why can this be a problem? Because often we don't suspect that a narrowing – information destroying – conversion is taking place. Consider:

```
double x = 2.7;
// ... lots of code ...
int y = x;              // y becomes 2
```

By the time we assign **x** to **y** we may have forgotten that **x** was a **double**, or that a **double**-to-**int** conversion *truncate*s (always rounds down, toward zero) rather than using the conventional 4/5 rounding (rounding towards the nearest integer). What happens is well-defined, but there is nothing in the **y = x;** to remind us that information (the **.7**) is thrown away.

To get a feel for conversions and an understanding why narrowing conversions must be avoided, experiment. Consider this program that shows how conversions from **double** to **int** and conversions from **int** to **char** are done on your machine:

```
int main()
{
     double d = 0;
     while (cin>>d) {             // repeat the statements below as long as we type in numbers
          int i = d;              // try to squeeze a floating-point value into an integer value
          char c = i;             // try to squeeze an integer into a char
          cout << "d==" << d                  // the original double
               << " i=="<< i                  // double converted to int
               << " c==" << c                 // int value of char
               << " char(" << c << ")\n";     // the char
     }
}
```

TRY THIS

Run this program with a variety of inputs:

- Small values (e.g., 2 and 3).
- Large values (larger than 127, larger than 1000).
- Negative values.
- 56, 89, and 128.
- Non-integer values (e.g., 56.9 and 56.2).

You'll find that many inputs produce "unreasonable" results when converted. Basically, we are trying to put a gallon into a pint pot (about 4 liters into a 500ml glass).

CC Why do people accept the problem of narrowing conversions? The major reason is history: C++ inherited narrowing conversions from its ancestor language, C, so from day one of C++, there existed much code that depended on narrowing conversions. Also, many such conversions don't actually cause problems because the values involved happen to be in range, and many programmers object to "compilers telling them what to do." In particular, the problems with narrowing conversions are often manageable in small programs and for experienced programmers. They can be a source of errors in larger programs, though, and a significant cause of problems for novice programmers. Fortunately, compilers can warn about narrowing conversions – and many do. Adhere to those warnings.

When we really need narrowing, we can use **narrow<T>(x)** to check that **x** can be narrowed to a **T** without loss of information (§7.4.7). When we want rounding, we can use **round_to<int>(x)**. Both are supplied by **PPP_support**.

CC For historical and practical reasons, C++ offers four notations for initialization: For example:

```
int x0 = 7.8;         // narrows, some compilers warn
int x1 {7.8};         // error: {} doesn't narrow
int x2 = {7.8};       // error: ={} doesn't narrow (the redundant = is allowed)
int x3 (7.8);         // narrows, some compilers warn
```

The = and ={} notations go back to the early days of C. We use the = notation when an initialization simply copies its initializer and the {} and ={} notations for more complex initializations and when we want compile-time protection against narrowing.

```
int x = 7;
double d = 7.7;
string s = "Hello, World\n";

vector v = {1, 2, 3, 5, 8 };     // see §17.3
pair p {"Hello",17};             // see §20.2.2
```

We reserve () initialization to a few very special cases (§17.3).

2.10 Type deduction: auto

You may have noticed a bit of repetitiveness in definitions. Consider:

```
int x = 7;
double d = 7.7;
```

We know that 7 is an integer and that 7.7 is a floating-point number, and so does the compiler. Why then do we have to say int and double? Well, we don't have to unless we want to; we can let the compiler deduce the type from the type of the initializer:

```
auto x = 7;          // x is an int (because 7 is)
auto d = 7.7;        // d is a double (because 7.7 is)
```

This version using auto means *exactly* the same as the one with explicit types. We use auto when, and *only* when, the type is obvious from the initializer and we don't want any conversion. AA

When we use longer type names (§18.5.2, §20.2.1) and in generic programming (§18.1.2) the notational convenience of auto becomes significant. For example:

```
auto z = complex<double>{1.3,3.4};
auto p = make_unique<Pair<string,int>>{"Harlem",10027};    // a unique_ptr<Pair<string,int>> (§18.5.2)
auto b = lst.begin();                                      // lst.begin is a vector<int>::iterator (§19.3.2)
```

Until then, resist the temptation to overuse auto. Overuse of auto can make code obscure so that we get unpleasant surprises.

Drill

After each step of this drill, run your program to make sure it is really doing what you expect it to. Keep a list of what mistakes you make so that you can try to avoid those in the future.

[1] Write a program that produces a simple form letter based on user input. Begin by typing the code from §2.1 prompting a user to enter his or her first name and writing "Hello, first_name" where first_name is the name entered by the user. Then modify your code as follows: change the prompt to "Enter the name of the person you want to write to" and change the output to "Dear first_name,". Don't forget the comma.

[2] Add an introductory line or two, like "How are you? I am fine. I miss you." Be sure to indent the first line. Add a few more lines of your choosing – it's your letter.

[3] Now prompt the user for the name of another friend and store it in friend_name. Add a line to your letter: "Have you seen friend_name lately?"

[4] Prompt the user to enter the age of the recipient and assign it to an int variable age. Have your program write "I hear you just had a birthday and you are age years old." If age is 0 or less or 110 or more, call simple_error("you're kidding!") using simple_error() from PPP_support.

[5] Add this to your letter:

> If your friend is under 12, write "Next year you will be age+1." If your friend is 17, write "Next year you will be able to vote." If your friend is over 70, write "Are you retired?"

Check your program to make sure it responds appropriately to each kind of value.

[6] Add "Yours sincerely," followed by two blank lines for a signature, followed by your name.

Review

[1] What is meant by the term *prompt*?
[2] Which operator do you use to read into a variable?
[3] What notations can you use to initialize an object?
[4] If you want the user to input an integer value into your program for a variable named **number**, what are two lines of code you could write to ask the user to do it and to input the value into your program?
[5] What is **\n** called and what purpose does it serve?
[6] What terminates input into a string?
[7] What terminates input into an integer?
[8] How would you write the following as a single line of code:

```
cout << "Hello, ";
cout << first_name;
cout << "!\n";
```

[9] What is an object?
[10] What is a literal?
[11] What kinds of literals are there?
[12] What is a variable?
[13] What are typical sizes for a **char**, an **int**, and a **double**?
[14] What measures do we use for the size of small entities in memory, such as **int**s and **string**s?
[15] What is the difference between = and ==?
[16] What is a definition?
[17] What is an initialization and how does it differ from an assignment?
[18] What is string concatenation and how do you make it work in C++?
[19] What operators can you apply to an **int**?
[20] Which of the following are legal names in C++? If a name is not legal, why not?

This_little_pig	This_1_is fine	2_For_1_special	latest thing
George@home	_this_is_ok	MineMineMine	number
correct?	stroustrup.com	$PATH	

[21] Give five examples of legal names that you shouldn't use because they are likely to cause confusion.
[22] What are some good rules for choosing names?
[23] What is type safety and why is it important?
[24] Why can conversion from **double** to **int** be a bad thing?
[25] Define a rule to help decide if a conversion from one type to another is safe or unsafe.
[26] How can we avoid undesirable conversions?
[27] What are the uses of **auto**?

Terms

assignment	definition	operation	cin
increment	operator	concatenation	initialization
type	conversion	name	type safety
declaration	narrowing	value	decrement
object	variable	widening	truncation
int	double	string	auto
==	!=	=	++
<	<=	>	>=

Exercises

[1] If you haven't done so already, do the **TRY THIS** exercises from this chapter.

[2] Write a program in C++ that converts from miles to kilometers. Your program should have a reasonable prompt for the user to enter a number of miles. Hint: A mile is1.609 kilometers.

[3] Write a program that doesn't do anything, but declares a number of variables with legal and illegal names (such as `int double = 0;`), so that you can see how the compiler reacts.

[4] Write a program that prompts the user to enter two integer values. Store these values in `int` variables named `val1` and `val2`. Write your program to determine the smaller, larger, sum, difference, product, and ratio of these values and report them to the user.

[5] Modify the program above to ask the user to enter floating-point values and store them in `double` variables. Compare the outputs of the two programs for some inputs of your choice. Are the results the same? Should they be? What's the difference?

[6] Write a program that prompts the user to enter three integer values, and then outputs the values in numerical sequence separated by commas. So, if the user enters the values `10 4 6`, the output should be `4, 6, 10`. If two values are the same, they should just be ordered together. So, the input `4 5 4` should give `4, 4, 5`.

[7] Do exercise 6, but with three string values. So, if the user enters the values `Steinbeck, Hemingway, Fitzgerald`, the output should be `Fitzgerald, Hemingway, Steinbeck`.

[8] Write a program to test an integer value to determine if it is odd or even. As always, make sure your output is clear and complete. In other words, don't just output `yes` or `no`. Your output should stand alone, like `The value 4 is an even number`. Hint: See the remainder (modulo) operator in §2.4.

[9] Write a program that converts spelled-out numbers such as "zero" and "two" into digits, such as 0 and 2. When the user inputs a number, the program should print out the corresponding digit. Do it for the values 0, 1, 2, 3, and 4 and write out `not a number I know` if the user enters something that doesn't correspond, such as `stupid computer!`.

[10] Write a program that takes an operation followed by two operands and outputs the result. For example:

```
+ 100 3.14
* 4 5
```

Read the operation into a string called **operation** and use an **if**-statement to figure out which operation the user wants, for example, **if (operation=="+")**. Read the operands into variables of type **double**. Implement this for operations called +, –, *, /, **plus**, **minus**, **mul**, and **div** with their obvious meanings.

[11] Write a program that prompts the user to enter some number of pennies (1-cent coins), nickels (5-cent coins), dimes (10-cent coins), quarters (25-cent coins), half dollars (50-cent coins), and one-dollar coins (100-cent coins). Query the user separately for the number of each size coin, e.g., "How many pennies do you have?" Then your program should print out something like this:

```
You have 23 pennies.
You have 17 nickels.
You have 14 dimes.
You have 7 quarters.
You have 3 half dollars.
The value of all of your coins is 573 cents.
```

Make some improvements: if only one of a coin is reported, make the output grammatically correct, e.g., **14 dimes** and **1 dime** (not **1 dimes**). Also, report the sum in dollars and cents, i.e., .73 instead of **573 cents**.

Postscript

Please don't underestimate the importance of the notion of type safety. Types are at the center of most notions of correct programs, and some of the most effective techniques for constructing programs rely on the design and use of types – as you'll see in Chapter 5 and Chapter 8, and indeed in most of the rest of the book.

3

Computation

If it doesn´t have
to produce correct results,
I can make it arbitrarily fast.
– Gerald M. Weinberg

This chapter presents the basics of computation. In particular, we discuss how to compute a value from a set of operands (*expression*), how to choose among alternative actions (*selection*), and how to repeat a computation for a series of values (*iteration*). We also show how a particular sub-computation can be named and specified separately (a *function*). Our primary concern is to express computations in ways that lead to correct and well-organized programs. To help you perform more realistic computations, we introduce the **vector** type to hold sequences of values.

§3.1 Computation
§3.2 Objectives and tools
§3.3 Expressions
Constant expressions; Operators
§3.4 Statements
Selection; Iteration
§3.5 Functions
Why bother with functions?; Function declarations
§3.6 **vector**
Traversing a **vector**; Growing a **vector**; A numeric example; A text example
§3.7 Language features

3.1 Computation

From one point of view, all that a program ever does is to compute; that is, it takes some inputs and produces some output. After all, we call the hardware on which the program runs "a computer." This view is reasonable as long as we take a broad view of what constitutes input and output:

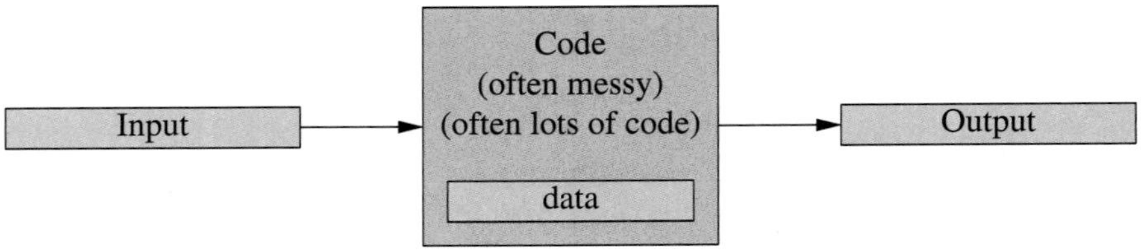

The input can come from a keyboard, from a mouse, from a touch screen, from files, from other input devices, from other programs, from other parts of a program. "Other input devices" is a category that contains really interesting input sources: music keyboards, video recorders, network connections, temperature sensors, image sensors, power supplies, etc.

To deal with input, a program usually contains some data, sometimes referred to as its *data structures* or its *state*. For example, a calendar program may contain lists of holidays in various countries and a list of your appointments. Some of that data is part of the program from the start; other data is built up as the program reads input and collects useful information from it. For example, the calendar program will probably build your list of appointments from the input you give it. For the calendar, the main inputs are the requests to see the months and days you ask for (probably using mouse clicks) and the appointments you give it to keep track of (probably by typing information on your keyboard). The output is the display of calendars and appointments, plus the buttons and prompts for input that the calendar program writes on your screen. In addition, the calendar may send you reminders and synchronize with other copies of the calendar programs.

Input comes from a wide variety of sources. Similarly, output can go to a wide variety of destinations. Output can be to a screen, to files, to network connections, to other output devices, to other programs, and to other parts of a program. Examples of output devices include network interfaces, music synthesizers, electric motors, light generators, heaters, etc.

From a programming point of view the most important and interesting categories are "to/from another program" and "to/from other parts of a program." Most of the rest of this book could be seen as discussing that last category: how do we express a program as a set of cooperating parts and how can they share and exchange data? These are key questions in programming. We can illustrate that graphically:

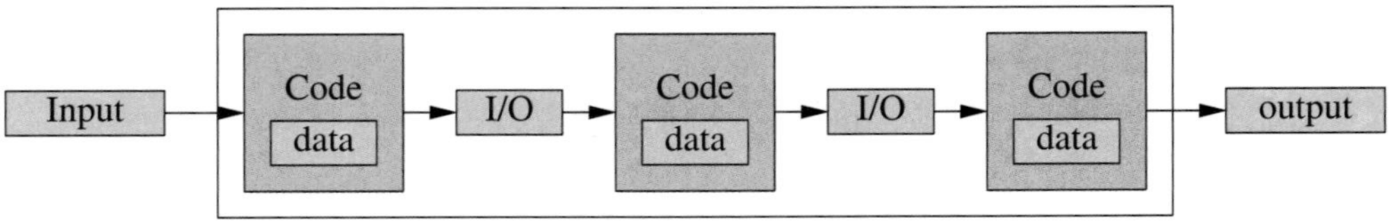

The abbreviation *I/O* stands for "input/output." In this case, the output from one part of code is the input for the next part. What such "parts of a program" share is data stored in main memory, on persistent storage devices (such as disks), or transmitted over network connections. By "parts of a program" we mean entities such as a function producing a result from a set of input arguments (e.g., a square root from a floating-point number), a function performing an action on a physical object (e.g., a function drawing a line on a screen), or a function modifying some table within the program (e.g., a function adding a name to a table of customers).

When we say "input" and "output" we generally mean information coming into and out of a computer, but as you see, we can also use the terms for information given to or produced by a part of a program. Inputs to a part of a program are often called *arguments* and outputs from a part of a program are often called *results*.

By *computation* we simply mean the act of producing some outputs based on some inputs, such as producing the result (output) `49` from the argument (input) `7` using the computation (function) `square` (see §3.5). As a possibly helpful curiosity, we note that until the 1950s a computer was defined as a person who did computations, such as an accountant, a navigator, or a physicist. Today, we simply delegate most computations to computers of various forms, such as smartphones.

3.2 Objectives and tools

Our job as programmers is to express computations CC

- Correctly
- Simply
- Efficiently

Please note the order of those ideals: it doesn't matter how fast a program is if it gives the wrong results. Similarly, a correct and efficient program can be so complicated that it must be thrown away or completely rewritten to produce a new version (release). Remember, useful programs will always be modified to accommodate new needs, new hardware, etc. Therefore a program – and any part of a program – should be as simple as possible to perform its task. For example, assume that you have written the perfect program for teaching basic arithmetic to children in your local school, and that its internal structure is a mess. Which language did you use to communicate with the children? English? English and Spanish? What if I'd like to use it in Finland? In Kuwait? How would you change the (natural) language used for communication with a child? If the internal structure of the program is a mess, the logically simple (but in practice almost always very difficult) operation of changing the natural language used to communicate with users becomes insurmountable.

Concerns about correctness, simplicity, and efficiency become ours the minute we start writing code for others and accept the responsibility to do that well; that is, we must accept that responsibility when we decide to become professionals. In practical terms, this means that we can't just throw code together until it appears to work; we must concern ourselves with the structure of code. Paradoxically, concerns for structure and "quality of code" are often the fastest ways of getting something to work. When programming is done well, such concerns minimize the need for the most frustrating part of programming: debugging; that is, good program structure during development can minimize the number of mistakes made and the time needed to search for such errors and to remove them. AA

CC Our main tool for organizing a program – and for organizing our thoughts as we program – is to break up a big computation into many little ones. This technique comes in two variations:

- *Abstraction:* Hide details that we don't need to use a facility ("implementation details") behind a convenient and general interface. For example, rather than considering the details of how to sort a phone book (thick books have been written about how to sort), we just call the sort algorithm from the C++ standard library. All we need to know to sort is how to invoke (call) that algorithm, so we can write sort(b) where b refers to the phone book; sort() is a version of the standard-library sort algorithm (§21.5). Another example is the way we use computer memory. Direct use of memory can be quite messy, so we access it through typed and named variables (§2.2), standard-library vectors (§3.6), maps (§20.2), etc.
- *Divide-and-conquer*: Here we take a large problem and divide it into several little ones. For example, if we need to build a dictionary, we can separate that job into three: read the data, sort the data, and output the data. Each of the resulting problems is significantly smaller than the original.

XX Why does this help? After all, a program built out of parts is likely to be slightly larger than a program where everything is optimally merged together. The reason is that we are not very good at dealing with large problems. The way we actually deal with those – in programming and elsewhere – is to break them down into smaller problems, and we keep breaking those into even smaller parts until we get something simple enough to understand and solve. In terms of programming, you'll find that a first attempt of a 1000-line program has far more than ten times as many errors as a 100-line program, so we try to compose the 1000-line program out of parts with fewer than 100 lines. For large programs, say 10,000,000 lines, applying abstraction and divide-and-conquer is not just an option, it's an essential requirement. We simply cannot write and maintain large monolithic programs. One way of looking at the rest of this book is as a long series of examples of problems that need to be broken up into smaller parts together with the tools and techniques needed to do so.

When we consider dividing up a program, we must always consider what tools we have available to express the parts and their communications. A good library, supplying useful facilities for expressing ideas, can crucially affect the way we distribute functionality into different parts of a program. We cannot just sit back and "imagine" how best to partition a program; we must consider what libraries we have available to express the parts and their communication. It is early days yet, but not too soon to point out that if you can use an existing library, such as the C++ standard library, you can save yourself a lot of work, not just on programming but also on testing and documentation. The iostreams save us from having to directly deal with the hardware's input/output ports. This is a first example of partitioning a program using abstraction. Every new chapter will provide more examples.

Note the emphasis on structure and organization: you don't get good code just by writing a lot of statements. Why do we mention this now? At this stage you (or at least many readers) have little idea about what code is, and it will be months before you are ready to write code upon which other people could depend for their lives or livelihood. We mention it to help you get the emphasis of your learning right. It is very tempting to dash ahead, focusing on the parts of programming that – like what is described in the rest of this chapter – are concrete and immediately useful and to ignore the "softer," more conceptual parts of the art of software development. However, good programmers and system designers know (often having learned it the hard way) that concerns about structure lie at the heart of good software and that ignoring structure leads to expensive messes.

Without structure, you are (metaphorically speaking) building with mud bricks. It can be done, but you'll never get to the tenth floor (classical mud bricks lack the structural strength for that). If you have the ambition to build something reasonably permanent or something large, you pay attention to matters of code structure and organization along the way, rather than having to come back and learn them after failures.

3.3 Expressions

The most basic building block of programs is an expression. An expression computes a value from a number of operands. The simplest expression is simply a literal value, such as 10, 'a', 3.14, or "Norah". CC

Names of variables are also expressions. A variable represents the object of which it is the name. Consider:

```
int length = 20;              // a literal integer (used to initialize a variable)
int width = 40;
int area = length*width;   // a multiplication
```

Here the literals 20 and 40 are used to initialize the variables length and width. Then, length and width are multiplied; that is, we multiply the values found in length and width. Here, length is simply shorthand for "the value found in the object named length." Consider also

```
length = 99;      // assign 99 to length
```

Here, as the left-hand operand of the assignment, length means "the object named length," so that the assignment expression is read "Put 99 into the object named length." We distinguish between length used on the left-hand side of an assignment or an initialization (the *lvalue* of length: "the object named length") and length used on the right-hand side of an assignment or initialization (the *rvalue* of length: "the value of the object named length," or just "the value of length"). In this context, we find it useful to visualize a variable as a box labeled by its name (§2.2, §2.5):

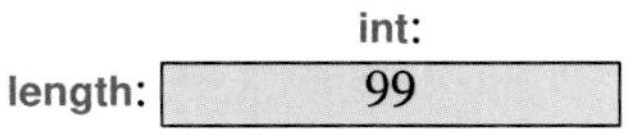

That is, length is the name of an object of type int containing the value 99. Sometimes (as an lvalue) length refers to the box (object) and sometimes (as an rvalue) length refers to the value in that box.

We can make more complicated expressions by using operators, such as + and *, in just the way that we are used to. When needed, we can use parentheses to group expressions:

```
int perimeter = (length+width)*2;          // add then multiply
```

Without parentheses, we'd have had to say

```
int perimeter = length*2+width*2;
```

which is clumsy, and we might even have made this mistake:

```
int perimeter = length+width*2;          // add width*2 to length
```

This last error is logical and cannot be found by the compiler. All the compiler sees is a variable called **perimeter** initialized by a valid expression. If the result of that expression is nonsense, that's your problem. You know the mathematical definition of a perimeter, but the compiler doesn't.

The usual mathematical rules of operator precedence apply, so **length+width*2** means **length+(width*2)**. Similarly **a*b+c/d** means **(a*b)+(c/d)** and not **a*(b+c)/d**. See cppreference (§0.4.1) for an operator precedence table.

The first rule for the use of parentheses is simply "If in doubt, parenthesize," but please do learn enough about expressions so that you are not in doubt about **a*b+c/d**. Overuse of parentheses, as in **(a*b)+(c/d)**, decreases readability.

Why should you care about readability? Because you and possibly others will read your code. Ugly code slows down reading and comprehension. Ugly code is not just hard to read, it is also much harder to get correct. Ugly code often hides logical errors. Don't write absurdly complicated expressions such as

```
a*b+c/d*(e/-f/g)/h+7        // too complicated
```

and always try to choose meaningful names.

3.3.1 Constant expressions

Programs typically use a lot of constants. For example, a geometry program might use **pi** and an inch-to-centimeter conversion program will use a conversion factor such as **2.54**. Obviously, we want to use meaningful names for those constants (as we did for **pi**; we didn't say **3.14159**). Similarly, we don't want to change those constants accidentally. Consequently, C++ offers the notion of a symbolic constant, that is, a named object to which you can't give a new value after it has been initialized. For example:

```
constexpr double pi = 3.14159;
pi = 7;                      // error: assignment to constant
double c = 2*pi*r;           // OK: we just read pi; we don't try to change it
```

Such constants are useful for keeping code readable. You might have recognized **3.14159** as an approximation to **pi** if you saw it in some code, but would you have recognized **299792458**? Also, if someone asked you to change some code to use **pi** with the precision of 12 digits for your computation, you could search for **3.14** in your code, but if someone incautiously had used **22/7**, you probably wouldn't find it. It would be much better just to change the definition of **pi** to use the more appropriate value:

```
constexpr double pi = 3.14159265359;
```

AA Consequently, we prefer not to use literals (except very obvious ones, such as **0** and **1**) in most places in our code. Instead, we use constants with descriptive names. Non-obvious literals in code (outside definitions of symbolic constants) are derisively referred to as *magic constant*. And by the way, **299792458** is one of the fundamental constants of the universe: the speed of light in vacuum measured in meters per second. If you didn't instantly recognize that, why would you expect not to be confused and slowed down by other literals embedded in code? Avoid magic constants!

A **constexpr** symbolic constant must be given a value that is known at compile time (a *constant expression*). For example: XX

```
constexpr int max = 100;
int n;
cin >> n;

constexpr int c1 = max+7;       // OK: c1 is 107
constexpr int c2 = n+7;         // error: we don't know the value of n
```

To handle cases where the value of a constant that is initialized with a value that is not known at compile time but never changes after initialization, C++ offers a second form of constant (a **const**):

```
int n;
cin >> n;

const int c3 = n;               // OK
c3 = 7;                         // error: c3 is a const
```

Such "**const** variables" are very common for two reasons:

- C++98 did not have **constexpr**, so people used **const**.
- "Variables" that are not constant expressions (their value is not known at compile time) but do not change values after initialization are in themselves widely useful.

3.3.2 Operators

We just used the simplest operators. However, you will soon need more as you want to express more complex operations. Most operators are conventional, so we'll just explain them later as needed and you can look up details if and when you find a need. Here are some common operators:

Example	Name	Comment
lval=a	assignment	not to be confused with **==**
++lval	pre-increment	increment and use the incremented value
--lval	pre-decrement	decrement and use the decremented value
!a	not	result is **bool**
-a	unary minus	
a*b	multiply	
a/b	divide	
a%b	modulo (remainder)	only for integer types
a+b	add	
a-b	subtract	
out<<b	write **b** to **out**	where **out** is an **ostream**
in>>b	read from **in** into **b**	where **in** is an **istream**
lval*=a	compound assignment	**lval = lval*a**; also for **/**, **%**, **+**, **-**
f(a)	function call	pass **a** to **f** as an argument (§3.5)
f<T>(a)	function template call	pass **a** to **f<T>** as an argument (§21.2)
[](a){S}	lambda expression	create a function object taking **a** as an argument (§21.2.3)

We used lval (short for lvalue, that is a value that can appear on the left-hand side of an assignment) where the operator modifies an operand.

Example	Name	Comment
a<b	less than	result is bool
a<=b	less than or equal	result is bool
a>b	greater than	result is bool
a>=b	greater than or equal	result is bool
a==b	equal	not to be confused with =
a!=b	not equal	result is bool
a&&b	logical and	result is bool
a||b	logical or	result is bool
T{a}	widening conversion	result is the value of a converted to type T

See cppreference (§0.4.1) for a complete list of operators. For examples of the use of the logical operators && (and), || (or), and ! (not), see §4.5.1, §6.7, and §9.3.1.

XX Note that a<b<c means (a<b)<c and that a<b evaluates to a Boolean value: true or false. So, a<b<c will be equivalent to either true<c or false<c. In particular, a<b<c does not mean "Is b between a and c?" as many have naively (and not unreasonably) assumed. Thus, a<b<c is basically a useless expression. Don't write such expressions with two comparison operations, and be very suspicious if you find such an expression in someone else's code – it is most likely an error.

An increment can be expressed in at least three ways:

```
++a
a+=1
a=a+1
```

AA Which notation should we use? Why? We prefer the first version, ++a, because it more directly expresses the idea of incrementing. It says what we want to do (increment a) rather than how to do it (add 1 to a and then write the result to a). In general, a way of saying something in a program is better than another if it more directly expresses an idea. The result is more concise and easier for a reader to understand. If we wrote a=a+1, a reader could easily wonder whether we really meant to increment by 1. Maybe we just mistyped a=b+1, a=a+2, or even a=a−1; with ++a there are far fewer opportunities for such doubts. Please note that this is a logical argument about readability and correctness, not an argument about efficiency. Contrary to popular belief, modern compilers tend to generate exactly the same code from a=a+1 as for ++a when a is one of the built-in types. Similarly, we prefer a*=scale over a=a*scale.

3.4 Statements

An expression computes a value from a set of operands using operators like the ones mentioned in §3.3. What do we do when we want to produce several values? When we want to do something many times? When we want to choose among alternatives? When we want to get input or produce output? In C++, as in many languages, you use language constructs called *statements* to express those things.

So far, we have seen two kinds of statements: expression statements and declarations. An expression statement is simply an expression followed by a semicolon. For example:

```
a = b;
++c;
```

Those are two expression statements. Note that the assignment = is an operator so that a=b is an expression and we need the terminating semicolon to make a=b; a statement. Why do we need those semicolons? The reason is largely technical. Consider:

```
a = b
++ c;     // syntax error: missing semicolon
```

Without the semicolon, the compiler doesn't know whether we mean a=b++; c; or a=b; ++c;. Such problems are not restricted to computer languages; consider the exclamation "man eating tiger!" Who is eating whom? Punctuation exists to eliminate such problems: "man-eating tiger!"

When statements follow each other, the computer executes them in the order in which they are written. For example:

```
int a = 7;
cout << a << '\n';
```

Here the declaration, with its initialization, is executed before the output expression statement.

In general, we want a statement to have some effect. Statements without effect are typically useless. For example:

```
1+2;      // do an addition, but don't use the sum
a*b;      // do a multiplication, but don't use the product
```

Such statements without effects are typically logical errors, and compilers often warn against them. Thus, expression statements are typically assignments, I/O statements, or function calls.

We will mention one more type of statement: the "empty statement." Consider the code:

```
if (x == 5);
     y = 3;
```

This looks like an error, and it almost certainly is. The ; in the first line is not supposed to be there. XX
But, unfortunately, this is a legal construct in C++. It is called an *empty statement*, a statement doing nothing. An empty statement before a semicolon is rarely useful.

What will happen if this code is run? The compiler will test x to see if it has the value 5. If this condition is true, the following statement (the empty statement) will be executed, with no effect. Then the program continues to the next line, assigning the value 3 to y (which is what you wanted to have happen if x equals 5). If, on the other hand, x does not have the value 5, the compiler will not execute the empty statement (still no effect) and will continue as before to assign the value 3 to y (which is not what you wanted to have happen unless x equals 5). In other words, the if-statement doesn't matter; y is going to get the value 3 regardless. This is a common error for novice programmers, and it can be difficult to spot, so watch out for it and hope your compiler warns.

The next section is devoted to statements used to alter the order of evaluation to allow us to express more interesting computations than those we get by just executing statements in the order in which they were written.

3.4.1 Selection

In programs, as in life, we often have to select among alternatives. In C++, that is done using either an **if**-statement or a **switch**-statement.

3.4.1.1 if-statements

The simplest form of selection is an **if**-statement, which selects between two alternatives. For example:

```
int a = 0;
int b = 0;
cout << "Please enter two integers\n";
cin >> a >> b;

if (a<b)      // condition
        cout << a << " is smaller than " << b << '\n';                  // 1st alternative (if condition is true)
else
        cout << a << " is larger than or equal to " << b << '\n';    // 2nd alternative (if condition is false)
```

CC An **if**-statement chooses between two alternatives. If its condition is true, the first statement is executed; otherwise, the second statement is. This notion is simple. Most basic programming language features are. In fact, most basic facilities in a programming language are just new notation for things you learned in primary school – or even before that. For example, you were probably told in kindergarten that to cross the street at a traffic light, you had to wait for the light to turn green: "If the traffic light is green, go" and "If the traffic light is red, wait." In C++ that becomes something like

```
if (traffic_light==green)
        go();
```

and

```
if (traffic_light==red)
        wait();
```

So, the basic notion is simple, but it is also easy to use **if**-statements in a too-simple-minded manner. Consider what's wrong with this:

```
// convert from inches to centimeters or centimeters to inches
// a suffix 'i' or 'c' indicates the unit of the input

constexpr double cm_per_inch = 2.54;        // number of centimeters in an inch
double length = 1;                          // length in inches or centimeters
char unit = ' ';
cout<< "Please enter a length followed by a unit (c or i):\n";
cin >> length >> unit;
```

```
if (unit == 'i')
      cout << length << "in == " << length*cm_per_inch << "cm\n";
else
      cout << length << "cm == " << length/cm_per_inch << "in\n";
```

Actually, this program works roughly as advertised: enter **1i** and you get **1in == 2.54cm**; enter **2.54c** and you'll get **2.54cm == 1in**. Just try it; it's good practice.

The snag is that we didn't test for bad input. The program assumes that the user enters proper input. The condition **unit=='i'** distinguishes between the case where the unit is **'i'** and all other cases. It never looks for a **'c'**.

What if the user entered **15f** (for feet) "just to see what happens"? The condition (**unit == 'i'**) would fail and the program would execute the **else** part (the second alternative), converting from centimeters to inches. Presumably that was not what we wanted when we entered **'f'**.

We must always test our programs with "bad" input, because someone will eventually – intentionally or accidentally – enter bad input. A program should behave sensibly even if its users don't. **AA**

Here is an improved version of the **if** statement:

```
if (unit == 'i')
      cout << length << "in == " << length*cm_per_inch << "cm\n";
else if (unit == 'c')
      cout << length << "cm == " << length/cm_per_inch << "in\n";
else
      cout << "Sorry, I don't know a unit called '" << unit << "'\n";
```

We first test for **unit=='i'** and then for **unit=='c'** and if it isn't (either) we say, "Sorry." It may look as if we used an "**else-if**-statement," but there is no such thing in C++. Instead, we combined two **if**-statements. The general form of an **if**-statement is

if (*expression* **)**
    statement
else
    statement

That is, an **if**, followed by an *expression* in parentheses, followed by a *statement*, followed by an **else**, followed by a *statement*. We used an **if**-statement as the **else** part of an **if**-statement:

if (*expression* **)**
    statement
else if (*expression* **)**
    statement
else
    statement

For our program that gives this structure:

```
if (unit == 'i')
      ...              // 1st alternative
else if (unit == 'c')
      ...              // 2nd alternative
else
      ...              // 3rd alternative
```

AA In this way, we can write arbitrarily complex tests and associate a statement with each alternative. However, please remember that one of the ideals for code is simplicity, rather than complexity. You don't demonstrate your cleverness by writing the most complex program. Rather, you demonstrate competence by writing the simplest code that does the job.

> TRY THIS
>
> Use the example above as a model for a program that converts yen ('y'), kroner ('k'), and pounds ('p') into dollars. If you like realism, you can find conversion rates on the Web.

3.4.1.2 switch-statements

Actually, the comparison of unit to 'i' and to 'c' is an example of the one of the most common forms of selection: a selection based on comparison of a value against several constants. Such selection is so common that C++ provides a special statement for it: the switch-statement. We can rewrite the selection part of our unit example as

```
switch (unit) {
case 'i':
        cout << length << "in == " << length*cm_per_inch << "cm\n";
        break;
case 'c':
        cout << length << "cm == " << length/cm_per_inch << "in\n";
        break;
default:
        cout << "Sorry, I don't know a unit called '" << unit << "'\n";
        break;
}
```

AA The switch-statement syntax is archaic but still clearer than nested if-statements, especially when we compare against many constants. The value presented in parentheses after the switch is compared to a set of constants. Each constant is presented as part of a case label. If the value equals the constant in a case label, the statement for that case is chosen. Each case is terminated by a break. If the value doesn't match any of the case labels, the statement identified by the default label is chosen. You don't have to provide a default, but it is a good idea to do so unless you are absolutely certain that you have listed every alternative. If you don't already know, programming will teach you that it's hard to be absolutely certain (and right) about anything.

3.4.1.3 Switch technicalities

Here are some technical details about switch-statements:

[1] The value on which we switch must be of an integer, char, or enumeration (§8.5) type. In particular, you cannot switch on a string or a floating-point value.

[2] The values in the case labels must be constant expressions (§3.3). In particular, you cannot use a variable in a case label.

[3] You cannot use the same value for two case labels.

[4] You can use several case labels for a single case.

[5] Don't forget to end each case with a break. Unfortunately, the compiler probably won't warn you if you forget.

For example:

```
// you can switch only on integers, etc.:

cout << "Do you like fish?\n";
string s;
cin >> s;

switch (s) {     // error: the value must be of integer, char, or enum type
case "no":
      // ...
      break;
case "yes":
      // ...
      break;
}
```

To select based on a string you have to use an if-statement or a map (Chapter 19).

A switch-statement generates optimized code for comparing against a set of constants. For larger sets of constants, this typically yields more efficient code than a collection of if-statements. However, this means that the case label values must be distinct and constants. For example:

```
// case labels must be distinct and constants:

int y = 'y';          // this is going to cause trouble
constexpr char n = 'n';

cout << "Do you like fish?\n";
char a = 0;
cin >> a;

switch (a) {
case n:
      // ...
      break;
case y:             // error: variable in case label
      // ...
      break;
case 'n':           // error: duplicate case label (n's value is 'n')
      // ...
      break;
default:
      // ...
      break;
}
```

Often you want the same action for a set of values in a switch. It would be tedious to repeat the action so you can label a single action by a set of **case** labels. For example:

```
// you can label a statement with several case labels:

cout << "Please enter a digit\n";
char a = 0;
cin >> a;

switch (a) {
case '0': case '2': case '4': case '6': case '8':
        cout << "is even\n";
        break;
case '1': case '3': case '5': case '7': case '9':
        cout << "is odd\n";
        break;
default:
        cout << "is not a digit\n";
        break;
}
```

XX The most common error with **switch**-statements is to forget to terminate a **case** with a **break**. For example:

```
switch (unit) {
case 'i':
        cout << length << "in == " << length*cm_per_inch << "cm\n";
case 'c':
        cout << length << "cm == " << length/cm_per_inch << "in\n";
}
```

Unfortunately, the compiler will accept this, and when you have finished case **'i'** you'll just "fall through" into case **'c'**, so that if you enter **2i** the program will output

```
2in == 5.08cm
2cm == 0.787402in
```

You have been warned!

In the rare case where you want to fall through to the next case, you can and should say so:

```
switch (check) {
case checked:
        if (val<0)
                val = 0;
        [[fallthrough]];
case unchecked:
        // ... use val ...
        break;
}
```

The **[[fallthrough]]** is an *attribute* making our intent explicit.

TRY THIS

Rewrite your currency converter program from the previous **TRY THIS** to use a **switch**-statement. Add a conversion from Swiss francs. Which version of the program is easier to write, understand, and modify? Why?

3.4.2 Iteration

We rarely do something only once. Therefore, programming languages provide convenient ways of doing something several times. Doing the same thing to a series of objects is called *iteration*.

3.4.2.1 while-statements

As an example of iteration, consider the first program ever to run on a stored-program computer (the EDSAC). It was written and run by David J. Wheeler in the computer laboratory in Cambridge University, England, on May 6, 1949, to calculate and print a simple list of squares like this:

```
0	0
1	1
2	4
3	9
4	16
 ...
98	9604
99	9801
```

Each line is a number followed by a "tab" character ('\t'), followed by the square of the number. A C++ version looks like this:

```
int main()
	// calculate and print a table of squares 0-99
{
	int i = 0;			// start from 0
	while (i<100) {
		cout << i << '\t' << square(i) << '\n';
		++i;		// increment i (that is, i becomes i+1)
	}
}
```

The notation **square(i)** simply means the square of **i**. Later, we will explain how to get it to mean that (§3.5).

No, this first modern program wasn't actually written in C++, but the logic was as is shown:

- We start with **0**.
- We see if we have reached **100**, and if so we are finished.
- Otherwise, we print the number and its square, separated by a tab ('\t'), increase the number, and try again.

Clearly, to do this we need

- A way to repeat some statement (to *loop*)
- A variable to keep track of how many times we have been through the loop (a *loop variable* or a *control variable*), here the **int** called **i**

- An initializer for the loop variable, here 0
- A termination criterion, here that we want to go through the loop 100 times
- Something to do each time around the loop (the *body* of the loop)

The language construct we used is called a while-statement. Just following its distinguishing keyword, while, it has a condition "on top" followed by its body:

```
while (i<100)          // the loop condition testing the loop variable i
{
        cout << i << '\t' << square(i) << '\n';
        ++i;           // increment the loop variable i
}
```

The loop body is a block (delimited by curly braces) that writes out a row of the table and increments the loop variable, i. We start each pass through the loop by testing if i<100. If so, we are not yet finished, and we can execute the loop body. If we have reached the end, that is, if i is 100, we leave the while-statement and execute what comes next. In this program the end of the program is next, so we leave the program.

The loop variable for a while-statement must be defined and initialized outside (before) the while-statement. If we fail to define it, the compiler will give us an error. If we define it, but fail to initialize it, most compilers will warn us, saying something like "local variable i not set," but would be willing to let us execute the program if we insisted. Don't insist! Compilers are almost certainly right when they warn about uninitialized variables. Uninitialized variables are a common source of errors. In this case, we wrote

```
int i = 0;    // start from 0
```

so all is well.

Basically, writing a loop is simple. Getting it right for real-world problems can be tricky, though. In particular, it can be hard to express the condition correctly and to initialize all variables so that the loop starts correctly.

> TRY THIS
>
> The character 'b' is char('a'+1), 'c' is char('a'+2), etc. Use a loop to write out a table of characters with their corresponding integer values:
>
> ```
> a    97
> b    98
>  ...
> z    122
> ```

3.4.2.2 Blocks

Note how we grouped the two statements that the while had to execute:

```
while (i<100) {
        cout << i << '\t' << square(i) << '\n';
        ++i;        // increment i (that is, i becomes i+1)
}
```

A sequence of statements delimited by curly braces { and } is called a *block statement* or a *compound statement*. A block is a kind of statement. The empty block { } is sometimes useful for expressing that nothing is to be done. For example: CC

```
if (a<=b) {
        // do nothing
}
else {       // swap a and b:
        int t = a;
        a = b;
        b = t;
}
```

3.4.2.3 for-statements

Iterating over a sequence of numbers is so common that C++, like most other programming languages, has a special syntax for it. A for-statement is like a while-statement except that the management of the control variable is concentrated at the top where it is easy to see and understand. We could have written the "first program" like this:

```
int main()
        // calculate and print a table of squares 0-99
{
        for (int i = 0; i<100; ++i)
                cout << i << '\t' << square(i) << '\n';
}
```

This means "Execute the body with i starting at 0 incrementing i after each execution of the body until we reach 100." A for-statement is always equivalent to some while-statement. In this case

```
for (int i = 0; i<100; ++i)
        cout << i << '\t' << square(i) << '\n';
```

means

```
{
        int i = 0;                                      // the for-statement initializer
        while (i<100) {                                 // the for-statement condition
                cout << i << '\t' << square(i) << '\n'; // the for-statement body
                ++i;                                    // the for-statement increment
        }
}
```

Some novices prefer while-statements and some novices prefer for-statements. However, using a for-statement yields more easily understood and more maintainable code whenever a loop can be defined as a for-statement with a simple initializer, condition, and increment operation. Use a while-statement only when that's not the case. AA

Never modify the loop variable inside the body of a for-statement. That would violate every reader's reasonable assumption about what a loop is doing. Consider: XX

```
// bad code:

for (int i = 0; i<100; ++i) {          // for i in the [0:100) range
        cout << i << '\t' << square(i) << '\n';
        ++i;                            // what's going on here? It smells like an error!
}
```

Anyone looking at this loop would reasonably assume that the body would be executed 100 times. However, it isn't. The **++i** in the body ensures that **i** is incremented twice each time around the loop so that we get an output only for the 50 even values of **i**. If we saw such code, we would assume it to be an error, probably caused by a sloppy conversion from a **while**-statement. If you want to increment by 2, say so:

```
// calculate and print a table of squares of even numbers in the [0:100) range:

for (int i = 0; i<100; i+=2)
        cout << i << '\t' << square(i) << '\n';
```

AA Please note that the cleaner, more explicit version is shorter than the messy one. That's typical.

> TRY THIS
>
> Rewrite the character value example from the previous **TRY THIS** to use a **for**-statement. Then modify your program to also write out a table of the integer values for uppercase letters and digits.

There is also a simpler "range-**for**-loop" for traversing collections of data, such as **vector**s; see §3.6.

3.5 Functions

In the program above, what was **square(i)**? It is a call of a function. In particular, it is a call of the function called **square** with the argument **i**. A *function* is a named sequence of statements. A function can return a result (also called a **return**-value). The standard library provides a lot of useful functions, such as the square root function **sqrt()** that we used in §2.4. However, we write many functions ourselves. Here is a plausible definition of **square**:

```
int square(int x)
        // return the square of x
{
        return x*x;
}
```

The first line of this definition tells us that this is a function (that's what the parentheses mean), that it is called **square**, that it takes an **int** argument (here, called **x**), and that it returns an **int** (the type of the result comes first in a function declaration); that is, we can use it like this:

```
cout << square(2) << ' ' < square(10) << '\n';          // print 4 100
```

We don't have to use the result of a function call, but we do have to give a function exactly the arguments it requires. Consider:

```
square(2);                  // probably a mistake: unused return value
int v1 = square();          // error: argument missing
int v2 = square;            // error: parentheses missing
int v3 = square(1,2);       // error: too many arguments
int v4 = square("two");     // error: wrong type of argument; int expected
```

Many compilers warn against unused results, and all give errors as indicated. You might think that a computer should be smart enough to figure out that by the string "two" you really meant the integer 2. However, a C++ compiler deliberately isn't that smart. It is the compiler's job to do exactly what you tell it to do after verifying that your code is well formed according to the definition of C++. If the compiler guessed about what you meant, it would occasionally guess wrong, and you – or the users of your program – would be quite annoyed. You'll find it hard enough to predict what your code will do without having the compiler "help" by second-guessing you. CC

The *function body* is the block (§3.4.2.2) that actually does the work.

```
{
        return x*x;     // return the square of x
}
```

For square, the work is trivial: we produce the square of the argument and return that as our result. Saying that in C++ is easier than saying it in English. That's typical for simple ideas. After all, a programming language is designed to state such simple ideas simply and precisely.

The syntax of a *function definition* can be described like this:

function-definition:
    type-identifier function-identifier (*parameter-list*) *function-body*

That is, a type (the return type), followed by an identifier (the name of the function), followed by a list of parameters in parentheses, followed by the body of the function (the statements to be executed). The list of arguments required by the function is called a *parameter list* and its elements are called *parameters* (or *formal arguments*). The list of parameters can be empty, and if we don't want to return a result we give void (meaning "nothing") as the return type. For example:

```
void write_sorry()
        // take no argument; return no value
{
        cout << "Sorry\n";
}
```

The language-technical aspects of functions will be examined more closely in Chapter 7.

3.5.1 Why bother with functions?

We define a function when we want a separate computation with a name because doing so CC

- Makes the computation logically separate
- Makes the program text clearer (by naming the computation)
- Makes it possible to use the function in more than one place in our program
- Eases testing

We'll see many examples of each of those reasons as we go along, and we'll occasionally mention a reason. Note that real-world programs use thousands of functions, some even hundreds of thousands of functions. Obviously, we would never be able to write or understand such programs if their parts (e.g., computations) were not clearly separated and named. Also, you'll soon find that many functions are repeatedly useful and you'd soon tire of repeating equivalent code. For example, you might be happy writing `x*x` and `7*7` and `(x+7)*(x+7)`, etc. rather than `square(x)` and `square(7)` and `square(x+7)`, etc. However, that's only because `square` is a very simple computation. Consider square root (called `sqrt` in C++): you prefer to write `sqrt(x)` and `sqrt(7)` and `sqrt(x+7)`, etc. rather than repeating the (somewhat complicated and many lines long) code for computing square root. Even better: you don't have to even look at the computation of square root because knowing that `sqrt(x)` gives the square root of `x` is sufficient.

In §7.4, we address many function technicalities, but for now, we'll just give another example.

If we had wanted to make the loop in `main()` in the "first program" (§3.4.2.3) really simple, we could have written

```
void print_square(int v)
{
        cout << v << '\t' << v*v << '\n';
}

int main()
{
        for (int i = 0; i<100; ++i)
                print_square(i);
}
```

Why didn't we use the version using `print_square()`? That version is not significantly simpler than the version using `square()`, and note that

- `print_square()` is a rather specialized function that we could not expect to be able to use later, whereas `square()` is an obvious candidate for other uses
- `square()` hardly requires documentation, whereas `print_square()` obviously needs explanation

The underlying reason for both is that `print_square()` performs two logically separate actions:

- It prints.
- It calculates a square.

AA Programs are usually easier to write and to understand if each function performs a single logical action. Basically, the `square()` version is the better design.

Finally, why did we use `square(i)` rather than simply `i*i` in the first version of the problem? Well, one of the purposes of functions is to simplify code by separating out complicated calculations as named functions, and for the 1949 version of the program there was no hardware that directly implemented "multiply." Consequently, in the 1949 version of the program, `i*i` was actually a fairly complicated calculation, similar to what you'd do by hand using a piece of paper. Also, the writer of that original version, David Wheeler, was the inventor of the function (then called a subroutine) in modern computing, so it seemed appropriate to use it here.

> TRY THIS
>
> Implement **square()** without using the multiplication operator; that is, do the **x*x** by repeated addition (start a variable result at **0** and add **x** to it **x** times). Then run some version of "the first program" using that **square()**.

3.5.2 Function declarations

Did you notice that all the information needed to call a function was in the first line of its definition? For example:

```
int square(int x)
```

Given that, we know enough to say

```
int x = square(44);
```

We don't really need to look at the function body. In real programs, we most often don't want to look at a function body. Why would we want to look at the body of the standard-library **sqrt()** function? We know it calculates the square root of its argument. Why would we want to see the body of our **square()** function? Of course we might just be curious. But almost all of the time, we are just interested in knowing how to call a function – seeing the definition would just be distracting. Fortunately, C++ provides a way of supplying that information separate from the complete function definition. It is called a *function declaration*:

```
int square(int);          // declaration of square
double sqrt(double);      // declaration of sqrt
```

Note the terminating semicolons. A semicolon is used in a function declaration instead of the body used in the corresponding function definition:

```
int square(int x)         // definition of square
{
        return x*x;
}
```

So, if you just want to use a function, you simply write – or more commonly **import** or **#include** – its declaration. The function definition can be elsewhere. We'll discuss where that "elsewhere" might be in §7.3–§7.7.1. This distinction between declarations and definitions becomes essential in larger programs where we use declarations to keep most of the code out of sight to allow us to concentrate on a single part of a program at a time (§3.2).

3.6 vector

To do just about anything of interest in a program, we need a collection of data to work on. For example, we might need a list of phone numbers, a list of members of a football team, a list of courses, a list of books read over the last year, a catalog of songs for download, a set of payment options for a car, a list of the weather forecasts for the next week, a list of prices for a camera in different Web stores, etc. The possibilities are literally endless and therefore ubiquitous in programs. We'll get to see a variety of ways of storing collections of data (a variety of containers of data; see Chapter 19 and Chapter 20). Here we will start with one of the simplest, and arguably the most useful, ways of storing data: a **vector**.

CC

A **vector** is simply a sequence of elements that you can access by an index. For example, here is a **vector** called **v**:

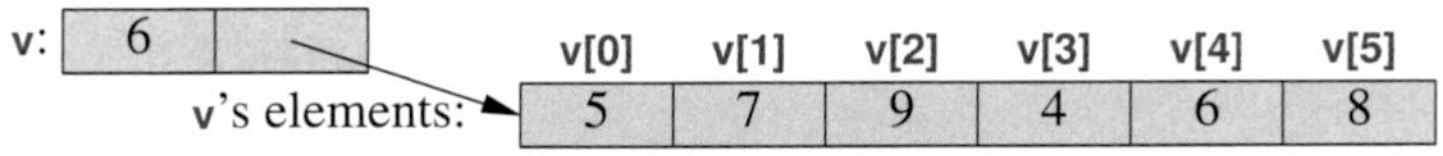

That is, the first element has index 0, the second index 1, and so on. We refer to an element by subscripting the name of the **vector** with the element's index, so here the value of **v[0]** is **5**, the value of **v[1]** is **7**, and so on. Indices for a **vector** always start with 0 and increase by 1. This should look familiar: the standard-library **vector** is simply the C++ standard library's version of an old and well-known idea. I have drawn the vector so as to emphasize that it "knows its size"; that is, a **vector** doesn't just store its elements, it also stores its size.

We could make such a **vector** like this:

```
vector<int> v = {5, 7, 9, 4, 6, 8};        // vector of 6 ints
```

We specify the type of the elements and the initial set of elements. The element type comes after **vector** in angle brackets (**< >**), here **<int>**. Here is another example:

```
vector<string> philosopher = {"Kant", "Plato", "Hume", "Kierkegaard"};   // vector of 4 strings
```

Naturally, a **vector** will only accept elements of its declared element type:

```
philosopher[2] = 99;        // error: trying to assign an int to a string
v[2] = "Hume";              // error: trying to assign a string to an int
```

We can also define a **vector** of a given size without specifying the element values. In that case, we use the **(n)** notation where **n** is the number of elements, and the elements are given a default value according to the element type. For example:

```
vector<int> vi(6);          // vector of 6 ints initialized to 0
vector<string> vs(4);       // vector of 4 strings initialized to ""
```

The string with no characters **""** is called the empty string.

Please note that you cannot simply refer to a nonexistent element of a **vector**:

```
vi[20000] = 44;    // run-time error
```

We will discuss run-time errors and subscripting in the next chapter.

3.6.1 Traversing a vector

A **vector** "knows" its size, so we can print the elements of a **vector** like this:

```
vector<int> v = {5, 7, 9, 4, 6, 8};
for (int i = 0; i<v.size(); ++i)
        cout << v[i] << '\n';
```

The call **v.size()** gives the number of elements of the **vector** called **v**. In general, **v.size()** gives us the ability to access elements of a **vector** without accidentally referring to an element outside the **vector**'s range. The range for a **vector v** is [**0**:**v.size()**). That's the mathematical notation for a half-open sequence of elements. The first element of **v** is **v[0]** and the last **v[v.size()−1]**. If **v.size()==0**, **v** has no elements, that is, **v** is an empty **vector**. This notion of half-open sequences is used throughout C++ and the C++ standard library (§19.2, §20.7).

The language takes advantage of the notion of a half-open sequence to provide a simple loop over all the elements of a sequence, such as the elements of a **vector**. For example:

```
vector<int> v = {5, 7, 9, 4, 6, 8};
for (int x : v)                // for each x in v
        cout << x << '\n';
```

This is called a range-**for**-loop because the word *range* is often used to mean the same as "sequence of elements." We read **for (int x : v)** as "for each **int x in v**" and the meaning of the loop is exactly like the equivalent loop over the subscripts [**0**:**v.size()**). We use the range-**for**-loop for simple loops over all the elements of a sequence looking at one element at a time. More complicated loops, such as looking at every third element of a **vector**, looking at only the second half of a **vector**, or comparing elements of two **vector**s, are usually better done using the more complicated and more general traditional **for**-statement (§3.4.2.3).

3.6.2 Growing a vector

CC

Often, we start a **vector** empty and grow it to its desired size as we read or compute the data we want in it. The key operation here is **push_back()**, which adds a new element to a **vector**. The new element becomes the last element of the **vector**. For example:

```
vector<double> v;      // v starts off empty; that is, v has no elements
```

```
v.push_back(2.7);      // add an element 2.7 to v at the end (back)
```

```
v.push_back(5.6);      // add an element 5.6 to v at the end (back)
```

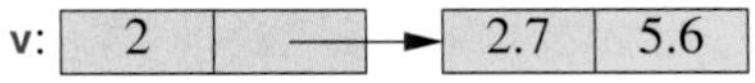

Note the syntax for a call of **push_back()**. It is called a *member function call*; **push_back()** is a member function of **vector** and must be called using this dot notation:

member-function-call:
  object-name . *member-function-name* (*argument-list*)

The size of a **vector** can be obtained by a call to another of **vector**'s member functions: **size()**. Initially **v.size()** was **0**, and after the second call of **push_back()**, **v.size()** has become **2**.

If you have programmed before, you will note that a **vector** is similar to an array in C and other languages. However, you need not specify the size (length) of a **vector** in advance, and you can add as many elements as you like. As we go along, you'll find that the C++ standard **vector** has other useful properties.

3.6.3 A numeric example

Let's look at a more realistic example. Often, we have a series of values that we want to read into our program so that we can do something with them. The "something" could be producing a graph of the values, calculating the mean and median, finding the largest element, sorting them, combining them with other data, searching for "interesting" values, comparing them to other data, etc. There is no limit to the range of computations we might perform on data, but first we need to get it into our computer's memory. Here is the basic technique for getting an unknown – possibly large – amount of data into a computer. As a concrete example, we chose to read in floating-point numbers representing temperatures:

```
int main()
     // read some temperatures into a vector
{
     vector<double> temps;               // temperatures
     for (double temp; cin>>temp; )      // read into temp
          temps.push_back(temp);         // put temp into vector
     // . . . do something . . .
}
```

So, what goes on here? First we declare a **vector** to hold the data:

```
vector<double> temps;   // temperatures
```

This is where the type of input we expect is mentioned. We read and store **double**s.

Next comes the actual read loop:

```
for (double temp; cin>>temp; )      // read into temp
     temps.push_back(temp);         // put temp into vector
```

We define a variable **temp** of type **double** to read into. The **cin>>temp** reads a **double**, and that **double** is pushed into the **vector** (placed at the back). We have seen those individual operations before. What's new here is that we use the input operation, **cin>>temp**, as the condition for a **for**-statement. Basically, **cin>>temp** is true if a value was read correctly and false otherwise, so that **for**-statement will read all the **double**s we give it and stop when we give it anything else. For example, if you typed

```
1.2 3.4 5.6 7.8 9.0 |
```

then **temps** would get the five elements **1.2**, **3.4**, **5.6**, **7.8**, **9.0** (in that order, for example, **temps[0]==1.2**). We used the character **'|'** to terminate the input – anything that isn't a **double** can be used. In §9.4 we discuss how to terminate input and how to deal with errors in input.

To limit the scope of our input variable, **temp**, to the loop, we used a **for**-statement, rather than a **while**-statement:

```
double temp;
while (cin>>temp)             // read
     temps.push_back(temp);   // put into vector
// ... temp might be used here ...
```

As usual, a **for**-loop shows what is going on "up front" so that the code is easier to understand and accidental errors are harder to make.

Once we get data into a **vector** we can easily manipulate it. As an example, let's calculate the mean and median temperatures:

```
int main()
	// compute mean and median temperatures
{
	vector<double> temps;				// temperatures
	for (double temp; cin>>temp; )		// read into temp
		temps.push_back(temp);			// put temp into vector

	// compute mean temperature:
	double sum = 0;
	for (double x : temps)
		sum += x;
	cout << "Average temperature: " << sum/temps.size() << '\n';

	// compute median temperature:
	ranges::sort(temps);					// sort the temperatures
	cout << "Median temperature: " << temps[temps.size()/2] << '\n';
}
```

We calculate the average (the mean) by simply adding all the elements into **sum**, and then dividing the sum by the number of elements (that is, **temps.size()**):

```
// compute average temperature:
double sum = 0;
for (double x : temps)
	sum += x;
cout << "Average temperature: " << sum/temps.size() << '\n';
```

Note how the **+=** operator comes in handy.

To calculate a median (a value chosen so that half of the values are lower and the other half are higher) we need to sort the elements. For that, we use a variant of the standard-library **sort** algorithm, **sort()**:

```
// compute median temperature:
ranges::sort(temps);					// sort the temperatures
cout << "Median temperature: " << temps[temps.size()/2] << '\n';
```

We will explain the standard-library algorithms much later (Chapter 21). Once the temperatures are sorted, it's easy to find the median: we just pick the middle element, the one with index **temps.size()/2**. If you feel like being picky (and if you do, you are starting to think like a programmer), you could observe that the value we found may not be a median according to the definition we offered above. Exercise 3 at the end of this chapter is designed to solve that problem.

We deliberately left a potentially worse problem in that code. Did you spot it? What happens if we don't enter any temperature values? In that case, all is well until we try to output the median temperature. Then, we try to read **temps[temps.size()/2]** but **temp.size()** is zero, so there is no element to read! Fortunately, if you use an implementation of **vector** that does range checking, the error is caught and reported. If you use our PPP support that's what happens. Forgetting the case of no elements is a common problem when iterating; always consider that possibility.

3.6.4 A text example

We didn't present the temperature example because we were particularly interested in temperatures. Many people – such as meteorologists, agronomists, and oceanographers – are very interested in temperature data and values based on it, such as means and medians. However, we are not. From a programmer's point of view, what's interesting about this example is its generality: the **vector** and the simple operations on it can be used in a huge range of applications. It is fair to say that whatever you are interested in, if you need to analyze data, you'll use **vector** (or a similar data structure; see Chapter 15). As an example, let's build a simple dictionary:

```
int main()
    // simple dictionary: list of sorted words
{
    vector<string> words;
    for(string temp; cin>>temp; )              // read whitespace-separated words
        words.push_back(temp);                 // put into vector
    cout << "Number of words: " << words.size() << '\n';

    ranges::sort(words);                       // sort the words

    for (int i = 0; i<words.size(); ++i)
        if (i==0 || words[i-1]!=words[i])      // is this a new word?
            cout << words[i] << "\n";
}
```

If we feed some words to this program, it will write them out in order without repeating a word. For example, given

```
a man a plan a canal panama
```

it will write

```
a
canal
man
panama
plan
```

How do we stop reading string input? In other words, how do we terminate the input loop?

```
for (string temp; cin>>temp; )      // read
    words.push_back(temp);          // put into vector
```

When we read numbers (in §3.6.2), we just gave some input character that wasn't a number. We can't do that here because every (ordinary) character can be read into a **string**. Fortunately, there are characters that are "not ordinary." As mentioned in §2.5.1, Ctrl+Z terminates an input stream under Windows and Ctrl+D does that under Linux.

Most of this program is remarkably similar to what we did for the temperatures. In fact, we wrote the "dictionary program" by cutting and pasting from the "temperature program." The only thing that's new is the test

```
if (i==0 || words[i-1]!=words[i])    // is this a new word?
```

If you deleted that test the output would be

```
a
a
a
canal
man
panama
plan
```

We didn't like the repetition, so we eliminated it using that test. What does the test do? It looks to see if the previous word we printed is different from the one we are about to print (**words[i–1]!=words[i]**) and if so, we print that word; otherwise, we do not. Obviously, we can't talk about a previous word when we are about to print the first word (**i==0**), so we first test for that and combine those two tests using the || (or) operator:

```
if (i==0 || words[i-1]!=words[i])    // is this a new word?
```

Note that we can compare strings. We use **!=** (not equals) here; **==** (equals), **<** (less than), **<=** (less than or equal), **>** (greater than), and **>=** (greater than or equal) also work for strings. The **<**, **>**, etc. operators use the usual lexicographical ordering, so **"Ape"** comes before **"Apple"** and **"Chimpanzee"**.

> TRY THIS
>
> Write a program that "bleeps" out words that you don't like; that is, you read in words using **cin** and print them again on **cout**. If a word is among a few you have defined, you write out **BLEEP** instead of that word. Start with one "disliked word" such as
>
> ```
> string disliked = "Broccoli";
> ```
>
> When that works, add a few more.

3.7 Language features

The temperature and dictionary programs used most of the fundamental language features we presented in this chapter: iteration (the **for**-statement and the **while**-statement), selection (the **if**-statement), simple arithmetic (the **++** and **+=** operators), comparisons and logical operators (the **==**, **!=**, and || operators), variables, and functions (e.g., **main()**, **sort()**, and **size()**). In addition, we used standard-library facilities, such as **vector** (a container of elements), **cout** (an output stream), and **sort()** (an algorithm).

If you count, you'll find that we actually achieved quite a lot with rather few features. That's **CC** the ideal! Each programming language feature exists to express a fundamental idea, and we can combine them in a huge (really, infinite) number of ways to write useful programs. This is a key notion: a computer is not a gadget with a fixed function. Instead, it is a machine that we can program to do any computation we can think of, and given that we can attach computers to gadgets that interact with the world outside the computer, we can in principle get it to do anything.

Drill

Go through this drill step by step. Do not try to speed up by skipping steps. Test each step by entering at least three pairs of values – more values would be better.

[1] Write a program that consists of a while-loop that (each time around the loop) reads in two ints and then prints them. Exit the program when a terminating '|' is entered.

[2] Change the program to write out the smaller value is: followed by the smaller of the numbers and the larger value is: followed by the larger value.

[3] Augment the program so that it writes the line the numbers are equal (only) if they are equal.

[4] Change the program so that it uses doubles instead of ints.

[5] Change the program so that it writes out the numbers are almost equal after writing out which is the larger and the smaller if the two numbers differ by less than 1.0/100.

[6] Now change the body of the loop so that it reads just one double each time around. Define two variables to keep track of which is the smallest and which is the largest value you have seen so far. Each time through the loop write out the value entered. If it's the smallest so far, write the smallest so far after the number. If it is the largest so far, write the largest so far after the number.

[7] Add a unit to each double entered; that is, enter values such as 10cm, 2.5in, 5ft, or 3.33m. Accept the four units: cm, m, in, ft. Assume conversion factors 1m==100cm, 1in==2.54cm, 1ft==12in. Read the unit indicator into a string. You may consider 12 m (with a space between the number and the unit) equivalent to 12m (without a space).

[8] Reject values without units or with "illegal" representations of units, such as y, yard, meter, km, and gallons.

[9] Keep track of the sum of values entered (as well as the smallest and the largest) and the number of values entered. When the loop ends, print the smallest, the largest, the number of values, and the sum of values. Note that to keep the sum, you have to decide on a unit to use for that sum; use meters.

[10] Keep all the values entered (converted into meters) in a vector. At the end, write out those values.

[11] Before writing out the values from the vector, sort them (that'll make them come out in increasing order).

Review

[1] What is a computation?

[2] What do we mean by inputs and outputs to a computation? Give examples.

[3] What are the three requirements a programmer should keep in mind when expressing computations?

[4] What does an expression do?

[5] What is the difference between a statement and an expression, as described in this chapter?

[6] What is an lvalue? List the operators that require an lvalue. Why do these operators, and not the others, require an lvalue?

[7] What is a constant expression?

[8] What is a literal?
[9] What is a symbolic constant and why do we use them?
[10] What is a magic constant? Give examples.
[11] What are some operators that we can use for integers and floating-point values?
[12] What operators can be used on integers but not on floating-point numbers?
[13] What are some operators that can be used for strings?
[14] When would a programmer prefer a switch-statement to an if-statement?
[15] What are some common problems with switch-statements?
[16] What is the function of each part of the header line in a for-loop, and in what sequence are they executed?
[17] When should the for-loop be used and when should the while-loop be used?
[18] Describe what the line char foo(int x) means in a function definition.
[19] When should you define a separate function for part of a program? List reasons.
[20] What can you do to an int that you cannot do to a string?
[21] What can you do to a string that you cannot do to an int?
[22] What is the index of the third element of a vector?
[23] How do you write a for-loop that prints every element of a vector?
[24] What does vector<char> alphabet(26); do?
[25] Describe what push_back() does to a vector.
[26] What does vector's member size() do?
[27] What makes vector so popular/useful?
[28] How do you sort the elements of a vector?

Terms

abstraction	range-for-statement	push_back()	for-statement
function	repetition	computation	if-statement
rvalue	conditional statement	increment	selection
declaration	input	size()	definition
iteration	sort()	divide-and-conquer	loop
statement	else	lvalue	switch-statement
while-statement	member function	vector	expression
output			

Exercises

[1] If you haven't already, do the TRY THIS exercises from this chapter.
[2] Write a program that reads a string from input and then, for each character read, prints out the character and its integer value on a line.
[3] If we define the median of a sequence as "a number so that exactly as many elements come before it in the sequence as come after it," fix the program in §3.6.3 so that it always prints out a median. Hint: A median need not be an element of the sequence.

[4] Read a sequence of **double** values into a **vector**. Think of each value as the distance between two cities along a given route. Compute and print the total distance (the sum of all distances). Find and print the smallest and greatest distance between two neighboring cities. Find and print the mean distance between two neighboring cities.

[5] Write a program to play a numbers guessing game. The user thinks of a number between 1 and 100 and your program asks questions to figure out what the number is (e.g., "Is the number you are thinking of less than 50?"). Your program should be able to identify the number after asking no more than seven questions.

[6] Write a program that performs as a very simple calculator. Your calculator should be able to handle the four basic math operations – add, subtract, multiply, and divide – on two input values. Your program should prompt the user to enter three arguments: two **double** values and a character to represent an operation. If the entry arguments are **35.6**, **24.1**, and **'+'**, the program output should be **The sum of 35.6 and 24.1 is 59.7**. In Chapter 5 and Chapter 6, we look at a much more sophisticated simple calculator.

[7] Make a **vector** holding the ten **string** values **"zero"**, **"one"**, . . . **"nine"**. Use that in a program that converts a digit to its corresponding spelled-out value; e.g., the input **7** gives the output **seven**. Have the same program, using the same input loop, convert spelled-out numbers into their digit form; e.g., the input **seven** gives the output **7**.

[8] Modify the "mini calculator" from exercise 6 to accept (just) single-digit numbers written as either digits or spelled out.

[9] There is an old story that the emperor wanted to thank the inventor of the game of chess and asked the inventor to name his reward. The inventor asked for one grain of rice for the first square, 2 for the second, 4 for the third, and so on, doubling for each of the 64 squares. That may sound modest, but there wasn't that much rice in the empire! Write a program to calculate how many squares are required to give the inventor at least 1000 grains of rice, at least 1,000,000 grains, and at least 1,000,000,000 grains. You'll need a loop, of course, and probably an **int** to keep track of which square you are at, an **int** to keep the number of grains on the current square, and an **int** to keep track of the grains on all previous squares. We suggest that you write out the value of all your variables for each iteration of the loop so that you can see what's going on.

[10] Try to calculate the number of rice grains that the inventor asked for in exercise 9 above. You'll find that the number is so large that it won't fit in an **int** or a **double**. Observe what happens when the number gets too large to represent exactly as an **int** and as a **double**. What is the largest number of squares for which you can calculate the exact number of grains (using an **int**)? What is the largest number of squares for which you can calculate the approximate number of grains (using a **double**)?

[11] Write a program that plays the game "Rock, Paper, Scissors." If you are not familiar with the game do some research (e.g., on the Web using Google). Research is a common task for programmers. Use a **switch**-statement to solve this exercise. Also, the machine should give random answers (i.e., select the next rock, paper, or scissors randomly). Real randomness is too hard to provide just now, so just build a **vector** with a sequence of values to be used as "the next value." If you build the **vector** into the program, it will always play the same game, so maybe you should let the user enter some values. Try variations to make it less easy for the user to guess which move the machine will make next.

[12] Create a program to find all the prime numbers between 1 and 100. One way to do this is to write a function that will check if a number is prime (i.e., see if the number can be divided by a prime number smaller than itself) using a **vector** of primes in order (so that if the **vector** is called **primes**, **primes[0]==2**, **primes[1]==3**, **primes[2]==5**, etc.). Then write a loop that goes from 1 to 100, checks each number to see if it is a prime, and stores each prime found in a **vector**. Write another loop that lists the primes you found. You might check your result by comparing your **vector** of prime numbers with **primes**. Consider 2 the first prime.

[13] Create a program to find all the prime numbers between 1 and 100. There is a classic method for doing this, called the "Sieve of Eratosthenes." If you don't know that method, get on the Web and look it up. Write your program using this method.

[14] Write a program that takes an input value **n** and then finds the first **n** primes.

[15] In the drill, you wrote a program that, given a series of numbers, found the max and min of that series. The number that appears the most times in a sequence is called the *mode*. Create a program that finds the mode of a set of positive integers.

[16] Write a program that finds the min, max, and mode of a sequence of **string**s.

[17] Write a program to solve quadratic equations. A quadratic equation is of the form $ax^2 + bx + c = 0$. If you don't know the formula for solving such an expression, do some research. Remember, researching how to solve a problem is often necessary before a programmer can teach the computer how to solve it. Use **double**s for the user inputs for **a**, **b**, and **c**. Since there are two solutions to a quadratic equation, output both **x1** and **x2**.

[18] Write a program where you first enter a set of name-and-value pairs, such as **Joe 17** and **Barbara 22**. For each pair, add the name to a **vector** called **names** and the number to a **vector** called **scores** (in corresponding positions, so that if **names[7]=="Joe"** then **scores[7]==17**). Terminate input with **NoName 0**. Check that each name is unique and terminate with an error message if a name is entered twice. Write out all the (name,score) pairs, one per line.

[19] Modify the program from the previous exercise so that once you have entered the name-and-value pairs, you ask for values: In a loop, when you enter a name, the program will output the corresponding score or **name not found**.

[20] Modify the program from the previous exercise so that once you have entered the name-and-value pairs, you ask for names: In a loop, when you enter a value, the program will output all the names with that score or **score not found**.

Postscript

From a philosophical point of view, you can now do everything that can be done using a computer – the rest is details! Among other things, this shows the value of "details" and the importance of practical skills, because clearly you have barely started as a programmer. But we are serious. The tools presented so far do allow you to express every computation: you have as many variables (including **vector**s and **string**s) as you want, you have arithmetic and comparisons, and you have selection and iteration. Every computation can be expressed using those primitives. You have text and numeric input and output, and every input or output can be expressed as text (even graphics). You can even organize your computations as sets of named functions. What is left for you to do is "just" to learn to write good programs, that is, to write programs that are correct, maintainable, and reasonably efficient. Importantly, you must try to learn to do so with a reasonable amount of effort.

4

Errors!

I realized that from now on a large part
of my life would be spent finding and
correcting my own mistakes.
– Maurice Wilkes, 1949

In this chapter, we discuss correctness of programs, errors, and error handling. If you are a genuine novice, you'll find the discussion a bit abstract at times and painfully detailed at other times. Can error handling really be this important? It is, and you'll learn that one way or another before you can write programs that others are willing to use. What we are trying to do is to show you what "thinking like a programmer" is about. It combines fairly abstract strategy with painstaking analysis of details and alternatives.

§4.1 Introduction
§4.2 Sources of errors
§4.3 Compile-time errors
  Syntax errors; Type errors
§4.4 Link-time errors
§4.5 Run-time errors
  The caller deals with errors; The callee deals with errors; Error reporting
§4.6 Exceptions
  Bad arguments; Range errors; Bad input
§4.7 Avoiding and finding errors
  Estimation; Debugging; Assertions; Testing; Random numbers

4.1 Introduction

We have referred to errors repeatedly in the previous chapters, and – having done the drills and some exercises – you have some idea why. Errors are simply unavoidable when you develop a program, yet the final program must be free of errors, or at least free of errors that we consider unacceptable for it.

CC There are many ways of classifying errors. For example:

- *Compile-time errors*: Errors found by the compiler. We can further classify compile-time errors based on which language rules they violate, for example:
  - Syntax errors
  - Type errors
- *Link-time errors*: Errors found by the linker when it is trying to combine object files into an executable program.
- *Run-time errors*: Errors found by checks in a running program. We can further classify run-time errors as
  - Errors detected by the computer (hardware and/or operating system)
  - Errors detected by a library (e.g., the standard library)
  - Errors detected by user code

  Such errors are also called *Logic errors*.

This list is actually a bit optimistic. We "forgot" to mention two of the nastiest kind of errors:

- Undetected logic errors leading to crashes or wrong results.
- Mismatches between what the user needs and what the code delivers.

AA It is tempting to say that our job as programmers is to eliminate all errors. That is of course the ideal, but often that's not feasible. In fact, for real-world programs it can be hard to know exactly what "all errors" means. If we kicked out the power cord from your computer while it executed your program, would that be an error that you were supposed to handle? In many cases, the answer is "Obviously not," but what if we were talking about a medical monitoring program or the control program for a telephone switch? In those cases, a user could reasonably expect that something in the system of which your program was a part will do something sensible even if your computer lost power or a cosmic ray damaged the memory holding your program. The key question becomes:

Is my program supposed to detect that error?

Unless we specifically say otherwise, we will assume that your program

[1] Should produce the desired results for all legal inputs
[2] Should give reasonable error messages for all illegal inputs
[3] Need not worry about misbehaving hardware
[4] Need not worry about misbehaving system software
[5] Is allowed to terminate after finding an error

Essentially all programs for which assumptions 3, 4, or 5 do not hold can be considered advanced and beyond the scope of this book. However, assumptions 1 and 2 are included in the definition of basic professionalism, and professionalism is one of our goals. Even if we don't meet that ideal 100% of the time, it must be the ideal.

When we write programs, errors are natural and unavoidable; the question is: How do we deal with them? Our guess is that avoiding, finding, and correcting errors takes 90% or more of the effort when developing serious software. For safety-critical programs, the effort can be greater still.

You can do much better for small programs; on the other hand, you can easily do worse if you're sloppy.

Basically, we offer three approaches to producing acceptable software: AA

- Organize software to minimize errors.
- Eliminate most of the errors we made through debugging and testing.
- Make sure the remaining errors are not serious.

None of these approaches can completely eliminate errors by itself; we have to use all three.

Experience matters immensely when it comes to producing reliable programs, that is, programs that can be relied on to do what they are supposed to do with an acceptable error rate. Please don't forget that the ideal is that our programs always do the right thing. We are usually able only to approximate that ideal, but that's no excuse for not trying very hard.

4.2 Sources of errors

Here are some sources of errors: CC

- *Poor specification*: If we are not specific about what a program should do, we are unlikely to adequately examine the "dark corners" and make sure that all cases are handled (i.e., that every input gives a correct answer or an adequate error message).
- *Incomplete programs*: During development, there are obviously cases that we haven't yet taken care of. That's unavoidable. What we must aim for is to know when we have handled all cases.
- *Unexpected arguments*: Functions take arguments. If a function is given an argument we don't handle, we have a problem. An example is calling the standard-library square root function with -1.2: **sqrt(−1.2)**. Since **sqrt()** of a **double** returns a **double**, there is no possible correct return value. §4.5 and §4.7.3.1 discuss this kind of problem.
- *Unexpected input*: Programs typically read data (from a keyboard, from files, from GUIs, from network connections, etc.). A program makes many assumptions about such input, for example, that the user will input a number. What if the user inputs "aw, shut up!" rather than the expected integer? §4.5 and §9.4 discuss this kind of problem.
- *Unexpected state*: Most programs keep a lot of data ("state") around for use by different parts of the system. Examples are address lists, phone directories, and **vector**s of temperature readings. What if such data is incomplete or wrong? The various parts of the program must still manage. PPP2.26.3.5 discusses this kind of problem.
- *Logical errors*: That is, code that simply doesn't do what it was supposed to do; we'll just have to find and fix such problems. §5.6 and §5.7 give examples of finding such problems.

This list has a practical use. We can use it as a checklist when we are considering how far we have come with a program. No program is complete until we have considered all of these potential sources of errors. In fact, it is prudent to keep them in mind from the very start of a project, because it is most unlikely that a program that is just thrown together without thought about errors can have its errors found and removed without a serious rewrite.

4.3 Compile-time errors

When you are writing programs, your compiler is your first line of defense against errors. Before generating code, the compiler analyzes code to detect syntax errors and type errors. Only if it finds that the program conforms to the language specification will it allow you to proceed. Many of the errors that the compiler finds are simply "silly errors" caused by mistyping or incomplete edits of the source code. Others result from flaws in our understanding of the way parts of our program interact. To a beginner, the compiler often seems petty, but as you learn to use the language facilities – and especially the type system – to directly express your ideas, you'll come to appreciate the compiler's ability to detect problems that would otherwise have caused you hours of tedious searching for bugs.

As an example, we will look at some calls of this simple function:

```
int area(int length, int width);    // calculate area of a rectangle
```

4.3.1 Syntax errors

What if we were to call area() like this:

```
int s1 = area(7,2;          // error: ) missing
int s2 = area(7,2)          // error: ; missing
Int s3 = area(7,2);         // error: Int (with a capitalized 'i') is not a type
int s4 = area('7,2);        // error: non-terminated character '; terminating ' is missing)
```

AA Each of those lines has a syntax error; that is, they are not well formed according to the C++ grammar, so the compiler will reject them. Unfortunately, syntax errors are not always easy to report in a way that you, the programmer, find easy to understand. That's because the compiler may have to read a bit further than the error to be sure that there really is an error. The effect of this is that even though syntax errors tend to be completely trivial (you'll often find it hard to believe you have made such a mistake once you find it), the reporting is often cryptic and occasionally refers to a line further on in the program. So, for syntax errors, if you don't see anything wrong with the line the compiler points to, also look at earlier lines in the program.

Note that the compiler has no idea what you are trying to do, so it cannot report errors in terms of your intent, only in terms of what you did. For example, given the error in the declaration of s3 above, a compiler is unlikely to say

You misspelled int*; don't capitalize the* i.

Rather, it'll say something like

*Syntax error: missing ';' before identifier '*s3*'*
*'*s3*' missing storage-class or type identifiers*
*'*Int*' missing storage-class or type identifiers*

Such messages tend to be cryptic, until you get used to them, and to use a vocabulary that can be hard to penetrate. Different compilers can give very different-looking error messages for the same code. Fortunately, you soon get used to reading such stuff. After all, a quick look at those cryptic lines can be read as

There was a syntax error before s3*, and it had something to do with the type of* Int *or* s3.

Given that, it's not rocket science to find the problem.

> TRY THIS
>
> Try to compile those examples and see how the compiler responds.

4.3.2 Type errors

Once you have removed syntax errors, the compiler will start reporting type errors; that is, it will report mismatches between the types you declared (or forgot to declare) for your variables, functions, etc. and the types of values or expressions you assign to them, pass as function arguments, etc. For example:

```
int x0 = arena(7,2);            // error: undeclared function
int x1 = area(7);               // error: wrong number of arguments
int x2 = area("seven",2);       // error: 1st argument has a wrong type
```

Let's consider these errors.

- For **arena(7,2)**, we misspelled **area** as **arena**, so the compiler thinks we want to call a function called **arena**. (What else could it "think"? That's what we said.) Assuming there is no function called **arena()**, you'll get an error message complaining about an undeclared function. If there is a function called **arena**, and if that function accepts **(7,2)**, you have a worse problem: the program will compile but do something you didn't expect it to (that's a logical error; see §4.5).
- For **area(7)**, the compiler detects the wrong number of arguments. In C++, every function call must provide the expected number of arguments, of the right types, and in the right order. When the type system is used appropriately, this can be a powerful tool for avoiding run-time errors (§12.1).
- For **area("seven",2)**, you might hope that the computer would look at **"seven"** and figure out that you meant the integer **7**. It won't. If a function needs an integer, you can't give it a string. C++ does support some implicit type conversions (see §2.9) but not **string** to **int**. The compiler does not try to guess what you meant. What would you have expected for **area("Hovel lane",2)**, **area("7,2")**, and **area("sieben","dos")**?

These are just a few examples. There are many more errors that the compiler will find for you.

> TRY THIS
>
> Try to compile those examples and see how the compiler responds. Try thinking of a few more errors yourself and try those.

As you work with the compiler, you'll wish that it was smart enough to figure out what you meant; that is, you'd like some of the errors it reports not to be errors. That's natural. More surprisingly, as you gain experience, you'll begin to wish that the compiler would reject more code, rather than less. Consider:

```
int x4 = area(10,–7);           // OK: but what is a rectangle with a width of minus 7?
int x5 = area(10.7,9.3);        // OK: but calls area(10,9)
char x6 = area(100,9999);       // OK: but truncates the result
```

For **x4** we get no error message from the compiler. From the compiler's point of view, **area(10,–7)** is fine: **area()** asks for two integers and you gave them to it; nobody said that those arguments had to be positive.

For **x5**, a good compiler will warn about the truncation of the floating-point values **10.7** and **9.3** into the integers **10** and **9** (see §2.9). However, the (ancient) language rules state that you can implicitly convert a **double** to an **int**, so the compiler is not allowed to reject the call **area(10.7,9.3)**. If you really mean to narrow, do so explicitly (§7.4.7).

As you gain experience, you'll learn how to get the most out of the compiler's ability to detect errors and to dodge its known weaknesses. However, don't get overconfident: "my program compiled" doesn't mean that it will run correctly. Even when it does run, it typically gives wrong results at first until you find the flaws in your logic.

Furthermore, there are many tools that will help by detecting and reporting constructs that are not obviously violating language rules, but that we'd like caught. Many such tools are domain specific because what's acceptable in some kind of program may not be in some other kind. The programs enforcing the C++ Core Guidelines [CG] are examples of such tools.

4.4 Link-time errors

CC A program consists of several separately compiled parts, called *translation units* or *modules*. Every function in a program must be declared with exactly the same type in every translation unit in which it is used. Every function must also be defined exactly once in a program. If either of these rules is violated, the linker will give an error. We discuss how to avoid link-time errors in §7.6 and §7.7. For now, here is an example of a program that might give a typical linker error:

```
int area(int length, int width);          // calculate area of a rectangle

int main()
{
        int x = area(2,3);
}
```

Unless we somehow have defined **area()** in another source file and linked the code generated from that source file to this code, the linker will complain that it didn't find a definition of **area()**.

The definition of **area()** must have exactly the same types (both the return type and the argument types) as we used in our file, that is:

```
int area(int x, int y) { /* ... */ }                 // "our" area()
```

Functions with the same name but different types will not match and will be ignored:

```
double area(double x, double y) { /* ... */ }      // not "our" area()
int area(int x, int y, char unit) { /* ... */ }     // not "our" area()
```

Note that a misspelled function name doesn't usually give a linker error. Instead, the compiler gives an error immediately when it sees a call to an undeclared function. That's good: compile-time errors are found earlier than link-time errors and are typically easier to fix.

The linkage rules for functions, as stated above, also hold for all other entities of a program, such as variables and types: there has to be exactly one definition of an entity with a given name, but there can be many declarations, and all have to agree exactly on its type. See also §7.2 and §7.3.

4.5 Run-time errors

Once we have removed the initial compiler and linker errors, the program runs. Typically, what happens next is that no output is produced or that the output produced by the program is just wrong. This can occur for a number of reasons. Maybe your understanding of the underlying program logic is flawed; maybe you didn't write what you thought you wrote; or maybe you made some "silly error" in one of your **if**-statements, or whatever. Such logic errors are usually the most difficult to find and eliminate, because at this stage the computer does exactly what you asked it to. Your job now is to figure out why what you wrote wasn't really what you meant. Basically, a computer is a very fast moron. It does exactly what you tell it to do, and that can be most humbling. When you write the program you are able to detect errors, but it is not always easy to know what to do with an error once you catch it at run time. Consider:

```
int area(int length, int width)
        // calculate area of a rectangle
{
        return length*width;
}

int framed_area(int x, int y)
        // calculate area within frame
{
        return area(x-2,y-2);
}

void test(int x, int y, int z)
{
        int area1 = area(x,y);
        int area2 = framed_area(1,z);
        int area3 = framed_area(y,z);
        double ratio = double(area1)/area3;        // convert to double to get floating-point division
        // ...
}
```

We know that dividing one integer with another gives an integer result (§2.4), so instead of plain **area1/area3**, we converted **area1** to a **double** to get a proper ratio. AA

Now we can test:

```
int main()
{
        test(-1,2,3);
}
```

We separated the definition of the values **-1**, **2**, and **3** from their use in **test()** to make the problems less obvious to the human reader and harder for the compiler to detect. However, these calls lead to negative values, representing areas, being assigned to **area1** and **area2**. Should we accept such erroneous results, which violate most notions of math and physics? If not, who should detect the errors: the caller of **area()** or the function itself? And how should such errors be reported?

Before answering those questions, look at the calculation of the **ratio** in the code above. It looks innocent enough. Did you notice something wrong with it? If not, look again: **area3** will be **0**, so that **double(area1)/area3** divides by zero. This leads to a hardware-detected error that terminates the program with some cryptic message relating to hardware. This is the kind of error that you – or your users – will have to deal with if you don't detect and deal sensibly with run-time errors. Most people have low tolerance for such "hardware violations" because to anyone not intimately familiar with the program all the information provided is "Something went wrong somewhere!" That's insufficient for any constructive action, so we feel angry and would like to yell at whoever supplied the program.

So, let's tackle the problem of argument errors with **area()**. We have two obvious alternatives:

- Let the caller of **area()** deal with bad arguments.
- Let **area()** (the called function) deal with bad arguments.

4.5.1 The caller deals with errors

Let's try the first alternative ("Let the user beware!") first. That's the one we'd have to choose if **area()** was a function in a library where we couldn't modify it. For better or worse, this is the most common approach.

Protecting the call of **area(x,y)** in **main()** is relatively easy:

```
if (x<=0)
      error("non-positive x");
if (y<=0)
      error("non-positive y");
int area1 = area(x,y);
```

Really, the only question is what to do if we find an error. Here, we have called a function **error()** which we assume will do something sensible. In fact, in **PPP_support** we supply an **error()** that by default terminates the program with a system error message plus the string we passed as an argument to **error()**. If you prefer to write out your own error message or take other actions, you catch **runtime_error** (§4.6.3, §6.3, §6.7). This approach suffices for most student programs and is an example of a style that can be used for more sophisticated error handling.

If we didn't need separate error messages about each argument, we would simplify:

```
if (x<=0 || y<=0)                    // || means "or"
      error("non-positive area() argument");
int area1 = area(x,y);
```

To complete protecting **area()** from bad arguments, we have to deal with the calls through **framed_area()**. We could write

```
if (z<=2)
      error("non-positive 2nd area() argument called by framed_area()");
int area2 = framed_area(1,z);
// ...
if (y<=2 || z<=2)
      error("non-positive area() argument called by framed_area()");
int area3 = framed_area(y,z);
```

This is messy, but there is also something fundamentally wrong. We could write this only by knowing exactly how framed_area() used area(). We had to know that framed_area() subtracted 2 from each argument. We shouldn't have to know such details! What if someone modified framed_area() to use 1 instead of 2? Someone doing that would have to look at every call of framed_area() and modify the error-checking code correspondingly. Such code is called "brittle" because it breaks easily. This is also an example of a "magic constant" (§3.3.1). We could make the code less brittle by giving the value subtracted by framed_area() a name:

```
constexpr int frame_width = 2;

int framed_area(int x, int y)
    // calculate area within frame
{
    return area(x−frame_width,y−frame_width);
}
```

That name could be used by code calling framed_area():

```
if (1−frame_width<=0 || z−frame_width<=0)
    error("non−positive argument for area() called by framed_area()");
int area2 = framed_area(1,z);
if (y−frame_width<=0 || z−frame_width<=0)
    error("non−positive argument for area() called by framed_area()");
int area3 = framed_area(y,z);
```

Look at that code! Are you sure it is correct? Do you find it pretty? Is it easy to read? Actually, we find it very ugly (and therefore error-prone). We have more than tripled the size of the code and exposed an implementation detail of framed_area(). There has to be a better way!

Look at the original code:

```
int area2 = framed_area(1,z);
int area3 = framed_area(y,z);
```

It may be wrong, but at least we can see what it is supposed to do. We can keep this code if we put the check inside framed_area().

4.5.2 The callee deals with errors

Checking for valid arguments within framed_area() is easy, and error() can still be used to report a problem:

```
int framed_area(int x, int y)
    // calculate area within frame
{
    constexpr int frame_width = 2;
    if (x−frame_width<=0 || y−frame_width<=0)
        error("non−positive area() argument called by framed_area()");
    return area(x−frame_width,y−frame_width);
}
```

This is rather nice, and we no longer have to write a test for each call of **framed_area()**. For a useful function that we call 500 times in a large program, that can be a huge advantage. Furthermore, if anything to do with the error handling changes, we only have to modify the code in one place.

Note something interesting: we almost unconsciously slid from the "caller must check the arguments" approach to the "function must check its own arguments" approach (also called "the callee checks" because a called function is often called "a callee"). One benefit of the latter approach is that the argument-checking code is in one place. We don't have to search the whole program for calls. Furthermore, that one place is exactly where the arguments are to be used, so all the information we need is easily available for us to do the check.

Let's apply this solution to **area()**:

```
int area(int length, int width)
     // calculate area of a rectangle
{
     if (length<=0 || width<=0)
          error("non-positive area() argument");
     return length*width;
}
```

This will catch all errors in calls to **area()**, so we no longer need to check in **framed_area()**. We might want to, though, to get a better – more specific – error message.

Checking arguments in the function seems so simple, so why don't people do that always? Inattention to error handling is one answer, sloppiness is another, but there are also respectable reasons:

- *We can't modify the function definition*: The function is in a library that for some reason can't be changed. Maybe it's used by others who don't share your notions of what constitutes good error handling. Maybe it's owned by someone else and you don't have the source code. Maybe it's in a library where new versions come regularly so that if you made a change in your copy, you'd have to repeat your change again for each new release of the library.
- *The called function doesn't know what to do in case of error*: This is typically the case for library functions. The library writer can detect the error, but only you (the caller) know what is to be done when an error occurs.
- *The called function doesn't know where it was called from*: When you get an error message, it tells you that something is wrong, but not how the executing program got to that point. Sometimes, you want an error message to be more specific.
- *Performance:* For a small function the cost of a check can be more than the cost of calculating the result. For example, that's the case with **area()**, where the check also more than doubles the size of the function (that is, the number of machine instructions that need to be executed, not just the length of the source code). For some programs, that can be critical, especially if the same information is checked repeatedly as functions call each other, passing information along more or less unchanged.

So what should you do? Check your arguments in a function unless you have a good reason not to.

AA After examining a few related topics, we'll return to the question of how to deal with bad arguments in §4.6.1.

4.5.3 Error reporting

Let's consider a slightly different question: Once you have checked a set of arguments and found an error, what should you do? Sometimes you can return an "error value." For example:

```
char ask_user(string question)
	// ask user for a yes-or-no answer;
	// return 'b' to indicate a bad answer (i.e., not yes or no)
{
	cout << question << "? (yes or no)\n";
	string answer;
	cin >> answer;
	if (answer =="y" || answer=="yes")
		return 'y';
	if (answer =="n" || answer=="no")
		return 'n';
	return 'b';			// 'b' for "bad answer"
}

int area(int length, int width)
	// calculate area of a rectangle;
	// return -1 to indicate a bad argument
{
	if (length<=0 || width <=0)
		return -1;
	return length*width;
}
```

That way, we can have the called function do the detailed checking, while letting each caller handle the error as desired. This approach seems like it could work, but it has a couple of problems that make it unusable in many cases:

- Now both the called function and all callers must test. The caller has only a simple test to do but must still write that test and decide what to do if it fails.
- A caller can forget to test. That can lead to unpredictable behavior further along in the program.
- Many functions do not have an "extra" return value that they can use to indicate an error. For example, a function that reads an integer from input (such as **cin**'s operator **>>**) can obviously return any **int** value, so there is no **int** that it could return to indicate failure.

The second case above – a caller forgetting to test – can easily lead to surprises. For example:

```
int f(int x, int y, int z)
{
	int area1 = area(x,y);
	if (area1<=0)
		error("non-positive area");
	int area2 = framed_area(1,z);
	int area3 = framed_area(y,z);
	double ratio = double(area1)/area3;
	// ...
}
```

Do you see the errors? This kind of error is hard to find because there is no obvious "wrong code" to look at: the error is the absence of a test.

> TRY THIS
>
> Test this program with a variety of values. Print out the values of area1, area2, area3, and ratio. Insert more tests until all errors are caught. How do you know that you caught all errors? This is not a trick question. In this particular example, you can give a valid argument for having caught all errors.

There is another solution that deals with that problem: using exceptions.

4.6 Exceptions

Like most modern programming languages, C++ provides a mechanism to help deal with errors: exceptions. The fundamental idea is to separate detection of an error (which should be done in a called function) from the handling of an error (which should be done in the calling function) while ensuring that a detected error cannot be ignored; that is, exceptions provide a mechanism that allows us to combine the best of the various approaches to error handling we have explored so far. Nothing makes error handling easy, but exceptions make it easier.

CC The basic idea is that if a function finds an error that it cannot handle and it cannot expect its immediate called to handle, it does not return normally; instead, it throws an exception indicating what went wrong. Any direct or indirect caller can catch the exception, that is, specify what to do if the called code used throw. A function expresses interest in exceptions by using a try-block (as described in the following subsections) listing the kinds of exceptions it wants to handle in the catch parts of the try-block. If no caller catches an exception, the program terminates.

AA We'll come back to exceptions much later (§18.3, §18.4, §18.5) to see how to use them in more advanced ways. For now, just use them to report errors that cannot be handled locally. That is, use exceptions for errors that are considered "exceptional." That does not mean every problem that a function cannot handle. For example, when we try to open a file, it is not exceptional for the file not being available or not being usable in the way we requested. So, the function trying to open the file must be ready to handle such an error; see §9.3.

4.6.1 Bad arguments

Here is a version of area() using exceptions:

```
class Bad_area { };    // a type specifically for reporting errors from area()

int area(int length, int width)
     // calculate area of a rectangle;
     // throw a Bad_area exception in case of a bad argument
{
     if (length<=0 || width<=0)
          throw Bad_area{};
     return length*width;
}
```

That is, if the arguments are OK, we return the area as always; if not, we get out of area() using the throw, hoping that some catch will provide an appropriate response. Bad_area is a new type we define with no other purpose than to provide something unique to throw from area() so that some catch can recognize it as the kind of exception thrown by area(). User-defined types (classes and enumeration) will be discussed in Chapter 9. The notation Bad_area{} means "Make an object of type Bad_area with the default value," so throw Bad_area{} means "Make an object of type Bad_area and throw it."

We can now write

```
void test(int x, int y, int z)
{
        int area1 = area(x,y);
        int area2 = framed_area(1,z);
        int area3 = framed_area(y,z);
        double ratio = area1/area3;
}

int main()
try {
        test(-1,2,4);
}
catch (Bad_area) {
        cout << "Oops! bad arguments to area()\n";
}
```

First note that this handles all calls to area(), both the one in main() and the two through framed_area(). Second, note how the handling of the error is cleanly separated from the detection of the error: main() knows nothing about which function did a throw Bad_area{}, and area() knows nothing about which function (if any) cares to catch the Bad_area exceptions it throws. This separation is especially important in large programs written using many libraries. In such programs, nobody can "just deal with an error by putting some code where it's needed," because nobody would want to modify code in both the application and in all of the libraries.

4.6.2 Range errors

Most real-world code deals with collections of data; that is, it uses all kinds of tables, lists, etc. of data elements to do a job. In the context of C++, we often refer to "collections of data" as *containers*. The most common and useful standard-library container is the vector we introduced in §3.6. A vector holds a number of elements, and we can determine that number by calling the vector's size() member function. The general notation [low:high) means indices from low to high-1, that is, including low but not high:

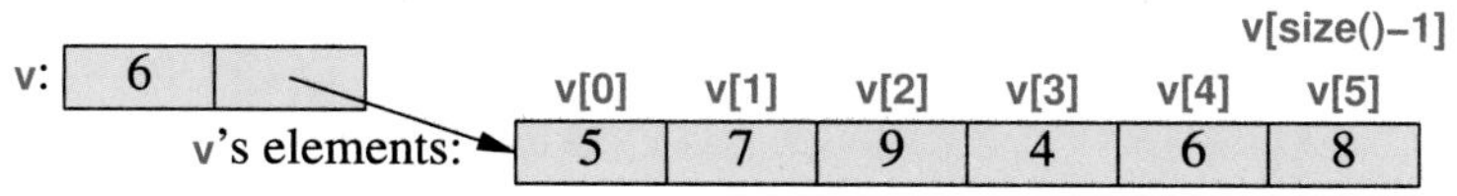

What happens if we try to use an element with an index (subscript) that isn't in the valid range [0:v.size())? Before answering that question, we should pose another question:

Why would you do that?

After all, you know that a subscript for v should be in the range [0,v.size()), so just be sure that's always so! As it happens, that's easy to say but sometimes hard to do. Consider this plausible code:

```
vector<int> v;                          // a vector of ints
for (int i; cin>>i; )
        v.push_back(i);                 // get values
for (int i = 0; i<=v.size(); ++i)       // print values
        cout << "v[" << i <<"] == " << v[i] << '\n';
```

Do you see the error? Please try to spot it before reading on. It's not an uncommon error. We have made such errors ourselves – especially late at night when we were tired. Errors are always more common when you are tired or rushed. We use 0 and size() to try to make sure that i is always in range when we do v[i].

XX Unfortunately, we made a mistake. Look at the for-loop: the termination condition is i<=v.size() rather than the correct i<v.size(). This has the unfortunate consequence that if we read in five integers we'll try to write out six. We try to read v[5], which is one beyond the end of the vector. This kind of error is so common and "famous" that it has several names: it is an example of an *off-by-one error*, a *range error* because the index (subscript) wasn't in the range required by the vector, and a *bounds error* because the index was not within the limits (bounds) of the vector.

Why didn't we use a range-for-statement to express that loop? With a range-for, we cannot get the end of the loop wrong. However, for this loop, we wanted not only the value of each element but also the indices (subscripts). A range-for doesn't give that without extra effort.

Here is a simpler version that produces the same range error as the loop:

```
vector<int> v(5);
int x = v[5];
```

However, we doubt that you'd have considered that realistic and worth serious attention.

So what actually happens when we make such a range error? The subscript operation of vector knows the size of the vector, so it can check (and the vector we are using does; see §3.6 and §18.3). If that check fails, the subscript operation throws an exception of type out_of_range. So, if the off-by-one code above had been part of a program that caught exceptions, we would at least have gotten a decent error message:

```
int main()
try {
        vector<int> v;                          // a vector of ints
        for (int x; cin>>x; )
                v.push_back(x);                 // set values
        for (int i = 0; i<=v.size(); ++i)       // print values
                cout << "v[" << i <<"] == " << v[i] << '\n';
}
```

```
catch (out_of_range) {
        cerr << "Oops! Range error\n";
        return 1;
}
catch (...) {                                   // catch all other exceptions
        cerr << "Exception: something went wrong\n";
        return 2;
}
```

Note that a range error is really a special case of the argument errors we discussed in §4.5.2. We didn't trust ourselves to consistently check the range of **vector** indices, so we told **vector**'s subscript operation to do it for us. For the reasons we outline, **vector**'s subscript function (called **vector::operator[]**) reports finding an error by throwing an exception. What else could it do? It has no idea what we would like to happen in case of a range error. The author of **vector** couldn't even know what programs the **vector** code would be part of.

4.6.3 Bad input

We'll postpone the detailed discussion of what to do with bad input until §9.4. However, once bad input is detected, it is dealt with using the same techniques and language features as argument errors and range errors. Here, we'll just show how you can tell if your input operations succeeded. Consider reading a floating-point number:

```
double d = 0;
cin >> d;
```

We can test if the last input operation succeeded by testing **cin**:

```
if (cin) {
    // ... all is well, and we can try reading again ...
}
else {
    // ... the last read didn't succeed, so we take some other action ...
}
```

There are several possible reasons for that input operation's failure. The one that should concern you right now is that there wasn't a **double** for **>>** to read.

During the early stages of development, we often want to indicate that we have found an error but aren't yet ready to do anything particularly clever about it; we just want to report the error and terminate the program. Later, maybe, we'll come back and do something more appropriate. For example:

```
double some_function()
{
        double d = 0;
        cin >> d;
        if (!cin)
                error("couldn't read a double in 'some_function()'");
        // ... use d ...
}
```

The condition !cin ("not cin," that is, cin is not in a good state) means that the previous operation on cin failed.

The string passed to error() can then be printed as a help to debugging or as a message to the user. How can we write error() so as to be useful in a lot of programs? It can't return a value because we wouldn't know what to do with that value; instead error() is supposed to terminate the program after getting its message written. In addition, we might want to take some minor action before exiting, such as keeping a window alive long enough for us to read the message. That's an obvious job for an exception (see §6.3).

AA The standard library defines a few types of exceptions, such as the out_of_range thrown by vector. It also supplies runtime_error which is pretty ideal for our needs because it holds a string that can be used by an error handler. So, we can write our simple error() like this:

```
void error(string s)
{
        throw runtime_error{s};
}
```

When we want to deal with runtime_error we simply catch it. For simple programs, catching runtime_error in main() is ideal:

```
int main()
try {
        // ... our program ...
        return 0;         // 0 indicates success
}
catch (runtime_error& e) {
        cerr << "runtime error: " << e.what() << '\n';
        return 1;         // 1 indicates failure
}
```

The call e.what() extracts the error message from the runtime_error. The & in

```
catch(runtime_error& e) {
```

is an indicator that we want to "pass the exception by reference." For now, please treat this as simply an irrelevant technicality. In §7.4.5, we explain what it means to pass something by reference.

Note that we used cerr rather than cout for our error output: cerr is exactly like cout except that it is meant for error output. By default, both cerr and cout write to the screen, but cerr isn't optimized so it is more resilient to errors, and on some operating systems it can be diverted to a different target, such as a file. Using cerr also has the simple effect of documenting that what we write relates to errors. Consequently, we use cerr for error messages.

As it happens, out_of_range is not a runtime_error, so catching runtime_error does not deal with the out_of_range errors that we might get from misuse of vectors and other standard-library container types. However, both out_of_range and runtime_error are "exceptions," so we can catch exception to deal with both:

```
int main()
try {
        // our program
        return 0;          // 0 indicates success
}
catch (exception& e) {
        cerr << "error: " << e.what() << '\n';
        return 1;          // 1 indicates failure
}
catch (...) {
        cerr << "Oops: unknown exception!\n";
        return 2;          // 2 indicates failure
}
```

We added catch(...) to handle exceptions of any type whatsoever.

Dealing with exceptions of both type out_of_range and type runtime_error through a single type exception, said to be a common base (supertype) of both, is a useful and general technique that we will explore in Chapter 12 and elsewhere.

Note again that the return value from main() is passed to "the system" that invoked the program. Some systems (such as Linux) often use that value, whereas others (such as Windows) typically ignore it. A zero indicates successful completion and a nonzero return value from main() indicates some sort of failure.

When you use error(), you'll often wish to pass two pieces of information along to describe the problem. In that case, just concatenate the strings describing those two pieces of information. This is so common that we provide a second version of error() for that:

```
void error(string s1, string s2)
{
        throw runtime_error{s1+s2};
}
```

This simple error handling will do for a while, until our needs increase significantly and our sophistication as designers and programmers increases correspondingly. Note that we can use error() independently of how many function calls we have done on the way to the error: error() will find its way to the nearest catch of runtime_error, typically the one in main(). For examples of the use of exceptions and error(), see §6.3 and §6.7. If you don't catch an exception, you'll get a default system error (an "uncaught exception" error).

> TRY THIS
>
> To see what an uncaught exception error looks like, run a small program that uses error() without catching any exceptions.

4.7 Avoiding and finding errors

We know that our first attempt at a program won't be perfect. So we must develop our skills at finding problems and fixing them (§4.7.1, §4.7.2, §4.7.4). A major part of that is to organize our code to make it harder for bugs to hide (§7.3, §4.7.3). AA

4.7.1 Estimation

Imagine you have written a program that does a simple calculation, say, computing the area of a hexagon. You run it and it gives the area -34.56. You just know that's wrong. Why? Because no shape has a negative area. So, you fix that bug (whatever it was) and get 21.65685. Is that right? That's harder to say because we don't usually keep the formula for the area of a hexagon in our heads. What we must do before making fools of ourselves by delivering a program that produces ridiculous results is just to check that the answer is plausible. In this case, that's easy. A hexagon is much like a square. We scribble our regular hexagon on a piece of paper and eyeball it to be about the size of a 3-by-3 square. Such a square has the area 9. Bummer, our 21.65685 can't be right! So we work over our program again and get 10.3923. Now, that just might be right!

AA The general point here has nothing to do with hexagons. The point is that unless we have some idea of what a correct answer will be like – even ever so approximately – we don't have a clue whether our result is reasonable. Always ask yourself this question:

- *Is this answer to this particular problem plausible?*

You should also ask the more general (and often far harder) question:

- How would I recognize a plausible result?

Here, we are not asking, "What's the exact answer?" or "What's the correct answer?" That's what we are writing the program to tell us. All we want is to know that the answer is not ridiculous. Only when we know that we have a plausible answer does it make sense to proceed with further work.

Estimation is a noble art that combines common sense and some very simple arithmetic applied to a few facts. Some people are good at doing estimates in their heads, but we prefer scribbles "on the back of an envelope" because we find we get confused less often that way. What we call estimation here is an informal set of techniques that are sometimes (humorously) called *guesstimation* because they combine a bit of guessing with a bit of calculation.

> TRY THIS
>
> Our hexagon was regular with 2cm sides. Did we get that answer right? Just do the "back of the envelope" calculation. Take a piece a paper and scribble on it. Don't feel that's beneath you. Many famous scientists have been greatly admired for their ability to come up with an approximate answer using a pencil and the back of an envelope (or a napkin). This is an ability – a simple habit, really – that can save us a lot of time and confusion.

Often, making an estimate involves coming up with estimates of data that are needed for a proper calculation, but that we don't yet have. Imagine you have to test a program that estimates driving times between cities. Is a driving time of 15 hours and 33 minutes plausible for New York City to Denver? From London to Nice? Why or why not? What data do you have to "guess" to answer these questions? Often, a quick Web search can be most helpful. For example, 2000 miles is not a bad guess on the road distance from New York City to Denver, and it would be hard (and illegal) to maintain an average speed of 130m/hr, so 15 hours is not plausible (15*130 is just a bit less than 2000). You can check: we overestimated both the distance and the average speed, but for a check of plausibility, we don't have to be exactly right; we just have to guess well enough.

> TRY THIS
>
> Estimate those driving times. Also, estimate the corresponding flight times (using ordinary commercial air travel). Then, try to verify your estimates by using appropriate sources, such as maps and timetables. We'd use online sources.

4.7.2 Debugging

When you have written (drafted?) a program, it'll have errors. Small programs do occasionally compile and run correctly the first time you try. But if that happens for anything but a completely trivial program, you should at first be very, very suspicious. If it really did run correctly the first time, go tell your friends and celebrate – because this won't happen every year.

So, when you have written some code, you have to find and remove the errors. That process is usually called *debugging* and the errors *bugs*. The term *bug* is often claimed to have originated from a hardware failure caused by insects in the electronics in the days when computers were racks of vacuum tubes and relays filling rooms. Several people have been credited with the discovery and the application of the word *bug* to errors in software. The most famous of those is Grace Murray Hopper, the inventor of the COBOL programming language (PPP2.§22.2.2.2). Whoever invented the term more than 50 years ago, *bug* is evocative and ubiquitous. The activity of deliberately searching for errors and removing them is called *debugging*.

Debugging works roughly like this:

[1] Get the program to compile.
[2] Get the program to link.
[3] Get the program to do what it is supposed to do.

Basically, we go through this sequence again and again: hundreds of times, thousands of times, again and again for years for really large programs. Each time something doesn't work we have to find what caused the problem and fix it. I consider debugging the most tedious and time-wasting aspect of programming and will go to great lengths during design and programming to minimize the amount of time spent hunting for bugs. Others find that hunt thrilling and the essence of programming – it can be as addictive as any video game and keep a programmer glued to the computer for days and nights (I can vouch for that from personal experience also).

Here is how *not* to debug: XX

```
while (the program doesn't appear to work) {     // pseudo code
      Randomly look through the program for something that "looks odd"
      Change it to look better
}
```

Why do we bother to mention this? It's obviously a poor algorithm with little guarantee of success. AA
Unfortunately, that description is only a slight caricature of what many people find themselves doing late at night when feeling particularly lost and clueless, having tried "everything else." The key question in debugging is

How would I know if the program actually worked correctly?

If you can't answer that question, you are in for a long and tedious debug session, and most likely your users are in for some frustration. We keep returning to this point because anything that helps answer that question minimizes debugging and helps produce correct and maintainable programs.

Basically, we'd like to design our programs so that bugs have nowhere to hide. That's typically too much to ask for, but we aim to structure programs to minimize the chance of error and maximize the chance of finding the errors that do creep in.

4.7.2.1 Practical debug advice

AA Start thinking about debugging before you write the first line of code. Once you have a lot of code written it's too late to try to simplify debugging.

Decide how to report errors: "Use **error()** and catch **exception** in **main()**" (§4.6) will be your default answer in this book.

AA Make the program easy to read so that you have a chance of spotting the bugs:

- Comment your code well. That doesn't simply mean "Add a lot of comments." You don't say in English what is better said in code. Rather, you say in the comments – as clearly and briefly as you can – what can't be said clearly in code:
  - The name of the program
  - The purpose of the program
  - Who wrote this code and when
  - Version numbers
  - What complicated code fragments are supposed to do
  - What the general design ideas are
  - How the source code is organized
  - What assumptions are made about inputs
  - What parts of the code are still missing and what cases are still not handled
  - References to supporting material (e.g., to a book explaining the algorithms used)
- Use meaningful names.
  - That doesn't simply mean "Use long names."
- Use a consistent layout of code.
  - Your IDE tries to help, but it can't do everything, and you are the one responsible.
  - The style used in this book is a reasonable starting point.
- Break code into small functions, each expressing a logical action.
  - Try to avoid functions longer than a page or two; most functions will be much shorter.
- Avoid complicated code sequences.
  - Try to avoid nested loops, nested **if**-statements, complicated conditions, etc. Unfortunately, you sometimes need those, but remember that complicated code is where bugs can most easily hide.
- Use library facilities rather than your own code when you can.
  - A library is likely to be better thought out and better tested than what you could produce as an alternative while busily solving your main problem.

This is pretty abstract just now, but we'll show you example after example as we go along.

AA Get the program to compile. Obviously, your compiler is your best help here. Its error messages are usually helpful – even if we always wish for better ones – and, unless you are a real expert, assume that the compiler is always right; if you are a real expert, this book wasn't written for you. Occasionally, you will feel that the rules the compiler enforces are stupid and unnecessary (they rarely are) and that things could and ought to be simpler (indeed, but they are not). However, as they say, "a poor craftsman curses his tools." A good craftsman knows the strengths and weaknesses of his tools and adjusts his work accordingly. See §4.3 for common compile-time errors and §4.4 for some link-time errors.

After the program compiles and links, next comes what is typically the hardest part: figuring out why the program doesn't do what it's supposed to. You look at the output and try to figure out how your code could have produced that. Actually, first you often look at a blank screen (or window), wondering how your program could have failed to produce any output.

When looking for a bug, carefully follow the code statement by statement from the last point that you are sure it was correct. Pretend you're the computer executing the program. Does the output match your expectations? Of course not, or you wouldn't be debugging.

Often, when we don't see the problem, the reason is that we "see" what we expect to see rather than what was written. Consider: AA

```
for (int i = 0; 0<=max; ++i) {            // oops!
      for (int j = 0; j<v.size(); ++i);          // print the elements of v
            cout << "v[" << j << "]==" << v[j] << '\n';
      // ...
}
```

This last example is equivalent to code from a real program written by a experienced programmer. We expect it was written very late some night.

Often when we do not see the problem, the reason is that there is too much code being executed between the point where the program produced the last good output and the next output (or lack of output). Most programming environments provide a way to execute ("step through") the statements of a program one by one. Eventually, you'll learn to use such facilities, but for simple problems and simple programs, you can just temporarily put in a few extra output statements (using the error-reporting output stream cerr) to help you see what's going on. For example:

```
int my_fct(int a, double d)
{
      cerr << "my_fct(" << a << "," << d << ")\n";
      int res = 0;
      // ... misbehaving code here ...
      cerr << "my_fct() returns " << res << '\n';
      return res;
}
```

Insert statements that check invariants (that is, conditions that should always hold; see §4.7.3 and §8.4) in sections of code suspected of harboring bugs. For example:

```
int my_complicated_function(int a, int b, int c)
      // the arguments are positive and a < b < c
{
      if (!(0<a && a<b && b<c))            // ! means "not" and && means "and"
            error("bad arguments for mcf");
      // ...
}
```

If that doesn't have any effect, insert invariant checks in sections of code not suspected of harboring bugs; if you can't find a bug, you are almost certainly looking in the wrong place.

4.7.3 Assertions

A statement that states (asserts) an invariant is called an *assertion* (or just an *assert*) and sometimes a *contract*.

AA Interestingly enough, there are many effective ways of programming. Different people successfully use dramatically different techniques. Many differences in debugging technique come from differences in the kinds of programs people work on; others seem to have to do with differences in the ways people think. To the best of our knowledge, there is no one best way to debug. One thing should always be remembered, though: messy code can easily harbor bugs. By keeping your code as simple, logical, and well formatted as possible, you decrease your debug time.

4.7.3.1 Preconditions

CC Now, let us return to the question of how to deal with bad arguments to a function. The call of a function is basically the best point to think about correct code and to catch errors: this is where a logically separate computation starts (and ends on the return). Look at what we did in the piece of advice above:

```
int my_complicated_function(int a, int b, int c)
    // the arguments are positive and a < b < c
{
    if (!(0<a && a<b && b<c))       // ! means "not" and && means "and"
        error("bad arguments for mcf");
    // ...
}
```

First, we stated (in a comment) what the function required of its arguments, and then we checked that this requirement held (throwing an exception if it did not).

This is a good basic strategy. A requirement of a function upon its argument is often called a *precondition*: it must be true for the function to perform its action correctly. The question is just what to do if the precondition is violated (doesn't hold). We basically have two choices:

[1] Ignore it (hope/assume that all callers give correct arguments).
[2] Check it (and report the error somehow).

Looking at it this way, argument types are just a way of having the compiler check the simplest preconditions for us and report them at compile time. For example:

```
my_complicated_function(1, 2, "horsefeathers")
```

Here, the compiler will catch that the requirement (precondition) that the third argument be an integer was violated. Basically, what we are talking about here is what to do with the requirements/preconditions that the compiler can't check.

AA Our suggestion is to always document preconditions in comments (so that a caller can see what a function expects). A function with no comments will be assumed to handle every possible argument value. But should we believe that callers read those comments and follow the rules? Sometimes we have to, but the "check the arguments in the callee" rule could be stated, "Let a function check its preconditions." We should do that whenever we don't see a reason not to. The reasons most often given for not checking preconditions are:

- Nobody would give bad arguments.
- It would slow down my code.
- It is too complicated to check.

The first reason can be reasonable only when we happen to know "who" calls a function – and in real-world code that can be very hard to know.

The second reason is valid far less often than people think and should most often be ignored as an example of "premature optimization." You can always remove checks if they really turn out to be a burden. You cannot easily gain the correctness they ensure or get back the nights' sleep you lost looking for bugs those tests could have caught.

The third reason is the serious one. It is easy (once you are an experienced programmer) to find examples where checking a precondition would take significantly more work than executing the function. An example is a lookup in a dictionary: a precondition is that the dictionary entries are sorted – and verifying that a dictionary is sorted can be far more expensive than a lookup. Sometimes, it can also be difficult to express a precondition in code and to be sure that you expressed it correctly. However, when you write a function, always consider if you can write a quick check of the preconditions, and do so unless you have a good reason not to.

4.7.3.2 expect()

Writing preconditions (even as comments) also has a significant benefit for the quality of your programs: it forces you to think about what a function requires. If you can't state that simply and precisely in a couple of comment lines, you probably haven't thought hard enough about what you are doing. Experience shows that writing those precondition comments and precondition tests help you avoid many design mistakes. We did mention that we hated debugging; explicitly stating preconditions helps in avoiding design errors as well as catching usage errors early. Writing

```
int my_complicated_function(int a, int b, int c)
    // the arguments are positive and a < b < c
{
    if (!(0<a && a<b && b<c))          // ! means "not" and && means "and"
        error("bad arguments for mcf");
    // ...
}
```

saves you time and grief compared with the apparently simpler

```
int my_complicated_function(int a, int b, int c)
{
    // ...
}
```

Following the advice of checking preconditions soon leads to a couple of problems:

- Some preconditions cannot be checked simply and cheaply. For those, stay with the comments and check only what can be checked simply and cheaply.
- We can't see whether an **if**-statement checks an invariant or is part of the ordinary logic of the function.

To deal with the second problem, we introduce a function called expect to do the checking. As arguments expect() takes a function to test and a string used to report errors:

```
bool ordered_positive(int a, int b, int c)
{
        return 0<a && a<b && b<c;
}

int my_complicated_function(int a, int b, int c)
        // the arguments are positive and a < b < c
{
        expect(ordered_positive(a,b,c), "bad arguments for mcf");
        // ...
}
```

now we can see what my_complicated_function() expects from its arguments, but for tests we don't use often in our source code, we'd rather have them expressed directly where they are used. We can do that:

```
int my_complicated_function(int a, int b, int c)
        // the arguments are positive and a < b < c
{
        expect([&]{ return 0<a && a<b && b<c; }, "bad arguments for mcf");
        // ...
}
```

The construct

```
[&]{ return 0<a && a<b && b<c; }
```

is called a lambda expression and will be explained in §21.2.3. The syntax isn't as clean as we might like, but it constructs a function that tests

```
0<a && a<b && b<c
```

for expect() to call. If that test fails,

```
error("bad arguments for mcf")
```

is called exactly as when we used the named function ordered_positive().

4.7.3.3 Postconditions

Stating preconditions and inserting calls to expect() help us improve our design and catch usage errors early. Can this idea of explicitly stating requirements be used elsewhere? Yes, one more place immediately springs to mind: the return value! After all, we typically have to state what a function returns; that is, if we return a value from a function, we are *always* making a promise about the return value (how else would a caller know what to expect?). Let's look at our area function (from §4.6.1) again:

```
int area(int length, int width)
    // calculate area of a rectangle
    // the arguments are positive
{
    expect([&]{ return 0<length && 0<width; }, "bad arguments to area()");
    return length*width;
}
```

It checks its precondition, but just assumes that the computation is correct (that's probably OK for such a trivial computation). A check on the correctness is called a *postcondition*. For area() the postcondition would be that the result really was the area. We can't check the complete postcondition, but we can check that the result should be positive:

```
int area(int length, int width)
    // the arguments are positive
{
    expect([&]{ return 0<length && 0<width; }, "bad arguments to area()");
    int a = length*width;
    expect([&]{ return 0<a; }, "bad area() result");
    return a;
}
```

This code looks rather bloated compared to the straightforward

```
int area(int length, int width)
{
    return length*width;
}
```

but it illustrates a technique that can be enormously useful when writing programs where correct results are critically important.

> TRY THIS
>
> Find a pair of values so that the precondition of this version of area holds, but the postcondition doesn't.

Preconditions and postconditions provide basic sanity checks in code. As such they are closely connected to the notion of invariants (§8.4.3), correctness (§3.2, §4.2), and testing (§4.7.4).

Note that error() and expect() are not part of the ISO C++ standard library. They are just part of the PPP_support module. There is work going on in the standards committee for direct support for preconditions and postconditions, but at the time of writing, that work is not complete. CC

4.7.4 Testing

How do we know when to stop debugging? Well, we keep debugging until we have found all the bugs – or at least we try to. How do we know that we have found the last bug? We don't. "The last bug" is a programmers' joke: there is no such creature; we never find "the last bug" in a large program. By the time we might have, we are busy modifying the program for some new use.

In addition to debugging, we need a systematic way to search for errors. This is called *testing* and we'll get back to that in §6.3 and the exercises in Chapter 9. Basically, testing is executing a CC program with a large and systematically selected set of inputs and comparing the results to what was expected. A run with a given set of inputs is called a *test case*. Realistic programs can require millions of test cases, so systematic testing cannot be done by humans typing in one test after another. Tools necessary to properly approach testing are available but are beyond the scope of this book. For now, approach testing with the attitude that finding errors is good. Consider:

- *Attitude 1: I'm smarter than any program! I'll break that @#%^ code!*
- *Attitude 2: I polished this code for two weeks. It's perfect!*

AA Who do you think will find more errors? Of course, the very best is an experienced person with a bit of "attitude 1" who coolly, calmly, patiently, and systematically works through the possible failings of the program. Good testers are worth their weight in gold.

We try to be systematic in choosing our test cases and always try both correct and incorrect inputs. §6.3 gives the first example of this.

For industrial use, programs called *test frameworks* are integrated with other development support and are almost universally used. Examples are Boost.Test, Catch2, CTest, Google Test, Microsoft Unit Testing Framework for C++, and UnitTest++. They all allow you to write a set of code examples and for each to say what is the expected result of executing it, such as producing a specific result or throwing a specific exception. Once you know a bit more about programming and C++, we encourage you to try and use such a framework. As with all tools, it would be best if you can get an experienced developer to help you get started.

4.7.5 Random numbers

A random number is a number from a sequence of numbers where given the previous numbers, it's hard (or even impossible) to determine the next. Some random sequences are really random, e.g., the readout of background radiation from a Geiger counter, but most are *pseudo random*, that is, generated from a mathematical formula.

Random numbers are important in many fields of computing, such as simulation, games, cryptography, security, and testing. That is, where we want unpredictable results or inputs. For example, when testing a function it can be useful to call it with a series of random inputs to see if it responds appropriately. The C++ standard-library provides a sophisticated random number component that has been described as "what every random-number library wants to be when it grows up" but here we just describe the general idea and a couple of simple examples.

We start by generating a series of random values. That's done by an *engine*:

```
default_random_engine engine;                    // the simplest engine
```

The **default_random_engine** is good enough for most uses and the only one we will use here. The standard library offers several engines for professional uses.

To be useful, the random numbers from the engine must be transformed into the *distribution* we require, such as integers in the [1:6] range to model a die (a dice):

```
uniform_int_distribution<int> dist(1,6);         // the distribution we want
for (int i=0; i<10; ++i)
     cout << dist(engine) << ' ';                // get a value from the distribution using the engine
```

If all values in the range appear at the same frequency when we throw the die many times – as they will for an unloaded die – the distribution is called a **uniform_int_distribution**. The standard library offers many of the most useful distributions including **normal_distribution** to model variation around a mean and **exponential_distribution** for modeling waiting times.

Typically, we want to choose the engine and distribution in one place and then just use them through a simple interface. We have done so in **PPP_support** by providing a couple of access functions:

```
int random_int(int min, int max);        // get an int from the range [min:max]
int random_int(int max);                 // get an int from the range [0:max]
```

We can now say:

```
for (int i=0; i<10; ++i)
    cout << random_int(1,6) << ' ';      // get a value from the distribution using the engine
```

In §20.4 we will show how that's done. It's quite simple but requires several features that we have yet to explain.

Once we have random numbers, we can generate random sequences of values of other types. For example, this generates random strings that we might use to test algorithms over containers of strings:

```
string random_letters(int n, int m)
    // generate a string with between 4 and 24 random lower-case characters
{
    string s(random_int(n, m),'x');                   // a string with a size in the [n:m] range
    for (char& ch : s)
        ch = narrow<char>(random_int('a','z'));       // a lower-case letter
    return s;
}
```

When constructing a **string** of a given size, its characters must be initialized to something; here, we chose '**x**'. Also, we used **narrow** to be explicit about narrowing the **int** returned by **random_int()** to the **char** we needed (§7.4.7).

Like **random_int()**, **random_letters()** can be found in **PPP_support**. We might use that to generate a **vector** of (name,value) pairs for testing:

```
vector<pair<string, int>> generate(int n)
    // generate n random (name,value) pairs
{
    vector <pair<string, int>> res;
    for (int i = 0; i < n; ++i)
        res.push_back({random_letters(4,24),random_int(1'000'000)});
    return res;
}
```

A random number generator delivers the same sequence every time it is created and used. That's very useful for debugging and testing where we want repeatable results, but undesirable when we want unpredictable outputs. For example, in a game, we don't want the monster to always be a troll who attacks in the same place, same time, and in the same way every time we play.

To get different sequences from an engine, we *seed* it:

```
default_random_engine engine2(7777);        // use 7777 instead of the default starting value
// ...
engine2.seed(9876);                         // start a new sequence from 9876
```

To make a sequence unpredictable, seed it with something unpredictable, such as the time of creation. In PPP_support, we provide a function seed() to seed the engine used by random_int():

```
void seed(int s);           // seed with s
void seed();        // seed with a really unpredictable value
```

The random_int() and seed() functions expose just a tiny fraction of the sophisticated random component of the standard library, but it is simple and is sufficient for a wide range of uses.

Drill

Below are 25 code fragments. Each is meant to be inserted into this "scaffolding":

```
#include "PPP.h"

int main()
try {
        <<your code here>>
        return 0;
}
catch (exception& e) {
        cerr << "error: " << e.what() << '\n';
        return 1;
}
catch (...) {
        cerr << "Oops: unknown exception!\n";
        return 2;
}
```

Each has zero or more errors. Your task is to find and remove all errors in each program. When you have removed those bugs, the resulting program will compile, run, and write "Success!" Even if you think you have spotted an error, you still need to enter the (original, unimproved) program fragment and test it; you may have guessed wrong about what the error is, or there may be more errors in a fragment than you spotted. Also, one purpose of this drill is to give you a feel for how your compiler reacts to different kinds of errors. Do not enter the scaffolding 25 times – that's a job for cut and paste or some similar "mechanical" technique. Do not fix problems by simply deleting a statement; repair them by changing, adding, or deleting a few characters.

[1] `Cout << "Success!\n";`

[2] `cout << "Success!\n;`

[3] `cout << "Success" << !\n"`

[4] `cout << success << '\n';`

[5] `string res = 7; vector<int> v(10); v[5] = res; cout << "Success!\n";`

[6] `vector<int> v(10); v(5) = 7; if (v(5)!=7) cout << "Success!\n";`

[7] if (cond) cout << "Success!\n"; else cout << "Fail!\n";
[8] bool c = false; if (c) cout << "Success!\n"; else cout << "Fail!\n";
[9] string s = "ape"; boo c = "fool"<s; if (c) cout << "Success!\n";
[10] string s = "ape"; if (s=="fool") cout << "Success!\n";
[11] string s = "ape"; if (s=="fool") cout < "Success!\n";
[12] string s = "ape"; if (s+"fool") cout < "Success!\n";
[13] vector<char> v(5); for (int i = 0; 0<v.size(); ++i) ; cout << "Success!\n";
[14] vector<char> v(5); for (int i = 0; i<=v.size(); ++i) ; cout << "Success!\n";
[15] string s = "Success!\n"; for (int i = 0; i<6; ++i) cout << s[i];
[16] if (true) then cout << "Success!\n"; else cout << "Fail!\n";
[17] int x = 2000; char c = x; if (c==2000) cout << "Success!\n";
[18] string s = "Success!\n"; for (int i = 0; i<10; ++i) cout << s[i];
[19] vector v(5); for (int i = 0; i<=v.size(); ++i) ; cout << "Success!\n";
[20] int i = 0; int j = 9; while (i<10) ++j; if (j<i) cout << "Success!\n";
[21] int x = 2; double d = 5/(x–2); if (d==2*x+0.5) cout << "Success!\n";
[22] string<char> s = "Success!\n"; for (int i = 0; i<=10; ++i) cout << s[i];
[23] int i = 0; while (i<10) ++j; if (j<i) cout << "Success!\n";
[24] int x = 4; double d = 5/(x–2); if (d=2*x+0.5) cout << "Success!\n";
[25] cin << "Success!\n";

Review

[1] Name four major types of errors and briefly define each one.
[2] What kinds of errors can we ignore in student programs?
[3] What guarantees should every completed project offer?
[4] List three approaches we can take to eliminate errors in programs and produce acceptable software.
[5] Why do we hate debugging?
[6] What is a syntax error? Give five examples.
[7] What is a type error? Give five examples.
[8] What is a linker error? Give three examples.
[9] What is a logic error? Give three examples.
[10] List four potential sources of program errors discussed in the text.
[11] How do you know if a result is plausible? What techniques do you have to answer such questions?
[12] How do you test if an input operation succeeded?
[13] Compare and contrast having the caller of a function handle a run-time error vs. having the called function handle the run-time error.
[14] When is throwing an exception preferable to returning an "error value"?
[15] When is returning an "error value" preferable to throwing an exception?
[16] Describe the process of how exceptions are thrown and caught.
[17] Why, with a vector called v, is v[v.size()] a range error? What would be the result of calling this?

[18] What is an assertion?
[19] Define *precondition* and *postcondition*; give an example (that is not the **area()** function from this chapter), preferably a computation that requires a loop.
[20] When would you *not* test a precondition?
[21] When would you *not* test a postcondition?
[22] What are the steps in debugging a program?
[23] Why does commenting help when debugging?
[24] How does testing differ from debugging?
[25] What is a random number?
[26] How do we use **random_int()** and **seed()**?

Terms

argument error	exception	requirement	assertion
invariant	run-time error	**catch**	link-time error
syntax error	compile-time error	logic error	testing
container	postcondition	**throw**	debugging
precondition	type error	error	range error
expect()	**random_int()**	**seed()**	distribution

Exercises

[1] If you haven't already, do the **TRY THIS** exercises from this chapter.
[2] The following program takes in a temperature value in Celsius and converts it to Kelvin. This code has many errors in it. Find the errors, list them, and correct the code.

```
double ctok(double c)           // converts Celsius to Kelvin
{
        int k = c + 273.25;
        return int
}

int main()
{
        double c = 0;           // declare input variable
        cin >> d;               // retrieve temperature to input variable
        double k = ctok("c");   // convert temperature
        Cout << k << '/n' ;     // print out temperature
}
```

[3] Absolute zero is the lowest temperature that can be reached; it is -273.15C, or 0K. The above program, even when corrected, will produce erroneous results when given a temperature below this. Place a check in the main program that will produce an error if a temperature is given below -273.15C.

[4] Do exercise 3 again, but this time handle the error inside **ctok()**.

[5] Add to the program so that it can also convert from Kelvin to Celsius.

[6] Write a program that converts from Celsius to Fahrenheit and from Fahrenheit to Celsius. Use estimation (§4.7.1) to see if your results are plausible.

[7] Quadratic equations are of the form $a*x^2 + b*x + c = 0$. To solve these, one uses the quadratic formula: $x = \frac{-b \pm \sqrt{b^2 - 4ac}}{2a}$. There is a problem, though: if $b^2 - 4ac$ is less than zero, then it will fail. Write a program that can calculate x for a quadratic equation. Create a function that prints out the roots of a quadratic equation, given a, b, c. When the program detects an equation with no real roots, have it print out a message. How do you know that your results are plausible? Can you check that they are correct?

[8] Write a program that reads and stores a series of integers and then computes the sum of the first *N* integers. First ask for *N*, then read the values into a **vector**, then calculate the sum of the first *N* values. For example:

> Please enter the number of values you want to sum: **3**
> Please enter some integers (press '|' to stop): **12 23 13 24 15 |**
> The sum of the first **3** numbers (**12 23 13**) is **48**

Handle all inputs. For example, make sure to give an error message if the user asks for a sum of more numbers than there are in the vector.

[9] Modify the program from the previous exercise to write out an error if the result cannot be represented as an **int**.

[10] Modify the program from the previous exercise to use **double** instead of **int**. Also, make a **vector** of **doubles** containing the *N-1* differences between adjacent values and write out that **vector** of differences.

[11] Write a program that writes out the first N values of the Fibonacci series, that is, the series that starts with 1 1 2 3 5 8 13 21 34. The next number of the series is the sum of the two previous ones. Find the largest Fibonacci number that fits in an **int**.

[12] Implement a little guessing game called (for some obscure reason) "Bulls and Cows." The program has a **vector** of four different integers in the range 0 to 9 (e.g., 1234 but not 1122) and it is the user's task to discover those numbers by repeated guesses. Say the number to be guessed is 1234 and the user guesses 1359; the response should be "1 bull and 1 cow" because the user got one digit (1) right and in the right position (a bull) and one digit (3) right but in the wrong position (a cow). The guessing continues until the user gets four bulls, that is, has the four digits correct and in the correct order.

[13] The program is a bit tedious because the answer is hard-coded into the program. Make a version where the user can play repeatedly (without stopping and restarting the program) and each game has a new set of four digits. You can get four random digits by calling the random number generator **random_int(0,9)** from **PPP_support** (and §4.7.5) four times. You will note that if you run that program repeatedly, it will pick the same sequence of four digits each time you start the program. To avoid that, ask the user to enter a number (any number) and call **seed(n)**, also from **PPP_support**, where **n** is the number the user entered before calling **random_int(0,10)**. Such an **n** is called a *seed*, and different seeds give different sequences of random numbers.

[14] Read (day-of-the-week,value) pairs from standard input. For example:

```
Tuesday 23 Friday 56 Tuesday –3 Thursday 99
```

Collect all the values for each day of the week in a vector<int>. Write out the values of the seven day-of-the-week vectors. Print out the sum of the values in each vector. Ignore illegal days of the week, such as Funday, but accept common synonyms such as Mon and monday. Write out the number of rejected values.

Postscript

XX Do you think we overemphasize errors? As novice programmers, we would have thought so. The obvious and natural reaction is "It simply can't be that bad!" Well, it is that bad. Many of the world's best brains have been astounded and confounded by the difficulty of writing correct programs. In our experience, good mathematicians are the people most likely to underestimate the problem of bugs, but we all quickly exceed our natural capacity for writing programs that are correct the first time. You have been warned! Fortunately, after 70 years or so, we have a lot of experience in organizing code to minimize problems, and techniques to find the bugs that we – despite our best efforts – inevitably leave in our programs as we first write them. The techniques and examples in this chapter are a good start.

5

Writing a Program

Programming is understanding.
– Kristen Nygaard

Writing a program involves gradually refining our ideas of what we want to do and how we want to express them. In this chapter and the next, we will develop a program from a first vague idea through stages of analysis, design, implementation, testing, redesign, and re-implementation. Our aim is to give you some idea of the kind of thinking that goes on when you develop a piece of code. In the process, we discuss program organization, user-defined types, and input processing.

§5.1 A problem
§5.2 Thinking about the problem
  Stages of development; Strategy
§5.3 Back to the calculator!
  First attempt; Tokens; Implementing tokens; Using tokens
§5.4 Back to the drawing board
  Grammars; Writing a grammar
§5.5 Turning a grammar into code
  Implementing grammar rules; Expressions; Terms; Primary expressions
§5.6 Trying the first version
§5.7 Trying the second version
§5.8 Token streams
  Implementing Token_stream; Reading tokens; Reading numbers
§5.9 Program structure

5.1 A problem

AA Writing a program starts with a problem; that is, you have a problem that you'd like a program to help solve. Understanding that problem is key to a good program. After all, a program that solves the wrong problem is likely to be of little use to you, however elegant it may be. There are happy accidents when a program just happens to be useful for something for which it was never intended, but let's not rely on such rare luck. What we want is a program that simply and cleanly solves the problem we decided to solve.

At this stage, what would be a good program to look at? A program that

- Illustrates design and programming techniques
- Gives us a chance to explore the kinds of decisions that a programmer must make and the considerations that go into such decisions
- Doesn't require too many new programming language constructs
- Is complicated enough to require thought about its design
- Allows for many variations in its solution
- Solves an easily understood problem
- Solves a problem that's worth solving
- Has a solution that is small enough to completely present and completely comprehend

We chose "Get the computer to do ordinary arithmetic on expressions we type in"; that is, we want to write a simple calculator. Such programs are clearly useful; every personal computer and modern phone comes with such a program.

For example, if you enter

```
2+3.1*4
```

the program should respond

```
14.4
```

Unfortunately, such a calculator program doesn't give us anything we don't already have available on our computer, but that would be too much to ask from a first program.

5.2 Thinking about the problem

So how do we start? Basically, think a bit about the problem and how to solve it. First think about what the program should do and how you'd like to interact with it. Later, you can think about how the program could be written to do that. Try writing down a brief sketch of an idea for a solution and see what's wrong with that first idea. Maybe discuss the problem and how to solve it with a friend. Trying to explain something to a friend is a marvelous way of figuring out what's wrong with ideas, even better than writing them down; paper (or a computer) doesn't talk back at you and challenge your assumptions. Ideally, design isn't a lonely activity.

Unfortunately, there isn't a general strategy for problem solving that works for all people and all problems. There are whole books that claim to help you be better at problem solving and another huge branch of literature that deals with program design. We won't go there. Instead, we'll present a page's worth of suggestions for a strategy for the kind of smaller problems an individual might face. After that, we'll quickly proceed to try out these suggestions on our tiny calculator problem.

When reading our discussion of the calculator program, we recommend that you adopt a more than usually skeptical attitude. For realism, we evolve our program through a series of versions, presenting the reasoning that leads to each version along the way. Obviously, much of that reasoning must be incomplete or even faulty, or we would finish the chapter early. As we go along, we provide examples of the kinds of concerns and reasoning that designers and programmers deal with all the time. We don't reach a version of the program that we are happy with until the end of the next chapter.

Please keep in mind that for this chapter and the next, the way we get to the final version of the program – the journey through partial solutions, ideas, and mistakes – is at least as important as that final version and more important than the language-technical details we encounter along the way (we will get back to those later).

5.2.1 Stages of development

Here is a bit of terminology for program development. As you work on a problem you repeatedly go through these stages: CC

- *Analysis*: Figure out what should be done and write a description of your (current) understanding of that. Such a description is called a *set of requirements* or a *specification*. We will not go into details about how such requirements are developed and written down. That's beyond the scope of this book, but it becomes increasingly important as the size of problems increases.
- *Design*: Create an overall structure for the system, deciding which parts the implementation should have and how those parts should communicate. As part of the design consider which tools – such as libraries – can help you structure the program.
- *Implementation*: Write the code, debug it, and test that it does what it is supposed to do.

5.2.2 Strategy

Here are some suggestions that – when applied thoughtfully and with imagination – help with many programming projects: AA

[1] What is the problem to be solved? The first thing to do is to try to be specific about what you are trying to accomplish. This typically involves constructing a description of the problem or – if someone else gave you such a statement – trying to figure out what it really means. At this point you should take the user's point of view (not the programmer/implementer's view); that is, you should ask questions about what the program should do, not about how it is going to do it. Ask: "What can this program do for me?" and "How would I like to interact with this program?" Remember, most of us have lots of experience as users of computers on which to draw.

- Is the problem statement clear? For real problems, it never is. Even for a student exercise, it can be hard to be sufficiently precise and specific. So we try to clarify it. It would be a pity if we solved the wrong problem. Another pitfall is to ask for too much. When we try to figure out what we want, we easily get too greedy/ambitious. It is almost always better to ask for less to make a program easier to specify, easier to understand, easier to use, and (hopefully) easier to implement. Once it works, we can always build a fancier "version 2.0" based on our experience.

- Does the problem seem manageable, given the time, skills, and tools available? There is little point in starting a project that you couldn't possibly complete. If there isn't sufficient time to implement (including testing) a program that does all that is required, it is usually wise not to start. Instead, acquire more resources (especially more time) or (best of all) modify the requirements to simplify your task.

[2] Try breaking the program into manageable parts. Even the smallest program for solving a real problem is large enough to be subdivided.

- Do you know of any tools, libraries, etc. that might help? The answer is almost always yes. Even at the earliest stage of learning to program, you have parts of the C++ standard library. Later, you'll know large parts of that standard library and how to find more. You'll have graphics and GUI libraries, and more. Once you have gained a little experience, you will be able to find thousands of libraries by simple Web searches. Remember: There is little value in reinventing the wheel when you are building software for real use. When learning to program it is a different matter; then, reinventing the wheel to see how that is done is often a good idea. Any time you save by using a good library can be spent on other parts of your problem, or on rest. How do you know that a library is appropriate for your task and of sufficient quality? That's a hard problem. Part of the solution is to ask colleagues, to ask in discussion groups, and to try small examples before committing to use a library.
- Look for parts of a solution that can be separately described (and potentially used in several places in a program or even in other programs). To find such parts requires experience, so we provide many examples throughout this book. We have already used `vector`, `string`, and `iostreams` (`cin` and `cout`). This chapter gives the first complete examples of design, implementation, and use of program parts provided as user-defined types (`Token` and `Token_stream`). Chapter 7, Chapter 11 – Chapter 14 present many more examples together with their design rationales. For now, consider an analogy: If we were to design a car, we would start by identifying parts, such as wheels, engine, computers, seats, door handles, etc., on which we could work separately before assembling the complete car. There are tens of thousands of such parts of a modern car. A real-world program is no different in that respect, except of course that the parts are all code. We would not try to build a car directly out of raw materials, such as iron, plastics, and wood. Nor would we try to build a major program directly out of (just) the expressions, statements, and types provided by the language. Designing and implementing such parts is a major theme of this book and of software development in general; see the discussions of user-defined types (Chapter 8), class hierarchies (Chapter 12), and generic types (Chapter 19).

[3] Build a small, limited version of the program that solves a key part of the problem. When we start, we rarely know the problem well. We often think we do (don't we all know what a calculator program is?), but we don't. Only a combination of thinking about the problem (analysis) and experimentation (design and implementation) gives us the solid understanding that we need to write a good program. So first, we build a small, limited version.

- To bring out problems in our understanding, ideas, and tools.

- To see if details of the problem statement need changing to make the problem manageable. It is rare to find that we had anticipated everything when we analyzed the problem and made the initial design. We should take advantage of the feedback that writing code and testing give us.

Sometimes, such a limited initial version aimed at experimentation is called a *prototype*. If (as is likely) our first version doesn't work or is so ugly and awkward that we don't want to work with it, we throw it away and make another limited version based on our experience. Repeat until we find a version that we are happy with. Do not proceed with a mess; messes just grow with time.

[4] Build a full-scale solution, ideally by using parts of the initial version. The ideal is to grow a program from working parts rather than writing all the code at once. The alternative is to hope that by some miracle an untested idea will work and do what we want.

5.3 Back to the calculator!

How do we want to interact with the calculator? That's easy: we know how to use **cin** and **cout**, but graphical user interfaces (GUIs) are not explained until Chapter 14, so we'll stick to the keyboard and a console window. Given expressions as input from the keyboard, we evaluate them and write out the resulting value to the screen. For example:

```
Expression: 2+2
Result: 4
Expression: 2+2*3
Result: 8
Expression: 2+3−25/5
Result: 0
```

The expressions, e.g., **2+2** and **2+2*3**, should be entered by the user; the rest is produced by the program. We chose to output **Expression:** to prompt the user. We could have chosen **Please enter an expression followed by a newline** but that seemed verbose and pointless. On the other hand, a pleasantly short prompt, such as **>**, seemed too cryptic. Sketching out such examples of use early on is important. They provide a very practical definition of what the program should minimally do. When discussing design and analysis, such examples of use are called *use cases*.

When faced with the calculator problem for the first time, most people come up with a first idea like this for the main logic of the program:

```
read_a_line
calculate        // do the work
write_result
```

This kind of "scribbles" clearly isn't code; it's called *pseudo code*. We tend to use it in the early stages of design when we are not yet certain exactly what our notation means. For example, is "calculate" a function call? If so, what would be its arguments? It is simply too early to answer such questions.

5.3.1 First attempt

At this point, we are not really ready to write the calculator program. We simply haven't thought hard enough, but thinking is hard work and – like most programmers – we are anxious to write some code. So let's take a chance, write a simple calculator, and see where it leads us. The first idea is something like

```
#include "PPP.h"

int main()
{
        cout << "Please enter expression (we can handle + and –): ";
        int lval = 0;
        int rval = 0;
        char op = 0;
        int res = 0;
        cin >> lval >> op >> rval;          // read something like 1 + 3

        if (op=='+')
                res = lval + rval;          // addition
        else if (op=='–')
                res = lval – rval;          // subtraction
        cout << "Result: " << res << '\n';
}
```

That is, read a pair of values separated by an operator, such as 2+2, compute the result (in this case 4), and print the resulting value. We chose the variable names lval for left-hand value and rval for right-hand value.

This (sort of) works! So what if this program isn't quite complete? It feels great to get something running! Maybe this programming and computer science stuff is easier than the rumors say. Well, maybe, but let's not get too carried away by an early success. Let's

[1] Clean up the code a bit
[2] Add multiplication and division (e.g., 2*3)
[3] Add the ability to handle more than one operand (e.g., 1+2+3)

In particular, we know that we should always check that our input is reasonable (in our hurry, we "forgot") and that testing a value against many constants is best done by a switch-statement rather than an if-statement.

The "chaining" of operations, such as 1+2+3+4, we will handle by adding the values as they are read; that is, we start with 1, see +2 and add 2 to 1 (getting an intermediate result 3), see +3 and add that 3 to our intermediate result (3), and so on. After a few false starts and after correcting a few syntax and logic errors, we get

```
#include "PPP.h"

int main()
{
        cout << "Please enter expression (we can handle +, –, *, and /)\n";
        cout << "add an x to end expression (e.g., 1+2*3x): ";
```

```
        int lval = 0;
        int rval = 0;
        cin>>lval;                          // read left-most operand
        if (!cin)
                error("no first operand");

        for (char op; cin>>op; ) {          // read operator and right-hand operand repeatedly
                if (op!='x')
                        cin>>rval;
                if (!cin)
                        error("no second operand");
                switch(op) {
                case '+':
                        lval += rval;       // add: lval = lval + rval
                        break;
                case '-':
                        lval -= rval;       // subtract: lval = lval - rval
                        break;
                case '*':
                        lval *= rval;       // multiply: lval = lval * rval
                        break;
                case '/':
                        lval /= rval;       // divide: lval = lval / rval
                        break;
                default:                    // not another operator: print result
                        cout << "Result: " << lval << '\n';
                        return 0;
                }
        }
        error("bad expression");
}
```

This isn't bad, but then we try **1+2*3** (really **1+2*3x**, but let's ignore the terminating **x** for now) and see that the result is **9** and not the **7** our arithmetic teacher told us was the right answer. Similarly, **1–2*3** gives **–3** rather than the **–5** we expected. We are doing the operations in the wrong order: **1+2*3** is calculated as **(1+2)*3** rather than as the conventional **1+(2*3)**. Similarly, **1–2*3** is calculated as **(1–2)*3** rather than as the conventional **1–(2*3)**. Bummer! We might consider the convention that "multiplication binds tighter than addition" as a silly old convention, but hundreds of years of convention will not disappear just to simplify our programming.

5.3.2 Tokens

So (somehow), we have to "look ahead" on the line to see if there is a * (or a /). If so, we have to (somehow) adjust the evaluation order from the simple and obvious left-to-right order. Unfortunately, trying to barge ahead here, we immediately hit a couple of snags:

[1] We don't actually need for an expression to be on one line. For example:

```
1
+
2
```

works perfectly with our code so far.

[2] How do we search for a * (or a /) among digits, plusses, minuses, and parentheses on several input lines?

[3] How do we remember where a * was?

[4] How do we handle evaluation that's not strictly left-to-right (e.g., **1+2*3**)?

Having decided to be super-optimists, we'll solve problems 1-3 first and not worry about 4 until later.

Also, we'll ask around for help. Surely someone will know a conventional way of reading "stuff," such as numbers and operators, from input and storing it in a way that lets us look at it in convenient ways. The conventional and very useful answer is "tokenize": first input characters are read and assembled into *tokens*, so if you type in

```
45+11.5/7
```

the program should produce a list of tokens representing

```
45
+
11.5
/
7
```

CC A *token* is a sequence of characters that represents something we consider a unit, such as a number or an operator. That's the way a C++ compiler deals with its source. Actually, "tokenizing" in some form or another is the way most analysis of text starts. Following the example of C++ expression, we see the need for three kinds of tokens:

- Floating-point-literals: as defined by C++, e.g., **3.14**, **0.274e2** (i.e., $0.274*10^2$), and **42**
- Operators: e.g., **+**, **–**, *****, **/**, and **%**
- Parentheses: **(** and **)**

The floating-point-literals look as if they may become a problem: reading **12** seems much easier than reading **12.3e–4** (i.e., $12.3*10^{-4}$; i.e, 12.3/10000), but calculators do tend to do floating-point arithmetic. Similarly, we suspect that we'll have to accept parentheses to have our calculator deemed useful.

How do we represent such tokens in our program? We could try to keep track of where each token started (and ended), but that gets messy. Also, if we keep a number as a string of characters, we later have to figure out what its value is; that is, if we see **42** and store the characters **4** and **2** somewhere, we then later have to figure out that those characters represent the numerical value **42** (i.e., **4*10+2**). The obvious – and conventional – solution is to represent each token as a (*kind,value*) pair. The *kind* tells us if a token is a number, an operator, or a parenthesis. For a number, and in this example only for a number, we use its numerical value as its *value*.

CC So how do we express the idea of a (*kind,value*) pair in code? We define a type **Token** to represent tokens. Why? Remember why we use types: they hold the data we need and give us useful operations on that data. For example, **int**s hold integers and give us addition, subtraction, multiplication, division, and remainder, whereas **strings** hold sequences of characters and give us concatenation and subscripting. The C++ language and its standard library give us many types such as **char**, **int**, **double**, **string**, **vector**, and **ostream**, but not a **Token** type. In fact, there is a huge number of types – thousands or tens of thousands – that we would like to have, but the language and its standard library do not supply them. Among our favorite types that are not supported are **Matrix** (see PPP2.Ch24), **Shape** (see Chapter 10) and infinite precision integers (try searching the Web for **Bignum**). If you think about it for a second, you'll realize that a language cannot supply tens of thousands of types: who would define them, who would implement them, how would you find them, and how thick would the manual have to be? Like most modern languages, C++ escapes that problem by letting us define our own types (*user-defined types*) when we need them.

5.3.3 Implementing tokens

What should a token look like in our program? In other words, what would we like our **Token** type to be? A **Token** must be able to represent operators, such as **+** and **–**, and numeric values, such as **42** and **3.14**. The obvious implementation is something that can represent what "kind" a token is and hold the numeric value for tokens that have one:

There are many ways that this idea could be represented in C++ code. Here is the simplest that we found useful:

```
class Token {          // a very simple user-defined type
public:
      char kind;
      double value;
};
```

A **Token** is a type (like **int** or **char**), so it can be used to define variables and hold values. It has two parts (called *members*): **kind** and **value**. The keyword **class** means "user-defined type"; it indicates that a type with zero or more members is being defined. The first member, **kind**, is a character, **char**, so that it conveniently can hold **'+'** and **'*'** to represent + (plus) and * (multiply). We can use it to make types like this:

```
Token t;               // t is a Token
t.kind = '+';          // t represents a +
Token t2;              // t2 is another Token
t2.kind = '8';         // we use the digit 8 as the "kind" for numbers
t2.value = 3.14;
```

We use the member access notation to access a member:

object_name . *member_name*

You can read **t.kind** as "**t**'s **kind**" and **t2.value** as "**t2**'s **value**." We can copy **Tokens** just as we can copy **ints**:

```
Token tt = t;                  // copy initialization
if (tt.kind != t.kind)
      error("impossible!");
t = t2;                        // assignment
cout << t.value;               // will print 3.14
```

We can represent the expression **(1.5+4)*11** using seven **Tokens**:

'('	'8'	'+'	'8'	')'	'*'	'8'
	1.5		4			11

Note that for simple tokens, such as **+**, we don't need the value, so we don't use its **value** member. We needed a character to mean "number" and picked **'8'** just because **'8'** obviously isn't an operator or a punctuation character. Using **'8'** to mean "number" is a bit cryptic, but it'll do for now.

Token is an example of a C++ user-defined type. A user-defined type can have member functions (operations) as well as data members. Here, we just provide two functions to make it more convenient to initialize a **Token**.

```
class Token {
public:
      char kind;                                           // what kind of token
      double value;                                        // for numbers: a value
      Token(char k) :kind{k}, value{0.0} {}                // construct from one value
      Token(char k, double v) :kind{k}, value{v} {}        // construct from two values
};
```

We can now initialize ("construct") **Tokens**. For example:

```
Token t1 {'+'};           // initialize t1 so that t1.kind = '+'
Token t2 {'8',11.5};      // initialize t2 so that t2.kind = '8' and t2.value = 11.5
Token t3;                 // error: initializer missing for t3
```

For more about initializing class objects, see §8.4.2 and §8.7.

5.3.4 Using tokens

So, maybe now we can complete our calculator! However, maybe a small amount of planning ahead would be worthwhile. How would we use **Tokens** in the calculator? We can read input into a **vector** of **Tokens**:

```
Token get_token();        // function to read a token from cin

vector<Token> tok;        // we'll put the tokens here
```

```
int main()
{
      // ...
      while (cin) {
            Token t = get_token();
            tok.push_back(t);
      }
      // ...
}
```

Now we can read an expression first and evaluate later. For example, for 11*12, we get

'8'	'*'	'8'
11		12

We can look at that to find the multiplication and its operands. Having done that, we can easily perform the multiplication because the numbers 11 and 12 are stored as numeric values and not as strings.

Now let's look at more complex expressions. Given 1+2*3, tok will contain five Tokens:

'8'	'+'	'8'	'*'	'8'
1		2		3

Now we could find the multiply operation by a simple loop:

```
for (int i = 0; i<tok.size(); ++i) {
      if (tok[i].kind=='*') {                   // we found a multiply!
            double d = tok[i−1].value*tok[i+1].value;
            // now what?
      }
}
```

Yes, but now what? What do we do with that product d? How do we decide in which order to evaluate the sub-expressions? Well, + comes before * so we can't just evaluate from left to right. We could try right-to-left evaluation! That would get 1+2*3 right but not 1*2+3. Worse still, consider 1+2*3+4. This example has to be evaluated "inside out": 1+(2*3)+4. And how will we handle parentheses, as we eventually will have to do? We seem to have hit a dead end. We need to back off, stop programming for a while, and think about how we read and understand an input string and evaluate it as an arithmetic expression.

So, this first enthusiastic attempt to solve the problem (writing a calculator) ran out of steam. That's not uncommon for first tries, and it serves the important role of helping us understand the problem. In this case, it even gave us the useful notion of a token, which itself is an example of the notion of a (*name,value*) pair that we will encounter again and again. However, we must always make sure that such relatively thoughtless and unplanned "coding" doesn't steal too much time. We should do very little programming before we have done at least a bit of analysis (understanding the problem) and design (deciding on an overall structure of a solution). CC

TRY THIS

On the other hand, why shouldn't we be able to find a simple solution to this problem? It doesn't seem to be all that difficult. If nothing else, trying would give us a better appreciation of the problem and the eventual solution. Consider what you might do right away. For example, look at the input 12.5+2. We could tokenize that, decide that the expression was simple, and compute the answer. That may be a bit messy, but straightforward, so maybe we could proceed in this direction and find something that's good enough! Consider what to do if we found both a + and a * in the line 2+3*4. That too can be handled by "brute force." How would we deal with a complicated expression, such as 1+2*3/4%5+(6–7*(8))? And how would we deal with errors, such as 2+*3 and 2&3? Consider this for a while, maybe doodling a bit on a piece of paper trying to outline possible solutions and interesting or important input expressions.

5.4 Back to the drawing board

Now, we will look at the problem again and try not to dash ahead with another half-baked solution. One thing that we did discover was that having the program (calculator) evaluate only a single expression was tedious. We would like to be able to compute several expressions in a single invocation of our program; that is, our pseudo code grows to

```
while (not_finished) {
    read_a_line
    calculate        // do the work
    write_result
}
```

Clearly this is a complication, but when we think about how we use calculators, we realize that doing several calculations is very common. Could we let the user invoke our program several times to do several calculations? We could, but program startup is unfortunately (and unreasonably) slow on many modern operating systems, so we'd better not rely on that.

As we look at this pseudo code, our early attempts at solutions, and our examples of use, several questions – some with tentative answers – arise:

[1] If we type in 45+5/7, how do we find the individual parts 45, +, 5, /, and 7 in the input? (Tokenize!)

[2] What terminates an input expression? A newline, of course! (Always be suspicious of "of course": "of course" is not a reason.)

[3] How do we represent 45+5/7 as data so that we can evaluate it? Before doing the addition we must somehow turn the characters 4 and 5 into the integer value 45 (i.e., 4*10+5). (So tokenizing is part of the solution.)

[4] How do we make sure that 45+5/7 is evaluated as 45+(5/7) and not as (45+5)/7?

[5] What's the value of 5/7? About .71, but that's not an integer. Based on experience with calculators, we know that people would expect a floating-point result. Should we also allow floating-point inputs? Sure!

[6] Can we have variables? For example, could we write

```
v=7
m=9
v*m
```

Good idea, but let's wait until later. Let's first get the basics working.

XX

Possibly the most important decision here is the answer to question 6. In §6.8, you'll see that if we had said yes we'd have almost doubled the size of the initial project. That would have more than doubled the time needed to get the initial version running. Our guess is that if you really are a novice, it would have at least quadrupled the effort needed and most likely pushed the project beyond your patience. It is most important to avoid "feature creep" early in a project. Instead, always first build a simple version, implementing the essential features only. Once we have something running, we can get more ambitious. It is far easier to build a program in stages than all at once. Saying yes to question 6 would have had yet another bad effect: it would have made it hard to resist the temptation to add further "neat features" later. How about adding the usual mathematical functions? How about adding loops? Once we start adding "neat features" it is hard to stop.

From a programmer's point of view, questions 1, 3, and 4 are the most bothersome. They are also related, because once we have found a 45 or a +, what do we do with them? That is, how do we store them in our program? Obviously, tokenizing is an essential part of the solution, but only one part.

AA

What would an experienced programmer do? When we are faced with a tricky technical question, there often is a standard answer. We know that people have been writing calculator programs for at least as long as there have been computers taking symbolic input from a keyboard. That is at least for 70 years. There has to be a standard answer! In such a situation, the experienced programmer consults colleagues and/or the literature. It would be silly to barge on, hoping to beat 70 years of experience in a morning.

5.4.1 Grammars

There is a standard answer to the question of how to make sense of expressions: first input characters are read and assembled into tokens (as we discovered). So if you type in

```
45+11.5/7
```

the program should produce a list of tokens representing

```
45
+
11.5
/
7
```

A token is a sequence of characters that represents something we consider a unit, such as a number or an operator.

CC

After tokens have been produced, the program must ensure that complete expressions are understood correctly. For example, we know that 45+11.5/7 means 45+(11.5/7) and not (45+11.5)/7, but how do we teach the program that useful rule (division "binds tighter" than addition)? The standard answer is that we write a *grammar* defining the syntax of our input and then write a program that implements the rules of that grammar. For example:

```
// a simple expression grammar:
Expression:
    Term
    Expression "+" Term        // addition
    Expression "–" Term        // subtraction
Term:
    Primary
    Term "*" Primary           // multiplication
    Term "/" Primary           // division
    Term "%" Primary           // remainder (modulo)
Primary:
    Number
    "(" Expression ")"         // grouping
Number:
    floating–point–literal
```

This is a set of simple rules. The last rule is read "A **Number** is a **floating–point–literal**." The next-to-last rule says, "A **Primary** is a **Number** or a '(' followed by an **Expression** followed by a ')'." The rules for **Expression** and **Term** are similar; each is defined in terms of rules and tokens.

As seen in §5.3.2, our tokens – as borrowed from the C++ definition – are

- **floating–point–literal** (as defined by C++, e.g., **3.14**, **0.274e2**, or **42**)
- **+**, **–**, *****, **/**, **%** (the operators)
- **(**, **)** (the parentheses)

From our first tentative pseudo code to this approach, using tokens and a grammar is actually a huge conceptual jump. It's the kind of jump we hope for but rarely manage without help. This is what experience, the literature, and Mentors are for.

At first glance, a grammar probably looks like complete nonsense. Technical notation often does. However, please keep in mind that it is a general and elegant (as you will eventually appreciate) notation for something you have been able to do since middle school (or earlier). You have no problem calculating **1–2*3** and **1+2–3** and **3*2+4/2**. It seems hardwired in your brain. However, could you explain how you do it? Could you explain it well enough for someone who had never seen conventional arithmetic to grasp? Could you do so for every combination of operators and operands? To articulate an explanation in sufficient detail and precisely enough for a computer to understand, we need a notation – and a grammar is a most powerful and conventional tool for that.

How do we read a grammar? Basically, given some input, we start with the "top rule," **Expression**, and search through the rules to find a match for the tokens as they are read. That strategy is called *top-down*. Alternatively, we can look at a token and see which grammar rules might make sense, then look at the next token to see which still makes sense until we find a unique answer. That strategy is called *bottom-up*.

Reading a stream of tokens according to a grammar is called *parsing,* and a program that does that is often called a *parser* or a *syntax analyzer*. There are thick books written about how to express grammars and how to write parsers for them. There are programs, *parser generators*, for generating parsers from grammars. However, our topic here is programming and we deliberately muddle along without a deep understanding of parser theory, exploring design and programming techniques.

Our parser reads the tokens from left to right, just like we type them and read them. Let's try something really simple: Is 2 an expression?

2 is a floating-point-literal which is a Number which is a Primary which is a Term which is an Expression

So yes, according to our grammar, 2 is an expression.

Let's try something a bit more complicated: Is 2+3 an Expression? Naturally, much of the reasoning is the same as for 2:

Next, we see a +:

- is the left-hand side an Expression? Yes, 2 is an Expression.
- is the right-hand side of the + a Term? Yes, 3 is a Term.

The real reason we are interested in grammars is that they can solve our problem of how to correctly parse expressions with both + and ∗, so let's try 45+11.5∗7. However, "playing computer" following the rules in detail as we did above is tedious, so let's skip some of the intermediate steps that we have already gone through for 2 and 2+3. Obviously, 45, 11.5, and 7 are all floating-point-literals which are Numbers, which are Primarys, so we can ignore all rules below Primary. So we get:

[1] 45 is an Expression followed by a +, so we look for a Term to finish the Expression+Term rule.

[2] 11.5 is a Term followed by ∗, so we look for a Primary to finish the Term∗Primary rule. Yes, 11.5∗7 is a Term.

[3] Now we can see that 45+11.5∗7 is an Expression according to the Expression+Term rule. In particular, it is an Expression that first does the multiplication 11.5∗7 and then the addition 45+11.5∗7, just as if we had written 45+(11.5∗7).

You may find this logic hard to follow at first but simple grammars are not particularly hard to understand. However, we are not really trying to teach *you* to understand 2+3 or 45+11.5∗7. Obviously, you know that already. We are trying to find a way for the computer to "understand" 45+11.5∗7 and all the other complicated expressions you might give it to evaluate. Actually, complicated grammars are not fit for humans to read, but computers are good at it. They follow grammar rules quickly and correctly with the greatest of ease. Following precise rules is exactly what computers are good at.

5.4.2 Writing a grammar

How did we pick those expression grammar rules? "Experience" is the honest answer. The way we do it is simply the way people usually write expression grammars. However, writing a simple grammar is pretty straightforward: we need to know how to **AA**

[1] Distinguish a rule from a token
[2] Put one rule after another (*sequencing*)
[3] Express alternative patterns (*alternation*)
[4] Express a repeating pattern (*repetition*)
[5] Recognize the grammar rule to start with

Different textbooks and different parser systems use different notational conventions and different terminology. For example, some call tokens *terminals* and rules *non-terminals* or *productions*. We simply put tokens in (double) quotes and start with the first rule. Alternatives are put on separate lines. For example:

```
List:
    "{" Sequence "}"
Sequence:
    Element
    Element "," Sequence
Element:
    "A"
    "B"
```

So a **Sequence** is either an **Element** or an **Element** followed by a **Sequence** using a comma for separation. An **Element** is either the letter **A** or the letter **B**. A **List** is a **Sequence** in "curly brackets." We can generate these **Lists** (how?):

```
{ A }
{ B }
{ A,B }
{ A,A,A,A,B }
```

However, these are not **Lists** (why not?):

```
{ }
A
{ A,A,A,A,B
{ A,A,C,A,B }
{ A B C }
{ A,A,A,A,B, }
```

This sequence rule is not one you learned in kindergarten or have hardwired into your brain, but it is still not rocket science. See §6.4 and §6.8.1 for examples of how we work with a grammar to express syntactic ideas.

5.5 Turning a grammar into code

There are many ways of getting a computer to follow a grammar. We'll use the simplest one: we simply write one function for each grammar rule and use our type **Token** to represent tokens. A program that implements a grammar is often called a *parser*.

5.5.1 Implementing grammar rules

To implement our calculator, we need four functions: one to read tokens plus one for each rule in our grammar:

```
get_token()      // read characters and compose tokens;   uses cin
expression()     // deal with + and -;                    calls term() and get_token()
term()           // deal with *, /, and %;                calls primary() and get_token()
primary()        // deal with numbers and parentheses;    calls expression() and get_token()
```

AA Note: Each function deals with a specific part of an expression and leaves everything else to other functions; this radically simplifies each function. This is much like a group of humans dealing with problems by letting each person handle problems in his or her own specialty, handing all other problems over to colleagues.

What should such a parsing function return? How about the answer we really wanted? For example, for 2+3, expression() could return 5. After all, the information is all there. That's what we'll try! Doing so will save us from answering one of the hardest questions from our list: "How do I represent 45+5/7 as data so that I can evaluate it?" Instead of storing a representation of 45+5/7 in memory, we simply evaluate it as we read it from input. This little idea is really a major break-through! It will keep the program to a quarter of the size it would have been if we had expression() return something complicated for later evaluation. We just saved ourselves about 80% of the work.

The "odd man out" is get_token(): because it deals with tokens, not expressions, it can't return the value of a sub-expression. For example, + and (are not expressions. So, it must return a Token. We conclude that we want functions to match the grammar rules:

```
Token get_token();          // read characters and compose tokens
double expression();        // deal with + and -
double term();              // deal with *, /, and %
double primary();           // deal with numbers and parentheses
```

5.5.2 Expressions

Let's first write expression(). The grammar looks like this:

```
Expression:
      Term
      Expression "+" Term
      Expression "–" Term
```

Since this is our first attempt to turn a set of grammar rules into code, we'll proceed through a couple of false starts. That's the way it usually goes with new techniques, and we learn useful things along the way. In particular, a novice programmer can learn a lot from looking at the dramatically different behavior of similar pieces of code. Reading code is a useful skill to cultivate.

5.5.2.1 Expressions: first try

Looking at the Expression "+" Term rule, we try first calling expression(), then looking for + (and –) and then term():

```
double expression()
{
      double left = expression();          // read and evaluate an Expression
      Token t = get_token();               // get the next token
      switch (t.kind) {                    // see which kind of token it is
      case '+':
            return left + term();          // read and evaluate a Term, then do an add
      case '–':
            return left – term();          // read and evaluate a Term, then do a subtraction
      default:
            return left;                   // return the value of the Expression
      }
}
```

It looks good. It is almost a trivial transcription of the grammar. It is quite simple, really: first read an Expression and then see if it is followed by a + or a –, and if it is, read the Term.

Unfortunately, that doesn't really make sense. How do we know where the expression ends so that we can look for a + or a –? Remember, our program reads left to right and can't peek ahead to see if a + is coming. In fact, this expression() will never get beyond its first line: expression() starts by calling expression() which starts by calling expression() and so on "forever." This is called an *infinite recursion* and will in fact terminate after a short while when the computer runs out of memory to hold the "never-ending" sequence of calls of expression(). The term *recursion* is used to describe what happens when a function calls itself. Not all recursions are infinite, and recursion is a very useful programming technique (see §7.4.8).

5.5.2.2 Expressions: second try

So what do we do? Every Term is an Expression, but not every Expression is a Term; that is, we could start looking for a Term and look for a full Expression only if we found a + or a –. For example:

```
double expression()
{
        double left = term();                    // read and evaluate a Term
        Token t = get_token();                   // get the next token
        switch (t.kind) {                        // see which kind of token that is
        case '+':
                return left + expression();      // read and evaluate an Expression, then do an add
        case '–':
                return left – expression();      // read and evaluate an Expression, then do a subtraction
        default:
                return left;                     // return the value of the Term
        }
}
```

This actually – more or less – works. We have tried it in the finished program and it parses every correct expression we throw at it (and no illegal ones). It even correctly evaluates most expressions. For example, 1+2 is read as a Term (with the value 1) followed by + followed by an Expression with the value 2) and gives the answer 3. Similarly, 1+2+3 gives 6.

We could go on for quite a long time about what works, but to make a long story short: How about 1–2–3? This expression() will read the 1 as a Term, then proceed to read 2–3 as an Expression (consisting of the Term 2 followed by the Expression 3). It will then subtract the value of 2–3 from 1. In other words, it will evaluate 1–(2–3). The value of (2–3) is –1 so the value of 1–(2–3) is 0. However, we were taught (in primary school or even earlier) that 1–2–3 means (1–2)–3 and therefore has the value –4 (negative four).

XX So we got a very nice program that just didn't do the right thing. That's dangerous. It is especially dangerous because it gives the right answer in many cases. For example, 1+2+3 gives the right answer (6) because 1+(2+3) equals (1+2)+3.

What, fundamentally, from a programming point of view, did we do wrong? We should always ask ourselves this question when we have found an error. That way we might avoid making the same mistake again, and again, and again.

Fundamentally, we just looked at the code and guessed. That's rarely good enough! We have to understand what our code is doing and we have to be able to explain why it does the right thing.

Analyzing our errors is often also the best way to find a correct solution. What we did here was to define **expression()** to first look for a **Term** and then, if that **Term** is followed by a **+** or a **–**, look for an **Expression**. Our code actually implements a slightly different grammar:

```
Expression:
        Term
        Term "+" Expression          // addition
        Term "–" Expression          // subtraction
```

The difference from our desired grammar is exactly that we wanted **1–2–3** to be the **Expression 1–2** followed by **–** followed by the **Term 3**, but what we got here was the **Term 1** followed by **–** followed by the **Expression 2–3**. That is, we wanted **1–2–3** to mean **(1–2)–3** but we got **1–(2–3)**.

Yes, debugging can be tedious, tricky, and time-consuming, but in this case, we are really working through rules you learned in primary school and learned to apply without too much trouble. The snag is that we have to teach the rules to a computer – and a computer is a far slower learner than you are.

We could have defined **1–2–3** to mean **1–(2–3)** rather than **(1–2)–3** and avoided this discussion altogether. Often, the trickiest programming problems come when we must match conventional rules that were established by and for humans long before we started using computers.

5.5.2.3 Expressions: third time lucky

So, what now? Look again at the grammar (the correct grammar in §5.5.2): any **Expression** starts with a **Term** and such a **Term** can be followed by a **+** or a **–**. So, we have to look for a **Term**, see if it is followed by a **+** or a **–**, and keep doing that until there are no more plusses or minuses. For example:

```
double expression()
{
        double left = term();                   // read and evaluate a Term
        Token t = get_token();                  // get the next token
        while (t.kind=='+' || t.kind=='–') {    // look for a + or a -
                if (t.kind == '+')
                        left += term();         // evaluate Term and add
                else
                        left –= term();         // evaluate Term and subtract
                t = get_token();
        }
        return left;                            // finally: no more + or -; return the answer
}
```

This is a bit messier: we had to introduce a loop to keep looking for plusses and minuses. We also got a bit repetitive: we test for **+** and **–** twice and twice call **get_token()**. Because it obscures the logic of the code, let's just get rid of the duplication of the test for **+** and -:

```
double expression()
{
	double left = term();          // read and evaluate a Term
	Token t = get_token();         // get the next token
	while (true) {
		switch (t.kind) {
		case '+':
			left += term();        // evaluate Term and add
			t = get_token();
			break;
		case '–':
			left –= term();        // evaluate Term and subtract
			t = get_token();
			break;
		default:
			return left;           // finally: no more + or -; return the answer
		}
	}
}
```

Note that – except for the loop – this is actually rather similar to our first try (§5.6). What we have done is to remove the mention of **expression()** within **expression()** and replace it with a loop. In other words, we translated the **Expression** in the grammar rules for **Expression** into a loop looking for a **Term** followed by a **+** or a **–**.

5.5.3 Terms

The grammar rule for **Term** is very similar to the **Expression** rule:

```
Term:
	Primary
	Term "*" Primary
	Term "/' Primary
	Term "%" Primary
```

Consequently, the code should be very similar also. Here is a first try:

```
double term()
{
	double left = primary();
	Token t = get_token();
	while (true) {
		switch (t.kind) {
		case '*':
			left *= primary();
			t = get_token();
			break;
```

```
            case '/':
                  left /= primary();
                  t = get_token();
                  break;
            case '%':
                  left %= primary();
                  t = get_token();
                  break;
            default:
                  return left;
            }
      }
}
```

Unfortunately, this doesn't compile: the remainder operation (%) is not defined for floating-point numbers. The compiler kindly tells us so. When we answered question 5 in §5.4 – "Should we also allow floating-point inputs?" – with a confident "Sure!" we actually hadn't thought the issue through and fell victim to *feature creep*. That *always* happens! So what do we do about it? We could at run time check that both operands of % are integers and give an error if they are not. Or we could simply leave % out of our calculator. Let's take the simplest choice for now. We can always add % later (§6.5). XX

After we eliminate the % case, the function works: terms are correctly parsed and evaluated. However, an experienced programmer will notice an undesirable detail that makes **term()** unacceptable. What would happen if you entered **2/0**? You can't divide by zero. If you try, the computer hardware will detect it and terminate your program with a somewhat unhelpful error message. An inexperienced programmer will discover this the hard way. So, we'd better check and give a decent error message:

```
double term()
{
      double left = primary();
      Token t = get_token();
      while (true) {
            switch (t.kind) {
            case '*':
                  left *= primary();
                  t = get_token();
                  break;
            case '/':
            {     double d = primary();
                  if (d == 0)
                        error("divide by zero");
                  left /= d;
                  t = get_token();
                  break;
            }
```

```
            default:
                return left;
            }
        }
}
```

Why did we put the statements handling / into a block? (§3.4.2.2, between curly braces '{' '}'). The compiler insists. If you want to define and initialize variables within a **case** of a **switch**-statement, you must place them inside a block.

5.5.4 Primary expressions

The grammar rule for primary expressions is also simple:

```
Primary:
        Number
        "(" Expression ")"
```

The code that implements it is a bit messy because there are more opportunities for syntax errors:

```
double primary()
{
        Token t = get_token();
        switch (t.kind) {
        case '(':                       // handle '(' expression ')'
        {       double d = expression();
                t = get_token();
                if (t.kind != ')')
                        error("')' expected");
                return d;
        }
        case '8':                       // we use '8' to represent a number
                return t.value;         // return the number's value
        default:
                error("primary expected");
        }
}
```

Basically there is nothing new compared to **expression()** and **term()**. We use the same language primitives, the same way of dealing with **Token**s, and the same programming techniques.

5.6 Trying the first version

To run these calculator functions, we need to implement **get_token()** and provide a **main()**. The **main()** is trivial: we just keep calling **expression()** and printing out its result:

```
int main()
try {
        while (cin)
                cout << expression() << '\n';
}
catch (exception& e) {
        cerr << e.what() << '\n';
        return 1;
}
catch (...) {
        cerr << "exception \n";
        return 2;
}
```

The error handling is the usual "boilerplate" (§4.6.3). Let us postpone the description of the implementation of get_token() to §5.8 and test this first version of the calculator.

> TRY THIS
>
> This first version of the calculator program (including get_token()) is available as file calculator00.cpp. Get it to run and try it out.

Unsurprisingly, this first version of the calculator doesn't work quite as we expected. So we shrug and ask, "Why not?" or rather, "So, why does it work the way it does?" and "What does it do?" Type a 2 followed by a newline. No response. Try another newline to see if it's asleep. Still no response. Type a 3 followed by a newline. No response! Type a 4 followed by a newline. It answers 2! Now the screen looks like this:

```
2
3
4
2
```

We carry on by typing 5+6. The program responds with a 5, so that the screen looks like this:

```
2
3
4
2
5+6
5
```

Unless you have programmed before, you are most likely very puzzled! In fact, even an experienced programmer might be puzzled. What's going on here? At this point, you try to get out of the program. How do you do this? We "forgot" to program an exit command, but an error will cause the program to exit, so you type an x and the program prints Bad token and exits. Finally, something worked as planned!

However, we forgot to distinguish between input and output on the screen. Before we try to solve the main puzzle, let's just fix the output to better see what we are doing. Adding an = to indicate output will do for now:

```
while (cin)
        cout << "="<< expression() << '\n';    // version 2: '=' added
```

Now, entering the exact sequence of characters as before, we get

```
2
3
4
=2
5+6
=5
x
Bad token
```

Strange! Try to figure out what the program did. We tried another few examples, but let's just look at this. This is a puzzle:

- Why didn't the program respond after the first 2 and 3 and the newlines?
- Why did the program respond with 2, rather than 4, after we entered 4?
- Why did the program answer 5, rather than 11, after 5+6?

There are many possible ways of proceeding from such mysterious results. We'll examine some of those in the next chapter, but here, let's just think. Could the program be doing bad arithmetic? That's most unlikely; computers are good at arithmetic. Consider what happens when we enter

```
1 2 3 4+5 6+7 8+9 10 11 12
```

followed by a newline. We get

```
1 2 3 4+5 6+7 8+9 10 11 12
=1
=4
=6
=8
=10
```

Huh? No 2 or 3. Why 4 and not 9 (that is, 4+5)? Why 6 and not 13 (that is, 6+7)? Look carefully: the program is outputting every third token! Maybe the program "eats" some of our input without evaluating it? It does. Consider expression():

```
double expression()
{
        double left = term();            // read and evaluate a Term
        Token t = get_token();           // get the next token
        while (true) {
                switch (t.kind) {
                case '+':
                        left += term();  // evaluate Term and add
                        t = get_token();
                        break;
```

```
            case '-':
                  left -= term();          // evaluate Term and subtract
                  t = get_token();
                  break;
            default:
                  return left;              // finally: no more + or -; return the answer
            }
      }
}
```

When the **Token** returned by **get_token()** is not a **+** or a **-** we just return. We don't use that token and we don't store it anywhere for any other function to use later. That's not smart. Throwing away input without even determining what it is can't be a good idea. A quick look shows that **term()** has exactly the same problem. That explains why our calculator ate two tokens for each that it used.

Let us modify **expression()** so that it doesn't "eat" tokens. Where would we put that next token (**t**) when the program doesn't need it? We could think of many elaborate schemes, but let's jump to the obvious answer ("obvious" once you see it): that token is going to be used by some other function that is reading tokens from the input, so let's put the token back into the input stream so that it can be read again by some other function! Actually, you can put characters back into an **istream**, but that's not really what we want. We want to deal with tokens, not mess with characters. What we want is an input stream that deals with tokens and that you can put an already read token back into.

So, assume that we have a stream of tokens – a **Token_stream** – called **ts**. Assume further that a **Token_stream** has a member function **get()** that returns the next token and a member function **putback(t)** that puts a token **t** back into the stream. We'll implement that **Token_stream** in §5.8 as soon as we have had a look at how it needs to be used. Given **Token_stream**, we can rewrite **expression()** so that it puts a token that it does not use back into the **Token_stream**:

```
double expression()
{
      double left = term();           // read and evaluate a Term
      Token t = ts.get();             // get the next Token from the Token stream
      while (true) {
            switch (t.kind) {
            case '+':
                  left += term();      // evaluate Term and add
                  t = ts.get();
                  break;
            case '-':
                  left -= term();      // evaluate Term and subtract
                  t = ts.get();
                  break;
```

```
                default:
                        ts.putback(t);          // put t back into the token stream
                        return left;            // finally: no more + or -; return the answer
                }
        }
}
```

In addition, we must make the same change to **term()**:

```
double term()
{
        double left = primary();
        Token t = ts.get();                     // get the next Token from the Token stream
        while (true) {
                switch (t.kind) {
                case '*':
                        left *= primary();
                        t = ts.get();
                        break;
                case '/':
                {       double d = primary();
                        if (d == 0)
                                error("divide by zero");
                        left /= d;
                        t = ts.get();
                        break;
                }
                default:
                        ts.putback(t);          // put t back into the Token stream
                        return left;
                }
        }
}
```

For our last parser function, **primary()**, we just need to change **get_token()** to **ts.get()**; **primary()** uses every token it reads.

The style of parser used here is called *recursive descent* and is quite popular at industrial scale for yielding compact code and giving good error messages.

5.7 Trying the second version

So, we are ready to test our second version. This second version of the calculator program (including **Token_stream**) is available as file **calculator01.cpp**. Get it to run and try it out. Type **2** followed by a newline. No response. Try another newline to see if it's asleep. Still no response. Type a **3** followed by a newline and it answers **2**. Try **2+2** followed by a newline and it answers **3**. Now your screen looks like this:

```
2

3
=2
2+2
=3
```

Hmm. Maybe our introduction of **putback()** and its use in **expression()** and **term()** didn't fix the problem. Let's try another test:

```
2 3 4 2+3 2*3
=2
=3
=4
=5
```

Yes! These are correct answers! But the last answer (**6**) is missing. We still have a token-look-ahead problem. However, this time the problem is not that our code "eats" characters, but that it doesn't get any output for an expression until we enter the following expression. The result of an expression isn't printed immediately; the output is postponed until the program has seen the first token of the next expression. Unfortunately, the program doesn't see that token until we hit Return after the next expression. The program isn't really wrong; it is just a bit slow responding.

How can we fix this? One obvious solution is to require a "print command." So, let's accept a semicolon after an expression to terminate it and trigger output. And while we are at it, let's add an "exit command" to allow for graceful exit. The character **q** (for "quit") would do nicely for an exit command. In **main()**, we have

```
while (cin)
        cout << "=" << expression() << '\n';        // version 2: '=' added
```

We can change that to the messier but more useful

```
double val = 0;                                   // version 3: 'q' and ';' added
while (cin) {
        Token t = ts.get();
        if (t.kind == 'q')              // 'q' for "quit"
                break;
        if (t.kind == ';')              // ';' for "print now"
                cout << "=" << val << '\n';
        else
                ts.putback(t);
        val = expression();
}
```

Now the calculator is actually usable. For example, we get

```
2;
=2
2+3;
=5
3+4*5;
=23
q
```

At this point we have a good initial version of the calculator. It's not quite what we said we wanted, but we have a program that we can use as the base for making a more acceptable version. Importantly, we can now correct problems and add features one by one while maintaining a working program as we go along.

5.8 Token streams

Before further improving our calculator, let us show the implementation of **Token_stream**. After all, nothing – nothing at all – works until we get correct input. We implemented **Token_stream** first of all but didn't want too much of a digression from the problems of calculation before we had shown a minimal solution.

Input for our calculator is a sequence of tokens, just as we showed for **(1.5+4)*11** above (§5.3.3). What we need is something that reads characters from the standard input, **cin**, and presents the program with the next token when it asks for it. In addition, we saw that we – that is, our calculator program – often read a token too many, so that we must be able to put it back for later use. This is typical and fundamental; when you see **1.5+4** reading strictly left to right, how could you know that the number **1.5** had been completely read without reading the **+**? Until we see the **+** we might be on our way to reading **1.55555**. So, we need a "stream" that produces a token when we ask for one using **get()** and where we can put a token back into the stream using **putback()**. Everything we use in C++ has a type, so we have to start by defining the type **Token_stream**.

You probably noticed the **public:** in the definition of **Token** in §5.3.3. There, it had no apparent purpose. For **Token_stream**, we need it and must explain its function. A C++ user-defined type often consists of two parts: the public interface (labeled **public:**) and the implementation details (labeled **private:**). The idea is to separate what a user of a type needs for convenient use from the details that we need in order to implement the type, but that we'd rather not have users mess with:

```
class Token_stream {
public:
        // user interface
private:
        // implementation details
        // (not directly accessible to users of Token_stream)
};
```

CC Obviously, users and implementers are often just us "playing different roles," but making the distinction between the (public) interface meant for users and the (private) implementation details used only by the implementer is a powerful tool for structuring code. The public interface should contain (only) what a user needs, which is typically a set of functions. The private implementation contains what is necessary to implement those public functions, typically data and functions dealing with messy details that the users need not know about and shouldn't directly use.

Let's elaborate the Token_stream type a bit. What does a user want from it? Obviously, we want get() and putback() functions – that's why we invented the notion of a token stream. The Token_stream is to make Tokens out of characters that it reads from input, so we need to define a Token_stream that reads from cin. Thus, the simplest Token_stream looks like this:

```
class Token_stream {
public:
        Token get();                    // get a Token
        void putback(Token t);          // put a Token back
private:
        // ... implementation details ...
};
```

That's all a user needs to use a Token_stream. Experienced programmers will wonder why cin is the only possible source of characters, but we decided to take our input from the keyboard. We'll revisit that decision in a Chapter 6 exercise.

Why do we use the "verbose" name putback() rather than the logically sufficient put()? We wanted to emphasize the asymmetry between get() and putback(); this is an input stream, not something that you can also use for general output. Also, istream has a putback() function: consistency in naming is a useful property of a system. It helps people remember and helps people avoid errors.

We can now make a Token_stream and use it:

```
Token_stream ts;            // a Token_stream called ts
Token t = ts.get();         // get next Token from ts
// ...
ts.putback(t);              // put the Token t back into ts
```

That's all we need to write the rest of the calculator.

5.8.1 Implementing Token_stream

Now, we need to implement those two Token_stream functions. How do we represent a Token_stream? That is, what data do we need to store in a Token_stream for it to do its job? We need space for any token we put back into the Token_stream. To simplify, let's say we can put back at most one token at a time. That happens to be sufficient for our program (and for many, many similar programs). That way, we just need space for one Token and an indicator of whether that space is full or empty:

```
class Token_stream {
public:
        Token get();                    // get a Token (get() is defined in §5.8.2)
        void putback(Token t);          // put a Token back
private:
        bool full = false;              // is there a Token in the buffer?
        Token buffer;                   // putback() saves its token here
};
```

Note the way we can initialize a data member inside the class itself. That's called *default member initialization* or *in-class initialization* (§8.4.2).

Now, we can define the two member functions. The **putback()** is easy, so we will define it first. The **putback()** member function puts its argument back into the **Token_stream**'s buffer:

```
void Token_stream::putback(Token t)
{
        buffer = t;        // copy t to buffer
        full = true;       // buffer is now full
}
```

The keyword **void** (meaning "nothing") is used to indicate that **putback()** doesn't return a value.

When we define a member of a class outside the class definition itself, we have to mention which class we mean the member to be a member of. We use the notation

class_name :: *member_name*

for that. In this case, we define **Token_stream**'s member **putback**.

Why would we define a member outside its class? The main answer is clarity: the class definition (primarily) states what the class can do. Member function definitions are implementations that specify how things are done. We prefer to put them "elsewhere" where they don't distract. Our ideal is to have every logical entity in a program fit on a screen. Class definitions typically do that if the member function definitions are placed elsewhere, but not if they are placed within the class definition ("in-class").

If we wanted to make sure that we didn't try to use **putback()** twice without reading what we put back in between (using **get()**), we could add a test:

```
void Token_stream::putback(Token t)
{
        if (full)
                error("putback() into a full buffer");
        buffer = t;                // copy t to buffer
        full = true;               // buffer is now full
}
```

The test of **full** checks the precondition (§4.7.3.1) "Is the buffer already full?"

Obviously, a **Token_stream** should start out empty. That is, **full** should be **false** until after the first call of **get()**. We achieve that by initializing the member **full** right in the definition of **Token_stream**.

5.8.2 Reading tokens

All the real work is done by **get()**. If there isn't already a **Token** in **Token_stream::buffer**, **get()** must read characters from **cin** and compose them into **Tokens**:

```
Token Token_stream::get()
{
        if (full) {                    // do we already have a Token ready?
                full = false;          // remove Token from buffer
                return buffer;
        }
        char ch = 0;
        if !(cin >> ch)                // note that >> skips whitespace (space, newline, tab, etc.)
                error("no input");

        switch (ch) {
        case ';':                              // for "print"
        case 'q':                              // for "quit"
        case '(': case ')': case '+': case '–': case '*': case '/':
                return Token{ch};              // let each character represent itself
        case '.':
        case '0': case '1': case '2': case '3': case '4':
        case '5': case '6': case '7': case '8': case '9':
        {       cin.putback(ch);               // put digit back into the input stream
                double val = 0;
                cin >> val;                    // read a floating-point number
                return Token{'8',val};         // let '8' represent "a number"
        }
        default:
                error("Bad token");
        }
}
```

Let's examine **get()** in detail. First we check if we already have a **Token** in the buffer. If so, we can just return that:

```
if (full) {                    // do we already have a Token ready?
        full = false;          // remove Token from buffer
        return buffer;
}
```

Only if **full** is **false** (that is, there is no token in the buffer) do we need to mess with characters. In that case, we read a character and deal with it appropriately. We look for parentheses, operators, and numbers. Any other character gets us the call of **error()** that terminates the program:

```
default:
        error("Bad token");
```

The **error()** function is described in §4.6.3 and we make it available in **PPP_support**.

We had to decide how to represent the different kinds of **Tokens**; that is, we had to choose values for the member **kind**. For simplicity and ease of debugging, we decided to let the **kind** of a **Token** be the parentheses and operators themselves. This leads to extremely simple processing of parentheses and operators:

```
case '(': case ')': case '+': case '–': case '*': case '/':
      return Token{ch};               // let each character represent itself
```

To be honest, we had forgotten ';' for "print" and 'q' for "quit" in our first version. We didn't add them until we needed them for our second solution.

5.8.3 Reading numbers

Now we just have to deal with numbers. That's actually not that easy. How do we really find the value of 123? Well, that's 100+20+3, but how about 12.34, and should we accept scientific notation, such as 12.34e5? We could spend hours or days to get this right, but fortunately, we don't have to. Input streams know what a C++ floating-point literal looks like and how to turn it into a value of type double. All we have to do is to figure out how to tell cin to do that for us inside get():

```
case '.':
case '0': case '1': case '2': case '3': case '4':
case '5': case '6': case '7': case '8': case '9':
{     cin.putback(ch);                // put digit back into the input stream
      double val = 0;
      cin >> val;                     // read a floating-point number
      return Token{'8',val};          // let '8' represent "a number"
}
```

We – somewhat arbitrarily – chose '8' to represent "a number" in a Token.

How do we know that a number is coming? Well, if we guess from experience or look in a C++ reference (§0.4.1), we find that a numeric literal must start with a digit or . (the decimal point). So, we test for that. Next, we want to let cin read the number, but we have already read the first character (a digit or dot), so just letting cin loose on the rest will give a wrong result. We could try to combine the value of the first character with the value of "the rest" as read by cin; for example, if someone typed 123, we would get 1 and cin would read 23 and we'd have to add 100 to 23. Yuck! And that's a trivial case. Fortunately (and not by accident), cin works much like Token_stream in that you can put a character back into it. So instead of doing any messy arithmetic, we just put the initial character back into cin and then let cin read the whole number.

AA Please note how we again and again avoid doing complicated work and instead find simpler solutions – often relying on library facilities. That's the essence of good programming: the continuing search for simplicity. Sometimes that's – somewhat facetiously – expressed as "Good programmers are lazy." In that sense (and only in that sense), we should be "lazy"; why write a lot of code if we can find a way of writing far less?

5.9 Program structure

Sometimes, the proverb says, it's hard to see the forest for the trees. Similarly, it is easy to lose sight of a program when looking at all its functions, classes, etc. So, let's have a look at the program with its details omitted:

```
#include "PPP.h"

class Token { /* ... */ };
class Token_stream { /* ... */ };

void Token_stream::putback(Token t) { /* ... */ }
Token Token_stream::get() { /* ... */ }

Token_stream ts;                    // provides get() and putback()
double expression();                // declaration so that primary() can call expression()

double primary() { /* ... */ }      // deal with numbers and parentheses
double term() { /* ... */ }         // deal with * and /
double expression() { /* ... */ }   // deal with + and -

int main() { /* ... */ }            // main loop and deal with errors
```

The order of the declarations is important. You cannot use a name before it has been declared, so **ts** must be declared before **ts.get()** uses it, and **error()** from **PPP_support** must be declared before the parser functions because they all use it. CC

We can represent that graphically (leaving out calls to **error()** – everyone calls **error()**):

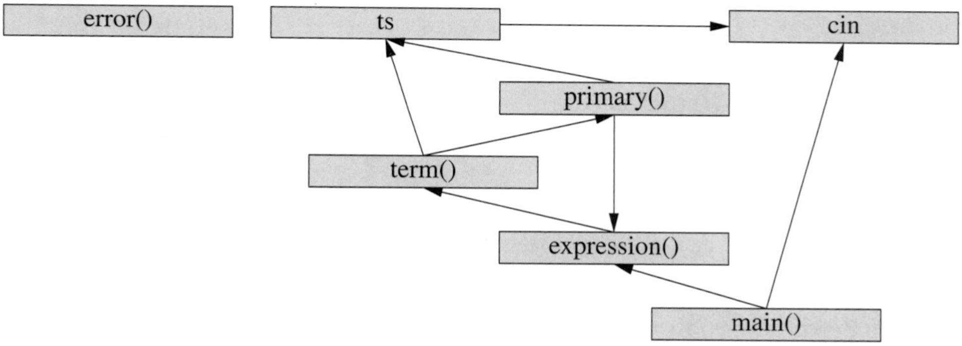

There is an interesting loop in the call graph: **expression()** calls **term()** which calls **primary()** which calls **expression()**. This means that we can't just define those three functions: there is no order that allows us to define every function before it is used. We need at least one declaration that isn't also a definition. We chose to declare ("forward declare") **expression()**.

But does this work? It does, for some definition of "work." It compiles, runs, correctly evaluates expressions, and gives decent error messages. But does it work in a way that we like? The unsurprising answer is "Not really." We tried the first version in §5.6 and removed a serious bug. This second version (§5.7) still has problems. But that's fine (and expected). It is good enough for its main purpose, which is to be something that we can use to verify our basic ideas and get feedback from. As such, it is a success, but try it: it'll (still) drive you nuts!

> TRY THIS
>
> Get the calculator as presented above to run, see what it does, and try to figure out why it works as it does.

Drill

This drill involves a series of modifications of a buggy program to turn it from something useless into something reasonably useful.

[1] Take the calculator from the file **calculator02buggy.cpp**. Get it to compile. You need to find and fix a few bugs. Those bugs are not in the text in the book. Find the three logic errors deviously inserted in **calculator02buggy.cpp** and remove them so that the calculator produces correct results.

[2] Change the character used as the exit command from **q** to **x**.

[3] Change the character used as the print command from ; to **=**.

[4] Add a greeting line in **main()**:

```
"Welcome to our simple calculator.
Please enter expressions using floating-point numbers."
```

[5] Improve that greeting by mentioning which operators are available and how to print and exit.

Review

[1] What do we mean by "Programming is understanding"?

[2] The chapter details the creation of a calculator program. Write a short analysis of what the calculator should be able to do.

[3] How do you break a problem up into smaller manageable parts?

[4] Why is creating a small, limited version of a program a good idea?

[5] Why is feature creep a bad idea?

[6] What are the three main phases of software development?

[7] What is a "use case"?

[8] What is the purpose of testing?

[9] According to the outline in the chapter, describe the difference between a **Term**, an **Expression**, a **Number**, and a **Primary**.

[10] In the chapter, an input was broken down into its components: **Term**s, **Expression**s, **Primary**s, and **Number**s. Do this for **(17+4)/(5–1)**.

[11] Why does the program not have a function called **number()**?

[12] What is a token?

[13] What is a grammar? A grammar rule?

[14] What is a class? What do we use classes for?

[15] How can we provide a default value for a member of a class?

[16] In the expression function, why is the default for the **switch**-statement to "put back" the token?

[17] What is "look-ahead"?
[18] What does putback() do and why is it useful?
[19] Why is the remainder (modulus) operation, %, difficult to implement in the term()?
[20] What do we use the two data members of the Token class for?
[21] Why do we (sometimes) split a class's members into private and public members?
[22] What happens in the Token_stream class when there is a token in the buffer and the get() function is called?
[23] Why were the ';' and 'q' characters added to the switch-statement in the get() function of the Token_stream class?
[24] When should we start testing our program?
[25] What is a "user-defined type"? Why would we want one?
[26] What is the interface to a C++ "user-defined type"?
[27] Why do we want to rely on libraries of code?

Terms

analysis	grammar	prototype	class
implementation	pseudo code	class member	interface
public	data member	member function	syntax analyzer
design	parser	token	divide by zero
private	use case	token stream	look-ahead

Exercises

[1] If you haven't already, do the TRY THIS exercises from this chapter.
[2] Add the ability to use {} as well as () in the program, so that {(4+5)*6} / (3+4) will be a valid expression.
[3] Add a factorial operator: use a suffix ! operator to represent "factorial." For example, the expression 7! means 7 * 6 * 5 * 4 * 3 * 2 * 1. Make ! bind tighter than * and /; that is, 7*8! means 7*(8!) rather than (7*8)!. Begin by modifying the grammar to account for a higher-level operator. To agree with the standard mathematical definition of factorial, let 0! evaluate to 1. Hint: The calculator functions deal with doubles, but factorial is defined only for ints, so just for x!, assign the x to an int and calculate the factorial of that int.
[4] Define a class Name_value that holds a string and a value. Rework exercise 20 in Chapter 3 to use a vector<Name_value> instead of two vectors.
[5] Write a grammar for bitwise logical expressions. A bitwise logical expression is much like an arithmetic expression except that the operators are ! (not), ~ (complement), & (and), | (or), and ^ (exclusive or). Each operator does its operation to each bit of its integer operands (see PPP2.§25.5). ! and ~ are prefix unary operators. A ^ binds tighter than a | (just as * binds tighter than +) so that x|y^z means x|(y^z) rather than (x|y)^z. The & operator binds tighter than ^ so that x^y&z means x^(y&z).
[6] Redo the "Bulls and Cows" game from exercise 12 in Chapter 4 to use four letters rather than four digits.

[7] Write a program that reads digits and composes them into integers. For example, `123` is read as the characters 1, 2, and 3. The program should output `123 is 1 hundred and 2 tens and 3 ones`. The number should be output as an `int` value. Handle numbers with one, two, three, or four digits. Hint: To get the integer value `5` from the character `'5'` subtract `'0'`, that is, `'5'–'0'==5`.

[8] A permutation is an ordered subset of a set. For example, say you wanted to pick a combination to a vault. There are 60 possible numbers, and you need three different numbers for the combination. There are $P(60,3)$ permutations for the combination, where P is defined by the formula $P(a,b) = (a!)/((a-b)!)$ where ! is used as a suffix factorial operator. For example, 4! is 4∗3∗2∗1.

Combinations are similar to permutations, except that the order of the objects doesn't matter. For example, if you were making a "banana split" sundae and wished to use three different flavors of ice cream out of five that you had, you probably wouldn't care if you put a scoop of vanilla at the beginning or the end or the serving dish. The formula for combinations is $C(a,b) = (P(a,b))/(b!)$

Design a program that asks users for two numbers, asks them whether they want to calculate permutations or combinations, and prints out the result. This will have several parts. Do an analysis of the above requirements. Write exactly what the program will have to do. Then, go into the design phase. Write pseudo code for the program and break it into subcomponents. This program should have error checking. Make sure that all erroneous inputs will generate good error messages.

Postscript

Making sense of input is one of the fundamental programming activities. Every program somehow faces that problem. Making sense of something directly produced by a human is among the hardest problems. For example, many aspects of voice recognition are still research problems. Simple variations of this problem, such as our calculator, cope by using a grammar to define the input.

6

Completing a Program

Keep it simple:
as simple as possible,
but no simpler.
– Albert Einstein

Writing a program involves gradually refining our ideas of what we want to do and how we want to express it. In Chapter 5, we produced the initial working version of a calculator program. Here, we'll refine it. Completing the program – that is, making it fit for users and maintainers – involves improving the user interface, doing some serious work on error handling, adding a few useful features, and restructuring the code for ease of understanding and modification.

§6.1 Introduction
§6.2 Input and output
§6.3 Error handling
§6.4 Negative numbers
§6.5 Remainder: %
§6.6 Cleaning up the code
Symbolic constants. Use of functions. Code layout. Commenting
§6.7 Recovering from errors
§6.8 Variables
Variables and definitions. Introducing names. Predefined names. Are we there yet?

6.1 Introduction

AA When your program first starts running "reasonably," you're probably about halfway finished. For a large program or a program that could do harm if it misbehaved, you will be nowhere near halfway finished. Once the program "basically works," the real fun begins! That's when we have enough working code to experiment with ideas.

In this chapter, we will guide you through the considerations a professional programmer might have trying to improve the calculator from Chapter 5. Note that the questions asked about the program and the issues considered here are far more interesting than the calculator itself. What we do is to give an example of how real programs evolve under the pressure of requirements and constraints and of how a programmer can gradually improve code.

6.2 Input and output

If you look back to the beginning of Chapter 5, you'll find that we decided to prompt the user with

```
Expression:
```

and to report back answers with

```
Result:
```

In the heat of getting the program to run, we forgot all about that. That's pretty typical. We can't think of everything all the time, so when we stop to reflect, we find that we have forgotten something or other.

For some programming tasks, the initial requirements cannot be changed. That's usually too rigid a policy and leads to programs that are unnecessarily poor solutions to the problems that they are written to solve. So, let's consider what we would do, assuming that we can change the specification of what exactly the program should do. Do we really want the program to write **Expression:** and **Result:**? How would we know? Just "thinking" rarely helps. We have to try and see what works best.

```
2+3; 5*7; 2+9;
```

currently gives

```
= 5
= 35
= 11
```

If we used **Expression:** and **Result:**, we'd get

```
Expression: 2+3; 5*7; 2+9;
Result : 5
Expression: Result: 35
Expression: Result: 11
Expression:
```

We are sure that some people will like one style and others will like the other. In such cases, we can consider giving people a choice, but for this simple calculator that would be overkill, so we must decide. We think that writing **Expression:** and **Result:** is a bit too "heavy" and distracting.

Using those, the actual expressions and results are only a minor part of what appears on the screen, and since expressions and results are what matter, nothing should distract from them. On the other hand, unless we somehow separate what the user types from what the computer outputs, the result can be confusing. During initial debugging, we added = as a result indicator. We would also like a short "prompt" to indicate that the program wants input. The > character is often used as a prompt:

```
> 2+3;
= 5
> 5*7;
= 35
>
```

This looks much better, and we can get it by a minor change to the main loop of **main()**:

```
double val = 0;
while (cin) {
        cout << "> ";                   // print prompt
        Token t = ts.get();
        if (t.kind == 'q') break;
        if (t.kind == ';')
                cout << "= " << val << '\n';            // print result
        else
                ts.putback(t);
        val = expression();
}
```

Unfortunately, the result of putting several expressions on a line is still messy:

```
> 2+3; 5*7; 2+9;
= 5
> = 35
> = 11
>
```

The basic problem is that we didn't think of multiple expressions on a line when we started out (at least we pretended not to). What we want is

```
> 2+3; 5*7; 2+9;
= 5
= 35
= 11
>
```

This looks right, but unfortunately there is no really obvious way of achieving it. We first looked at **main()**. Is there a way to write out > only if it is not immediately followed by a =? We cannot know! We need to write > before the **get()**, but we do not know if **get()** actually reads new characters or simply gives us a **Token** from characters that it had already read from the keyboard. In other words, we would have to mess with **Token_stream** to make this final improvement.

For now, we decide that what we have is good enough. If we find that we have to modify **Token_stream**, we'll revisit this decision. However, it is unwise to make major structural changes to gain a minor advantage, and we haven't yet thoroughly tested the calculator.

6.3 Error handling

CC The first thing to do once we have a program that "basically works" is to try to break it; that is, we try to feed it input in the hope of getting it to misbehave. We say "hope" because the challenge here is to find as many errors as possible, so that we can fix them before anybody else finds them. If you go into this exercise with the attitude that "my program works and I don't make errors!" you won't find many bugs and you'll feel bad when you do find one. You'd be playing head games with yourself! The right attitude when testing is "I'll break it! I'm smarter than any program – even my own!" So, we feed the calculator a mix of correct and incorrect expressions. For example:

```
1+2+3+4+5+6+7+8
1-2-3-4
!+2
;;;
(1+3;
(1+);
1*2/3%4+5-6;
();
1+;
+1
1++;
1/0
1/0;
1++2;
-2;
-2;;;;
1234567890123456;
'a';
q
1+q
1+2; q
```

> TRY THIS
>
> Feed a few such "problematic" expressions to the calculator and try to figure out in how many ways you can get it to misbehave. Can you get it to crash, that is, to get it past our error handling and give a machine error? We don't think you can. Can you get it to exit without a useful error message? You can.

Technically, this is known as *testing* (§4.7.4). There are people who do this – break programs – for a living. Testing is a very important part of software development and can actually be fun. One big question is: "Can we test the program systematically, so that we find all of the errors?" There is no general answer to this question; that is, there is no answer that holds for all programs. However, you can do rather well for many programs when you approach testing seriously. You try to create test cases systematically, and just in case your strategy for selecting tests isn't complete, you do some "unreasonable" tests, such as

```
Mary had a little lamb
srtvrqtiewcbet7rewaewre–wqcntrretewru754389652743nvcqnwq;
!@#%^&*()~:;
```

Once, when testing compilers, I got into the habit of feeding email that reported compiler errors straight to the compiler – mail headers, user's explanation, and all. That wasn't "sensible" because "nobody would do that." However, a program ideally catches all errors, not just the sensible ones, and soon that compiler was very resilient against "strange input." AA

The calculator takes input from the keyboard. That makes testing tedious: each time we make an improvement, we have to type in a lot of test cases (yet again!) to make sure we haven't broken anything. It would be much better if we could store our test cases somewhere and run them with a single command. Some operating systems (notably Unix) make it trivial to get **cin** to read from a file without modifying the program, and similarly to divert the output from **cout** to a file. If that's not convenient, we must modify the program to use a file (see §9).

Now consider:

```
1+2; q
```

and

```
1+2 q
```

We would like both to print the result (**3**) and then exit the program. Curiously enough,

```
1+2 q
```

does that, but the apparently cleaner

```
1+2; q
```

elicits a **Primary expected** error. Where would we look for this error? In **main()** where ; and **q** are handled, of course. We added those "print" and "quit" commands rather quickly to get the calculator to work (§5.7). Now we are paying for that haste. Consider again:

```
double val = 0;
while (cin) {
      cout << "> ";
      Token t = ts.get();
      if (t.kind == 'q')
            break;
      if (t.kind == ';')
            cout << "= " << val << '\n';
      else
            ts.putback(t);
      val = expression();
}
```

If we find a semicolon, we straightaway proceed to call **expression()** without checking for **q**. The first thing that **expression()** does is to call **term()**, which first calls **primary()**, which finds **q**. The letter **q** isn't a **Primary** so we get our error message. So, we should test for **q** after testing for a semicolon. While we were at it, we felt the need to simplify the logic a bit, so the complete **main()** reads

```
int main()
try
{
	while (cin) {
		cout << "> ";
		Token t = ts.get();
		while (t.kind == ';')
			t=ts.get();		// eat ';'
		if (t.kind == 'q')
			return 0;
		ts.putback(t);
		cout << "= " << expression() << '\n';
	}
	return 0;
}
catch (exception& e) {
	cerr << e.what() << '\n';
	return 1;
}
catch (...) {
	cerr << "exception \n";
	return 2;
}
```

This makes for reasonably robust error handling. So we can start considering what else we can do to improve the calculator.

6.4 Negative numbers

If you tested the calculator, you found that it couldn't handle negative numbers elegantly. For example, this is an error:

```
-1/2
```

We have to write

```
(0-1)/2
```

That's not acceptable.

AA Finding such problems during late debugging and testing is common. Only now do we have the opportunity to see what our design really does and get the feedback that allows us to refine our ideas. When planning a project, it is wise to try to preserve time and flexibility to benefit from the lessons we learn here. All too often, "release 1.0" is shipped without needed refinements because a tight schedule or a rigid project management strategy prevents "late" changes to the specification; "late" addition of "features" is especially dreaded. In reality, when a program is good enough for simple use by its designers but not yet ready to ship, it isn't "late" in the development sequence; it's the earliest time when we can benefit from solid experience with the program. A realistic schedule takes that into account.

In this case, we basically need to modify the grammar to allow unary minus. The simplest change seems to be in **Primary**. We have

```
Primary:
      Number
      "(" Expression ")"
```

and we need something like

```
Primary:
      Number
      "(" Expression ")"
      "–" Primary
      "+" Primary
```

We added unary plus because that's what C++ does. When we have unary minus, someone always tries unary plus and it's easier just to implement that than to explain why it is useless. The code that implements **Primary** becomes

```
double primary()
{
      Token t = ts.get();
      switch (t.kind) {
      case '(':                          // handle '(' expression ')'
      {
            double d = expression();
            t = ts.get();
            if (t.kind != ')')
                  error("')' expected");
            return d;
      }
      case '8':                          // we use '8' to represent a number
            return t.value;              // return the number's value
      case '–':
            return – primary();
      case '+':
            return primary();
      default:
            error("primary expected");
      }
}
```

That's so simple that it actually worked the first time.

6.5 Remainder: %

When we first analyzed the ideals for a calculator, we wanted the remainder (modulo) operator: %. However, % is not defined for floating-point numbers, so we backed off. Now we can consider it again. It should be simple:

[1] We add % as a Token.
[2] We define a meaning for %.

We know the meaning of % for integer operands. For example:

```
> 2%3;
= 2
> 3%2;
= 1
> 5%3;
= 2
```

But how should we handle operands that are not integers? Consider:

```
> 6.7%3.3;
```

What should be the resulting value? There is no perfect technical answer. However, modulo is often defined for floating-point operands. In particular, x%y can be defined as x%y==x−y∗int(x/y), so that 6.7%3.3==6.7−3.3∗int(6.7/3.3), that is, 0.1. This is easily done using the standard-library function fmod() (floating-point modulo) (PPP2.§24.8). We modify term() to include

```
case '%':
{       double d = primary();
        if (d == 0)
                error("%:divide by zero");
        left = fmod(left,d);
        t = ts.get();
        break;
}
```

Alternatively, we can prohibit the use of % on a floating-point argument. We check if the floating-point operands have fractional parts and give an error message if they do. The problem of ensuring int operands for % is a variant of the narrowing problem (§2.9), so we could solve it using narrow (§7.4.7):

```
case '%':
{       int i1 = narrow<int>(left);
        int i2 = narrow<int>(primary());
        if (i2 == 0)
                error("%: divide by zero");
        left = i1%i2;
        t = ts.get();
        break;
}
```

For a simple calculator, either solution will do.

6.6 Cleaning up the code

AA We have made several changes to the code. They are, we think, all improvements, but the code is beginning to look a bit messy. Now is a good time to review the code to see if we can make it clearer and shorter, add and improve comments, etc. In other words, we are not finished with the program until we have it in a state suitable for someone else to take over maintenance. Except for the almost total absence of comments, the calculator code really isn't that bad, but let's do a bit of cleanup.

6.6.1 Symbolic constants

Looking back, we find the use of '8' to indicate a Token containing a numeric value odd. It doesn't really matter what value is used to indicate a number Token as long as the value is distinct from all other values indicating different kinds of Tokens. However, the code looks a bit odd and we had to keep reminding ourselves in comments:

```
case '8':                  // we use '8' to represent a number
        return t.value;    // return the number's value
case '–':
        return – primary();
```

To be honest, we also made a few mistakes, typing '0' rather than '8', because we forgot which value we had chosen to use. In other words, using '8' directly in the code manipulating Tokens was sloppy, hard to remember, and error-prone; '8' is one of those "magic constants" we warned against in §3.3.1. What we should have done was to introduce a symbolic name for the constant we used to represent a number: XX

```
constexpr char number = '8';   // t.kind==number means that t is a number Token
```

The constexpr modifier (§3.3.1) simply tells the compiler that we are defining an object that is not supposed to change: for example, an assignment number='0' would cause the compiler to give an error message. Given that definition of number, we don't have to use '8' explicitly anymore. The code fragment from primary above now becomes

```
case number:
        return t.value;        // return the number's value
case '–':
        return – primary();
```

This requires no comment. We should not say in comments what can be clearly and directly said in code. Repeated comments explaining something are often an indication that the code should be improved. AA

Similarly, the code in Token_stream::get() that recognizes numbers becomes

```
case '.':
case '0': case '1': case '2': case '3': case '4':
case '5': case '6': case '7': case '8': case '9':
{       cin.putback(ch);           // put digit back into the input stream
        double val;
        cin >> val;                // read a floating-point number
                return Token{number,val};
}
```

We could consider symbolic names for all tokens, but that seems overkill. After all, '(' and '+' are about as obvious a notation for (and + as anyone could come up with. Looking through the tokens, only ';' for "print" (or "terminate expression") and 'q' for "quit" seem arbitrary. Why not 'p' and 'e'? In a larger program, it is only a matter of time before such obscure and arbitrary notation becomes a cause of a problem, so we introduce

```
constexpr char quit = 'q';       // t.kind==quit means that t is a quit Token
constexpr char print = ';';      // t.kind==print means that t is a print Token
```

Now we can write main()'s loop like this:

```
while (cin) {
        cout << "> ";
        Token t = ts.get();
        while (t.kind == print)
                t=ts.get();
        if (t.kind == quit)
                return 0;
        ts.putback(t);
        cout << "= " << expression() << '\n';
}
```

Introducing symbolic names for "print" and "quit" makes the code easier to read. In addition, it doesn't encourage someone reading main() to make assumptions about how "print" and "quit" are represented. For example, it should come as no surprise if we decide to change the representation of "quit" to 'e' (for "exit"). That would now require no change in main().

Now the strings "> " and "= " stand out. Why do we have these "magical" literals in the code? How would a new programmer reading main() guess their purpose? Maybe we should add a comment? Adding a comment might be a good idea, but introducing a symbolic name is more effective:

```
constexpr string prompt = "> ";
constexpr string result = "= ";      // used to indicate that what follows is a result
```

Should we want to change the prompt or the result indicator, we can just modify those constexprs. The loop now reads

```
while (cin) {
        cout << prompt;
        Token t = ts.get();
        while (t.kind ==print)
                t=ts.get();
        if (t.kind == quit)
                return 0;
        ts.putback(t);
        cout << result << expression() << '\n';
}
```

6.6.2 Use of functions

The functions we use should reflect the structure of our program, and the names of the functions should identify the logically separate parts of our code. Basically, our program so far is rather good in this respect: expression(), term(), and primary() directly reflect our understanding of the expression grammar, and get() handles the input and token recognition. Looking at main(), though, we notice that it does two logically separate things:

[1] main() provides general "scaffolding": start the program, end the program, and handle "fatal" errors.

[2] main() handles the calculation loop.

Ideally, a function performs a single logical action (§3.5.1). Having main() perform both of these actions obscures the structure of the program. The obvious solution is to make the calculation loop into a separate function calculate(): AA

```
void calculate()
        // expression evaluation loop
{
        while (cin) {
                cout << prompt;
                Token t = ts.get();
                while (t.kind == print)                        // first discard all "prints"
                        t=ts.get();
                if (t.kind == quit)
                        return;
                ts.putback(t);
                cout << result << expression() << '\n';
        }
}

int main()
try {
        calculate();
        return 0;
}
catch (runtime_error& e) {
        cerr << e.what() << '\n';
        return 1;
}
catch (...) {
        cerr << "exception \n";
        return 2;
}
```

This reflects the structure much more directly and is therefore easier to understand.

6.6.3 Code layout

Looking through the code for ugly code, we find

```
switch (ch) {
case 'q': case ';': case '%': case '(': case ')': case '+': case '–': case '*': case '/':
        return Token{ch};          // let each character represent itself
```

This wasn't too bad before we added 'q', ';', and '%', but now it's beginning to become obscure. Code that is hard to read is where bugs can more easily hide. Using one line per case and adding a couple of comments help. So, Token_stream's get() becomes

```
Token Token_stream::get()
        // read characters from cin and compose a Token
{
        if (full) {                    // check if we already have a Token ready
                full = false;
                return buffer;
        }
        char ch;
        cin >> ch;                     // note that >> skips whitespace (space, newline, tab, etc.)

        switch (ch) {
        case quit:
        case print:
        case '(':
        case ')':
        case '+':
        case '–':
        case '*':
        case '/':
        case '%':
                return Token{ch};                          // let each character represent itself
        case '.':                                          // a floating-point-literal can start with a dot
        case '0': case '1': case '2': case '3': case '4':
        case '5': case '6': case '7': case '8': case '9':  // numeric literal
        {       cin.putback(ch);                           // put digit back into the input stream
                double val;
                cin >> val;                                // read a floating-point number
                return Token{number,val};
        }
        default:
                error("Bad token");
        }
}
```

We could of course have put each digit case on a separate line also, but that didn't seem to buy us any clarity. Also, doing so would prevent **get()** from being viewed in its entirety on a screen at once. Our ideal is for each function to fit on the screen; one obvious place for a bug to hide is in the code that we can't see it because it's off the screen. Code layout matters.

Note also that we changed the plain **'q'** to the symbolic name **quit**. This improves readability.

AA When we clean up code, we might accidentally introduce errors. Always retest the program after cleanup. Better still, do a bit of testing after each set of minor improvements so that if something went wrong you can still remember exactly what you did. Remember: Test early and often.

6.6.4 Commenting

AA We added a few comments as we went along. Good comments are an important part of writing code. We tend to forget about comments in the heat of programming. When you go back to the code to clean it up is an excellent time to look at each part of the program to see if the comments you originally wrote are

[1] Still valid (you might have changed the code since you wrote the comment)
[2] Adequate for a reader (they usually are not)
[3] Not so verbose that they distract from the code

To emphasize that last concern: what is best said in code should be said in code. Avoid comments that explain something that's perfectly clear to someone who knows the programming language. For example: XX

```
x = b+c;    // add b and c and assign the result to x
```

You'll find such comments in this book, but only when we are trying to explain the use of a language feature that might not yet be familiar to you.

Comments are for things that code expresses poorly. An example is intent: code says what it does, not what it was intended to do (§4.7.2). Look at the calculator code. There is something missing: the functions show how we process expressions and tokens, but there is no indication (except the code) of what we meant expressions and tokens to be. The grammar is a good candidate for something to put in comments or into some documentation of the calculator.

```
/*
    Simple calculator

    Revision history:

    Revised by Bjarne Stroustrup (bjarne@stroustrup.com) November 2023
    Revised by Bjarne Stroustrup November 2013
    Revised by Bjarne Stroustrup May 2007
    Revised by Bjarne Stroustrup August 2006
    Revised by Bjarne Stroustrup August 2004
    Originally written by Bjarne Stroustrup (bs@cs.tamu.edu) Spring 2004.

    This program implements a basic expression calculator.
    Input from cin; output to cout.
    The grammar for input is:

    Statement:
        Expression
        Print
        Quit
    Print:
        ";"
    Quit:
        "q"
    Expression:
        Term
        Expression "+" Term
        Expression "-" Term
```

```
    Term:
        Primary
        Term "*" Primary
        Term "/" Primary
        Term "%" Primary
    Primary:
        Number
        "(" Expression ")"
        "-" Primary
        "+" Primary
    Number:
        floating-point-literal

    Input comes from cin through the Token_stream called ts.
*/
```

Here we used the block comment, which starts with a /* and continues until a */. In a real program, the revision history would contain indications of what corrections and improvements were made.

Note that the comments are not the code. In fact, this grammar simplifies a bit: compare the rule for **Statement** with what really happens (e.g., have a peek at the code in the following section). The comment fails to explain the loop in **calculate()** that allows us to do several calculations in a single run of the program. We'll return to that problem in §6.8.1.

6.7 Recovering from errors

Why do we exit when we find an error? That seemed simple and obvious at the time, but why? Couldn't we just write an error message and carry on? After all, we often make little typing errors and such an error doesn't mean that we have decided not to do a calculation. So let's try to recover from an error. That basically means that we have to catch exceptions and continue after we have cleaned up any messes that were left behind.

Until now, all errors have been represented as exceptions and handled by **main()**. If we want to recover from errors, **calculate()** must catch exceptions and try to clean up the mess before trying to evaluate the next expression:

```
void calculate()
{
    while (cin)
    try {
        cout << prompt;
        Token t = ts.get();
        while (t.kind == print)
            t=ts.get();                    // first discard all "prints"
        if (t.kind == quit)
            return;
        ts.putback(t);
        cout << result << expression() << '\n';
    }
```

```
        catch (exception& e) {
            cerr << e.what() << '\n';          // write error message
            clean_up_mess();
        }
    }
```

We simply made the **while**-loop's block into a **try**-block that writes an error message and cleans up the mess. Once that's done, we carry on as always.

What would "clean up the mess" entail? Basically, getting ready to compute again after an error has been handled means making sure that all our data is in a good and predictable state. In the calculator, the only data we keep outside an individual function is the **Token_stream**. So what we need to do is to ensure that we don't have tokens related to the aborted calculation sitting around to confuse the next calculation. For example,

```
1++2*3; 4+5;
```

will cause an error, and **2*3; 4+5** will be left in the **Token_stream**'s and **cin**'s buffers after the second **+** has triggered an exception. We have two choices:

[1] Purge all tokens from the **Token_stream**.

[2] Purge all tokens from the current calculation from the **Token_stream**.

The first choice discards all (including **4+5;**), whereas the second choice just discards **2*3;**, leaving **4+5** to be evaluated. Either could be a reasonable choice, and either could surprise a user. As it happens, both are about equally simple to implement. We chose the second alternative because it simplifies testing.

So we need to read input until we find a semicolon. This seems simple. We have **get()** to do our reading for us so we can write a **clean_up_mess()** like this:

```
void clean_up_mess()                   // naive
{
    while (true) {                     // skip until we find a print
        Token t = ts.get();
        if (t.kind == print)
            return;
    }
}
```

Unfortunately, that doesn't work all that well. Why not? Consider this input:

```
1@z; 1+3;
```

The **@** gets us into the **catch**-clause for the **while**-loop. Then, we call **clean_up_mess()** to find the next semicolon. Then, **clean_up_mess()** calls **get()** and reads the **z**. That gives another error (because **z** is not a token) and we find ourselves in **main()**'s **catch(...)** handler, and the program exits. Oops! We don't get a chance to evaluate **1+3**. Back to the drawing board!

We could try more elaborate **try**s and **catch**es, but basically we are heading into an even bigger mess. Many **try**-blocks is a sign of poor design; we have better techniques (§18.4.1, §18.4.2). Errors are hard to handle, and errors during error handling are even worse than other errors. So, let's try to devise some way to flush characters out of a **Token_stream** that couldn't possibly throw an exception. The only way of getting input into our calculator is **get()**, and that can – as we just discovered the hard way – throw an exception. So we need a new operation. The obvious place to put that is in Token_stream:

```
class Token_stream {
public:
        Token get();                    // get a Token
        void putback(Token t);          // put a Token back
        void ignore(char c);            // discard characters up to and including a c
private:
        bool full = false;              // is there a Token in the buffer?
        Token buffer = 0;               // putback() saves its token here
};
```

This ignore() function needs to be a member of Token_stream because it needs to look at Token_stream's buffer. We chose to make "the thing to look for" an argument to ignore() – after all, the Token_stream doesn't have to know what the calculator considers a good character to use for error recovery. We decided that argument should be a character because we don't want to risk composing Tokens – we saw what happened when we tried that. So we get

```
void Token_stream::ignore(char c)
        // c represents the kind of Token
{
        if (full && c==buffer.kind) {           // first look in buffer
                full = false;
                return;
        }
        full = false;

        // now search input:
        char ch = 0;
        while (cin>>ch)
                if (ch==c)
                        return;
}
```

This code first looks at the buffer. If there is a c there, we are finished after discarding that c; otherwise, we need to read characters from cin until we find a c.

We can now write clean_up_mess() rather simply:

```
void clean_up_mess()
{
        ts.ignore(print);
}
```

Dealing with errors is always tricky. It requires much experimentation and testing because it is extremely hard to imagine all the errors that can occur. Trying to make a program foolproof is always a very technical activity; amateurs typically don't care. Quality error handling is one mark of a professional.

6.8 Variables

Having worked on style and error handling, we can return to looking for improvements in the calculator functionality. We now have a program that works quite well; how can we improve it? The first wish list for the calculator included variables. Having variables gives us better ways of expressing longer calculations. Similarly, for scientific calculations, we'd like built-in named values, such as pi and e, just as we have on scientific calculators.

Adding variables and constants is a major extension to the calculator. It will touch most parts of the code. This is the kind of extension that we should not embark on without good reason and sufficient time. Here, we add variables and constants because it gives us a chance to look over the code again and try out some more programming techniques.

6.8.1 Variables and definitions

Obviously, the key to both variables and built-in constants is for the calculator program to keep (*name,value*) pairs so that we can access the value given the name. We can define a Variable like this:

```
class Variable {
public:
      string name;
      double value;
};
```

We will use the name member to identify a Variable and the value member to store the value corresponding to that name.

How can we store Variables so that we can search for a Variable with a given name string to find its value or to give it a new value? Looking back over the programming tools we have encountered so far, we find only one good answer: a vector of Variables:

```
vector<Variable> var_table;
```

We can put as many Variables as we like into the vector var_table and search for a given name by looking at the vector elements one after another. We can write a get_value() function that looks for a given name string and returns its corresponding value:

```
double get_value(string s)
      // return the value of the Variable named s
{
      for (const Variable& v : var_table)
            if (v.name == s)
                  return v.value;
      error("trying to read undefined variable ", s);
}
```

The code really is quite simple: go through every Variable in var_table (starting with the first element and continuing until the last) and see if its name matches the argument string s. If that is the case, return its value.

Similarly, we can define a set_value() function to give a Variable a new value:

```
void set_value(string s, double d)
      // set the Variable named s to d
{
      for (Variable& v : var_table)
            if (v.name == s) {
                  v.value = d;
                  return;
            }
      error("trying to write undefined variable ", s);
}
```

Did you notice the & in the last two functions? It means that v is a reference to a Variable in the var_table, rather than a copy of one. For set_value, that's essential because giving a new value to a copy, to something not in the table, would be useless. References are essential for many important programming techniques. They will be presented in detail in §7.4 and§16.2.

We can now read and write "variables" represented as Variables in var_table. How do we get a new Variable into var_table? What does a user of our calculator have to write to define a new variable and later to get its value? We could consider C++'s notation

```
double var = 7.2;
```

That would work, but all variables in this calculator hold double values, so saying "double" would be redundant. Could we make do without an explicit "declaration indicator"? For example:

```
var = 7.2;
```

Possibly, but then we would be unable to tell the difference between the declaration of a new variable and a spelling mistake:

```
var1 = 7.2;          // define a new variable called var1
var1 = 3.2;          // define a new variable called var2
```

Oops! Clearly, we meant var2 = 3.2; but we didn't say so (except in the comment). We could live with this, but we'll follow the tradition in languages, such as C++, that distinguishes declarations (with initializations) from assignments. We could use double, but for a calculator we'd like something short, so – drawing on another old tradition – we choose the keyword let:

```
let var = 7.2;
```

The grammar would be

```
Calculation:
      Statement
      Print
      Quit
      Calculation Statement

Statement:
      Declaration
      Expression
```

```
Declaration:
        "let" Name "=" Expression
```

Calculation is the new top production (rule) of the grammar. It expresses the loop (in calculate()) that allows us to do several calculations in a run of the calculator program. It relies on the Statement production to handle expressions and declarations. We can handle a statement like this:

```
double statement()
{
        Token t = ts.get();
        switch (t.kind) {
        case let:
                return declaration();
        default:
                ts.putback(t);
                return expression();
        }
}
```

We can now use statement() instead of expression() in calculate():

```
void calculate()
{
        while (cin)
                try {
                        cout << prompt;
                        Token t = ts.get();
                        while (t.kind == print)          // first discard all "prints"
                                t=ts.get();
                        if (t.kind == quit)              // quit
                                return;
                        ts.putback(t);
                        cout << result << statement() << '\n';
                }
                catch (exception& e) {
                        cerr << e.what() << '\n';        // write error message
                        clean_up_mess();
                }
}
```

We now have to define declaration(). What should it do? It should make sure that what comes after a let is a Name followed by a = followed by an Expression. That's what our grammar says. What should it do with the name? We should add a Variable with that name string and the value of the expression to our vector<Variable> called var_table. Once that's done we can retrieve the value using get_value() and change it using set_value(). However, before writing this, we have to decide what should happen if we define a variable twice. For example:

```
let v1 = 7;
let v1 = 8;
```

We chose to consider such a redefinition an error. Typically, it is simply a spelling mistake. Instead of what we wrote, we probably meant

```
let v1 = 7;
let v2 = 8;
```

There are logically two parts to defining a Variable with the name var with the value val:

[1] Check whether there already is a Variable called var in var_table.

[2] Add (var,val) to var_table.

We have no use for uninitialized variables. We defined the functions is_declared() and define_name() to represent those two logically separate operations:

```
bool is_declared(string var)
	// is var already in var_table?
{
	for (const Variable& v : var_table)
		if (v.name == var)
			return true;
	return false;
}

double define_name(string var, double val)
	// add {var,val} to var_table
{
	if (is_declared(var))
		error(var," declared twice");
	var_table.push_back(Variable{var,val});
	return val;
}
```

Adding a new Variable to a vector<Variable> is easy; that's what vector's push_back() member function does:

```
var_table.push_back(Variable{var,val});
```

The Variable{var,val} makes the appropriate Variable and push_back(), then adds that Variable to the end of var_table. Given that, and assuming that we can handle let and name tokens, declaration() is straightforward to write:

```
double declaration()
	// assume we have seen "let"
	// handle: name = expression
	// declare a variable called "name" with the initial value "expression"
{
	Token t = ts.get();
	if (t.kind != name)
		error ("name expected in declaration");

	Token t2 = ts.get();
	if (t2.kind != '=')
		error("= missing in declaration of ", t.name);
```

```
        double d = expression();
        define_name(t.name,d);
        return d;
}
```

Note that we returned the value stored in the new variable. That's useful when the initializing expression is nontrivial. For example:

```
let v = d/(t2–t1);
```

This declaration will define v and also print its value. Additionally, printing the value of a declared variable simplifies the code in calculate() because every statement() returns a value. General rules tend to keep code simple, whereas special cases tend to lead to complications.

This mechanism for keeping track of Variables is what is often called a *symbol table* and could be radically simplified by the use of a standard-library map; see PPP2.§21.6.1.

6.8.2 Introducing names

This is all very good, but unfortunately, it doesn't quite work. By now, that shouldn't come as a surprise. Our first cut never – well, hardly ever – works. Here, we haven't even finished the program – it doesn't yet compile. We have no '=' token, but that's easily handled by adding a case to Token_stream::get() (§6.6.3). But how do we represent let and name as tokens? Obviously, we need to modify get() to recognize these tokens. How? Here is one way:

```
const char name = 'a';              // name token
const char let = 'L';               // declaration token
const string declkey = "let";       // declaration keyword

Token Token_stream::get()
{
        if (full) {
                full = false;
                return buffer;
        }
        char ch;
        cin >> ch;
        switch (ch) {
                // ... as before ...
        default:
                if (isalpha(ch)) {
                        cin.putback(ch);
                        string s;
                        cin >> s;
                        if (s == declkey)
                                return Token{let};   // declaration keyword
                        return Token{name,s};
                }
                error("Bad token");
        }
}
```

Note first of all the call **isalpha(ch)**. This call answers the question "Is **ch** a letter?"; **isalpha()** is part of the standard library. For more character classification functions, see §9.10.4. The logic for recognizing names is the same as that for recognizing numbers: find a first character of the right kind (here, a letter), then put it back using **putback()** and read in the whole name using **>>**.

Unfortunately, this doesn't compile; we have no **Token** that can hold a **string**, so the compiler rejects **Token{name,s}**. To handle that, we must modify the definition of **Token** to hold either a **string** or a **double**, and handle three forms of initializers, such as

- Just a **kind**; for example, **Token{'*'}**
- A **kind** and a number; for example, **Token{number,4.321}**
- A **kind** and a **name**; for example, **Token{name,"pi"}**

We handle that by introducing three initialization functions, known as constructors because they construct objects:

```
class Token {
public:
        char kind;
        double value;
        string name;
        Token() :kind{0} {}                                        // default constructor
        Token(char ch) :kind{ch} { }                               // initialize kind with ch
        Token(char ch, double val) :kind{ch}, value{val} { }       // initialize kind and value
        Token(char ch, string n) :kind{ch}, name{n} { }            // initialize kind and name
};
```

Constructors add an important degree of control and flexibility to initialization. We will examine constructors in detail in §8.4.2 and §8.7.

We chose **'L'** as the representation of the **let** token and the string **let** as our keyword. Obviously, it would be trivial to change that keyword to **double**, **var**, **#**, or whatever by changing the string **declkey** that we compare **s** to.

Now we try the program again. If you type this, you'll see that it all works:

```
let x = 3.4;
let y = 2;
x + y * 2;
```

However, this doesn't work:

```
let x = 3.4;
let y = 2;
x+y*2;
```

What's the difference between those two examples? Have a look to see what happens.

The problem is that we were sloppy with our definition of **Name**. We even "forgot" to define our **Name** production in the grammar (§6.8.1). What characters can be part of a name? Letters? Certainly. Digits? Certainly, as long as they are not the starting character. Underscores? Eh? The **+** character? Well? Eh? Look at the code again. After the initial letter we read into a **string** using **>>**. That accepts every character until it sees whitespace. So, for example, **x+y*2;** is a single name – even the trailing semicolon is read as part of the name. That's unintended and unacceptable.

What must we do instead? First we must specify precisely what we want a name to be, and then we must modify get() to do that. Here is a workable specification of a name: a sequence of letters and digits starting with a letter. Given this definition,

```
a
ab
a1
Z12
asdsddsfdfdasfdsa434RTHTD12345dfdsa8fsd888fadsf
```

are names and

```
1a
as_s
#
as*
a car
```

are not. Except for leaving out the underscore, this is C++'s rule. We can implement that in the default case of get():

```
default:
      if (isalpha(ch)) {
            string s;
            s += ch;
            while (cin.get(ch) && (isalpha(ch) || isdigit(ch)))
                  s+=ch;
            cin.putback(ch);
            if (s == declkey)
                  return Token{let};    // declaration keyword
            return Token{name,s};
      }
      error("Bad token");
```

Instead of reading directly into the string s, we read characters and put those into s as long as they are letters or digits. The s+=ch statement adds (appends) the character ch to the end of the string s. The curious statement

```
while (cin.get(ch) && (isalpha(ch) || isdigit(ch)))
      s+=ch;
```

reads a character into ch (using cin's member function get()) and checks if it is a letter or a digit. If so, it adds ch to s and reads again. The get() member function works just like >> except that it doesn't by default skip whitespace.

6.8.3 Predefined names

Now that we have names, we can easily predefine a few common ones. For example, if we imagine that our calculator will be used for scientific calculations, we'd want pi and e. Where in the code would we define those? In main() before the call of calculate() or in calculate() before the loop. We'll put them in main() because those definitions really aren't part of any calculation:

```
int main()
try {
        // predefine names:
        define_name("pi",3.1415926535);
        define_name("e",2.7182818284);

        calculate();
        return 0;
}
catch (exception& e) {
        cerr << e.what() << '\n';
        return 1;
}
catch (...) {
        cerr << "exception \n";
        return 2;
}
```

6.8.4 Are we there yet?

Not really. We have made so many changes that we need to test everything again, clean up the code, and review the comments. Also, we could define more useful operations. For example, we "forgot" to provide an assignment operator (see exercise 2), and if we have an assignment we might want to distinguish between variables and constants (exercise 3).

Initially, we backed off from having named variables in our calculator. Looking back over the code that implements them, we may have two possible reactions:

[1] Implementing variables wasn't all that bad; it took only about three dozen lines of code.
[2] Implementing variables was a major extension. It touched just about every function and added a completely new concept to the calculator. It increased the size of the calculator by 45% and we haven't even implemented assignment!

AA In the context of a first program of significant complexity, the second reaction is the correct one. More generally, it's the right reaction to any suggestion that adds something like 50% to a program in terms of both size and complexity. When that has to be done, it is more like writing a new program based on a previous one than anything else, and it should be treated that way. In particular, if you can build a program in stages as we did with the calculator, and test it at each stage, you are far better off doing so than trying to do the whole program all at once.

Drill

[1] Starting from the file **calculator08buggy.cpp**, get the calculator to compile.
[2] Go through the entire program and add appropriate comments.
[3] As you commented, you found errors (deviously inserted especially for you to find). Fix them; they are not in the text of the book.
[4] Testing: prepare a set of inputs and use them to test the calculator. Is your list pretty complete? What should you look for? Include negative values, 0, very small, very large, and

"silly" inputs.

[5] Do the testing and fix any bugs that you missed when you commented.

[6] Add a predefined name k meaning 1000.

[7] Give the user a square root function sqrt(), for example, sqrt(2+6.7). Naturally, the value of sqrt(x) is the square root of x; for example, sqrt(9) is 3. Use the standard-library sqrt() function to implement that calculator sqrt(). Remember to update the comments, including the grammar.

[8] Catch attempts to take the square root of a negative number and print an appropriate error message.

[9] Allow the user to use pow(x,i) to mean "Multiply x with itself i times"; for example, pow(2.5,3) is 2.5*2.5*2.5. Require i to be an integer using the technique we used for % (§6.5).

[10] Change the "declaration keyword" from let to #.

[11] Change the "quit keyword" from quit to exit. That will involve defining a string for quit just as we did for let in §6.8.2.

Review

[1] What is the purpose of working on the program after the first version works? Give a list of reasons.

[2] Why does 1+2; q typed into the calculator not quit after it receives an error?

[3] Why did we choose to make a constant character called number?

[4] We split main() into two separate functions. What does the new function do and why did we split main()?

[5] Why do we split code into multiple functions? State principles.

[6] What is the purpose of commenting?

[7] What is the use of symbolic constants?

[8] Why do we care about code layout?

[9] How do we handle % (remainder) of floating-point numbers?

[10] What does is_declared() do and how does it work?

[11] The input representation for let is more than one character. How is it accepted as a single token in the modified code?

[12] What are the rules for what names can and cannot be in a calculator program?

[13] Why is it a good idea to build a program incrementally?

[14] When do you start to test?

[15] When do you retest?

[16] How do you decide what should be a separate function?

[17] How do you choose names for variables and functions? List possible reasons.

[18] What should be in comments and what should not?

[19] When do we consider a program finished?

Terms

code layout	maintenance	scaffolding	commenting
recovery	symbolic constant	error handling	revision history
testing	feature creep	magic constant	

Exercises

[1] Allow underscores in the calculator's variable names.

[2] Provide an assignment operator, =, so that you can change the value of a variable after you have introduced it using let. Discuss why that can be useful and how it can be a source of problems.

[3] Provide named constants that you really can't change the value of. Hint: You have to add a member to Variable that distinguishes between constants and variables and check for it in set_value(). If you want to let the user define constants (rather than just having pi and e defined as constants), you'll have to add a notation to let the user express that, for example, const pi = 3.14;.

[4] The get_value(), set_value(), is_declared(), and define_name() functions all operate on the variable var_table. Define a class called Symbol_table with a member var_table of type vector<Variable> and member functions get(), set(), is_declared(), and declare(). Rewrite the calculator to use a variable of type Symbol_table.

[5] Modify Token_stream::get() to return Token(print) when it sees a newline. This implies looking for whitespace characters and treating newline ('\n') specially. You might find the standard-library function isspace(ch), which returns true if ch is a whitespace character, useful.

[6] Part of what every program should do is to provide some way of helping its user. Have the calculator print out some instructions for how to use the calculator if the user presses the H key (both upper- and lowercase).

[7] Change the q and h commands to be quit and help, respectively.

[8] The grammar in §6.6.4 is incomplete (we did warn you against overreliance on comments); it does not define sequences of statements, such as 4+4; 5–6;, and it does not incorporate the grammar changes outlined in §6.8. Fix that grammar. Also add whatever you feel is needed for that comment as the first comment of the calculator program and its overall comment.

[9] Suggest three improvements (not mentioned in this chapter) to the calculator. Implement one of them.

[10] Modify the calculator to operate on ints (only); give errors for overflow and underflow. Hint: Use narrow (§6.5).

[11] Revisit two programs you wrote for the exercises in §3 or Chapter 4. Clean up that code according to the rules outlined in this chapter. See if you find any bugs in the process.

[12] Modify the calculator to accept input from any istream.

Postscript

As it happens, we have now seen a simple example of how a compiler works. The calculator analyzes input broken down into tokens and understood according to a grammar. That's exactly what a compiler does. After analyzing its input, a compiler then produces a representation (object code) that we can later execute. The calculator immediately executes the expressions it has analyzed; programs that do this are called interpreters rather than compilers.

7

Technicalities: Functions, etc.

No amount of genius can overcome
obsession with detail.
– Traditional

In this chapter and the next, we change our focus from programming to our main tool for programming: the C++ programming language. We present language-technical details to give a slightly broader view of C++'s basic facilities and to provide a more systematic view of those facilities. These chapters also act as a review of many of the programming notions presented so far and provide an opportunity to explore our tool without adding new programming techniques or concepts.

§7.1 Technicalities
§7.2 Declarations and definitions
Kinds of declarations; Variable and constant declarations; Default initialization
§7.3 Scope
§7.4 Function call and return
Declaring arguments and return type; Returning a value; Pass-by-value; Pass-by-**const**-reference; Pass-by-reference; Pass-by-value vs. pass-by-reference; Argument checking and conversion; Function call implementation; Compile-time computation; Suffix return type
§7.5 Order of evaluation
Expression evaluation; Global initialization
§7.6 Namespaces
using-declarations and **using**-directives
§7.7 Modules and headers
Modules; Header files

7.1 Technicalities

Given a choice, we'd much rather talk about programming than about programming language features; that is, we consider how to express ideas as code far more interesting than the technical details of the programming language that we use to express those ideas. To pick an analogy from natural languages: we'd much rather discuss the ideas in a good novel and the way those ideas are expressed than study the grammar and vocabulary of English. What matters are ideas and how those ideas can be expressed in code, not the individual language features.

CC However, we don't always have a choice. When you start programming, your programming language is a foreign language for which you need to look at "grammar and vocabulary." This is what we will do in this chapter and the next, but please don't forget:

- Our primary study is programming.
- Our output is programs/systems.
- A programming language is (only) a tool.

Keeping this in mind appears to be amazingly difficult. Many programmers come to care passionately about apparently minor details of language syntax and semantics. In particular, too many get the mistaken belief that the way things are done in their first programming language is "the one true way." Please don't fall into that trap. C++ is in many ways a very nice language, but it is not perfect; neither is any other programming language.

CC Most design and programming concepts are universal, and many such concepts are widely supported by popular programming languages. That means that the fundamental ideas and techniques we learn in a good programming course carry over from language to language. They can be applied – with varying degrees of ease – in all languages. The language technicalities, however, are specific to a given language. Fortunately, programming languages do not develop in a vacuum, so much of what you learn here will have reasonably obvious counterparts in other languages. In particular, C++ belongs to a group of languages that also includes C (PPP2.Ch27), Java, and C#, so quite a few technicalities are shared with those languages.

Note that when we are discussing language-technical issues, we deliberately use nondescriptive names, such as `f`, `g`, `X`, and `y`. We do that to emphasize the technical nature of such examples, to keep those examples very short, and to try to avoid confusing you by mixing language technicalities and genuine program logic. When you see nondescriptive names (such as should never be used in real code), please focus on the language-technical aspects of the code. Technical examples typically contain code that simply illustrates language rules. If you compiled and ran them, you'd get many "variable not used" warnings, and few such technical program fragments would do anything sensible.

Please note that what we write here is not a complete description of C++'s syntax and semantics – not even for the facilities we describe. The 2023 ISO C++ standard is about 1600 pages of dense technical language aimed at experienced programmers (about 3/4 defines the standard library). We do not try to compete with the standard in completeness and comprehensiveness; we compete in comprehensibility and value for time spent reading.

7.2 Declarations and definitions

A *declaration* is a statement that introduces a name into a scope (§7.3)

- Specifying a type for what is named (e.g., a variable or a function)
- Optionally, specifying an initializer (e.g., an initializer value or a function body)

For example:

```
int a = 7;                  // an int variable
const double cd = 8.7;      // a double-precision floating-point constant
double sqrt(double);        // a function taking a double argument and returning a double result
vector<Token> v;            // a vector-of-Tokens variable
```

Before a name can be used in a C++ program, it must be declared. Consider:

```
int main()
{
        std::cout << f(i) << '\n';
}
```

The compiler will give at least four "undeclared identifier" errors for this: **std**, **cout**, **f**, and **i** are not declared anywhere in this program fragment. We can get **cout** declared by **import**ing the standard-library module **std**, which contains its declaration:

```
import std;         // we find the declaration of cout in here

int main()
{
        std::cout << f(i) << '\n';
}
```

Now, we get only two "undefined" errors. As you write real-world programs, you'll find that most declarations are found in modules or headers (§7.7). That's where we define interfaces to useful facilities defined "elsewhere." Basically, a declaration defines how something can be used; it defines the interface of a function, variable, or class. Please note one obvious but invisible advantage of this use of declarations: we didn't have to look at the details of how **cout** and its **<<** operators were defined; we just **import**ed their declarations. We didn't even have to look at their declarations; from textbooks, manuals, code examples, or other sources, we just know how **cout** is supposed to be used. The compiler reads the declarations in the header that it needs to "understand" our code.

However, we still have to declare **f** and **i**. We could do that like this:

```
import std;                 // we find the declaration of cout in here

int f(int);                 // declaration of f

int main()
{
        int i = 7;          // declaration of i
        cout << f(i) << '\n';
}
```

This will compile because every name has been declared, but it will not link (§1.4) because we have not defined f(); that is, nowhere have we specified what f() actually does.

> TRY THIS
>
> Compile the three examples above to see how the compiler complains. Then add a definition of f() to get a running version.

A declaration that (also) fully specifies the entity declared is called a *definition*. For example:

```
int a = 7;
vector<double> v;
double sqrt(double d) { /* ... */ }
```

Every definition is (by definition) also a declaration, but only some declarations are also definitions. Here are some examples of declarations that are not definitions; if the entity it refers to is used, each must be matched by a definition elsewhere in the code:

```
double sqrt(double);        // no function body here
extern int a;               // "extern plus no initializer" means "not definition"
```

When we contrast definitions and declarations, we follow convention and use *declarations* to mean "declarations that are not definitions" even though that's slightly sloppy terminology.

A definition specifies exactly what a name refers to. In particular, a definition of a variable sets aside memory for that variable. Consequently, you can't define something twice. For example:

```
double sqrt(double d) { /* ... */ }         // definition
double sqrt(double d) { /* ... */ }         // error: double definition

int a;                  // definition
int a;                  // error: double definition
```

In contrast, a declaration that isn't also a definition simply tells how you can use a name; it is just an interface and doesn't allocate memory or specify a function body. Consequently, you can declare something as often as you like as long as you do so consistently:

```
int x = 7;                  // definition
extern int x;               // declaration
extern int x;               // another declaration

double sqrt(double);                    // declaration
double sqrt(double d) { /* ... */ }     // definition
double sqrt(double);                    // another declaration of sqrt
double sqrt(double);                    // yet another declaration of sqrt

int sqrt(double);                       // error: inconsistent declarations of sqrt
```

Why is that last declaration an error? Because there cannot be two functions called sqrt taking an argument of type double and returning different types (int and double).

The extern keyword used in the second declaration of x simply states that this declaration of x isn't a definition. It is rarely useful. We recommend that you don't use it, but you'll see it in other people's code, especially code that uses too many global variables (see §7.3 and §7.5.2).

We can represent the difference between definitions and declarations that are not definitions graphically:

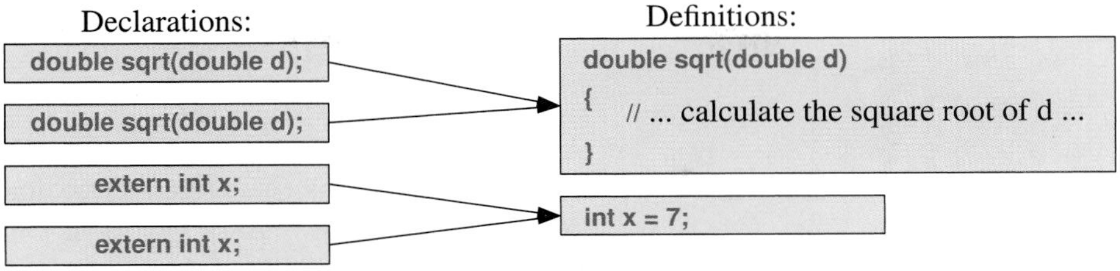

Why does C++ offer both declarations and definitions? The declaration/definition distinction reflects the fundamental distinction between what we need to use something (an interface) and what we need for that something to do what it is supposed to (an implementation). For a variable, a declaration supplies the type but only the definition supplies the object (the memory). For a function, a declaration again provides the type (argument types plus return type) but only the definition supplies the function body (the executable statements). Note that function bodies are stored in memory as part of the program, so it is fair to say that function and variable definitions consume memory, whereas declarations don't. CC

The declaration/definition distinction allows us to separate a program into many parts that can be compiled separately. The declarations allow each part of a program to maintain a view of the rest of the program without bothering with the definitions in other parts. As all declarations (including the one definition) must be consistent, the use of names in the whole program will be consistent. We'll discuss that further in §7.7. Here, we'll just remind you of the expression parser from Chapter 5: **expression()** calls **term()** which calls **primary()** which calls **expression()**. Since every name in a C++ program has to be declared before it is used, there is no way we could just define those three functions:

```
double expression();      // just a declaration, not a definition

double primary()
{
      // ...
      expression();
      // ...
}

double term()
{
      // ...
      primary();
      // ...
}
```

```
double expression()
{
    // ...
    term();
    // ...
}
```

We can order those four functions any way we like; there will always be one call to a function defined below it. Somewhere, we need a "forward" declaration. Therefore, we declared **expression()** before the definition of **primary()** and all is well. Such cyclic call chains are very common.

Why does a name have to be declared before it is used? Couldn't we just require the language implementation to read the program (just as we do) and find the definition to see how a function must be called? We could, but that would lead to "interesting" technical problems, especially in large programs, so we decided against that. The C++ definition requires declaration before use (except for class members; see §8.4.4). Also, this is the convention for ordinary (non-program) writing: when you read a textbook, you expect the author to define terminology before using it; otherwise, you have to guess or go to the index all the time. Having to know the declarations only of what we use saves us (and the compiler) from looking through huge amounts of program text.

7.2.1 Kinds of declarations

There are many kinds of entities that a programmer can define in C++. The most interesting are

- Variables and constants (§7.2.2)
- Functions (§7.4)
- Namespaces (§7.6)
- Modules (§7.7)
- Types (classes and enumerations; Chapter 8)
- Templates (Chapter 18)
- Concepts (§18.1.3)

7.2.2 Variable and constant declarations

The declaration of a variable or a constant specifies a name, a type, and optionally an initializer:

```
int a;                      // no initializer
double d = 7;               // initializer using the = syntax
vector<int> vi(10);         // initializer using the ( ) syntax
vector<int> vi2 {1,2,3,4};  // initializer using the { } syntax
```

Constants have the same declaration syntax as variables. They differ in having **const** or **constexpr** as part of their type and requiring an initializer (§3.3.1):

```
const int x = 7;      // initializer using the = syntax
const int x2 {9};     // initializer using the {} syntax
const int y;          // error: no initializer
```

AA The reason for requiring an initializer for a **const** is obvious: how could a **const** be a constant if it didn't have a value? It is almost always a good idea to initialize variables also; an uninitialized variable is a recipe for obscure bugs. For example:

```
void f(int z)
{
	int x;	// uninitialized
	// ...
	x = 7;	// give x a value
	// ...
}
```

This looks innocent enough, but what if the first ... included a use of x? For example:

```
void f(int z)
{
	int x;	// uninitialized
	// ... no assignment to x here ...
	if (z>x) {
		// ...
	}
	x = 7;	// give x a value
	// ...
}
```

Because x is uninitialized, the result of executing z>x would be undefined. The comparison z>x could give different results on different machines and different results in different runs of the program on the same machine. In principle, z>x might cause the program to terminate with a hardware error, but most often that doesn't happen. Instead we get unpredictable results.

Naturally, we wouldn't do something like that deliberately, but if we don't consistently initialize variables it will eventually happen by mistake. Remember, most "silly mistakes" (such as using an uninitialized variable before it has been assigned to) happen when you are busy or tired. Compilers try to warn, but in complicated code – where such errors are most likely to occur – compilers are not smart enough to catch all such errors. There are people who are not in the habit of initializing their variables. Some refrain because they learned to program in languages that didn't allow or encourage consistent initialization. Others are used to languages where every variable is initialized to a default value (which may or may not be appropriate in all cases). Therefore, you'll see examples of uninitialized variables in other people's code. Please just don't add to the problem by forgetting to initialize the variables you define yourself.

We have a preference for the = syntax for initializations that just copy a value and for the { } initializer syntax for initializations that do more complex construction.

7.2.3 Default initialization

You might have noticed that we often don't provide an initializer for strings and vectors. For example:

```
vector<string> v;
string s;
while (cin>>s)
	v.push_back(s);
```

This is not an exception to the rule that variables must be initialized before use. What is going on here is that **string** and **vector** are defined so that variables of those types are initialized with a default value whenever we don't supply one explicitly. Thus, **v** is empty (it has no elements) and **s** is the empty string ("") before we reach the loop. The mechanism for guaranteeing default initialization is called a *default constructor* (§8.4.2).

Unfortunately, the language doesn't allow us to make such guarantees for built-in types. However, uninitialized variables are a significant bug source and the Core Guidelines ban them [CG: ES.20]. You have been warned!

7.3 Scope

CC A *scope* is a region of program text. A name is declared in a scope and is valid (is "in scope") from the point of its declaration until the end of the scope in which it was declared. For example:

```
void f()
{
        g();                    // error: g() isn't (yet) in scope
}

void g()
{
        f();                    // OK: f() is in scope
}

void h()
{
        int x = y;              // error: y isn't (yet) in scope
        int y = x;              // OK: x is in scope
        g();                    // OK: g() is in scope
}
```

Names in a scope can be seen from within scopes nested within it. For example, the call of f() is within the scope of g() which is "nested" in the global scope. The global scope is the scope that's not nested in any other. The rule that a name must be declared before it can be used still holds, so f() cannot call g().

There are several kinds of scopes that we use to control where our names can be used:

- The *global scope:* the area of text outside any other scope
- A *module scope*: the area of text within a module (§7.7.1)
- A *namespace scope*: a named scope nested in the global scope or in another namespace (§7.6)
- A *class scope*: the area of text within a class (§8.2)
- A *local scope*: between { ... } braces of a block or in a function argument list
- A *statement scope*: e.g., in a **for**-statement

The main purpose of a scope is to keep names local, so that they won't interfere with names declared elsewhere. For example:

```
int max(int a, int b)          // max is global; a and b are local
{
        int m;                 // m is local
        if (a>=b)
                m = a;
        else
                m = b;
        return m;
}

int abs(int a)                 // abs is global; a is local
{
        return (a>=0) ? a : –a;
}
```

Or graphically:

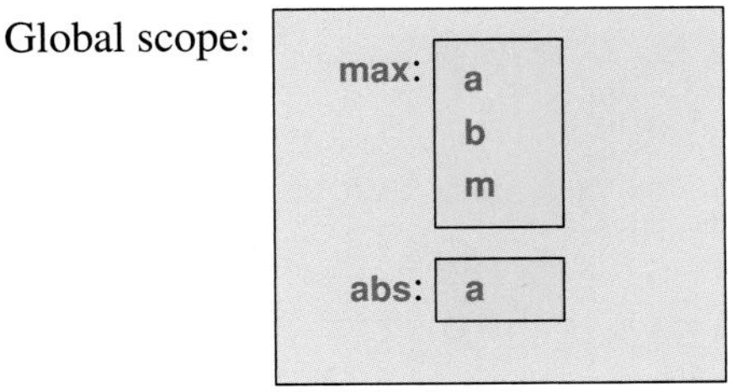

The a in max() is different from the a in abs(). They don't "clash" because they are in different scopes. Two incompatible declarations in the same scope is often referred to as a *clash*.

The ?: construct used in abs() is called an *arithmetic if* or a *conditional expression*. The value of (a>=0)?a:–a is a if a>=0 and –a otherwise. In many cases, a conditional expression saves us from writing long-winded code using if like the one in max(). It also saves us from the temptation to have an uninitialized variable because "we are just about to assign to it." You find max() and abs() in the standard library, so you don't have to write them yourself.

So, with the notable exception of the global scope, a scope keeps names local. For most purposes, locality is good, so keep names as local as possible. When I declare my variables, functions, etc. within functions, classes, namespaces, etc., they won't interfere with yours. Remember: Real programs have *many* thousands of named entities. To keep such programs manageable, most names have to be local. AA

Here is a larger technical example illustrating how names go out of scope at the end of statements and blocks (including function bodies):

```
// no r, i, or v here
class My_vector {
        vector<int> v;                    // v is in class scope
```

```
public:
        int largest()
        {
                int r = 0;                           // r is local
                for (int i = 0; i<v.size(); ++i)
                        r = max(r,abs(v[i]));        // i is in the for's statement scope
                // ... no i here ...
                return r;
        }
        // ... no r here ...
};
// no v here

int x = 0;                  // a global variable – avoid those where you can
int y = 0;

int f()
{
        int x = 0;          // a local variable, hides the global x
        x = 7;              // the local x
        {
                int x = y;  // local x initialized by global y, hides the previous local x
                ++x;        // the x from the previous line
        }
        ++x;                // the x from the first line of f()
        return x;
}
```

Whenever you can, avoid such complicated nesting and hiding. Remember: "Keep it simple!"

The larger the scope of a name is, the longer and more descriptive its name should be: **x**, **y**, and **f** are horrible as global names. The main reason that you don't want global variables in your program is that it is hard to know which functions modify them. In large programs, it is basically impossible to know which functions modify a global variable. Imagine that you are trying to debug a program and you find that a global variable has an unexpected value. Who gave it that value? Why? What functions write to that value? How would you know? The function that wrote a bad value to that variable may be in a source file you have never seen! A good program will have only very few (say, one or two), if any, global variables. For example, the calculator in Chapter 5 and Chapter 6 has two global variables: the token stream, **ts**, and the symbol table, **names**.

Note that most C++ constructs that define scopes nest:

- Functions within classes: member functions (see §8.4.2)

```
class C {
public:
        void f();
        void g() { /* ... */ }      // a member function can be defined within its class
        // ...
};
```

```
void C::f()                    // a member definition can be outside its class
{
    // ...
}
```

This is the most common and useful case.

- Classes within classes: member classes (also called nested classes)

```
class C {
public:
    class M {
        // ...
    };
    // ...
};
```

This tends to be useful only in complicated classes; remember that the ideal is to keep classes small and simple.

- Classes within functions: local classes

```
void f()
{
    class L {
        // ...
    };
    // ...
}
```

- Functions within functions: local functions (also called nested functions)

```
void f()
{
    void g() { /* ... */ }     // error: nested function
    // ...
}
```

Function nesting is not legal in C++. Instead, use a lambda (§13.3.3, §21.2.3).

- Blocks within functions and other blocks: nested blocks

```
void f(int x, int y)
{
    if (x>y) {
        // ...
    }
    else {
        // ...
        {
            // ...
        }
        // ...
    }
}
```

XX Nested blocks are unavoidable, but be suspicious of complicated nesting: it can easily hide errors. Similarly, if you feel the need for a local class, your function is probably far too long.

AA We use indentation to indicate nesting. Without consistent indentation, nested constructs become unreadable. Consider:

```
// dangerously ugly code
struct X {
void f(int x) {
struct Y {
int f() { return 1; } int m; };
int m;
m=x; Y m2;
return f(m2.f()); }
int m; void g(int m) {
if (0<m) f(m+2); else {
g(m+2.3); }}
X() { } int m3() {
}

void main() {
X a; a.f(2);}
};
```

Hard-to-read code usually hides bugs. When you use an IDE, it tries to automatically make your code properly indented (according to some definition of "properly"), and there exist "code beautifiers" that will reformat a source code file for you (often offering you a choice of formats). However, the ultimate responsibility for your code being readable rests with you.

> TRY THIS
>
> Type in the example above and indent it properly. What suspicious constructs and bugs can you now find?

7.4 Function call and return

CC Functions are the way we represent actions and computations. Whenever we want to do something that is worthy of a name, we write a function. The C++ language gives us operators (such as + and *) with which we can produce new values from operands in expressions, and statements (such as **for** and **if**) with which we can control the order of execution. To organize code made out of these primitives, we have functions.

To do its job, a function usually needs arguments, and many functions return a result. This section focuses on how arguments are specified and passed.

7.4.1 Declaring arguments and return type

Functions are what we use in C++ to name and represent computations and actions. A function declaration consists of a return type followed by the name of the function followed by a list of parameters in parentheses. For example:

```
double fct(int a, double d);            // declaration of fct (no body)

double fct(int a, double d)             // definition of fct
{
      return a*d;
}
```

A definition contains the function body (the statements to be executed by a call), whereas a declaration that isn't a definition just has a semicolon. Parameters are often called *formal arguments*. If you don't want a function to take arguments, just leave out the formal arguments. For example:

```
int current_power();                    // current_power doesn't take an argument
```

If you don't want to return a value from a function, give void as its return type. For example:

```
void increase_power_to(int level);  // increase_power_to() doesn't return a value
```

Here, void means "doesn't return a value" or "return nothing."

You can name a parameter or not as it suits you in both declarations and definitions. For example:

```
int my_find(vector<string> vs, string s, int hint);    // naming arguments: search starting from hint

int my_find(vector<string>, string, int);              // not naming arguments
```

CC

In declarations, formal argument names are not logically necessary, just very useful for writing good comments. From a compiler's point of view, the second declaration of my_find() is just as good as the first: it has all the information necessary to call my_find().

Usually, we name all the arguments in the definition. For example:

```
int my_find(vector<string> vs, string s, int hint)
      // search for s in vs starting at hint
{
      if (hint<0 || vs.size()<=hint)
            hint = 0;
      for (int i = hint; i<vs.size(); ++i)        // search starting from hint
            if (vs[i]==s)
                  return i;
      for (int i = 0; i<hint; ++i)                // if we didn't find s, so search before hint
            if (vs[i]==s)
                  return i;
      return -1;
}
```

The hint complicates the code quite a bit, but the hint was provided under the assumption that users could use it to good effect by knowing roughly where in the vector a string will be found. However, imagine that we had used my_find() for a while and then discovered that callers rarely used hint well, so that it actually hurts performance. Now we don't need hint anymore, but there is lots of code "out there" that calls my_find() with a hint. We don't want to rewrite that code (or can't because it is someone else's code), so we don't want to change the declaration(s) of my_find(). Instead, we just don't use the last argument. Since we don't use it we can leave it unnamed:

```
int my_find(vector<string> vs, string s, int)    // 3rd argument unused
{
        for (int i = 0; i<vs.size(); ++i)
                if (vs[i]==s) return i;
        return -1;
}
```

7.4.2 Returning a value

We return a value from a function using a **return**-statement:

```
T f()    // f() returns a T
{
        V v;
        // ...
        return v;
}
```

Here, the value returned is exactly the value we would have gotten by initializing a variable of type **T** with a value of type **V**:

```
V v;
// ...
T t(v);      // initialize t with v
```

That is, value return is a form of initialization. Unfortunately, it is the potentially narrowing form of initialization (§2.9), but compilers often warn and the Core Guidelines will catch narrowing.

A function declared to return a value must return a value. In particular, it is an error to "fall through the end of the function":

```
double my_abs(int x)      // warning: buggy code
{
        if (x < 0)
                return -x;
        else if (x > 0)
                return x;
}       // error: no value returned if x is 0
```

Actually, the compiler probably won't notice that we "forgot" the case **x==0**. In principle it could, but few compilers are that smart. For complicated functions, it can be impossible for a compiler to know whether or not you return a value, so be careful. Here, "being careful" means to make really sure that you have a **return**-statement or an **error()** for every possible way out of the function.

For historical reasons, **main()** is a special case. Falling through the bottom of **main()** is equivalent to returning the value **0**, meaning "successful completion" of the program.

In a function that does not return a value, we can use **return** without a value to cause a return from the function. For example:

```
void print_until(vector<string> v, string quit)
        // print until the string called "quit" is found
{
        for (string s : v) {
                if (s==quit)
                        return;
                cout << s << '\n';
        }
}
```

As you can see, it is acceptable to "drop through the bottom" of a **void** function. This is equivalent to a **return;**.

7.4.3 Pass-by-value

The simplest way of passing an argument to a function is to give the function a copy of the value you use as the argument. An argument of a function **f()** is a local variable in **f()** that's initialized each time **f()** is called. For example: CC

```
// pass-by-value (give the function a copy of the value passed)
int f(int x)
{
        x = x+1;            // give the local x a new value
        return x;
}

int xx = 0;
cout << f(xx) << '\n';       // write: 1
cout << xx << '\n';          // write: 0; f() doesn't change xx

int yy = 7;
cout << f(yy) << '\n';       // write: 8
cout << yy << '\n';          // write: 7; f() doesn't change yy
```

Since a copy is passed, the **x=x+1** in **f()** does not change the values **xx** and **yy** passed in the two calls. We can illustrate a pass-by-value argument passing like this:

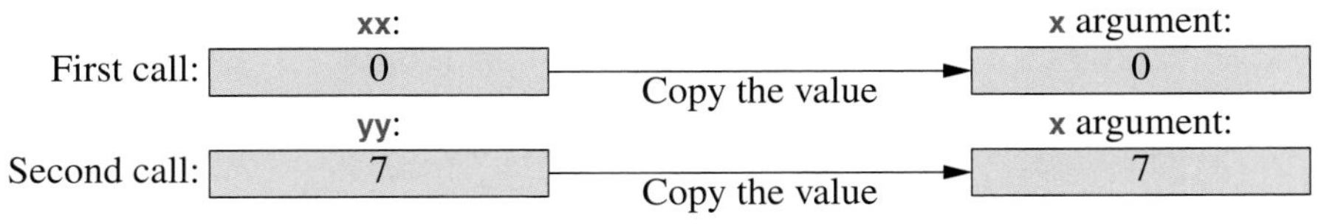

Pass-by-value is pretty straightforward, and its cost is the cost of copying the value.

7.4.4 Pass-by-const-reference

Pass-by-value is simple, straightforward, and efficient when we pass small values, such as an int, a double, or a Token (§5.3.2). But what if a value is large, such as an image (often, several million bits), a large table of values (say, thousands of integers), or a long string (say, hundreds of characters)? Then, copying can be costly. We should not be obsessed by cost, but doing unnecessary work can be embarrassing because it is an indication that we didn't directly express our idea of what we wanted. For example, we could write a function to print out a vector of floating-point numbers like this:

```
void print(vector<double> v)          // pass-by-value; appropriate?
{
        cout << "{ ";
        for (int i = 0; i<v.size(); ++i) {
                cout << v[i];
                if (i!=v.size()-1)
                        cout << ", ";
        }
        cout << " }\n";
}
```

We could use this print() for vectors of all sizes. For example:

```
void f(int x)
{
        vector<double> vd1(10);              // small vector
        vector<double> vd2(1000000);         // large vector
        vector<double> vd3(x);               // vector of some unknown size

        // ... fill vd1, vd2, vd3 with values ...

        print(vd1);
        print(vd2);
        print(vd3);
}
```

CC This code works, but the first call of print() has to copy ten doubles (probably 80 bytes), the second call has to copy a million doubles (probably 8 megabytes), and we don't know how much the third call has to copy. The question we must ask ourselves here is: "Why are we copying anything at all?" We just wanted to print the vectors, not to make copies of their elements. Obviously, there has to be a way for us to pass a variable to a function without copying it. As an analogy, if you were given the task to make a list of books in a library, the librarians wouldn't ship you a copy of the library building and all its contents; they would send you the address of the library, so that you could go and look at the books. So, we need a way of giving our print() function "the address" of the vector to print() rather than the copy of the vector. Such an "address" is called a *reference* and is used like this:

```
void print(const vector<double>& v)            // pass-by-const-reference
{
        cout << "{ ";
        for (int i = 0; i<v.size(); ++i) {
                cout << v[i];
                if (i!=v.size()-1)
                        cout << ", ";
        }
        cout << " }\n";
}
```

The & means "reference" and the const is there to stop print() from modifying its argument by accident. Apart from the change to the argument declaration, all is the same as before; the only change is that instead of operating on a copy, print() now refers back to the argument through the reference. Note the phrase "refer back"; such arguments are called references because they "refer" to objects defined elsewhere. We can call this print() exactly as before:

```
void f(int x)
{
        vector<double> vd1(10);                // small vector
        vector<double> vd2(1000000);           // large vector
        vector<double> vd3(x);                 // vector of some unknown size

        // ... fill vd1, vd2, vd3 with values ...
        print(vd1);
        print(vd2);
        print(vd3);
}
```

We can illustrate that graphically:

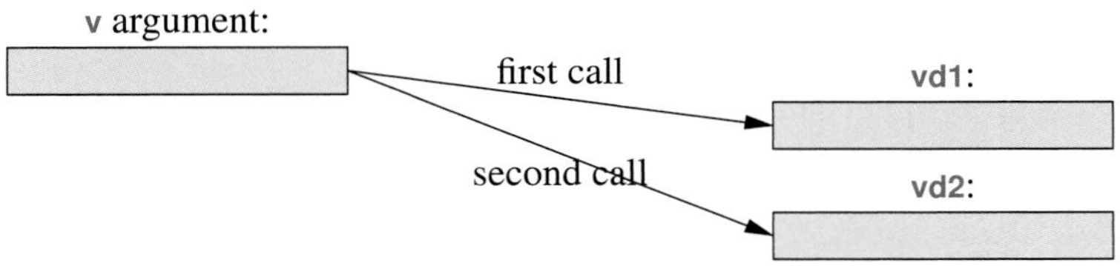

Compare to the pass-by-value example in §7.4.3.

A const reference has the useful property that we can't accidentally modify the object passed. For example, if we made a silly error and tried to assign to an element from within print(), the compiler would catch it:

```
void print(const vector<double>& v)            // pass-by-const-reference
{
        // ...
        v[i] = 7;                 // error: v is a const (is not mutable)
        // ...
}
```

Pass-by-const-reference is a useful and popular mechanism. Consider again the my_find() function (§7.4.1) that searches for a string in a vector of strings. Pass-by-value could be unnecessarily costly:

```
int my_find(vector<string> vs, string s); // pass-by-value: copy
```

If the vector contained many thousands of strings, you might notice the time spent even on a fast computer. So, we could improve my_find() by making it take its arguments by const reference:

```
int my_find(const vector<string>& vs, const string& s); // pass-by-const-reference: no copy, read-only
```

7.4.5 Pass-by-reference

But what if we did want a function to modify its arguments? Sometimes, that's a perfectly reasonable thing to wish for. For example, we might want an init() function that assigns values to vector elements:

```
void init(vector<double>& v)          // pass-by-reference
{
        for (int i = 0; i<v.size(); ++i)
                v[i] = i;
}

void g(int x)
{
        vector<double> vd1(10);              // small vector
        vector<double> vd2(1000000);         // large vector
        vector<double> vd3(x);               // vector of some unknown size

        init(vd1);
        init(vd2);
        init(vd3);
}
```

Here, we wanted init() to modify the argument vector, so we did not copy (did not use pass-by-value) or declare the reference const (did not use pass-by-const-reference) but simply passed a "plain reference" to the vector.

Let us consider references from a more technical point of view. A reference is a construct that allows us to declare a new name for an object. For example, int& is a reference to an int, so we can write

```
int x = 7;
int& r = x;
```

Or graphically:

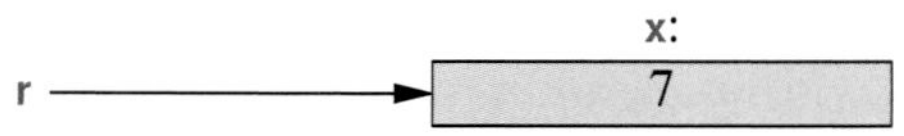

That is, any use of r is really a use of x.

References can be useful as shorthand. For example, we might have a

```
vector< vector<double> > v;  // vector of vector of double
```

and we need to refer to some element v[f(x)][g(y)] several times. Clearly, v[f(x)][g(y)] is a complicated expression that we don't want to repeat more often than we have to. If we just need its value, we could write

```
double val = v[f(x)][g(y)];        // val is the value of v[f(x)][g(y)]
```

and use val repeatedly. But what if we need to both read from v[f(x)][g(y)] and write to v[f(x)][g(y)]? Then, a reference comes in handy:

```
double& var = v[f(x)][g(y)];       // var is a reference to v[f(x)][g(y)]
```

Now we can read and write v[f(x)][g(y)] through var. For example:

```
var = var/2+sqrt(var);
```

This key property of references, that a reference can be a convenient shorthand for some object, is what makes them useful as arguments as shown for print() in §7.4.4.

Pass-by-reference is clearly a very powerful mechanism: we can have a function operate directly on any object to which we pass a reference. For example, swapping two values is an immensely important operation in many algorithms, such as sorting. Using references, we can write a function that swaps doubles like this: CC

```
void swap(double& d1, double& d2)
{
        double temp = d1;          // copy d1's value to temp
        d1 = d2;                   // copy d2's value to d1
        d2 = temp;                 // copy d1's old value to d2
}

int main()
{
        double x = 1;
        double y = 2;
        cout << "x == " << x << " y== " << y << '\n';        // write: x==1 y==2
        swap(x,y);
        cout << "x == " << x << " y== " << y << '\n';        // write: x==2 y==1
}
```

The standard library provides a swap() for every type that you can copy, so you don't have to write swap() yourself for each type.

7.4.6 Pass-by-value vs. pass-by-reference

When should you use pass-by-value, pass-by-reference, and pass-by-const-reference? Consider first a technical example:

```
void f(int a, int& r, const int& cr)
{
        ++a;          // change the local a
        ++r;          // change the object referred to by r
        ++cr;         // error: cr is const
}
```

If you want to change the value of the object passed, you must use a non-**const** reference: pass-by-value gives you a copy and pass-by-**const**-reference prevents you from changing the value of the object passed. So we can try

```
void g(int a, int& r, const int& cr)
{
        ++a;                // change the local a
        ++r;                // change the object referred to by r
        int x = cr;         // read the object referred to by cr
}

int main()
{
        int x = 0;
        int y = 0;
        int z = 0;

        g(x,y,z);           // x==0; y==1; z==0
        g(1,2,3);           // error: reference argument r needs a variable to refer to
        g(1,y,3);           // OK: since cr is const we can pass a literal
}
```

So, if you want to change the value of an object passed by reference, you have to pass an object. Technically, the integer literal **2** is just a value (an rvalue), rather than an object holding a value. What you need for **g()**'s argument **r** is an lvalue, that is, something that could appear on the left-hand side of an assignment.

Note that a **const** reference doesn't need an lvalue. It can perform conversions exactly as initialization or pass-by-value. Basically, what happens in that last call, **g(1,y,3)**, is that the compiler sets aside an **int** for **g()**'s argument **cr** to refer to:

```
g(1,y,3);     // means: int compiler_generated = 3; g(1,y, compiler_generated)
```

Such a compiler-generated object is called a *temporary object* or just a *temporary*.

AA Our rule of thumb is:

[1] Use pass-by-value to pass very small objects.
[2] Use pass-by-**const**-reference to pass large objects that you don't need to modify.
[3] Return a result rather than modifying an object through a reference argument.
[4] Use pass-by-reference only when you have to.

These rules lead to the simplest, least error-prone, and most efficient code. By "very small" we mean one or two **int**s, one or two **double**s, or something like that.

That third rule reflects that you have a choice when you want to use a function to change the value of a variable. Consider:

```
int incr1(int a) { return a+1; }        // return the new value as the result
void incr2(int& a) { ++a; }             // modify object passed as reference

int x = 7;
x = incr1(x);           // pretty obvious
incr2(x);               // pretty obscure
```

Why do we ever use non-const-reference arguments? Occasionally, they are essential CC

- For manipulating containers (e.g., vector) and other large objects
- For functions that change several objects

For example:

```
void larger(vector<int>& v1, vector<int>& v2)
        // make each element in v1 the larger of the corresponding elements in v1 and v2;
        // similarly, make each element of v2 the smaller
{
        if (v1.size()!=v2.size())
                error("larger(): different sizes");
        for (int i=0; i<v1.size(); ++i)
                if (v1[i]<v2[i])
                        swap(v1[i],v2[i]);
}
```

Using pass-by-reference arguments (or logical equivalents; §19.3.2) is the only reasonable choice for a function like larger().

If we use a reference simply to avoid copying, we use a const reference. Consequently, when we see a non-const-reference argument, we assume that the function changes the value of its argument; that is, when we see a pass-by-non-const-reference we assume that not only can that function modify the argument passed, but it will, so that we have to look extra carefully at the call to make sure that it does what we expect it to. AA

7.4.7 Argument checking and conversion

Passing an argument is the initialization of the function's formal argument with the actual argument specified in the call. Consider:

```
void f(T x);
f(y);
T x = y;                // initialize x with y (see §7.2.2)
```

The call f(y) is legal whenever the initialization T x = y; is, and when it is legal both xs get the same value. For example:

```
void f(double x);

void g(int y)
{
        f(y);
        double x = y;           // initialize x with y (see §7.2.2)
}
```

Note that to initialize x with y, we have to convert an int to a double. The same happens in the call of f(). The double value received by f() is the same as the one stored in x.

XX Conversions are often useful, but occasionally they give surprising results (see §2.9). Consequently, we have to be careful with them and hope for compiler warnings. For example:

```
g(7.8);          // truncate 7.8 to 7; did you really mean to do that?
int x = 7.8;     // truncate 7.8 to 7; did you really mean to do that?
```

If you really mean to truncate a double value to an int, say so explicitly [CG: ES.46]. We can use narrowing operations from the Core Guideline support library, provided as part of PPP_support: narrow<T>(x): checks x and throws narrowing_error if there would be a loss of information after converting x to a T. For example:

```
void conv1(double y)
{
        int x = narrow<int>(y);          // checked conversion
}
```

That way, the next programmer to look at this code can see that you thought about the potential problem and you'll get an error if information is lost. When, on the other hand, we want rounding, we can use round_to() from PPP_support. For example:

```
void conv2(double y)
{
        int x = round_to<int>(y);        // 4/5 rounding
}
```

In scientific calculations, we often have to convert from integers to floating point values and back. You can find examples in our graphics library (§11.7.5 and §13.3). For conversions from int to double, we use the double(i) notation: For example:

```
void conv3(int x, int y)
{
        double z = double(x)/y;          // x/y would have truncated
}
```

> TRY THIS
>
> Try examples like the ones above converting all combinations of an int, a double, and a char. Use values 1001, 7.7, and 'x'. Try with implicit conversion and narrow. Write out the results for the cases where the program compiles. What errors and warnings did you get?

7.4.8 Function call implementation

But how does a computer really do a function call? The expression(), term(), and primary() functions from Chapter 5 and Chapter 6 are perfect for illustrating this except for one detail: they don't take any arguments, so we can't use them to explain how arguments are passed. But wait! They *must* take some input; if they didn't, they couldn't do anything useful. They do take an implicit argument: they use a Token_stream called ts to get their input; ts is a global variable. That's a bit sneaky. We can improve these functions by letting them take a **Token_stream&** argument. Here they are with a **Token_stream&** parameter added and everything that doesn't concern function call implementation removed.

First, **expression()** is completely straightforward; it has one argument (**ts**) and two local variables (**left** and **t**):

```
double expression(Token_stream& ts)
{
        double left = term(ts);
        Token t = ts.get();
        // ...
}
```

Second, **term()** is much like **expression()**, except that it has an additional local variable (**d**) that it uses to hold the result of a divisor for '/':

```
double term(Token_stream& ts)
{
        double left = primary(ts);
        Token t = ts.get();
        // ...
                case '/':
                {
                        double d = primary(ts);
                        // ...
                }
        // ...
}
```

Third, **primary()** is much like **term()** except that it doesn't have a local variable **left**:

```
double primary(Token_stream& ts)
{
        Token t = ts.get();
        switch (t.kind) {
        case '(':
                {       double d = expression(ts);
                        // ...
                }
                // ...
        }
}
```

Now they don't use any "sneaky global variables" and are perfect for our illustration: they have an argument, they have local variables, and they call each other. You may want to take the opportunity to refresh your memory of what the complete **expression()**, **term()**, and **primary()** look like, but the salient features as far as function call is concerned are presented here.

When a function is called, the language implementation sets aside a data structure, called a *function activation record*, containing a copy of all its parameters and local variables. For example, when **expression()** is first called, the compiler ensures that a structure like this is created: CC

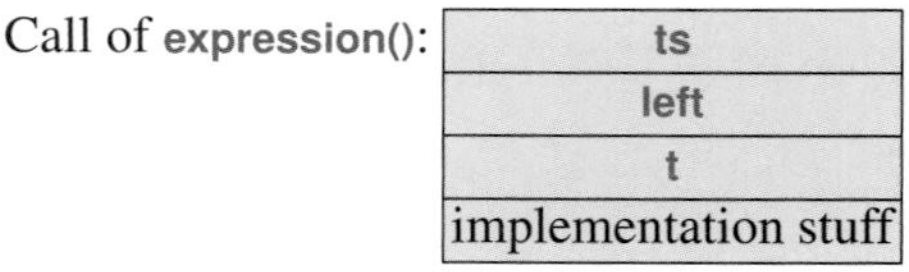

The "implementation stuff" varies from implementation to implementation, but that's basically the information that the function needs to return to its caller and to return a value to its caller. Each function has its own detailed layout of its activation record. Note that from the implementation's point of view, a parameter is just another local variable.

So far, so good, and now **expression()** calls **term()**, so the compiler ensures that an activation record for this call of **term()** is generated:

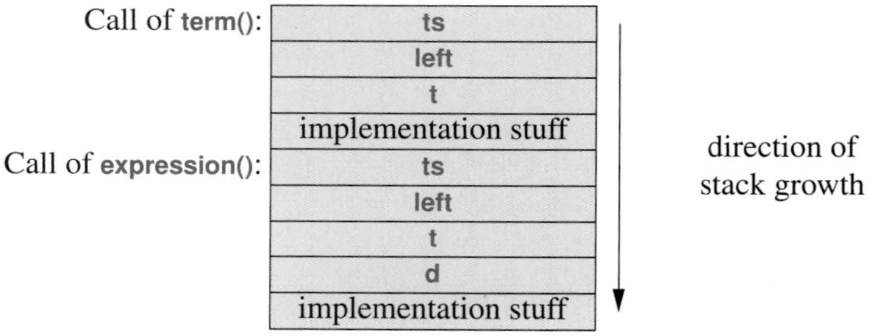

Note that **term()** has an extra variable **d** that needs to be stored, so we set aside space for that in the call even though the code may never get around to using it. That's OK. For reasonable functions (such as every function we directly or indirectly use in this book), the run-time cost of laying down a function activation record doesn't depend on how big it is. The local variable **d** will be initialized only if we execute its **case** '/'. Next, **term()** calls **primary()** and we get

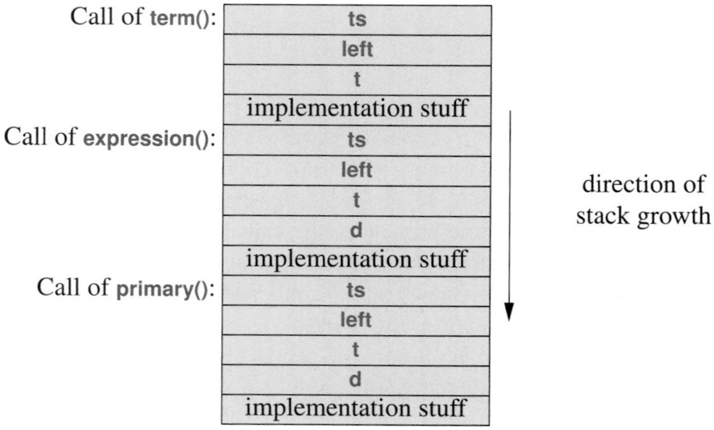

This is starting to get a bit repetitive, but now primary() calls expression():

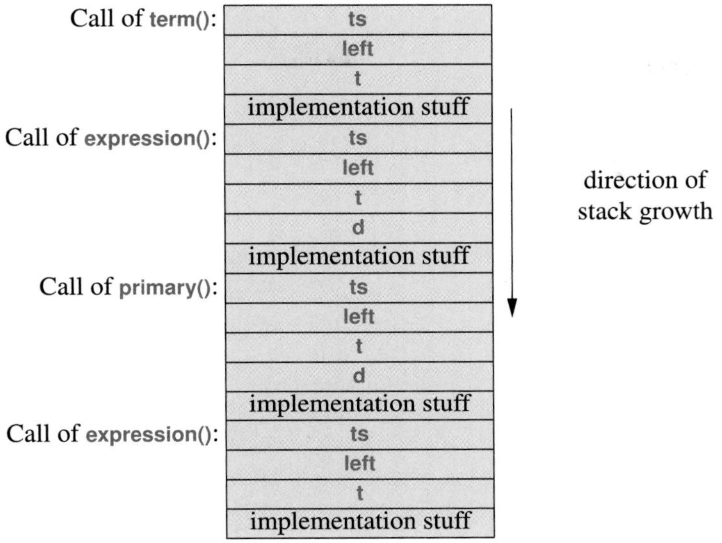

So this call of expression() gets its own activation record, different from the first call of expression(). CC
That's good or else we'd be in a terrible mess, since left and t will be different in the two calls. A function that directly or (as here) indirectly calls itself is called *recursive*.

So, each time we call a function the *stack of activation records*, usually just called the *stack*, grows by one record. Conversely, when the function returns, its record is no longer used. For example, when that last call of expression() returns to primary(), the stack will revert to this:

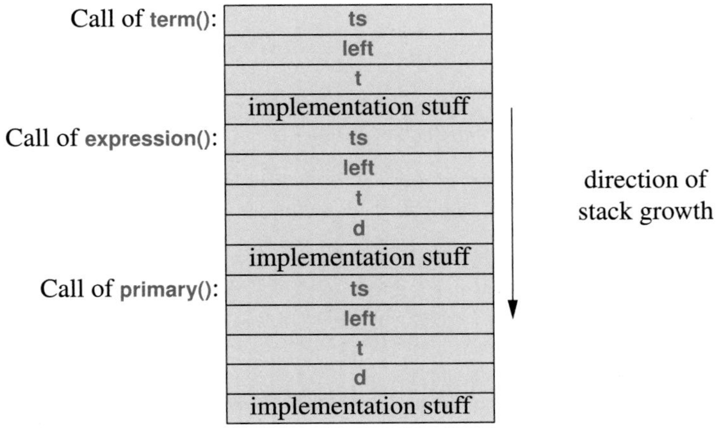

And when that call of **primary()** returns to **term()**, we get back to

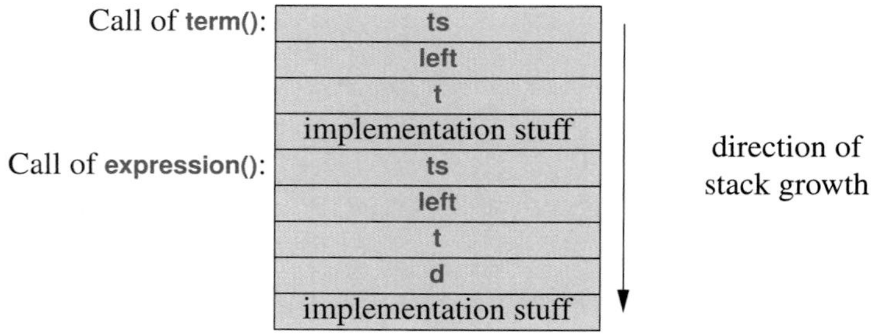

And so on. The stack, also called the *call stack*, is a data structure that grows and shrinks at one end according to the rule "Last in, first out."

Please remember that the details of how a call stack is implemented and used vary from C++ implementation to C++ implementation, but the basics are as outlined here. Do you need to know how function calls are implemented to use them? Of course not! You have done well enough before this implementation subsection, but many programmers like to know and many use phrases like "activation record" and "call stack," so it's better to know what they mean.

7.4.9 Compile-time computation

A function represents a calculation, and sometimes we want to do a calculation at compile time. The reason to want a calculation to be evaluated by the compiler is usually to avoid having the same calculation done millions of times at run time. We use functions to make our calculations comprehensible, so naturally we sometimes want to use a function in a constant expression. We convey our intent to have a function evaluated by the compiler by declaring the function **constexpr** (§3.3.1). A **constexpr** function can be evaluated by the compiler if it is given constant expressions as arguments. For example:

```
constexpr double xscale = 10;     // scaling factors
constexpr double yscale = 0.8;

constexpr Point scale(Point p) { return {xscale*p.x,yscale*p.y}; };
```

Assume that **Point** is a simple **struct** with members **x** and **y** representing 2D coordinates. Now, when we give **scale()** a **Point** argument, it returns a **Point** with coordinates scaled according to the factors **xscale** and **yscale**. For example:

```
void user(int x, int y)
{
        Point p1 {x,y};                     // at compile time, we don't know the value of p1
        constexpr Point p2 {10,10};

        Point p3 = scale(p1);               // OK: p3 == {100,8}; run-time evaluation is fine
        constexpr Point p4 = scale(p2);     // OK: p4 == {100,8}; scale(p2) is a constant
```

```
        constexpr Point p5 = scale(p1);      // error: scale (p1) is not a constant expression
        // ...
}
```

A constexpr function behaves just like an ordinary function until you use it where a constant is needed. Then, it is calculated at compile time and its arguments must be constant expressions (e.g., p2) and gives an error if they are not (e.g., p1). To enable that, a constexpr function must be so simple that the compiler (every standard-conforming compiler) can evaluate it. That includes simple loops and local variables. For example:

```
constexpr int sum(const vector<int>& v)
{
        int s = 0;
        for (int x : v)
                s += x;
        return s;
}
```

When called in a constant expression, a constexpr function cannot have side effects; that is, it cannot change the value of objects outside its own body. At compile time, such objects do not exist.

If you want a function that can be evaluated only at compile time, declare it consteval rather than constexpr. For example:

```
consteval half(double d) { return d/2; }

double x1 = half(7);        // OK: 7 is a constant
double x2 = half(x1);       // error: x1 is a non-const variable
```

7.4.10 Suffix return type

The traditional function declaration syntax that we have used so far is:

type-identifier function-identifier (*parameter-list*)

For example:

```
double expression(Token_stream& ts);          // double is the result of calling expression(ts)
```

However, there is another notation that puts the return type to the end where it arguably belongs:

auto *function-identifier* (*parameter-list*) -> *type-identifier*

For example:

```
auto expression(Token_stream& ts) -> double;      // call expression(ts) and get a double
```

This is called the *suffix return type* notation or the *trailing return* notation. It is occasionally essential when the return type is expressed in terms of the argument types and has the nice property that names align. For example:

```
auto Token_stream::get() -> Token;
auto statement() -> double;
auto find_all(string s) -> vector<Variable>;
```

as opposed to

```
Token Token_stream::get();
double statement();
vector<Variable> find_all(string s);
```

The difference becomes more noticeable when the return names become longer and more elaborate.

When using auto to introduce a function definition, the return type can be deduced from the return-statement:

```
auto expression(Token_stream& ts)        // deduce the return type from the definition
{
        double left = term(ts);
        // ...
        return left;
}
```

Like in auto object definitions (§2.10), the return type is deduced from the initializer (here, the function body). This deduction mechanism shouldn't be overused, like auto in general shouldn't, because it could lead to harder-to-read code. Worse, the type of a function could be unintentionally changed as the result of a change of its implementation.

7.5 Order of evaluation

CC The evaluation of a program – also called the execution of a program – proceeds through the statements according to the language rules. When this "thread of execution" reaches the definition of a variable, the variable is constructed; that is, memory is set aside for the object and the object is initialized. When the variable goes out of scope, the variable is destroyed; that is, the object it refers to is in principle removed and the compiler can use its memory for something else. For example:

```
string program_name = "silly";
vector<string> v;                        // v is global

void f()
{
        string s;                        // s is local to f
        while (cin>>s && s!="quit") {
                string stripped;         // stripped is local to the loop
                string not_letters;
                for (char x : s)         // x has statement scope
                        if (isalpha(x))
                                stripped += x;
                        else
                                not_letters += x;
                v.push_back(stripped);
        }
        // ... we can still use s here ...
}
```

Global variables, such as program_name and v, are initialized before the first statement of main() is executed. They "live" until the program terminates, and then they are destroyed. They are constructed in the order in which they are defined (that is, program_name before v) and destroyed in the reverse order (that is, v before program_name).

When someone calls f(), first s is constructed; that is, s is initialized to the empty string. It will live until we return from f().

Each time we enter the block that is the body of the while-statement, stripped and not_letters are constructed. Since stripped is defined before not_letters, stripped is constructed before not_letters. They live until the end of the loop, where they are destroyed in the reverse order of construction (that is, not_letters before stripped) before the condition is reevaluated. So, if ten strings are seen before we encounter the string quit, stripped and not_letters will each be constructed and destroyed ten times.

Each time we reach the for-statement, x is constructed. Each time we exit the for-statement, x is destroyed before we reach the v.push_back(stripped); statement.

Please note that compilers (and linkers) are clever beasts and they are allowed to – and do – optimize code as long as the results are equivalent to what we have described here. In particular, compilers are clever at not allocating and deallocating memory more often than is really necessary. For example, only one stripped is ever used at any time, so the stack frame for f() will contain space for just one stripped which will be reused repeatedly.

7.5.1 Expression evaluation

The order of evaluation of sub-expressions is governed by rules designed to please an optimizer rather than to make life simple for the programmer. That's unfortunate, but you should avoid complicated expressions anyway, and there is a simple rule that can keep you out of trouble: if you change the value of a variable in an expression, don't read or write it twice in that same expression. For example: XX

```
f(++i,++i);             // don't: undefined order of evaluation
x = ++i + i;            // don't: undefined order of evaluation
z = f(x)+g(y)           // don't if the order of f(x) and g(y) matters
h(f(x),g(y))            // don't if the order of f(x) and g(y) matters
```

Unfortunately, not all compilers warn if you write such bad code; it's bad because you can't rely on the results being the same if you move your code to another computer, use a different compiler or use a different optimizer setting. Compilers really differ for such code; just don't do it.

Fortunately, some order has been imposed. The order of evaluation is left-to-right for x.y, x–>y, x(y), x[y], x<<y, x>>y, x,y, x&&y, and x||y. For assignments (e.g., x=y and x+=y), the order is right-to-left. That actually makes most sensible constructs behave as one would naively expect. For example:

```
if (0<=x && v[x]!=0) ...    // v[x] will never be executed for x<0
v[i] = ++i;                 // i will be incremented before being used as a subscript
cout << ++i << ' ' << ++i;  // will print "2 3" if invoked with i==1
```

For &&, the second (right-hand) operand is not executed unless the first (left-hand) operand is true. Similarly, for ||, the second operand is not executed unless the first operand is false. This is sometimes called *short-circuit evaluation*.

7.5.2 Global initialization

XX Using a global variable in anything but the most limited circumstances is usually not a good idea. The programmer has no really effective way of knowing which parts of a large program read and/or write a global variable (§7.3). Unfortunately, global variables are common in older code.

Global variables (and namespace variables; see §7.6) in a single translation unit (§7.7.1) are initialized in the order in which they appear. For example:

```
// file f1.cpp
int x1 = 1;
int y1 = x1+2;          // y1 becomes 3
```

This initialization logically takes place "before the code in **main()** is executed." However, the order of initialization of global variables in different translation units is not defined. For example:

```
// file f2.cpp
extern int y1;
int y2 =y1+2;           // y2 becomes 2 or 5
```

Such code is to be avoided for several reasons: it uses global variables, it gives the global variables short names, and it uses complicated initialization of the global variables. If the globals in file **f1.cpp** are initialized before the globals in **f2.cpp**, **y2** will be initialized to **5** (as a programmer might naively and reasonably expect). However, if the globals in file **f2.cpp** are initialized before the globals in **f1.cpp**, **y2** will be initialized to **2** (because the memory used for global variables is initialized to **0** before complicated initialization is attempted). Avoid such code, and be very suspicious when you see global variables with nontrivial initializers. For global variables, consider any initializer that isn't a constant expression complicated.

But what can we do when we really need a global variable (or constant) with a complicated initializer? A plausible example would a **Date** initialized to today's date at program startup every morning.

```
const Date today = get_date_from_clock();          // suspicious definition
```

How do we know that **today** is never used before it was initialized? Basically, we can't know, so we shouldn't write that definition. The technique that we use most often is to call a function that returns the value. For example:

```
const Date today()
{
        return get_date_from_clock();          // return today's date
}
```

AA This constructs a **Date** every time we call **today()**. If **today()** is called often and if a call to **get_date_from_clock()** is expensive, we'd like to construct that **Date** once only. We can do that by using a **static** local variable:

```
const Date& today()
{
        static const Date today = get_date_from_clock();          // initialize today the first time we get here
        return today;
}
```

This **Date** is initialized (constructed) the first time its function is called (only). Note that we returned a reference to eliminate unnecessary copying. In particular, we returned a **const** reference to prevent the calling function from accidentally changing the value. The arguments about how to pass an argument (§7.4.6) also apply to returning values.

7.6 Namespaces

We use blocks to organize code within a function (§7.3). We use classes to organize functions, data, and types into a type (Chapter 8). A function and a class both do two things for us:

- They allow us to define a number of "entities" without worrying that their names clash with other names in our program.
- They give us a name to refer to what we have defined.

What we lack so far is something to organize classes, functions, data, and types into an identifiable and named part of a program without defining a type. The language mechanism for such grouping of declarations is a *namespace*. For example, we might like to provide a graphics library with classes called **Color**, **Shape**, **Line**, **Function**, and **Text** (see Chapter 11): CC

```
namespace Graph_lib {
        struct Color { /* ... */ };
        struct Shape { /* ... */ };
        struct Line : Shape { /* ... */ };
        struct Function : Shape { /* ... */ };
        struct Text : Shape { /* ... */ };
        // ...
        int gui_main() { /* ... */ }
}
```

Most likely somebody else in the world has used those names, but now that doesn't matter. You might define something called **Text**, but our **Text** doesn't interfere. **Graph_lib::Text** is one of our classes and your **Text** is not. We have a problem only if you have a class or a namespace called **Graph_lib** with **Text** as its member. **Graph_lib** is a slightly ugly name; we chose it because the "pretty and obvious" name **Graphics** had a greater chance of already being used somewhere.

Let's say that your **Text** was part of a text manipulation library. The same logic that made us put our graphics facilities into namespace **Graph_lib** should make you put your text manipulation facilities into a namespace called something like **TextLib**:

```
namespace TextLib {
        class Text { /* ... */ };
        class Glyph { /* ... */ };
        class Line { /* ... */ };
        // ...
}
```

Had we both used the global namespace, we could have been in real trouble. Someone trying to use both of our libraries would have had really bad name clashes for **Text** and **Line**. Worse, if we both had users for our libraries, we would not have been able to change our names, such as **Line** and **Text**, to avoid clashes. We avoided that problem by using namespaces; that is, our **Text** is

Graph_lib::Text and yours is TextLib::Text. A name composed of a namespace name (or a class name) and a member name combined by :: is called a *fully qualified name*.

7.6.1 Using-declarations and using-directives

Writing fully qualified names can be tedious. For example, the facilities of the C++ standard library are defined in namespace std and can be used like this:

```
import std;            // get the ISO C++ standard library

int main()
{
	std::string name;
	std::cout << "Please enter your first name\n";
	std::cin >> name;
	std::cout << "Hello, " << name << '\n';
}
```

Having seen the standard-library string and cout thousands of times, we don't really want to have to refer to them by their "proper" fully qualified names std::string and std::cout all the time. A solution is to say that "by string, I mean std::string," "by cout, I mean std::cout," etc.:

```
using std::string;          // from here on, string means std::string
using std::cout;            // from here on, cout means std::cout
// ...
```

That construct is called a using declaration; it is the programming equivalent to using plain "Greg" to refer to Greg Hansen, when there are no other Gregs in the room.

Sometimes, we prefer an even stronger "shorthand" for the use of names from a namespace: "If you don't find a declaration for a name in this scope, look in std." The way to say that is to use a using directive:

```
using namespace std;          // make names from std directly accessible
```

So we get this common style:

```
import std;               // get the ISO C++ standard library
using namespace std;      // make names from std directly accessible

int main()
{
	string name;
	cout << "Please enter your first name\n";
	cin >> name;
	cout << "Hello, " << name << '\n';
}
```

The cin is std::cin, the string is std::string, etc. As long as you use PPP_support, you don't need to worry about standard headers and the std namespace.

XX It is usually a good idea to avoid using directives for any namespace except for a namespace, such as std, that's extremely well known in an application area. The problem with overuse of using directives is that you lose track of which names come from where, so that you again start to get name clashes. Explicit qualification with namespace names and **using** declarations doesn't suffer from that problem. So, putting a **using** directive in a header file (so that users can't avoid it) is a very bad habit. However, to simplify our initial code we did place a **using** directive for **std** in **PPP_support**. That allows us to write

```
import PPP_import;

int main()
{
	string name;
	cout << "Please enter your first name\n";
	cin >> name;
	cout << "Hello, " << name << '\n';
}
```

7.7 Modules and headers

How do we manage our declarations and definitions? After all, they have to be consistent, and in real-world programs there can be tens of thousands of declarations; programs with hundreds of thousands of declarations are not rare. Typically, when we write a program, most of the definitions we use are not written by us. For example, the implementations of **cout** and **sqrt()** were written by someone else many years ago. We just use them.

The keys to managing declarations of facilities defined "elsewhere" in C++ are the module and the header. CC

- *The header*: an old and established mechanism for composing programs out of files.
- *The module*: a modern language mechanism for directly expressing modularity.

The module is by far the superior mechanism for ensuring modularity and thereby speeding up compilation. However, header files have been used for more than 50 years and there are billions of lines of code using them, so we must know how to use them well.

7.7.1 Modules

Imagine that we wanted to package the **Token_stream** abstraction as a separate facility that people could import as a whole, classes, functions, and all, into their program. We could enable that by defining a **module** called **Tokenstream**:

```
module Tokenstream;      // we are defining a module called "Tokenstream"

import std;              // implementation "details"
using namespace std;     // implicitly accessing std - only within Tokenstream
```

```
export class Token {
public:
	char kind;		// what kind of token
	double value;		// for numbers: a value
	Token(char k) :kind{k}, value{0.0} {}		// construct from one value
	Token(char k, double v) :kind{k}, value{v} {}	// construct from two values
};

export class Token_stream {
public:
	Token get();			// get a Token (get() is defined in §5.8.2)
	void putback(Token t);		// put a Token back
private:
	bool full = false;		// is there a Token in the buffer?
	Token buffer;			// putback() saves its token here
};

void Token_stream::putback(Token t)
{
	if (full)
		error("Token_stream::putpack() into a full buffer");
	buffer = t;		// copy t to buffer
	full = true;		// buffer is now full
}

Token Token_stream::get()
{
	if (full) {			// do we already have a Token ready?
		full = false;		// remove Token from buffer
		return buffer;
	}

	// ... use iostream and create a Token ...
}
```

This is of course a very tiny module. Modules like **std** and **PPP_support** offer far more significant benefits, but **Tokenstream** serves as a manageable example.

The definitions marked **export** are made available to users that **import** the module. A module can itself **import** the modules it needs, as is done here for **std**. Importantly, only **exported** declarations are made available to uses, so in this case the user of **Tokenstream** is not implicitly burdened by all of the standard library from the imported module **std**.

We can represent a use of **Tokenstream** graphically:

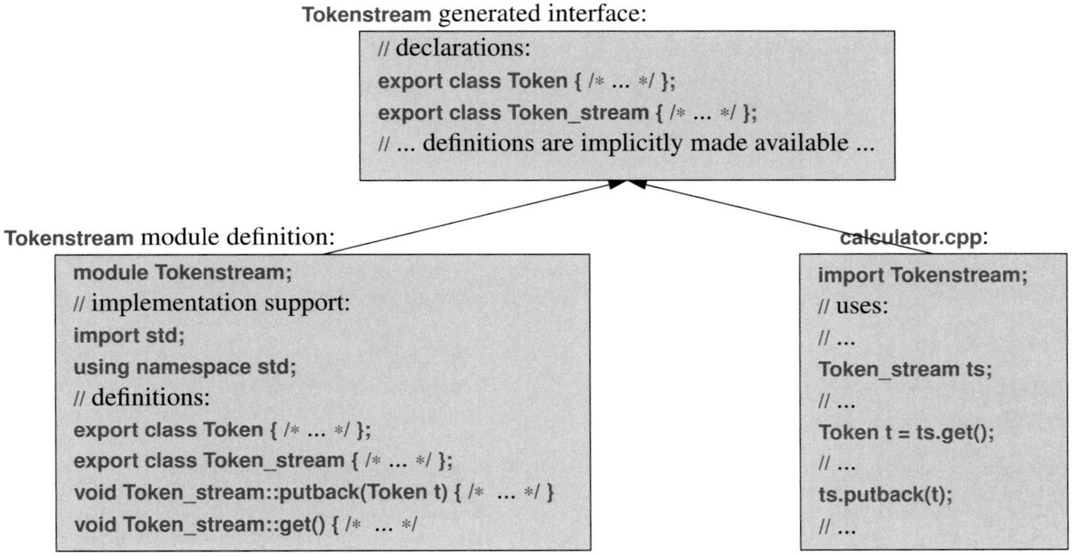
Tokenstream generated interface:
// declarations:
export class Token { /* ... */ };
export class Token_stream { /* ... */ };
// ... definitions are implicitly made available ...
Tokenstream module definition:
module Tokenstream;
// implementation support:
import std;
using namespace std;
// definitions:
export class Token { /* ... */ };
export class Token_stream { /* ... */ };
void Token_stream::putback(Token t) { /* ... */ }
void Token_stream::get() { /* ... */
calculator.cpp:
import Tokenstream;
// uses:
// ...
Token_stream ts;
// ...
Token t = ts.get();
// ...
ts.putback(t);
// ...

Unfortunately, there is no standardized suffix for module definition (Microsoft uses **.ixx**, GCC **.cxx**, and Clang **.cppm**). To compile and use modules, you need to know how your specific C++ implementation handles that; **cppreference.com** and **www.stroustrup.com/programming.html** may offer some help (§0.4.1).

The generated module interface is not meant to be seen by programmers, just to be **import**ed.

Modules offer many benefits, including fast compilation – much faster compilation than alternatives – and better isolation of concerns. That is, "implementation details" such as the use of the **iostream** library within **Tokenstream** is not visible to **import**ing code. This has important implications, such as that modules can be **import**ed in any order:

```
import m1;
import m2;
```

means the same as

```
import m2;
import m1;
```

That is a great help to both compilers and human readers.

7.7.2 Header files

At the time of writing, modules are still rather new in C++. Before that, for 50 years, modularity was "simulated" through file manipulation using the notion of a *header file*. Given that billions of lines of code use header files and millions of programmers are familiar with them, they will be in use for many more years.

Basically, a *header* is a collection of declarations, typically defined in a file, so a header is also called a *header file*. Such headers are then **#included** in our source files. For example, we might decide to improve the organization of the source code for our calculator (Chapter 5 and Chapter 6) by separating out the token management. We could define a header file **token.h** containing declarations needed to use **Token** and **Token_stream**:

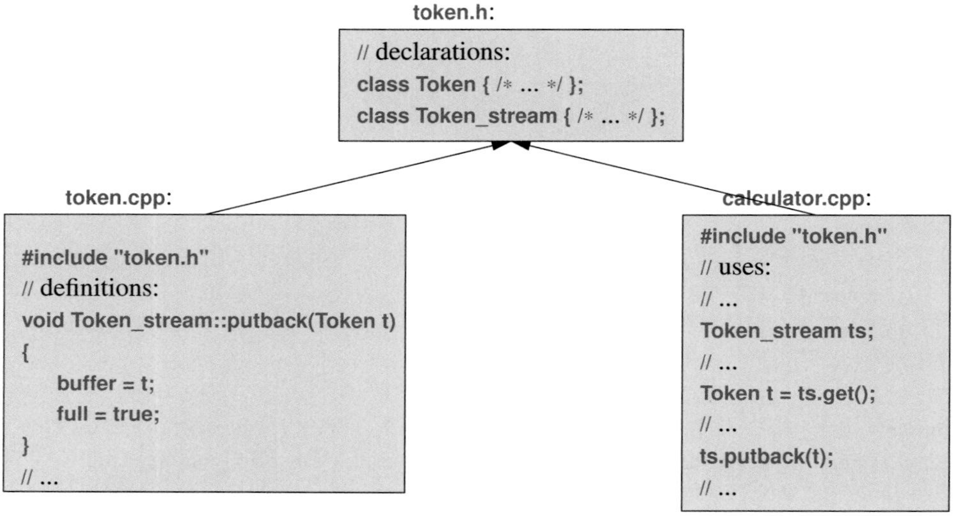

The declarations of **Token** and **Token_stream** are in the header **token.h**. Their definitions are in **token.cpp**. The **.h** suffix is the most common for C++ headers, and the **.cpp** suffix is the most common for C++ source files. Actually, the C++ language doesn't care about file suffixes, but some compilers and most program development environments insist, so please use this convention for your source code.

In principle, **#include "file.h"** simply copies the declarations from **file.h** into your file at the point of the **#include**. For example, we could write a header **f.h**:

```
// f.h
int f(int);
```

and include it in our file **user.cpp**:

```
// user.cpp
#include "f.h"

int g(int i)
{
      return f(i);
}
```

When compiling **user.cpp** the compiler would do the **#include** and compile

```
int f(int);

int g(int i)
{
      return f(i);
}
```

Since #includes logically happen before anything else a compiler does, handling #includes is part of what is called *preprocessing* (PPP2.§27.8).

To ease consistency checking, we #include a header both in source files that use its declarations and in source files that provide definitions for those declarations. That way, the compiler catches errors as soon as possible. For example, imagine that the implementer of Token_stream::putback() made mistakes: **AA**

```
Token Token_stream::putback(Token t)
{
      buffer.push_back(t);
      return t;
}
```

This looks innocent enough. Fortunately, the compiler catches the mistakes because it sees the (#included) declaration of Token_stream::putback(). Comparing that declaration with our definition, the compiler finds that putback() should not return a Token and that buffer is a Token, rather than a vector<Token>, so we can't use push_back(). Such mistakes occur when we work on our code to improve it, but don't quite get a change consistent throughout a program.

Similarly, consider these mistakes:

```
Token t = ts.gett();    // error: no member gett
// ...
ts.putback();           // error: argument missing
```

The compiler would immediately give errors; the header token.h gives it all the information it needs for checking.

A header will typically be included in many source files. That means that a header should only contain declarations that can be duplicated in several files (such as function declarations, class definitions, and definitions of numeric constants). **AA**

In §10.8.1, we offer a slightly more realistic example of header use.

Drill

[1] Write three functions swap_v(int,int), swap_r(int&,int&), and swap_cr(const int&, const int&). Each should have the body

```
{ int temp; temp = a, a=b; b=temp; }
```

where a and b are the names of the arguments.

Try calling each swap like this

```
int x = 7;
int y = 9;
swap_?(x,y);          // replace ? by v, r, or cr
swap_?(7,9);
const int cx = 7;
const int cy = 9;
swap_?(cx,cy);
swap_?(7.7,9.9);
double dx = 7.7;
double dy = 9.9;
swap_?(dx,dy);
swap_?(7.7,9.9);
```

Which functions and calls compiled, and why? After each swap that compiled, print the value of the arguments after the call to see if they were actually swapped. If you are surprised by a result, consult §7.5.

[2] Write a program using a single file containing three namespaces X, Y, and Z so that the following main() works correctly:

```
int main()
{
        X::var = 7;
        X::print();           // print X's var
        using namespace Y;
        var = 9;
        print();              // print Y's var
        {
                using Z::var;
                using Z::print;
                var = 11;
                print();      // print Z's var
        }
        print();              // print Y's var
        X::print(); // print X's var
}
```

Each namespace needs to define a variable called var and a function called print() that outputs the appropriate var using cout.

[3] Create a module foo with the suffix appropriate to your system:

```
int foo = 0;
export void print_foo() { ... };
export void set_foo(int x} { foo = x; }
export int get_foo() { return x; }
```

Add what it takes to get the ... part to print foo. Write file use.cpp that imports foo and tests it. Get the resulting program to compile and run.

[4] Create a header file: foo.h:

```
extern int foo;
void print_foo();
void print(int);
```

Write a file foo.cpp that implements the functions declared in foo.h. Write file use.cpp that #includes foo.h and tests it. Get the resulting program to compile and run.

Review

[1] What is the difference between a declaration and a definition?
[2] How do we syntactically distinguish between a function declaration and a function definition?
[3] How do we syntactically distinguish between a variable declaration and a variable definition?
[4] Why can't you use the functions in the calculator program from Chapter 5 without declaring one or more of them first?
[5] Is int a; a definition or just a declaration?
[6] Why is it a good idea to initialize variables as they are declared?
[7] What can a function declaration consist of?
[8] What is the *suffix return type* notation, and why might you use it?
[9] What good does indentation do?
[10] What is the scope of a declaration?
[11] What kinds of scope are there? Give an example of each.
[12] What is the difference between a class scope and local scope?
[13] Why should a programmer minimize the number of global variables?
[14] What is the difference between pass-by-value and pass-by-reference?
[15] What is the difference between pass-by-reference and pass-by-const-reference?
[16] What is a swap()?
[17] Would you ever define a function with a vector<double> as a by-value parameter?
[18] Give an example of undefined order of evaluation. Why can undefined order of evaluation be a problem?
[19] What do x&&y and x||y, respectively, mean?
[20] Which of the following is standard-conforming C++: functions within functions, functions within classes, classes within classes, classes within functions?
[21] What goes into an activation record?
[22] What is a call stack and why do we need one?
[23] What is the purpose of a namespace?
[24] How does a namespace differ from a class?
[25] What is a using declaration?
[26] Why should you avoid using directives in a header?
[27] What is namespace std?

Terms

activation record	function	pass-by-reference	argument
function definition	pass-by-value	argument passing	global scope
recursion	call stack	header file	`return`
class scope	initializer	return value	`const`
local scope	scope	`constexpr`	`namespace`
statement scope	declaration	namespace scope	technicalities
definition	nested block	undeclared identifier	`extern`
parameter	`using` declaration	forward declaration	pass-by-`const`-reference
`using` directive	`auto`	`->`	suffix return type

Exercises

[1] Modify the calculator program from Chapter 6 to make the input stream an explicit parameter (as shown in §7.4.8), rather than simply using `cin`. Also give the `Token_stream` constructor (§6.8.2) an `istream&` parameter so that when we figure out how to make our own `istreams` (e.g., attached to files), we can use the calculator for those. Hint: Don't try to copy an `istream`.

[2] Write a function `print()` that prints a `vector` of `ints` to `cout`. Give it two arguments: a `string` for "labeling" the output and a `vector`.

[3] Create a `vector` of Fibonacci numbers and print them using the function from exercise 2. To create the `vector`, write a function, `fibonacci(x,y,v,n)`, where integers `x` and `y` are `ints`, `v` is an empty `vector<int>`, and `n` is the number of elements to put into `v`; `v[0]` will be `x` and `v[1]` will be `y`. A Fibonacci number is one that is part of a sequence where each element is the sum of the two previous ones. For example, starting with 1 and 2, we get 1, 2, 3, 5, 8, 13, 21, … . Your `fibonacci()` function should make such a sequence starting with its `x` and `y` arguments.

[4] An `int` can hold integers only up to a maximum number. Find an approximation of that maximum number by using `fibonacci()`.

[5] Write two functions that reverse the order of elements in a `vector<int>`. For example, 1, 3, 5, 7, 9 becomes 9, 7, 5, 3, 1. The first reverse function should produce a new `vector` with the reversed sequence, leaving its original `vector` unchanged. The other reverse function should reverse the elements of its `vector` without using any other `vectors` (hint: `swap`).

[6] Write versions of the functions from exercise 5, but with a `vector<string>`.

[7] Read five names into a `vector<string> name`, then prompt the user for the ages of the people named and store the ages in a `vector<double> age`. Then print out the five (`name[i]`,`age[i]`) pairs. Sort the names (`sort(name.begin(),name.end())`) and print out the (`name[i]`,`age[i]`) pairs. The tricky part here is to get the `age vector` in the correct order to match the sorted `name vector`. Hint: Before sorting `name`, take a copy and use that to make a copy of `age` in the right order after sorting `name`.

[8] Do the previous exercise but allow an arbitrary number of names.

[9] Write a function that given two `vector<double>`s `price` and `weight` computes a value (an "index") that is the sum of all `price[i]*weight[i]`. Make sure to have `weight.size()==price.size()`.

[10] Write a function maxv() that returns the largest element of a vector argument.

[11] Write a function that finds the smallest and the largest element of a vector argument and also computes the mean and the median. Do not use global variables. Either return a struct containing the results or pass them back through reference arguments. Which of the two ways of returning several result values do you prefer and why?

[12] Improve print_until_s() from §7.4.2. Test it. What makes a good set of test cases? Give reasons. Then, write a print_until_ss() that prints until it sees a second occurrence of its quit argument.

[13] Write a function that takes a vector<string> argument and returns a vector<int> containing the number of characters in each string. Also find the longest and the shortest string and the lexicographically first and last string. How many separate functions would you use for these tasks? Why?

[14] Can we declare a non-reference function argument const (e.g., void f(const int);)? What might that mean? Why might we want to do that? Why don't people do that often? Try it; write a couple of small programs to see what works.

Postscript

We could have put much of this chapter (and much of the next) into an appendix. However, you'll need most of the facilities described here in the rest of this book. You'll also encounter most of the problems that these facilities were invented to help solve very soon. Most simple programming projects that you might undertake will require you to solve such problems. So, to save time and minimize confusion, a somewhat systematic approach is called for, rather than a series of "random" visits to manuals and appendices.

8

Technicalities: Classes, etc.

Remember, things take time.
– Piet Hein

In this chapter, we keep our focus on our main tool for programming: the C++ programming language. We present language technicalities, mostly related to user-defined types, that is, to classes and enumerations. Much of the presentation of language features takes the form of the gradual improvement of a **Date** type. That way, we also get a chance to demonstrate some useful class design techniques.

§8.1 User-defined types
§8.2 Classes and members
§8.3 Interface and implementation
§8.4 Evolving a class: **Date**
  struct and functions; Member functions and constructors; Keep details private; Defining member functions; Referring to the current object; Reporting errors
§8.5 Enumerations
  "Plain" enumerations
§8.6 Operator overloading
§8.7 Class interfaces
  Argument types; Copying; Default constructors; **const** member functions; Member functions and helper functions; The ISO standard

8.1 User-defined types

CC The C++ language provides you with some built-in types, such as `char`, `int`, and `double`. A type is called built-in if the compiler knows how to represent objects of the type and which operations can be done on it (such as `+` and `*`) without being told by declarations supplied by a programmer in source code.

CC Types that are not built-in are called *user-defined types*. They can be standard-library types – available to all C++ programmers as part of every ISO standard C++ implementation – such as `string`, `vector`, and `ostream` (Chapter 9), or types that we build for ourselves, such as `Token` and `Token_stream` (§5.3.2 and §5.8). As soon as we get the necessary technicalities under our belt, we'll build graphics types such as `Shape`, `Line`, and `Text` (Chapter 11). The standard-library types are as much a part of the language as the built-in types, but we still consider them user-defined because they are built from the same primitives and with the same techniques as the types we built ourselves; the standard-library builders have no special privileges or facilities that you don't have. Like the built-in types, most user-defined types provide operations. For example, `vector` has `[ ]` and `size()` (§3.6.1), `ostream` has `<<` (§9), `Token_stream` has `get()` (§5.8), and `Shape` has `add(Point)` and `set_color()` (§12.2).

AA Why do we build types? The compiler does not know all the types we might like to use in our programs. It couldn't, because there are far too many useful types – no language designer or compiler implementer could know them all. We invent new ones every day. Why? What are types good for? Types are good for directly representing ideas in code. When we write code, the ideal is to represent our ideas directly in our code so that we, our colleagues, and the compiler can understand what we wrote. When we want to do integer arithmetic, `int` is a great help; when we want to manipulate text, `string` is a great help; when we want to manipulate calculator input, `Token` and `Token_stream` are a great help. The help comes in two forms:

- *Representation*: A type "knows" how to represent the data needed in an object.
- *Operations*: A type "knows" what operations can be applied to objects.

Many ideas follow this pattern: "something" has data to represent its current value – sometimes called the current *state* – and a set of operations that can be applied. Think of a computer file, a Web page, a toaster, a music player, a coffee cup, an electric motor, a cell phone, a telephone directory; all can be characterized by some data and all have a more or less fixed set of standard operations that you can perform. In each case, the result of the operation depends on the data – the current state – of an object.

So, we want to represent such an "idea" or "concept" in code as a data structure plus a set of functions. The question is: "Exactly how?" This chapter presents the technicalities of the basic ways of doing that in C++.

CC C++ provides two kinds of user-defined types: classes and enumerations. The class is by far the most general and important, so we first focus on classes. A class directly represents a concept in a program. A *class* is a (user-defined) type that specifies how objects of its type are represented, how those objects can be created, how they can be used, and how they can be destroyed (Chapter 17). If you think of something as a separate entity, it is likely that you should define a class to represent that "thing" in your program. Examples are vector, matrix, input stream, string, FFT (fast Fourier transform), valve controller, robot arm, device driver, picture on screen, dialog box, graph, window, temperature reading, and clock.

In C++, a class is the key building block for large programs – and very useful for small ones as well, as we saw for our calculator (Chapter 5 and Chapter 6).

8.2 Classes and members

A class is a user-defined type. It is composed of built-in types, other user-defined types, and functions. The parts used to define the class are called *members*. A class has zero or more members. For example: CC

```
class X {
public:
        int m;                                          // data member
        int mf(int v) { int old = m; m=v; return old; } // function member
};
```

Members can be of various types. Most are either data members, which define the representation of an object of the class, or function members, which provide operations on such objects. We access members using the *object.member* notation. For example:

```
X var;                 // var is a variable of type X
var.m = 7;             // assign to var's data member m
int x = var.mf(9);     // call var's member function mf()
```

You can read var.m as var's m. Most people pronounce it "var dot m" or "var's m." The type of a member determines what operations we can do on it. For example, we can read and write an int member and call a member function.

A member function, such as X's mf(), does not need to use the var.m notation. It can use the plain member name (m in this example). Within a member function, a member name refers to the member of that name in the object for which the member function was called. Thus, in the call var.mf(9), the m in the definition of mf() refers to var.m.

8.3 Interface and implementation

Usually, we think of a class as having an interface plus an implementation. The interface is the part of the class's declaration that its users access directly. The implementation is that part of the class's declaration that its users access only indirectly through the interface. The public interface is identified by the label public: and the implementation by the label private:. You can think of a class declaration like this: CC

```
class X {        // this class's name is X
public:
        // the interface to users (accessible by all)
        // functions, types, and data (data is often best kept private)
private:
        // the implementation details (used by members of this class only)
        // functions, types, and data
};
```

Class members are private by default; that is,

```
class X {
        int mf(int);
        // ...
};
```

means

```
class X {
private:
        int mf(int);
        // ...
};
```

so that

```
X x;                    // variable x of type X
int y = x.mf();         // error: mf is private (i.e., inaccessible)
```

A user cannot directly refer to a private member. Instead, we have to go through a public function that can use it. For example:

```
class X {
        int m;
        int mf(int);
public:
        int f(int i) { m=i; return mf(i); }
};

X x;
int y = x.f(2);
```

We use **private** and **public** to represent the important distinction between an interface (the user's view of the class) and implementation details (the implementer's view of the class). We explain that and give lots of examples as we go along. Here we'll just mention that for something that's just data, this distinction doesn't make sense. So, there is a useful simplified notation for a class that has no private implementation details. A **struct** is a **class** where members are public by default:

```
struct X {
        int m;
        // ...
};
```

means

```
class X {
public:
        int m;
        // ...
};
```

structs are primarily used for data structures where the members can take any value; that is, we can't define any meaningful invariant (§8.4.3).

8.4 Evolving a class: Date

Let's illustrate the language facilities supporting classes and the basic techniques for using them by showing how – and why – we might evolve a simple data structure into a class with private implementation details and supporting operations. We use the apparently trivial problem of how to represent a date (such as August 14, 1954) in a program. The need for dates in many programs is obvious (commercial transactions, weather data, calendar programs, work records, inventory management, etc.). The only question is how we might represent them.

8.4.1 struct and functions

How would we represent a date? When asked, most people answer, "Well, how about the year, the month, and the day of the month?" That's not the only answer and not always the best answer, but it's good enough for our use here, so that's what we'll do. Our first attempt is a simple **struct**:

```
// simple Date (too simple?)
struct Date {
        int y;      // year
        int m;      // month in year
        int d;      // day of month
};

Date today;         // a Date variable (a named object)
```

A **Date** object, such as **today**, will simply be three **ints**:

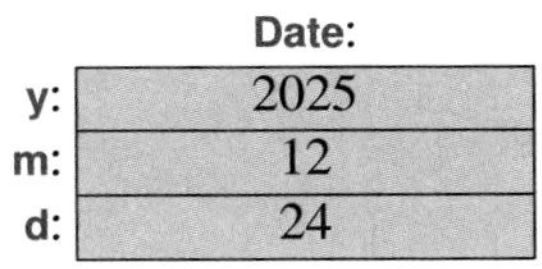

There is no "magic" relying on hidden data structures anywhere related to a **Date** – and that will be the case for every version of **Date** in this chapter.

So, we now have **Dates**; what can we do with them? We can do everything in the sense that we can access the members of **today** (and any other **Date**) and read and write them as we like. The snag is that nothing is really convenient. Just about anything that we want to do with a **Date** has to be written in terms of reads and writes of those members. For example:

```
today.y = 2025;     // set today to December 24, 2025
today.m = 24;
today.d = 12;
```

This is tedious and error prone. Did you spot the error? Everything that's tedious is error-prone! **AA**
Some errors are harder to spot. How about

```
Date y;             // set today to December 24, 2025:
y.y = 2000;
y.m = 2;
y.d = 29;
```

Was year 2000 a leap year? Are you sure?

What we do then is to provide some *helper functions* to do the most common operations for us. That way, we don't have to repeat the same code over and over again and we won't make, find, and fix the same mistakes over and over again. For just about every type, initialization and assignment are among the most common operations. For Date, increasing the value of the Date is another common operation, so we add those as helpers:

```
void init_day(Date& dd, int y, int m, int d)
{
        // ... check that (y,m,d) is a valid date. If it is, use it to initialize dd ...
}

void add_day(Date& dd, int n)
{
        // ... increase dd by n days ...
}
```

We can now try to use Date:

```
void f()
{
        Date today;
        init_day(today, 12, 24, 2025);    // oops! (no day 2025 in year 12)
        add_day(today,1);
}
```

AA First we note the usefulness of such "operations" – here implemented as helper functions. Checking that a date is valid is sufficiently difficult and tedious that if we didn't write a checking function once and for all, we'd skip the check occasionally and get buggy programs. Whenever we define a type, we want some operations for it. Exactly how many operations we want and of which kind will vary. Exactly how we provide them (as functions, member functions, or operators) will also vary, but whenever we decide to provide a type, we ask ourselves, "Which operations would we like for this type?"

8.4.2 Member functions and constructors

We provided an initialization function for Dates, one that provided an important check on the validity of Dates. However, checking functions are of little use if we fail to use them. For example, assume that we have defined the output operator << for a Date:

```
void f()
{
        Date today;
        // ...
        cout << today << '\n';          // use today
        // ...
        init_day(today,2008,3,30);
        // ...
```

```
        Date tomorrow;
        tomorrow.y = today.y;
        tomorrow.m = today.m;
        tomorrow.d = today.d+1;         // add 1 to today

        cout << tomorrow << '\n';       // use tomorrow
}
```

Here, we "forgot" to immediately initialize **today** and "someone" used it before we got around to calling **init_day()**. "Someone else" decided that it was a waste of time to call **add_day()** – or maybe hadn't heard of it – and constructed **tomorrow** by hand. As it happens, this is bad code – very bad code. Sometimes, probably most of the time, it works, but small changes lead to serious errors. For example, writing out an uninitialized **Date** will produce garbage output, and incrementing a day by simply adding **1** to its member **d** is a time bomb: when **today** is the last day of the month, the increment yields an invalid date. The worst aspect of this "very bad code" is that it doesn't look bad.

This kind of thinking leads to a demand for an initialization function that can't be forgotten and for operations that are less likely to be overlooked. The basic tool for that is *member functions*, that is, functions declared as members of the class within the class body. For example:

```
// simple Date
// guarantee initialization with constructor and provide some notational convenience
struct Date {
        int y, m, d;                    // year, month, day
        Date(int y, int m, int d);      // check for valid date and initialize
        void add_day(int n);            // increase the Date by n days
};
```

A member function with the same name as its class is special. It is called a *constructor* and will be used for initialization ("construction") of objects of the class. It is an error – caught by the compiler – to forget to initialize an object of a class that has a constructor that requires an argument, and there is a special convenient syntax for doing such initialization:

```
Date birthday;                          // error: birthday not initialized
Date today {12,24,2027};                // oops! run-time error
Date last {2005,12,31};                 // OK (colloquial style)
Date next = {2014,2,14};                // also OK (slightly verbose)
Date Beethoven = Date{1770,12,16};      // also OK (verbose style)
```

The attempt to declare **birthday** fails because we didn't specify the required initial value. The attempt to declare **today** will pass the compiler, but the checking code in the constructor will catch the illegal date at run time (**{12,24,2027}** – there is no day 2027 of the 24th month of year 12).

The definition of **last** provides the initial value – the arguments required by **Date**'s constructor – as a **{ }** list immediately after the name of the variable. That's the most common style of initialization of variables of a class that has a constructor requiring arguments. We can also use the more verbose style where we explicitly create an object (here, **Date{1976,12,24}**) and then use that to initialize the variable using the **=** initializer syntax. Unless you actually like typing, you'll soon tire of that.

We can now try to use our newly defined variables:

```
last.add_day(1);
add_day(2);                    // error: what date?
```

Note that the member function **add_day()** is called for a particular **Date** using the dot member-access notation. We'll show how to define member functions in §8.4.4.

In C++98, people used parentheses to delimit the initializer list, so you will see a lot of code like this:

```
Date last(2000,12,31);         // OK (old style)
```

We prefer { } for initializer lists because that clearly indicates when initialization (construction) is done, and also because that notation is more widely useful. Logically, even built-in types have constructors so we can write:

```
int x {7};                     // OK (initializer list style)
x = int{9};
```

When we get to write functions that can be used for a mixture of built-in types and user-defined types (Chapter 18), the ability to use a uniform notation becomes essential.

8.4.3 Keep details private

We still have a problem: What if someone forgets to use the member function **add_day()**? What if someone decides to change the month directly? After all, we "forgot" to provide a facility for that:

```
Date birthday {1960,12,31};    // December 31, 1960
++birthday.d;                  // ouch! Invalid date (birthday.d==32 makes birthday invalid)

Date today {1924,2,3};
today.m = 14;                  // ouch! Invalid date (today.m==14 makes today invalid)
```

XX As long as we leave the representation of **Date** accessible to everybody, somebody will – by accident or design – mess it up; that is, someone will do something that produces an invalid value. In these examples, we gave **Dates** values that don't correspond to days on the calendar. Such invalid objects are time bombs; it is just a matter of time before someone innocently uses the invalid value and gets a run-time error or – usually worse – produces a bad result.

Such concerns lead us to conclude that the representation of **Date** should be inaccessible to users except through the public member functions that we supply. Here is a first cut:

```
// simple Date (control access)
class Date {
        int y, m, d;                    // year, month, day
public:
        Date(int y, int m, int d);      // check for valid date and initialize
        void add_day(int n);            // increase the Date by n days
        int month() { return m; }
        int day() { return d; }
        int year() { return y; }
};
```

We can use it like this:

```
Date birthday {1970, 12, 30};          // OK
birthday.m = 14;                       // error: Date::m is private
cout << birthday.month() << '\n';      // we provided a way to read m
```

The notion of a "valid **Date**" is an important special case of the idea of a valid value. We try to design our types so that values are guaranteed to be valid; that is, we hide the representation, provide a constructor that creates only valid objects, and design all member functions to expect valid values and leave only valid values behind when they return. The value of an object is often called its *state*, so the idea of a valid value is often referred to as a *valid state* of an object. AA

The alternative is for us to check for validity every time we use an object, or just hope that nobody left an invalid value lying around. Experience shows that "hoping" can lead to "pretty good" programs. However, producing "pretty good" programs that occasionally produce erroneous results and occasionally crash is no way to win friends and respect as a professional. We prefer to write code that can be demonstrated to be correct.

A rule for what constitutes a valid value is called an *invariant*. The invariant for **Date** ("A **Date** must represent a day in the past, present, or future") is unusually hard to state precisely: remember leap years, the Gregorian calendar, time zones, etc. However, for simple realistic uses of **Date**s we can do it. For example, if we are analyzing internet logs, we need not be bothered with the Gregorian, Julian, or Mayan calendars. If we can't think of a good invariant, we are probably dealing with plain data. If so, use a **struct**. CC

8.4.4 Defining member functions

So far, we have looked at **Date** from the point of view of an interface designer and a user. But sooner or later, we have to implement those member functions. First, here is a subset of **Date** reorganized to suit the common style of providing the public interface first:

```
// simple Date (many people prefer implementation details last)
class Date {
public:
        Date(int y, int m, int d);    // constructor: check for valid date and initialize
        void add_day(int n);          // increase the Date by n days
        int month();
        // ...
private:
        int y, m, d;                  // year, month, day
};
```

Many put the public interface first because the interface is what most people are interested in. In principle, a user need not look at the implementation details. In reality, we are typically curious and have a quick look to see if the implementation looks reasonable and if the implementer used some technique that we could learn from. However, unless we are the implementers, we do tend to spend much more time with the public interface. The compiler doesn't care about the order of class function and data members; it takes the declarations in any order you care to present them.

When we define a member outside its class, we need to say which class it is a member of. We do that using the *class_name* :: *member_name* notation:

```
Date::Date(int yy, int mm, int dd)     // constructor
        :y{yy}, m{mm}, d{dd}           // note: member initializers
{
}

void Date::add_day(int n)
{
        // ...
}

int month()             // oops: we forgot Date::
{
        return m; // not the member function, can't access m
}
```

The :y{yy}, m{mm}, d{dd} notation is called a (member) initializer list. We use such lists to explicitly initialize members. We could have written

```
Date::Date(int yy, int mm, int dd)  // constructor
{
        y = yy;
        m = mm;
        d = dd;
}
```

However, we would then in principle first have default initialized the members and then assigned values to them. We would then also open the possibility of accidentally using a member before it was initialized. The :y{yy}, m{mm}, d{dd} notation more directly expresses our intent. The distinction is exactly the same as the one between

```
int x;      // first define the variable x
// ...
x = 2;      // later assign to x
```

and

```
int x = 2;  // define and immediately initialize with 2
```

We can also define member functions right in the class definition:

```
class Date {
public:
        Date(int yy, int mm, int dd)
                :y{yy}, m{mm}, d{dd}
        {
        }

        void add_day(int n)
        {
                // ...
        }
```

```
        int month() { return m; }

        // ...
private:
        int y, m, d;    // year, month, day
};
```

The first thing we notice is that the class declaration became larger and "messier." In this example, the code for the constructor and add_day() could be a dozen or more lines each. This makes the class declaration several times larger and makes it harder to find the interface among the implementation details. Consequently, we don't define large functions within a class declaration.

However, look at the definition of month(). That's straightforward and shorter than the version that places Date::month() out of the class declaration. For such short, simple functions, we might consider writing the definition right in the class declaration.

Note that month() can refer to m even though m is defined after (below) month(). A member can refer to a function or data member of its class independently of where in the class that other member is declared. The rule that a name must be declared before it is used is relaxed within the limited scope of a class.

Writing the definition of a member function within the class definition has three effects: CC

- The function will be *inline*; that is, the compiler will try to generate code for the function at each point of call rather than using function-call instructions to use common code. This can be a significant performance advantage for functions, such as month(), that hardly do anything but are used a lot.
- All uses of the class will have to be recompiled whenever we make a change to the body of an inlined function. If the function body is out of the class declaration, recompilation of users is needed only when the class declaration is itself changed. Not recompiling when the body is changed can be a huge advantage in large programs.
- The class definition gets larger. Consequently, it can be harder to find the members among the member function definitions.

The obvious rule of thumb is: Don't put member function bodies in the class declaration unless you know that you need the performance boost from inlining tiny functions. Large functions, say five or more lines of code, don't benefit from inlining and make a class declaration harder to read. We rarely inline a function that consists of more than one or two expressions. AA

TRY THIS

Get some example uses of a version of Date so far to run. For that, we need an output operator for Date. There is one in PPP_support, but for now use

```
ostream& operator<<(ostream& os, Date d)
{
        return os << d.year() << '/' << d.month() << '/' << d.day();
}
```

Chapter 9 explains why and how that works.

8.4.5 Referring to the current object

Consider a simple use of the **Date** class so far:

```
class Date {
        // ...
        int month() { return m; }
        // ...
private:
        int y, m, d;     // year, month, day
};

void f(Date d1, Date d2)
{
        cout << d1.month() << ' ' << d2.month() << '\n';
}
```

How does **Date::month()** know to return the value of **d1.m** in the first call and **d2.m** in the second? Look again at **Date::month()**; its declaration specifies no function argument! How does **Date::month()** know for which object it was called? A class member function, such as **Date::month()**, has an implicit argument which it uses to identify the object for which it is called. So in the first call, **m** correctly refers to **d1.m** and in the second call it refers to **d2.m**. See §15.8 for more uses of this implicit argument.

8.4.6 Reporting errors

CC What do we do when we find an invalid date? Where in the code do we look for invalid dates? From §4.6, we know that the answer to the first question is "Throw an exception," and the obvious place to look is where we first construct a **Date**. If we don't create invalid **Date**s and also write our member functions correctly, we will never have a **Date** with an invalid value. So, we'll prevent users from ever creating a **Date** with an invalid state:

```
// simple Date (prevent invalid dates)
class Date {
public:
        class Invalid { };                 // to be used as exception
        Date(int y, int m, int d);         // check for valid date and initialize
        // ...
        bool is_valid();                   // return true if date is valid
private:
        int y, m, d;                       // year, month, day
};
```

We put the testing of validity into a separate **is_valid()** function because checking for validity is logically distinct from initialization and because we might want to have several constructors. As you can see, we can have private functions as well as private data:

```
Date::Date(int yy, int mm, int dd)
      : y{yy}, m{mm}, d{dd}           // initialize data members
{
      if (!is_valid())                 // check for validity
            throw Invalid{};
}

bool Date::is_valid()                  // return true if date is valid
{
      return 0<m && m<13;              // very incomplete check
}
```

Given that definition of Date, we can write

```
void f(int x, int y)
try {
      Date dxy {2024,x,y};
      cout << dxy << '\n';
      dxy.add_day(2);
}
catch(Date::Invalid) {
       error("f(): invalid date");     // error() defined in §4.6.3
}
```

We now know that << and add_day() will have a valid Date on which to operate.

Before completing the evolution of our Date class (§8.7), we take a detour to describe a couple of general language facilities that we need to do that well: enumerations and operator overloading.

8.5 Enumerations

An enum (an *enumeration*) is a very simple user-defined type, specifying its set of values (its *enumerators*) as symbolic constants. For example: CC

```
enum class Month {
      jan=1, feb, mar, apr, may, jun, jul, aug, sep, oct, nov, dec
};
```

The "body" of an enumeration is simply a list of its enumerators. The class in enum class means that the enumerators are in the scope of the enumeration. That is, to refer to jan, we have to say Month::jan.

You can give a specific representation value for an enumerator, as we did for jan here, or leave it to the compiler to pick a suitable value. If you leave it to the compiler to pick, it'll give each enumerator the value of the previous enumerator plus one. Thus, our definition of Month gave the months consecutive values starting with 1. We could equivalently have written

```
enum class Month {
      jan=1, feb=2, mar=3, apr=4, may=5, jun=6, jul=7, aug=8, sep=9, oct=10, nov=11, dec=12
};
```

However, that's tedious and opens the opportunity for errors. It is better to let the compiler do simple, repetitive "mechanical" things. The compiler is better at such tasks than we are, and it doesn't get bored.

If we don't initialize the first enumerator, the count starts with **0**. For example:

```
enum class Day {
      monday, tuesday, wednesday, thursday, friday, saturday, sunday
};
```

Here **monday** is represented as **0** and **sunday** is represented as **6**. Starting with **0** is often a good choice.

We can use our **Month** like this:

```
Month m1 = Month::feb;
Month m2 = feb;                  // error: feb is not in scope
Month m3 = 7;                    // error: can't assign an int to a Month
Month m4 = Month{7};             // OK: explicit conversion
Month m5 {7};                    // OK: explicit initialization

int x1 = m1;                     // error: can't assign a Month to an int
int x2 = int{m1};                // error: narrowing conversion
int x3 = to_int(m1);             // convert Month to int; see below
```

Month is a separate type from its "underlying type" **int**. Every **Month** has an equivalent integer value, but most **int**s do not have a **Month** equivalent. For example, we really do want this initialization to fail:

```
Month bad = 9999;           // error: can't convert an int to a Month
```

XX The explicit **Month{7}** conversion is unchecked so use it only when you are certain that the value to be converted really fits your idea of a **Month**. We cannot define a constructor for an enumeration to check initializer values, but it is trivial to write a simple checking function:

```
Month int_to_month(int x)
      // checked conversion
{
      if (x<to_int(Month::jan) || to_int(Month::dec)<x)
            error("bad month");
      return Month{x};
}
```

We use the **to_int(Month::jan)** notation to get the **int** representation of **Month::jan**. For example:

```
void f(int m)
{
      Month mm = int_to_month(m);
      // ...
}
```

The ways of converting a **Month** to its underlying type **int** are a bit messy, so in **PPP_support**, we define a function to do it:

```
int to_int(Month m)
{
	return static_cast<int>(m);
}
```

What do we use enumerations for? Basically, an enumeration is useful whenever we need a set of related named integer constants. That happens all the time when we try to represent sets of alternatives (up, down; yes, no, maybe; on, off; n, ne, e, se, s, sw, w, nw) or distinctive values (red, blue, green, yellow, maroon, crimson, black).

8.5.1 "Plain" enumerations

In addition to the enum classes, also known as *scoped enumerations*, there are "plain" enumerations that differ from scoped enumerations by implicitly "exporting" their enumerators to the scope of the enumeration and allowing implicit conversions to int. For example:

```
enum Month {			// note: no "class"
	jan=1, feb, mar, apr, may, jun, jul, aug, sep, oct, nov, dec
};

Month m1 = feb;			// OK: feb in scope
Month m2 = Month::feb;		// also OK
Month m3 = 7;			// error: can't assign an int to a Month
Month m4 = Month{7};		// OK: explicit conversion

int x1 = m1;			// OK: we can assign a Month to an int
```

Obviously, "plain" enums are less strict than enum classes. Their enumerators can "pollute" the scope in which their enumerator is defined. That can be a convenience, but it occasionally leads to surprises. For example, if you try to use this Month together with the iostream formatting mechanisms (§9.10.1), you will find that dec for December clashes with dec for decimal.

Similarly, having an enumeration value convert to int can be a convenience by saving us from being explicit when we want a conversion to int. However, when we don't want such implicit conversion, it can lead to surprises and errors. For example:

```
void bad_code(Month m)
{
	if (m==17)			// huh: 17th month?
		do_something();
	if (m==monday)			// huh: compare month to Monday?
		do_something_else();
}
```

If Month is an enum class, neither condition will compile. If Month is a plain class and monday is an enumerator of a "plain" enum, rather than an enum class, both comparisons will succeed, most likely with undesirable results.

Prefer the simpler and safer enum classes to "plain" enums, but expect to find "plain" enums in older code: enum classes were new in C++11.

8.6 Operator overloading

You can define almost all C++ operators for class or enumeration operands. That's often called *operator overloading*. We use it when we want to provide conventional notation for a type we design. For example, we can provide an increment operator for our **Month** type:

```
enum class Month {
      jan=1, feb, mar, apr, may, jun, jul, aug, sep, oct, nov, dec
};

Month operator++(Month& m)          // prefix increment operator
{
      m = (m==Month::dec) ? Month::jan : Month{to_int(m)+1};      // "wrap around"
      return m;
}
```

The **? :** construct is an "arithmetic if": **m** becomes **Jan** if **(m==Dec)** and **Month(to_int(m)+1)** otherwise. It is a reasonably elegant way of expressing the fact that months "wrap around" after December. The **Month** type can now be used like this:

```
Month m = Month::oct;
++m;        // m becomes nov
++m;        // m becomes dec
++m;        // m becomes jan ("wrap around")
```

You might not think that incrementing a **Month** is common enough to warrant a special operator. That may be so, but how about an output operator? We can define one like this:

```
vector<string> month_tbl = {"Not a month", "January", "February", "March", /* ... */ };

ostream& operator<<(ostream& os, Month m)
{
      return os << month_tbl[to_int(m)];
}
```

We gave **Month::jan** the conventional integer value **1**, so **month_tbl[0]** does not represent a month.

We can now control the appearance of a month on output by changing **month_tbl**. For example, we could set **month_tbl[to_int(Month::mar)]** to **"marzo"** or some other suitable name for that month; see §9.9.3.

CC We can define just about any operator provided by C++ for our own types, but only existing operators, such as **+**, **–** *, **/**, **%**, **[ ]**, **( )**, **^**, **!**, **&**, **<**, **<=**, **>**, and **>=**. We cannot define our own operators; we might like to have ** or **@=** as operators in our program, but C++ won't let us. We can define operators only with their conventional number of operands. For example, we can define unary **–**, but not unary **<=** (less than or equal), and binary **+**, but not binary **!** (not). Basically, the language allows us to use the existing syntax for the types you define, but not to extend that syntax.

An overloaded operator must have at least one user-defined type as operand:

```
int operator+(int,int);                              // error: you can't overload built-in +
Vector operator+(const Vector&, const Vector &);     // OK
Vector operator+=(const Vector&, int);               // OK
```

It is generally a good idea *not* to define operators for a type unless you are really certain that it makes a big positive change to your code. Also, define operators only with their conventional meaning: + should be addition, binary * multiplication, [ ] access, ( ) call, etc. This is just advice, not a language rule, but it is good advice: conventional use of operators, such as + for addition, can significantly help us understand a program. After all, such use is the result of hundreds of years of experience with mathematical notation. Conversely, obscure operators and unconventional use of operators can be a significant distraction and a source of errors. We will not elaborate on this point. Instead, in the following chapters, we will simply use operator overloading in a few places where we consider it appropriate.

Note that the most interesting operators to overload aren't +, –, *, and / as people often assume, but = (assignment), == (equality), < (less than), –> (dereference), [ ] (subscript), and ( ) (call).

> TRY THIS
>
> Write, compile, and run a small example using ++ and << for **Month**.

8.7 Class interfaces

We have argued that the public interface and the implementation parts of a class should be separated. As long as we leave open the possibility of using **structs** for types that are just collections of data, few professionals would disagree. However, how do we design a good interface? What distinguishes a good public interface from a mess? Part of that answer can be given only by example, but there are a few general principles that we can list and that are given some support in C++:

- Keep interfaces complete.
- Keep interfaces minimal.
- Provide constructors.
- Support copying (or prohibit it) (see §12.4.1).
- Use types to provide good argument checking.
- Identify nonmodifying member functions (see §8.7.4).
- Free all resources in the destructor (see §15.5).

See also §4.5 (how to detect and report run-time errors).

The first two principles can be combined to

- Keep the interface as small as possible, but no smaller.

We want our interface to be small because a small interface is easy to learn and easy to remember, and the implementer doesn't waste a lot of time implementing unnecessary and rarely used facilities. A small interface also means that when something is wrong, there are only a few functions to check to find the problem. On average, the more public member functions a class has, the harder it is to find bugs. But of course, we want a complete interface; otherwise, it would be useless. We couldn't use an interface that didn't allow us to do all we really needed. For operations beyond the minimal set, use "helper functions" (§8.7.5).

Let's look at the other – less abstract and more directly supported – ideals.

8.7.1 Argument types

When we defined the constructor for **Date** in §8.4.3, we used three **ints** as the arguments. That caused some problems:

```
Date d1 {4,5,2005};    // oops: year 4, day 2005
Date d2 {2005,4,5};    // April 5 or May 4?
```

The first problem (an illegal day of the month) is easily dealt with by a test in the constructor. The second problem is simply that the conventions for writing month and day-in-month differ; for example, 4/5 is April 5 in the United States and May 4 in England. We can't calculate our way out of this, so we must do something else. The obvious solution is to use a **Month** type:

```
enum class Month {
     jan=1, feb, mar, apr, may, jun, jul, aug, sep, oct, nov, dec
};

// simple Date (use Month type)
class Date {
public:
     Date(int y, Month m, int d);          // check for valid date and initialize
     // . . .
private:
     int y;          // year
     Month m;
     int d;          // day
};
```

When we use a **Month** type, the compiler will catch us if we swap month and day, and using an enumeration as the **Month** type also gives us symbolic names to use. It is usually easier to read and write symbolic names than to play around with numbers, and therefore, less error-prone:

```
Date dx1 {1998, 4, 3};                // error: 2nd argument not a Month
Date dx2 {1998, 4, Month::mar};       // error: 2nd argument not a Month
Date dx3 {4, Month::mar, 1998};       // oops: run-time error: day 1998
Date dx4 {Month::mar, 4, 1998};       // error: 2nd argument not a Month
Date dx5 {1998, Month::mar, 30};      // OK
```

This takes care of most "accidents." Note the use of the qualification of the enumerator **mar** with the enumeration name: **Month::mar**. We don't say **Month.mar** because **Month** isn't an object (it's a type) and **mar** isn't a data member (it's an enumerator – a symbolic constant). Use :: after the name of a class, enumeration, or namespace (§7.6.1) and **.** (dot) after an object name.

AA When we have a choice, we catch errors at compile time rather than at run time. We prefer for the compiler to find the error rather than for us to try to figure out exactly where in the code a problem occurred. Importantly, errors caught at compile time don't require us to write tests and error-handling code. Catching errors at compile time makes code simpler and faster.

Thinking like that, could we catch the swap of the day of the month and the year also? We could, but the solution is not as simple or as elegant as for **Month**; after all, there was a year 4 and you might want to represent it. Even if we restricted ourselves to modern times there would probably be too many relevant years for us to list them all in an enumeration.

Probably the best we could do (without knowing quite a lot about the intended use of Date) would be a minimal Year type:

```
struct Year {
      int y;
};

class Date {
public:
      Date(Year y, Month m, int d);          // check for valid date and initialize
      // ...
private:
      Year y;
      Month m;
      int d;             // day
};
```

Now we get

```
Date dx1 {Year{1998}, 4, 3};                  // error: 2nd argument not a Month
Date dx2 {Year{1998}, 4, Month::mar};         // error: 2nd argument not a Month
Date dx3 {4, Month::mar, Year{1998}};         // error: 1st argument not a Year
Date dx4 {Month::mar, 4, Year{1998}};         // error: 2nd argument not a Month
Date dx5 {Year{1998}, Month::mar, 30};        // OK
Date dx6 {Year{4}, Month::mar, 1998};         // run-time error: Year::Invalid
```

We could modify Year to check for unlikely years, but would the extra work be worthwhile? Naturally, that depends on the constraints on the kind of problem you are solving using Date.

When we program, we always have to ask ourselves what is good enough for a given application. We usually don't have the luxury of being able to search "forever" for the perfect solution after we have already found one that is good enough. Search further, and we might even come up with something that's so elaborate that it is worse than the simple early solution. This is one meaning of the saying "The best is the enemy of the good" (Voltaire). AA

8.7.2 Copying

We always have to create objects; that is, we must always consider initialization and constructors. Arguably they are the most important members of a class: to write them, you have to decide what it takes to initialize an object and what it means for a value to be valid (what is the invariant?). Just thinking about initialization will help you avoid errors.

The next thing to consider is often: Can we copy our objects? And if so, how do we copy them?

For Date or Month, the answer is that we obviously want to copy objects of that type and that the meaning of *copy* is trivial: just copy all of the members. Actually, this is the default case. So as long as you don't say anything else, the compiler will do exactly that. For example, if you copy a Date as an initializer or right-hand side of an assignment, all its members are copied:

```
Date holiday {Year{1978}, Month::jul, 4};      // initialization
Date d2 = holiday;
Date d3 = Date{Year{1978}, Month::jul, 4};
```

```
holiday = Date{Year{1978}, Month::dec, 24};        // assignment
d3 = holiday;
```

This will all work as expected. The Date{Year{1978}, Month::dec, 24} notation makes the appropriate unnamed Date object, which you can then use appropriately. For example:

```
cout << Date{Year{1978}, Month::dec, 24};
```

This is a use of a constructor that acts much as a literal for a class type. It often comes in as a handy alternative to first defining a variable or const and then using it once.

What if we don't want the default meaning of copying? We can either define our own (§17.4) or delete the copy constructor and copy assignment (§12.4.1).

8.7.3 Default constructors

CC Uninitialized variables can be a serious source of errors. To counter that problem, we have the notion of a constructor to guarantee that every object of a class is initialized. For example, we declared the constructor Date::Date(int,Month,int) to ensure that every Date is properly initialized. In the case of Date, that means that the programmer must supply three arguments of the right types. For example:

```
Date d0;                        // error: no initializer
Date d1 {};                     // error: empty initializer
Date d2 {Year{1998}};           // error: too few arguments
Date d3 {Year{1},2,3,4};        // error: too many arguments
Date d4 {Year{1},"jan",2};      // error: wrong argument type
Date d5 {Year{1},Month::jan,2}; // OK: use the three-argument constructor
Date d6 {d5};                   // OK: use the copy constructor
```

Note that even though we defined a constructor for Date, we can still copy Dates.

Many classes have a good notion of a default value; that is, there is an obvious answer to the question "What value should it have if I didn't give it an initializer?" For example:

```
string s1;              // default value: the empty string ""
vector<string> v1;      // default value: the empty vector; no elements
```

This looks reasonable. It even works the way the comments indicate. That is achieved by giving vector and string each a *default constructor* that implicitly provide the desired initialization. A constructor that can be called with no arguments is called a default constructor.

Using a default constructor is not just a matter of looks. Just imagine the errors we could get if we could have an uninitialized string or vector:

```
string s;                           // imagine that s could be uninitialized
for (int i = 0; i<s.size(); ++i)    // oops: loop an undefined number of times
        s[i] = toupper(s[i]);       // oops: read and write a random memory location

vector<string> v;                   //imagine that v could be uninitialized
v.push_back("bad");                 // oops: write to random address
```

If the values of s and v were genuinely undefined, s and v would have no notion of how many elements they contained or (using the common implementation techniques; see Chapter 17) where those elements were supposed to be stored. The results would be use of random addresses – and that can lead to the worst kind of errors. Basically, without a constructor, we cannot establish an invariant – we cannot ensure that the values in those variables are valid (§8.4.3). We must insist that such variables are initialized. We could insist on an initializer and then write

```
string s2 = "";
vector<string> v2 {};
```

That's not particularly pretty and a bit verbose. However, "empty" is a reasonable and useful default for string and vector, so the standard provides it.

However, for many types, it is not easy to find a reasonable notation for a default value. For many types, it is better to define a constructor that gives meaning to the creation of an object without an explicit initializer.

There isn't an obvious default value for dates. That's why we haven't defined a default constructor for Date so far, but let's provide one (just to show we can). We have to pick a default date. The first day of the 21st century might be a reasonable choice:

```
class Date {
public:
        Date()                  // default constructor (takes no arguments)
                :y{Year{2001}}, m{Month::jan}, d{1}
        {
        }
        // ...
}
```

Now we can write:

```
Date d;         // d = {Year{2001},Month::jan,1}
```

Instead of placing the default values for members in the constructor, we could place them on the members themselves:

```
class Date {
public:
        // ...
        Date() {}
        Date(Year y, Month m, int d);
        Date(Year y);                   // January 1 of year y
        // ...
        bool is_valid();
private:
        Year y {2001};
        Month m = Month::jan;
        int d = 1;
};
```

That way, the default values are available to every constructor. For example:

```
Date::Date(Year yy)          // January 1 of year y
      :y{yy}
{
}
```

Because Date(int) does not explicitly initialize the month (m) or the day (d), the specified initializers (Month::jan and 1) are implicitly used. Because we didn't place any constraints on the value of Date::y, we don't need to call is_valid().

An initializer for a class member specified as part of the member declaration is called a *default member initializer* or an *in-class initializer*.

CC For a type T, T{} is the notation for the default value, as defined by the default constructor, so we could write

```
string{};                // default value: the empty string ""
vector<string>{};        // default value: the empty vector;      no elements
```

However, in initializations, we prefer the colloquial

```
string s1;               // default value: the empty string ""
vector<string> v1;       // default value: the empty vector; no elements
```

For built-in types, such as int and double, the default constructor notation means 0, so int{} is a complicated way of saying 0, and double{} a long-winded way of saying 0.0. However, {} can be used to shorten initialization of variables:

```
void test()
{
      double x0;         // uninitialized; don't do that
      double x1 {0};     // initialize to 0
      double x2 = 0;     // initialize to 0
      double x3 {};      // initialize to 0
}
```

8.7.4 const member functions

Some variables are meant to be changed – that's why we call them "variables" – but some are not; that is, we have "variables" representing immutable values. Those, we typically call *constant variables* (sic!), *constants* or just consts. Consider:

```
Date d;
const Date start_of_term;

int a = d.day();                      // OK
int b = start_of_term.day();          // should be OK (why?), but isn't

d.add_day(3);                         // OK
start_of_term.add_day(3);             // error
```

Here, d is mutable, but start_of_term in a const. It is not acceptable to change the value of start_of_term. So far, so good, but then why is it OK to read the day of start_of_term using day()? As the definition of Date stands so far, start_of_term.day() is an error because the compiler does not know that day() doesn't change its Date. We never told it, so the compiler assumes that day() may modify its Date, just like add_day() does, and reports an error.

AA We deal with this problem by classifying operations on a class as modifying and nonmodifying. That's a fundamental distinction that helps us understand a class. It also has practical importance: operations that do not modify the object can be invoked for const objects. For example:

```
class Date {
public:
        // . . .
        int day() const;                // const member: can't modify the object
        Month month() const;            // const member: can't modify the object
        Year year() const;              // const member: can't modify the object

        void add_day(int n);            // non-const member: can modify the object
        void add_month(int n);          // non-const member: can modify the object
        void add_year(int n);           // non-const member: can modify the object
private:
        Year y;
        Month m;
        int d;                          // day of month
};

Date d {2000, Month::jan, 20};
const Date cd {2001, Month::feb, 21};
cout << d.day() << " – " << cd.day() << '\n';    // OK
d.add_day(1);                                     // OK
cd.add_day(1);                                    // error: cd is a const
```

We use const right after the argument list in a member function declaration to indicate that the member function can be called for a const object. Once we have declared a member function const, the compiler holds us to our promise not to modify the object. For example:

```
int Date::day() const
{
        ++d;        // error: attempt to change object from const member function
        return d;
}
```

Naturally, we don't deliberately try to "cheat" in this way. However, the compiler helps the class implementer by protecting against accidental violations.

8.7.5 Member functions and helper functions

AA When we design our interfaces to be minimal (though complete), we have to leave out lots of operations that are merely useful. A function that can be simply, elegantly, and efficiently implemented as a freestanding function (that is, as a nonmember function) should be implemented outside the class. That way, a bug in that function cannot directly corrupt the data in a class object. Not accessing the representation is important because the usual debug technique is "Round up the usual suspects"; that is, when something goes wrong with a class, we first look at the functions that directly access the representation: one of those almost certainly did it. If there are a dozen such functions, we will be much happier than if there were 50.

Fifty functions for a **Date** class! You must wonder if we are kidding. We are not: a few years ago I surveyed a number of commercially used **Date** libraries and found them full of member functions like **next_Sunday()**, **next_workday()**, etc. Fifty is not an unreasonable number for a class designed for the convenience of the users rather than for ease of comprehension, implementation, and maintenance.

Note also that if the representation changes, only the functions that directly access the representation need to be rewritten. That's another strong practical reason for keeping interfaces minimal. In our **Date** example, we might decide that an integer representing the number of days since January 1, 1900, is a much better representation for our uses than (year,month,day). Only the member functions would have to be changed.

Here are some examples of *helper functions*:

```
Date next_Sunday(const Date& d)
{
        // access d using d.day(), d.month(), and d.year()
        // make new Date to return
}

Date next_weekday(const Date& d) { /* . . . */ }

bool leapyear(int y) { /* . . . */ }

bool operator==(const Date& a, const Date& b)
{
        return a.year()==b.year()
                && a.month()==b.month()
                && a.day()==b.day();
}

bool operator!=(const Date& a, const Date& b)
{
        return !(a==b);
}
```

CC Helper functions are also called *convenience functions*, *auxiliary functions*, and many other things. The distinction between these functions and other nonmember functions is logical; that is, "helper function" is a design concept, not a programming language concept. The helper functions often take arguments of the classes that they are helpers of. There are exceptions, though: note **leapyear()**. Often, we use namespaces to identify a group of helper functions; see §7.6:

```
namespace Chrono {
        enum class Month { /* ... */ };
        class Date { /* . . . */ };
        bool is_date(int y, Month m, int d);                    // true for valid date
```

```
        Date next_Sunday(const Date& d) { /* . . . */ }
        Date next_weekday(const Date& d) { /* . . . */ }

        bool leapyear(int y) { /* . . . */ }                    // see exercise 10
        bool operator==(const Date& a, const Date& b) { /* . . . */ }
        // ...
}
```

Note the == and != functions. They are typical helpers. For many classes, == and != make obvious sense, but since they don't make sense for all classes, the compiler can't write them for you the way it writes the copy constructor and copy assignment.

Note also that we introduced a helper function is_date(). That function replaces Date::is_valid() because checking whether a date is valid is largely independent of the representation of a Date. For example, we don't need to know how Date objects are represented to know that "January 30, 2028" is a valid date and "February 30, 2028" is not. There still may be aspects of a date that depend on the representation (e.g., can we represent "October 14, 1066"?), but (if necessary) Date's constructor can take care of that.

8.7.6 The ISO standard

Our Date isn't bad, but it is nowhere near as sophisticated as the facilities for handling time, dates, and time zones in the ISO C++ standard libraries. However, now you know most of the language facilities and design techniques used in the standard-library's chrono component (§20.4) where the equivalent to our Date is called year_month_date. Using that, you can write

```
auto birthday = December/16/1770;       // year_month_day{year{1770},December,day{16}}
```

Date is one of those types that it is useful to build as an exercise, but it is important to throw it away afterwards: The standard's version is not just better designed: importantly, it is also implemented by experts, extensively documented, extensively tested, and known by millions of programmers. Other such useful "exercise classes" with standard-library versions are string and vector. We visit more of the standard library in Chapter 15, Chapter 19, Chapter 20, and Chapter 21.

Drill

Write Day, Month, and their associated functions as described above. Complete the final version of Date with default constructor, is_valid(), Month, Year, etc. Define a Date called today initialized to February 2, 2020. Then, define a Date called tomorrow and give it a value by copying today into it and increasing its day by one using add_day(). Finally, output today and tomorrow using a << defined as in §9.6 and §9.7.

Your check for a valid date, is_valid(), may be very simple. Feel free to ignore leap years. However, don't accept a month that is not in the [1,12] range or a day of the month that is not in the [1,31] range. Test each version with at least one invalid date (e.g., 2004, 13, -5).

Review

[1] What are the two parts of a class, as described in the chapter?
[2] What is the difference between the interface and the implementation in a class?
[3] What are the limitations and problems of the struct Date from §8.4.1?
[4] Why is a constructor used for the Date type instead of an init_day() function?
[5] What is an invariant? Give examples.
[6] When should functions be put in the class definition, and when should they be defined outside the class? Why?
[7] What is a default constructor and when do we need one?
[8] What is a default member initializer?
[9] When should operator overloading be used in a program? Give a list of operators that you might want to overload (each with a reason). Which ones can you define in C++?
[10] Why should the public interface to a class be as small as possible?
[11] What does adding const to a member function do?
[12] Why are "helper functions" best placed outside the class definition?
[13] How does an enum class differ from a "plain" enum?

Terms

built-in types	enumerator	representation	class
helper function	struct	const	implementation
structure	constructor	in-class initializer	user-defined types
destructor	inlining	valid state	enum
interface	enumeration	invariant	enum class
operator overloading	default member initializer		

Exercises

[1] List plausible operations for the examples of real-world objects in §8.1 (e.g., a toaster).
[2] Design and implement a Name_pairs class holding (name,age) pairs where name is a string and age is a double. Represent that as a vector<string> (called name) and a vector<double> (called age) member. Provide an input operation read_names() that reads a series of names. Provide a read_ages() operation that prompts the user for an age for each name. Provide a print() operation that prints out the (name[i],age[i]) pairs (one per line) in the order determined by the name vector. Provide a sort() operation that sorts the name vector in alphabetical order and reorganizes the age vector to match. Implement all "operations" as member functions. Test the class (of course: test early and often).
[3] Replace Name_pair::print() with a (global) operator << and define == and != for Name_pairs.
[4] Do the previous exercise again but implement Name_pairs using a Name_pair class.
[5] This exercise and the next few require you to design and implement a Book class, such as you can imagine as part of software for a library. Class Book should have members for the ISBN, title, author, and copyright date. Also store data on whether or not the book is checked out. Create functions for returning those data values. Create functions for checking a book in and

out. Do simple validation of data entered into a Book; for example, accept ISBNs only of the form n–n–n–x where n is an integer and x is a digit or a letter. Store an ISBN as a string.

[6] Add operators for the Book class. Have the == operator check whether the ISBN numbers are the same for two books. Have != also compare the ISBN numbers. Have a << print out the title, author, and ISBN on separate lines.

[7] Create an enumerated type for the Book class called Genre. Have the types be fiction, nonfiction, periodical, biography, and children. Give each book a Genre and make appropriate changes to the Book constructor and member functions.

[8] Create a Patron class for the library. The class will have a user's name, library card number, and library fees (if owed). Have functions that access this data, as well as a function to set the fee of the user. Have a helper function that returns a Boolean (bool) depending on whether or not the user owes a fee.

[9] Create a Library class. Include vectors of Books and Patrons. Include a struct called Transaction to record when a book is checked out. Have it include a Book, a Patron, and a Date. Make a vector of Transactions to keep a record of which books are out. Create functions to add books to the library, add patrons to the library, and check out books. Whenever a user checks out a book, have the library make sure that both the user and the book are in the library. If they aren't, report an error. Then check to make sure that the user owes no fees. If the user does, report an error. If not, create a Transaction, and place it in the vector of Transactions. Also write a function that will return a vector that contains the names of all Patrons who owe fees.

[10] Implement leapyear(int).

[11] Design and implement a set of useful helper functions for the Date class with functions such as next_workday() (assume that any day that is not a Saturday or a Sunday is a workday) and week_of_year() (assume that week 1 is the week with January 1 in it and that the first day of a week is a Sunday).

[12] Change the representation of a Date to be the number of days since January 1, 1970 (known as day 0), represented as a long int (that is, an int that can hold much larger integers than plain int), and re-implement the Date member functions from §8.4.2. Be sure to reject dates outside the range we can represent that way (feel free to reject days before day 0, i.e., no negative days).

[13] Design and implement a rational number class, Rational. A rational number has two parts: a numerator and a denominator, for example, 5/6 (five-sixths, also known as approximately .83333). Look up the definition if you need to. Provide assignment, addition, subtraction, multiplication, division, and equality operators. Also, provide a conversion to double. Why would people want to use a Rational class?

[14] Design and implement a Money class for calculations involving dollars and cents where arithmetic has to be accurate to the last cent using the 4/5 rounding rule (.5 of a cent rounds up; anything less than .5 rounds down). Represent a monetary amount as a number of cents in a long int, but input and output as dollars and cents, e.g., $123.45. Do not worry about amounts that don't fit into a long int.

[15] Refine the Money class by adding a currency (given as a constructor argument). Accept a floating-point initializer as long as it can be exactly represented as a long int. Don't accept illegal operations. For example, Money*Money doesn't make sense, and USD1.23+DKK5.00

makes sense only if you provide a conversion table defining the conversion factor between U.S. dollars (USD) and Danish kroner (DKK).

[16] Define an input operator (>>) that reads monetary amounts with currency denominations, such as USD1.23 and DKK5.00, into a Money variable. Also define a corresponding output operator (<<).

[17] Give an example of a calculation where a Rational gives a mathematically better result than Money.

[18] Give an example of a calculation where a Rational gives a mathematically better result than double.

Postscript

There is a lot to user-defined types, much more than we have presented here. User-defined types, especially classes, are the heart of C++ and the key to many of the most effective design techniques. Most of the rest of the book is about the design and use of classes. A class – or a set of classes – is the mechanism through which we represent our concepts in code. Here we primarily introduced the language-technical aspects of classes; elsewhere we focus on how to elegantly express useful ideas as classes.

For a good example of an industrial-strength date library, see the standard-library chrono. For example, look it up in cppreference.com. It is part of the std module. Please don't look too hard. It uses a few advanced features that have yet to be presented.

Part II
Input and Output

Part II first describes how to get numeric and text data from the keyboard and from files, and how to produce corresponding output to the screen and to files. Then, we show how to present numeric data, text, and geometric shapes as graphical output, and how to get input into a program from a graphical user interface (GUI). As part of that, we introduce the fundamental principles and techniques of object-oriented programming.

Chapter 9: Input and Output Streams
Chapter 10: A Display Model
Chapter 11: Graphics Classes
Chapter 12: Class Design
Chapter 13: Graphing Functions and Data
Chapter 14: Graphical User Interfaces

9

Input and Output Streams

Science is what we have learned about
how to keep from fooling ourselves.
– Richard P. Feynman

In this chapter, we present the C++ standard-library facilities for handling input and output from a variety of sources: I/O streams. We show how to read and write files, how to deal with errors, how to deal with formatted input, and how to provide and use I/O operators for user-defined types. This chapter focuses on the basic model: how to read and write individual values, and how to open, read, and write whole files.

§9.1 Input and output
§9.2 The I/O stream model
§9.3 Files
Opening a file; Reading and writing a file
§9.4 I/O error handling
§9.5 Reading a single value
Breaking the problem into manageable parts; Separating dialog from function
§9.6 User-defined output operators
§9.7 User-defined input operators
§9.8 A standard input loop
§9.9 Reading a structured file
In-memory representation; Reading structured values; Changing representations
§9.10 Formatting
Integer I/O; Floating-point I/O; String I/O; Character I/O; Extend I/O; format()
§9.11 String streams

9.1 Input and output

Without data, computing is pointless. We need to get data into our program to do interesting computations and we need to get the results out again. In §3.1, we mentioned the bewildering variety of data sources and targets for output. If we don't watch out, we'll end up writing programs that can receive input only from a specific source and deliver output only to a specific output device. That may be acceptable (and sometimes even necessary) for specialized applications, such as a digital camera or a heat sensor, but for more common tasks, we need a way to separate the way our program reads and writes from the actual input and output devices used. If we had to directly address each kind of device, we'd have to change our program each time a new screen or disk came on the market, or limit our users to the screens and disks we happen to like. That would be absurd.

Most modern operating systems separate the detailed handling of I/O devices into device drivers, and programs then access the device drivers through an I/O library that makes I/O from/to different sources appear as similar as possible. Generally, the device drivers are deep in the operating system where most users don't see them, and the I/O library provides an abstraction of I/O so that the programmer doesn't have to think about devices and device drivers:

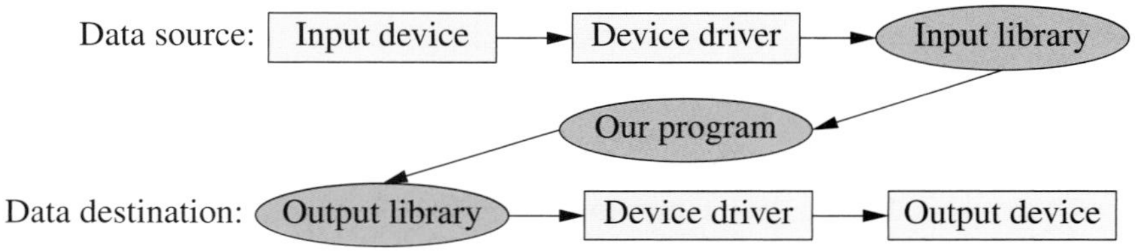

When a model like this is used, input and output can be seen as streams of bytes (characters) handled by the input/output library. More complex forms of I/O require specialized expertise and are beyond the scope of this book. Our job as programmers of an application then becomes

[1] To set up I/O streams to the appropriate data sources and destinations

[2] To read and write from/to those streams

The details of how our characters are actually transmitted to/from the devices are dealt with by the I/O library and the device drivers. In this chapter, we'll see how I/O consisting of streams of formatted data is done using the C++ standard library.

From the programmer's point of view there are many different kinds of input and output. One classification is

- Streams of (many) data items (usually to/from files, network connections, recording devices, or display devices)
- Interactions with a user at a keyboard
- Interactions with a user through a graphical interface (outputting objects, receiving mouse clicks, etc.)

This classification isn't the only classification possible, and the distinction between the three kinds of I/O isn't as clear as it might appear. For example, if a stream of output characters happens to be an HTTP document aimed at a browser, the result looks remarkably like user interaction and can contain graphical elements. Conversely, the results of interactions with a GUI (graphical user interface) may be presented to a program as a sequence of characters. However, this classification fits our tools: the first two kinds of I/O are provided by the C++ standard-library I/O streams and supported rather directly by most operating systems. We have been using the iostream library since Chapter 1 and will focus on that for this and the next chapter. The graphical output and graphical user interactions are served by a variety of different libraries, and we will focus on that kind of I/O in Chapter 10 to Chapter 14.

9.2 The I/O stream model

The C++ standard library provides the type **istream** to deal with streams of input and the type **ostream** to deal with streams of output. We have used the standard **istream** called **cin** and the standard **ostream** called **cout**, so we know the basics of how to use this part of the standard library (usually called the iostream library).

CC

An **ostream**

- Turns values of various types into character sequences
- Sends those characters "somewhere" (such as to a console, a file, the main memory, or another computer)

We can represent an **ostream** graphically like this:

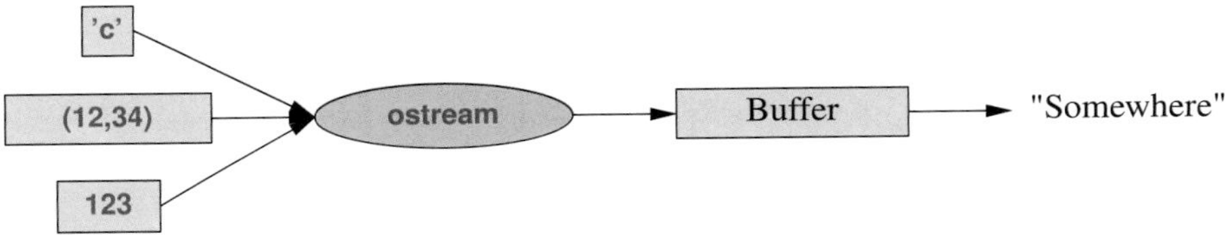

The buffer is a data structure that the **ostream** uses internally to store the data you give it while communicating with the operating system. If you notice a "delay" between your writing to an **ostream** and the characters appearing at their destination, it's usually because they are still in the buffer. Buffering is important for performance, and performance is important if you deal with large amounts of data.

CC

An **istream**

[1] Gets characters from somewhere (such as a console, a file, the main memory, or another computer)

[2] Turns those character sequences into values of various types

We can represent an **istream** graphically like this:

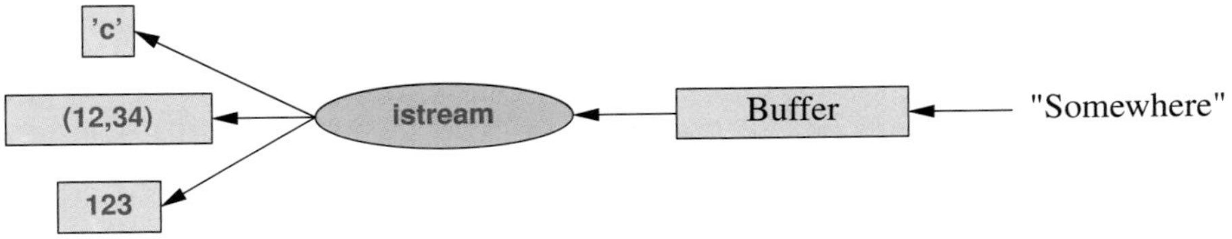

As with an **ostream**, an **istream** uses a buffer to communicate with the operating system. With an

istream, the buffering can be quite visible to the user. When you use an istream that is attached to a keyboard, what you type is left in the buffer until you hit Enter (return/newline), and you can use the erase (Backspace) key "to change your mind" (until you hit Enter).

One of the major uses of output is to produce data for humans to read. Think of email messages, scholarly articles, Web pages, billing records, business reports, contact lists, tables of contents, equipment status readouts, etc. Therefore, ostreams provide many features for formatting text to suit various tastes. Similarly, much input is written by humans or is formatted to make it easy for humans to read it. Therefore, istreams provide features for reading the kind of output produced by ostreams. We'll discuss formatting in §9.10. Most of the complexity related to input has to do with how to handle errors. To be able to give more realistic examples, we'll start by discussing how the iostream model relates to files of data.

9.3 Files

CC We typically have much more data than can fit in the main memory of our computer, so we store most of it on disks or other large-capacity storage devices. Such devices also have the desirable property that data doesn't disappear when the power is turned off – the data is *persistent*. At the most basic level, a file is simply a sequence of bytes numbered from 0 upward:

A file has a format; that is, it has a set of rules that determine what the bytes mean. For example, if we have a text file, the first 4 bytes will be the first four characters. On the other hand, if we have a file that uses a binary representation of integers, those very same first 4 bytes will be taken to be the (binary) representation of the first integer. The format serves the same role for files on disk as types serve for objects in main memory. We can make sense of the bits in a file if (and only if) we know its format.

CC For a file, an ostream converts objects in main memory into streams of bytes and writes them to disk. An istream does the opposite; that is, it takes a stream of bytes from disk and composes objects from them:

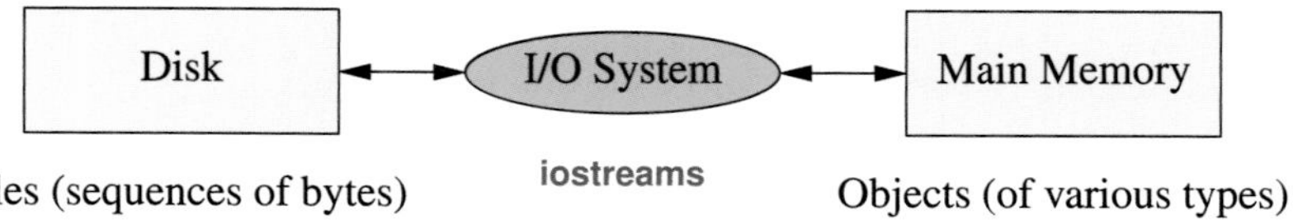

Most of the time, we assume that these "bytes on disk" are in fact characters in our usual character set. That is not always so, but we can get an awfully long way with that assumption, and other representations are not that hard to deal with. We also talk as if all files were on some form of permanent storage (that is, on rotating-magnetic storage or solid-state storage). Again, that's not always so (think files stored remotely), but at this level of programming the actual storage makes no difference. That's one of the beauties of the file and stream abstractions.

To read a file, we must

[1] Know its name
[2] Open it (for reading)
[3] Read in the characters
[4] Close it (though that is typically done implicitly)

To write a file, we must

[1] Name it
[2] Open it (for writing) or create a new file of that name
[3] Write out our objects
[4] Close it (though that is typically done implicitly)

We already know the basics of reading and writing because an **ostream** attached to a file behaves exactly as **cout** for what we have done so far, and an **istream** attached to a file behaves exactly as **cin** for what we have done so far. We'll present operations that can only be done for files in PPP2.§11.3.3, but for now we'll just see how to open files and then concentrate on operations and techniques that apply to all **ostreams** and all **istreams**.

9.3.1 Opening a file

If you want to read from a file or write to a file, you have to open a stream specifically for that file. An **ifstream** is an **istream** for reading from a file, an **ofstream** is an **ostream** for writing to a file, and an **fstream** is an **iostream** that can be used for both reading and writing. Before a file stream can be used it must be attached to a file. For example: **AA**

```
cout << "Please enter input file name: ";
string iname;
cin >> iname;
ifstream ist {iname};              // ist is an input stream for the file named name
if (!ist)
      error("can't open input file ",iname);
```

Defining an **ifstream** with a name string opens the file of that name for reading. The test of **!ist** checks if the file was properly opened. After that, we can read from the file exactly as we would from any other **istream**. For example, assuming that the input operator, **>>**, was defined for a type **Point**, we could write **AA**

```
vector<Point> points;
for (Point p; ist>>p; )
      points.push_back(p);
```

Output to files is handled in a similar fashion by **ofstreams**. For example:

```
cout << "Please enter name of output file: ";
string oname;
cin >> oname;
ofstream ost {oname};              // ost is an output stream for a file named oname
if (!ost)
      error("can't open output file ",oname);
```

Defining an **ofstream** with a name string opens the file with that name for writing. The test of **!ost** checks if the file was properly opened. After that, we can write to the file exactly as we would to any other ostream. For example:

```
for (Point p: points)
        ost << '(' << p.x << ',' << p.y << ")\n";
```

When a file stream goes out of scope its associated file is closed. When a file is closed its associated buffer is "flushed"; that is, the characters from the buffer are written to the file.

It is usually best to open files early in a program before any serious computation has taken place. After all, it is a waste to do a lot of work just to find that we can't complete it because we don't have anywhere to write our results.

Opening the file implicitly as part of the creation of an **ostream** or an **istream** is ideal, and a file stream implicitly closes its file upon scope exit; see §15.5. For example:

```
void fill_from_file(vector<Point>& points, string& name)
{
        ifstream ist {name};                // open file for reading
        if (!ist)
                error("can't open input file ",name);
        // ... use ist ...
        // the file is implicitly closed when we leave the function
}
```

Don't forget to test a stream after opening it.

You can also use explicit **open()** and **close()** operations. For example:

```
ifstream ifs;
ifs.open(name,ios::in);                 // open file named name for reading
// ...
ifs.close();                            // close file
```

However, that's verbose. Also, relying on scope to control when the file is open minimizes the chances of someone trying to use it before it has been opened or after it was closed.

Why would you use **open()** or **close()** explicitly? Well, occasionally the lifetime of a connection to a file isn't conveniently limited by a scope so you have to. But that's rare enough for us not to have to worry about it here. More to the point, you'll find such use in code written by people using styles from languages and libraries that don't have the scoped idiom used by **iostreams** (and the rest of the C++ standard library, §18.4.2).

9.3.2 Reading and writing a file

Consider how you might read a set of results of some measurements from a file and represent them in memory. These might be the temperature readings from a weather station:

```
0 60.7
1 60.6
2 60.3
3 59.22
...
```

This data file contains a sequence of (hour,temperature) pairs. The hours are numbered 0 to 23 and the temperatures are in Fahrenheit. No further formatting is assumed; that is, the file does not contain any special header information (such as where the reading was taken), units for the values, punctuation (such as parentheses around each pair of values), or termination indicator. This is the simplest case.

We could represent a temperature reading by a **Reading** type:

```
struct Reading {                // a temperature reading
      int hour;                        // hour after midnight [0:23]
      double temperature;              // in Fahrenheit
};
```

Given that, we could read like this:

```
vector<Reading> temps;                 // store the readings here
int hour;
double temperature;
while (ist >> hour >> temperature) {
      if (hour < 0 || 23 <hour)
            error("hour out of range");
      temps.push_back(Reading{hour,temperature});
}
```

This is a typical input loop. The **istream** called **ist** could be an input file stream an (**ifstream**) as shown in the previous section, (an alias for) the standard input stream (**cin**), or any other kind of **istream**. For code like this, it doesn't matter exactly from where the **istream** gets its data. All that our program cares about is that **ist** is an **istream** and that the data has the expected format. The next section addresses the interesting question of how to detect errors in the input data and what we can do after detecting a format error.

Writing to a file is usually simpler than reading from one. Again, once a stream is initialized, we don't have to know exactly what kind of stream it is. In particular, we can use the output file stream (**ost**) from the section above just like any other **ostream**. For example, we might want to output the readings with each pair of values in parentheses:

```
for (Reading x : temps)
      ost << '(' << x.hour << ',' << x.temperature << ")\n";
```

The resulting program would then be reading the original temperature reading file and producing a new file with the data in (hour,temperature) format.

Because the file streams automatically close their files when they go out of scope, the complete program becomes **AA**

```
struct Reading {                // a temperature reading
      int hour;                 // hour after midnight [0:23]
      double temperature;       // in Fahrenheit
};
```

```
int main()
{
	cout << "Please enter input file name: ";
	string iname;
	cin >> iname;
	ifstream ist {iname};			// ist reads from the file named iname
	if (!ist)
		error("can't open input file ",iname);

	string oname;
	cout << "Please enter name of output file: ";
	cin >> oname;
	ofstream ost {oname};			// ost writes to a file named oname
	if (!ost)
		error("can't open output file ",oname);

	vector<Reading> temps;			// store the readings here
	int hour = -1;
	double temperature = -700;
	while (ist >> hour >> temperature) {
		if (hour < 0 || 23 <hour)
			error("hour out of range");
		temps.push_back(Reading{hour,temperature});
	}

	for (int x : temps)
		ost << '(' << x.hour << ',' << x.temperature << ")\n";
}
```

9.4 I/O error handling

When dealing with input we must expect errors and deal with them. What kind of errors? And how? Errors occur because humans make mistakes (misunderstanding instructions, mistyping, letting the cat walk on the keyboard, etc.), because files fail to meet specifications, because we (as programmers) have the wrong expectations, etc. The possibilities for input errors are limitless! However, an istream reduces all to four possible cases, called the stream state:

Stream states	
good()	The operations succeeded.
eof()	We hit end of input (“end-of-file” aka "eof").
fail()	Something unexpected happened (e.g., we looked for a digit and found 'x').
bad()	Something unexpected and serious happened (e.g., a disk read error).

CC Unfortunately, the distinction between fail() and bad() is not precisely defined and subject to varying opinions among programmers defining I/O operations for new types. However, the basic idea is simple: If an input operation encounters a simple format error, it lets the stream fail(), assuming that you (the user of our input operation) might be able to recover. If, on the other hand, something really nasty, such as a bad disk read, happens, the input operation lets the stream go bad(), assuming that there is nothing much you can do except to abandon the attempt to get data from that stream. A stream that is bad() is also fail(). This leaves us with this general logic:

```
int i = 0;
cin >> i;
if (!cin) {                          // we get here (only) if an input operation failed
      if (cin.bad())                 // stream corrupted
            error("cin is bad");     // let's get out of here!
      if (cin.eof()) {               // no more input:
            // ... this is often how we want a sequence of input operations to end ...
      }
      if (cin.fail()) {              // stream encountered something unexpected
            cin.clear();             // make ready for more input
            // ... somehow recover ...
      }
}
```

The !cin can be read as "cin is not good" or "Something went wrong with cin" or "The state of cin is not good()." It is the opposite of "The operation succeeded." Note the cin.clear() where we handle fail(). When a stream has failed, we might be able to recover. To try to recover, we explicitly take the stream out of the fail() state, so that we can look at characters from it again; clear() does that – after cin.clear() the state of cin is good().

Here is an example of how we might use the stream state. Consider how to read a sequence of integers that may be terminated by the character * or an "end-of-file" (Ctrl+Z on Windows, Ctrl+D on Linux) into a vector. For example:

```
1 2 3 4 5 *
```

This could be done using a function like this:

```
void fill_vector(istream& ist, vector<int>& v, char terminator)
      // read integers from ist into v until we reach eof() or terminator
{
      for (int x; ist>>x; )
            v.push_back(x);
      if (ist.eof())                        // fine: we found the end of file
            return;
      if (ist.bad())                        // stream corrupted;
            error("ist is bad");            // let's get out of here!
      if (ist.fail()) {                     // clean up the mess as best we can and report the problem
            ist.clear();                    // clear stream state, so that we can look for terminator
            char c = 0;
            ist >> c;                       // read a character, hopefully terminator
            if (c != terminator) {          // unexpected character
                  ist.unget();              // put that character back
                  ist.clear(ios::failbit);  // set the state to fail()
            }
      }
}
```

Note that when we didn't find the terminator, we still returned. After all, we may have collected some data and the caller of fill_vector() may be able to recover from a fail(). Since we cleared the state to be able to examine the character, we have to set the stream state back to fail(). We do that with ist.clear(ios::failbit). The ios that appears here and there is the part of an iostream that holds constants such as failbit and other useful stuff to control the behavior of the stream. You refer to them using the :: operator, for example, ios::badbit. The use of clear() with an argument is potentially confusing; clear() sets the iostream state flags (bits) mentioned and clears flags not mentioned.

By setting the state to fail(), we indicate that we encountered a format error, rather than something more serious. We put the character back into ist using unget(); the caller of fill_vector() might have a use for it. The unget() function is a shorter version of putback() (§5.8) that relies on the stream remembering which character it last produced, so that you don't have to mention it.

If you called fill_vector() and want to know what terminated the read, you can test for fail() and eof(). You could also catch the runtime_error exception thrown by error(), but it is understood that getting more data from istream in the bad() state is unlikely. Most callers won't bother. This implies that in almost all cases the only thing we want to do if we encounter bad() is to throw an exception. To make life easier, we can tell an istream to do that for us:

```
ist.exceptions(ist.exceptions()|ios::badbit);          // make ist throw if it goes bad
```

The notation may seem odd, but the effect is simply that from that statement onward, ist will throw the standard-library exception ios::failure if it goes bad(). We need to execute that exceptions() call for an istream only once in a program. That'll allow us to simplify all input loops on ist by ignoring bad():

```
void fill_vector(istream& ist, vector<int>& v, char terminator)
     // read integers from ist into v until we reach eof() or terminator
{
     for (int x; ist>>x; )
          v.push_back(x);
     if (ist.eof())                              // fine: we found the end of file
          return;

     // if we get here ist is not good(), bad(), nor eof(), so ist must be fail()
     ist.clear();                                // clear stream state
     char c = 0;
     ist >> c;                                   // read a character, hopefully terminator
     if (c != terminator) {                      // ouch: not the terminator, so we must fail
          ist.unget();                           // maybe the caller can use that character
          ist.clear(ios::failbit);// set the state to fail()
     }
}
```

Sometimes, we don't want to try recover locally from formatting errors. Then, we can ask for the stream to throw on fail() also:

```
ist.exceptions(ist.exceptions()|ios::badbit|ios::failbit);   // throw on any failure
```

If we want a really minimal fill_vector(), we can also eliminate the check for a terminator and get the simple and obvious loop:

```
void fill_vector(istream& ist, vector<int>& v)
        // read integers from ist into v until we reach eof()
{
        for (int x; ist>>x; )
                v.push_back(x);
}
```

For programs where output devices have a significant chance of being unavailable, filled, or broken, we can test after each output operation just as we test after each input operation. An **ostream** has exactly the same states as an **istream**: **good()**, **fail()**, **eof()**, and **bad()**. However, for output we can often simplify our code by having **bad()** and **fail()** throw exceptions.

9.5 Reading a single value

So, we know how to read a series of values ending with the end-of-file or a terminator. We'll show more examples as we go along, but let's just have a look at the ever-popular idea of repeatedly asking for a value until an acceptable one is entered. This example will allow us to examine several common design choices. We'll discuss these alternatives through a series of alternative solutions to the simple problem of "how to get an acceptable value from the user." We start with an unpleasantly messy obvious "first try" and proceed through a series of improved versions. Our fundamental assumption is that we are dealing with interactive input where a human is typing input and reading the messages from the program. Let's ask for an integer in the range 1 to 10 (inclusive):

```
int get10()
{
        cout << "Please enter an integer in the range 1 to 10 (inclusive):\n";
        int n = 0;
        while (cin>>n) {                    // read
                if (1<=n && n<=10)          // check range
                        return n;
                cout << "Sorry " << n << " is not in the [1:10] range; please try again\n";
        }
}
```

This is pretty ugly, but it "sort of works." Why does it only "sort of work"? It works if the user carefully enters integers. If the user is a poor typist and hits **t** rather than **6** (**t** is just below **6** on many keyboards), the program will leave the loop without changing the value of **n**, so that **n** will have an out-of-range value. We wouldn't call that quality code. A joker (or a diligent tester) might also send an end-of-file from the keyboard. Again, we'd leave the loop with **n** out of range. In other words, to get a robust read we have to deal with three problems:

[1] The user typing an out-of-range value
[2] Getting no value (end-of-file)
[3] The user typing something of the wrong type (here, not an integer)

What do we want to do in those three cases? That's often the question when writing a program: What do we really want? Here, for each of those three errors, we have three alternatives:

[1] Handle the problem in the code doing the read.
[2] Throw an exception to let someone else handle the problem (potentially terminating the program).
[3] Ignore the problem.

AA As it happens, those are three very common alternatives for dealing with an error condition. Thus, this is a good example of the kind of thinking we have to do about errors.

It is tempting to say that the third alternative, ignoring the problem, is always unacceptable, but that would be patronizing. If I'm writing a trivial program for my own use, I can do whatever I like, including forgetting about error checking with potential nasty results. However, for a program that I might want to use for more than a few hours after I wrote it, I would probably be foolish to leave such errors, and if I want to share that program with anyone, I should not leave such holes in the error checking in the code. Please note the use of first-person singular here; "we" would be misleading. We do not consider alternative 3 acceptable even when just two people are involved.

The choice between alternatives 1 and 2 is genuine; that is, in a given program there can be good reasons to choose either way. First we note that in most programs there is no local and elegant way to deal with no input from a user sitting at the keyboard: after the input stream is closed, there isn't much point in asking the user to enter a number. We could reopen **cin** (using **cin.clear()**), but the user is unlikely to have closed that stream by accident (how would you hit Ctrl+Z by accident?). If the program wants an integer and finds end-of-file, the part of the program trying to read the integer must usually give up and hope that some other part of the program can cope; that is, our code requesting input from the user must throw an exception.

The deeper question is what to consider a valid input. For example, where should we reject "December 32, 202"? Typically, an input routine can handle only relatively simple, format related, problems. Problems related to the meaning of input must typically be handled at a higher-level of a program where the intended use of the data is known. For example, in most programs, year 202 would be a bad ("out of possible range") year, but in a program analyzing historical data it might be a perfectly good value. We will return to such questions repeatedly because validating input is a key part of writing a good program.

9.5.1 Breaking the problem into manageable parts

Let's try handling both an out-of-range input and an input of the wrong type locally:

```
int get10()
{
     cout << "Please enter an integer in the range 1 to 10 (inclusive):\n";
     int n = 0;
     while (true) {
          cin >> n;
          if (cin) {                         // we got an integer; now check it
               if (1<=n && n<=10)
                    return n;
               cout << "Sorry " << n << " is not in the [1:10] range; please try again\n";
          }
```

```
		else if (cin.fail()) {			// we found something that wasn't an integer
			cin.clear();			// set the state back to good(); we want to look at the characters
			cout << "Sorry, that was not a number; please try again\n";
			for (char ch; cin>>ch && !isdigit(ch); )		// throw away non-digits
				/* nothing */ ;
			if (!cin)			// we didn't find a digit: give up
				error("no input");
			cin.unget();			// put the digit back, so that we can read the number
		}
		else
			error("no input");		// bad: give up
	}
}
```

This is messy, and rather long-winded. In fact, it is so messy that we could not recommend that people write such code each time they needed an integer from a user. On the other hand, we do need to deal with the potential errors because people do make them, so what can we do? The reason that the code is messy is that code dealing with several different concerns is all mixed together: XX

- Reading values
- Prompting the user for input
- Writing error messages
- Skipping past "bad" input characters
- Testing the input against a range

The way to make code clearer is often to separate logically distinct concerns into separate functions. For example, we can separate out the code for recovering after seeing a "bad" (i.e., unexpected) character: AA

```
void skip_to_int()
{
	if (cin.fail()) {				// we found something that wasn't an integer
		cin.clear();				// we'd like to look at the characters
		for (char ch; cin>>ch; ) {		// throw away non-digits
			if (isdigit(ch) || ch=='-') {
				cin.unget();		// put the digit back, so that we can read the number
				return;
			}
		}
	}
	error("no input");				// eof or bad: give up
}
```

Given the skip_to_int() "utility function," we can write:

```
int get10()
{
	cout << "Please enter an integer in the range 1 to 10 (inclusive):\n";
	int n = 0;
```

```
        while (true) {
                if (cin>>n) {           // we got an integer; now check it
                        if (1<=n && n<=10)
                                return n;
                        cout << "Sorry " << n << " is not in the [1:10] range; please try again\n";
                }
                else {
                        cout << "Sorry, that was not a number; please try again\n";
                        skip_to_int();
                }
        }
}
```

This code is better, but it is still too long, too messy, and too special purpose (e.g., why [1:10]?).

What operation would we really like to have? One plausible answer is "a function that reads an int, any int, and another that reads an int of a given range":

```
int get_int();                          // read an int from cin
int get_int(int low, int high);         // read an int in [low:high] from cin
```

If we had those, we could use them simply and correctly. They are not that hard to write:

```
int get_int()
{
        int n = 0;
        while (true) {
                if (cin >> n)
                        return n;
                cout << "Sorry, that was not a number; please try again\n";
                skip_to_int();
        }
}
```

Basically, get_int() stubbornly keeps reading until it finds some digits that it can interpret as an integer. If we want to get out of get_int(), we must supply an integer or end-of-file (and end-of-file will cause skip_to_int() to throw an exception).

Using that general get_int(), we can write the range-checking get_int():

```
int get_int(int low, int high)
{
        cout << "Please enter an integer in the range "
                << low << " to " << high << " (inclusive):\n";
        while (true) {
                int n = get_int();
                if (low<=n && n<=high)
                        return n;
                cout << "Sorry "
                        << n << " is not in the [" << low << ':' << high
                        << "] range; please try again\n";
        }
}
```

This get_int() is as stubborn as the other. It keeps getting ints from the non-range get_int() until the int it gets is in the expected range.

We can now reliably read integers like this:

```
int n = get_int(1,10);
cout << "n: " << n << '\n';

int m = get_int(2,300);
cout << "m: " << m << '\n';
```

Don't forget to catch exceptions somewhere, though, if you want decent error messages for the (probably rare) case when get_int() really couldn't read a number for us.

9.5.2 Separating dialog from function

The get_int() functions still mix up reading with writing messages to the user. That's probably good enough for a simple program, but in a large program we might want to vary the messages written to the user. We might want to call get_int() like this:

```
int strength = get_int(1,10, "enter strength", "Not in range, try again");
cout << "strength: " << strength << '\n';

int altitude = get_int(0,50000, "Please enter altitude in feet", "Not in range, please try again");
cout << "altitude: " << altitude << "f above sea level\n";
```

We could implement that like this:

```
int get_int(int low, int high, const string& greeting, const string& sorry)
{
	cout << greeting << ": [" << low << ':' << high << "]\n";

	while (true) {
		int n = get_int();
		if (low<=n && n<=high)
			return n;
		cout << sorry << ": [" << low << ':' << high << "]\n";
	}
}
```

It is hard to compose arbitrary messages, so we "stylized" the messages. That's often acceptable, and composing really flexible messages, such as are needed to support many natural languages (e.g., Arabic, Bengali, Chinese, Danish, English, and French), is not a task for a novice.

Note that our solution is still incomplete: the get_int() without a range still "blabbers." The deeper point here is that "utility functions" that we use in many parts of a program shouldn't have messages "hardwired" into them. Further, library functions that are meant for use in many programs shouldn't write to the user at all – after all, the library writer may not even know that the program in which the library runs is used on a machine with a human watching. That's one reason that our error() function doesn't just write an error message (§4.6.3); in general, we wouldn't know where to write.

9.6 User-defined output operators

Defining the output operator, <<, for a given type is typically trivial. The main design problem is that different people might prefer the output to look different, so it is hard to agree on a single format. However, even if no single output format is good enough for all uses, it is often a good idea to define << for a user-defined type. That way, we can at least trivially write out objects of the type during debugging and early development. Later, we might provide a more sophisticated << that allows a user to provide formatting information. Also, if we want output that looks different from what a << provides, we can simply bypass the << and write out the individual parts of the user-defined type the way we happen to like them in our application.

Here is a simple output operator for the Date from §8.7.4 that simply prints the year, month, and day comma-separated in parentheses:

```
ostream& operator<<(ostream& os, const Date& d)
{
        return os << '(' << d.year()
                        << ',' << as_int(d.month())
                        << ',' << d.day() << ')';
}
```

This will print August 30, 2004, as (2004,8,30). This simple list-of-elements representation is what we tend to use for types with a few members unless we have a better idea or more specific needs.

In §8.6, we mention that a user-defined operator is handled by calling a function. Here, we have an example of how that's done: Given the definition of << for Date, the meaning of

```
cout << d1;
```

where d1 is a Date is the call

```
operator<<(cout,d1);
```

Note how operator<<() takes an ostream& as its first argument and returns it again as its return value. That's the way the output stream is passed along so that you can "chain" output operations. For example, we could output two dates like this:

```
cout << d1 << d2;
```

This will be handled by first resolving the first << and after that the second <<:

```
cout << d1 << d2;          // means operator<<(cout,d1) << d2;
                           // means operator<<(operator<<(cout,d1),d2);
```

That is, first output d1 to cout and then output d2 to the output stream that is the result of the first output operation (that is cout). In fact, we can use any of those three variants to write out d1 and d2. We know which one is easier to read, though.

9.7 User-defined input operators

Defining the input operator, >>, for a given type and input format is basically an exercise in error handling. It can therefore be quite tricky.

Here is a simple input operator for the **Date** from §8.7.4 that will read dates as written by the output << operator defined above:

```
istream& operator>>(istream& is, Date& dd)
{
        int y, m, d;
        char ch1, ch2, ch3, ch4;
        is >> ch1 >> y >> ch2 >> m >> ch3 >> d >> ch4;
        if (!is)
                return is;
        if (ch1!='(' || ch2!=',' || ch3!=',' || ch4!=')') {       // oops: format error
                is.clear(ios::failbit);
                return is;
        }
        dd = Date{y,Month(m),d};                                  // update dd
        return is;
}
```

This >> will read items like (2004,8,20) and try to make a Date out of those three integers. As ever, input is harder to deal with than output. There is simply more that can – and often does – go wrong with input than with output.

If this >> doesn't find something in the *(integer , integer , integer)* format, it will leave the stream in a not-good state (**fail**, **eof**, or **bad**) and leave the target **Date** unchanged. The **clear()** member function is used to set the state of the **istream**. Obviously, **ios::failbit** puts the stream into the **fail()** state. Leaving the target **Date** unchanged in case of a failure to read is the ideal; it tends to lead to cleaner code. The ideal is for an **operator>>()** not to consume (throw away) any characters that it didn't use, but that's too difficult in this case: we might have read lots of characters before we caught a format error. As an example, consider (2004, 8, 30}. Only when we see the final } do we know that we have a format error on our hands, and we cannot in general rely on putting back many characters. One character **unget()** is all that's universally guaranteed. If this **operator>>()** reads an invalid **Date**, such as **(2004,8,32)**, **Date**'s constructor will throw an exception, which will get us out of this **operator>>()**.

9.8 A standard input loop

In §9.3.2, we saw how we could read and write files. However, that was before we looked more carefully at errors (§9.4), so the input loop simply assumed that we could read a file from its beginning until end-of-file. That can be a reasonable assumption, because we often apply separate checks to ensure that a file is valid. However, we often want to check our reads as we go along. Here is a general strategy, assuming that **ist** is an **istream**:

```
for (My_type var; ist>>var; ) {        // read until end-of-file
        // ... maybe check that var is valid ...
        // ... do something with var ...
}
```

```
// we can rarely recover from bad; don't try unless you really have to:
if (ist.bad())
      error("bad input stream");

if (ist.fail()) {
      // .. was it an acceptable terminator? ...
}
// carry on: we found end-of-file
```

That is, we read a sequence of values into variables and when we can't read any more values, we check the stream state to see why. As in §9.4, we can improve this a bit by letting the **istream** throw an exception of type failure if it goes bad. That saves us the bother of checking for it all the time:

```
// somewhere: make ist throw an exception if it goes bad:
ist.exceptions(ist.exceptions()|ios::badbit);
```

We could also decide to designate a character as a terminator:

```
for (My_type var; ist>>var; ) {          // read until end-of-file
      // ... maybe check that var is valid ...
      // ... do something with var ...
}

if (ist.fail()) {                        // use '|' as terminator and/or separator
      ist.clear();
      char ch;
      if (!(ist>>ch && ch=='|'))
            error("bad termination of input");
}
// carry on: we found end-of-file or a terminator
```

If we don't want to accept a terminator – that is, to accept only end-of-file as the end – we simply delete the test before the call of **error()**. However, terminators are very useful when you read files with nested constructs, such as a file of monthly readings containing daily readings, containing hourly readings, etc., so we'll keep considering the possibility of a terminating character.

Unfortunately, that code is still a bit messy. In particular, it is tedious to repeat the terminator test if we read many values. We could write a function to deal with that:

```
void end_of_loop(istream& ist, char term, const string& message)
{
      if (ist.fail()) {                  // use term as terminator and/or separator
            ist.clear();
            char ch = 0;
            if (ist>>ch && ch==term)
                  return;                // all is fine
            error(message);
      }
}
```

This reduces the input loop to

```
for (My_type var; ist>>var; ) {                    // read until end-of-file
        // ... maybe check that var is valid ...
        // ... do something with var ...
}
end_of_loop(ist,'|',"bad termination of file");     // test if we can continue

// carry on: we found end-of-file or a terminator
```

The end_of_loop() does nothing unless the stream is in the fail() state. We consider that simple enough and general enough for many purposes.

9.9 Reading a structured file

Let's try to use this "standard loop" for a concrete example. As usual, we'll use the example to illustrate widely applicable design and programming techniques. Assume that you have a file of temperature readings that has been structured like this:

- A file holds years (of months of readings). A year starts with { year followed by an integer giving the year, such as 1900, and ends with }.
- A year holds months (of days of readings). A month starts with { month followed by a three-letter month name, such as jan, and ends with }.
- A reading holds a time and a temperature. A reading starts with a (followed by day of the month, hour of the day, and temperature and ends with a).

For example:

```
{ year 1990 }
{year 1991 { month jun }}
{ year 1992 { month jan ( 1 0 61.5) } {month feb (1 1 64) (2 2 65.2) } }
{year 2000
        { month feb (1 1 68 ) (2 3 66.66 ) ( 1 0 67.2)}
        {month dec (15 15 –9.2 ) (15 14 –8.8) (14 0 –2) }
}
```

This format is somewhat peculiar. File formats often are. There is a move toward more regular and hierarchically structured files (such as HTML, XML, and JSON files) in the industry, but the reality is still that we can rarely control the input format offered by the files we need to read. The files are the way they are, and we just have to read them. If a format is too awful or files contain too many errors, we can write a format conversion program to produce a format that suits our main program better. On the other hand, we can typically choose the in-memory representation of data to suit our needs, and we can often pick output formats to suit needs and tastes. AA

So, let's assume that we have been given the temperature reading format above and have to live with it. Fortunately, it has self-identifying components, such as years and months (a bit like HTML or XML). On the other hand, the format of individual readings is somewhat unhelpful. For example, there is no information that could help us if someone flipped a day-of-the-month value with an hour of day or if someone produced a file with temperatures in Celsius and the program expected them in Fahrenheit or vice versa. We just have to cope.

9.9.1 In-memory representation

How should we represent this data in memory? The obvious first choice is three classes, Year, Month, and Reading, to exactly match the input. Year and Month are obviously useful when manipulating the data; we want to compare temperatures of different years, calculate monthly averages, compare different months of a year, compare the same month of different years, match up temperature readings with sunshine records and humidity readings, etc. Basically, Year and Month match the way we think about temperatures and weather in general: Month holds a month's worth of information and Year holds a year's worth of information. But what about Reading? That's a low-level notion matching some piece of hardware (a sensor). The data of a Reading (day of month, hour of day, temperature) is "odd" and makes sense only within a Month. It is also unstructured: we have no promise that readings come in day-of-the-month or hour-of-the-day order. Basically, whenever we want to do anything of interest with the readings we have to sort them.

For representing the temperature data in memory, we make these assumptions:

- If we have any readings for a month, then we tend to have many readings for that month.
- If we have any readings for a day, then we tend to have many readings for that day.

When that's the case, it makes sense to represent a Year as a vector of 12 Months, a Month as a vector of about 30 Days, and a Day as 24 temperatures (one per hour). That's simple and easy to manipulate for a wide variety of uses. So, Day, Month, and Year are simple data structures, each with a constructor. Since we plan to create Months and Days as part of a Year before we know what temperature readings we have, we need to have a notion of "not a reading" for an hour of a day for which we haven't (yet) read data.

```
const int not_a_reading = −7777;          // less than absolute zero
```

Similarly, we noticed that we often had a month without data, so we introduced the notion "not a month" to represent that directly, rather than having to search through all the days to be sure that no data was lurking somewhere:

```
const int not_a_month = −1;
```

The three key classes then become

```
struct Day {
     vector<double> temp = vector<double>(24,not_a_reading);          // note: parentheses
};
```

That is, a Day has temperatures for 24 hours, each initialized to not_a_reading.

```
struct Month {          // a month of temperature readings
     int month = not_a_month;                         // [0:11] January is 0
     vector<Day> day = vector<Day>(32);               // [1:31] one vector of readings per day
};
```

We "waste" day[0] to keep the code simple.

```
struct Year {          // a year of temperature readings, organized by month
     int year;                                        // positive == A.D.
     vector<Month> month = vector<Month>(12);         // [0:11] January is 0
};
```

Each class is basically a simple vector of "parts," and Month and Year have an identifying member month and year, respectively.

XX

There are several "magic constants" here (for example, 24, 32, and 12). We try to avoid such literal constants in code. These are pretty fundamental (the number of months in a year rarely changes) and will not be used in the rest of the code. However, we left them in the code primarily so that we could remind you of the problem with "magic constants"; symbolic constants are almost always preferable (§6.6.1). Using 32 for the number of days in a month definitely requires explanation; 32 is obviously "magic" here.

Why didn't we write

```
struct Day {
        vector<double> temp {24,not_a_reading};            // note: curly brackets
};
```

That would have been simpler, but unfortunately, we would have gotten a vector of two elements (24 and -7777). When we want to specify the number of elements for a vector for which an integer can be converted to the element type, we unfortunately have to use the ( ) initializer syntax (§7.2.2).

9.9.2 Reading structured values

The Reading class will be used only for reading input and is trivial:

```
struct Reading {
        int day;
        int hour;
        double temperature;
};

istream& operator>>(istream& is, Reading& r)
        // read a temperature reading from is into r. format: ( 3 4 9.7 )
        // check format, but don't bother with data validity
{
        char ch1;
        if (is>>ch1 && ch1!='(') {                                  // could it be a Reading?
                is.unget();
                is.clear(ios::failbit);
                return is;
        }

        char ch2;
        if ((is >> r.day >> r.hour >> r.temperature >> ch2) && ch2!=')')        // messed-up Reading?
                error("bad reading");
        return is;
}
```

Basically, we check if the format begins plausibly. If it doesn't, we set the file state to fail() and return. This allows us to try to read the information in some other way. On the other hand, if we find the format wrong after having read some data so that there is no real chance of recovering, we bail out with error().

The Month input operation is much the same, except that it has to read an arbitrary number of Readings rather than a fixed set of values (as Reading's >> did):

```
istream& operator>>(istream& is, Month& m)
        // read a month from is into m. format: { month feb . . . }
{
        char ch = 0;
        if (is >> ch && ch!='{') {
                is.unget();
                is.clear(ios::failbit);                 // we failed to read a Month
                return is;
        }

        string month_marker;
        string mm;
        is >> month_marker >> mm;
        if (!is || month_marker!="month")
                error("bad start of month");
        m.month = month_to_int(mm);

        int duplicates = 0;
        int invalids = 0;
        for (Reading r; is >> r; ) {
                if (is_valid(r)) {
                        if (m.day[r.day].hour[r.hour] != not_a_reading)
                                ++duplicates;
                        m.day[r.day].hour[r.hour] = r.temperature;
                }
                else
                        ++invalids;
        }
        if (invalids)
                error("invalid readings in month",invalids);
        if (duplicates)
                error("duplicate readings in month", duplicates);
        end_of_loop(is,'}',"bad end of month");
        return is;
}
```

We'll get back to month_to_int() later; it converts the symbolic notation for a month, such as jun, to a number in the [0:11] range. Note the use of end_of_loop() from §9.8 to check for the terminator. We keep count of invalid and duplicate Readings; someone might be interested.

Month's >> does a quick check that a Reading is plausible before storing it:

```
constexpr int implausible_min = -200;
constexpr int implausible_max = 200;
```

```
bool is_valid(const Reading& r)
      // a rough test
{
      if (r.day<1 || 31<r.day)
            return false;
      if (r.hour<0 || 23<r.hour)
            return false;
      if (r.temperature<implausible_min|| implausible_max<r.temperature)
            return false;
      return true;
}
```

Finally, we can read Years. Year's >> is similar to Month's >>:

```
istream& operator>>(istream& is, Year& y)
      // read a year from is into y. format: { year 1972 ... }
{
      char ch = 0;
      is >> ch;
      if (ch!='{') {
            is.unget();
            is.clear(ios::failbit);
            return is;
      }

      string year_marker;
      int yy = -1;
      is >> year_marker >> yy;
      if (!is || year_marker!="year")
            error("bad start of year");
      y.year = yy;

      while(true) {
            Month m;        // get a clean m each time around
            if(!(is >> m))
                  break;
            y.month[m.month] = m;
      }

      end_of_loop(is,'}',"bad end of year");
      return is;
}
```

We would have preferred "boringly similar" to just "similar," but there is a significant difference. Have a look at the read loop. Did you expect something like the following?

```
for (Month m; is >> m; )
      y.month[m.month] = m;
```

You probably should have, because that's the way we have written all the read loops so far. That's actually what we first wrote, and it's wrong. The problem is that operator>>(istream& is, Month& m) doesn't assign a brand-new value to m; it simply adds data from Readings to m. Thus, the repeated is>>m would have kept adding to our one and only m. Oops! Each new month would have gotten all the readings from all previous months of that year. We need a brand-new, clean Month to read into each time we do is>>m. The easiest way to do that was to put the definition of m inside the loop so that it would be initialized each time around. The alternatives would have been for operator>>(istream& is, Month& m) to assign an empty Month to m before reading into it, or for the loop to do that:

```
for (Month m; is >> m; ) {
      y.month[m.month] = m;
      m = Month{};          // "reinitialize" m
}
```

Let's try to use it:

```
// open an input file:
cout << "Please enter input file name\n";
string iname;
cin >> iname;
ifstream ifs {iname};
if (!ifs)
      error("can't open input file",iname);

ifs.exceptions(ifs.exceptions()|ios::badbit);          // throw for bad()

// open an output file:
cout << "Please enter output file name\n";
string oname;
cin >> oname;
ofstream ofs {oname};
if (!ofs)
      error("can't open output file",oname);

// read an arbitrary number of years:
vector<Year> ys;
while(true) {
      Year y;               // get a freshly initialized Year each time around
      if (!(ifs>>y))
            break;
      ys.push_back(y);
}
cout << "read " << ys.size() << " years of readings\n";

for (Year& y : ys)
      print_year(ofs,y);
```

We leave print_year() as an exercise.

9.9.3 Changing representations

To get Month's >> to work, we need to provide a way of reading symbolic representations of the month. For symmetry, we'll provide a matching write using a symbolic representation. The tedious way would be to write an if-statement convert:

```
if (s=="jan")
      m = 1;                // Months start at 1
else if (s=="feb")
      m = 2;
...
```

This is not just tedious; it also builds the names of the months into the code. It would be better to have those in a table somewhere so that the main program could stay unchanged even if we had to change the symbolic representation. We decided to represent the input representation as a vector<string> plus an initialization function and a lookup function:

```
vector<string> month_input_tbl = {
      "-not a month-",
      "jan", "feb", "mar", "apr", "may", "jun", "jul", "aug", "sep", "oct", "nov", "dec"
};

int month_to_int(string s)
      // is s the name of a month? If so return its index [1:12] otherwise -1
{
      for (int i=1; i<13; ++i)
            if (month_input_tbl[i]==s)
                  return i;
      return 0;
}
```

In case you wonder: the C++ standard library does provide a simpler way to do this. See §20.2 for a map<string,int>.

When we want to produce output, we have the opposite problem. We have an int representing a month and would like a symbolic representation to be printed. Our solution is fundamentally similar, but instead of using a table to go from string to int, we use one to go from int to string:

```
vector<string> month_print_tbl = {
      "-not a month-",
      "January", "February", "March", "April", "May", "June", "July",
      "August", "September", "October", "November", "December"
};

string int_to_month(int i)
      // months [1:12]
{
      if (i<1 || 12<=i)
            error("bad month index");
      return month_print_tbl[i];
}
```

So, did you actually read all of that code and the explanations? Or did your eyes glaze over and skip to the end? Remember that the easiest way of learning to write good code is to read a lot of code. Believe it or not, the techniques we used for this example are simple, but not trivial to discover without help. Reading data is fundamental. Writing loops correctly (initializing every variable used correctly) is fundamental. Converting between representations is fundamental. That is, you will learn to do such things. The only questions are whether you'll learn to do them well and whether you learn the basic techniques before losing too much sleep.

9.10 Formatting

The iostream library – the input/output part of the ISO C++ standard library – provides a unified and extensible framework for input and output of text. By "text" we mean just about anything that can be represented as a sequence of characters. Thus, when we talk about input and output we can consider the integer 1234 as text because we can write it using the four characters 1, 2, 3, and 4.

So far, we worked on the assumption that the type of an object completely determined the layout of its input and output. That's not quite right and wouldn't be sufficient. For example, we often want to specify the number of digits used to represent a floating-point number on output (its precision). This section presents a number of ways in which we can tailor input and output to our needs.

People care a lot about apparently minor details of the output they have to read. For example, to a physicist 1.25 (rounded to two digits after the dot) can be very different from 1.24670477, and to an accountant (1.25) can be legally different from (1.2467) and totally different from 1.25 (in financial documents, parentheses are sometimes used to indicate losses, that is, negative values). As programmers, we aim to make our output as clear and as close as possible to the expectations of the "consumers" of our program. Output streams (ostreams) provide a variety of ways for formatting the output of built-in types. For user-defined types, it is up to the programmer to define suitable << operations.

CC

The details of I/O seem infinite. They probably are, since they are limited only by human inventiveness and capriciousness. For example, we have not considered the complexity implied by natural languages. What is written as 12.35 in English will be conventionally represented as 12,35 in most European languages. Naturally, the C++ standard library provides facilities for dealing with that and many other natural-language-specific aspects of I/O. How do you write Chinese characters? How do you compare strings written using Malayalam characters? There are answers, but they are far beyond the scope of this book. If you need to know, look in more specialized or advanced books and in library and system documentation. Look for "locale"; that's the term usually applied to facilities for dealing with natural language differences.

Another source of complexity and flexibility is buffering: the standard-library iostreams rely on a concept called streambuf. For advanced work – whether for performance or functionality – with iostreams these streambufs are unavoidable. If you feel the need to define your own iostreams or to tune iostreams to new data sources/sinks, look them up.

9.10.1 Integer I/O

Integer values can be output textually as binary (base-2), octal (base-8), decimal (our usual base-10 number system), and hexadecimal (base-16). Most output uses decimal. Hexadecimal is popular for outputting hardware-related information. The reason is that a hexadecimal digit exactly represents a 4-bit value. Thus, two hexadecimal digits can be used to present the value of an 8-bit byte, four hexadecimal digits give the value of 2 bytes (that's often a half word), and eight hexadecimal digits can present the value of 4 bytes (that's often the size of an **int**). When C++'s ancestor C was first designed (in the 1970s), octal was popular for representing bit patterns, but now it's rarely used.

For example:

```
int x = 1234;
cout << x << " - " << hex << x << " - " << oct << x << " - " << dec << x << '\n';
```

This prints

```
1234 - 4d2 - 2322 - 1234
```

The notation **<< hex** does not output values. Instead, **hex** informs the stream that any further integer values should be displayed in hexadecimal. They are known as *manipulators* because they manipulate the state of a stream. We also have **dec** and **oct** manipulators.

> TRY THIS
>
> Output your birth year in decimal, hexadecimal, and octal form. Label each value. Line up your output in columns using the tab character. Now output your age.

By default, >> assumes that numbers use the decimal notation:

```
int a = 0;
int b = 0;
int c = 0;
cin >> a >> hex >> b >> oct >> c;
cout << dec;
cout << a << '\t' << b << '\t' << c << '\n';
cout << hex;
cout << a << '\t' << b << '\t' << c << '\n';
```

The '\t' character is called "tab" (short for "tabulation character" – a leftover from the days of mechanical typewriters).

If you type in

```
1234 4d2 2322
```

This prints:

```
1234 1234 1234
4d2  4d2  4d2
```

Note that the operators, such as **hex**, controlling formatting are "sticky"; that is, they persist until changed so that we can set them once for a stream and have their effect persist for many operations. We don't have to apply them repeatedly.

There is no standard bin manipulator to give us binary output. If we want binary output, we have to write one ourselves or use format() (§9.10.6).

9.10.2 Floating-point I/O

In scientific computation and many other fields, we deal with the formatting of floating-point values. They are handled using iostream manipulators in a manner very similar to that of integer values. For example:

```
constexpr double d = 1234.56789;

cout << "format: " << d << " - "              // use the default format for d
     << hexfloat << d << " - "                // use hexadecimal notation for d
     << scientific << d << " - "              // use 1.123e2 style format for d
     << fixed << d << " - "                   // use 123.456 style format for d
     << defaultfloat << d << '\n';            // use the default format for d
```

This prints

```
format: 1234.57 - 0x1.34a4584f4c6e7p+10 - 1.234568e+03 - 1234.567890 - 1234.57
```

The basic floating-point output-formatting manipulators are:

Floating-point formats	
fixed	use fixed-point notation
scientific	use mantissa and exponent notation; the mantissa is always in the [1:10) range; that is, there is a single nonzero digit before the decimal point
defaultfloat	choose fixed or scientific to give the numerically most accurate representation
hexfloat	use scientific notation with hexadecimal for mantissa and exponent

A key property we often want to control is *precision*; that is how many digits are used when printing a floating-point number. The precision is defined as:

Floating-point precision	
defaultfloat	precision is the total number of digits
scientific	precision is the number of digits after the decimal point
fixed	precision is the number of digits after the decimal point

Use the default (defaultfloat format with precision 6) unless there is a reason not to. The usual reason not to is "Because we need greater accuracy of the output."

Floating-point values are rounded rather than just truncated, and precision() doesn't affect integer output. For example:

```
cout << "precision: " << d << " - " << setprecision(8) << d << " - " << setprecision(16) << d << '\n';
```

This prints:

```
precision: 1234.57 - 1234.5679 - 1234.56789
```

When printing a lot of numbers, we often want them presented in neat rows and columns. This can be achieved by specifying the width of the field into which a value is written using setw(n). For example:

```
cout << "width: " << d << " – " << setw(8) << d <<  " – " << setw(16) << d << '\n';
```

This prints:

```
width: 1234.57 – 1234.57 –         1234.57
```

Note that setw applies just to its following number or string. There are more such controls. If you need them, look them up.

9.10.3 String I/O

A >> operator reads into objects of a given type according to that type's standard format. For example, when reading into an int, >> will read until it encounters something that's not a digit, and when reading into a string, >> will read until it encounters whitespace. The standard-library istream library also provides facilities for reading whole lines. Consider:

```
string name;
cin >> name;                    // input: Dennis Ritchie
cout << name << '\n';           // output: Dennis
```

What if we want to read everything on that line at once and decide how to format it later? That can be done using the function getline(). For example:

```
string name;
getline(cin,name);              // input: Dennis Ritchie
cout << name << '\n';           // output: Dennis Ritchie
```

Now we have the whole line. Why would we want that? A good answer would be "Because we want to do something that can't be done by >>." Often, the answer is a poor one: "Because the user typed a whole line." If that's the best you can think of, stick to >>, because once you have the line entered, you usually have to parse it somehow.

9.10.4 Character I/O

Usually, we read integers, floating-point numbers, words, etc. as defined by format conventions. CC
However, we can – and sometimes must – go down a level of abstraction and read individual characters. That's more work, but when we read individual characters, we have full control over what we are doing. Consider tokenizing an expression (§5.8.2). There, we wanted 1+4*x<=y/z*5 to be separated into the eleven tokens

```
1 + 4 * x <= y / z * 5
```

We could use >> to read the numbers, but trying to read the identifiers as strings would cause x<=y to be read as one string (since < and = are not whitespace characters) and z* to be read as one string (since * isn't a whitespace character either). Instead, we could write

```
for (char ch; cin.get(ch); ) {
        if (isspace(ch)) {
                // do nothing; i.e., skip whitespace (e.g. space or tab)
        }
        else if (isdigit(ch)) {
                // .. read a number ...
        }
        else if (isalpha(ch)) {
                // ... read an identifier ...
        }
        else {
                // ... deal with operators ...
        }
}
```

The **istream::get()** function reads a single character into its argument. It does not skip whitespace. Like **>>**, **get()** returns a reference to its **istream** so that we can test its state.

When we read individual characters, we usually want to classify them: Is this character a digit? Is this character uppercase? And so forth. There is a set of standard-library functions for that:

Character classification	
isspace(c)	Is **c** whitespace (' ', '\t', '\n', etc.)?
isalpha(c)	Is **c** a letter ('**a**'..'**z**', '**A**'..'**Z**') (note: not '_')?
isdigit(c)	Is **c** a decimal digit ('**0**'..'**9**')?
isxdigit(c)	Is **c** a hexadecimal digit (decimal digit or '**a**'..'**f**' or '**A**'..'**F**')?
isupper(c)	Is **c** an uppercase letter?
islower(c)	Is **c** a lowercase letter?
isalnum(c)	Is **c** a letter or a decimal digit?
iscntrl(c)	Is **c** a control character (ASCII 0..31 and 127)?
ispunct(c)	Is **c** not a letter, digit, whitespace, or invisible control character?
isprint(c)	Is **c** printable (ASCII ' '..'~')?
isgraph(c)	Is **isalpha(c)** or **isdigit(c)** or **ispunct(c)** (note: not space)?

Note that the classifications can be combined using the "or" operator (**||**). For example, **isalnum(c)** means **isalpha(c)||isdigit(c)**; that is, "Is **c** either a letter or a digit?"

In addition, the standard library provides two useful functions for getting rid of case differences:

Character case	
x=toupper(c)	**x** becomes **c** or **c**'s uppercase equivalent
x=tolower(c)	**x** becomes **c** or **c**'s lowercase equivalent

These are useful when you want to ignore case differences. For example, in input from a user **Right**, **right**, and **rigHT** most likely mean the same thing (**rigHT** most likely being the result of an unfortunate hit on the Caps Lock key). After applying **tolower()** to each character in each of those strings, we get **right** for each. We can do that for an arbitrary **string**:

```
void tolower(string& s)          // put s into lowercase
{
      for (char& x : s)
            x = tolower(x);
}
```

We use pass-by-reference (§7.4.5) to actually change the **string**. Had we wanted to keep the old string we could have written a function to make a lowercase copy. Prefer **tolower()** to **toupper()** because that works better for text in some natural languages, such as German, where not every lowercase character has an uppercase equivalent. AA

Possibly the most common reason to look at individual characters in a string or an input stream is to separate items; see §20.2.

9.10.5 Extend I/O

The stream I/O is extensible, so we can define << for our own (user-defined) types (§9.7, §9.6). Fortunately, the standard library defines << and >> for quite a few types. In addition to the basic numbers, strings, and characters, << can also handle time and dates: **duration**, **time_point**, **year_month_date**, **weekday**, **month**, and **zoned_time** (§20.4, §20.4.1). For example:

```
cout << "birthday: " << November/28/2021 << '\n';
cout << "zt: " << zoned_time{current_zone(), system_clock::now()} << '\n';
```

This produced:

```
birthday: 2021-11-28
zt: 2021-12-05 11:03:13.5945638 EST
```

The standard also defines << for **complex** numbers, **bitset**s (PPP2.§25.5.2), error codes, **bool**s, and pointers (§15.3, §15.4).

9.10.6 format()

It has been credibly argued that **printf()** is the most popular function in C and a significant factor in C's success. For example:

```
printf("an int %g and a string '%s'\n", 123, "Hello!");
```

This "format string followed by arguments"-style was adopted into C from BCPL and has been followed by many languages. Naturally, **printf()** has always been part of the C++ standard library, but it suffers from lack of type safety and lack of extensibility to handle user-defined types.

However, the standard library provides a type-safe and extensible **printf()**-style formatting mechanism. The function, **format()** produces a **string**:

```
string s = format("Hello, {}!\n", val);
```

"Ordinary characters" in the *format string* are simply put into the output **string**. On the other hand, characters delimited by **{** and **}** specify how arguments following the format string are to be inserted into the output **string**. The simplest format string is the empty string, **{}**, that takes the next argument from the argument list and inserts it according to its << default (if any). So, if **val** is **"World"**, we get the iconic **"Hello, World!\n"**. If **val** is **127** we get **"Hello, 127!\n"**.

The most common use of format() is to output its result:

```
cout << format("Hello, {}\n", val);
```

To see how this works, let's first repeat the examples from (§9.10.1):

```
int x = 1234;
cout << format("{} – {:x} – {:o} – {:d} – {:b}\n", x, x, x, x, x);
```

This gives the same output as the integer example in §9.10.1, except that I added b for binary which is not directly supported by ostream:

```
1234 – 4d2 – 2322 – 1234 – 10011010010
```

A formatting directive is preceded by a colon. The integer formatting alternatives are

- x: hexadecimal
- o: octal
- d: decimal
- b: binary
- none: d

The format string relies on a whole little programming language for specifying how a value is presented. Explaining all of that is beyond the scope of this book. If you need more see some more detailed source, such as https://en.cppreference.com/w/cpp/utility/format/formatter.

For floating-point numbers, the choices described in §9.10.2 are represented by

- a: hexfloat
- e: scientific
- f: fixed
- g: general, with precision 6
- none: general, with default precision

For example:

```
constexpr double d = 1234.56789;
cout << format("format: {} – {:a} – {:e} – {:f} – {:g}\n", d, d, d, d, d);
```

This prints

```
format: 1234.56789 – 1.34a4584f4c6e7p+10 – 1.234568e+03 – 1234.567890 – 1234.57
```

We can also specify how many character positions are used for a value. The "width example" from §9.10.2 can be written like this:

```
cout << format("width: {} – {:8} – {:20} –\n", d, d, d);
```

This prints:

```
width: 1234.56789 – 1234.56789 –           1234.56789 –
```

Precision is specified by a number after a dot:

```
cout << format("precision: {} – {:.8} – {:.20} –\n", d, d, d);
```

This prints:

```
precision: 1234.56789 – 1234.57 – 1234.567890000000034 –
```

You can combine formatting directives. For example:

```
cout << format("– {:12} – {:12.8f} – {:30.20e} –\n", d, d, d);
```

> TRY THIS
>
> See what that last statement prints, and explain it. Try some other formats.

9.11 String streams

You can use a **string** as the source of an **istream** or the target for an **ostream**. An **istream** that reads from a **string** is called an **istringstream** and an **ostream** that stores characters written to it in a **string** is called an **ostringstream**. For example, an **istringstream** is useful for extracting values from a formatted **string**: CC

```
Point get_coordinates(const string& s)  // extract {x,y} from "(x,y)"
{
        istringstream is {s};        // make a stream so that we can read from s
        Point xy;
        char left_paren, ch, right_paren;
        is >> left_paren >> xy.x >> ch >> xy.y >> right_paren;
        if (!is || left_paren !='(' || ch!=',' || right_paren!=')')
                error("format error: ",s);
        return xy;
}

// testing:
auto c1 = get_coordinates("(2,3)");
auto c2 = get_coordinates("(   200, 300) ");
auto c3 = get_coordinates("100,400");            // will call error()
```

If we try to read beyond the end of an **istringstream**'s string, the **istringstream** will go into **eof()** state. This means that we can use "the usual input loop" for an **istringstream**; an **istringstream** really is a kind of **istream**.

The **stringstreams** are generally used when we want to separate actual I/O from processing. For example, a **string** argument for **get_coordinates()** will usually originate from a file (e.g., a Web log), a GUI library, or a keyboard. Similarly, the message we composed in **my_code()** will eventually end up written to an area of a screen. AA

A simple use of an **ostringstream** is to construct strings by concatenation. For example:

```
int seq_no = get_next_number();           // get the number of a log file
ostringstream name;
name << "myfile" << seq_no << ".log";     // e.g., myfile17.log
ofstream logfile{name.str()};             // e.g., open myfile17.log
```

For logfiles, people often want fixed-length file names. In such cases, we can pad the names with the appropriate number of leading zeros:

```
name << "myfile" << setw(6) << setfill('0') << seq_no << ".log";      // e.g., myfile000017.log
```

Yes, external constraints can make I/O messy.

Usually, we initialize an **istringstream** with a string and then read the characters from that string using input operations. Conversely, we typically initialize an **ostringstream** to the empty string and then fill it using output operations.

Drill

[1] Start a program called **Test_output.cpp**. Declare an integer **birth_year** and assign it the year you were born.

[2] Output your **birth_year** in decimal, hexadecimal, and octal form.

[3] Label each value with the name of the base used.

[4] Did you line up your output in columns using the tab character? If not, do it.

[5] Now output your age.

[6] Was there a problem? What happened? Fix your output to decimal.

[7] Go back to 2 and cause your output to show the base for each output.

[8] Try reading as octal, hexadecimal, etc.:

```
cin >> a >>oct >> b >> hex >> c >> d;
cout << a << '\t'<< b << '\t'<< c << '\t'<< d << '\n';
```

Run this code with the input

```
1234 1234 1234 1234
```

Explain the results.

[9] Write some code to print the number **1234567.89** three times, first using **defaultfloat**, then **fixed**, then **scientific** forms. Which output form presents the user with the most accurate representation? Explain why.

[10] Make a simple table including last name, first name, telephone number, and email address for yourself and at least five of your friends. Use **string**s to hold all values, even for the phone numbers. Experiment with different field widths until you are satisfied that the table is well presented.

[11] Defining a data type **Point** that has two coordinate members **x** and **y**. Define **<<** and **>>** for **Point** as discussed in §9.3.1.

[12] Using the code and discussion in §9.3.1, prompt the user to input seven (x,y) pairs. As the data is entered, store it in a **vector<Point>** called **original_points**.

[13] Print the data in **original_points** to see what it looks like.

[14] Open an **ofstream** and output each point to a file named **mydata.txt**. We suggest the **.txt** suffix to make it easier to look at the data with an ordinary text editor if you are using Windows.

[15] Open an **ifstream** for **mydata.txt**. Read the data from **mydata.txt** and store it in a new vector called **processed_points**.

[16] Print the data elements from both `vectors`.
[17] Compare the two `vectors` and print "Something's wrong!" if the number of elements or the values of elements differ.

Review

[1] Why is I/O tricky for a programmer?
[2] What does the notation `<< hex` do?
[3] What are hexadecimal numbers used for in computer science? Why?
[4] Name some of the options you may want to implement for formatting integer output.
[5] What is a manipulator?
[6] What is the default output format for floating-point values?
[7] Explain what `setprecision()` and `setw()` do.
[8] Which of the following manipulators do not "stick": `hex`, `scientific`, `setprecision()`, `setw()`?
[9] In `format()`, how do you specify where an argument is placed on output?
[10] Give two examples where a `stringstream` can be useful.
[11] When would you prefer line-oriented input to type-specific input?
[12] What does `isalnum(c)` do?
[13] When dealing with input and output, how is the variety of devices dealt with in most modern computers?
[14] What, fundamentally, does an `istream` do?
[15] What, fundamentally, does an `ostream` do?
[16] What, fundamentally, is a file?
[17] What is a file format?
[18] Name four different types of devices that can require I/O for a program.
[19] What are the four steps for reading a file?
[20] What are the four steps for writing a file?
[21] Name and define the four stream states.
[22] Discuss how the following input problems can be resolved:
   a. The user typing an out-of-range value
   b. Getting no value (end-of-file)
   c. The user typing something of the wrong type
[23] In what way is input usually harder than output?
[24] In what way is output usually harder than input?
[25] Why do we (often) want to separate input and output from computation?
[26] What are the two most common uses of the `istream` member function `clear()`?
[27] What are the usual function declarations for `<<` and `>>` for a user-defined type `X`?
[28] How do you specify where an argument is inserted into a format string in `format()`?
[29] What is the notation for bases of decimal values in `format()`?
[30] How do you specify the precision of floating-point values in `format()`?

Terms

binary	hexadecimal	octal	getline()
character classification	output formatting	decimal	line-oriented input
defaultfloat	manipulator	scientific	get()
setprecision()	fixed	<<	>>
bad()	good()	ostream	buffer
ifstream	output device	clear()	input device
output operator	close()	input operator	stream state
device driver	iostream	structured file	eof()
istream	terminator	fail()	ofstream
unget()	file	open()	format()
tolower()	setw()	setfill()	isdigit()
isalpha()			

Exercises

[1] Write a program that reads a text file and converts its input to all lowercase, producing a new file.

[2] Write a program that given a file name and a word will output each line that contains that word together with the line number. Hint: getline().

[3] Write a program that removes all vowels from a file (“disemvowels”). For example, Once upon a time! becomes nc pn tm!. Surprisingly often, the result is still readable; try it on your friends.

[4] Write a program called multi_input.cpp that prompts the user to enter several integers in any combination of octal, decimal, or hexadecimal, using the 0 and 0x base prefixes; interprets the numbers correctly; and converts them to decimal form. Then your program should output the values in properly spaced columns like this:

```
0x43    hexadecimal   converts to   67   decimal
0123    octal         converts to   83   decimal
  65    decimal       converts to   65   decimal
```

[5] Write a program that reads strings and for each string outputs the character classification of each character, as defined by the character classification functions presented in §9.10.3. Note that a character can have several classifications (e.g., x is both a letter and an alphanumeric).

[6] Write a program that replaces punctuation with whitespace. Consider . (dot), ; (semicolon), , (comma), ? (question mark), - (dash), ' (single quote) punctuation characters. Don't modify characters within a pair of double quotes ("). For example, “ - don't use the as-if rule.” becomes “ don t use the as if rule ”.

[7] Modify the program from the previous exercise so that it replaces don't with do not, can't with cannot, etc.; leaves hyphens within words intact (so that we get “ do not use the as-if rule ”); and converts all characters to lowercase.

[8] Use the program from the previous exercise to make a sorted list of words. Run the result on a multi-page text file, look at the result, and see if you can improve the program to make a

better list.

[9] Write a function vector<string> split(const string& s) that returns a vector of whitespace-separated substrings from the argument s.

[10] Write a function vector<string> split(const string& s, const string& w) that returns a vector of whitespace-separated substrings from the argument s, where whitespace is defined as "ordinary whitespace" plus the characters in w.

[11] Reverse the order of characters in a text file. For example, asdfghjkl becomes lkjhgfdsa. Warning: There is no really good, portable, and efficient way of reading a file backward.

[12] Reverse the order of words (defined as whitespace-separated strings) in a file. For example, Norwegian Blue parrot becomes parrot Blue Norwegian. Assume that all the strings from the file will fit into memory at once.

[13] Write a program that reads a text file and writes out how many characters of each character classification (§9.10.3) are in the file.

[14] Write a program that reads a file of whitespace-separated numbers and outputs a file of numbers using scientific format and precision 8 in four fields of 20 characters per line.

[15] Write a program to read a file of whitespace-separated numbers and output them in order (lowest value first), one value per line. Write a value only once, and if it occurs more than once write the count of its occurrences on its line. For example, 7 5 5 7 3 117 5 should give

```
3
5  3
7  2
117
```

[16] Write a program that produces the sum of all the numbers in a file of whitespace-separated integers.

[17] Write a program that creates a file of data in the form of the temperature Reading type defined in §9.3.2. For testing, fill the file with at least 50 "temperature readings." Call this program store_temps.cpp and the file it creates raw_temps.txt.

[18] Write a program that reads the data from raw_temps.txt created in exercise 2 into a vector and then calculates the mean and median temperatures in your data set. Call this program temp_stats.cpp.

[19] Modify the store_temps.cpp program from exercise 2 to include a temperature suffix c for Celsius or f for Fahrenheit temperatures. Then modify the temp_stats.cpp program to test each temperature, converting the Celsius readings to Fahrenheit before putting them into the vector.

[20] Write the function print_year() mentioned in §9.9.2.

[21] Define a Roman_int class for holding Roman numerals (as ints) with a << and >>. Provide Roman_int with an as_int() member that returns the int value, so that if r is a Roman_int, we can write cout << "Roman" << r << " equals " << r.as_int() << '\n';.

[22] Make a version of the calculator from Chapter 6 that accepts Roman numerals rather than the usual Arabic ones, for example, XXI + CIV == CXXV.

[23] Write a program that accepts two file names and produces a new file that is the contents of the first file followed by the contents of the second; that is, the program concatenates the two files.

[24] Write a program that takes two files containing sorted whitespace-separated words and merges them, preserving order.

[25] Add a command `from x` to the calculator from Chapter 6 that makes it take input from a file `x`. Add a command `to y` to the calculator that makes it write its output (both standard output and error output) to file `y`. Write a collection of test cases based on ideas from §6.3 and use that to test the calculator. Discuss how you would use these commands for testing.

[26] Write a program that produces the sum of all the whitespace-separated integers in a text file. For example, bears: 17 elephants 9 end should output 26.

Postscript

Much of computing involves moving lots of data from one place to another, for example, copying text from a file to a screen or moving music from a computer onto an MP3 player. Often, some transformation of the data is needed on the way. The iostream library is a way of handling many such tasks where the data can be seen as a sequence (a stream) of values. Input and output can be a surprisingly large part of common programming tasks. This is partly because we (or our programs) need a lot of data and partly because the point where data enters a system is a place where lots of errors can happen. So, we must try to keep our I/O simple and try to minimize the chances that bad data "slips through" into our system.

CC Input and output are messy because our human tastes and conventions have not followed simple-to-state rules and straightforward mathematical laws. As programmers, we are rarely in a position to dictate that our users must depart from their preferences, and when we are, we should typically be less arrogant than to think that we can provide a superior alternative to conventions built up over decades or centuries. Consequently, we must expect, accept, and adapt to a certain messiness of input and output while still trying to keep our programs as simple as possible – but no simpler.

10

A Display Model

The world was black and white then.
It didn´t turn color
until sometime in the 1930s.
– Calvin´s dad

This chapter presents a display model (the output part of GUI), giving examples of use and fundamental notions such as screen coordinates, lines, and color. **Line**, **Lines**, **Polygons**, **Axis**, and **Text** are examples of **Shape**s. A **Shape** is an object in memory that we can display and manipulate on a screen. The next two chapters will explore these classes further, with Chapter 11 focusing on their implementation and Chapter 12 on design issues.

§10.1 Why graphics?
§10.2 A display model
§10.3 A first example
§10.4 Using a GUI library
§10.5 Coordinates
§10.6 **Shape**s
§10.7 Using **Shape** primitives
Graphics headers and **main**; **Axis**; Graphing a function; **Polygons**; **Rectangle**s; Fill; **Text**; **Image**s; And much more
§10.8 Getting the first example to run
Source files; Putting it all together

10.1 Why graphics?

Why do we spend four chapters on graphics and one on GUIs (graphical user interfaces)? After all, this is a book about programming, not a graphics book. There is a huge number of interesting software topics that we don't discuss, and we can at best scratch the surface on the topic of graphics. So, "Why graphics?" Basically, graphics is a subject that allows us to explore several important areas of software design, programming, and programming language facilities:

- *Graphics are useful.* There is much more to programming than graphics and much more to software than code manipulated through a GUI. However, in many areas good graphics are either essential or very important. For example, we wouldn't dream of studying scientific computing, data analysis, or just about any quantitative subject without the ability to graph data. Chapter 13 gives simple (but general) facilities for graphing data. Also consider browsers, games, animation, scientific visualization, phones, and control displays.
- *Graphics are fun.* There are few areas of computing where the effect of a piece of code is as immediately obvious and – when finally free of bugs – as pleasing. We'd be tempted to play with graphics even if it wasn't useful!
- *Graphics provide lots of interesting code to read.* Part of learning to program is to read lots of code to get a feel for what good code is like. Similarly, the way to become a good writer of English involves reading a lot of books, articles, and quality newspapers. Because of the direct correspondence between what we see on the screen and what we write in our programs, simple graphics code is more readable than most kinds of code of similar complexity. This chapter will prove that you can read graphics code after a few minutes of introduction; Chapter 11 will demonstrate how you can write it after another couple of hours.
- *Graphics are a fertile source of design examples.* It is actually hard to design and implement a good graphics and GUI library. Graphics are a very rich source of concrete and practical examples of design decisions and design techniques. Some of the most useful techniques for designing classes, designing functions, separating software into layers (of abstraction), and constructing libraries can be illustrated with a relatively small amount of graphics and GUI code.
- *Graphics provide a good introduction to what is commonly called object-oriented programming and the language features that support it.* Despite rumors to the contrary, object-oriented programming wasn't invented to be able to do graphics (see PPP2.§22.2.4), but it was soon applied to that, and graphics provide some of the most accessible and tangible examples of object-oriented designs.
- *Some of the key graphics concepts are nontrivial.* So they are worth teaching, rather than leaving it to your own initiative (and patience) to seek out information. If we did not show how graphics and GUI were done, you might consider them "magic," thus violating one of the fundamental aims of this book.

10.2 A display model

The iostream library is oriented toward reading and writing streams of characters as they might appear in a list of numeric values or a book. The only direct supports for the notion of graphical position are the newline and tab characters. You can embed notions of color and two-dimensional positions, etc. in a one-dimensional stream of characters. That's what layout (typesetting, "markup") languages such as Troff, TeX, Word, Markup, HTML, and XML (and their associated graphical packages) do. For example:

```
<hr>
<h2>
Organization
</h2>
This list is organized in three parts:
<ul>
    <li><b>Proposals</b>, numbered EPddd, ...</li>
    <li><b>Issues</b>, numbered EIddd, ...</li>
    <li><b>Suggestions</b>, numbered ESddd, ...</li>
</ul>
<p>We try to ...
<p>
```

This is a piece of HTML specifying a header (<h2> ... </h2>), a list (<ul> ... </ul>) with list items (<li> ... </li>), and a paragraph (<p>). We left out most of the actual text because it is irrelevant here. The point is that you can express layout notions in plain text, but the connection between the characters written and what appears on the screen is indirect, governed by a program that interprets those "markup" commands. Such techniques are fundamentally simple and immensely useful (just about everything you read has been produced using them), but they also have their limitations.

In this chapter and the next four, we present an alternative: a notion of graphics and of graphical user interfaces that is directly aimed at a computer screen. The fundamental concepts are inherently graphical (and two-dimensional, adapted to the rectangular area of a computer screen), such as coordinates, lines, rectangles, and circles. The aim from a programming point of view is a direct correspondence between the objects in memory and the images on the screen.

CC

The basic model is as follows: We compose objects with basic objects provided by a graphics system, such as lines. We "attach" these graphics objects to a window object, representing our physical screen. A program that we can think of as the display itself, as "a display engine," as "our graphics library," as "the GUI library," or even (humorously) as "the small gnome sitting behind the screen," then takes the objects we have attached to our window and draw them on the screen:

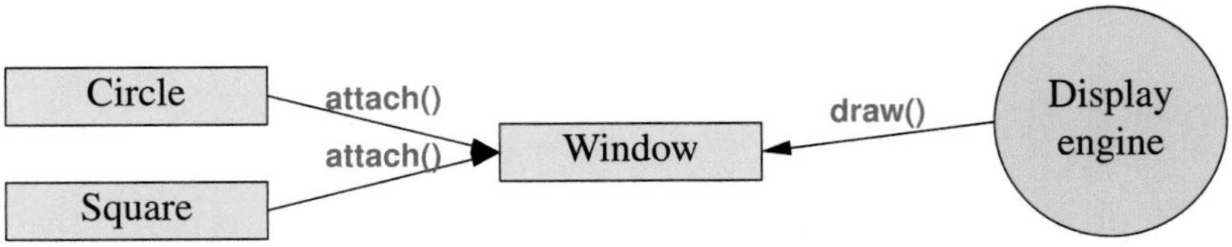

The "display engine" draws lines on the screen, places strings of text on the screen, colors areas of the screen, etc. For simplicity, we'll use the phrase "our GUI library" or even "the system" for the display engine even though our GUI library does much more than just drawing the objects. In the same way that our code lets the GUI library do most of the work for us, the GUI library delegates much of its work to the operating system.

10.3 A first example

Our job is to define classes from which we can make objects that we want to see on the screen. For example, we might want to draw a graph as a series of connected lines. Here is a small program presenting a very simple version of that:

```
#include "Simple_window.h"                // get access to our window library
#include "Graph.h"                        // get access to our graphics library facilities

int main()
{
        using namespace Graph_lib;                    // our graphics facilities are in Graph_lib

        Application app;                              // start a Graphics/GUI application

        Point tl {900,500};                           // to become top left corner of window

        Simple_window win {tl,600,400,"Canvas"};      // make a simple window

        Polygon poly;                                 // make a shape (a polygon)
        poly.add(Point{300,200});                     // add a point
        poly.add(Point{350,100});                     // add another point
        poly.add(Point{400,200});                     // add a third point
        poly.set_color(Color::red);                   // adjust properties of poly

        win.attach (poly);                            // connect poly to the window

        win.wait_for_button();                        // give control to the display engine
}
```

When we run this program, the screen looks something like this:

AA In the background of our window, we see a laptop screen (cleaned up for the occasion). For people who are curious about irrelevant details, we can tell you that my background is a famous painting by the Danish painter Peder Severin Krøyer. The ladies are Anna Ancher and Marie Krøyer, both well-known painters. If you look carefully, you'll notice that we have the Microsoft C++ compiler running, but we could just as well have used some other compiler (such as GCC or Clang). Let's go through the program line by line to see what was done.

First we #include our graphics interface library:

```
#include "Simple_window.h"      // get access to our window library
#include "Graph.h"              // get access to our graphics library facilities
```

Why don't we use a module Graph_lib (§7.7.1)? One reason is at the time of writing not all implementations are up to using modules for this relatively complex task. For example, the system we use to implement our graphics library, Qt, exports its facilities using header files (§7.7.2). Another reason is that there is so much C++ code "out there" using header files (§7.7.2) that we need to show a realistic example somewhere.

Then, in main(), we start by telling the compiler that our graphics facilities are to be found in Graph_lib:

```
using namespace Graph_lib;                 // our graphics facilities are in Graph_lib
```

Then we start our display engine (§10.2):

```
Application app;                           // start a Graphics/GUI application
```

Then, we define a point that we will use as the top left corner of our window:

```
Point tl {900,500};                        // to become top left corner of window
```

Next, we create a window on the screen:

```
Simple_window win {tl,600,400,"Canvas"};   // make a simple window
```

We use a class called Simple_window to represent a window in our Graph_lib interface library . The name of this particular Simple_window is win; that is, win is a variable of class Simple_window. The initializer list for win starts with the point to be used as the top left corner, tl, followed by 600 and 400. Those are the width and height, respectively, of the window, as displayed on the screen, measured in pixels. We'll explain in more detail later, but the main point here is that we specify a rectangle by giving its width and height. The string "Canvas" is used to label the window. If you look, you can see the word Canvas in the top left corner of the window's frame.

Next, we put an object in the window:

```
Polygon poly;                     // make a shape (a polygon)
poly.add(Point{300,200});         // add a point
poly.add(Point{350,100});         // add another point
poly.add(Point{400,200});         // add a third point
```

We define a polygon, poly, and then add points to it. In our graphics library, a Polygon starts empty and we can add as many points to it as we like. Since we added three points, we get a triangle. A point is simply a pair of values giving the x and y (horizontal and vertical) coordinates within a window.

Just to show off, we then color the lines of our polygon red:

```
poly.set_color(Color::red);              // adjust properties of poly
```

Finally, we attach poly to our window, win:

```
win.attach(poly);                    // connect poly to the window
```

If the program wasn't so fast, you would notice that so far nothing had happened to the screen: nothing at all. We created a window (an object of class Simple_window, to be precise), created a polygon (called poly), painted that polygon red (Color::red), and attached it to the window (called win), but we have not yet asked for that window to be displayed on the screen. That's done by the final line of the program:

```
win.wait_for_button();               // give control to the display engine
```

To get a GUI system to display objects on the screen, you have to give control to "the system." Our wait_for_button() does that, and it also waits for you to "press" ("click") the "Next" button in the top right corner of our Simple_window before proceeding. This gives you a chance to look at the window before the program finishes and the window disappears. When you press the button, the program terminates, closing the window.

For the rest of the Graphics-and-GUI chapters, we eliminate the distractions around our window and just show the window itself:

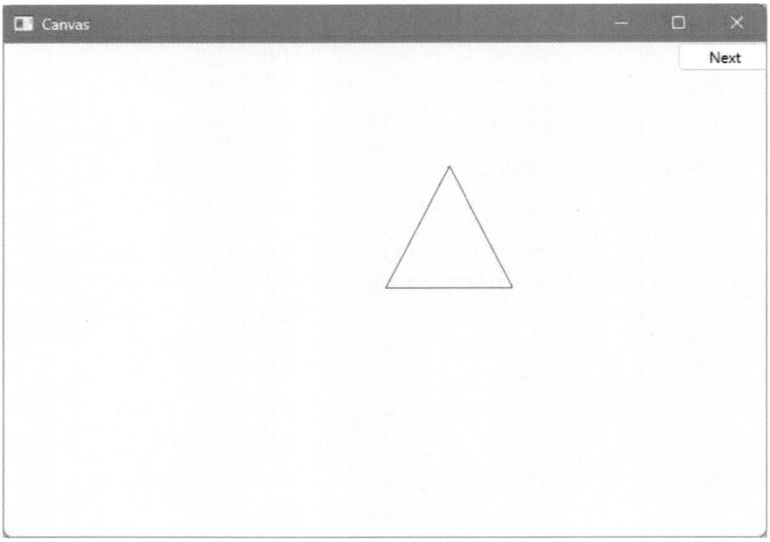

You'll notice that we "cheated" a bit. Where did that button labeled "Next" come from? We built it into our Simple_window class. In Chapter 14, we'll move from Simple_window to "plain" Window, which has no potentially spurious facilities built in, and show how we can write our own code to control interaction with a window.

For the next three chapters, we'll simply use that "Next" button to move from one "display" to the next when we want to display information in stages ("frame by frame").

The pictures in this and the following chapters were produced on a Microsoft Windows system, so you get the usual three buttons on the top right "for free." This can be useful: if your program gets in a real mess (as it surely will sometimes during debugging), you can kill it by hitting the X button. When you run your program on another system, a different frame will be added to fit that system's conventions. Our only contribution to the frame is the label (here, Canvas).

10.4 Using a GUI library

In this book, we will not use the operating system's graphical and GUI (graphical user interface) facilities directly. Doing so would limit our programs to run on a single operating system and would also force us to deal directly with a lot of messy details. As with text I/O, we'll use a library to smooth over operating system differences, I/O device variations, etc. and to simplify our code. Unfortunately, C++ does not provide a standard GUI library the way it provides the standard stream I/O library, so we use one of the many available C++ GUI libraries. So as not to tie you directly into one of those GUI libraries, and to save you from hitting the full complexity of a GUI library all at once, we use a set of simple interface classes that can be implemented in a couple of hundred lines of code for just about any GUI library. CC

The GUI toolkit that we are using (indirectly for now) is called Qt from www.qt.io. Our code is portable wherever Qt is available (Windows, Mac, Linux, many embedded systems, phones, browsers, etc.). Our interface classes can also be re-implemented using other toolkits, so code using them is potentially even more portable.

The programming model presented by our interface classes is far simpler than what common toolkits offer. For example, our complete graphics and GUI interface library is about 600 lines of C++ code, whereas the Qt documentation is thousands of pages. You can download Qt from www.qt.io, but we don't recommend you do that just yet. You can do without that level of detail for a while. The general ideas presented in Chapter 10 – Chapter 14 can be used with any popular GUI toolkit. We will of course explain how our interface classes map to Qt so that you will (eventually) see how you can use that (and similar toolkits) directly, if necessary.

We can illustrate the parts of our "graphics world" like this: CC

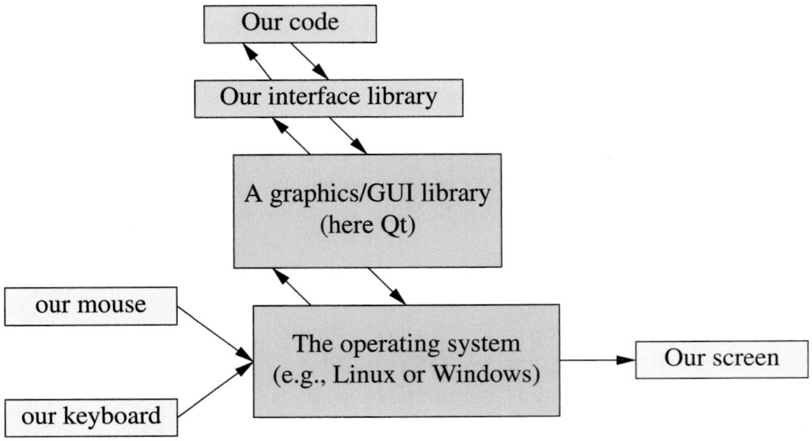

Our interface classes provide a simple and user-extensible basic notion of two-dimensional shapes with limited support for the use of color. To drive that, we present a simple notion of GUI based on "callback" functions triggered by the use of user-defined buttons, etc. on the screen (Chapter 14).

10.5 Coordinates

CC A computer screen is a rectangular area composed of pixels. A pixel is a tiny spot that can be given some color. The most common way of modeling a screen in a program is as a rectangle of pixels. Each pixel is identified by an *x* (horizontal) coordinate and a *y* (vertical) coordinate. The *x* coordinates start with 0, indicating the leftmost pixel, and increase (toward the right) to the rightmost pixel. The *y* coordinates start with 0, indicating the topmost pixel, and increase (toward the bottom) to the lowest pixel:

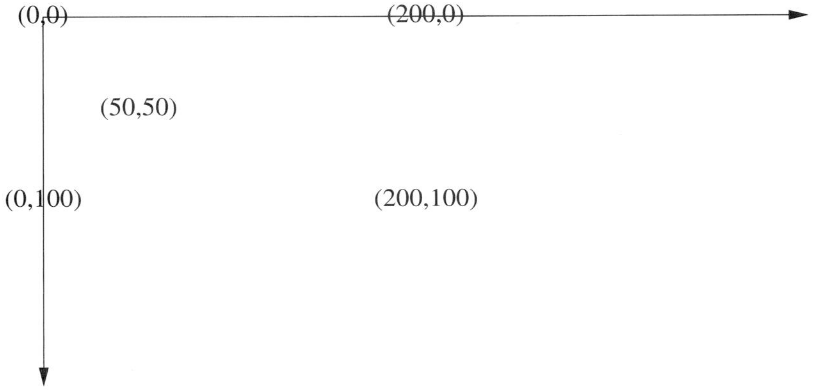

XX Please note that *y* coordinates "grow downward." Mathematicians, in particular, find this odd, but screens (and windows) come in many sizes, and the top left point is about all that they have in common.

The number of pixels available depends on the screen and varies a lot (e.g., 600-by-1024, 1280-by-1024, 1920-by-1080, 2412-by-1080, and 2880-by-1920).

In the context of interacting with a computer using a screen, a window is a rectangular region of the screen devoted to some specific purpose and controlled by a program. A window is addressed exactly like a screen. Basically, we see a window as a small screen. For example, when we said

```
Simple_window win {tl,600,400,"Canvas"};
```

we requested a rectangular area 600 pixels wide and 400 pixels high that we can address as 0–599 (left to right) and 0–399 (top to bottom). The area of a window that you can draw on is commonly referred to as a *canvas*. The 600-by-400 area refers to "the inside" of the window, that is, the area inside the system-provided frame; it does not include the space the system uses for the title bar, quit button, etc.

10.6 Shapes

Our basic toolbox for drawing on the screen consists of about a dozen classes, including:

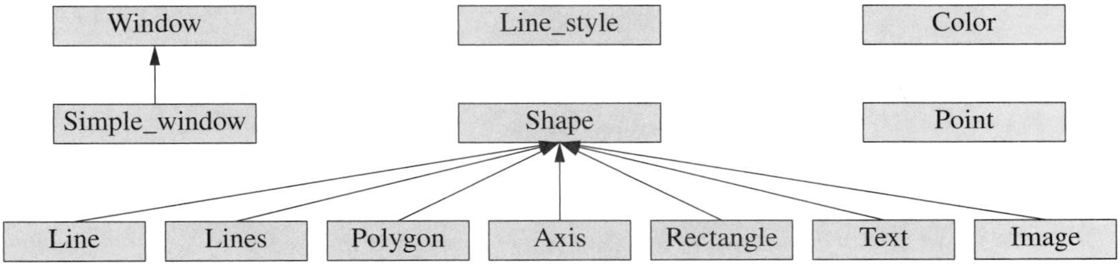

An arrow indicates that the class pointing can be used where the class pointed to is required. For example, a **Polygon** can be used where a **Shape** is required; that is, a **Polygon** is a kind of **Shape**.

We will start out presenting and using

- **Simple_window**, **Window**
- **Shape**, **Text**, **Polygon**, **Line**, **Lines**, **Rectangle**, **Function**, **Circle**, **Ellipse**, etc.
- **Color**, **Line_style**, **Point**
- **Axis**

Later (Chapter 14), we'll add GUI (user interaction) classes:

- **Button**, **In_box**, **Menu**, etc.

We could easily add many more classes (for some definition of "easy"), such as

- **Spline**, **Grid**, **Block_chart**, **Pie_chart**, etc.

However, defining or describing a complete GUI framework with all its facilities is beyond the scope of this book.

10.7 Using Shape primitives

In this section, we will walk you through some of the primitive facilities of our graphics library: **Simple_window**, **Window**, **Shape**, **Text**, **Polygon**, **Line**, **Lines**, **Rectangle**, **Color**, **Line_style**, **Point**, **Axis**. The aim is to give you a broad view of what you can do with those facilities, but not yet a detailed understanding of any of those classes. In the next chapters, we explore the design of each.

We will now walk through a simple program, explaining the code line by line and showing the effect of each on the screen. When you run the program, you'll see how the image changes as we add shapes to the window and modify existing shapes. Basically, we are "animating" the progress through the code by looking at the program as it is executed.

10.7.1 Axis

An almost blank window isn't very interesting, so we'd better add some information. What would we like to display? Just to remind you that graphics is not all fun and games, we will start with something serious and somewhat complicated, an axis. A graph without axes is usually a disgrace. You just don't know what the data represents without axes. Maybe you explained it all in some accompanying text, but it is far safer to add axes; people often don't read the explanation and often a nice graphical representation gets separated from its original context. So, a graph needs axes:

```
Axis xa {Axis::x, Point{20,300}, 280, 10, "x axis"};  // make an Axis
        // an Axis is a kind of Shape
        // Axis::x means horizontal
        // starting at (20,300)
        // 280 pixels long
        // with 10 "notches"
        // label the axis "x axis"

win.attach(xa);                   // attach xa to the window, win
win.set_label("X axis");          // re-label the window
win.wait_for_button();            // display!
```

The sequence of actions is: make the axis object, add it to the window, and finally display it:

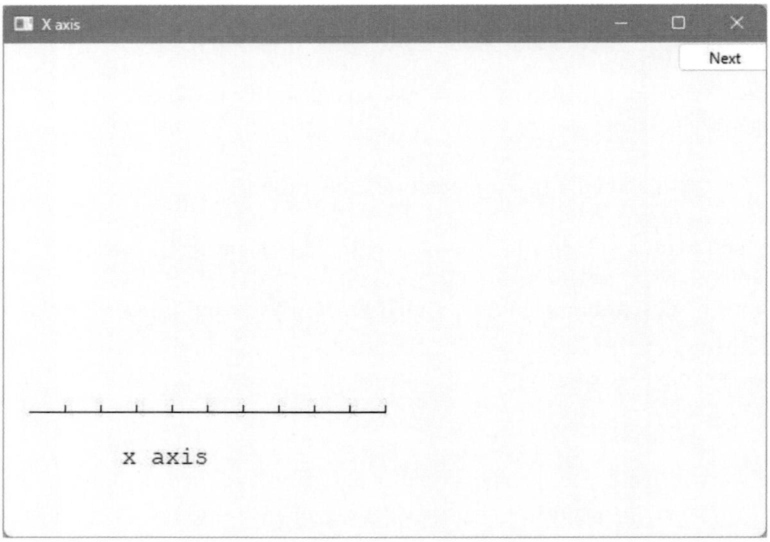

We can see that an **Axis::x** is a horizontal line. We see the required number of "notches" (10) and the label "x axis." Usually, the label will explain what the axis and the notches represent. Naturally, we chose to place the *x* axis somewhere near the bottom of the window. In real life, we'd represent the height and width by symbolic constants so that we could refer to "just above the bottom" as something like **y_max−bottom_margin** rather than by a "magic constant," such as **300** (§3.3.1, §13.6.3).

To help identify our output we relabeled the screen to **X axis** using **Window**'s member function **set_label()**.

Now, let's add a *y* axis:

```
Axis ya {Axis::y, Point{20,300}, 280, 10, "y axis"};
ya.set_color(Color::cyan);                // choose a color for the y axis
ya.label.set_color(Color::dark_red);      // choose a color for the text
```

```
win.attach(ya);
win.set_label("Y axis");
win.wait_for_button();                    // display!
```

Just to show off some facilities, we colored our *y* axis cyan and our label dark red.

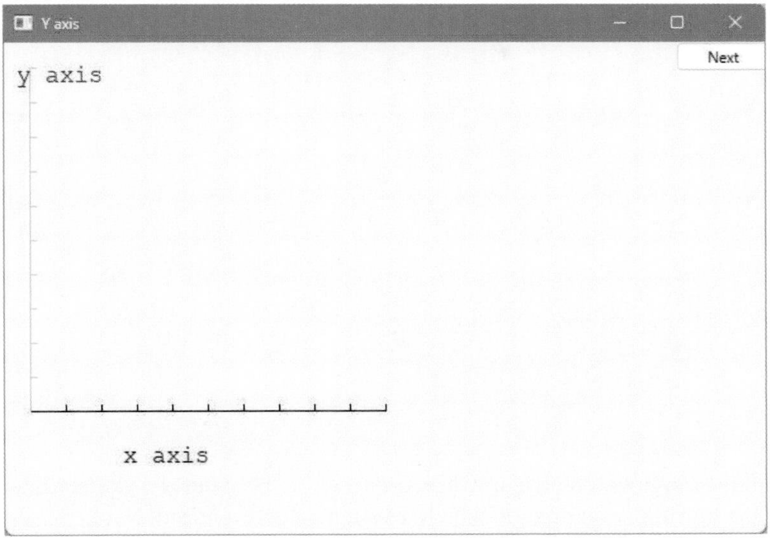

We don't actually think that it is a good idea to use different colors for *x* and *y* axes. We just wanted to show you how you can set the color of a shape and of individual elements of a shape. Using lots of color is not necessarily a good idea. In particular, novices often use color with more enthusiasm than taste.

10.7.2 Graphing a function

What next? We now have a window with axes, so it seems a good idea to graph a function. We make a shape representing a sine function and attach it:

```
double dsin(double d) { return sin(d); }  // chose the right sin() (§13.3)

Function sine {dsin,0,100,Point{20,150},1000,50,50};     // sine curve
        // plot sin() in the range [0:100) with (0,0) at (20,150)
        // using 1000 points; scale x values *50, scale y values *50

win.attach(sine);
win.set_label("Sine");
win.wait_for_button();
```

Here, the Function named sine will draw a sine curve using the standard-library function sin(double) to generate values. We explain details about how to graph functions in §13.3. For now, just note that to graph a function we have to say where it starts (a **Point**) and for what set of input values we want to see it (a range), and we need to give some information about how to squeeze that information into our window (scaling):

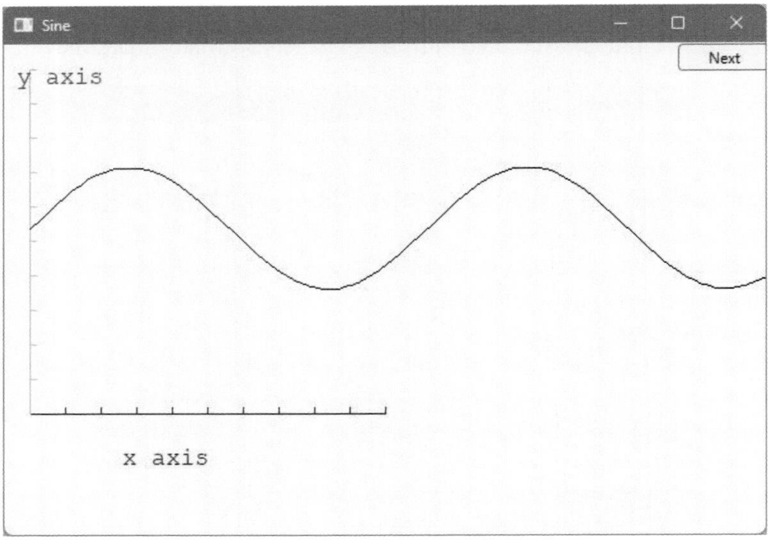

Note how the curve simply stops when it hits the edge of the window. Points drawn outside our window rectangle are simply ignored by the GUI system and never seen.

10.7.3 Polygons

A graphed function is an example of data presentation. We'll see much more of that in Chapter 11. However, we can also draw different kinds of objects in a window: geometric shapes. We use geometric shapes for graphical illustrations, to indicate user interaction elements (such as buttons), and generally to make our presentations more interesting. A **Polygon** is characterized by a sequence of points, which the **Polygon** class connects by lines. The first line connects the first point to the second, the second line connects the second point to the third, and the last line connects the last point to the first:

```
sine.set_color(Color::blue);          // we changed our mind about sine's color

Polygon poly;                         // a polygon; a Polygon is a kind of Shape
poly.add(Point{300,200});             // three points make a triangle
poly.add(Point{350,100});
poly.add(Point{400,200});
poly.set_color(Color::red);
```

```
win.attach(poly);
win.set_label("Triangle");
win.wait_for_button();
```

This time we change the color of the sine curve (**sine**) just to show how. Then, we add a triangle, just as in our first example from §10.3, as an example of a polygon. Again, we set a color, and finally, we set a style. The lines of a **Polygon** have a "style." By default, that is solid, but we can also make those lines dashed, dotted, etc. as needed (§11.5). We get

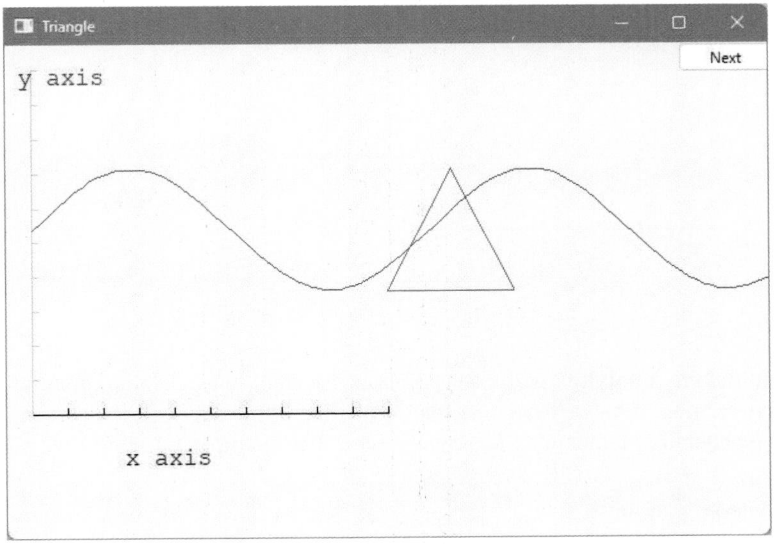

10.7.4 Rectangles

A screen is a rectangle, a window is a rectangle, and a piece of paper is a rectangle. In fact, an awful lot of the shapes in our modern world are rectangles (or at least rectangles with rounded corners). There is a reason for this: a rectangle is the simplest shape to deal with. For example, it's easy to describe (top left corner plus width plus height, or top left corner plus bottom right corner, or whatever), it's easy to tell whether a point is inside a rectangle or outside it, and it's easy to get hardware to draw a rectangle of pixels fast. CC

So, most higher-level graphics libraries deal better with rectangles than with other closed shapes. Consequently, we provide **Rectangle** as a class separate from the **Polygon** class. A **Rectangle** is characterized by its top left corner plus a width and height:

```
Rectangle r {Point{200,200}, 100, 50};          // top left corner, width, height

win.attach(r);
win.set_label("Rectangle");
win.wait_for_button();
```

From that, we get

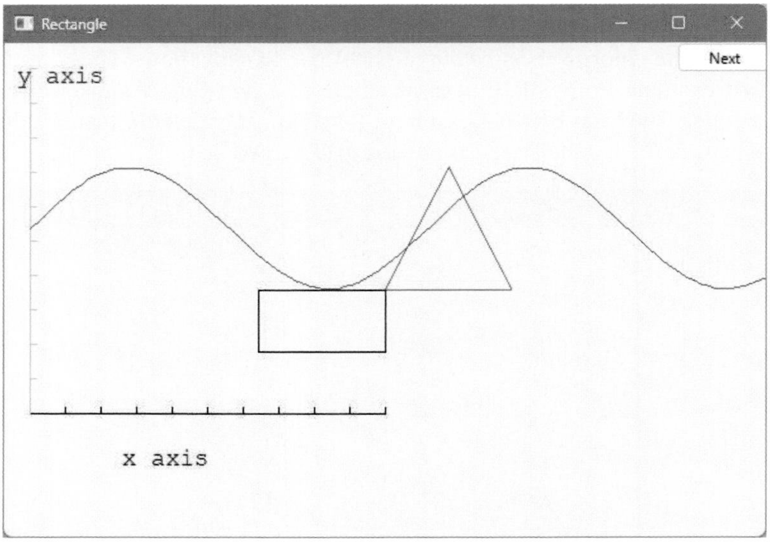

Please note that making a polyline with four points in the right places is not enough to make a Rectangle. It is easy to make a Closed_polyline that looks like a Rectangle on the screen (you can even make an Open_polyline that looks just like a Rectangle). For example:

```
Closed_polyline poly_rect;
poly_rect.add(Point{100,50});
poly_rect.add(Point{200,50});
poly_rect.add(Point{200,100});
poly_rect.add(Point{100,100});

win.set_label("Polyline");
win.attach(poly_rect);
win.wait_for_button();
```

That polygon looks exactly – to the last pixel – like a rectangle:

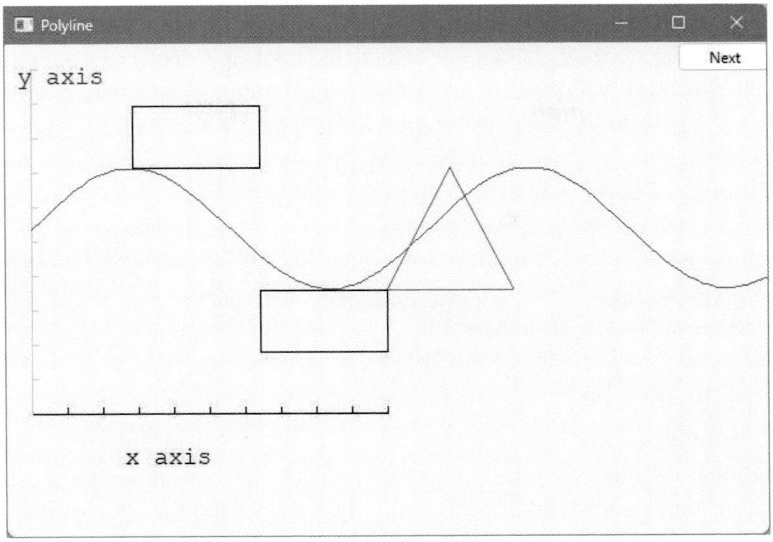

However, it only looks like a **Rectangle**. No **Rectangle** has four points:

```
poly_rect.add(Point{50,75});
win.set_label("Polyline 2");
win.wait_for_button();
```

No rectangle has five points:

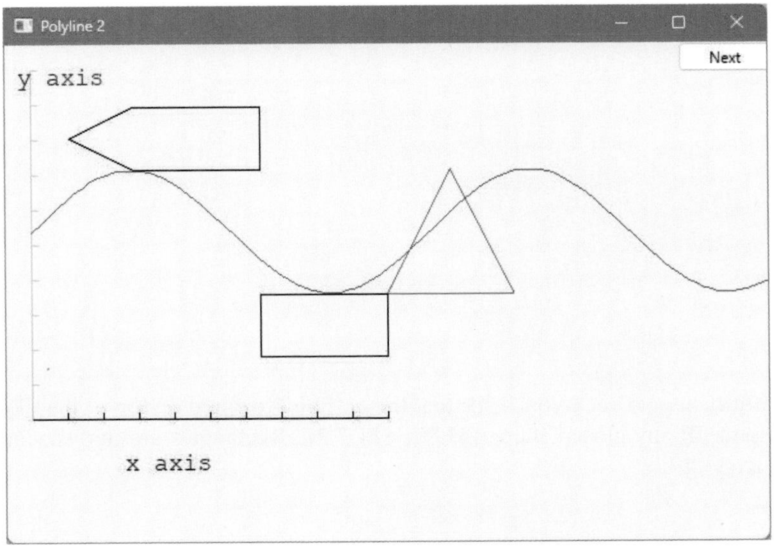

CC In fact, the *image* on the screen of the 4-point **poly_rect** *is* a rectangle. However, the **poly_rect** object in memory is not a **Rectangle** and it does not "know" anything about rectangles.

It is important for our reasoning about our code that a **Rectangle** doesn't just happen to look like a rectangle on the screen; it maintains the fundamental guarantees of a rectangle (as we know them from geometry). We write code that depends on a **Rectangle** really being a rectangle on the screen and staying that way.

10.7.5 Fill

We have been drawing our shapes as outlines. We can also "fill" a rectangle with color:

```
r.set_fill_color(Color::yellow);        // color the inside of the rectangle
poly.set_style(Line_style(Line_style::dash,4));
poly_rect.set_style(Line_style(Line_style::dash,2));
poly_rect.set_fill_color(Color::green);
win.set_label("Fill");
win.wait_for_button();
```

We also decided that we didn't like the line style of our triangle (**poly**), so we set its line style to "fat (thickness four times normal) dashed." Similarly, we changed the style of **poly_rect** (now no longer looking like a rectangle) and filled it with green:

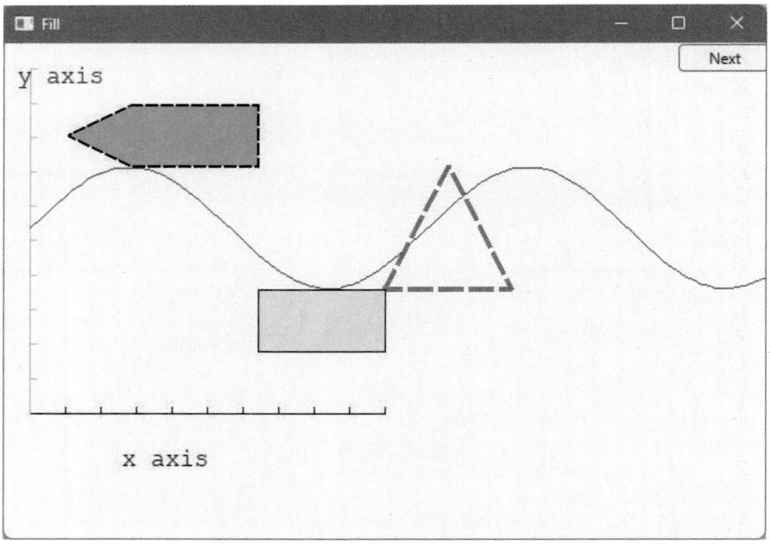

If you look carefully at **poly_rect**, you'll see that the outline is printed on top of the fill.

It is possible to fill any closed shape (§11.7, §11.7.2). Rectangles are just special in how easy (and fast) they are to fill.

10.7.6 Text

CC

Finally, no system for drawing is complete without a simple way of writing text – drawing each character as a set of lines just doesn't cut it. We label the window itself, and axes can have labels, but we can also place text anywhere using a **Text** object:

```
Text t {Point{150,150}, "Hello, graphical world!"};
win.attach(t);
win.set_label("Text");
win.wait_for_button();
```

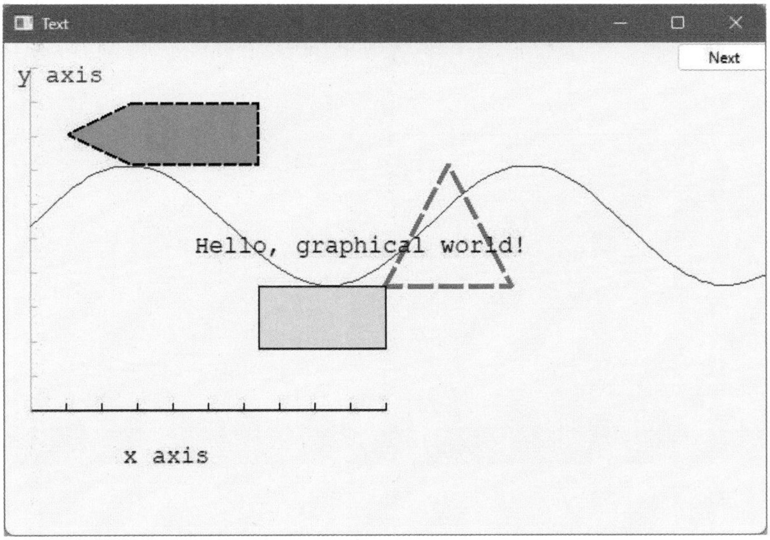

From the primitive graphics elements you see in this window, you can build displays of just about any complexity and subtlety. For now, just note a peculiarity of the code in this chapter: there are no loops, no selection statements, and all data was "hardwired" in. The output was just composed of primitives in the simplest possible way. Once we start composing these primitives, using data and algorithms, things will start to get interesting.

We have seen how we can control the color of text: the label of an **Axis** (§10.7.1) is simply a **Text** object. In addition, we can choose a font and set the size of the characters:

```
t.set_font(Font::times_bold);
t.set_font_size(20);
win.set_label("Bold text");
win.wait_for_button();
```

We enlarged the characters of the **Text** string **Hello, graphical world!** to point size 20 and chose the Times font in bold:

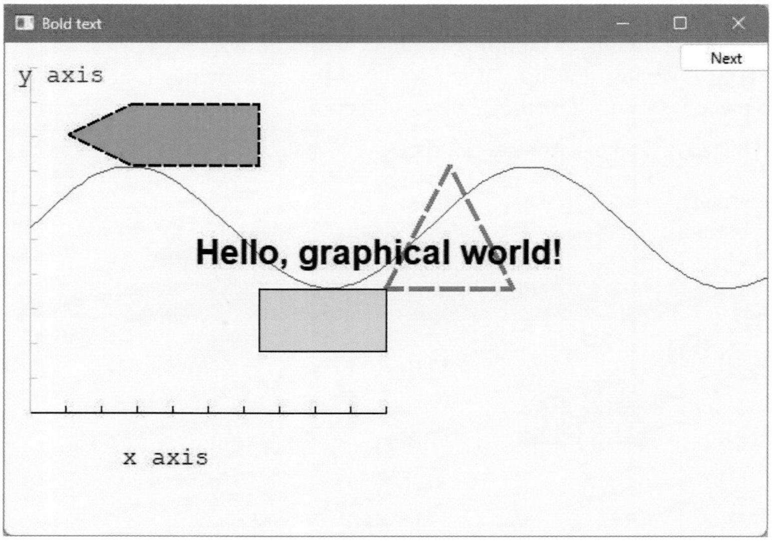

10.7.7 Images

We can also load images from files:

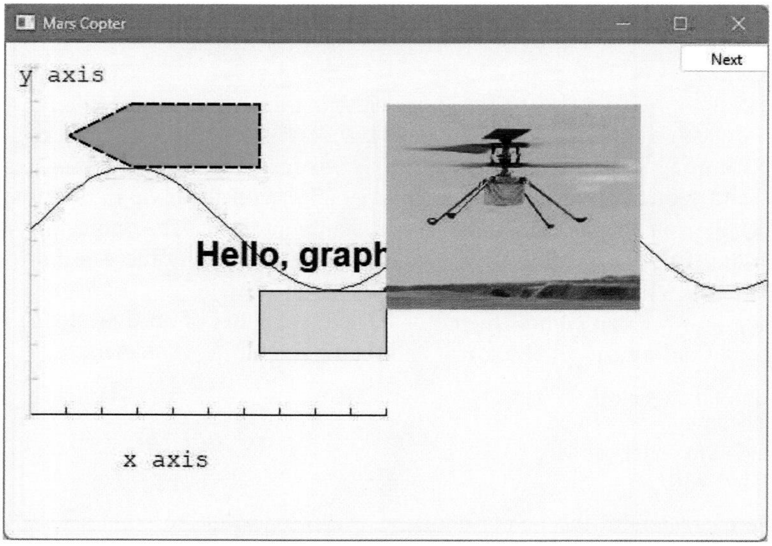

This was done by:

```
Image copter {Point{100,50},"mars_copter.jpg"};
win.attach(copter);
win.set_label("Mars copter");
win.wait_for_button();
```

That photo is relatively large, and we placed it right on top of our text and shapes. So, to clean up our window a bit, let us move it a bit out of the way:

```
copter.move(100,250);
win.set_label("Move");
win.wait_for_button();
```

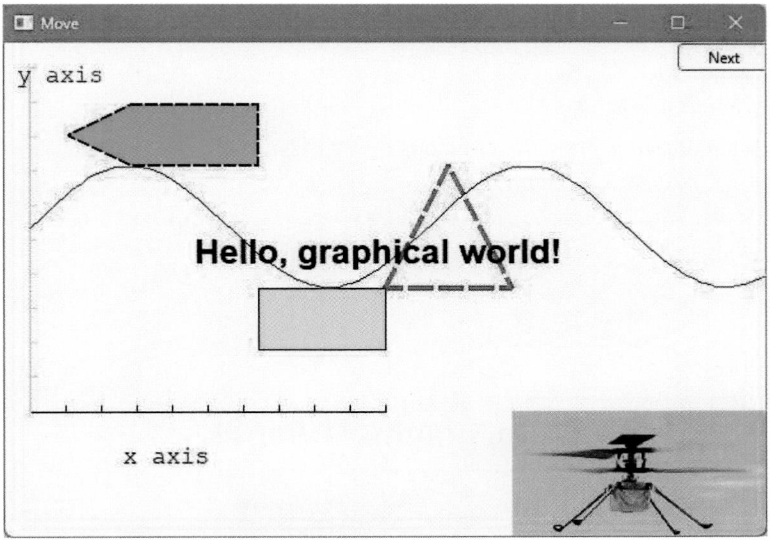

Note how the parts of the photo that didn't fit in the window are simply not represented. What would have appeared outside the window is "clipped" away.

10.7.8 And much more

And here, without further comment, is some more code:

```
Circle c {Point{100,200},50};

Ellipse e {Point{100,200}, 75,25};
e.set_color(Color::dark_red);

Mark m {Point{100,200},'x'};
m.set_color(Color::red);
```

```
ostringstream oss;
oss << "screen size: " << x_max() << "*" << y_max()
        << "; window size: " << win.x_max() << "*" << win.y_max();
Text sizes {Point{100,20},oss.str()};

Image scan{ Point{275,225},"scandinavia.jfif" };
scan.scale(150,200);

win.attach(c);
win.attach(m);
win.attach(e);

win.attach(sizes);
win.attach(scan);
win.set_label("Final!");
win.wait_for_button();
```

Can you guess what this code does? Is it obvious?

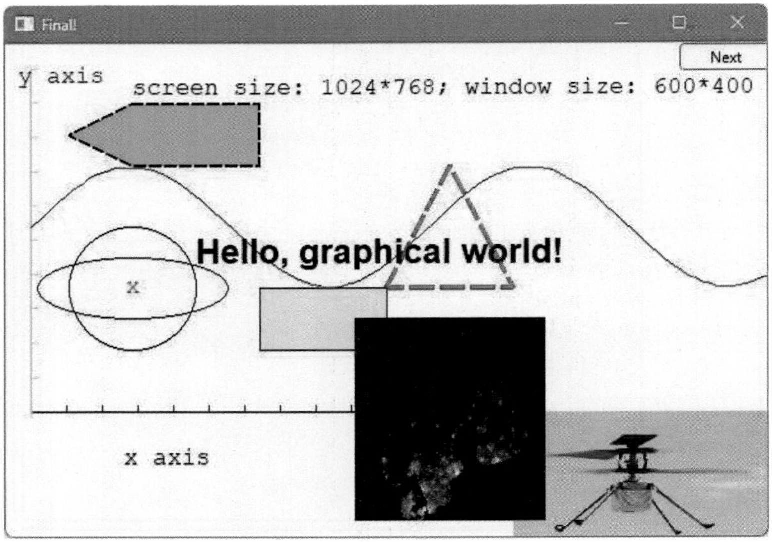

AA The connection between the code and what appears on the screen is direct. If you don't yet see how that code caused that output, it soon will become clear.

Note the way we used an **ostringstream** (§9.11) to format the text object displaying sizes. The string composed in **oss** is referred to as **oss.str()**.

10.8 Getting the first example to run

We have seen how to make a window and how to draw various shapes in it. In the following chapters, we'll see how those **Shape** classes are defined and show more ways of using them.

Getting this program to run requires more than the programs we have presented so far. In addition to our code in **main()**, we need to get the interface library code compiled and linked to our code, and finally, nothing will run unless the GUI system we use is installed and correctly linked to ours. Previous editions of the PPP code used the FLTK library; the current version uses the more modern Qt library. Both work over a wide range of systems.

One way of looking at the program is that it has four distinct parts:

- Our program code (**main()**, etc.)
- Our interface library (**Window**, **Shape**, **Polygon**, etc.)
- The Qt library
- The C++ standard library

Indirectly, we also use the operating system.

10.8.1 Source files

Our graphics and GUI interface library consists of just five header files:

- Headers meant for users (aka "user-facing headers"):
  - **Point.h**
  - **Window.h**
  - **Simple_window.h**
  - **Graph.h**
  - **GUI.h**
- To implement the facilities offered by those headers, a few more files are used. Implementation headers:
  - Qt headers
  - **GUI_private.h**
  - **Image_private.h**
  - **Colormap.h**
- Code files:
  - **Window.cpp**
  - **Graph.cpp**
  - **GUI.cpp**
  - **GUI_private.cpp**
  - **Image_private.cpp**
  - **Colormap.cpp**
  - Qt code

We can represent the user-facing headers like this:

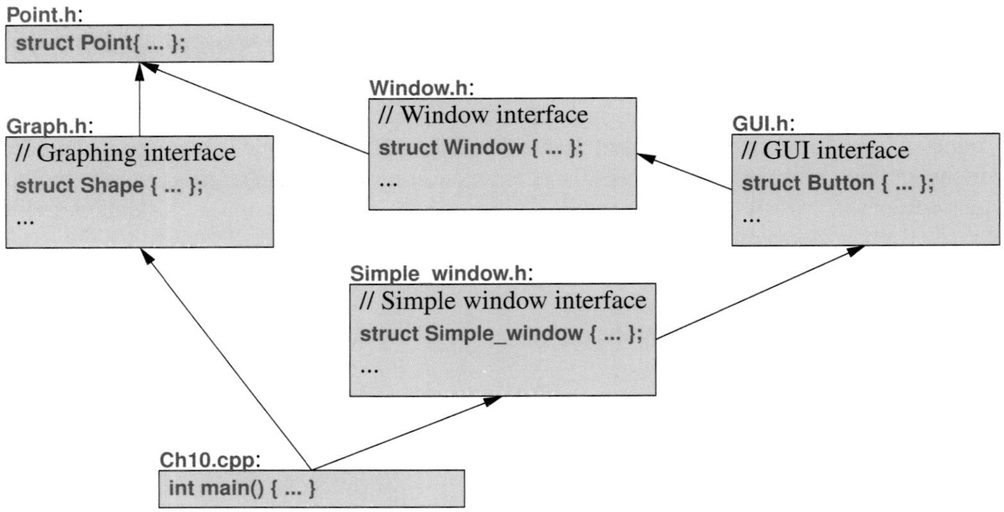

An arrow represents a **#include**. Until Chapter 14 you can ignore the GUI header.

A code file implementing a user-facing header **#includes** that header plus any headers needed for its code. For example, we can represent **Window.cpp** like this

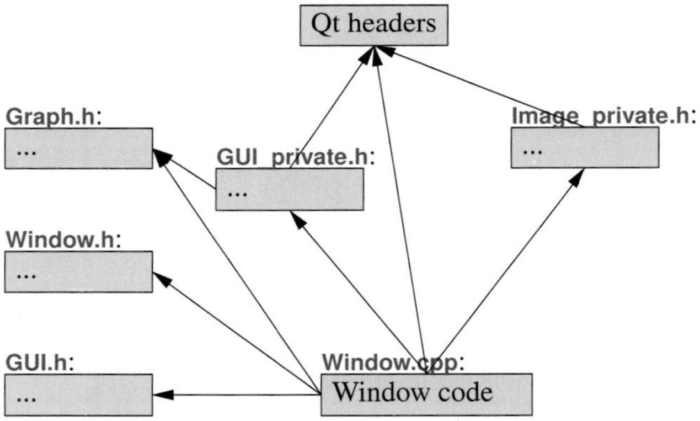

In this way, we use files to separate what a user sees (the user-facing headers, such as **Window.h**) and what the implementation of such headers uses (e.g., Qt headers and **GUI_private.h**. In modules, that distinction is controlled by **export** specifiers (§7.7.1).

This "mess of files" is *tiny* compared to industrial systems, where many thousands of files are common, not uncommonly tens of thousands of files. That's one reason we prefer modules; they help organize code. Fortunately, we don't have to think about more than a few files at a time to get work done. This is what we have done here: the many files of the operating system, the C++ standard library, and Qt are invisible to us as users of our graphics interface library.

10.8.2 Putting it all together

Different systems (such as Windows, Mac, and Linux) have different ways of installing a library (such as Qt) and compiling and linking a program (such as ours). Worse, such set-up procedures change over time. Therefore, we place the instructions on the Web: www.stroustrup.com/programming.html and try to keep those descriptions up to date. When setting up your first project, be careful and be prepared for possible frustration. Setting up a relatively complex system like this can be very simple, but there are usually "things" that are not obvious to a novice. If you are part of a course, your teacher or teaching assistant can help, and might even have found an easier way to get you started. In any case, installing a new system or library is exactly where a more experienced person can be of significant help.

Drill

The drill is the graphical equivalent to the "Hello, World!" program. Its purpose is to get you acquainted with the simplest graphical output tools.

[1] Get an empty Simple_window with the size 600 by 400 and a label My window compiled, linked, and run. Note that you have to link the Qt library, #include Graph.h and Simple_window.h in your code, and compile and link Graph.cpp and Window.cpp into your program.

[2] Now add the examples from §10.7 one by one, testing between each added subsection example.

[3] Go through and make one minor change (e.g., in color, in location, or in number of points) to each of the subsection examples.

Review

[1] Why do we use graphics?
[2] When do we try not to use graphics?
[3] Why is graphics interesting for a programmer?
[4] What is a window?
[5] In which namespace do we keep our graphics interface classes (our graphics library)?
[6] What header files do you need to do basic graphics using our graphics library?
[7] What is the simplest window to use?
[8] What is the minimal window?
[9] What's a window label?
[10] How do you label a window?
[11] How do screen coordinates work? Window coordinates? Mathematical coordinates?
[12] What are examples of simple "shapes" that we can display?
[13] What command attaches a shape to a window?
[14] Which basic shape would you use to draw a hexagon?
[15] How do you write text somewhere in a window?
[16] How would you put a photo of your best friend in a window (using a program you wrote yourself)?

[17] You made a Window object, but nothing appears on your screen. What are some possible reasons for that?

[18] What library do we use to implement our graphics/GUI interface library? Why don't we use the operating system directly?

Terms

color	graphic	JPEG	coordinates
GUI	line style	display	PPP_graphics
library	software layer	fill	Shape
color	HTML	window	Qt
image	XML	Simple_window	

Exercises

We recommend that you use Simple_window for these exercises.

[1] Draw a rectangle as a Rectangle and as a Polygon. Make the lines of the Polygon red and the lines of the Rectangle blue.

[2] Draw a 100-by-30 Rectangle and place the text "Howdy!" inside it.

[3] Draw your initials 150 pixels high. Use a thick line. Draw each initial in a different color.

[4] Draw a 3-by-3 tic-tac-toe board of alternating white and red squares.

[5] Draw a red 1/4-inch frame around a rectangle that is three-quarters the height of your screen and two-thirds the width.

[6] What happens when you draw a Shape that doesn't fit inside its window? What happens when you draw a Window that doesn't fit on your screen? Write two programs that illustrate these two phenomena.

[7] Draw a two-dimensional house seen from the front, the way a child would: with a door, two windows, and a roof with a chimney. Feel free to add details; maybe have "smoke" come out of the chimney.

[8] Draw the Olympic five rings. If you can't remember the colors, look them up.

[9] Display an image on the screen, e.g., a photo of a friend. Label the image both with a title on the window and with a caption in the window.

[10] Draw the source file diagram from §10.8.1.

[11] Draw a series of regular polygons, one inside the other. The innermost should be an equilateral triangle, enclosed by a square, enclosed by a pentagon, etc. For the mathematically adept only: let all the points of each N-polygon touch sides of the (N+1)-polygon. Hint: The trigonometric functions are found in <cmath> and module std (PPP2.§24.8).

[12] A superellipse is a two-dimensional shape defined by the equation

$$\left|\frac{x}{a}\right|^m + \left|\frac{y}{b}\right|^n = 1; \text{ where } m > 0 \text{ and } n > 0.$$

Look up *superellipse* on the Web to get a better idea of what such shapes look like. Write a program that draws "starlike" patterns by connecting points on a superellipse.

Take a, b, m, n, and N as arguments. Select N points on the superellipse defined by a, b, m, and n. Make the points equally spaced for some definition of "equal." Connect each of those N points to one or more other points (if you like you can make the number of points to which to connect a point another argument or just use N–1, i.e., all the other points).

[13] Find a way to add color to the lines from the previous exercise. Make some lines one color and other lines another color or other colors.

Postscript

The ideal for program design is to have our concepts directly represented as entities in our program. So, we often represent ideas by classes, real-world entities by objects of classes, and actions and computations by functions. Graphics is a domain where this idea has an obvious application. We have concepts, such as circles and polygons, and we represent them in our program as class Circle and class Polygon. Where graphics is unusual is that when writing a graphics program, we also have the opportunity to see objects of those classes on the screen; that is, the state of our program is directly represented for us to observe – in most applications we are not that lucky. This direct correspondence between ideas, code, and output is what makes graphics programming so attractive. Please do remember, though, that graphics/GUI is just an illustration of the general idea of using classes to directly represent concepts in code. That idea is far more general and useful: just about anything we can think of can be represented in code as a class, an object of a class, or a set of classes. AA

11

Graphics Classes

A language that doesn't
change the way you think
isn't worth learning.
– Traditional

Chapter 10 gave an idea of what we could do in terms of graphics using a set of simple interface classes, and how we can do it. This chapter presents many of the classes offered. The focus here is on the design, use, and implementation of individual interface classes such as **Point**, **Color**, **Polygon**, and **Open_polyline** and their uses. The following chapter will present ideas for designing sets of related classes and will also present more implementation techniques.

§11.1 Overview of graphics classes

§11.2 **Point** and **Line**

§11.3 **Lines**

Initialization

§11.4 **Color**

§11.5 **Line_style**

§11.6 Polylines

Open_polyline; **Closed_polyline**; **Marked_polyline**; **Marks**

§11.7 Closed shapes

Polygon; **Rectangle**; Managing unnamed objects; **Circle**; **Ellipse**

§11.8 **Text**

§11.9 **Mark**

§11.10 **Image**

11.1 Overview of graphics classes

Graphics and GUI libraries provide lots of facilities. By "lots" we mean hundreds of classes, often with dozens of functions applying to each. Reading a description, manual, or documentation is a bit like looking at an old-fashioned botany textbook listing details of thousands of plants organized according to obscure classifying traits. It is daunting! It can also be exciting – looking at the facilities of a modern graphics/GUI library can make you feel like a child in a candy store, but it can be hard to figure out where to start and what is really good for you.

One purpose of our interface library is to reduce the shock delivered by the complexity of a full-blown graphics/GUI library. We present just two dozen classes with hardly any operations. Yet they allow you to produce useful graphical output. A closely related goal is to introduce key graphics and GUI concepts through those classes. Already, you can write programs displaying results as simple graphics. After this chapter, your range of graphics programs will have increased to exceed most people's initial requirements. After Chapter 14, you'll understand most of the design techniques and ideas involved so that you can deepen your understanding and extend your range of graphical expressions as needed. You can do so either by adding to the facilities described here or by adopting a full-scale C++ graphics/GUI library.

The key interface classes are:

Graphics interface classes (in Graph.h)	
Color	used for lines, text, and filling shapes
Line_style	used to draw lines
Point	used to express locations on a screen and within a Window
Mark	a point marked by a character (such as x or o)
Line	a line as we see it on the screen, defined by its two end Points
Lines	a set of Lines defined by pairs of Points
Open_polyline	a sequence of connected Lines defined by a sequence of Points
Closed_polyline	like an Open_polyline, except that a Line connects the last Point to the first
Marks	a sequence of points indicated by marks (such as x and o)
Marked_polyline	an Open_polyline with its points indicated by marks
Polygon	a Closed_polyline where no two Lines intersect
Rectangle	a common shape optimized for quick and convenient display
Circle	a circle defined by a center and a radius
Ellipse	an ellipse defined by a center and two axes
Function	a function of one variable graphed in a range
Axis	a labeled axis
Text	a string of characters
Image	the contents of an image file

Chapter 13 examines Function and Axis. Chapter 14 presents the main GUI interface classes:

Window interface classes	
Window	an area of the screen in which we display our graphics objects. In Window.h.
Simple_window	a window with a "Next" button. In Simple_window.h.
Application	the class that provides our interface to Qt

Every GUI/graphics program needs to start by defining an Application object.

GUI interface classes (in GUI.h)	
Button	a rectangle, usually labeled, in a window that we can press to run one of our functions
In_box	a box, usually labeled, in a window into which a user can type a string
Out_box	a box, usually labeled, in a window into which our program can write a string
Menu	a vector of Buttons

This Graphics/GUI library is presented as module PPP_graphics. At the time of writing not every C++ implementation has excellent module support, so we also make the library source code available as source files organized as described in §10.8.1.

In addition to the graphics classes, we present a class that happens to be useful for holding collections for Shapes or Widgets:

A container of Shapes or Widgets. In Graph.h.	
Vector_ref	a vector with an interface that makes it convenient for holding unnamed elements

When you read the following sections, please don't move too fast. There is little that isn't pretty obvious, but the purpose of this chapter isn't just to show you some pretty pictures – you see prettier pictures on your computer screen, television, and phone every day. The main points of this chapter are

- To show the correspondence between code and the pictures produced.
- To get you used to reading code and thinking about how the code works.
- To get you to think about the design of code – in particular to think about how to represent concepts as classes in code. Why do those classes look the way they do? How else could they have looked? We made many, many design decisions, most of which could reasonably have been made differently, in some cases radically differently.

So please don't rush. If you do, you'll miss something important and you might then find the exercises unnecessarily hard.

11.2 Point and Line

The most basic part of any graphics system is the point. To define *point* is to define how we organize our geometric space. Here, we use a conventional, computer-oriented layout of two-dimensional points defined by (*x*,*y*) integer coordinates. As described in §10.5, *x* coordinates go from 0 (representing the left-hand side of the screen) to x_max() (representing the right-hand side of the screen); *y* coordinates go from 0 (representing the top of the screen) to y_max() (representing the bottom of the screen).

A **Point** is simply a pair of **int**s (the coordinates):

```
struct Point {
      int x, y;
};

bool operator==(Point a, Point b) { return a.x==b.x && a.y==b.y; }
bool operator!=(Point a, Point b) { return !(a==b); }
```

Whatever appears in a Window is a **Shape**, which we describe in detail in Chapter 12. So a **Line** is a **Shape** that connects two **Point**s with a line:

```
struct Line : Shape {                  // a Line is a Shape defined by two Points
      Line(Point p1, Point p2);        // construct a Line from two Points
};
```

A **Line** is a kind of **Shape**. That's what **: Shape** means. **Shape** is called a *base class* for **Line** or simply a *base* of **Line**. **Shape** provides the facilities needed to make the definition of **Line** simple. Once we have a feel for the particular shapes, such as **Line** and **Open_polyline**, we'll explain what that implies (§12.2).

A **Line** is defined by two **Point**s. We can create lines and cause them to be drawn like this:

```
#include "PPP.h"
#include "PPP/Simple_window.h"
#include "PPP/Graph.h"

using namespace Graph_lib;

int main()
      // draw two lines
{
      constexpr Point x {100,100};

      Simple_window win {x,600,400,"two lines"};

      Line horizontal {x,Point{200,100}};                // make a horizontal line
      Line vertical {Point{150,50},Point{150,150}};      // make a vertical line

      win.attach(horizontal);                            // attach the lines to the window
      win.attach(vertical);

      win.wait_for_button();                             // display!
}
catch (...) {
      cout << "something went wrong\n";
}
```

As a reminder, we left in the "scaffolding" (**#include**s, etc., as described in §10.3).

Executing that, we get

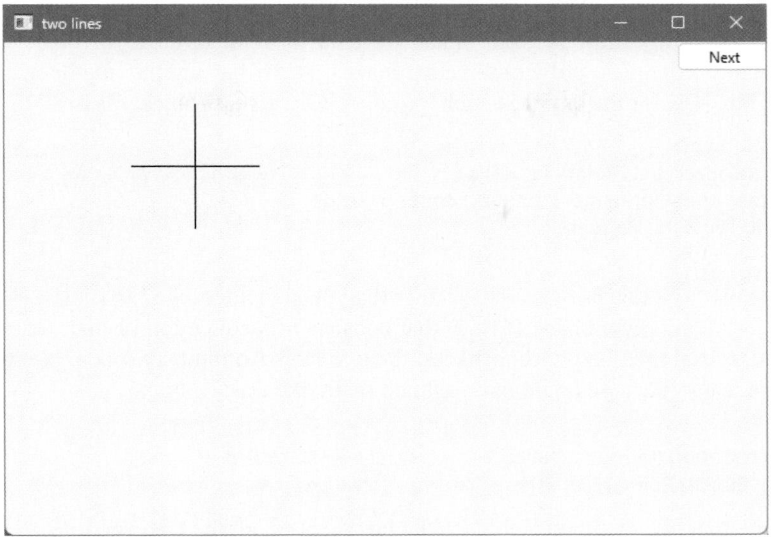

As a user interface designed for simplicity, **Line** works quite well. You don't need to be Einstein to guess that

```
Line vertical {Point{150,50},Point{150,150}};
```

creates a (vertical) line from (150,50) to (150,150). There are, of course, implementation details, but you don't have to know those to make **Lines**. The implementation of **Line**'s constructor is correspondingly simple:

```
Line::Line(Point p1, Point p2)  // construct a line from two points
{
        add(p1);         // add p1 to this shape
        add(p2);         // add p2 to this shape
}
```

That is, it simply "adds" two points. Adds to what? And how does a **Line** get drawn in a window? The answer lies in the **Shape** class. As we'll describe in Chapter 12, **Shape** can hold points defining lines, knows how to draw lines defined by pairs of **Points**, and provides a function **add()** that allows an object to add a **Point** to its **Shape**. The key point (*sic!*) here is that defining **Line** is trivial. Most of the implementation work is done by "the system" so that we can concentrate on writing simple classes that are easy to use.

From now on we'll also leave out the definition of the **Simple_window** (§14.3) and the calls of **attach()** and **set_label()**. Those are just more "scaffolding" that we need for a complete program but that adds little to the discussion of specific **Shapes**.

11.3 Lines

As it turns out, we rarely draw just one line. We tend to think in terms of objects consisting of many lines, such as triangles, polygons, paths, mazes, grids, bar graphs, mathematical functions, graphs of data, etc. One of the simplest such "composite graphical object classes" is **Lines**:

```
struct Lines : Shape {          // related lines
     Lines(initializer_list<Point> lst = {});          // by default, an empty list
     void draw_specific(Painter& painter) const override;
     void add(Point p1, Point p2);
};
```

The **override** means "use this **draw_specific** rather than **Shape**'s for **Lines**" (§12.3.3).

A **Lines** object is simply a **Shape** (§12.2) that consists of a collection of lines, each defined by a pair of **Points**. For example, had we considered the two lines from the **Line** example in §11.2 as part of a single graphical object, we could have defined them like this:

```
Lines y;
y.add(Point{100,100}, Point{200,100});          // first line: horizontal
y.add(Point{150,50}, Point{150,150});           // second line: vertical
```

This gives output that is indistinguishable (to the last pixel) from the **Line** version:

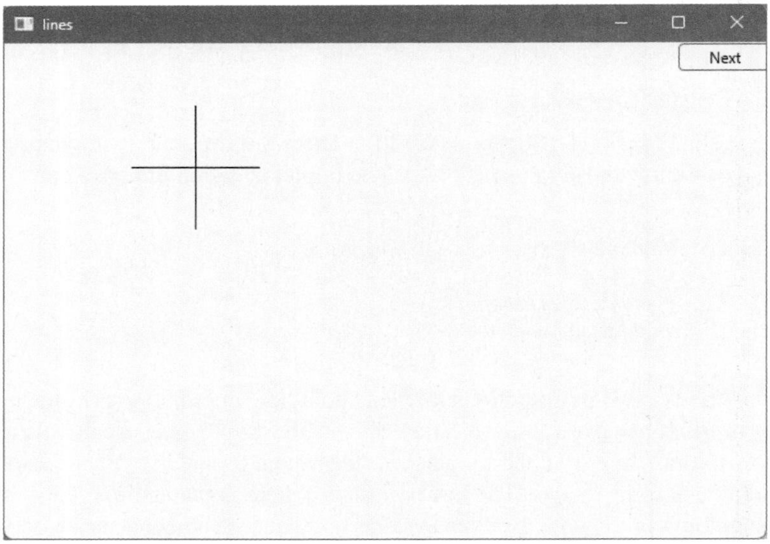

The only way we can tell that this is a different window is that we labeled them differently.

CC The difference between a set of **Line** objects and a set of lines in a **Lines** object is completely one of our view of what's going on. By using **Lines**, we have expressed our opinion that the two lines belong together and should be manipulated together. For example, we can change the color of all lines that are part of a **Lines** object with a single command. On the other hand, we can give lines that are individual **Line** objects different colors. As a more realistic example, consider how to define a grid. A grid consists of a number of evenly spaced horizontal and vertical lines. However, we think of a grid as one "thing," so we define those lines as part of a **Lines** object:

```
int x_size = win3.x_max();                    // get the size of our window
int y_size = win3.y_max();
int x_grid = 80;
int y_grid = 40;

Lines grid;
for (int x=x_grid; x<x_size; x+=x_grid)
     grid.add(Point{x,0},Point{x,y_size});    // vertical line
for (int y = y_grid; y<y_size; y+=y_grid)
     grid.add(Point{0,y},Point{x_size,y});    // horizontal line
```

Note how we get the dimensions of our window using **x_max()** and **y_max()**. This is also the first example where we are writing code that computes which objects we want to display. It would have been unbearably tedious to define this grid by defining one named variable for each grid line. From that code, we get

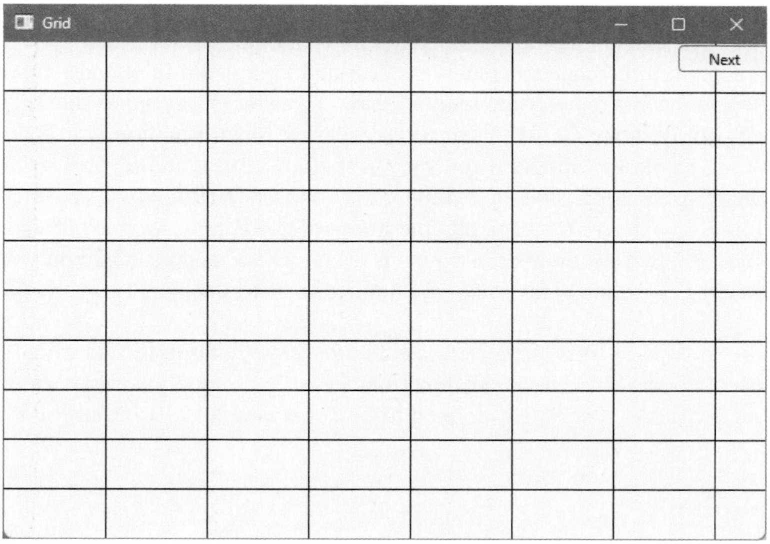

Let's return to the design of **Lines**. How are the member functions of class **Lines** implemented? **Lines** provides just two constructors and two operations.

The **add()** function simply adds a line defined by a pair of points to the set of lines to be displayed, and asks for the modified object to be redrawn in the **Window**:

```
void Lines::add(Point p1, Point p2)
{
        Shape::add(p1);
        Shape::add(p2);
        redraw();
}
```

Yes, the Shape:: qualification is needed because otherwise the compiler would see add(p1) as an (illegal) attempt to call Lines' add() rather than Shape's add().

The draw_specific() function draws the lines defined using add():

```
void Lines::draw_specific(Painter& painter) const
{
        if (color().visibility())
                for (int i=1; i<number_of_points(); i+=2)
                        painter.draw_line(point(i−1),point(i));
}
```

That is, Lines::draw_specific() takes two points at a time (starting with points 0 and 1) and draws the line between them using the underlying library's line-drawing function (Painter::draw_line()). A Painter is an object that holds the information about how an object is to be displayed on a screen. It defines the mapping from the concepts (such as Color and Line_style) in our interface library to the Qt versions of such concepts represented as a QPainter. QPainter is a complex and highly optimized class that we will not describe. Efficient quality rendering of information is a non-trivial art and here we will just use painters in simple ways, such as to draw a straight line.

For this example, we simply used the default color (black). Visibility is a property of the Lines' Color object (§11.4), so we have to check that the lines are meant to be visible before drawing them. We don't need to check that the number of points is even – Lines' add() can add only pairs of points. The functions number_of_points() and point() are defined in class Shape (§12.2) and have their obvious meaning.

As we explain in §12.2.3, draw_specific() is called by draw() that in turn is called "the system" when a Shape needs to appear. These two functions provide read-only access to a Shape's points. The member function draw_specific() is defined to be const (see §8.7.4) because it doesn't modify the shape.

11.3.1 Initialization

AA The Lines constructor takes an initializer_list of pairs of Points, each defining a line. Given that initializer-list constructor (§17.3), we can simply define Lines starting out with 0, 1, 2, 3, . . . lines. For example, the first Lines example could be written like this:

```
Lines x = {
        {Point{100,100}, Point{200,100}},        // first line: horizontal
        {Point{150,50}, Point{150,150}}          // second line: vertical
};
```

or even like this:

```
Lines x = {
      {{100,100}, {200,100}},           // first line: horizontal
      {{150,50}, {150,150}}             // second line: vertical
};
```

The initializer-list constructor is easily defined; just check that the number of points is even and let **Shape**'s list constructor do the work:

```
void Lines::Lines(initializer_list<pair<Point,Point>> lst)
      : Shape{lst}
{
      if (lst.size() % 2)
            error("odd number of points for Lines");
}
```

The **initializer_list** type is defined in the standard library (§17.3, §20.2.2).

The default constructor, **Lines{}**, simply sees an empty list **{}** and creates an empty object (containing no lines): the model of starting out with no points and then **add()**ing pairs of points as needed is more flexible than any constructor could be. In particular, it allows us to add **lines** later.

11.4 Color

Color is the type we use to represent color. We can use **Color** like this:

```
grid.set_color(Color::red);
```

This colors the lines defined in **grid** red so that we get

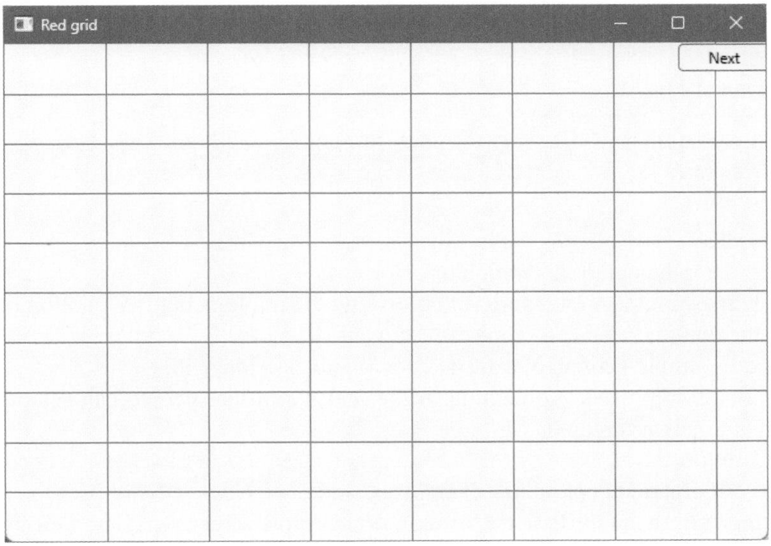

Color defines the notion of a color and gives symbolic names to a few of the more common colors:

```
struct Color {
	enum Color_type {
		red, blue, green,
		yellow, white, black,
		magenta, cyan, dark_red,
		dark_green, dark_yellow, dark_blue,
		dark_magenta, dark_cyan,
		palette_index,
		rgb
	};
	enum Transparency { invisible = 0, visible=255 };

	Color(Color_type cc) :c{cc}, ct{cc}, v{visible} { }                    // named colors
	Color(Color_type cc, Transparency vv) :c{cc}, ct{cc}, v{vv} { }
	Color(int cc)                     // choose from palette of 256 popular colors
		:c{cc}, ct{Color_type::palette_index}, v{visible} { }
	Color(Transparency vv) :c{}, ct{Color_type::black}, v{vv} { }
	Color(int r, int g, int b) :c{}, ct{Color_type::rgb}, rgb_color{r,g,b}, v{visible} {}  // RGB

	int as_int() const { return c; }
	int red_component() const { return rgb_color.r; }
	int green_component() const { return rgb_color.g; }
	int blue_component() const { return rgb_color.b; }
	Color_type type() const { return ct; }

	char visibility() const { return v; }
	void set_visibility(Transparency vv) { v=vv; }
private:
	int c = 0;
	Color_type ct = black;
	struct Rgb { int r; int g; int b; };
	Rgb rgb_color = {0,0,0};
	Transparency v;
};
```

The purpose of Color is

- To hide the implementation's notion of color
- To map between integer encodings of colors and the implementation's notion of color
- To give the color constants a scope
- To provide a simple version of transparency (visible and invisible)

As ever, when a class represents something in the real world that people can see and care about, complexity and alternatives creep in.

You can pick colors

- From the list of named colors, for example, Color::dark_blue.
- By picking from a small "palette" of colors that most screens display well by specifying a value in the range 0–255; for example, Color(99) is a dark green (§11.7.3).

- By picking a value in the RGB (red, green, blue) system, which we will not explain here. Look it up if you need it. In particular, a search for "RGB color" on the Web gives many sources, such as **http://en.wikipedia.org/wiki/RGB_color_model**. See also exercise 6.

Note the use of constructors to allow **Color**s to be created either from the **Color_type** or from a plain **int**. The member **c** is initialized by each constructor. You could argue that **c** is too short and too obscure a name to use, but since it is used only within the small scope of **Color** and not intended for general use, that's probably OK. We made the member **c** private to protect it from direct use from our users. For our representation of the data member **c** we use a plain **int** which we use appropriately for the **color_type**. We supplied readout functions, such as **as_int()** and **red_component()** to allow users to determine what color a **Color** object represents. Such functions don't change the **Color** object that they are used for so we declared them **const**. AA

The transparency is represented by the member **v** which can hold the values **Color::visible** and **Color::invisible**, with their obvious meaning. It may surprise you that an "invisible color" can be useful, but it can be most useful to have part of a composite shape invisible. This design allows us to extend the design to support many degrees of transparency, should we find the need to.

11.5 Line_style

When we draw several lines in a window, we can distinguish them by color, by style, or by both. A line style is the pattern used to outline the line. Like **set_color()**, **set_style()** applies to all lines of a shape. We can use **Line_style** like this:

```
grid.set_style(Line_style::dot);
```

This displays the lines in **grid** as a sequence of dots rather than a solid line:

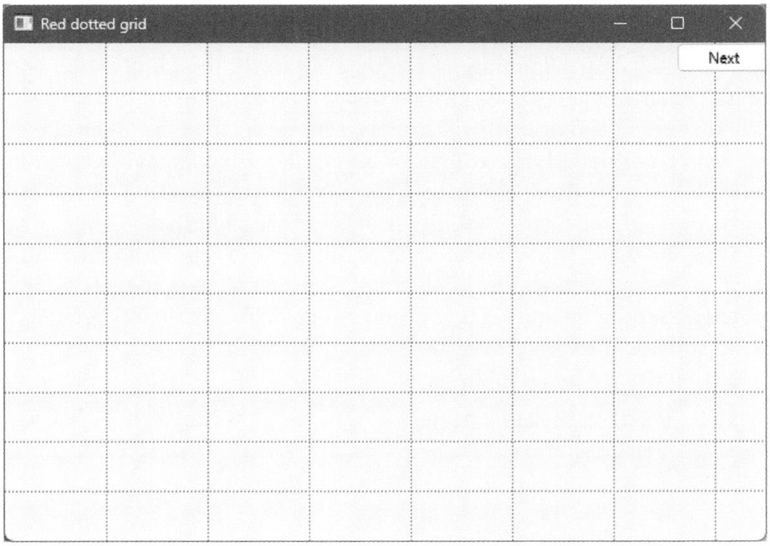

That “thinned out” the grid a bit, making it more discreet.

The Line_style type looks like this:

```
struct Line_style {
      enum Line_style_type {
            solid,                    // -------
            dash,                     // - - - -
            dot,                      // .......
            dashdot,                  // - . - .
            dashdotdot                // -..-..
      };
      Line_style(Line_style_type ss) :s{ss} { }
      Line_style(Line_style_type ss, int ww) :s{ss}, w(ww) { }
      Line_style() {}

      int width() const { return w; }
      int style() const { return s; }
private:
      int s = solid;
      int w = 1;
};
```

Line_style has two “components”:

- The style proper (e.g., use dashed or solid lines).
- The width (the thickness of the line used). The default width is 1, meaning one pixel.

> TRY THIS
>
> Replicate the grid example as above but use a different color and a different line style.

The programming techniques for defining Line_style are exactly the same as the ones we used for Color. Here, we hide the fact that Qt uses its own QFont type to represent line styles. Why is something like that worth hiding? Because it is exactly such a detail that might change as a library evolves or if we change our underlying graphics library. In particular, earlier editions of this book used FLTK where plain ints are used to represent fonts, so hiding that detail saved us from updating user code. In real-world software, such stability is of immense importance.

AA Most of the time, we don’t worry about style at all; we just rely on the default (default width and solid lines). This default line width is defined by the constructors in the cases where we don’t specify one explicitly. Setting defaults is one of the things that constructors are good for, and good defaults can significantly help users of a class.

We can request a fat dashed line like this:

```
grid.set_style(Line_style{Line_style::dash,2});
```

This produces:

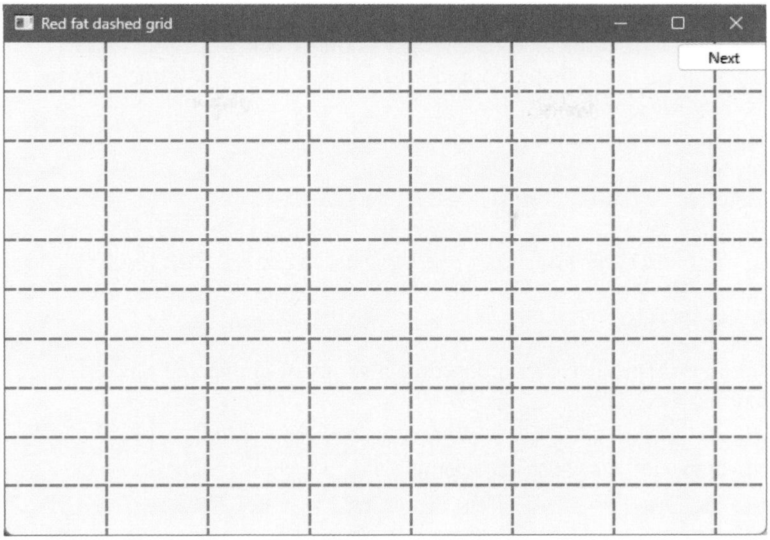

When we want to control the color or style for lines separately, we must define them as separate Lines as we did in §11.2. For example:

```
horizontal.set_color(Color::red);
vertical.set_color(Color::green);
```

This gives us

11.6 Polylines

A polyline is a sequence of connected lines. *Poly* is the Greek word for "many," and *polyline* is a fairly conventional name for a shape composed of many lines. Polylines are the basis for many shapes and especially for graphs.

In this shape library, we support:

- Open_polyline
- Closed_polyline
- Marked_polyline
- Marks

11.6.1 Open_polyline

An Open_polyline is a shape that is composed of a series of connected Lines defined by a series of points. For example:

```
Open_polyline opl = {
        {100,100}, {150,200}, {250,250}, {300,200}
};
```

This draws the shape that you get by connecting the four points:

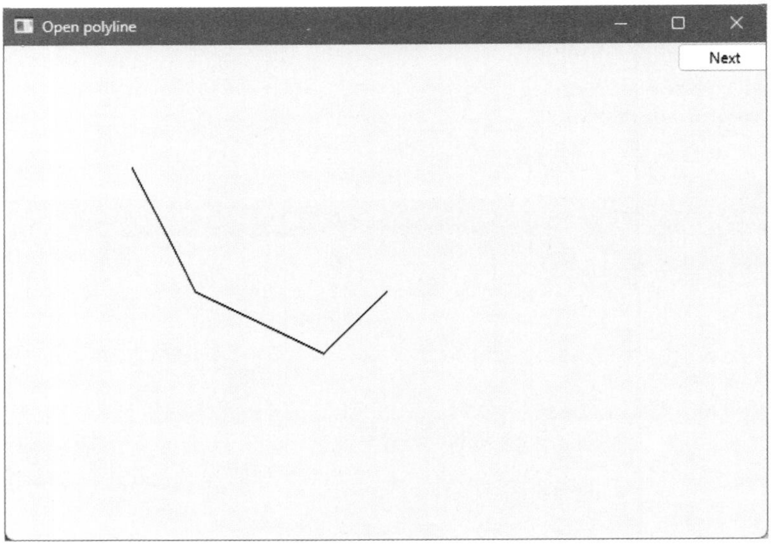

Basically, an Open_polyline is a fancy word for what we encountered in kindergarten playing "Connect the Dots."

Class Open_polyline is defined like this:

```
struct Open_polyline : Shape {                // open sequence of lines
      Open_polyline(initializer_list<Point> lst = {}) : Shape(lst) {}
      void add(Point p) { Shape::add(p); redraw(); }
      void draw_specific(Painter& painter) const override;
};
```

Open_polyline inherits from **Shape**. **Open_polyline**'s **add()** function is there to allow the users of an **Open_polyline** to access the **add()** from **Shape** (that is, **Shape::add()**). For **Open_polyline**, **draw_specific()** is the function that connects the dots with **Lines**:

```
void Open_polyline::draw_specific()(Painter& painter) const
{
      if (color().visibility())
            for (int int i=1; i<number_of_points(); ++i)
                  painter.draw_line(point(i-1),point(i));
}
```

Painter is the class that maps from our drawing functions to Qt's functions for "painting" the screen. It is never used directly by the users of our Graphics/GUI classes.

11.6.2 Closed_polyline

A **Closed_polyline** is just like an **Open_polyline**, except that we also draw a line from the last point to the first. For example, we could use the same points we used for the **Open_polyline** in §11.6.1 for a **Closed_polyline**:

```
Closed_polyline cpl = {    {100,100}, {150,200}, {250,250}, {300,200} };
```

The result is (of course) identical to that of §11.6.1 except for that final closing line:

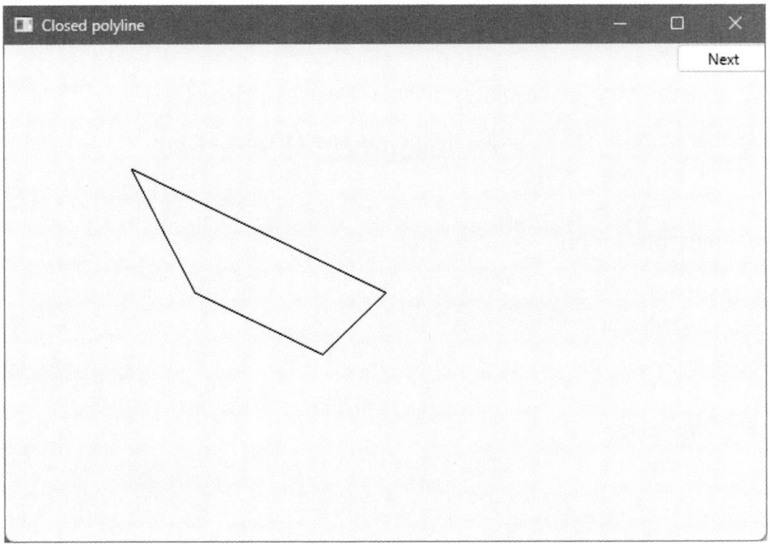

The definition of Closed_polyline is

```
struct Closed_polyline : Open_polyline {// closed sequence of lines
	using Open_polyline::Open_polyline;
	void draw_specific(Painter& painter) const override;
};

void Closed_polyline::draw_specific(Painter& painter) const
{
	painter.draw_polygon(*this);
}
```

The using declaration (§7.6.1) says that Closed_polyline has the same constructors as Open_polyline. Closed_polyline needs its own draw_specific() to draw that closing line connecting the last point to the first. It turns out that Qt has an optimized function for that, so we use it.

We only have to do the little detail where Closed_polyline differs from what Open_polyline offers. That's important and is sometimes called "programming by difference." We need to program only what's different about our derived class (here, Closed_polyline) compared to what a base class (here, Open_polyline) offers.

So how do we draw that closing line? We don't. The Qt library QPainter knows how to draw polygons. So, our Painter simply invokes this underlying graphics library. However, as in every other case, the mention of Qt is kept within the implementation of our class rather than being exposed to our users. No user code needs to use painter. If we wanted to, we could replace Qt with another GUI library with very little impact on our users' code.

11.6.3 Marked_polyline

We often want to "label" points on a graph. One way of displaying a graph is as an open polyline, so what we need is an open polyline with "marks" at the points. A Marked_polyline does that. For example:

```
Marked_polyline mpl {"1234", {{100,100}, {150,200}, {250,250}, {300,200}}};
```

The "1234" is the characters we use to labe the points and the second initlizer is a list of points.

We could have defined mpl like this:

```
Marked_polyline mpl{ "1234" };
mpl.add(Point{100,100});
mpl.add(Point{150,200});
mpl.add(Point{250,250});
mpl.add(Point{300,200});
```

That's verbose, but it shows how we can add points after the initial definition of a Marked_polyline object.

Either way, this produces:

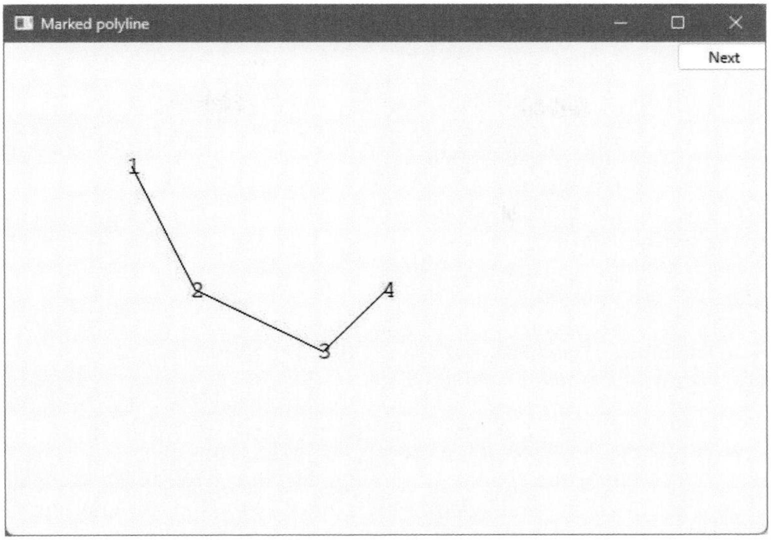

The definition of Marked_polyline is

```
struct Marked_polyline : Open_polyline {
    Marked_polyline(const string& m, initializer_list<Point> lst = {});

    void set_font(Font f) { fnt = f; redraw(); }
    Font font() const { return fnt; }

    void set_font_size(int s) { fnt_sz = s; redraw(); }
    int font_size() const { return fnt_sz; }

    void set_color(Color col) { Shape::set_color(col); set_mark_color(col); }
    void set_mark_color(Color c) { m_color = c; redraw();}
    Color mark_color() const { return m_color;}

    void draw_specifics(Painter& painter) const override;
protected:
    void hide_lines(bool hide = true);   // make the lines invisible or visible
private:
    string mark;
    Font fnt = Font::courier;
    int fnt_sz = 14;         // at least 14 point
    Color m_color;
};
```

By deriving from Open_polyline, we get the handling of Points "for free"; all we have to do is to deal with the marks. We wanted to control the appearance of the marks and that meant adding functions to manipulate the font, color, and size. The alternative would have been to leave those data members public. However, fonts and colors are exactly the kinds of properties for which implementations are likely to change over time, so we hide them behind a functional interface. In particular, draw_specific() becomes

```
void Marked_polyline::draw_specific(Painter& painter) const
{
        Open_polyline::draw_specifics(painter);

        painter.set_line_style(style());
        painter.set_color(m_color);
        painter.set_font(font());
        painter.set_font_size(font_size());

        for (int i=0; i<number_of_points(); ++i)
                draw_mark(painter, point(i),mark[i%mark.size()]);
}
```

The call Open_polyline::draw_specific() takes care of the style of the lines, so we just have to deal with the "marks." We supply the marks as a string of characters and use them in order: the marks[i%marks.size()] selects the character to be used next by cycling through the characters supplied when the Marked_polyline was created. The % is the modulo (remainder) operator. This draw_specific() uses a little helper function draw_mark() to actually output a letter at a given point:

```
void draw_mark(Painter& painter, Point xy, char c)
{
        string m(1,c);
        painter.draw_centered_text(xy, m);
}
```

The string m is constructed to contain the single character c.

The constructor that takes an initializer list simply forwards the list Open_polyline's initializer-list constructor:

```
Marked_polyline::Marked_polyline(const string& m, initializer_list<Point> lst)
        : Open_polyline{lst}, mark{(m=="") ? "*" : m}
{
}
```

The ?: test for the empty string is needed to avoid draw_specific() trying to access a character that isn't there.

11.6.4 Marks

Sometimes, we want to display marks without lines connecting them. We provide the class Marks for that. For example, we can mark the four points we have used for our various examples without connecting them with lines:

```
Marks pp {"x", {{100,100}, {150,200}, {250,250}, {300,200}}};
```

This produces:

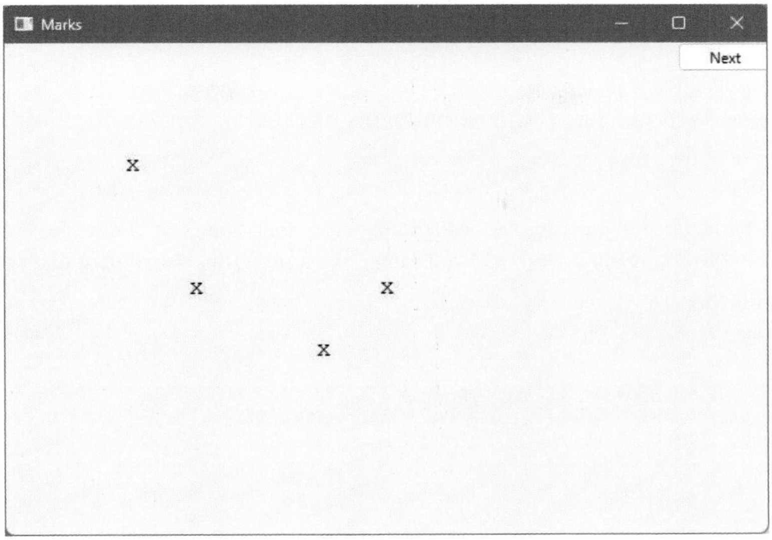

One obvious use of **Marks** is to display data that represents discrete events so that drawing connecting lines would be inappropriate. An example would be (height, weight) data for a group of people.

A **Marks** is simply a **Marked_polyline** where the lines are invisible:

```
struct Marks : Marked_polyline {
    Marks(const string& m, initializer_list<Point> lst = {})
        : Marked_polyline{ m,lst }
    {
        Color orig = color();
        Marked_polyline::set_color(Color::invisible); // hide the lines
        set_mark_color(orig);
    }

    void set_color(Color col) { set_mark_color(col); }
};
```

The **: Marked_polyline{m}** notation is used to initialize the **Marked_polyline** part of a **Marks** object. This notation is a variant of the syntax used to initialize members (§8.4.4).

All we need to do is to make the lines invisible and to provide a way for the user to set the color of the characters used as marks.

11.7 Closed shapes

A closed shape differs from a polyline by having a well-defined inside and outside. We can color the inside of a closed shape, but a polyline – even a **closed_polyline** – may not have an inside to color. In this shape library, we support:

- **Polygon**
- **Rectangle**
- **Circle**
- **Ellipse**

These **Shapes** support the notion of *fill color* (§12.2).

11.7.1 Polygon

The difference between **Polygons** and **Closed_polylines** is that **Polygons** don't allow lines to cross. For example, the **Closed_polyline** from §11.6.2 looks like a polygon, but we can add another point:

```
cpl.add(Point{100,250});
```

The result is

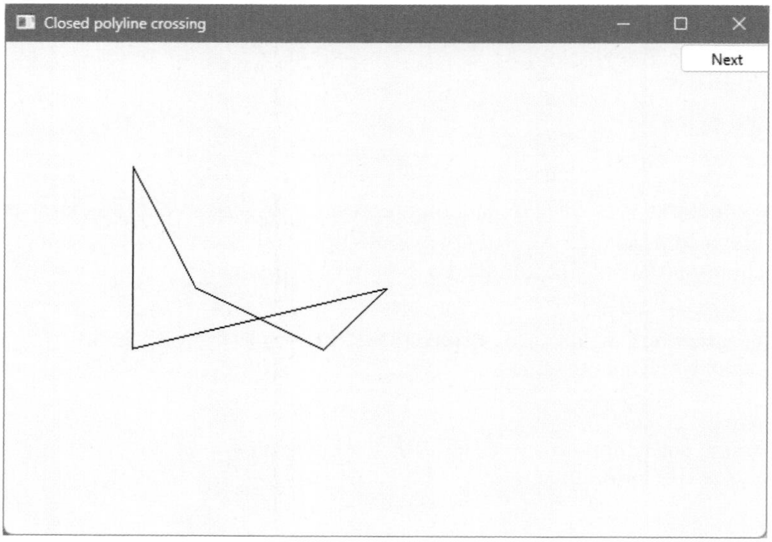

According to classical definitions, this **Closed_polyline** is not a polygon. How do we define **Polygon** so that we correctly capture the relationship to **Closed_polyline** without violating the rules of geometry? The presentation above contains a strong hint. A **Polygon** is a **Closed_polyline** where lines do not cross. Alternatively, we could emphasize the way a shape is built out of points and say that a **Polygon** is a **Closed_polyline** where we cannot add a **Point** that defines a **Line** that intersects one of the existing lines of the **Polygon**.

Given that idea, we define **Polygon** like this:

```
struct Polygon : Closed_polyline {          // closed sequence of nonintersecting lines
      using Closed_polyline::Closed_polyline;      // use Closed_polyline's constructors
      void add(Point p);
      void draw_specific(Painter& painter) const override;
};
```

```
void Polygon::add(Point p)
{
        // ... check that the new line doesn't intersect existing lines (code not shown) ...
        Closed_polyline::add(p);
}
```

Here we inherit Closed_polyline's definition of draw_specific(), thus saving a fair bit of work and avoiding duplication of code. Unfortunately, we have to check each add(). That yields an inefficient (order *N-squared*) Algorithm: defining a Polygon with *N* points requires *N∗(N-1)/2* calls of intersect(). In effect, we have made the assumption that the Polygon class will be used for polygons of a low number of points. For example, creating a Polygon with 24 Points involves 24∗(24-1)/2 == 276 calls of intersect(). That's probably acceptable, but if we wanted a polygon with 2000 points it would cost us about 2,000,000 calls, and we might look for a better algorithm, which might require a modified interface.

Using the initializer-list constructor (§17.3), we can create a polygon like this:

```
Polygon poly = {
        {100,100}, {150,200}, {250,250}, {300,200}
};
```

Obviously, this creates a Polygon that (to the last pixel) is identical to our original Closed_polyline:

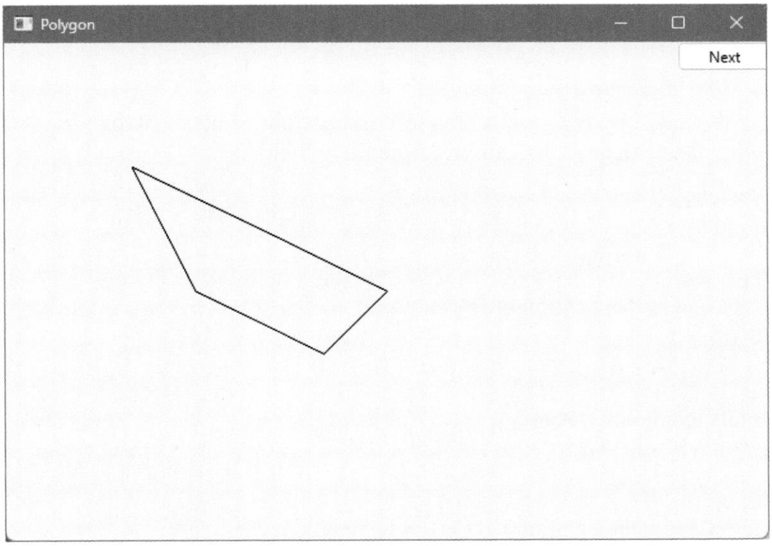

Ensuring that a Polygon really represents a polygon turned out to be surprisingly messy. The check for intersection that we left out of Polygon::add() is arguably the most complicated in the whole graphics library. If you are interested in fiddly coordinate manipulation of geometry, have a look at the code.

AA The trouble is that Polygon's invariant "the points represent a polygon" can't be verified until all points have been defined; that is, we are not – as strongly recommended – establishing Polygon's invariant in its constructor. We considered removing add() and requiring that a Polygon always be completely specified by an initializer list with at least three points, but that would have complicated uses where a program generated a sequence of points.

11.7.2 Rectangle

The most common shape on a screen is a rectangle. The reasons for that are partly cultural (most of our doors, windows, pictures, walls, bookcases, pages, etc. are also rectangular) and partly technical (keeping a coordinate within rectangular space is simpler than for any other shaped space). Anyway, rectangles are so common that GUI systems support them directly rather than treating them simply as polygons that happen to have four corners and right angles.

```
struct Rectangle : Shape {
        Rectangle(Point xy, int ww, int hh);
        Rectangle(Point x, Point y);

        void draw_specific(Painter& painter) const override;

        int height() const { return h; }
        int width() const { return w; }
private:
        int w;                    // width
        int h;                    // height
};
```

We can specify a rectangle by two points (top left and bottom right) or by one point (top left) and a width and a height. The constructors can be defined like this:

```
Rectangle::Rectangle(Point xy, int ww, int hh)
        :w{ ww }, h{ hh }
{
        if (h<=0 || w<=0)
                error("Bad rectangle: non-positive side");
        add(xy);
}

Rectangle::Rectangle(Point x, Point y)
        :w{ y.x - x.x }, h{ y.y - x.y }
{
        if (h<=0 || w<=0)
                error("Bad rectangle: first point is not top left");
        add(x);
}
```

Each constructor initializes the members h and w appropriately (using the member initialization syntax; see §8.2) and stores away the top left corner point in the Rectangle's base Shape (using add()). In addition, it does a simple sanity check: we don't really want Rectangles with non-positive width or height.

One of the reasons that some graphics/GUI systems treat rectangles as special is that the algorithm for determining which pixels are inside a rectangle is far simpler – and therefore far faster – than for other shapes, such as **Polygons** and **Circles**. CC

The notion of fill color is common to all closed **Shapes** so it is provided by **Shape**. We can set the fill color in a constructor or by the operation **set_fill_color()**:

```
Rectangle rect00 {Point{150,100},200,100};
Rectangle rect11 {Point{50,50},Point{250,150}};
Rectangle rect12 {Point{50,150},Point{250,250}};    // just below rect11
Rectangle rect21 {Point{250,50},200,100};           // just to the right of rect11
Rectangle rect22 {Point{250,150},200,100};          // just below rect21

rect00.set_fill_color(Color::yellow);
rect11.set_fill_color(Color::blue);
rect12.set_fill_color(Color::red);
rect21.set_fill_color(Color::green);
```

This produces:

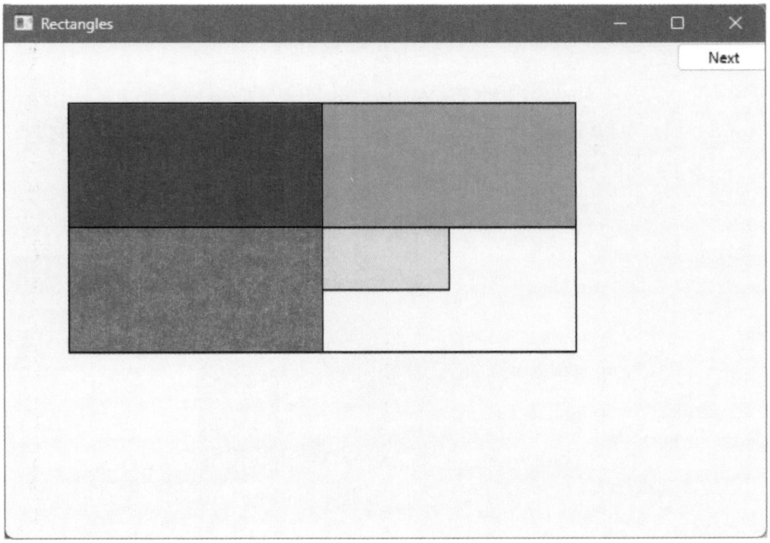

When you don't have a fill color, the rectangle is transparent; that's how you can see a corner of the yellow **rect00**.

We can move shapes around in a window (§12.2.3). For example:

```
rect11.move(400,0);             // to the right of rect21
rect11.set_fill_color(Color::white);
```

This produces:

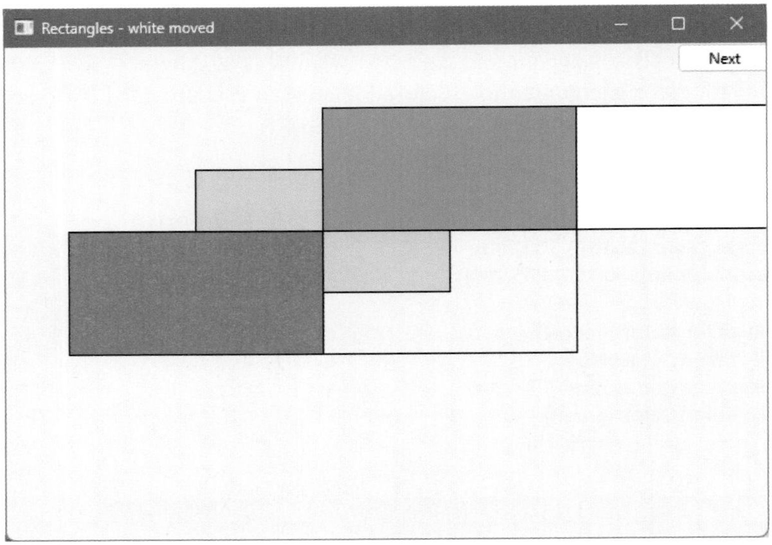

CC Note also how shapes are placed one on top of another. This is done just like you would put sheets of paper on a table. The first one you put will be on the bottom. For example:

```
win12.put_on_top(rect00);
```

This produces:

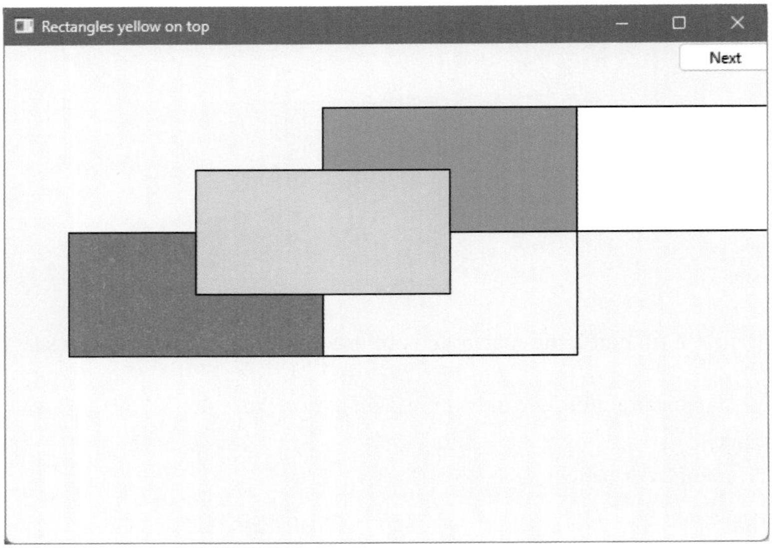

Note how only part of the white **rect11** fits in the window. What doesn't fit is "clipped"; that is, it is not shown anywhere on the screen.

Note that we can see the lines that make up the rectangles even though we have filled (all but one of) them. If we don't like those outlines, we can remove them:

```
rect00.set_color(Color::invisible);
rect11.set_color(Color::invisible);
rect12.set_color(Color::invisible);
rect21.set_color(Color::invisible);
rect22.set_color(Color::invisible);
```

We get

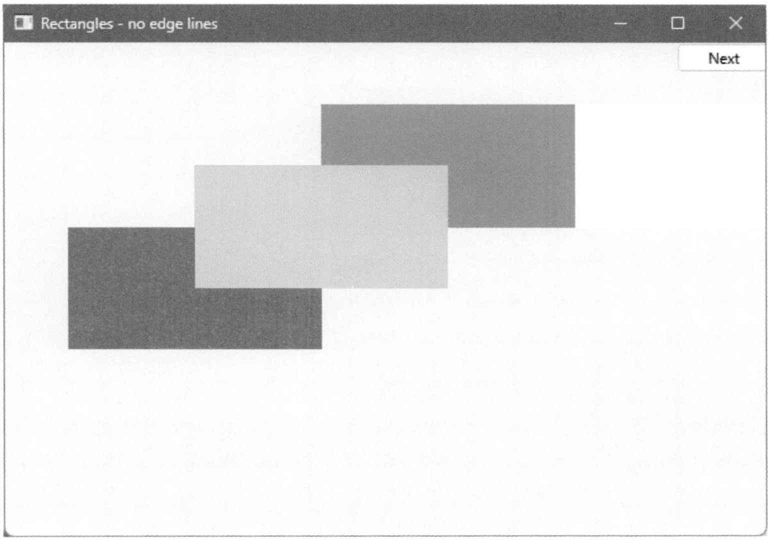

Note that with both fill color and line color set to **invisible**, **rect22** can no longer be seen.

Because it has to deal with both line color and fill color, **Rectangle**'s **draw_specific()** is a bit messy:

```
void Rectangle::draw_specific(Painter& painter) const
{
      painter.draw_rectangle(point(0), w, h);
}
```

As you can see, Qt's **Painter** provides functions for drawing rectangles. By default, we draw the lines/outline on top of the fill.

11.7.3 Managing unnamed objects

So far, we have named all our graphical objects. When we want lots of objects, this becomes infeasible. As an example, let us draw a simple color chart of the 256 colors in a palette; that is, let's make 256 colored squares and draw them in a 32-by-8 matrix with a set of popular colors and ranges of colors. First, here is the result:

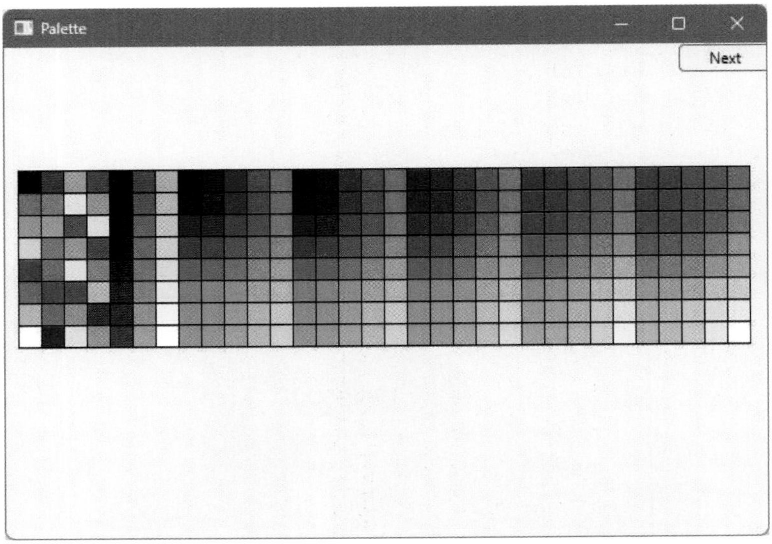

AA

Naming those 256 squares would not only be tedious, it would be silly. The obvious "name" of the top left square is its location in the matrix (0,0), and any other square is similarly identified ("named") by a coordinate pair (*i,j*). What we need for this example is the equivalent of a matrix of objects. We thought of using a **vector<Rectangle>**, but that turned out to be not quite flexible enough. For example, it can be useful to have a collection of unnamed objects (elements) that are not all of the same type. We discuss that flexibility issue in §12.3. Here, we'll just present our solution: a **vector** type that can hold named and unnamed objects:

AA

```
template<class T>
class Vector_ref {
        // ...
public:
        Vector_ref() {}
        Vector_ref(T& a);
        Vector_ref(unique_ptr<T> x);

        void push_back(T& s);                       // add a named variable
        void push_back(unique_ptr<T> x);            // add an unnamed object

        T& operator[](int i);
        const T& operator[](int i);
```

```
        int size() const;
        // ...
};
```

The way you use it is very much like a standard-library **vector**:

```
Vector_ref<Rectangle> rect;

Rectangle x {Point{100,200},Point{200,300}};
rect.push_back(x);                                                          // add a named variable

rect.push_back(make_unique<Rectangle>(Point{50,60},Point{80,90}));           // add an unnamed object

for (int i=0; i<rect.size(); ++i)
        rect[i].move(10,10);                // use rect
```

We explain the standard-library **make_unique()** in §15.5.2 and §18.5.2. For now, it is sufficient to know that we can use it to hold unnamed objects. **AA**

Experienced programmers will be relieved to hear that we did not introduce a memory leak (§15.4.5) in this example. Also, **Vector_ref** offers the support needed for **range**-for loops (§17.6).

Given **Rectangle** and **Vector_ref**, we can play with colors. For example, we can draw a simple color chart of the 256 colors shown above:

```
Vector_ref<Rectangle> vr;

const int max = 32;          //number of columns
const int side = 18;         // size of color rectangle
const int left = 10;         // left edge
const int top = 100;         // top edge
int color_index = 0;

for (int i = 0; i < max; ++i) {              // all columns
        for (int j = 0; j < 8; ++j) {        // 8 rows in each column
                vr.push_back(make_unique<Rectangle>(Point{ i*side+left,j*side+top }, side, side));
                vr[vr.size()−1].set_fill_color(color_index);
                ++color_index;               // move to the next color
                win.attach(vr[vr.size()−1]);
        }
}
```

We make a **Vector_ref** of 256 **Rectangle**s, organized graphically in the **Window** as a 32-by-8 matrix, reflecting its possible use. We give the **Rectangle**s the colors 0, 1, 2, 3, 4, and so on. After each **Rectangle** is created, we attach it to the window, so that it will be displayed:

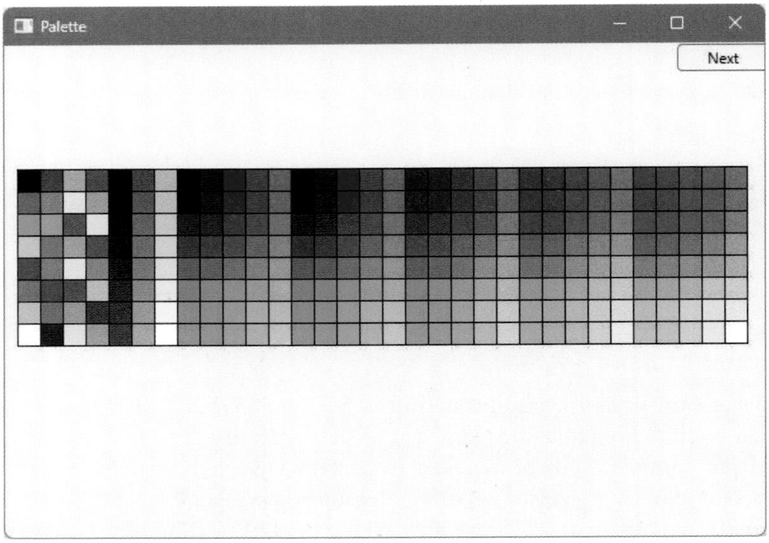

The colors in the palette were chosen to provide easy access to popular colors and ranges of popular colors.

11.7.4 Circle

Just to show that the world isn't completely rectangular, we provide class **Circle** and class **Ellipse**. A **Circle** is defined by a center and a radius:

```
struct Circle : Shape {
	Circle(Point p, int rr)		// center and radius
		:r{ rr }
	{
		add(Point{ p.x - r, p.y - r });
	}

	void draw_specific(Painter& painter) const override;

	Point center() const { return { point(0).x + r, point(0).y + r }; }

	void set_radius(int rr) { r=rr; redraw(); }
	int radius() const { return r; }
private:
	int r;
};
```

We can use **Circle** like this:

```
Circle c1 {Point{100,200},50};
Circle c2 {Point{150,200},100};
c2.set_fill_color(Color::red);
win.c1.put_on_top();
Circle c3 {Point{200,200},150};
```

This produces three circles of different sizes aligned with their centers in a horizontal line:

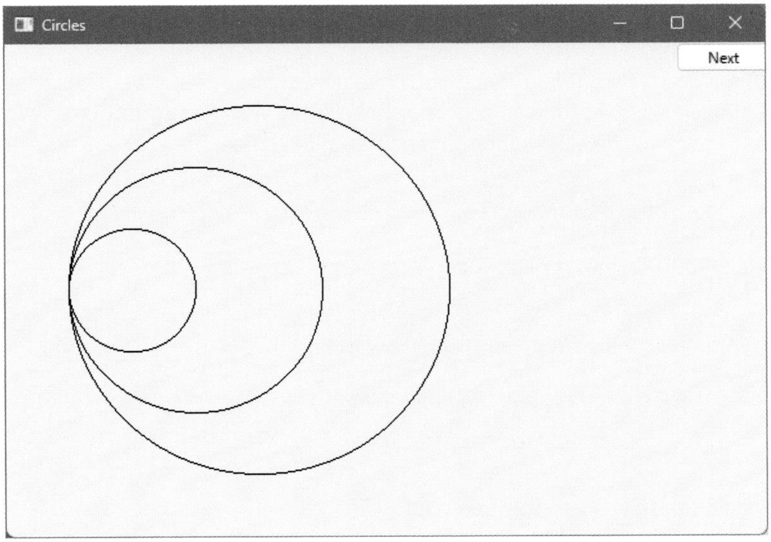

The main peculiarity of Circle's implementation is that the point stored is not the center, but the top left corner of the square bounding the circle. That way, Circle provides another example of how a class can be used to present a different (and supposedly nicer) view of a concept than its implementation:

```
Circle::Circle(Point p, int rr)          // center and radius
      :r{rr}
{
      add(Point{p.x-r,p.y-r});   // store top left corner
}

Point Circle::center() const
{
      return {point(0).x+r, point(0).y+r};
}
```

```
void Circle::draw_specific(Painter& painter) const
{
	painter.draw_ellipse(center(), r, r);
}
```

Note the use of the Painter to draw the circle. Qt offers an optimized function for drawing ellipses so we use that.

11.7.5 Ellipse

An ellipse is similar to Circle but is defined with a major and a minor axis, instead of a radius; that is, to define an ellipse, we give the center's coordinates, the distance from the center to a point on the *x* axis, and the distance from the center to a point on the *y* axis:

```
struct Ellipse : Shape {
	Ellipse(Point p, int ww, int hh) // center, min, and max distance from center
	:w{ ww }, h{ hh } {
		add(Point{ p.x - ww, p.y - hh });
	}

	void draw_specific(Painter& painter) const override;

	Point center() const { return{ point(0).x+w, point(0).y+h }; }
	Point focus1() const;
	Point focus2() const;

	void set_major(int ww) { w=ww; redraw(); }
	int major() const { return w; }
	void set_minor(int hh) { h=hh; redraw(); }
	int minor() const { return h; }
private:
	int w;
	int h;
};
```

We can use Ellipse like this:

```
Ellipse e1 {Point{200,200},50,50};
Ellipse e2 {Point{200,200},100,50};
Ellipse e3 {Point{200,200},100,150};
```

This gives us three ellipses with a common center but different-size axes:

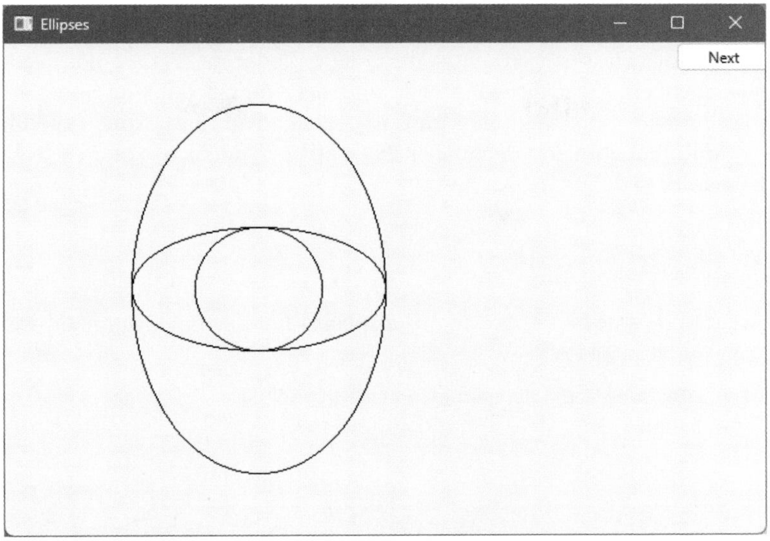

Note that an **Ellipse** with **major()==minor()** looks exactly like a circle.

For an ellipse there are two points on the long axis, so that the sum of distances from any point on the ellipse to those two points, called focus points, is the same. Given an **Ellipse**, we can compute a focus. For example:

```
Point focus1() const
{
    return{ center().x + round_to<int>(sqrt(w*w-h*h)), center().y };
}

Point focus2() const
{
    return{ center().x - round_to<int>(sqrt(w*w-h*h)), center().y };
}
```

Why is a **Circle** not an **Ellipse**? Geometrically, every circle is an ellipse, but not every ellipse is a circle. In particular, a circle is an ellipse where the two foci are equal. Imagine that we defined our **Circle** to be an **Ellipse**. We could do that at the cost of needing an extra value in its representation (a circle is defined by a point and a radius; an ellipse needs a center and a pair of axes). We don't like space overhead where we don't need it, but the primary reason for our **Circle** not being an **Ellipse** is that we couldn't define it so without somehow disabling **set_major()** and **set_minor()**. After all, it would not be a circle (as a mathematician would recognize it) if we could use **set_major()** to get **major()!=minor()** – at least it would no longer be a circle after we had done that. We can't have an object that is of one type sometimes (i.e., when **major()!=minor()**) and another type some other time (i.e., when **major()==minor()**). What we can have is an object (an **Ellipse**) that can look like a circle sometimes. A **Circle**, on the other hand, never morphs into an ellipse with two unequal axes. CC

AA When we design classes, we have to be careful not to be too clever and not to be deceived by our "intuition" into defining classes that don't make sense as classes in our code. Conversely, we have to take care that our classes represent some coherent concept and are not just a collection of data and function members. Just throwing code together without thinking about what ideas/concepts we are representing is "hacking" and leads to code that we can't explain and that others can't maintain. If you don't feel altruistic, remember that "others" might be you in a few months' time. Such code is also harder to debug.

11.8 Text

Obviously, we want to be able to add text to our displays. For example, we might want to label our "odd" **Closed_polyline** from §11.6.2:

```
Text t {Point{150,200},"A closed polyline that isn't a polygon"};
t.set_color(Color::blue);
```

We get

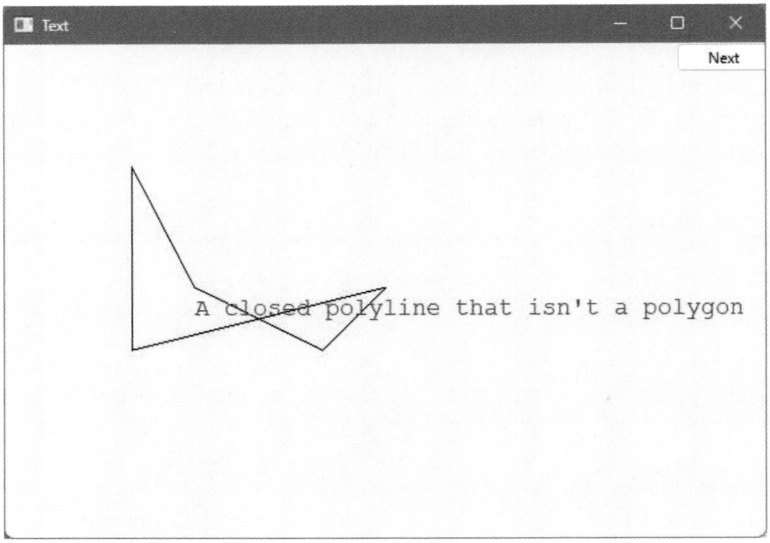

Basically, a **Text** object defines a line of text starting at a **Point**. The **Point** will be the bottom left corner of the text. The reason for restricting the string to be a single line is to ensure portability across systems. Don't try to put in a newline character; it may or may not be represented as a newline in your window. String streams (§9.11) are useful for composing **string**s for display in **Text** objects (examples in §10.7.8, §14.5). **Text** is defined like this:

```
struct Text : Shape {
    Text(Point x, const string& s) : lab{ s } { add(x); }    // the point is the bottom left of the first letter
```

```
        void draw_specific(Painter& painter) const override;

        void set_label(const string& s) { lab = s; redraw(); }
        string label() const { return lab; }

        void set_font(Font f) { fnt = f; redraw(); }
        Font font() const { return Font(fnt); }

        void set_font_size(int s) { fnt_sz = s; redraw(); }
        int font_size() const { return fnt_sz; }
private:
        string lab;                     // label
        Font fnt = Font::courier;
        int fnt_sz = 14;                // font size in the conventional "point" unit
};
```

If you want the font character size to be different from the default (14), you have to explicitly set it. This is an example of a test protecting a user from possible variations in the behavior of an underlying library. In this case, in an earlier version of our interface library, an update of the FLTK library that we used then changed its default in a way that broke existing programs by making the characters tiny. We decided to prevent that problem.

We provide the initializers for fnt and fnt_sz as member initializers, rather than as part of the constructors' initializer lists, because the initializers do not depend on constructor arguments.

Text has its own draw_specific() because only the Text class knows how its string is stored:

```
void Text::draw_specific(Painter& painter) const
{
        painter.set_font(font());
        painter.set_font_size(font_size());
        painter.draw_text(point(0), lab);
}
```

The color of the characters is determined exactly like the lines in shapes composed of lines (such as Open_polyline and Circle), so you can choose a color for them using set_color() and see what color is currently used by color(). The character size and font are handled analogously. There is a small number of predefined fonts:

```
struct Font {
        enum Font_type {
                helvetica, helvetica_bold, helvetica_italic, helvetica_bold_italic,
                courier, courier_bold, courier_italic, courier_bold_italic,
                times, times_bold, times_italic, times_bold_italic,
                symbol,
                screen, screen_bold,
                zapf_dingbats
        };
```

```
        Font(Font_type ff) :f(ff) { }

        int as_int() const { return f; }
private:
        int f = courier;
};
```

The style of class definition used to define **Font** is the same as we used to define **Color** (§11.4) and **Line_style** (§11.5).

We can use that to make our text more prominent:

```
t.set_font(Font::helvetica_bold_italic);
t.set_color(Color::blue);
```

This produces:

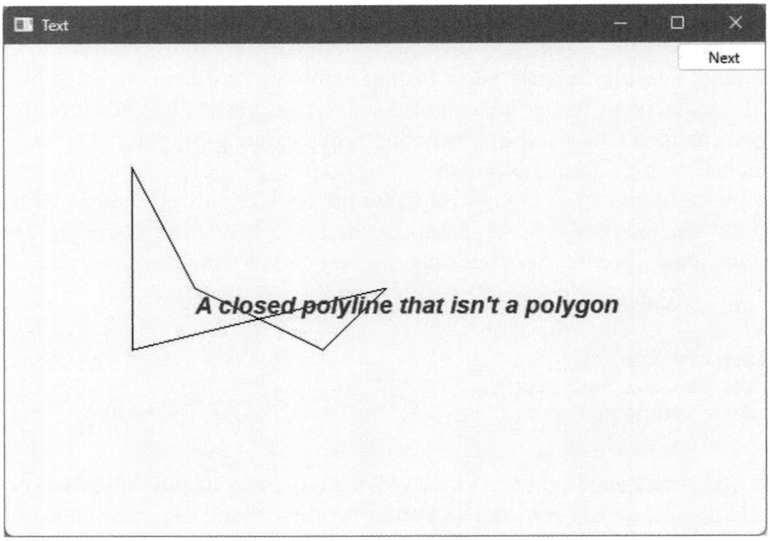

11.9 Mark

A **Point** is simply a location in a **Window**. It is not something we draw or something we can see. If we want to mark a single **Point** so that we can see it, we can indicate it by a pair of lines as in §11.2 or by using **Marks** (§11.6.4). That's a bit verbose, so we have a simple version of **Marks** that is initialized by a point and a character. For example, we could mark the centers of our circles from §11.7.4 like this:

```
Mark m1 {Point{100,200},'x'};
Mark m2 {Point{150,200},'y'};
Mark m3 {Point{200,200},'z'};
```

```
c1.set_color(Color::blue);
c2.set_color(Color::red);
c3.set_color(Color::green);

m1.set_mark_color(Color::blue);
m2.set_mark_color(Color::red);
m3.set_mark_color(Color::green);
```

This produces:

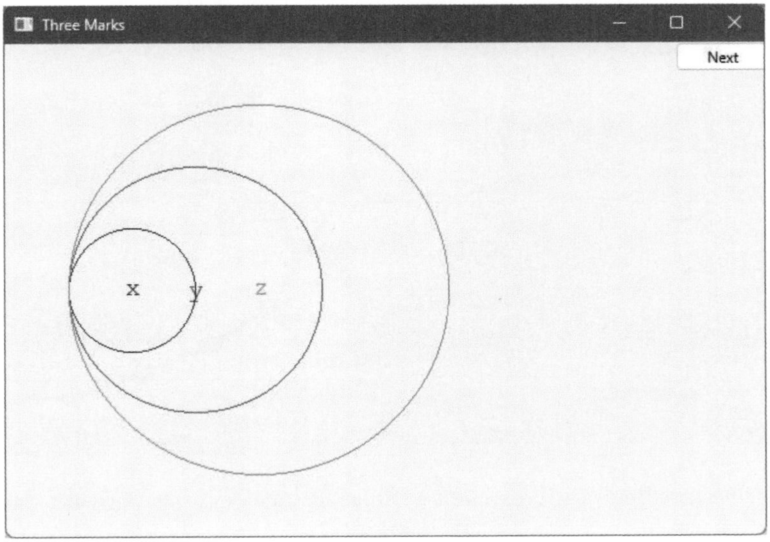

A **Mark** is simply a **Marks** with its initial (and typically only) point given immediately:

```
struct Mark : Marks {
        Mark(Point xy, char c) : Marks{string(1,c)}
        {
                add(xy);
        }
};
```

The **string{1,c}** is a constructor for **string**, initializing the **string** to contain the single character **c**.

All **Mark** provides is a convenient notation for creating a **Marks** object with a single point marked with a single character. Is **Mark** worth our effort to define it? Or is it just "spurious complication and confusion"? There is no clear, logical answer. We went back and forth on this question, but in the end decided that it was useful for users and the effort to define it was minimal.

Why use a character as a "mark"? We could have used any small shape, but characters provide a useful and simple set of marks. It is often useful to be able to use a variety of "marks" to distinguish different sets of points. Characters such as **x**, **o**, **+**, and * are pleasantly symmetric around a center.

11.10 Image

The average personal computer holds thousands of images in files and can access millions more over the Web. Naturally, we want to display some of those images in even quite simple programs. For example, here is an image (**rita_path.gif**) of the projected path of Hurricane Rita as it approached the Texas Gulf Coast:

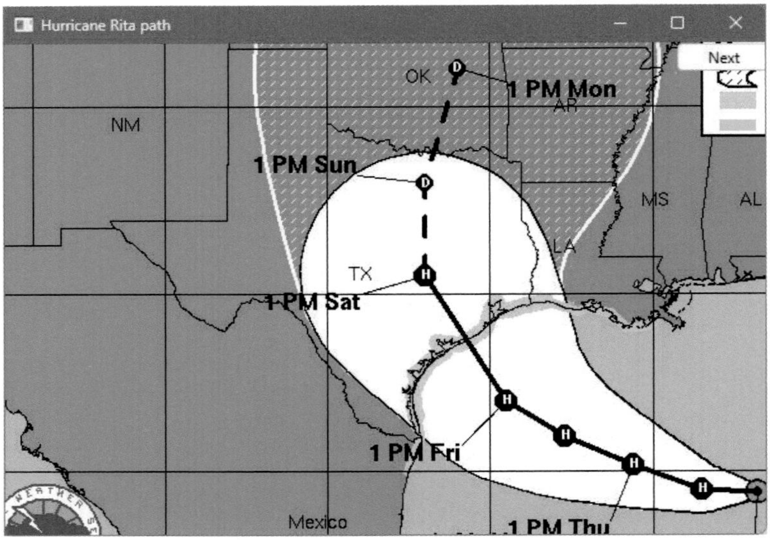

In our graphics interface library, we represent an image in memory as an object of class **Image**:

```
class ImagePrivate; // Implementation class that provides the interface to Qt classes

struct Image : Shape {
	Image(Point xy, string s);
	~Image() {};

	void set_mask(Point xy, int ww, int hh) { w=ww; h=hh; cx=xy.x; cy=xy.y; redraw(); }
	void move(int dx,int dy) override { Shape::move(dx,dy); redraw(); }
	void scale(int ww, int hh, bool keep_aspect_ratio = true);

	ImagePrivate& get_impl() const { return *impl; }
	void draw_specific(Painter& painter) const override;
private:
	int w,h,cx,cy;		// define "masking box" within image relative to position (cx,cy)
	Text fn;
	std::unique_ptr<ImagePrivate> impl;
};
```

The **Image** constructor tries to open a file with the name given to it. The handling of images within a graphics library is quite complicated, but the main complexity of our graphics interface class

Image is in the file handling in the constructor:

```
Image::Image(Point xy, string s)
	:w(0), h(0), fn(xy,""), impl(std::make_unique<ImagePrivate>())
{
	add(xy);

	if (!can_open(s)) {
		fn.set_label("cannot open \"" + s + '\"');
		return;
	}
	impl->load(s);
}
```

If the image cannot be displayed (e.g., because the file wasn't found), the **Image** displays a **Text** including the name of the file it failed to open. That way, we can see the problem right there on the screen, rather than trying to find the problem in the code. This is a common technique in GUI libraries.

Images can be encoded in a bewildering variety of formats, such as JPEG and GIF. We use the file's suffix, e.g. **jpg** or **gif**, to pick the kind of object we create to hold the image.

That mapping from our interface library to Qt's facilities is done by **ImagePrivate**. We access an **ImagePrivate** using a **unique_ptr** that takes care of its proper deletion (§18.5)

Now, we just have to implement **can_open()** to test if we can open a named file for reading:

```
bool can_open(const string& s)
	// check if a file named s exists and can be opened for reading
{
	ifstream ff(s);
	return ff.is_open();
}
```

Opening a file and then closing it again is a fairly clumsy way of portably separating errors related to "can't open the file" from errors related to the format of the data in the file.

> TRY THIS
>
> Write, compile, and run a simple program displaying a picture of your choice. Did it fit in your window? If not, what happened?

We selected part of that image file and added a photo of Rita as seen from space (**rita.jpg**):

```
Image path{ Point{0,0},"rita_path.gif" };
path.set_mask(Point{ 50,250 }, 600, 400);	// select likely landfall

Image rita{ Point{0,0},"rita.jpg" };
rita.scale(300, 200);
```

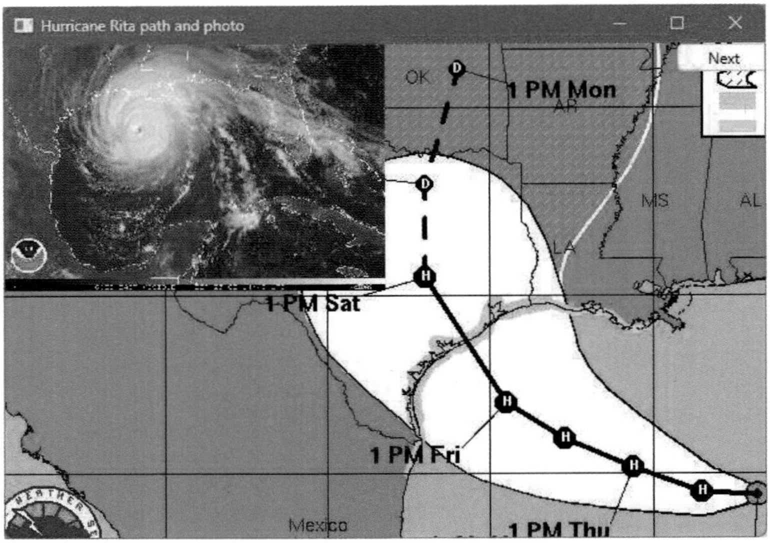

The **set_mask()** operation selects a sub-picture of an image to be displayed. Here, we selected a (600,400)-pixel image from **rita_path.gif** (loaded as **path**) with its top leftmost point at **path**'s point (50,250). Selecting only part of an image for display is so common that we chose to support it directly.

Shapes are laid down in the order they are attached, like pieces of paper on a desk, so we got **path** "on the bottom" simply by attaching it before **rita**.

Drill

[1] Make an 800-by-1000 **Simple_window**.

[2] Put an 8-by-8 grid on the leftmost 800-by-800 part of that window (so that each square is 100 by 100).

[3] Make the eight squares on the diagonal starting from the top left corner red (use **Rectangle**).

[4] Find a 200-by-200-pixel image (JPEG or GIF) and place three copies of it on the grid (each image covering four squares). If you can't find an image that is exactly 200 by 200, use **set_mask()** to pick a 200-by-200 section of a larger image. Don't obscure the red squares.

[5] Add a 100-by-100 image. Have it move around from square to square when you click the "Next" button. Just put **wait_for_button()** in a loop with some code that picks a new square for your image.

Review

[1] Why don't we "just" use a commercial or open-source graphics library directly?
[2] About how many classes from our graphics interface library do you need to do simple graphics output?
[3] What are the header files needed to use the graphics interface library?
[4] What classes define closed shapes?
[5] Why don't we just use **Line** for every shape?
[6] What do the arguments to **Point** indicate?
[7] What are the components of **Line_style**?
[8] What are the components of **Color**?
[9] What is RGB?
[10] What are the differences between two **Lines** and a **Lines** containing two lines?
[11] What properties can you set for every **Shape**?
[12] How many sides does a **Closed_polyline** defined by five **Points** have?
[13] What do you see if you define a **Shape** but don't attach it to a **Window**?
[14] How does a **Rectangle** differ from a **Polygon** with four **Points** (corners)?
[15] How does a **Polygon** differ from a **Closed_polyline**?
[16] What's on top: fill or outline?
[17] Why didn't we bother defining a **Triangle** class (after all, we did define **Rectangle**)?
[18] How do you move a **Shape** to another place in a **Window**?
[19] How do you label a **Shape** with a line of text?
[20] What properties can you set for a text string in a **Text**?
[21] What is a font and why do we care?
[22] What is **Vector_ref** for and how do we use it?
[23] What is the difference between a **Circle** and an **Ellipse**?
[24] What happens if you try to display an **Image** given a file name that doesn't refer to a file containing an image?
[25] How do you display part of an **Image**?
[26] How do you scale an **Image**?

Terms

closed shape	**Image**	**Point**	**Shape**
Color	image encoding	**Polygon**	**Text**
Ellipse	invisible	polyline	**Open_polyline**
fill	JPEG	unnamed object	**Closed_polyline**
Font	**Line**	**Vector_ref**	**Lines**
font size	**Line_style**	visible	**Marked_polyline**
GIF	open shape	**Rectangle**	**Mark**

Exercises

For each "define a class" exercise, display a couple of objects of the class to demonstrate that they work.

[1] Define a class **Arrow**, which draws a line with an arrowhead.

[2] Define functions **n()**, **s()**, **e()**, **w()**, **center()**, **ne()**, **se()**, **sw()**, and **nw()**. Each takes a **Rectangle** argument and returns a **Point**. These functions define "connection points" on and in the rectangle. For example, **nw(r)** is the northwest (top left) corner of a **Rectangle** called **r**.

[3] Define the functions from exercise 2 for a **Circle** and an **Ellipse**. Place the connection points on or outside the shape but not outside the bounding rectangle.

[4] Write a program that draws a class diagram like the one in §10.6. It will simplify matters if you start by defining a **Box** class that is a rectangle with a text label.

[5] Make an RGB color chart (e.g., search the Web for "RGB color chart").

[6] Define a class **Regular_hexagon** (a regular hexagon is a six-sided polygon with all sides of equal length). Use the center and the distance from the center to a corner point as constructor arguments.

[7] Tile a part of a window with **Regular_hexagons** (use at least eight hexagons).

[8] Define a class **Regular_polygon**. Use the center, the number of sides (>2), and the distance from the center to a corner as constructor arguments.

[9] Draw a 300-by-200-pixel ellipse. Draw a 400-pixel-long *x* axis and a 300-pixel-long *y* axis through the center of the ellipse. Mark the foci. Mark a point on the ellipse that is not on one of the axes. Draw the two lines from the foci to the point.

[10] Draw a circle. Move a mark around on the circle (let it move a bit each time you hit the "Next" button).

[11] Draw the color matrix from §11.7.3, but without lines around each color.

[12] Define a right triangle class. Make an octagonal shape out of eight right triangles of different colors.

[13] "Tile" a window with small right triangles.

[14] Do the previous exercise, but with hexagons.

[15] Do the previous exercise, but using hexagons of a few different colors.

[16] Define a class **Poly** that represents a polygon but checks that its points really do make a polygon in its constructor. Hint: You'll have to supply the points to the constructor.

[17] Define a class **Star**. One parameter should be the number of points. Draw a few stars with differing numbers of points, differing line colors, and differing fill colors.

[18] There is an **Arc** class in **Graph.h**. Find it and use it to define a box with rounded corner.

Postscript

Chapter 10 showed how to be a user of classes. This chapter moves us one level up the "food chain" of programmers: here we become tool builders in addition to being tool users.

12

Class Design

Functional, durable, beautiful.
– Vitruvius

The purpose of the graphics chapters is dual: we want to provide useful tools for displaying information, but we also use the family of graphical interface classes to illustrate general design and implementation techniques. In particular, this chapter presents some ideas of interface design and the notion of inheritance. Along the way, we have to take a slight detour to examine the language features that most directly support object-oriented programming: class derivation, virtual functions, and access control. We don't believe that design can be discussed in isolation from use and implementation, so our discussion of design is rather concrete. Ypu could think of this chapter as "Class Design and Implementation" or even "Object-Oriented Programming."

§12.1 Design principles
Types; Operations; Naming; Mutability
§12.2 **Shape**
An abstract class; Access control; Drawing shapes
§12.3 Base and derived classes
Object layout; Deriving classes and defining virtual functions; Overriding; Access; Pure virtual functions
§12.4 Other **Shape** functions
Copy; Moving **Shapes**
§12.5 Benefits of object-oriented programming

12.1 Design principles

This chapter focuses on the techniques usually referred to as *Object-Oriented Programming*. To complement, we have concrete classes (Chapter 8, Chapter 17) and parameterized classes (Chapter 18) and their associated techniques.

12.1.1 Types

What are the design principles for our graphics interface classes? First: What kind of question is that? What are "design principles" and why do we need to look at those instead of getting on with the serious business of producing neat pictures?

CC Graphics is an example of an application domain. So, what we are looking at here is an example of how to present a set of fundamental application concepts and facilities to programmers (like us). If the concepts are presented confusingly, inconsistently, incompletely, or in other ways poorly represented in our code, the difficulty of producing graphical output is increased. We want our graphics classes to minimize the effort of a programmer trying to learn and to use them.

CC Our ideal of program design is to represent the concepts of the application domain directly in code. That way, if you understand the application domain, you understand the code and vice versa. For example:

- **Window** – a window as presented by the operating system
- **Line** – a line as you see it on the screen
- **Point** – a coordinate point
- **Color** – as you see it on the screen
- **Shape** – what's common for all shapes in our graphics/GUI view of the world

The last example, **Shape**, is different from the rest in that it is a generalization, a purely abstract notion. We never see just a shape on the screen; we see a particular shape, such as a line or a hexagon. You'll find that reflected in the definition of our types: try to make a **Shape** variable and the compiler will stop you.

The set of our graphics interface classes is a library; the classes are meant to be used together and in combination. They are meant to be used as examples to follow when you define classes to represent other graphical shapes and as building blocks for such classes. We are not just defining a set of unrelated classes, so we can't make design decisions for each class in isolation. Together, our classes present a view of how to do graphics. We must ensure that this view is reasonably elegant and coherent. Given the size of our library and the enormity of the domain of graphical applications, we cannot hope for completeness. Instead, we aim for simplicity and extensibility.

In fact, no class library directly models all aspects of its application domain. That's not only impossible; it is also pointless. Consider writing a library for displaying geographical information. Do you want to show vegetation? National, state, and other political boundaries? Road systems? Railroads? Rivers? Highlight social and economic data? Seasonal variations in temperature and humidity? Wind patterns in the atmosphere above? Airline routes? Mark the locations of schools? The locations of fast-food "restaurants"? Local beauty spots? "All of that!" may be a good answer for a comprehensive geographical application, but it is not an answer for a single display. It may be an answer for a library supporting such geographical applications, but it is unlikely that such a library could also cover other graphical applications such as freehand drawing, editing photographic images, scientific visualization, and aircraft control displays.

So, as ever, we have to decide what's important to us. In this case, we have to decide which kind of graphics/GUI we want to do well. Trying to do everything is a recipe for failure. A good library directly and cleanly models its application domain from a particular perspective, emphasizes some aspects of the application and deemphasizes others. CC

The classes we provide here are designed for simple graphics and simple graphical user interfaces. They are primarily aimed at users who need to present data and graphical output from numeric/scientific/engineering applications. You can build your own classes "on top of" ours. If that is not enough, we expose sufficient Qt details in our implementation for you to get an idea of how to use that (or a similar "full-blown" industrial graphics/GUI library) directly, should you so desire. However, if you decide to go that route, wait until you have absorbed Chapter 15, Chapter 16, and Chapter 17. Those chapters contain information about pointers and memory management that you need for successful direct use of most graphics/GUI libraries.

One key decision is to provide a lot of "little" classes with few operations. For example, we provide **Open_polyline**, **Closed_polyline**, **Polygon**, **Rectangle**, **Marked_polyline**, **Marks**, and **Mark** where we could have provided a single class (possibly called "polyline") with a lot of arguments and operations that allowed us to specify which kind of polyline an object was and possibly even mutate a polyline from one kind to another. The extreme of this kind of thinking would be to provide every kind of shape as part of a single class **Shape**. We think that AA

- Using many small classes most closely and most usefully models our domain.
- A single class providing "everything" would leave the user messing with data and options without a framework to help understanding, debugging, and performance.
- Large classes and large functions are harder to get correct than a collection of smaller ones.
- The "many small classes" model simplifies adding new classes to a library.

For example, imagine what it would take to add a **Spline** or a **Clock_face** in the two alternative ways to representing **Shape**s.

12.1.2 Operations

We provide a minimum of operations as part of each class. Our ideal is the minimal interface that allows us to do what we want. Where we want greater convenience, we can always provide it in the form of added nonmember functions or yet another class. CC

We want the interfaces of our classes to show a common style. For example, all functions performing similar operations in different classes have the same name, take arguments of the same types, and where possible require those arguments in the same order. Consider the constructors: if a shape requires a location, it takes a **Point** as its first argument: AA

```
Line ln {Point{100,200},Point{300,400}};
Mark m {Point{100,200},'x'};                // display a single point as an 'x'
Circle c {Point{200,200},250};
```

All functions that deal with points use class **Point** to represent them. That would seem obvious, but many libraries exhibit a mixture of styles. For example, imagine a function for drawing a line. We could use one of two styles:

```
void draw_line(Point p1, Point p2);                 // from p1 to p2 (our style)
void draw_line(int x1, int y1, int x2, int y2);     // from (x1,y1) to (x2,y2)
```

We could even allow both, but for consistency, improved type checking, and improved readability we use the first style exclusively. Using **Point** consistently also saves us from confusion between coordinate pairs and the other common pair of integers: width and height. For example, consider:

```
draw_rectangle(Point{100,200}, 300, 400);        // our style
draw_rectangle(100,200,300,400);                  // an alternative
```

The first call draws a rectangle with a point, width, and height. That's reasonably easy to guess, but how about the second call? Is that a rectangle defined by points (100,200) and (300,400)? A rectangle defined by a point (100,200), a width 300, and a height 400? Something completely different (though plausible to someone)? Using the **Point** type consistently avoids such confusion.

Incidentally, if a function requires a width and a height, they are always presented in that order (just as we always give an *x* coordinate before a *y* coordinate). Getting such little details consistent makes a surprisingly large difference to the ease of use and the avoidance of run-time errors.

AA Logically identical operations have the same name. For example, every function that adds points, lines, etc. to any kind of shape is called **add()**. Such uniformity helps us remember (by offering fewer details to remember) and helps us when we design new classes ("just do the usual"). Sometimes, it even allows us to write code that works for many different types, because the operations on those types have an identical pattern. Such code is called *generic*; see Chapter 19, Chapter 20, and Chapter 21.

12.1.3 Naming

AA Logically different operations have different names. Again, that would seem obvious, but consider: why do we "attach" a **Shape** to a **Window**, but "add" a **Line** to a **Shape**? In both cases, we "put something into something," so shouldn't that similarity be reflected by a common name? No. The similarity hides a fundamental difference. Consider:

```
Open_polyline opl;
opl.add(Point{100,100});
opl.add(Point{150,200});
opl.add(Point{250,250});
```

Here, we copy three points into **opl**. The shape **opl** does not care about "our" points after a call to **add()**; it keeps its own copies. In fact, we rarely keep copies of the points – we leave that to the shape. On the other hand, consider:

```
win.attach(opl);
```

Here, we create a connection between the window **win** and our shape **opl**; **win** does not make a copy of **opl** – it keeps a reference to **opl**. We can update **opl** and the next time **win** comes to draw **opl**, our changes will appear on the screen.

We can illustrate the difference between **attach()** and **add()** graphically:

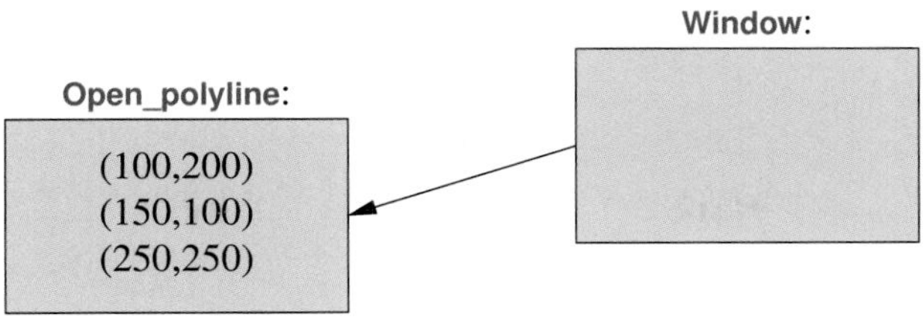

Basically, add() uses pass-by-value (copies) and attach() uses pass-by-reference (shares a single object). We could have chosen to copy graphical objects into Windows. However, that would have given a different programming model, which we would have indicated by using add() rather than attach(). As it is, we just "attach" a graphics object to a Window. That has important implications. For example, we can't create an object, attach it, allow the object to be destroyed, and expect the resulting program to work:

```
void f(Simple_window& w)
{
        Rectangle r {Point{100,200},50,30};
        w.attach(r);
        // oops, the lifetime of r ends here
}

int main()
{
        Simple_window win {Point{100,100},600,400,"My window"};
        // ...
        f(win);                 // asking for trouble
        // ...
        win.wait_for_button();
}
```

By the time we have exited from f() and reached wait_for_button(), there is no r for the win to refer to and display. In Chapter 15, we'll show how to create objects within a function and have them survive after the return from the function. Until then, we must avoid attaching objects that don't survive until the call of wait_for_button(). We have Vector_ref (§11.7.3) to help with that. XX

Note that had we declared f() to take its Window as a const reference argument (as recommended in §7.4.6), the compiler would have prevented our mistake. However, we can't attach(r) to a const Window because attach() needs to make a change to the Window to record the Window's interest in r.

12.1.4 Mutability

When we design a class, "Who can modify the data (representation)?" and "How?" are key questions that we must answer. We try to ensure that modification to the state of an object is done only by its own class. The public/private distinction is key to this, but we'll show examples where a more flexible/subtle mechanism (protected) is employed. This implies that we can't just give a class a data member, say a string called label; we must also consider if it should be possible to modify it after construction, and if so, how. We must also decide if code other than our class's member CC functions needs to read the value of **label**, and if so, how. For example:

```
struct Circle {
      // ...
private:
      int r;      // radius
};

Circle c {Point{100,200},50};
c.r = -9;         // OK? No, compile-time error: Circle::r is private
```

AA As you might have noticed in Chapter 11, we decided to prevent direct access to most data members. Not exposing the data directly gives us the opportunity to check against "silly" values, such as a **Circle** with a negative radius. For simplicity of implementation, we don't take full advantage of this opportunity to check against errors, so do be careful with your values. The decision not to consistently and completely check reflects a desire to keep the code short for presentation and the knowledge that if a user (you, us) supplies "silly" values, the result is simply a messed-up image on the screen and not corruption of precious data.

We treat the screen (seen as a set of **Windows**) purely as an output device. We can display new objects and remove old ones, but we never ask "the system" for information that we don't (or couldn't) know ourselves from the data structures we have built up representing our images.

12.2 Shape

Class **Shape** represents the general notion of something that can appear in a **Window** on a screen:

- It is the notion that ties our graphical objects to our **Window** abstraction, which in turn provides the connection to the operating system and the physical screen.
- It is the class that deals with color and the style used to draw lines. To do that it holds a **Line_style**, a **Color** for lines, and a **Color** for fill.
- It can hold a sequence of **Points** and has a basic notion of how to draw them.

Experienced designers will recognize that a class doing three things probably has problems with generality. However, here, we need something far simpler than the most general solution.

We'll first present the complete class and then discuss its details:

```
struct Shape {            // deals with color and style, and holds sequence of lines
      virtual ~Shape() { }                                    // destructor: see §15.5.2

      Shape(const Shape&) = delete;                           // prevent copying: see §12.4.1
      Shape& operator=(const Shape&) = delete;

      virtual void move(int dx, int dy);                      // move the shape +=dx and +=dy

      void set_color(Color col) { lcolor = col; redraw(); }   // write
      Color color() const { return lcolor; }                  // read
```

```
        void set_style(Line_style sty) { ls = sty; redraw(); }
        Line_style style() const { return ls; }

        void set_fill_color(Color col) { fcolor = col; redraw(); }
        Color fill_color() const { return fcolor; }

        Point point(int i) const { return points[i]; }
        int number_of_points() const { return naro<int>(points.size()); }

        void set_window(Window* win) { parent_window = win; }

        void draw(Painter& painter) const;                // deal with color and draw_specifics
protected:
        Shape(std::initializer_list<Point> lst = {});     // add() the Points to this Shape

        void add(Point p){ points.push_back(p); redraw(); }
        void set_point(int i, Point p) { points[i] = p; redraw(); }

        void redraw();
private:
        virtual void draw_specifics(Painter& painter) const = 0; // draw this specific shape

        Window* parent_window = nullptr;                  // The window in which the Shape appears
        vector<Point> points;                             // not used by all shapes
        Color lcolor = Color::black;
        Line_style ls;                                    // use the default line style
        Color fcolor = Color::invisible;                  // fill color
};
```

This is a relatively complex class designed to support a wide variety of graphics classes and to represent the general concept of a shape on the screen. However, it still has only 5 data members and 19 functions. Furthermore, those functions are all close to trivial so that we can concentrate on design issues. For the rest of this section, we will go through the members one by one and explain their role in the design.

12.2.1 An abstract class

Consider first **Shape**'s constructor:

```
protected:
        Shape(initializer_list<Point> lst = {});     // add() the Points to this Shape
```

The constructor **add()**s the elements of its argument list to the **Shape**'s **vector<Point>**:

```
Shape::Shape(initializer_list<Point> lst)
{
        for (Point p : lst)
                add(p);
}
```

If we don't provide a set of **Points**, we default to the empty **initializer_list**.

The constructor is **protected**. That means that it can only be used directly from classes derived from **Shape** using the **:Shape** notation. That is, for specific shapes, such as **Circle** and **Closed_polyline**, rather than for the general notion of a shape. Classes defined using the **:Shape** notation are called *derived classes* and **Shape** is called their *base class* (§12.3). The purpose of that **protected:** is to ensure that we don't make **Shape** objects directly. For example:

```
Shape ss;        // error: cannot construct Shape
```

CC By prohibiting the direct creation of **Shape** objects, we directly model the idea that we cannot have/see a general shape, only particular shapes, such as **Circle** and **Closed_polyline**. Think about it! What does a shape look like? The only reasonable response is the counter question "What shape?" The notion of a shape that we represent by **Shape** is an abstract concept. That's an important and frequently useful design notion, so we don't want to compromise it in our program. Allowing users to directly create **Shape** objects would do violence to our ideal of classes as direct representations of concepts.

CC A class is *abstract* if it can be used only as a base class. The other – more common – way of achieving that is called a *pure virtual function* (§12.3.5). A class that can be used to create objects – that is, the opposite of an abstract class – is called a *concrete* class. Note that *abstract* and *concrete* are simply technical words for an everyday distinction. We might go to the store to buy a camera. However, we can't just ask for a camera and take it home. What type of camera? What brand of camera? Which particular model camera? The word "camera" is a generalization; it refers to an abstract notion. An Olympus E-M5 refers to a specific kind of camera, which we (in exchange for a large amount of cash) might acquire a particular instance of: a particular camera with a unique serial number. So, "camera" is much like an abstract (base) class; "Olympus E-M5" is much like a concrete (derived) class, and the actual camera in my hand (if I bought it) would be much like an object of that class.

12.2.2 Access control

Class **Shape** declares all data members **private**:

```
private:
     Window* parent_window = nullptr;       // The window in which the Shape appears
     vector<Point> points;                  // not used by all shapes
     Color lcolor = Color::black;           // color for lines and characters (with default)
     Line_style ls;                         // use the default line style
     Color fcolor = Color::invisible;       // fill color (default: no color)
```

The initializers for the data members don't depend on constructor arguments, so we specified them in the data member declarations. As ever, the default value for a vector is "empty" so we didn't have to be explicit about that. The constructor will apply those default values.

AA Since the data members of **Shape** are declared **private**, we need to provide access functions. There are several possible styles for doing this. We chose one that we consider simple, convenient, and readable. If we have a member representing a property **X**, we provide a pair of functions **X()** and **set_X()** for reading and writing, respectively. For example:

```
void Shape::set_color(Color col)
{
	lcolor = col;
}

Color Shape::color() const
{
	return lcolor;
}
```

The main inconvenience of this style is that you can't give the member variable the same name as its readout function. As ever, we chose the most convenient names for the functions because they are part of the public interface. It matters far less what we call our **private** variables. Note the way we use **const** to indicate that the readout functions do not modify their **Shape** (§8.7.4).

Shape keeps a vector of **Points**, called **points**, that a **Shape** maintains in support of its derived classes. We provide the function **add()** for adding **Points** to **points**:

```
void Shape::add(Point p)	// protected
{
	points.push_back(p);
}
```

Naturally, **points** starts out empty. We decided to provide **Shape** with a complete functional interface rather than giving users – even member functions of classes derived from **Shape** – direct access to data members. To some, providing a functional interface is a no-brainer, because they feel that making any data member of a class **public** is bad design. To others, our design seems overly restrictive because we don't allow direct write access to all members of derived classes.

A shape derived from **Shape**, such as **Circle** and **Polygon**, knows what its points mean. The base class **Shape** does not "understand" the points; it only stores them. Therefore, the derived classes need control over how points are added. For example:

- **Circle** and **Rectangle** do not allow a user to add points; that just wouldn't make sense. What would be a rectangle with an extra point? (§10.7.4, §11.7.5).
- **Lines** allows only pairs of points to be added (and not an individual point; §11.3).
- **Open_polyline** and **Marks** allow any number of points to be added.
- **Polygon** allows a point to be added only by an **add()** that checks for intersections (§11.7.1).

We made **add() protected** (that is, accessible from a derived class only) to ensure that derived classes take control over how points are added. Had **add()** been **public** (everybody can add points) or **private** (only **Shape** can add points), this close match of functionality to our idea of shapes would not have been possible. **AA**

Similarly, we made **set_point() protected**. In general, only a derived class can know what a point means and whether it can be changed without violating an invariant (§8.4.3). For example, if we have a **Regular_hexagon** class defined as a set of six points, changing just a single point would make the resulting figure "not a regular hexagon." In fact, we didn't find a need for **set_point()** in our example classes and code, so **set_point()** is provided just to ensure that the rule that we can read and set every attribute of a **Shape** holds. For example, if we wanted a **Mutable_rectangle**, we could derive it from **Rectangle** and provide operations to change the points.

We made the vector of **Points**, **points**, **private** to protect it against undesired modification. To make it useful, we also need to provide access to it:

```
void Shape::set_point(int i, Point p)       // not used; not necessary so far
{
      points[i] = p;
}

Point Shape::point(int i) const
{
      return points[i];
}

int Shape::number_of_points() const
{
      return points.size();
}
```

In derived class member functions, these functions are used like this:

```
void Lines::draw_specifics(Painter& painter) const          // draw lines connecting pairs of points
{
      if (color().visibility())
            for (int i=1; i<number_of_points(); i+=2)
                  painter.draw_line(point(i–1),point(i));
}
```

CC You might worry about all those trivial access functions. Are they not inefficient? Do they slow down the program? Do they increase the size of the generated code? No, they will all be compiled away ("inlined") by the compiler. For example, calling **number_of_points()** will take up exactly as many bytes of memory and execute exactly as many instructions as calling **points.size()** directly.

These access control considerations and decisions are important. We could have provided this close-to-minimal version of **Shape**:

```
struct Shape {              // close-to-minimal definition - too simple - not used
      Shape(initializer_list<Point> = {});
      void draw() const;                                       // deal with color and call draw_specifics
      virtual void draw_specifics(Painter& painter) const;     // draw this specific shape
      virtual void move(int dx, int dy);                       // move the shape +=dx and +=dy
      virtual ˜Shape();

      Window∗ parent_window;
      vector<Point> points;                                    // not used by all shapes
      Color lcolor;
      Line_style ls;
      Color fcolor;
};
```

CC What value did we add by those extra 14 member functions and two lines of access specifications (**private:** and **protected:**)? The basic answer is that protecting the representation ensures that it doesn't change in ways unanticipated by a class designer so that we can write better classes with less effort. This is the argument about "invariants" (§8.4.3). Here, we'll point out such advantages as we define classes derived from **Shape**. One simple example is that earlier versions of **Shape** used

```
Fl_Color lcolor;      // earlier: use FLTK's color type
int line_style;       // earlier: use a plain integer to represent a line style
```

This turned out to be too limiting (an **int** line style doesn't elegantly support line width, and **Fl_Color** doesn't accommodate **invisible**) and led to some messy code. Had these two variables been **public** and used in a user's code, we could have improved our interface library only at the cost of breaking that code (because it mentioned the names **lcolor** and **line_style**).

In addition, the access functions often provide notational convenience. For example, **s.add(p)** is easier to read and write than **s.points.push_back(p)**. AA

We could simplify **Shape** even further by removing everything not needed by all shapes. For example, a **Line** doesn't use fill color and a **Circle** uses only a single **Point**, rather than a **vector** of **Points**. That would make **Shape** a pure interface as described in §12.3.5, but would also force us to repeat a lot of code in implementations of specific shapes.

12.2.3 Drawing shapes

We have now described almost all but the real heart of class **Shape**:

```
void draw(Painter& painter) const;                      // deal with color and style and call draw_specifics
virtual void draw_specifics(Painter& painter) const;    // draw this specific shape appropriately
```

Shape's most basic job is to draw shapes. We could remove all other functionality from **Shape** or leave it with no data of its own without doing major conceptual harm (§12.5), but drawing is **Shape**'s essential business. It does so using Qt and the operating system's basic machinery, but from a user's point of view, it provides just two functions:

- **draw()** chooses color and style; then calls **draw_specifics()**; then restores color and style.
- **draw_specifics()** puts pixels on the screen for a specific **Shape**.

The **draw()** function doesn't use any novel techniques. It simply calls Qt functions to set the color and style to what is specified in the **Shape**, calls **draw_specifics()** to do the actual drawing on the screen, and then restores color and style to what they were before the call:

```
void Shape::draw(Painter& painter) const
{
        painter.save();
        painter.set_line_style(style());
        painter.set_color(color());
        painter.set_fill_color(fill_color());
        draw_specifics(painter);
        painter.restore();
}
```

Shape::draw() doesn't directly handle fill color or the visibility of lines. Those are handled by the individual **draw_specifics()** functions that have a better idea of how to interpret them. For example **set_fill_color()** is a "no op", does nothing, for shapes that are not closed (§11.7). In principle, all color and style handling could be delegated to the individual **draw_specifics()** functions, but that would be quite repetitive.

CC Now consider how we might handle draw_specifics(). If you think about it for a bit, you'll realize that it would be hard for a Shape function to draw all that needs to be drawn for every kind of shape. To do so would require that every last pixel of each shape should somehow be stored in the Shape object. If we kept the vector<Point> model, we'd have to store an awful lot of points. Worse, "the screen" (that is, the graphics hardware) already does that – and does it better.

CC To avoid that extra work and extra storage, Shape takes another approach: it gives each Shape (that is, each class derived from Shape) a chance to define what it means to draw it. A Text, Rectangle, or Circle class may have a clever way of drawing itself. In fact, most such classes do. After all, such classes "know" exactly what they are supposed to represent. For example, a Circle is defined by a point and a radius, rather than, say, a lot of line segments. Generating the required bits for a Circle from the point and radius if and when needed isn't really all that hard or expensive. So Circle defines its own draw_specifics() which we want to call instead of Shape's draw_specifics(). That's what the virtual in the declaration of Shape::draw_specifics() means:

```
struct Shape {
     // ...
     virtual void draw_specifics(Painter& painter) const;      // draw this specific shape appropriately
     // ...
};

struct Circle : Shape {
     // ...
     void draw_specifics(Painter& painter) const override;
     // ...
};
```

So, Shape's draw_specifics() must somehow invoke Circle's draw_specifics() if the Shape is a Circle and Rectangle's draw_specifics() if the Shape is a Rectangle. That's what the word virtual in the draw_specifics() declaration ensures: Circle has defined its own draw_specifics() (with the same type as Shape's draw_specifics()), so that Circle::draw_specifics() will be called. Chapter 13 shows how that's done for Text, Circle, Closed_polyline, etc. Defining a function in a derived class so that it can be used through the interfaces provided by a base is called *overriding*.

Note that despite its central role in Shape, draw_specifics() is protected; it is not meant to be called by "the general user" – that's what draw() is for – but simply as an "implementation detail" used by draw() and the classes derived from Shape.

This completes our display model from §10.2. The system that drives the screen knows about Window. Window knows about Shape and can call Shape's draw(). Finally, draw() invokes the draw_specifics() for the particular kind of shape.

If we make a change to a Shape, we call redraw() to inform the Window that it must refresh its image on the screen accordingly.

A call of Application's gui_main() in our user code starts the display engine.

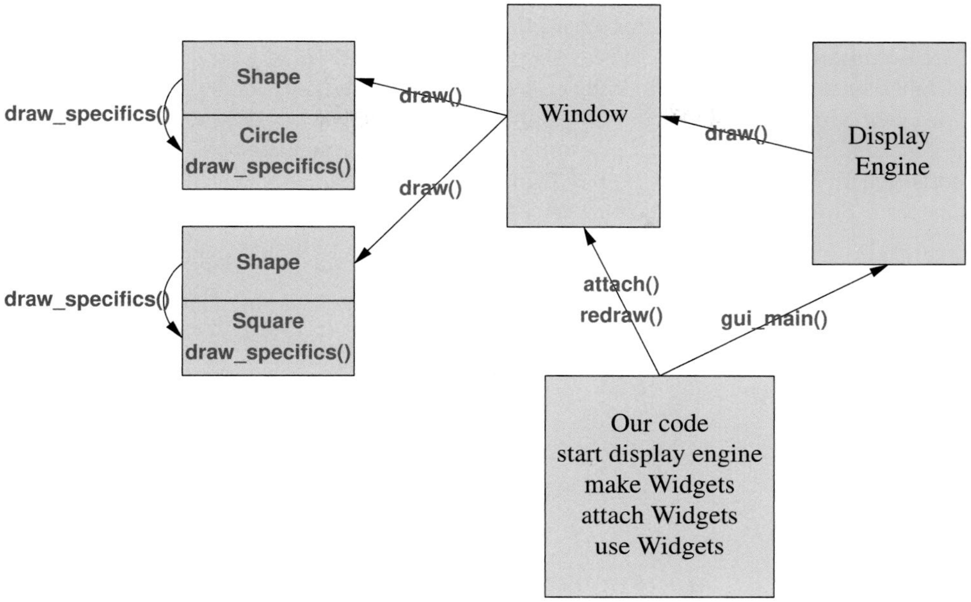

What gui_main()? So far, we haven't actually seen gui_main() in our code (§14.7). Instead we use wait_for_button(), which implicitly invokes the display engine in a more simple-minded manner.

12.3 Base and derived classes

Let's take a more technical view of base and derived classes; that is, let us for this section (only) change the focus of discussion from programming, application design, and graphics to programming language features. When designing our graphics interface library, we relied on three key language mechanisms: CC

- *Derivation:* a way to build one class from another so that the new class can be used in place of the original. For example, Circle is derived from Shape, or in other words, "a Circle is a kind of Shape" or "Shape is a base of Circle." The derived class (here, Circle) gets all of the members of its base (here, Shape) in addition to its own. This is often called *inheritance* because the derived class "inherits" all of the members of its base. In some contexts, a derived class is called a *subclass* and a base class is called a *superclass*.
- *Virtual functions:* the ability to define a function in a base class and have a function of the same name and type in a derived class called when a user calls the base class function. For example, when Window calls draw_specifics() (through draw()) for a Shape that is a Circle, it is the Circle's draw_specifics() that is executed, rather than Shape's own draw_specifics(). This is often called *run-time polymorphism*, *dynamic dispatch*, or *run-time dispatch* because the function called is determined at run time based on the type of the object used.

- *Private and protected members*: We kept the implementation details of our classes private to protect them from direct use that could complicate maintenance (§12.2.2). That's often called *encapsulation*.

The use of inheritance, run-time polymorphism, and encapsulation is the most common definition of *object-oriented programming*. Thus, C++ directly supports object-oriented programming in addition to other programming styles. For example, in Chapter 20 and Chapter 21, we'll see how C++ supports generic programming. C++ borrowed – with explicit acknowledgments – its key mechanisms from Simula67, the first language to directly support object-oriented programming (PPP2.Ch22).

That was a lot of technical terminology! But what does it all mean? And how does it actually work on our computers? Let's first draw a simple diagram of our graphics interface classes showing their inheritance relationships:

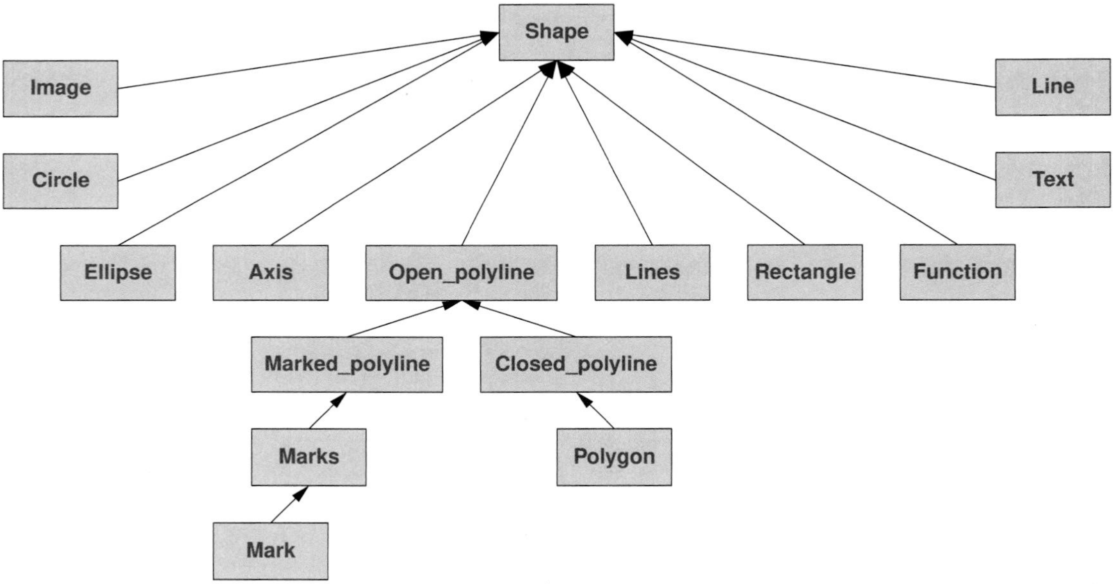

The arrows point from a derived class to its base. Such diagrams help visualize class relationships and often decorate the whiteboards of programmers. Compared to commercial frameworks, this is a tiny *class hierarchy* with only 16 classes, and only in the case of **Open_polyline**'s many descendants is the hierarchy more than one deep. Clearly the common base (**Shape**) is the most important class here, even though it represents an abstract concept so that we never directly make a shape.

12.3.1 Object layout

CC How are objects laid out in memory? As we saw in §8.4.1, members of a class define the layout of objects: data members are stored one after another in memory. When inheritance is used, the data members of a derived class are simply added after those of a base. For example:

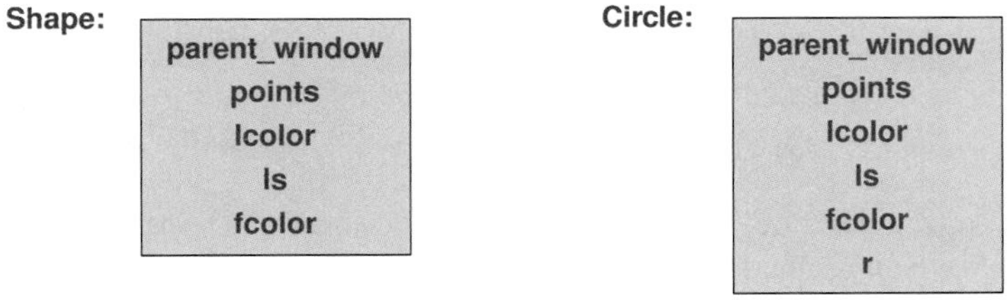

A **Circle** has the data members of a **Shape** (after all, it is a kind of **Shape**) and can be used as a **Shape**. In addition, **Circle** has "its own" data member **r** placed after the inherited data members.

CC

To handle a virtual function call, we need (and have) one more piece of data in a **Shape** object: something to tell which function is really invoked when we call **Shape**'s **draw_specifics()**. The way that is usually done is to add the address of a table of functions. This table is usually referred to as the **vtbl** (for "virtual table" or "virtual function table") and its address is often called the **vptr** (for "virtual pointer"). We discuss pointers in Chapter 17 and Chapter 18; here, they act like references. A given implementation may use different names for **vtbl** and **vptr**. Adding the **vptr** and the **vtbl**s to the picture we get:

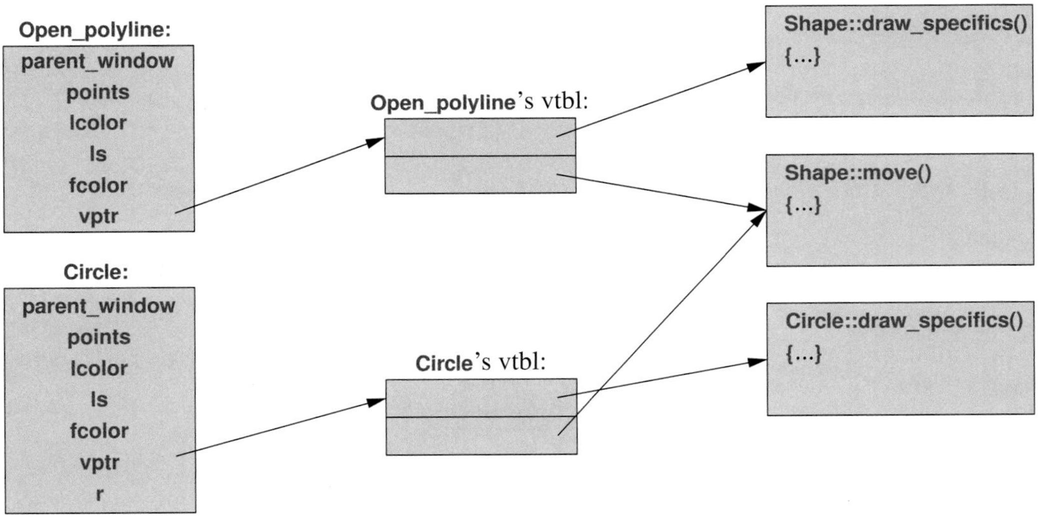

Since **draw_specifics()** is the first virtual function, it gets the first slot in the **vtbl**, followed by that of **move()**, the second virtual function. A class can have as many virtual functions as you want it to have; its **vtbl** will be as large as needed (one slot per virtual function). Now when we call **x.draw_specifics()**, the compiler generates a call to the function found in the **draw_specifics()** slot in the **vtbl** for **x**. Basically, the code just follows the arrows on the diagram. So if **x** is a **Circle**, **Circle::draw_specifics()** will be called. If **x** is of a type, say **Open_polyline**, that uses the **vtbl** exactly as **Shape** defined it, **Shape::draw_specifics()** will be called. Similarly, **Circle** didn't define its own **move()** so **x.move()** will call **Shape::move()** if **x** is a **Circle**. Basically, code generated for a virtual function call simply finds the **vptr**, uses that to get to the right **vtbl**, and calls the appropriate function there. The cost is about two memory accesses plus the cost of an ordinary function call. This is simple and fast.

Shape is an abstract class so you can't actually have an object that's just a **Shape**, but an **Open_polyline** will have exactly the same layout as a "plain shape" since it doesn't add a data member or define a virtual function. There is just one **vtbl** for each class with a virtual function, not one for each object, so the **vtbl**s tend not to add significantly to a program's object code size.

Note that we didn't draw any non-virtual functions in this picture. We didn't need to because there is nothing special about the way such functions are called and they don't increase the size of objects of their type.

Defining a function of the same name and type as a virtual function from a base class (such as **Circle::draw_specifics()**) so that the function from the derived class is put into the **vtbl** instead of the version from the base is called *overriding*. For example, **Circle::draw_specifics()** overrides **Shape::draw_specifics()**.

AA Why are we telling you about **vtbl**s and memory layout? Do you need to know about that to use object-oriented programming? No. However, many people strongly prefer to know how things are implemented (we are among those), and when people don't understand something, myths spring up. We have met people who were terrified of virtual functions "because they are expensive." Why? How expensive? Compared to what? Where would the cost matter? We explain the implementation model for virtual functions so that you won't have such fears. When we need to select among an unknown set of alternatives at run time, we can't code the functionality to be any faster or to use less memory by using other language features than a virtual function call. You can see that for yourself: measure before making statements about efficiency (§20.4).

12.3.2 Deriving classes and defining virtual functions

We specify that a class is to be a derived class by mentioning a base after the class name. For example:

```
struct Circle : Shape { /* ... */ };
```

CC By default, the members of a **struct** are **public** (§8.3), and that will include **public** members of a base. We could equivalently have said

```
class Circle : public Shape { public: /* ... */ };
```

These two declarations of **Circle** are completely equivalent, but you can have many long and fruitless discussions with people about which is better. We are of the opinion that time can be spent more productively on other topics.

Beware of forgetting **public** when you need it. For example:

```
class Circle : Shape { public: /* ... */ };      // probably a mistake
```

This would make **Shape** a **private** base of **Circle**, making **Shape**'s **public** functions inaccessible for a **Circle**. That's unlikely to be what you meant. A good compiler will warn about this likely error. There are uses for **private** base classes, but those are beyond the scope of this book.

A virtual function must be declared **virtual** in its class declaration, but the keyword **virtual** is neither required nor allowed outside the class. For example:

```
struct Shape {
        // ...
        virtual void draw_specifics(Painter& painter) const;
        virtual void move();
        // ...
};

virtual void Shape::draw_specifics(Painter& painter) const { /* ... */ }   // error: "virtual" outside class
void Shape::move() { /* ... */ }                                          // OK
```

12.3.3 Overriding

When you want to override a virtual function, you must use exactly the same name and type as in the base class. For example: XX

```
struct Circle : Shape {
        void draw_specifics(int) const;        // probably a mistake (int argument?)
        void drawlines() const;                // probably a mistake (misspelled name?)
        void draw_specifics();                 // probably a mistake (const missing?)
        void draw_specifics() const;           // probably a mistake (Painter& argument missing?)

        void draw_specifics(Painter&) const;             // OK: implicit override
        void draw_specifics(Painter&) const override;    // OK: explicit override

        // ...
};
```

Here, the compiler will see four functions that are independent of Shape::draw_specifics() (because they have a different name or a different type) and won't override them. A good compiler will warn about these likely mistakes.

The draw_specifics() example is real and can therefore be hard to follow in all details, so here is a purely technical example that illustrates overriding:

```
struct B {
        virtual void f() const { cout << "B::f "; }
        void g() const { cout << "B::g "; }          // not virtual
};

struct D : B {
        void f() const { cout << "D::f "; }          // overrides B::f
        void g() { cout << "D::g "; }
};

struct DD : D {
        void f() { cout << "DD::f "; }               // doesn't override D::f (not const)
        void g() const { cout << "DD::g "; }
};
```

Here, we have a small class hierarchy with (just) one virtual function **f()**. We can try using it. In particular, we can try to call **f()** and the non-virtual **g()**, which is a function that doesn't know what type of object it had to deal with except that it is a **B** (or something derived from **B**):

```
void call(const B& b)
        // a D is a kind of B, so call() can accept a D
        // a DD is a kind of D and a D is a kind of B, so call() can accept a DD
{
        b.f();
        b.g();
}

int main()
{
        B b;
        D d;
        DD dd;
        call(b);
        call(d);
        call(dd);

        b.f();
        b.g();

        d.f();
        d.g();

        dd.f();
        dd.g();
}
```

You'll get

```
B::f B::g D::f B::g D::f B::g B::f B::g D::f D::g DD::f DD::g
```

When you understand why, you know the mechanics of inheritance and virtual functions.

Obviously, it can be hard to keep track of which derived class functions are meant to override which base class functions. Fortunately, we can get compiler help to check. We can explicitly declare that a function is meant to override. Assuming that the derived class functions were meant to override, we can say so by adding **override** and the example becomes

```
struct B {
        virtual void f() const { cout << "B::f "; }
        void g() const { cout << "B::g "; }                    // not virtual
};
```

```
struct D : B {
      void f() const override { cout << "D::f "; }          // overrides B::f
      void g() override { cout << "D::g "; }                 // error: no virtual B::g to override
};

struct DD : D {
      void f() override { cout << "DD::f "; }                // error: doesn't override: D::f is not const
      void g() const override { cout << "DD::g "; }          // error: no virtual D::g to override
};
```

Explicit use of **override** is particularly useful in large, complicated class hierarchies.

12.3.4 Access

C++ provides a simple model of access to members of a class. A member of a class can be **CC**

- *Private*: If a member is **private**, its name can be used only by members of the class in which it is declared.
- *Protected*: If a member is **protected**, its name can be used only by members of the class in which it is declared and members of classes derived from that.
- *Public*: If a member is **public**, its name can be used by all functions.

Or graphically:

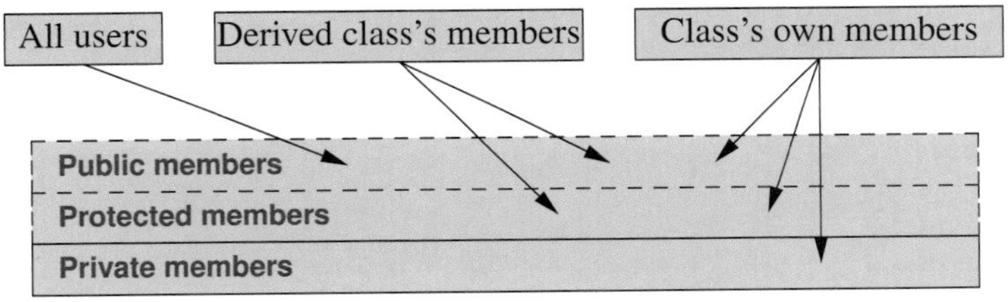

A base can also be **private**, **protected**, or **public**:

- If a base of class **D** is **private**, its **public** and **protected** member names can be used only by members of **D**.
- If a base of class **D** is **protected**, its **public** and **protected** member names can be used only by members of **D** and members of classes derived from **D**.
- If a base is **public**, its public member names can be used by all functions.

These definitions ignore the concept of "friend" and a few minor details, which are beyond the scope of this book. If you want to become a language lawyer, you need to study Stroustrup: *The Design and Evolution of C++* [DnE], the C++ *History of Programming Languages* papers [HOPL-4], and *The C++ Programming Language*. The official definition of C++ is *The ISO C++ standard*. We don't recommend becoming a language lawyer (someone knowing every little detail of the language definition); being a programmer (a software developer, an engineer, a user, whatever you prefer to call someone who actually uses the language) is much more fun and typically much more useful to society.

12.3.5 Pure virtual functions

CC An abstract class is a class that can be used only as a base class. We use abstract classes to represent concepts that are abstract; that is, we use abstract classes for concepts that are generalizations of common characteristics of related entities. Thick books of philosophy have been written trying to precisely define *abstract concept* (or *abstraction* or *generalization* or ...). However you define it philosophically, the notion of an abstract concept is immensely useful. Examples are "animal" (as opposed to any particular kind of animal), "device driver" (as opposed to the driver for any particular kind of device), and "publication" (as opposed to any particular kind of book or magazine). In programs, abstract classes usually define interfaces to groups of related classes (*class hierarchies*).

CC In §12.2.1, we saw how to make a class abstract by declaring its constructor **protected**. There is another – and much more common – way of making a class abstract: state that one or more of its **virtual** functions must be overridden in some derived class. For example:

```
class B {  // abstract base class
public:
        virtual void f() =0;    // pure virtual function
        virtual void g() =0;
};

B b;         // error: B is abstract
```

The curious **=0** notation says that the virtual functions **B::f()** and **B::g()** are "pure"; that is, they must be overridden in some derived class. Since **B** has pure virtual functions, we cannot create an object of class **B**. Overriding the pure virtual functions solves this "problem":

```
class D1 : public B {
public:
        void f() override;
        void g() override;
};

D1 d1;            // OK
```

Note that unless all pure virtual functions are overridden, the resulting class is still abstract:

```
class D2 : public B {
public:
        void f() override;
        // no g()
};

D2 d2;     // error: D2 is (still) abstract

class D3 : public D2 {
public:
        void g() override;
};
```

```
D3 d3;            // OK
```

AA

Classes with pure virtual functions tend to be pure interfaces; that is, they tend to have no data members (the data members will be in the derived classes) and consequently have no constructors (if there are no data members to initialize, a constructor is unlikely to be needed).

12.4 Other Shape functions

To complete **Shape**, we need to deal with copying **Shapes**. We also present how to move a **Shape** on the screen.

12.4.1 Copy

CC

The **Shape** class declared its copy constructor and the copy assignment **deleted**:

```
Shape(const Shape&) =delete;                    // prevent copying
Shape& operator=(const Shape&) =delete;
```

This eliminates the default copy operations for **Shapes** and for every class derived from **Shape** that hasn't defined its own copy operations (and we won't do that). Consider:

```
void copy_to(Circle& c, Rectangle& r)
{
        c = r;               // this doesn't look innocent at all (and fortunately it is an error)
        // ...
}
```

Assigning a **Rectangle** to a **Circle** doesn't make sense:

- A **Rectangle** is represented by two **Points**.
- A **Circle** is represented by a **Point** and an **int**.

Those two objects aren't even of the same size! If allowed, what space would the **Rectangle** be copied into (§12.3.1)? Also, **Circle** and **Rectangle** have completely different **draw_specifics()** functions.

So why would **c=r** have worked if we hadn't prohibited it? Had copying of **Shapes** been allowed, **Shape**'s copy assignment would have been called, treating the **Circle** and the **Rectangle** as **Shapes**:

```
Shape& operator=(const Shape&);          // copy assignment
```

Implementing that so that it makes sense is impossible in general. For example, assigning a **Circle** to a **Rectangle** simply doesn't make sense. For pairs of **Shapes**, where an assignment does make sense, we can define functions to handle those special cases.

XX

Basically, class hierarchies plus pass-by-reference and default copying do not mix. When you design a class that is meant to be a base class (i.e., has at least one **virtual** function), disable its copy constructor and copy assignment using **=delete** as was done for **Shape**. See also §12.3.

12.4.2 Moving Shapes

Shape's move() function simply moves every point stored relative to the current position:

```
void Shape::move(int dx, int dy)   // move the shape +=dx and +=dy
{
        for (auto& xy : points) {
                xy.x += dx;
                xy.y += dy;
        }
        redraw();
}
```

Like draw_specifics(), move() is virtual because a derived class may have data that needs to be moved and that Shape does not know about. For example, see Axis (§10.7.1, §13.4). Every class derived from Shape that doesn't store all its data in Shape must define its own move().

Note the call of redraw(). After a change to a Shape, we must tell the Window to refresh that Shape's image on the screen (§12.2.3).

12.5 Benefits of object-oriented programming

CC When we say that Circle is derived from Shape, or that Circle is a kind of Shape, we do so to obtain (either or both)

- *Interface inheritance*: A function expecting a Shape (usually as a reference argument) can accept a Circle (and can use a Circle through the interface provided by Shape).
- *Implementation inheritance*: When we define Circle and its member functions, we can take advantage of the facilities (such as data and member functions) offered by Shape.

XX A design that does not provide interface inheritance (that is, a design for which an object of a derived class cannot be used as an object of its public base class) is a poor and error-prone design. For example, we might define a class called Never_do_this with Shape as its public base. Then we could override Shape::draw_specifics() with a function that didn't draw the shape, but instead moved its center 100 pixels to the left. That "design" is fatally flawed because even though Never_do_this provides the interface of a Shape, its implementation does not maintain the semantics (meaning, behavior) required of a Shape. Never do that!

AA Interface inheritance gets its name because its benefits come from code using the interface provided by a base class ("an interface"; here, Shape) and not having to know about the derived classes ("implementations"; here, classes derived from Shape).

AA Implementation inheritance gets its name because the benefits come from the simplification in the implementation of derived classes (e.g., Circle) provided by the facilities offered by the base class (here, Shape).

Note that our graphics design critically depends on interface inheritance: the "graphics engine" calls Shape::draw() which in turn calls Shape's virtual function draw_specifics() to do the real work of putting images on the screen. Neither the "graphics engine" nor indeed class Shape knows which kinds of shapes exist. In particular, our "graphics engine" (for now, Qt plus the operating system's graphics facilities) was written and compiled years before our graphics classes! We just define particular shapes and attach() them to Windows as Shapes (Window::attach() takes a Shape&

argument). Furthermore, since class Shape doesn't know about your graphics classes, you don't need to recompile Shape each time you define a new graphics interface class.

In other words, we can add new Shapes to a program without modifying existing code. This is a holy grail of software design/development/maintenance: extension of a system without modifying it. There are limits to which changes we can make without modifying existing classes (e.g., Shape offers a rather limited range of services), and the technique doesn't apply well to all programming problems (see, for example, Chapter 15 – Chapter 18 where we define a Vector; inheritance has little to offer for that). However, interface inheritance is one of the most powerful techniques for designing and implementing systems that are robust in the face of change. CC

Similarly, implementation inheritance has much to offer, but it is no panacea. By placing useful services in Shape, we save ourselves the bother of repeating work over and over again in the derived classes. That can be most significant in real-world code. However, it comes at the cost that any change to the interface of Shape or any change to the layout of the data members of Shape necessitates a recompilation of all derived classes and their users. For a widely used library, such recompilation can be simply infeasible. Naturally, there are ways of gaining most of the benefits while avoiding most of the problems; see §12.3.5. XX

Drill

Unfortunately, we can't construct a drill for the understanding of general design principles, so here we focus on the language features that support object-oriented programming.

[1] Define a class B1 with a virtual function vf() and a non-virtual function f(). Define both of these functions within class B1. Implement each function to output its name (e.g., B1::vf()). Make the functions public. Make a B1 object and call each function.

[2] Derive a class D1 from B1 and override vf(). Make a D1 object and call vf() and f() for it.

[3] Define a reference to B1 (a B1&) and initialize that to the D1 object you just defined. Call vf() and f() for that reference.

[4] Now define a function called f() for D1 and repeat 1–3. Explain the results.

[5] Add a pure virtual function called pvf() to B1 and try to repeat 1–4. Explain the result.

[6] Define a class D2 derived from D1 and override pvf() in D2. Make an object of class D2 and invoke f(), vf(), and pvf() for it.

[7] Define a class B2 with a pure virtual function pvf(). Define a class D21 with a string data member and a member function that overrides pvf(); D21::pvf() should output the value of the string. Define a class D22 that is just like D21 except that its data member is an int. Define a function f() that takes a B2& argument and calls pvf() for its argument. Call f() with a D21 and a D22.

Review

[1] What is an application domain?

[2] What are ideals for naming?

[3] What can we name?

[4] What services does a Shape offer?

[5] How does an abstract class differ from a class that is not abstract?
[6] How can you make a class abstract?
[7] What is controlled by access control?
[8] What good can it do to make a data member **private**?
[9] What is a virtual function and how does it differ from a non-virtual function?
[10] What is a base class?
[11] What makes a class derived?
[12] What do we mean by object layout?
[13] What can you do to make a class easier to test?
[14] What is an inheritance diagram?
[15] What is the difference between a **protected** member and a **private** one?
[16] What members of a class can be accessed from a class derived from it?
[17] How does a pure virtual function differ from other virtual functions?
[18] Why would you make a member function virtual?
[19] Why would you *not* make a member function virtual?
[20] Why would you make a virtual member function pure?
[21] What does overriding mean?
[22] Why should you always suppress copy operations for a class in a class hierarchy?
[23] How does interface inheritance differ from implementation inheritance?
[24] What is object-oriented programming?

Terms

abstract class	mutability	**public**	access control
object layout	pure virtual function	base class	object-oriented
subclass	derived class	**override**	superclass
dispatch	polymorphism	**virtual** function	encapsulation
private	virtual function call	inheritance	**protected**
virtual function table	**=0**	OOP	**=delete**

Exercises

[1] Define two classes **Smiley** and **Frowny**, which are both derived from class **Circle** and have two eyes and a mouth. Next, derive classes from **Smiley** and **Frowny** which add an appropriate hat to each.
[2] Try to copy a **Shape**. What happens?
[3] Define an abstract class and try to define an object of that type. What happens?
[4] Define a class **Immobile_Circle**, which is just like **Circle** but can't be moved.
[5] Define a **Striped_rectangle** where instead of fill, the rectangle is "filled" by drawing one-pixel-wide horizontal lines across the inside of the rectangle (say, draw every second line like that). You may have to play with the width of lines and the line spacing to get a pattern you like.

[6] Define a Striped_circle using the technique from Striped_rectangle.

[7] Define a Striped_closed_polyline using the technique from Striped_rectangle (this requires some algorithmic inventiveness).

[8] Define a class Octagon to be a regular octagon. Write a test that exercises all of its functions (as defined by you or inherited from Shape).

[9] Define a class Rounded that is like a Rectangle, except that it has rounded corners. Use class Arc that you can find in the PPP support code on www.stroustrup.com/programming.html. Test it.

[10] Define a class Box that is a closed shape like a Rectangle (so it has fill color), except that it has rounded corners. Use class Pie that you can find in the PPP support code on www.stroustrup.com/programming.html.

[11] Define a Group to be a container of Shapes with suitable operations applied to the various members of the Group. Hint: Vector_ref. Use a Group to define a checkers (draughts) board where pieces can be moved under program control.

[12] Define a class Pseudo_window that looks as much like a Window as you can make it without heroic efforts. It should have rounded corners, a label, and control icons. Maybe you could add some fake "contents," such as an image. It need not actually do anything. It is acceptable (and indeed recommended) to have it appear within a Simple_window.

[13] Define a Binary_tree class derived from Shape. Give the number of levels as a parameter (levels==0 means no nodes, levels==1 means one node, levels==2 means one top node with two sub-nodes, levels==3 means one top node with two sub-nodes each with two sub-nodes, etc.). Let a node be represented by a small circle. Connect the nodes by lines (as is conventional). P.S. In computer science, trees conventionally grow downward from a top node (amusingly, but logically, often called the root).

[14] Modify Binary_tree to draw its nodes using a virtual function. Then, derive a new class from Binary_tree that overrides that virtual function to use a different representation for a node (e.g., a triangle).

[15] Modify Binary_tree to take a parameter (or parameters) to indicate what kind of line to use to connect the nodes (e.g., an arrow pointing down or a red arrow pointing up). Note how this exercise and the last use two alternative ways of making a class hierarchy more flexible and useful.

[16] Add an operation to Binary_tree that adds text to a node. You may have to modify the design of Binary_tree to implement this elegantly. Choose a way to identify a node; for example, you might give a string "lrrlr" for navigating left, right, right, left, and right down a binary tree (the root node would match both an initial l and an initial r).

[17] Define a class Controller with four virtual functions on(), off(), set_level(int), and show(). Derive at least two classes from Controller. One should be a simple test class where show() prints out whether the class is set to on or off and what is the current level. The second derived class should somehow control the line color of a Shape; the exact meaning of "level" is up to you. Try to find a third "thing" to control with such a Controller class.

[18] The exceptions defined in the C++ standard library, such as exception, runtime_error, and out_of_range (§4.6.3), are organized into a class hierarchy (with a virtual function what() returning a string supposedly explaining what went wrong). Search your information sources for the C++ standard exception class hierarchy and draw a class hierarchy diagram of it.

Postscript

AA The ideal for software is not to build a single program that does everything. The ideal is to build a lot of classes that closely reflect our concepts and that work together to allow us to build our applications elegantly, with minimal effort (relative to the complexity of our task), with adequate performance, and with confidence that the results produced are correct. Such programs are comprehensible and maintainable in a way that code that was simply thrown together to get a particular job done as quickly as possible is not. Classes, encapsulation (as supported by **private** and **protected**), inheritance (as supported by class derivation), and run-time polymorphism (as supported by virtual functions) are among our most powerful tools for structuring systems.

13

Graphing Functions and Data

The best is the enemy of the good.
– Voltaire

If you are in any empirical field, you need to graph data. If you are in any field that uses math to model phenomena, you need to graph functions. This chapter discusses basic mechanisms for such graphics. As usual, we show the use of the mechanisms and also discuss their design. The key examples are graphing a function of one argument and displaying values read from a file.

§13.1 Introduction
§13.2 Graphing simple functions
§13.3 **Function**
Default arguments; More examples; Lambda expressions
§13.4 **Axis**
§13.5 Approximation
§13.6 Graphing data
Reading a file; General layout; Scaling data; Building the graph

13.1 Introduction

AA Compared to the professional software systems you'll use if such visualization becomes your main occupation, the facilities presented here are primitive. Our primary aim is not elegance of output, but an understanding of how such graphical output can be produced and of the programming techniques used. You'll find the design techniques, programming techniques, and basic mathematical tools presented here of longer-term value than the graphics facilities presented. Therefore, please don't skim too quickly over the code fragments – they contain more of interest than just the shapes they compute and draw.

13.2 Graphing simple functions

Let's start. Let's look at examples of what we can draw and what code it takes to draw them. In particular, look at the graphics interface classes used. Here, first, are a parabola, a horizontal line, and a sloping line:

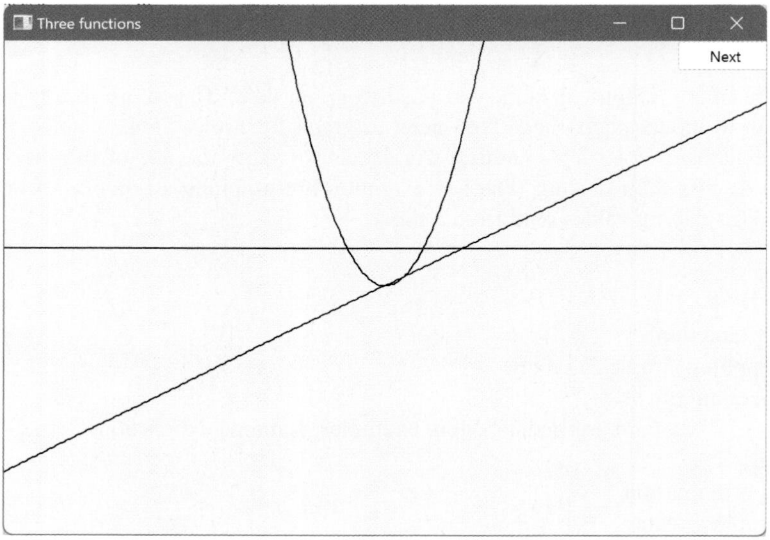

Actually, since this chapter is about graphing functions, that horizontal line isn't just a horizontal line; it is what we get from graphing the function

```
double one(double) { return 1; }
```

This is about the simplest function we could think of: it is a function of one argument that for every argument returns `1`. Since we don't need that argument to compute the result, we need not name it. For every `x` passed as an argument to `one()` we get the `y` value `1`; that is, the line is defined by `(x,y)==(x,1)` for all `x`.

Like all beginning mathematical arguments, this is somewhat trivial and pedantic, so let's look at a slightly more complicated function:

```
double slope(double x) { return 0.5*x; }          // the slope is 0.5
```

This is the function that generated the sloping line. For every x, we get the y value 0.5*x. In other words, (x,y)==(x,0.5*x). The point where the two lines cross is (2,1).

Now we can try something more slightly interesting, the square function that seems to reappear regularly in this book:

```
double square(double x) { return x*x; }
```

If you remember your high school geometry (and even if you don't), this defines a parabola with its lowest point at (0,0) and symmetric on the *y* axis. In other words, (x,y)==(x,x*x). So, the lowest point where the parabola touches the sloping line is (0,0).

Here is the code that drew those three functions:

```
constexpr int xmax = 600;                // window size
constexpr int ymax = 400;

constexpr int x_orig = xmax/2;           // position of (0,0) is center of window
constexpr int y_orig = ymax/2;
constexpr Point orig {x_orig,y_orig};

constexpr int r_min = -10;               // range [-10:11)
constexpr int r_max = 11;

constexpr int n_points = 400;            // number of points used in range

constexpr int x_scale = 30;              // scaling factors
constexpr int y_scale = 30;

Simple_window win {Point{100,100},xmax,ymax,"Three functions"};

Function s {one,r_min,r_max,orig,n_points,x_scale,y_scale};
Function s2 {slope,r_min,r_max,orig,n_points,x_scale,y_scale};
Function s3 {square,r_min,r_max,orig,n_points,x_scale,y_scale};

win.attach(s);
win.attach(s2);
win.attach(s3);
win.wait_for_button();
```

First, we define a bunch of constants so that we won't have to litter our code with "magic constants." Then, we make a window, define the functions, attach them to the window, and finally give control to the graphics system to do the actual drawing.

All of this is repetition and "boilerplate" except for the definitions of the three Functions, s, s2, and s3:

```
Function s {one,r_min,r_max,orig,n_points,x_scale,y_scale};
Function s2 {slope,r_min,r_max,orig,n_points,x_scale,y_scale};
Function s3 {square,r_min,r_max,orig,n_points,x_scale,y_scale};
```

Each **Function** specifies how its first argument (a function of one **double** argument returning a **double**) is to be drawn in a window. The second and third arguments give the range of **x** (the argument to the function to be graphed): [**r_min**:**r_max**). The fourth argument (here, **orig**) tells the **Function** where the origin **(0,0)** is to be located within the window.

XX If you think that the many arguments are confusing, we agree. Our ideal is to have as few arguments as possible, because having many arguments confuses and provides opportunities for bugs. However, here we need them. We'll explain the last three arguments later (§13.3). First, however, let's label our graphs:

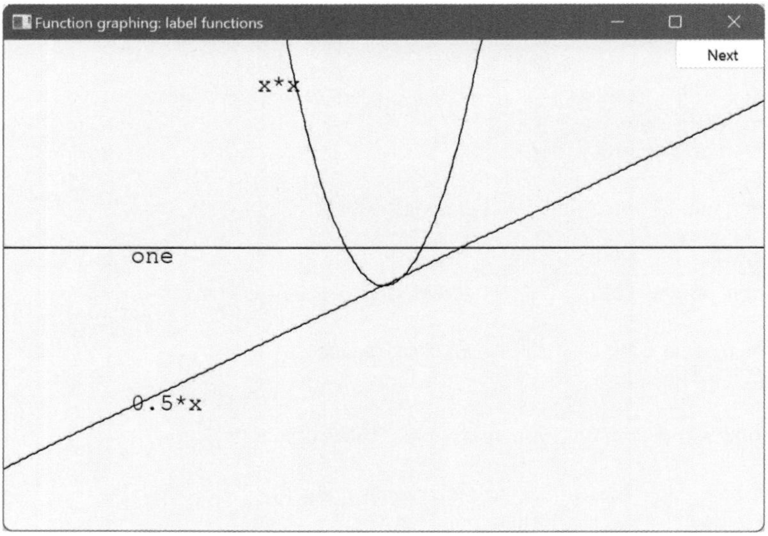

AA We always try to make our graphs self-explanatory. People don't always read the surrounding text and good diagrams get moved around, so that the surrounding text is "lost." Anything we put in as part of the picture itself is most likely to be noticed and – if reasonable – most likely to help the reader understand what we are displaying. Here, we simply put a label on each graph. The code for "labeling" was three **Text** objects (§11.8):

```
Text ts {Point{100,y_orig−40},"one"};
Text ts2 {Point{100,y_orig+y_orig/2−20},"0.5∗x"};
Text ts3 {Point{x_orig−100,20},"x∗x"};
win.set_label("Function graphing: label functions");
win.wait_for_button();
```

From now on in this chapter, we'll omit the repetitive code for attaching shapes to the window, labeling the window, and waiting for the user to hit "Next."

However, that picture is still not acceptable. We note that **0.5∗x** touches **x∗x** at **(0,0)** and that **one** crosses **0.5∗x** at **(2,1)** but that's far too subtle; we need axes to give the reader an unsubtle clue about what's going on. The code for the axes was two **Axis** objects (§13.4): AA

```
constexpr int xlength = xmax–40;   // make the axis a bit smaller than the window
constexpr int ylength = ymax–40;

Axis x {Axis::x,Point{20,y_orig}, xlength, xlength/x_scale, "one notch == 1"};
Axis y {Axis::y,Point{x_orig, ylength+20}, ylength, ylength/y_scale, "one notch == 1"};
```

Using **xlength/x_scale** as the number of notches ensures that a notch represents the values 1, 2, 3, etc. Having the axes cross at **(0,0)** is conventional. If you prefer them along the left and bottom edges as is conventional for the display of data (§13.6), you can of course do that instead.

To distinguish the axes from the data, we use color:

```
x.set_color(Color::red);
y.set_color(Color::red);
```

And we get

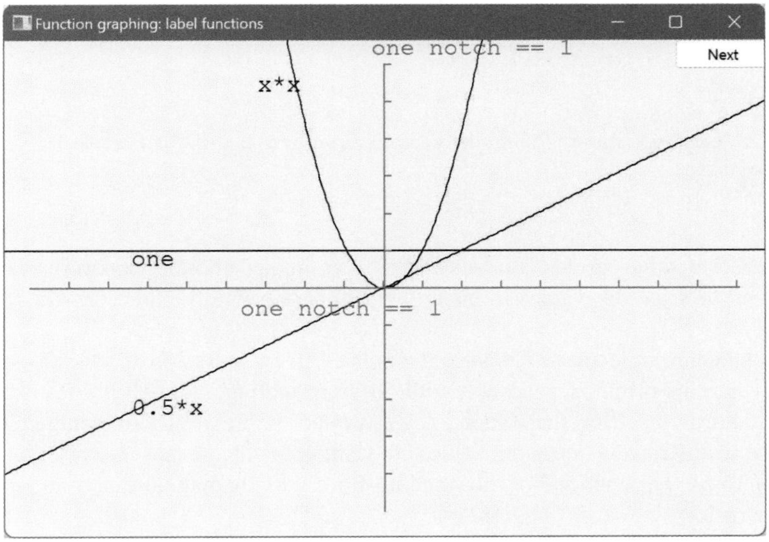

This is acceptable, though for aesthetic reasons, we'd probably want a bit of empty space at the top to match what we have at the bottom and sides. It might also be a better idea to push the label for the *x* axis further to the left. We left these blemishes so that we could mention them – there are always more aesthetic details that we can work on. One part of a programmer's art is to know when to stop and use the time saved on something better (such as learning new techniques or sleep). Remember: "The best is the enemy of the good." AA

13.3 Function

The Function graphics interface class is defined like this:

```
using Fct = std::function<double(double)>;    // function taking a double argument and returning a double

struct Function : Open_polyline {
    Function(Fct f, double r1, double r2, Point orig, int count = 100, double xscale = 25, double yscale = 25);
};
```

Function is a Shape with a constructor that generates a lot of line segments and stores them in its Shape part. Those line segments approximate the values of function f. The values of f are calculated count times for values equally spaced in the [r1:r2) range:

```
Function::Function(Fct f, double r1, double r2, Point xy, int count, double xscale, double yscale)
    // graph f(x) for x in [r1:r2) using count line segments with (0,0) displayed at xy
    // x coordinates are scaled by xscale and y coordinates scaled by yscale
{
    if (r2-r1<=0)
        error("bad graphing range");
    if (count<=0)
        error("non-positive graphing count");
    double dist = (r2-r1)/count;
    double r = r1;
    for (int i = 0; i<count; ++i) {
        add(Point{xy.x+round_to<int>(r*xscale),xy.y-round_to<int>(f(r)*yscale)});
        r += dist;
    }
}
```

The xscale and yscale values are used to scale the x coordinates and the y coordinates, respectively. We typically need to scale our values to make them fit appropriately into a drawing area of a window.

Note that a Function object doesn't store the values given to its constructors, so we can't later ask a function where its origin is, redraw it with different scaling, etc. All it does is to store points (in its Shape) and draw itself on the screen. If we wanted the flexibility to change a Function after construction, we would have to store the values we wanted to change (see exercise 2).

When trying to use Fct with one of the standard-library mathematical functions, say cos, we get an unpleasant surprise:

```
Function f3{ cos,r_min,r_max,orig,200,30,30 };        // error: can't deduce type of argument "cos"
```

The problem is that the standard library offers several cosine functions called cos so the compiler can't know which one we wanted. There are several ways to resolve this problem, but the simplest is to define a function that specifically does cos for the type we want, here double:

```
double dcos(double d) { return cos(d); }       // dcos() chooses cos(double)
// ...
Function f3{ dcos,r_min,r_max,orig,200,30,30 };
```

13.3.1 Default Arguments

Note the way the Function constructor arguments xscale and yscale were given initializers in the declaration. Such initializers are called *default arguments* and their values are used if a caller doesn't supply values. For example:

```
Function s {one, r_min, r_max,orig, n_points, x_scale, y_scale};
Function s2 {slope, r_min, r_max, orig, n_points, x_scale};          // no yscale
Function s3 {square, r_min, r_max, orig, n_points};                  // no xscale, no yscale
Function s4 {dsqrt, r_min, r_max, orig};                             // no count, no xscale, no yscale
```

This is equivalent to

```
Function s {one, r_min, r_max, orig, n_points, x_scale, y_scale};
Function s2 {slope, r_min, r_max,orig, n_points, x_scale, 25};
Function s3 {square, r_min, r_max, orig, n_points, 25, 25};
Function s4 {dsqrt, r_min, r_max, orig, 100, 25, 25};
```

Default arguments are used as an alternative to providing several overloaded functions. Instead of defining one constructor with three default arguments, we could have defined four constructors. That would have been more work, and with the four-constructor version, the nature of the default is hidden in the constructor definitions rather than being obvious from the declaration. Default arguments are frequently used for constructors but can be useful for all kinds of functions. You can only define default arguments for trailing parameters. For example: CC

```
Function(Fct f, double r1, double r2, Point orig,
                    int count = 100, double xscale, double yscale);         // error
```

If a parameter has a default argument, all subsequent parameters must also have one:

```
Function(Fct f, double r1, double r2, Point orig,
                    int count = 100, double xscale=25, double yscale=25);
```

Sometimes, picking good default arguments is easy. Examples of that are the default for string (the empty string) and the default for vector (the empty vector). In other cases, such as Function, choosing a default is less easy; we found the ones we used after a bit of experimentation and a failed attempt. Remember, you don't have to provide default arguments, and if you find it hard to provide one, just leave it to your user to specify that argument.

13.3.2 More examples

We added a couple more functions, a simple cosine (cos) from the standard library, and – just to show how we can compose functions – a sloping cosine that follows the 0.5*x slope:

```
double sloping_cos(double x) { return cos(x)+slope(x); }
```

Here is the result:

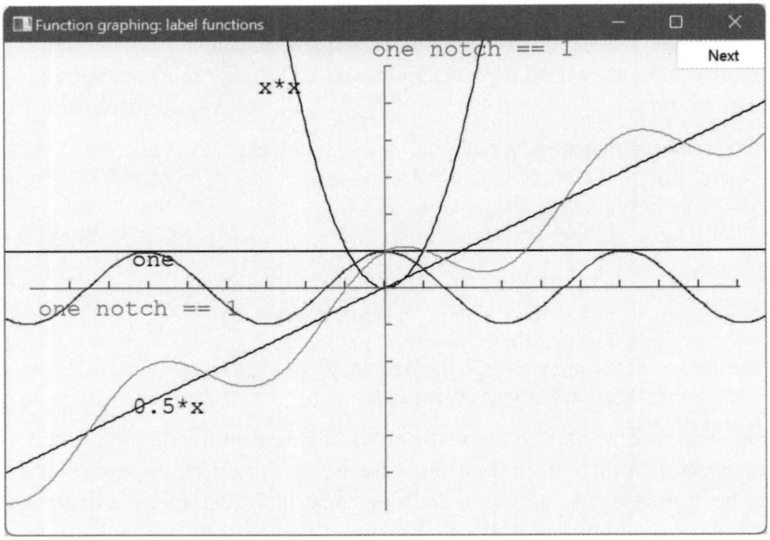

The code is

```
Function s4 {dcos,r_min,r_max,orig,400,30,30};
s4.set_color(Color::blue);

Function s5 {sloping_cos, r_min,r_max,orig,400,30,30};
s5.set_color(Color::green);

x.label.move(−160,0);
x.notches.set_color(Color::dark_red);
```

In addition to adding those two functions, we also moved the *x* axis's label and (just to show how) slightly changed the color of its notches.

Finally, we graph a log, an exponential, a sine, and a cosine:

```
Function f1 {dlog,0.000001,r_max,orig,200,30,30};     // log() logarithm, base e
Function f2 {dsin,r_min,r_max,orig,200,30,30};        // sin()
f2.set_color(Color::blue);

Function f3 {dcos,r_min,r_max,orig,200,30,30};        // cos()
Function f4 {dexp,r_min,r_max,orig,200,30,30};        // exp() exponential e^x
```

Since **log(0)** is undefined (mathematically, minus infinity), we started the range for **log** at a small positive number.

This is messy and only an example of what we can do, rather than a recommendation of style. Rather than labeling those functions we used color.

The result is

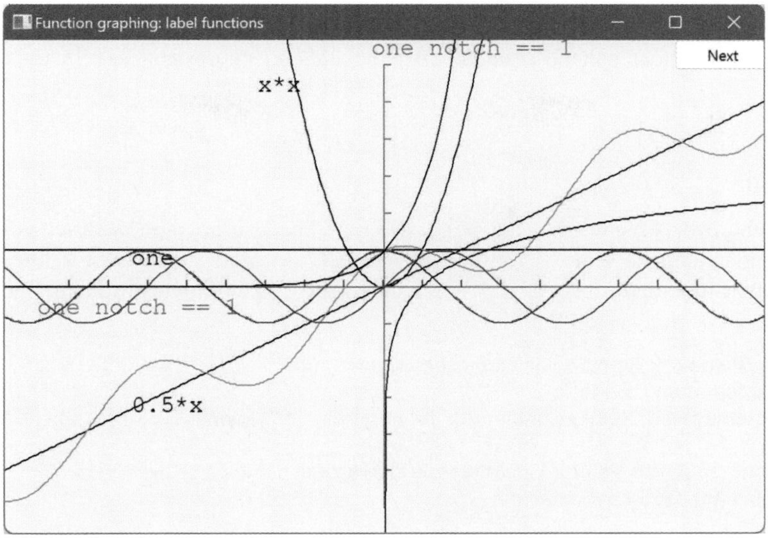

13.3.3 Lambda expressions

It can get tedious to define a function just to have it to pass as an argument to a **Function**. Consequently, C++ offers a notation for defining something that acts as a function in the argument position where it is needed. For example, we could define the **sloping_cos** shape like this:

```
Function s5 {[](double x) { return cos(x)+slope(x); },r_min,r_max,orig,400,30,30};
```

The **[](double x) { return cos(x)+slope(x); }** is a lambda expression; that is, it is an unnamed function that can be defined right where it is needed as an argument. The **[ ]** is called a *lambda introducer*. After the lambda introducer, the lambda expression specifies what arguments are required (the argument list) and what actions are to be performed (the function body). The return type can be deduced from the lambda body. Here, the return type is **double** because that's the type of **cos(x)+slope(x)**. Had we wanted to, we could have specified the return type explicitly using the suffix return type notation (§7.4.10):

```
Function s5 {[](double x) -> double { return cos(x)+slope(x); },r_min,r_max,orig,400,30,30};
```

In our **Function** example, we could have used lambdas, rather than named functions, to resolve the overloading problem (§13.3). For example:

```
Function f3{[](double d) { return cos(d); },r_min,r_max,orig,200,30,30 };     // use cos(double)
```

That would make sense if this was the only place we needed **cos(double)** but not if we needed it repeatedly.

Specifying the return type for a lambda expression is rarely necessary. The main reason for that is that lambda expressions should be kept simple to avoid becoming a source of errors and confusion. If a piece of code does something significant, it should be given a name and probably requires AA a comment to be comprehensible to people other than the original programmer. We recommend using named functions for anything that doesn't easily fit on a line or two.

The lambda introducer can be used to give the lambda expression access to local variables (§21.2.3).

13.4 Axis

We use **Axis** wherever we present data (e.g., §13.6.4) because a graph without information that allows us to understand its scale is most often suspect. An **Axis** consists of a line, a number of "notches" on that line, and a text label. The **Axis** constructor computes the axis line and (optionally) the lines used as notches on that line:

```
struct Axis : Shape {                    // representation left public
      enum Orientation { x, y, z };
      Axis(Orientation d, Point xy, int length, int nummber_of_notches=0, string label = "");

      void draw_specifics(Painter& painter) const override;
      void move(int dx, int dy) override;

      void set_color(Color c);

      Text label;
      Line line;
      Lines notches;
};
```

The **label** and **notches** objects are left public so that a user can manipulate them. For example, you can give the notches a different color from the line and **move()** the **label** to a more convenient location. **Axis** is an example of an object composed of several semi-independent objects.

The **Axis** constructor places the lines and adds the "notches" if **number_of_notches** is greater than zero:

```
Axis::Axis(Orientation d, Point xy, int length, int n, string lab)
      :label{Point{0,0},lab}, line{xy, (d==x) ? Point{xy.x+length,xy.y} : Point{xy.x,xy.y–length}}
{
      if (length<0) error("bad axis length");
      switch (d){
      case Axis::x:
            if (1<n) {                                    // add notches
                  int dist = length/n;
                  int x = xy.x+dist;
                  for (int i = 0; i<n; ++i) {
                        notches.add(Point{x,xy.y},Point{x,xy.y–5});
                        x += dist;
                  }
            }
```

```
            label.move(length/3,xy.y+20);              // put the label under the line
            break;
        case Axis::y:
            if (1<n) {                         // add notches
                int dist = length/n;
                int y = xy.y−dist;
                for (int i = 0; i<n; ++i) {
                    notches.add(Point{xy.x,y},Point{xy.x+5,y});
                    y −= dist;
                }
            }
            label.move(xy.x−10,xy.y−length−10);          // put the label at top
            break;
        case Axis::z:
            error("z axis not implemented");
        }
}
```

Compared to much real-world code, this constructor is very simple, but please have a good look at it because it isn't quite trivial and it illustrates a few useful techniques. Note how we store the line in the **Shape** part of the **Axis** (using **Shape::add()**) but the notches are stored in a separate object (**notches**). That way, we can manipulate the line and the notches independently; for example, we can give each its own color. Similarly, a label is placed in a fixed position relative to its axes, but since it is a separate object, we can always move it to a better spot. We use the enumeration **Orientation** to provide a convenient and non-error-prone notation for users.

Since an **Axis** has three parts, we must supply functions for when we want to manipulate an **Axis** as a whole. For example:

```
void Axis::draw_specific(Painter& painter) const
{
    line.draw_specific(painter);    // the line
    notches.draw(painter);          // the notches may have a different color from the line
    label.draw(painter);            // the label may have a different color from the line
}
```

We use **draw()** rather than **draw_specific()** for **notches** and **label** to be able to use the color stored in them. The line is stored in the **Axis::Shape** itself and uses the color stored there.

We can set the color of the line, the notches, and the label individually, but stylistically it's usually better not to, so we provide a function to set all three to the same:

```
void Axis::set_color(Color c)
{
    line.set_color(c);
    notches.set_color(c);
    label.set_color(c);
    redraw();
}
```

Similarly, **Axis::move()** moves all the parts of the **Axis** together:

```
void Axis::move(int dx, int dy)
{
	line.move(dx,dy);
	notches.move(dx,dy);
	label.move(dx,dy);
	redraw();
}
```

13.5 Approximation

Here we give another small example of graphing a function: we "animate" the calculation of an exponential function. The purpose is to help you get a feel for mathematical functions (if you haven't already), to show the way graphics can be used to illustrate computations, to give you some code to read, and finally to warn about a common problem with computations.

One way of computing an exponential function is to compute the series

$$e^x \equiv 1 + x + \frac{x^2}{2!} + \frac{x^3}{3!} + \frac{x^4}{4!} + \cdots$$

The more terms of this sequence we calculate, the more precise our value of e^x becomes; that is, the more terms we calculate, the more digits of the result will be mathematically correct. What we will do is to compute this sequence and graph the result after each term. The exclamation point here is used with the common mathematical meaning: factorial; that is, we graph these functions in order:

```
exp0(x) = 0                  // no terms
exp1(x) = 1                  // one term
exp2(x) = 1+x                // two terms; pow(x,1)/fac(1)==x
exp3(x) = 1+x+pow(x,2)/fac(2)
exp4(x) = 1+x+pow(x,2)/fac(2)+pow(x,3)/fac(3)
exp5(x) = 1+x+pow(x,2)/fac(2)+pow(x,3)/fac(3)+pow(x,4)/fac(4)
...
```

Each function is a slightly better approximation of e^x than the one before it. Here, `pow(x,n)` is the standard-library function that returns x^n. There is no factorial function in the standard library, so we must define our own:

```
int fac(int n)          // factorial(n); n!
{
	int r = 1;
	while (n>1) {
		r*=n;
		--n;
	}
	return r;
}
```

For an alternative implementation of fac(), see exercise 1. Given fac(), we can compute the nth term of the series like this:

```
double term(double x, int n) { return pow(x,n)/fac(n); }  // nth term of series
```

Given term(), calculating the exponential to the precision of n terms is now easy:

```
double exp_n(double x, int n)          // sum of n terms for x
{
        double sum = 0;
        for (int i=0; i<n; ++i)
                sum+=term(x,i);
        return sum;
}
```

Let's use that to produce some graphics. First, we'll provide some axes and the "real" exponential, the standard-library exp(), so that we can see how close our approximation using exp_n() is:

```
Function real_exp {exp,r_min,r_max,orig,200,x_scale,y_scale};
real_exp.set_color(Color::blue);
```

But how can we use exp_n()? From a programming point of view, the difficulty is that our graphing class, Function, takes a function of one argument and exp_n() needs two arguments. Given C++, as we have seen it so far, there is no really elegant solution to this problem. However, lambda expressions provide a way (§21.2.3). Consider:

```
for (int n = 0; n<50; ++n) {
        ostringstream ss;
        ss << "exp approximation; n==" << n ;
        win.set_label(ss.str());

        // get next approximation:
        Function e {[n](double x) { return exp_n(x,n); },r_min,r_max,orig,200,x_scale,y_scale};

        win.attach(e);
        win.wait_for_button();
        win.detach(e);
}
```

The lambda introducer, [n], says that the lambda expression may access the local variable n. That way, a call of exp_n(x,n) gets its n when its Function is created and its x from each call from within the Function.

Note the final detach(e) in that loop. The scope of the Function object e is the block of the for-statement. Each time we enter that block we get a new Function called e, and each time we exit the block that e goes away, to be replaced by the next. The window must not remember the old e because it will have been destroyed. Thus, detach(e) ensures that the window does not try to draw a destroyed object.

This first gives a window with just the axes and the "real" exponential rendered in blue:

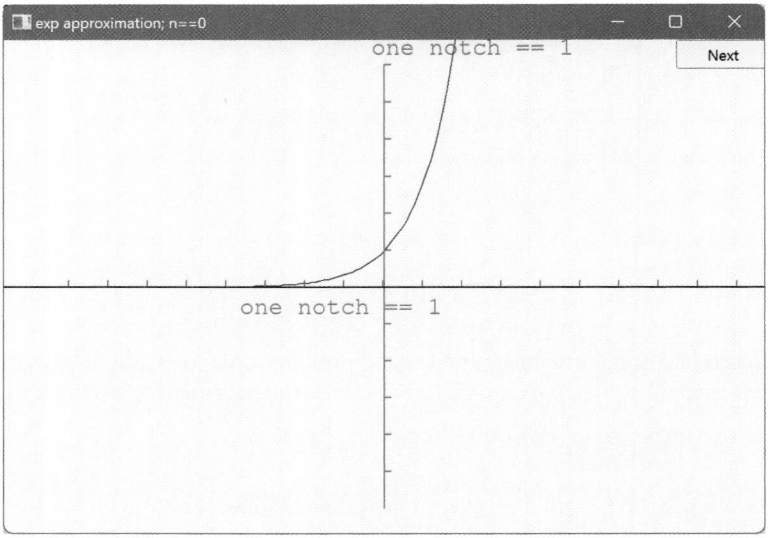

We see that **exp(0)** is **1** so that our blue "real exponential" crosses the *y* axis at **(0,1)**.

If you look carefully, you'll see that we actually drew the zero term approximation (**exp_n(x,0)==0**) as a black line right on top of the *x* axis. Hitting "Next," we get the approximation using just one term. Note that we display the number of terms used in the approximation in the window label:

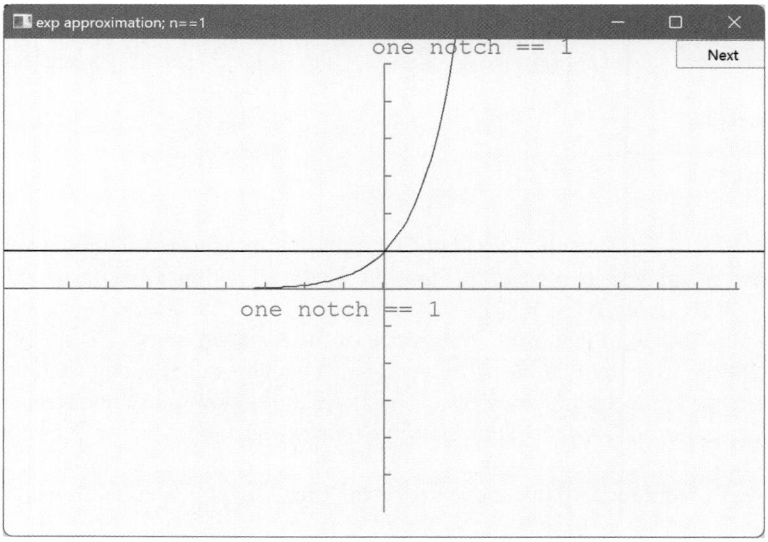

That's the function **exp_n(x,1)==1**, the approximation using just one term of the sequence. It matches the exponential perfectly at **(0,1)**, but we can do better:

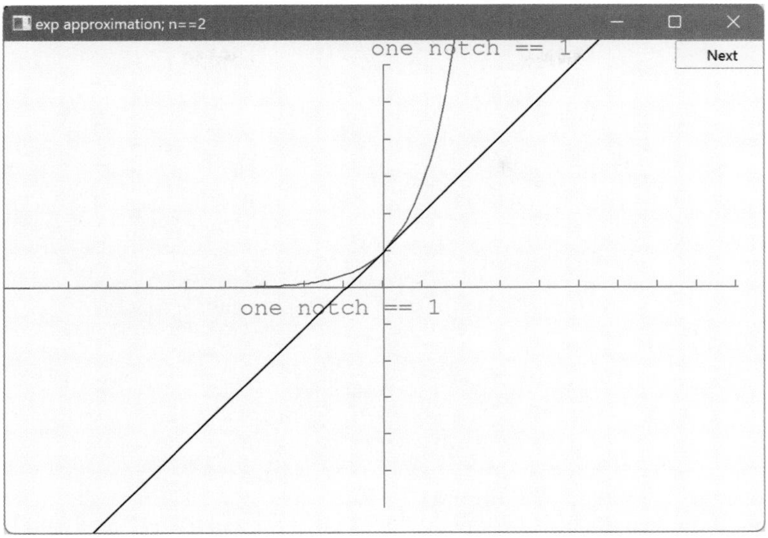

With two terms (**1+x**), we get the diagonal crossing the *y* axis at **(0,1)**. With three terms (**1+x+pow(x,2)/fac(2)**), we can see the beginning of a convergence:

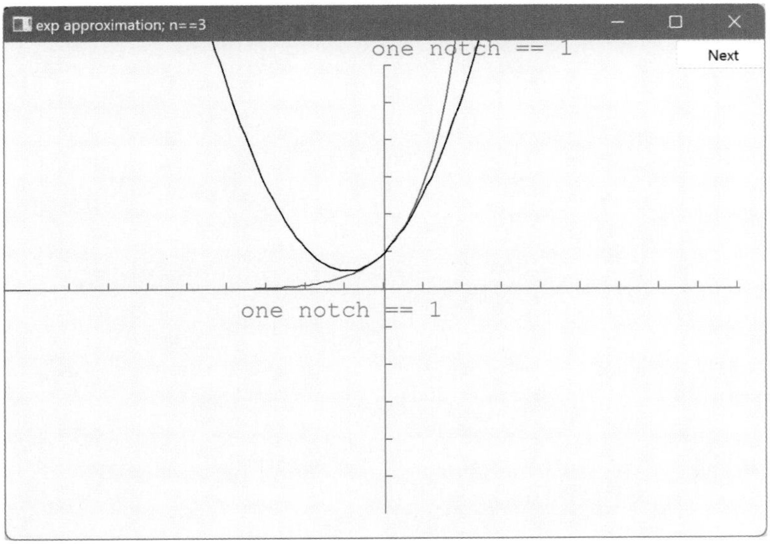

With ten terms we are doing rather well for values larger than -3:

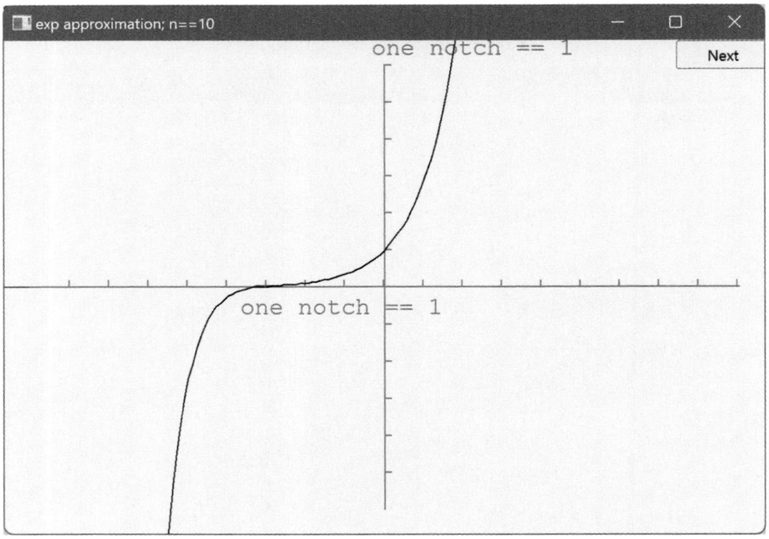

If we don't think too much about it, we might believe that we could get better and better approximations simply by using more and more terms. However, there are limits, and after 13 terms something strange starts to happen. First, the approximations start to get slightly worse, and at 18 terms vertical lines appear:

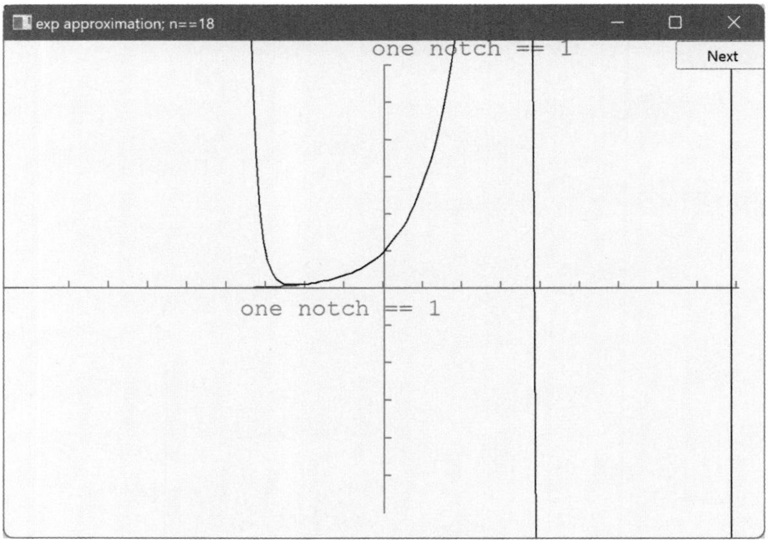

XX The computer's arithmetic is not pure math. Floating-point numbers are simply an approximation to real numbers for a fixed number of bits. An **int** overflows if you try to place a too-large integer in it, whereas a **double** stores an approximation. When I saw the strange output for larger numbers of terms, I first suspected that our calculation started to produce values that couldn't be represented as **doubles**, so that our results started to diverge from the mathematically correct answers. Later, I realized that **fac()** was producing values that couldn't be stored in an **int**. Modifying **fac()** to produce a **double** solved the problem. For more information, see exercise 10 of Chapter 6.

This last picture is also a good illustration of the principle that "it looks OK" isn't the same as "tested." Before giving a program to someone else to use, first test it beyond what at first seems reasonable. Unless you know better, running a program slightly longer or with slightly different data could lead to a real mess – as in this case.

13.6 Graphing data

Displaying data is a highly skilled and highly valued craft. When done well, it combines technical and artistic aspects and can add significantly to our understanding of complex phenomena. However, that also makes graphing a huge area that for the most part is unrelated to programming techniques. Here, we'll just show a simple example of displaying data read from a file. The data shown represents the age groups of Japanese people over some decades. The data to the right of the 2023 line is a projection: **AA**

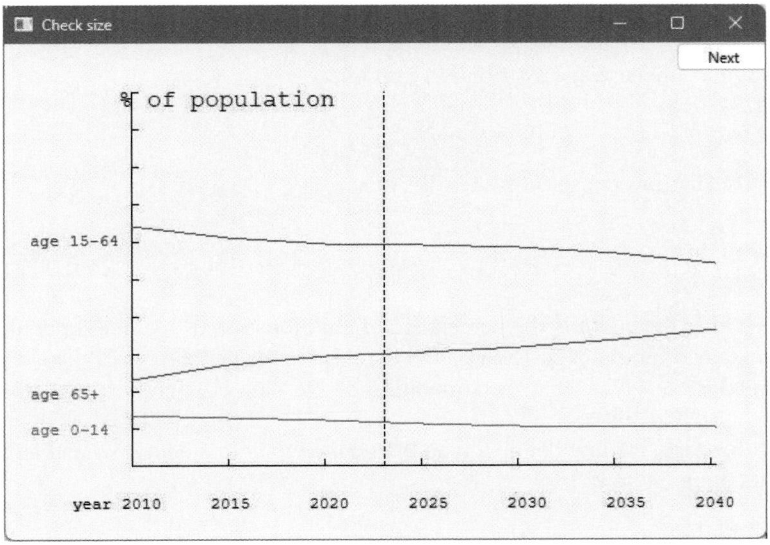

We'll use this example to discuss the programming problems involved in presenting such data:

- Reading a file
- Scaling data to fit the window
- Displaying the data
- Labeling the graph

We will not go into artistic details. Basically, this is "graphs for geeks," not "graphical art." Clearly, you can do better artistically when you need to.

Given a set of data, we must consider how best to display it. To simplify, we will only deal with data that is easy to display using two dimensions, but that's a huge part of the data most people deal with. Note that bar graphs, pie charts, and similar popular displays really are just two-dimensional data displayed in a fancy way. Three-dimensional data can often be handled by producing a series of two-dimensional images, by superimposing several two-dimensional graphs onto a single window (as is done in the "Japanese age" example), or by labeling individual points with information. If we want to go beyond that, we'll have to write new graphics classes or adopt another graphics library.

So, our data is basically pairs of values, such as **(year,number of children)**. If we have more data, such as **(year,number of children, number of adults,number of elderly)**, we simply have to decide which pair of values – or pairs of values – we want to draw. In our example, we simply graphed **(year,number of children)**, **(year,number of adults)**, and **(year,number of elderly)**.

AA There are many ways of looking at a set of **(x,y)** pairs. When considering how to graph such a set it is important to consider whether one value is in some way a function of the other. For example, for a **(year,steel production)** pair it would be quite reasonable to consider the steel production a function of the year and display the data as a continuous line. **Open_polyline** (§11.6.1) is the obvious choice for graphing such data. If **y** should not be seen as a function of **x**, for example **(gross domestic product per person,population of country)**, **Marks** (§11.6.4) can be used to plot unconnected points.

Now, back to our Japanese age distribution example.

13.6.1 Reading a file

The file of age distributions consists of lines like this:

```
{ 2010 : 13.1 63.8 23.0 }
{2015 : 12.5 60.7 26.8}
{2020 : 11.7 59.2 29.1}
```

The first number after the colon is the percentage of children (age 0–14) in the population, the second is the percentage of adults (age 15–64), and the third is the percentage of the elderly (age 65+). Our job is to read those. Note that the formatting of the data is slightly irregular. As usual, we have to deal with such details.

To simplify that task, we first define a type **Distribution** to hold a data item and an input operator to read such data items:

```
struct Distribution {
      int year;
      double young, middle, old;
};
```

```
istream& operator>>(istream& is, Distribution& d)
      // assume format: { year : young middle old }
{
      char ch1 = 0;
      char ch2 = 0;
      char ch3 = 0;
      Distribution dd;

      if (is >> ch1 >> dd.year
            >> ch2 >> dd.young >> dd.middle >> dd.old
            >> ch3) {
      if (ch1 != '{' || ch2 != ':' || ch3 != '}')   // format error
                  is.clear(ios_base::failbit);
            else
                  d = dd;
      }
      return is;
}
```

This is a straightforward application of the ideas from Chapter 9. If this code isn't clear to you, please review that chapter. We didn't need to define a **Distribution** type and a >> operator. However, it simplifies the code compared to a brute-force approach of "just read the numbers and graph them." Our use of **Distribution** splits the code up into logical parts to help comprehension and debugging. Don't be shy about introducing types "just to make the code clearer." We define classes to make the code correspond more directly to the way we think about the concepts in our code. Doing so even for "small" concepts that are used only very locally in our code, such as a line of data representing the age distribution for a year, can be most helpful.

First we need to open the file:

```
string file_name = "japanese-age-data.txt";
ifstream ifs {file_name};
if (!ifs) {
      Text err_label {Point{20,20},"Can't open file"};
      win.attach(err_label);
      win.wait_for_button();
      error("can't open ", file_name);
}
```

That is, we try to open the file **japanese-age-data.txt** and exit the program if we don't find that file. It is often a good idea *not* to "hardwire" a file name into the source code the way we did here, but we consider this program an example of a small "one-off" effort, so we don't burden the code with facilities that are more appropriate for long-lived applications. On the other hand, we did put **japanese-age-data.txt** into a named **string** variable so the program is easy to modify if we want to use it – or some of its code – for something else.

The error message turned out to be less helpful as the window disappeared, so we added a helpful text before exiting. Really, we needed a better error function for graphics programs; see also §11.10.

Given **Distribution**, the read loop becomes

```
for (Distribution d; ifs >> d; ) {
        if (d.year < base_year || end_year < d.year)
                error("year out of range");

        double all = d.young + d.middle + d.old;
        if (all-100 > 1.5 || 100-all>1.5 )        // take rounding errors into account
                error("percentages don't add up");

        // ... use the data ...
}
```

The read loop checks that the year read is in the expected range and that the percentages add up to about 100. That's a basic sanity check for the data. Date is often "dirty" so we always need to check. Since >> checks the format of each individual data item, we didn't bother with further checks in the main loop.

13.6.2 General layout

So what do we want to appear on the screen? You can see our answer at the beginning of §13.6. The data seems to ask for three **Open_polylines** – one for each age group. These graphs need to be labeled, and we decided to write a "caption" for each line at the left-hand side of the window. In this case, that seemed clearer than the common alternative: to place the label somewhere along the line itself. In addition, we use color to distinguish the graphs and associate their labels.

We want to label the *x* axis with the years. The vertical line through the year 2023 indicates where the graph goes from hard data to projected data.

We decided to just use the window's label as the title for our graph.

AA Getting graphing code both correct and good-looking can be surprisingly tricky. The main reason is that we have to do a lot of fiddly calculations of sizes and offsets. To simplify that, we start by defining a set of symbolic constants that defines the way we use our screen space:

```
constexpr int xmax = 600;     // window size
constexpr int ymax = 400;

constexpr int xoffset = 100; // distance from left-hand side of window to y axis
constexpr int yoffset = 60;  // distance from bottom of window to x axis

constexpr int xspace = 40;   // space beyond axis
constexpr int yspace = 40;

constexpr int xlength = xmax-xoffset-xspace;        // length of axes
constexpr int ylength = ymax-yoffset-yspace;
```

Basically this defines a rectangular space (the window) with another rectangle (defined by the axes) within it:

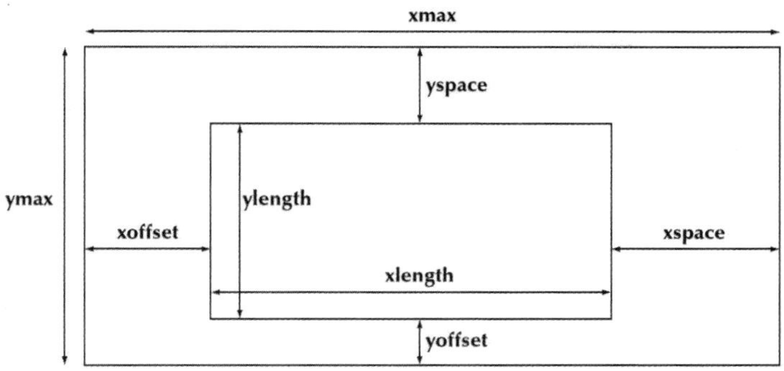

Without such a "schematic view" of where things are in our window and the symbolic constants that define it, we tend to get lost and become frustrated when our output doesn't reflect our wishes. **AA**

13.6.3 Scaling data

Next we need to define how to fit our data into that space. We do that by scaling the data so that it fits into the space defined by the axes. To do that we need the scaling factors that are the ratio between the data range and the axis range:

```
constexpr int base_year = 2010;
constexpr int end_year = 2040;

constexpr double xscale = double(xlength)/(end_year−base_year);
constexpr double yscale = double(ylength)/100;
```

We want our scaling factors (`xscale` and `yscale`) to be floating-point numbers – or our calculations could be subject to serious rounding errors. To avoid integer division, we convert our lengths to `double` before dividing (§7.4.7).

We can now place a data point on the x axis by subtracting its base value (`1960`), scaling with `xscale`, and adding the `xoffset`. A y value is dealt with similarly. We find that we can never remember to do that quite right when we try to do it repeatedly. It may be a trivial calculation, but it is fiddly and verbose. To simplify the code and minimize that chance of error (and minimize frustrating debugging), we define a little class to do the calculation for us:

```
class Scale {          // data value to coordinate conversion
        int cbase;     // coordinate base
        int vbase;     // base of values
        double scale;
public:
        Scale(int b, int vb, double s) :cbase{ b }, vbase{ vb }, scale{ s } { }
        int operator()(double v) const { return cbase+(v−vbase)*scale; }          // see §21.2
};
```

We want a class because the calculation depends on three constant values that we wouldn't like to unnecessarily repeat. Given that, we can define

```
Scale xs {xoffset,base_year,xscale};
Scale ys {ymax-yoffset,0,-yscale};
```

Note how we make the scaling factor for ys negative to reflect the fact that y coordinates grow downward whereas we usually prefer higher values to be represented by higher points on a graph. Now we can use xs to convert a year to an x coordinate. Similarly, we can use ys to convert a percentage to a y coordinate.

13.6.4 Building the graph

Finally, we have all the prerequisites for writing the graphing code in a reasonably elegant way. We start creating a window and placing the axes:

```
Simple_window win {Point{100,100},xmax,ymax,"Aging Japan"};

Axis x { Axis::x, Point{xoffset,ymax - yoffset}, xlength, (end_year-base_year)/5,    // one notch per 5 years
          "year "
          "2010    2015    2020    2025    "
          "2030     2035    2040"
    };
x.label.move(-100,0);
x.label.set_font_size(10);

Axis y {Axis::y, Point{xoffset,ymax-yoffset}, ylength, 10,"% of population"};

int now = 2023;
Line current_year {Point{xs(now),ys(0)},Point{xs(now),ys(100)}};
current_year.set_style(Line_style::dash);
```

The axes cross at Point{xoffset,ymax-yoffset} representing (1960,0). Note how the notches are placed to reflect the data. On the y axis, we have ten notches each representing 10% of the population. On the x axis, each notch represents five years, and the exact number of notches is calculated from base_year and end_year so that if we change that range, the axis will automatically be recalculated. This is one benefit of avoiding "magic constants" in the code. The label on the x axis violates that rule: it is simply the result of fiddling with the label string until the numbers were in the right position under the notches. To do better, we would have to look to a set of individual labels for individual "notches."

Please note the curious formatting of the label string. We used two adjacent string literals:

```
"year "
"2010    2015    2020    2025    "
"2030     2035    2040"
```

Adjacent string literals are concatenated by the compiler, so that's equivalent to

```
"year 2010    2015    2020    2025    2030    2035    2040"
```

That can be a useful "trick" for laying out long string literals to make our code more readable.

The current_year is a vertical line that separates hard data from projected data. Note how xs and ys are used to place and scale the line just right.

Given the axes, we can proceed to the data. We define three Open_polylines and fill them in the read loop:

```
Open_polyline children;
Open_polyline adults;
Open_polyline aged;

for (Distribution d; ifs>>d; ) {
	// ... data validation ...
	const int x = xs(d.year);
	children.add(Point{x,ys(d.young)});
	adults.add(Point{x,ys(d.middle)});
	aged.add(Point{x,ys(d.old)});
}
```

The use of xs and ys makes scaling and placement of the data trivial. "Little classes," such as Scale, can be immensely important for simplifying notation and avoiding unnecessary repetition – thereby increasing readability and increasing the likelihood of correctness.

To make the graphs more readable, we label each and apply color:

```
Text children_label {Point{20,children.point(0).y},"age 0-14"};
children.set_color(Color::red);
children_label.set_color(Color::red);
children_label.set_font_size(10);
children_label.set_style(Line_style::dash);

Text adults_label {Point{20,adults.point(0).y},"age 15-64"};
adults.set_color(Color::blue);
adults_label.set_color(Color::blue);
adults_label.set_font_size(10);
Text aged_label {Point{20,aged.point(0).y},"age 65+"};
aged.set_color(Color::dark_green);
aged_label.set_color(Color::dark_green);
aged_label.set_font_size(10);
aged_label.set_style(Line_style::dashdotdot);
```

Finally, we need to attach the various Shapes to the Window and start the GUI system (§12.2.3):

```
win.attach(children);
win.attach(adults);
win.attach(aged);

win.attach(children_label);
win.attach(adults_label);
win.attach(aged_label);

win.attach(x);
win.attach(y);
win.attach(current_year);

win.wait_for_button();
```

All the code could be placed inside **main()**, but we prefer to keep the helper classes **Scale** and **Distribution** outside together with **Distribution**'s input operator.

In case you have forgotten what we were producing, here is the output again:

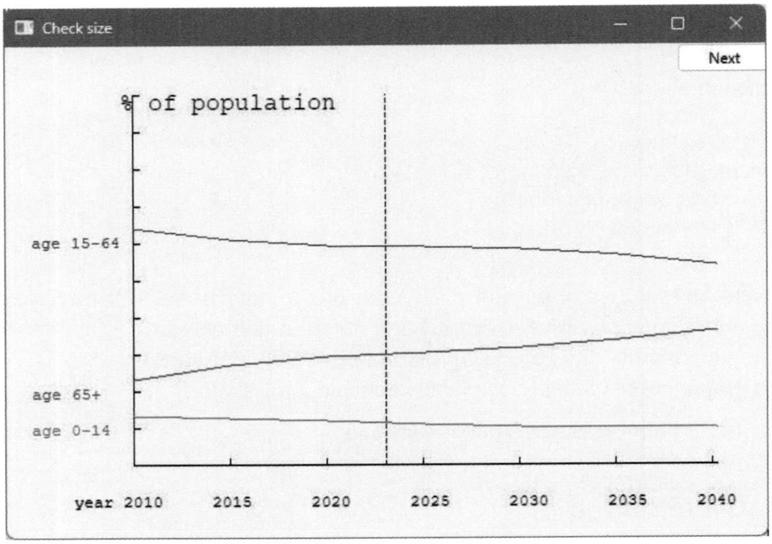

Drill

Graphing drill:

[1] Make an empty 600-by-600 **Window** labeled "Function graphs."
[2] Add an *x* axis and a *y* axis each of length 400, labeled "1 == 20 pixels" and with a notch every 20 pixels. The axes should cross at (300,300).
[3] Make both axes red.
[4] Graph the function **double one(double x) { return 1; }** in the range [-10,11] with (0,0) at (300,300) using 400 points and no scaling (in the window).
[5] Change it to use *x* scale 20 and *y* scale 20.
[6] From now on use that range, scale, etc. for all graphs.
[7] Add **double slope(double x) { return 0.5*x; }** to the window.
[8] Label the slope with a **Text "0.5x"** at a point just above its bottom left end point.
[9] Add **double square(double x) { return x*x; }** to the window.
[10] Add a cosine to the window (don't write a new function).
[11] Make the cosine blue.
[12] Write a function **sloping_cos()** that adds a cosine to **slope()** (as defined above) and add it to the window.

Class definition drill:

[13] Define a **struct Person** containing a **string** name and an **int** age.

[14] Define a variable of type **Person**, initialize it with "Goofy" and 63, and write it to the screen (**cout**).

[15] Define an input (>>) and an output (<<) operator for **Person**; read in a **Person** from the keyboard (**cin**) and write it out to the screen (**cout**).

[16] Give **Person** a constructor initializing **name** and **age**.

[17] Make the representation of **Person** private, and provide **const** member functions **name()** and **age()** to read the name and age.

[18] Modify >> and << to work with the redefined **Person**.

[19] Modify the constructor to check that **age** is [0:150) and that **name** doesn't contain any of the characters **; : " ' [ ] * & ^ % $ # @ !**. Use **error()** in case of error. Test.

[20] Read a sequence of **Person**s from input (**cin**) into a **vector<Person>**; write them out again to the screen (**cout**). Test with correct and erroneous input.

[21] Change the representation of **Person** to have **first_name** and **second_name** instead of **name**. Make it an error not to supply both a first and a second name. Be sure to fix >> and << also. Test.

Review

[1] What is a function of one argument?

[2] When would you use a (continuous) line to represent data? When do you use (discrete) points?

[3] What function (mathematical formula) defines a slope?

[4] What is a parabola?

[5] How do you make an *x* axis? A *y* axis?

[6] What is a default argument and when would you use one?

[7] How do you add functions together?

[8] How do you color and label a graphed function?

[9] What do we mean when we say that a series approximates a function?

[10] Why would you sketch out the layout of a graph before writing the code to draw it?

[11] How would you scale your graph so that the input will fit?

[12] How would you scale the input without trial and error?

[13] Why would you format your input rather than just having the file contain "the numbers"?

[14] How do you plan the general layout of a graph? How do you reflect that layout in your code?

Terms

approximation	**Function**	scaling	default argument
lambda expression	screen layout	**Axis**	overflow

Exercises

[1] Here is another way of defining a factorial function:

```
int fac(int n) { return n>1 ? n*fac(n-1) : 1; }    // factorial n!
```

It will do fac(4) by first deciding that since 4>1 it must be 4*fac(3), and that's obviously 4*3*fac(2), which again is 4*3*2*fac(1), which is 4*3*2*1. Try to see that it works. A function that calls itself is said to be *recursive*. The alternative implementation in §13.5 is called *iterative* because it iterates through the values (using while). Verify that the recursive fac() works and gives the same results as the iterative fac() by calculating the factorial of 0, 1, 2, 3, 4, up until and including 20. Which implementation of fac() do you prefer, and why?

[2] Define a class Fct that is just like Function except that it stores its constructor arguments. Provide Fct with "reset" operations, so that you can use it repeatedly for different ranges, different functions, etc.

[3] Modify Fct from the previous exercise to take an extra argument to control precision or whatever. Make the type of that argument a template parameter for extra flexibility.

[4] Graph a sine (sin()), a cosine (cos()), the sum of those (sin(x)+cos(x)), and the sum of the squares of those (sin(x)*sin(x)+cos(x)*cos(x)) on a single graph. Do provide axes and labels.

[5] "Animate" (as in §13.5) the series 1–/3+1/5–1/7+1/9–1/11+ ... . It is known as Leibniz's series and converges to pi/4.

[6] Design and implement a bar graph class. Its basic data is a vector<double> holding *N* values, and each value should be represented by a "bar" that is a rectangle where the height represents the value.

[7] Elaborate the bar graph class to allow labeling of the graph itself and its individual bars. Allow the use of color.

[8] Here is a collection of heights in centimeters together with the number of people in a group of that height (rounded to the nearest 5cm): (170,7), (175,9), (180,23), (185,17), (190,6), (195,1). How would you graph that data? If you can't think of anything better, do a bar graph. Remember to provide axes and labels. Place the data in a file and read it from that file.

[9] Find another data set of heights (an inch is 2.54cm) and graph them with your program from the previous exercise. For example, search the Web for "height distribution" or "height of people in the United States" and ignore a lot of rubbish or ask your friends for their heights. Ideally, you don't have to change anything for the new data set. Calculating the scaling from the data is a key idea. Reading in labels from input also helps minimize changes when you want to reuse code.

[10] What kind of data is unsuitable for a line graph or a bar graph? Find an example and find a way of displaying it (e.g., as a collection of labeled points).

[11] Find the average maximum temperatures for each month of the year for two or more locations (e.g., Cambridge, England, and Cambridge, Massachusetts; there are lots of towns called "Cambridge") and graph them together. As ever, be careful with axes, labels, use of color, etc.

Postscript

Graphical representation of data is important. We simply understand a well-crafted graph better than the set of numbers that was used to make it. Most people, when they need to draw a graph, use someone else's code – a library. How are such libraries constructed and what do you do if you don't have one handy? What are the fundamental ideas underlying "an ordinary graphing tool"? Now you know: it isn't magic or brain surgery. We covered only two-dimensional graphs; three-dimensional graphing is also very useful in science, engineering, marketing, etc. and can be even more fun. Explore it someday!

14

Graphical User Interfaces

Computing is not about
computers any more.
It is about living.
– Nicholas Negroponte

A graphical user interface (GUI) allows a user to interact with a program by pressing buttons, selecting from menus, entering data in various ways, and displaying textual and graphical entities on a screen. That's what we are used to when we interact with our computers and with Web sites. In this chapter, we show the basics of how code can be written to define and control a GUI application. In particular, we show how to write code that interacts with entities on the screen using callbacks. Our GUI facilities are built "on top of" system facilities. The low-level features and interfaces are presented in the code available on the Web, which uses features and techniques presented in Chapter 15 and Chapter 16. Here we focus on usage.

§14.1 User-interface alternatives
§14.2 The "Next" button
§14.3 A simple window
    A wait loop
§14.4 **Button** and other **Widgets**
    Widget; **Button**; **In_box** and **Out_box**; **Menu**
§14.5 An example: drawing lines
    Control inversion; Adding a menu
§14.6 Simple animation
§14.7 Debugging GUI code

14.1 User-interface alternatives

CC Every program has a user interface. A program running on a small gadget may be limited to input from a couple of push buttons and to a blinking light for output. Other computers are connected to the outside world only by a wire. Here, we will consider the common case in which our program communicates with a user who is watching a screen and using a keyboard and a pointing device (such as a mouse). In this case, we as programmers have three main choices:

- *Use console input and output*: This is a strong contender for technical/professional work where the input is simple and textual, consisting of commands and short data items (such as file names and simple data values). If the output is textual, we can display it on the screen or store it in files. The C++ standard-library **iostreams** (Chapter 9) provide suitable and convenient mechanisms for this. If graphical output is needed, we can use a graphics display library (as shown in Chapter 10 – Chapter 14) without making dramatic changes to our programming style.
- *Use a graphical user interface (GUI) library*: This is what we do when we want our user interaction to be based on the metaphor of manipulating objects on the screen (pointing, clicking, dragging and dropping, hovering, etc.). Often (but not always), that style goes together with a high degree of graphically displayed information. Anyone who has used a modern computer or phone knows examples where that is convenient. Anyone who wants to match the "feel" of Windows/Mac applications must use a GUI style of interaction.
- *Use a webbrowser interface*: For that, we need to use a markup (layout) language, such as HTML, and usually a scripting language, such as JavaScript, Python, and PHP. Showing how to do this is beyond the scope of this book, but it is often the ideal for applications that require remote access. In that case, the communication between the program and the screen is again textual (using streams of characters). A browser is a GUI application that translates some of that text into graphical elements and translates the mouse clicks, etc. into textual data that can be sent back to the program.

AA To many, the use of GUI is the essence of modern programming, and sometimes the interaction with objects on the screen is considered the central concern of programming. We disagree: GUI is a form of I/O, and separation of the main logic of an application from I/O is among our major ideals for software. Wherever possible, we prefer to have a clean interface between our main program logic and the parts of the program we use to get input and produce output. Such a separation allows us to change the way a program is presented to a user, to port our programs to use different I/O systems, and – most importantly – to think about the logic of the program and its interaction with users separately.

That said, GUI is important and interesting from several perspectives. This chapter explores both the ways we can integrate graphical elements into our applications and how we can keep interface concerns from dominating our thinking. Our Graphics/GUI library can run directly on a phone or a computer as well as in a browser.

14.2 The “Next” button

How did we provide that “Next” button that we used to drive the graphics examples in Chapter 10? There, we do graphics in a window using a button. Obviously, that is a simple form of GUI programming. In fact, it is so simple that we could argue that it isn’t “true GUI.” However, let’s see how it was done because it will lead directly into the kind of programming that everyone recognizes as GUI programming.

Our code in Chapter 10 – Chapter 13 is conventionally structured like this:

```
// ... create objects and/or manipulate objects, display them in Window win ...
win.wait_for_button();

// ... create objects and/or manipulate objects, display them in Window win ...
win.wait_for_button();

// ... create objects and/or manipulate objects, display them in Window win ...
win.wait_for_button();
```

Each time we reach `wait_for_button()`, we can look at our objects on the screen until we hit the button to get the output from the next part of the program. From the point of view of program logic, this is no different from a program that writes lines of output to a screen (a console window), stopping now and then to receive input from the keyboard. For example:

```
// ... define variables and/or compute values, produce output ...
cin >> var;     // wait for input

// ... define variables and/or compute values, produce output ...
cin >> var;     // wait for input

// ... define variables and/or compute values, produce output ...
cin >> var;     // wait for input
```

The implementations of these two kinds of programs are quite different. When your program executes `cin >> var`, it stops and waits for “the system” to bring back characters you typed. However, the system (the graphical user interface system) that looks after your screen and tracks the mouse as you use it works on a rather different model: the GUI keeps track of where the mouse is and what the user is doing with the mouse (clicking, etc.). When your program wants an action, it must CC

- Tell the GUI what to look for (e.g., “Someone clicked the ‘Next’ button”)
- Tell what is to be done when someone does that
- Wait until the GUI detects an action that the program is interested in

What is new and different here is that the GUI does not stop and wait for the user to respond; it is designed to respond in different ways to different user actions, such as clicking on one of many buttons, resizing windows, redrawing the window after it has been obscured by another, and popping up pop-up menus. This is called *control inversion* (see §14.5.1).

For starters, we just want to say, “Please wake me up when someone clicks my button”; that is, “Please stop executing my program until someone clicks the mouse button and the cursor is in the rectangular area where the image of my button is displayed. Then wake me up” This is just about the simplest action we could imagine. However, such an operation isn’t directly provided by “the system" so we wrote one ourselves. Seeing how that is done is the first step in understanding GUI programming.

14.3 A simple window

CC Basically, "the system" (which is a combination of a GUI library and the operating system) continuously tracks where the mouse is and whether its buttons are pressed or not. A program can express interest in an area of the screen and ask "the system" to call a function when "something interesting" happens. In this particular case, we ask the system to call one of our functions (a "callback function") when the mouse button is clicked "on our button." To do that we must

- Define a button
- Get it displayed
- Define a function for the GUI to call
- Tell the GUI about that button and that function
- Wait for the GUI to call our function

Let's do that. A button is part of a **Window**, so (in **Simple_window.h**) we define our class **Simple_window** to contain a member **next_button**:

```
struct Simple_window : Window {
      Simple_window(Point xy, int w, int h, const string& title );
      ~Simple_window() {}
      void wait_for_button();
private:
      Button next_button;
};
```

Obviously, **Simple_window** is derived from **Graph_lib**'s **Window**. All our windows must be derived directly or indirectly from **Graph_lib::Window** because it is the class that (through Qt) connects our notion of a window with the system's window implementation. For details of **Window**'s implementation, see **Window.h** on **www.stroustrup.com/programming.html**.

Our button is initialized in **Simple_window**'s constructor:

```
Simple_window::Simple_window(Point xy, int w, int h, const string& title)
      : Window(xy,w,h,title),
      next_button(Point{x_max()−70,0}, 70, 20, "Next", [](){})
{
      attach(next_button);
}
```

Unsurprisingly, **Simple_window** passes its location (**xy**), size (**w,h**), and title (**title**) on to **Graph_lib**'s **Window** to deal with. Next, the constructor initializes **next_button** with a location (**Point{x_max()−70,0}**; that's roughly the top right corner), a size (**70,20**), a label (**"Next"**), and an action **[](){}**. The first four parameters are exactly parallel to what we do for a **Window**: we place a rectangular shape on the screen and label it.

The **[](){}** is the minimal action. It is a lambda (§13.3.3, §21.2.3) indicating nothing is to be done. That implies that the processing simply continues after the button has been pressed ("clicked"). An action defined in our program that is invoked by the system in response to some user-action (e.g., "clicking" a button) is call a *callback*. That is the system calls back into our program. Here, **[]()** indicates " do nothing and proceed." Most callbacks do more.

Before showing that code, let's consider what is going on here:

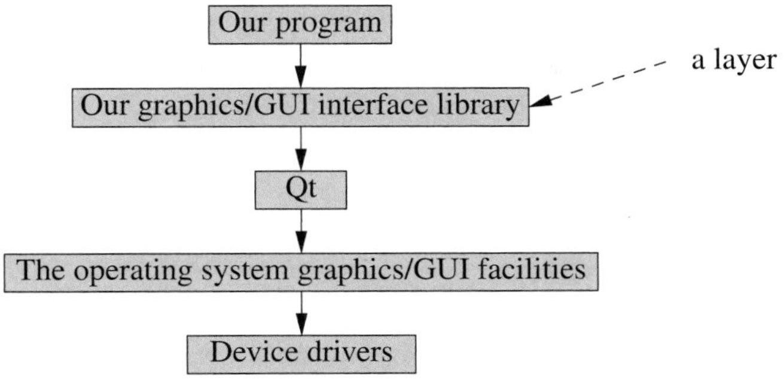

Our program runs on top of several *layers* of software. It directly uses our graphics/GUI library that we implemented using Qt. Qt in turn is implemented using operating system interfaces. In the operating system there are more layers until we reach the device drivers that put pixels on our screen and keep track of what our mouse is doing. Such layering helps us manage our complex system by letting us focus on one – or only a few – layers at a time.

14.3.1 A wait loop

So, in this – our simplest – case, what do we want done by **Simple_window** each time the button is "pressed"? We want to stop the execution of our program to give us a chance to see what we have done so far. Then, the program should wait for us to press the button to proceed:

```
// ... create some objects and/or manipulate some objects, display them in a window ...
win.wait_for_button();  // next() causes the program to proceed from here
// ... create some objects and/or manipulate some objects ...
```

Actually, that's easily done because we rely on Qt facilities, rather than the raw system:

```
void Simple_window::wait_for_button()          // wait for button to be pushed
{
        get_impl().wait_for_button(&next_button);     // pass &next_button to the Window's implementation
}
```

This looks simple, but there is significant complexity hidden here. For example, the code is portable across different operating systems, including MacOS, iOS, Linux, Android, and Windows. In our interface library, the Qt specific code is "hidden" in a class **WidgetPrivate** that is part of the implementation of our **Window** class. CC

Like most GUI systems, Qt provides a function that suspends (stops) a program until something happens. The Qt version is called **exec()** and it wakes up our program whenever anything that our program has expressed interest in happens. In this case, by **attaching next_button** to the **window** we expressed interest in "clicks" on the button. So, when someone clicks our "Next" button, **exec()** calls our **[]()** action and returns (to wait for more events).

14.4 Button and other Widgets

We define a **Button** like this:

```
using Callback = std::function<void()>;        // a callback takes no argument and returning nothing

struct Button : Widget {
      Button(Point xy, int w, int h, const string& label, Callback cb);
      void attach(Window&);
};
```

CC So, a **Button** is a **Widget** with a location (**xy**), a size (**w**,**h**), a text label (**label**), and a callback (**cb**). Basically, anything that appears on a screen with an action (e.g., a callback) associated is a **Widget**.

14.4.1 Widget

Yes, *widget* really is a technical term. A more descriptive, but less evocative, name for a widget is a *control*. We use widgets to define forms of interaction with a program through a GUI (graphical user interface). Our **Widget** interface class looks like this:

```
class Widget {
      // Widget is a handle to a QWidget - it is *not* a QWidget
      // We keep our interface classes at arm's length from Qt
public:
      Widget(Point xy, int w, int h, const string& s, Callback cb);

      Widget& operator=(const Widget&) = delete;        // don't copy Widgets
      Widget(const Widget&) = delete;

      virtual void move(int dx,int dy);
      virtual void hide();
      virtual void show();
      virtual void attach(Window&) = 0;

      Point loc;
      int width;
      int height;
      string label;
      Callback do_it;                                     // the action

      virtual ~Widget();

      WidgetPrivate& get_impl() const { return *impl; }
private:
      std::unique_ptr<WidgetPrivate> impl;
};
```

A **Widget** is similar to a **Shape** but differs in being able to perform actions involving users. It is thus a somewhat more complex mechanism with deeper integration with the GUI engine. Therefore, despite similarities in interface and use, a **Widget** is not a **Shape** or vice versa.

A Widget has two interesting functions that we can use for Button (and also for any other class derived from Widget, e.g., a Menu; see §14.5.2):

- hide() makes the Widget invisible.
- show() makes the Widget visible.

A Widget starts out visible.

Just like a Shape, we can move() a Widget in its Window, and we must attach() it to a Window before it can be used. Note that we declared attach() to be a pure virtual function (§12.3.5): every class derived from Widget must define what it means for it to be attached to a Window. In fact, it is in Window::attach() that the system-level widgets are created. The Widget::attach() and Shape::attach() functions are called from Window as part of its implementation of Window's own attach(). Basically, connecting a window and a widget is a delicate little dance where each has to do its own part. The result is that a window knows about its widgets and that each widget knows about its window:

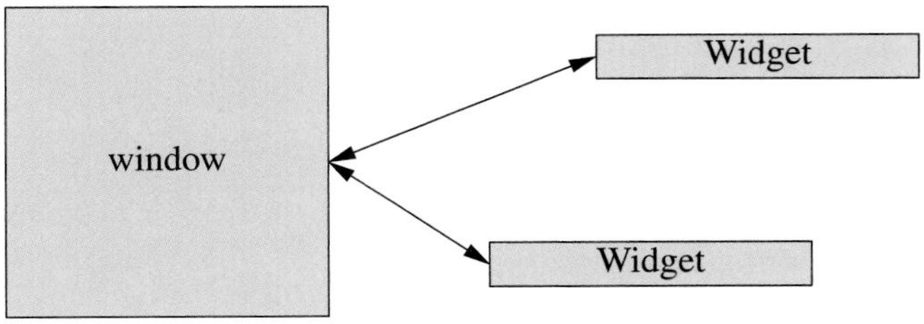

Note that a Window doesn't know what kind of Widgets it deals with. As described in §12.5, we are using basic object-oriented programming to ensure that a Window can deal with every kind of Widget. Similarly, a Widget doesn't know what kind of Window it deals with.

We have been slightly sloppy, leaving data members accessible. However, the alternative would have been to add 10 access functions with essentially no semantic benefits. The impl members are a Widget's link to its Qt implementation. Users of user-interface class Widget have no business messing with its implementation, so we keep it private. A Widget is an interface to a unique object that cannot be copied – it represents an area on the screen and the action associated with it – so we delete its copy operations (§12.4.1).

14.4.2 Button

A Button is the simplest Widget we deal with. All it does is to invoke a callback when we click on it:

```
class Button : public Widget {
public:
      Button(Point xy, int ww, int hh, const string& s, Callback cb);
      void attach(Window&) {}
};
```

```
Button::Button(Point xy, int w, int h, const string& label, Callback cb)
        :Widget(xy,w,h,label,cb)
{
        WidgetPrivate& w_impl = get_impl();
        QPushButton* button = new QPushButton();
        w_impl.widget = button;
        button->setText(QString::fromStdString(label));
        QObject::connect(button, &QPushButton::clicked, [this]{ do_it(); });
}
```

That's all. The constructor contains all the (relatively) messy code connecting to Qt. For now, please just note that defining a simple **Widget** isn't particularly difficult. The call of **connect()** it the most interesting: It says that when someone clicks the button the callback **do_it()** is invoked.

AA We do not deal with the somewhat complicated and messy issue of how buttons (and other **Widgets**) look on the screen. The problem is that there is a near infinity of choices and that some styles are mandated by certain systems. Also, from a programming technique point of view, nothing really new is needed for expressing the looks of buttons. If you get desperate, we note that placing a **Shape** on top of a button doesn't affect the button's ability to function – and you know how to make a shape look like anything at all.

14.4.3 In_box and Out_box

We provide a **Widget** for getting text into our program:

```
struct In_box : Widget {
        In_box(Point xy, int w, int h, const string& s, Callback cb);

        int get_int();
        string get_string();

        int get_int_keep_open();
        string get_string_keep_open();

        void attach(Window& win) override;

        void dismiss();
        void hide() override;
        void show() override;
        void hide_buttons();
        void show_buttons();

        enum State {idle, accepted, rejected};
        State last_result();
        void clear_last_result();
        string last_string_value();
        int last_int_value();
```

```
        struct ResultData {
              State state = idle;
              string last_string;
              int last_int = 0;
        };
  private:
        ResultData result;
        bool waiting = false;
  };
```

An **In_box** can accept text typed into it, and we can read that text as a string using **get_string()** or as an integer using **get_int()**. We can indicate that we are finished typing into the **In_box** by hitting keyboard return/enter key. Alternatively, we can bring up a button for the user to click when finished (using **show_buttons()**). A box that accepts input and generates output is often called a *dialog box*.

Our **In_box** is a bit complicated – apparently unnecessarily so – because it is written to support variations of dialog boxes that are beyond the scope of this book, such as pop-up dialog boxes. That's a common phenomenon in widely used libraries: they are written to serve many users, and many of those users have needs that differ from our current needs. We should be tolerant of such complexity because we might be among those "other users" next year or later.

An **Out_box** is used to present some message to a user. In analogy to **In_box**'s **get** functions, we can **put** either integers or strings into an **Out_box**:

```
  struct Out_box : Shape {
        enum Kind { horizontal, vertical };
        Out_box(Point p, const string& s, Kind k = horizontal);

        void set_parent_window(Window* win) override;

        void put(int);
        void put(const string&);
        void draw_specific(Painter& painter) const override;

        Text label;
        Text data;
        Kind orientation;            // does the Label come before or above the data?
  };
```

An **Out_box** is far simpler than an **In_box** because it doesn't require interaction with the user, it simply displays a value. Therefore, an **Out_box** is just a **Shape**, whereas an **In_box** is a **Widget**.

We could have provided **get_floating_point()**, **get_complex()**, etc., but we did not bother because you can take the string, stick it into a **stringstream**, and do any input formatting you like that way (§9.11). **AA**

§14.5 gives examples of the use of **In_box** and **Out_box**.

14.4.4 Menu

We offer a very simple notion of a menu:

```
struct Menu : Widget {
	enum Kind { horizontal, vertical };
	Menu(Point xy, int w, int h, Kind kk, const string& label);

	using Window::attach;                 // attach the menu to the window

	int attach(Button& b);                // attach a named buton to the menu
	int attach(unique_ptr<Button> p);     // attach an unnamed button to the menu

	void show()                           // show all buttons
	{
		for (auto&& x : selection)
			x->show();
	}

	void hide()                           // hide all buttons
	{
		for (auto&& x : selection)
			x->hide();
	}

	void move(int dx, int dy)             // move all buttons
	{
		for (auto&& x : selection)
			x->move(dx,dy);
	}

private:
	Vector_ref<Button> selection;
	Kind k;
	int offset;

	void layoutButtons(Button& b);        // horizontal or vertical
	void layoutMenu();                    // tells the Widget where the Menu is in the Window
};
```

A **Menu** is basically a vector of buttons. As usual, the **Point xy** is the top left corner. The width and height are used to resize buttons as they are added to the menu. For examples, see §14.5 and §14.5.2. Each menu button ("a menu item") is an independent **Widget** presented to the **Menu** as an argument to **attach()**. In turn, **Menu** provides an **attach()** operation to attach all of its **Buttons** to a **Window**. The **Menu** keeps track of its **Buttons** using a **Vector_ref** (§11.7.3). If you want a "pop-up" menu, you have to make it yourself; see §14.5.2.

14.5 An example: drawing lines

To get a better feel for the basic GUI facilities, consider the window for a simple application involving input, output, and a bit of graphics:

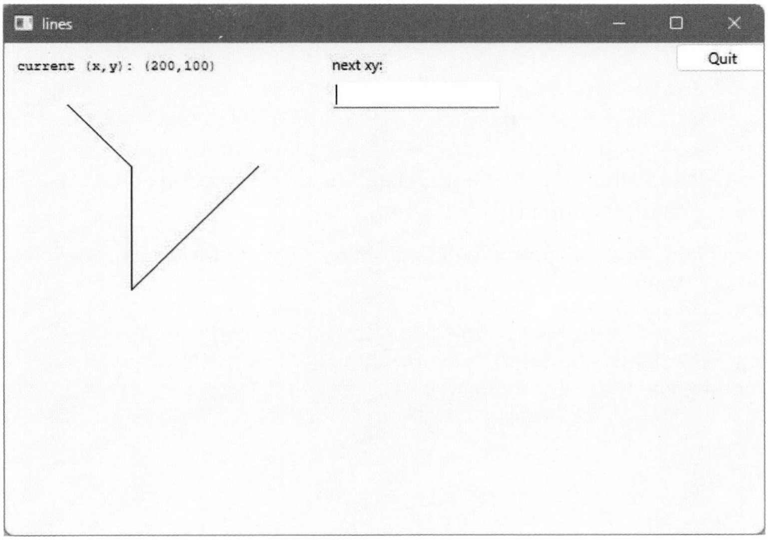

This program allows a user to display a sequence of lines (an open polyline; §11.6.1) specified as a sequence of coordinate pairs. The idea is that the user repeatedly enters (*x*, *y*) coordinates in the "next_xy" box For example, 100,200. Note that the comma is required and no parentheses are accepted. After each coordinate pair, the user hits return/enter keyboard key. The window above shows the result after entering four coordinate pairs: *(50,50)*, *(100,100)*, *(100,200)*, *(200,100)*.

Initially, the "current (x,y)" box is empty and the program waits for the user to enter the first coordinate pair. That done, the starting point appears in the "current (x,y)" box, and each new coordinate pair entered results in a line being drawn: a line from the current point (which has its coordinates displayed in the "current (x,y)" box) to the newly entered (*x*, *y*) is drawn, and that (*x*, *y*) becomes the new current point.

This draws an open polyline. When the user tires of this activity, there is the "Quit" button for exiting. That's pretty straightforward, and the program exercises several useful GUI facilities: text input and output, line drawing, and multiple buttons.

Let's define a class for representing such windows. It is pretty straightforward:

```
struct Lines_window : Window {
    Lines_window(Application& application, Point xy, int w, int h, const string& title);
    Open_polyline lines;
    void wait_for_button();
```

```
private:
      Application* app = nullptr;
      Button quit_button;              // a Widget
      In_box next_xy;                  // a Widget
      Out_box xy_out;                  // a Shape
      void next();
      void quit();
};
```

The line is represented as an **Open_polyline**. The buttons and boxes are declared (as **Buttons**, **In_boxes**, and **Out_boxes**), and for each button a member function implementing the desired action is defined. We decided to eliminate the "boilerplate" callback function and use lambdas instead.

Lines_window's constructor initializes everything:

```
Lines_window::Lines_window(Application& application, Point xy, int w, int h, const string & title)
      : Window{ xy,w,h,title },
            app(application),
            quit_button{ Point{x_max() – 70,0}, 70, 20, "Quit", [this]() { quit(); } },
            next_xy{ Point{250,0}, 50, 20, "next xy:", [this]() { next(); } },
            xy_out{ Point{10,10}, "current (x,y): " }
{
      attach(lines);
      attach(quit_button);

      next_xy.hide_buttons();                  // a Qt input box comes with buttons; we decided to hide them
      attach(next_xy);
      next_xy.show();                          // but we do want the box itself to show

      xy_out.label.set_font_size(8);           // use a smaller than default font
      xy_out.data.set_font_size(8);
      attach(xy_out);
}
```

AA That is, each **Widget** and **Shape** is constructed and then attached to the window. Note that the initializers are in the same order as the data member definitions. That's the proper order in which to write the initializers. In fact, member initializers are always executed in the order their data members were declared. Some compilers (helpfully) give a warning if a base or member constructor is specified out of order.

The "Quit" button deletes the **Window** using Qt facilities:

```
void Lines_window::quit()
{
      end_button_wait();         // don't wait anymore
      next_xy.dismiss();         // clean up
      app–>quit();
}
```

All the real work is done in the **next_xy** button's **next()**: it reads a pair of coordinates, updates the **Open_polyline**, and updates the position readout:

```
void Lines_window::next()          // the action performed by next_xy when woken up
{
        if (next_xy.last_result() == In_box::accepted) {      // check if the value has changed
                string s = next_xy.last_string_value();       // read coordinate pair
                istringstream iss{ s };
                int x = 0;
                char ch = 0;
                int y = 0;
                iss >> x >> ch >> y;
                lines.add(Point{ x,y });

                ostringstream oss;                            // update current position readout
                oss << '(' << x << ',' << y << ')';
                xy_out.put(oss.str());
        }
        next_xy.clear_last_result();                          // clear the box
}
```

We use an **istringstream** (§9.11) to read the integer coordinates from input and an **ostringstream** (§9.11) to format the string to be put into the **Out_box**. If a user enters something that isn't an integer coordinate value, we just default to zero. The test is there to handle the case where a user hits ESC rather than enter/return.

So what's odd and different about this program? Let's see its **main()**:

```
#include "GUI.h"

int main()
try {
        Application app;                                           // create a GUI application
        Lines_window win {app,Point{100,100},600,400,"lines"};     // our window
        return app.gui_main();                                     // start the GUI application
}
catch(exception& e) {
        cerr << "exception: " << e.what() << '\n';
        return 1;
}
catch ( ...) {
        cerr << "Some exception\n";
        return 2;
}
```

There is basically nothing there! The body of **main()** is just the definition of our window, **win**, preceded with the request to create a Qt GUI application and succeeded by a call to give control to the GUI system. There is not another function, **if**, **switch**, or loop – nothing of the kind of code we saw in Chapter 5 and Chapter 6 – just a definition of a variable and a call to the GUI system's main loop, **gui_main()**, which is simply the infinite loop.

Except for a few implementation details we have seen all of the code that makes our "lines" program run. We have seen all of the fundamental logic. So what happens?

14.5.1 Control inversion

CC What happened was that we moved the control of the order of execution from the program to the widgets: whichever widget the user activates, runs. For example, click on a button and its callback runs. When that callback returns, the program settles back, waiting for the user to do something else. Basically, a call **app.exec()** tells "the system" to look out for the widgets and invoke the appropriate callbacks. In theory, **app.exec()** could tell you, the programmer, which widget requested attention and leave it to you to call the appropriate function. However, in Qt and most other GUI systems, **app.exec()** simply invokes the appropriate callback, saving you the bother of writing code to select it.

A "conventional program" is organized like this:

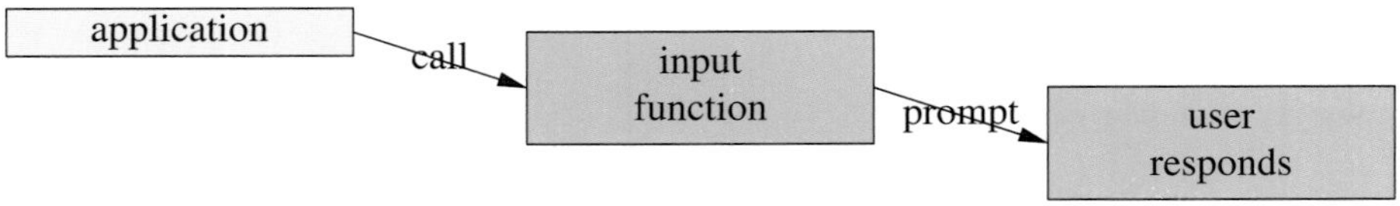

A "GUI program" is organized like this:

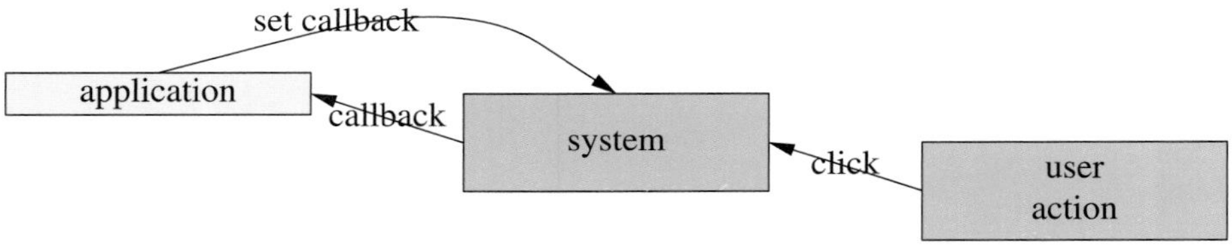

XX One implication of this "control inversion" is that the order of execution is completely determined by the actions of the user. This complicates both program organization and debugging. It is hard to imagine what a user will do and hard to imagine every possible effect of a random sequence of callbacks. This makes systematic testing a nightmare. The techniques for dealing with GUI testing are beyond the scope of this book, but we encourage you to be extra careful with code driven by users through callbacks. In addition to the obvious control flow problems, there are also problems of visibility and difficulties with keeping track of which widget is connected to what data. To minimize hassle, it is essential to keep the GUI portion of a program simple and to build a GUI program incrementally, testing at each stage. When working on a GUI program, it is almost essential to draw little diagrams of the objects and their interactions.

How does the code triggered by the various callbacks communicate? The simplest way is for the functions to operate on data stored in the window, as was done in the example in §14.5. There, the **Lines_window**'s **next()** function, invoked by pressing the "Next point" button, reads data from the **In_box** (**next_xy**) and updates the **lines** member variable and the **Out_box** (**xy_out**). Obviously, a function invoked by a callback can do anything: it could open files, connect to the Web, etc. However, for now, we'll just consider the simple case in which we hold our data in a window.

14.5.2 Adding a menu

Let's explore the control and communication issues raised by "control inversion" by providing a menu for our "lines" program. First, we'll simply provide a menu that allows the user to change the color of all lines in the lines member variable. We add the menu color_menu and its callbacks:

```
struct Color_window : Lines_window {
	Color_window(Application& app, Point xy, int w, int h, const string& title);
	void change(Color c) { lines.set_color(c); }
private:
	Button menu_button;
};
```

Having defined the color_menu member, we need to initialize it:

```
Color_window::Color_window(Application& app, Point xy, int w, int h, const string& title)
	: Lines_window{ app,xy,w,h,title },
		color_menu{ Point{x_max() – 70,40},70,20,Menu::vertical,"color" }
{
	color_menu.attach(make_unique<Button>( Point{0,0},0,0,"red", [&] { change(Color::red); } ));
	color_menu.attach(make_unique<Button>( Point{0,0},0,0,"blue",[&] { change(Color::blue); } ));
	color_menu.attach(make_unique<Button>( Point{0,0},0,0,"black",[&] { change(Color::black); } ));
	attach(color_menu);
}
```

The buttons are dynamically attached to the menu (using attach()) and can be removed and/or replaced as needed. Menu::attach() adjusts the size and location of the button and attaches it to the window. That's all. After entering a few coordinate pairs and pressing "red", we get:

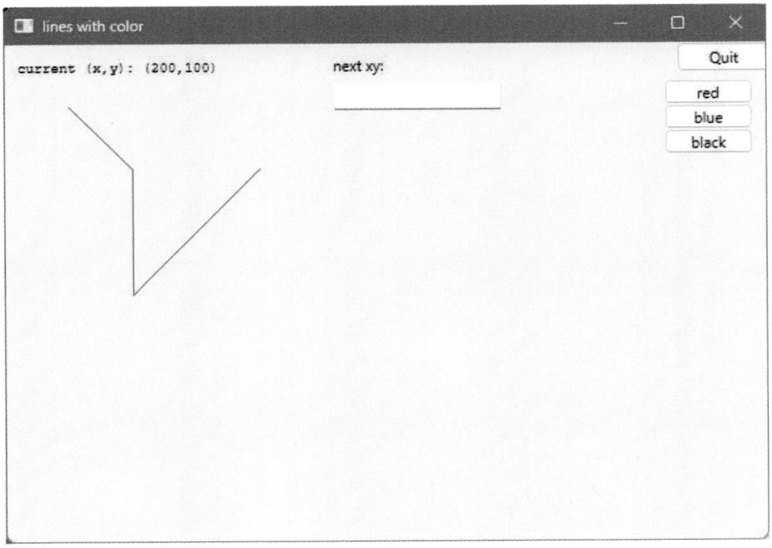

Having played with this for a while, we decided that what we really wanted was a "pop-up menu"; that is, we didn't want to spend precious screen space on a menu except when we are using it. So, we added a "color menu" button; press that, and up pops the color menu. When we have made a selection, the menu is again hidden, and the button appears.

Here first is the window after we have added a few lines:

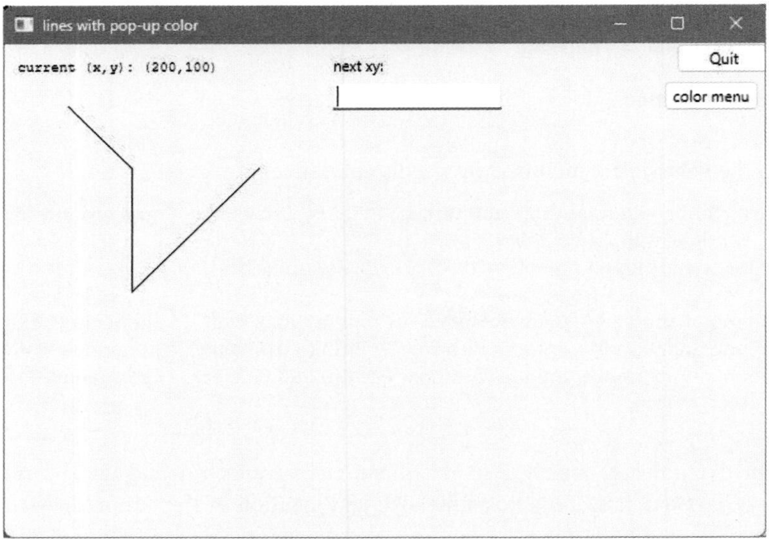

We see the new "color menu" button and some lines. Press "color menu" and the menu appears:

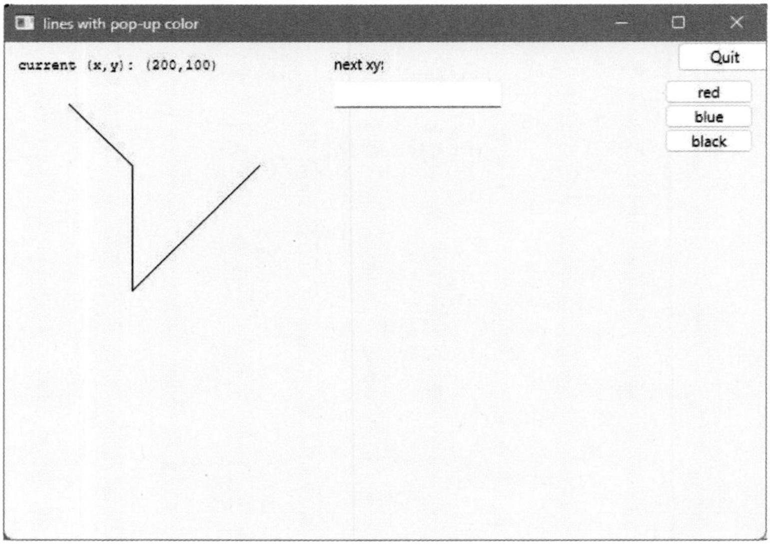

Note that the "color menu" button is now hidden. We don't need it until we are finished with the menu. Press "red" and we get

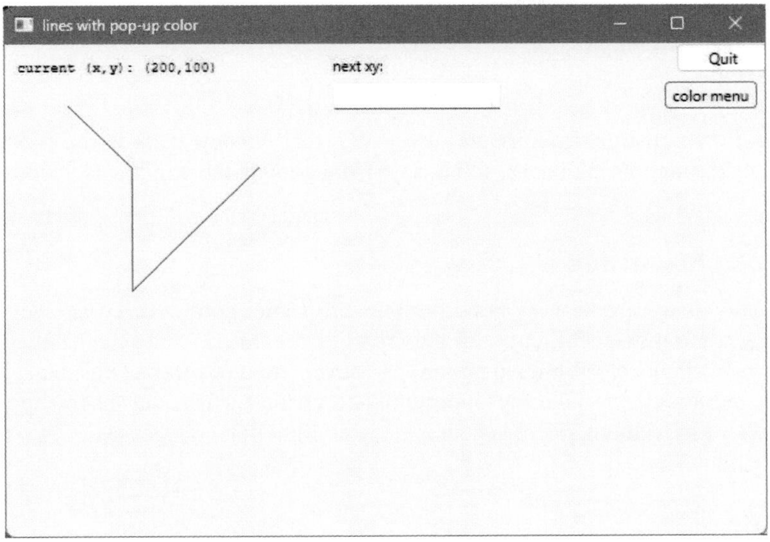

The lines are now red and the "color menu" button has reappeared.

To achieve this we added the "color menu" button and modified the "pressed" functions to adjust the visibility of the menu and the button. Here is the complete **Color_window** after all of our modifications:

```
struct Color_window : Lines_window {
      Color_window(Application& app, Point xy, int w, int h, const string& title);
private:
      void change(Color c) { lines.set_color(c); }
      void hide_menu() { color_menu.hide(); menu_button.show(); }

      Button menu_button;
      Menu color_menu;
};

Color_window::Color_window(Point xy, int w, int h, const string& title)
      :Lines_window{ xy,w,h,title },
      menu_button{ Point{x_max() – 80,30}, 80, 20, "color menu",
            [&] { menu_button.hide(); color_menu.show(); } },
      color_menu{ Point{x_max() – 70,40},70,20,Menu::vertical,"color" }
{
      attach(color_menu);
      color_menu.attach(make_unique< Button>(Point{0,0},0,0,"red",
            [&] { change(Color::red); hide_menu(); }));
```

```
        color_menu.attach(make_unique< Button>(Point{0,0},0,0,"blue",
              [&] { change(Color::blue); hide_menu(); }));
        color_menu.attach(make_unique< Button>(Point{0,0},0,0,"black",
              [&] { change(Color::black); hide_menu(); }));
        attach(menu_button);
        hide_menu();
}
```

Note how all but the constructor is private. Basically, that **Window** class is the program. All that happens, happens through its callbacks, so no code from outside the window is needed.

14.6 Simple animation

Buttons, **Texts**, and **Menus** are all very good but they are static: nothing moves! Well, we can load images that have some movement, but with the facilities presented so far, the best we can do is for something to move whenever we click a button. However, **Window** offers a mechanism to wait for a while and then redraw. If we take the opportunity to change what's on that window before that redraw, we can have movement. Here is a simple traffic light that changes every two seconds. First we define our window:

```
Window w{140, 240, "Traffic light"};

Rectangle r{{10, 10}, 120, 220};
r.set_fill_color(Color::black);

Circle red {{70, 50}, 30};
Circle amber {{70, 120}, 30};
Circle green {{70, 190}, 30};
```

Attach the four **Shapes** and we have a static **Window**. However, we can now add actions:

```
const int second = 1000;          // 1000 milliseconds == 1 second; the timer counts milliseconds
const int yellow_delay = 10*second;
const int red_green_delay = 120*second;

while (true)
   for (int i = 0; i < 3; ++i) {
      red.set_fill_color(Color::red);
      w.timer_wait(red_green_delay);

      amber.set_fill_color(Color::yellow);
      w.timer_wait(yellow_delay);

      red.set_fill_color(Color::black);
      amber.set_fill_color(Color::black);
      green.set_fill_color(Color::green);
      w.timer_wait(red_green_delay);
```

```
        amber.set_fill_color(Color::yellow);
        green.set_fill_color(Color::black);
        w.timer_wait(yellow_delay);

        amber.set_fill_color(Color::black);
    }
```

Now the traffic light slowly circles from red, to red and yellow, to green, to yellow:

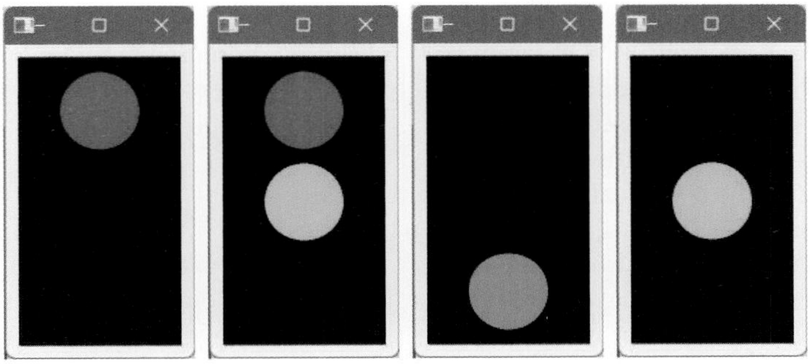

The w.timer_wait(yellow_delay) simply waits for 10,000 milliseconds (ten seconds):

```
void Window::timer_wait(int milliseconds)
{
        impl->timer_wait(milliseconds);
}
```

You can also add an action ("callback") as an argument. That action is invoked after the delay.

```
void Window::timer_wait(int milliseconds, std::function<void()> cb)
{
        impl->timer_wait(milliseconds, cb);
}
```

One of the nice things about the callback model is that "the system" still looks out for other user actions while the animation runs. That way, **Buttons**, **Menus**, and such still work.

The traffic light example was the simplest we could think of but we are confident that you can think of more interesting ones. Remember that an application can have many windows, so we can have several independent animations running simultaneously. Also, between timer_wait()s, we can update several different "animated objects."

14.7 Debugging GUI code

Once a GUI program starts working, it is often quite easy to debug: what you see is what you get. However, there is often a most frustrating period before the first shapes and widgets start appearing in a window or even before a window appears on the screen. Try this main():

```
int main()
{
	Application app;
	Lines_window {app,Point{100,100},600,400,"lines"};
	app.gui_main();
}
```

AA Do you see the error? Whether you see it or not, you should try it; the program will compile and run, but instead of the **Lines_window** giving you a chance to draw lines, you get at most a flicker on the screen. How do you find errors in such a program?

- By carefully using well-tried program parts (classes, function, libraries)
- By simplifying all new code, by slowly "growing" a program from its simplest version, by carefully looking over the code line by line
- By checking all linker settings
- By comparing the code to already working programs
- By explaining the code to a friend

XX The one thing that you will find it hard to do is to trace the execution of the code. If you have learned to use a debugger, you have a chance, but just inserting "output statements" will not work in this case – the problem is that no output appears. Even debuggers will have problems because there are several things going on at once ("multi-threading") – your code is not the only code trying to interact with the screen. Simplification of the code and a systematic approach to understanding the code are key.

So what was the problem? Here is the correct version (from §14.5):

```
int main()
{
	Application app;
	Lines_window win {app,Point{100,100},600,400,"lines"};
	app.gui_main();
}
```

We "forgot" the name of the **Lines_window**, **win**. Since we didn't actually need that name that seemed reasonable, but the compiler then decided that since we didn't use that window, it could immediately destroy it. Oops! That window existed for something on the order of a millisecond. No wonder we missed it.

XX Another common problem is to put one window *exactly* on top of another. This obviously (or rather not at all obviously) looks as if there is only one window. Where did the other window go? We can spend significant time looking for nonexistent bugs in the code. The same problem can occur if we put one shape on top of another.

XX Finally – to make matters still worse – exceptions don't always work as we would like them to when we use a GUI library. Since our code is managed by a GUI library, an exception we throw may never reach our handler – the library or the operating system may "eat" it. That is, they may rely on error-handling mechanisms that differ from C++ exceptions and may indeed be completely oblivious of C++).

AA Common problems found during debugging include **Shape**s and **Widget**s not showing because they were not attached and objects misbehaving because they have gone out of scope. Consider how a programmer might factor out the creation and attachment of buttons in a menu:

```
void load_disaster_menu(Menu& m)      // helper function for loading buttons into a menu
{
        Point orig {0,0};
        Button b1 {orig,0,0,"flood",cb_flood};
        Button b2 {orig,0,0,"fire",cb_fire};
        // ...
        m.attach(b1);
        m.attach(b2);
        // ...
}

int main()
{
        // ...
        Menu disasters {Point{100,100},60,20,Menu::horizontal,"disasters"};
        load_disaster_menu(disasters);
        win.attach(disasters);
        // ...
}
```

This will not work. All those buttons are local to the **load_disaster_menu** function and attaching them to a menu will not change that. The essence of the story is that after **load_disaster_menu()** has returned, those local objects have been destroyed and the **disasters** menu refers to nonexistent (destroyed) objects. The result is likely to be surprising and not pretty. Compilers can and should catch such errors, but unfortunately not all do. The solution is to use unnamed objects created by **make_unique** instead of named local objects:

```
void load_disaster_menu(Menu& m)
        // helper function for loading buttons into a menu
{
        Point orig {0,0};
        m.attach(make_unique<Button>(orig,0,0,"flood",cb_flood));
        m.attach(make_unique<Button>(orig,0,0,"fire",cb_fire));
        // ...
}
```

The correct solution is even simpler than the (all too common) bug.

Drill

[1] Make a completely new project with linker settings for Qt (**www.stroustrup.com/programming.html**).

[2] Using the facilities of **Graph_lib**, type in the line-drawing program from §14.5 and get it to run.

[3] Modify the program to use a pop-up menu as described in §14.5.2 and get it to run.

[4] Modify the program to have a second menu for choosing line styles and get it to run.

Review

[1] Why would you want a graphical user interface?
[2] When would you want a non-graphical user interface?
[3] What is a software layer?
[4] Why would you want to layer software?
[5] What is a callback?
[6] What is a widget?
[7] Is Qt an acronym?
[8] How do you pronounce Qt?
[9] What other GUI toolkits have you heard of?
[10] Which systems use the term *widget* and which prefer *control*?
[11] What are examples of widgets?
[12] When would you use an inbox?
[13] What is the type of the value stored in an inbox?
[14] When would you use a button?
[15] When would you use a menu?
[16] What is control inversion?
[17] What is the basic strategy for debugging a GUI program?
[18] Why is debugging a GUI program harder than debugging an "ordinary program using streams for I/O"?
[19] How do you animate a widget?

Terms

Button	dialog box	visible/hidden	callback
GUI	waiting for input	console I/O	GUI I/O
menu	wait loop	control	software
layer	widget	control inversion	user interface
browser I/O	Application	Qt	In_box
Out_box	animation	timer_wait()	

Exercises

[1] Make a My_window that's a bit like Simple_window except that it has two buttons, next and quit.
[2] Make a window (based on My_window) with a 4-by-4 checkerboard of square buttons. When pressed, a button performs a simple action, such as printing its coordinates in an output box, or turns a slightly different color (until another button is pressed).
[3] Place an Image on top of a Button; move both when the button is pushed. Use this random number generator from PPP__support to pick a new location for the "image button":

```
inline int rand_int(int min, int max)
{
      static default_random_engine ran;
      return uniform_int_distribution<>{min,max}(ran);
}
```

It returns a random int in the range [min,max).

[4] Make a menu with items that make a circle, a square, an equilateral triangle, and a hexagon, respectively. Make an input box (or two) for giving a coordinate pair, and place the shape made by pressing a menu item at that coordinate. Sorry, no drag and drop.

[5] Write a program that draws a shape of your choice and moves it to a new point each time you click "Next." The new point should be determined by a coordinate pair read from an input stream.

[6] Make an "analog clock," that is, a clock with hands that move. You get the time of day from the operating system through a library call. Hint: chrono::now(), sleep().

[7] Using the techniques developed in the previous exercises, make an image of an airplane "fly around" in a window. Have a "Start" and a "Stop" button.

[8] Provide a currency converter. Read the conversion rates from a file on startup. Enter an amount in an input window and provide a way of selecting currencies to convert to and from (e.g., a pair of menus).

[9] Modify the calculator from Chapter 6 to get its input from an input box and return its results in an output box.

[10] Provide a program where you can choose among a set of functions (e.g., sin() and log()), provide parameters for those functions, and then graph them.

Postscript

GUI is a huge topic. Much of it has to do with style and compatibility with existing systems. Furthermore, much has to do with a bewildering variety of widgets (such as a GUI library offering many dozens of alternative button styles) that would make a traditional botanist feel quite at home. However, little of that has to do with fundamental programming techniques, so we won't proceed in that direction. Other topics, such as scaling, rotation, morphing, three-dimensional objects, shadowing, etc., require sophistication in graphical and/or mathematical topics which we don't assume here.

One thing you should be aware of is that most GUI systems provide a "GUI builder" that AA
allows you to design your window layouts graphically and attach callbacks and actions to buttons, menus, etc. specified graphically. For many applications, such a GUI builder is well worth using to reduce the tedium of writing "scaffolding code" such as our callbacks. However, always try to understand how the resulting programs work. Sometimes, the generated code is equivalent to what you have seen in this chapter. Sometimes more elaborate and/or expensive mechanisms are used.

Part III
Data and Algorithms

Part III focuses on the C++ standard library's containers and algorithms framework (often referred to as the STL). It shows how containers (such as **vector**, **list**, and **map**) are implemented and used. In doing so, we introduce pointers, arrays, dynamic memory, exceptions, and templates. As part of that, we introduce the fundamental principles and techniques of generic programming. We also demonstrate the design and use of standard-library algorithms (such as **sort**, **find**, and **inner_product**).

Chapter 15: Vector and Free Store
Chapter 16: Arrays, Pointers, and References
Chapter 17: Essential Operations
Chapter 18: Templates and Exceptions
Chapter 19: Containers and Iterators
Chapter 20: Maps and Sets
Chapter 21: Algorithms

15

Vector and Free Store

Use vector *as the default!*
– Alex Stepanov

This chapter and the next five describe the containers and algorithms part of the C++ standard library, traditionally called the STL. We describe the key facilities from the STL and some of their uses. In addition, we present the key design and programming techniques used to implement the STL and some low-level language features used for that. Among those are pointers, arrays, and free store. The focus of this chapter and the next three is the design and implementation of the most common and most useful STL container: vector.

§15.1 Introduction
§15.2 vector basics
§15.3 Memory, addresses, and pointers
The sizeof operator
§15.4 Free store and pointers
Free-store allocation; Access through pointers; Initialization; The null pointer; Free-store deallocation
§15.5 Destructors
Generated destructors; Virtual destructors
§15.6 Access to elements
§15.7 An example: lists
List operations; List use
§15.8 The this pointer
More link use

15.1 Introduction

CC The most useful container in the C++ standard library is **vector**. A **vector** provides a sequence of elements of a given type. You can refer to an element by its index (subscript), extend the **vector** by using **push_back()** or **resize()**, ask a **vector** for the number of its elements using **size()**, and have access to the **vector** checked against attempts to access out-of-range elements. The standard library **vector** is a convenient, flexible, efficient (in time and space), statically type-safe container of elements. The standard **string** has similar properties, as have other useful standard container types, such as **list** and **map**, which we describe in Chapter 20. However, a computer's memory doesn't directly support such useful types. All that the hardware *directly* supports is sequences of bytes. For example, for a **vector<double>v**, the operation **v.push_back(2.3)** adds **2.3** to a sequence of **double**s and increases the element count of **v** (**v.size()**) by 1. At the lowest level, the computer knows nothing about anything as sophisticated as **push_back()**; all it knows is how to read and write a few bytes at a time.

In this and the following three chapters, we show how to build a **Vector** from the basic language facilities available to every programmer. Gradually, our **Vector** approximates the standard-library **vector**. This approach allows us to illustrate useful concepts and programming techniques, and to see how they are expressed using C++ language features. The language facilities and programming techniques we encounter in our **Vector** implementation are generally useful and very widely used.

Once we have seen how **vector** is designed, implemented, and used, we can proceed to look at other standard library containers, such as **map**, and examine the elegant and efficient facilities for their use provided by the C++ standard library (Chapter 20 and Chapter 21). These facilities save us from programming common tasks involving data ourselves. Instead, we can use what is available as part of every C++ implementation to ease the writing and testing of our code.

AA We approach the standard library **vector** through a series of increasingly sophisticated **Vector** implementations. First, we build an extremely simple **Vector**. Then, we see what's undesirable about that **Vector** and fix it. Please don't confuse the versions of **Vector** with the real **vector**. These versions are simplified to address a single issue at a time and therefore flawed. Be happy when you discover a flaw before we get around to mention and fix it in a later version. Spotting a flaw means that you are likely to recognize it when you see it in your own code or in that of others. When we have improved the seriously flawed early versions a few times, we reach a **Vector** that approximates the standard-library **vector** – shipped with your C++ compiler, the one that you have been using in the previous chapters. This process of gradual refinement mirrors the way we typically approach a new programming task. Along the way, we encounter and explore many classical problems related to the use of memory and data structures. The basic plan is this:

- *Chapter 15 (this chapter)*: How can we deal with varying amounts of memory? In particular, how can different **vector**s have different numbers of elements? This leads us to examine free store (also called *heap* and *dynamic memory*) and pointers. We introduce the crucial notion of a destructor.
- *Chapter 16*: We introduce arrays and explore their relation to pointers. We discuss the relationship between pointers and references. We present C-style strings. We offer **span**, **array**, and **string** as alternatives to the use of low-level constructs.
- *Chapter 17*: How can we copy **vector**s? How can we provide a subscript operation for them? How can we change the size of a **vector**? We introduce the notion of a set of

essential operations that a class needs for its lifetime and resources to be managed.

- *Chapter 18*: How can we have **vector**s with different element types? And how can we deal with out-of-range errors? To answer those questions, we explore the C++ template and exception facilities. We present a **Vector** that approximates the standard-library **vector** and also the resource-management pointers **unique_ptr** and **shared_ptr**.

In addition to the new language facilities and techniques that we introduce to handle the implementation of a flexible, efficient, and type-safe vector, we also use many of the language facilities and programming techniques we have already seen. Occasionally, we take the opportunity to give those a slightly more formal and technical definition.

So, this is the point at which we finally get to deal directly with memory. Why do we have to? Our **vector** and **string** are extremely useful and convenient; we can just use those. After all, containers, such as **vector** and **string**, are designed to insulate us from some of the unpleasant aspects of real memory. However, unless we are content to believe in magic, we must examine the lowest level of memory management. Why shouldn't you "just believe in magic"? Or – to put a more positive spin on it – why shouldn't you "just trust that the implementers of **vector** knew what they were doing"? After all, we don't suggest that you examine the device physics that allow our computer's memory to function. If so, we could skip right to Chapter 19.

Well, we are programmers (computer scientists, software developers, or whatever) rather than physicists. Had we been studying device physics, we would have had to look into the details of computer memory design. However, since we are studying programming, we must look into the detailed design of programs. In theory, we could consider the low-level memory access and management facilities "implementation details" just as we do the device physics. However, if we did that, we would not just have to "believe in magic"; we would be unable to implement a new container (should we need one, and that's not uncommon). Also, we would be unable to read huge amounts of C and older C++ code that directly uses memory. As we will see over the next few chapters, pointers (a low-level and direct way of referring to an object) are also useful for a variety of reasons not related to memory management. It is not easy to use C++ well without sometimes using pointers. **CC**

More philosophically, I am among the large group of computer professionals who are of the opinion that if you lack a basic and practical understanding of how a program maps onto a computer's memory and operations, you will have problems getting a solid grasp of higher-level topics, such as data structures, algorithms, and operating systems. **XX**

15.2 vector basics

We start our incremental design of our **Vector** by considering a very simple use of **vector**:

```
vector<double> age(4);        // a vector with 4 elements of type double
age[0]=0.33;
age[1]=22.0;
age[2]=27.2;
age[3]=54.2;
```

This creates a **vector** with four elements of type **double** and gives those four elements the values **0.33**, **22.0**, **27.2**, and **54.2**. The four elements are numbered 0, 1, 2, 3. The numbering of elements in

C++ standard library containers always starts from 0 (zero). Numbering from 0 is very common, and it is a universal convention among C++ programmers. The number of elements of a **vector** is called its size. So, the size of **age** is 4. The elements of a **vector** are numbered (indexed) from 0 to size-1. For example, the elements of **age** are numbered **0** to **age.size()–1**. We can represent **age** graphically like this:

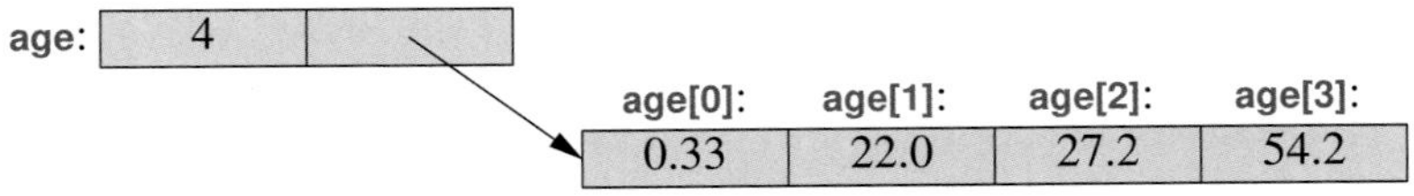

How do we make this "graphical design" real in a computer's memory? How do we get the values stored and accessed like that? Obviously, we have to define a class and we want to call this class **Vector**. Furthermore, it needs a data member to hold its size and one to hold its elements. But how do we represent a set of elements where the number of elements can vary? We could use a standard library **vector**, but that would – in this context – be cheating: we are building our own **Vector** here.

So, how do we represent that arrow in the drawing above? Consider doing without it. We could define a fixed-size data structure:

```
class Vector {
      int size;
      double age0, age1, age2, age3;
};
```

Ignoring some notational details, we'll have something like this:

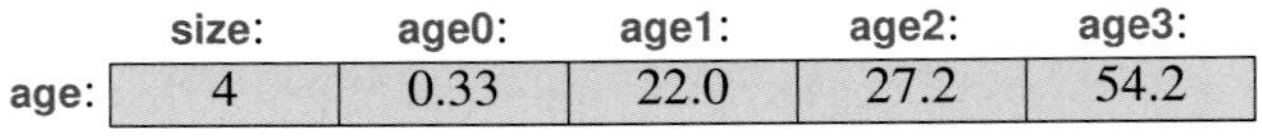

CC That's simple and nice, but the first time we try to add an element with **push_back()** we are sunk: we have no way of adding an element; the number of elements is fixed to four in the program text. We need something more than a data structure holding a fixed number of elements. Operations that change the number of elements of a **vector**, such as **push_back()**, can't be implemented if we defined our **Vector** to have a fixed number of elements. Basically, we need a data member that points to the set of elements so that we can make it point to a different set of elements when we need more space. We need something like the memory address of the first element. In C++, a data type that can hold an address is called a *pointer* and is syntactically distinguished by the suffix $*$, so that **double*** means "pointer to **double**." Given that, we can define our first version of a **Vector** class:

```
class Vector {          // a very simplified vector of doubles (like vector<double>)
      int sz;                          // the size
      double* elem;                    // pointer to the first element (of type double)
public:
      Vector(int s);                   // constructor: allocate s doubles,
                                       // let elem point to them and sz hold the size (s)
      int size() const { return sz; }  // the current size
};
```

Before proceeding with the Vector design, let us study the notion of "pointer" in some detail. The notion of "pointer" – together with its closely related notion of "array" – is key to C++'s notion of "memory" (§16.1).

15.3 Memory, addresses, and pointers

A computer's memory is a sequence of bytes. We can number the bytes from 0 to the last one. We call such "a number that indicates a location in memory" an *address*. You can think of an address as a kind of integer value. The first byte of memory has the address 0, the next the address 1, and so on. We can visualize a megabyte of memory like this: CC

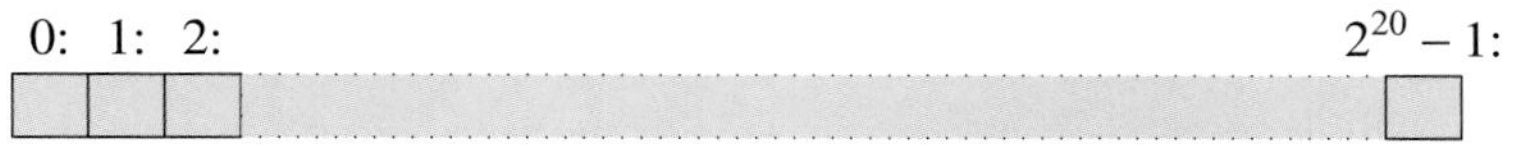

Everything we put in memory has an address. For example:

```
int var = 17;
```

This will set aside an "int-sized" piece of memory for var somewhere and put the value 17 into that memory. We can also store and manipulate addresses. An object that holds an address value is called a *pointer*. For example, the type needed to hold the address of an int is called a "pointer to int" or an "int pointer" and the notation is int*:

```
int* ptr = &var;        // ptr holds the address of var
```

The "address of" operator, unary &, is used to get the address of an object. So, if var happens to start at address 4096 (also known as 2^{12}), ptr will hold the value 4096:

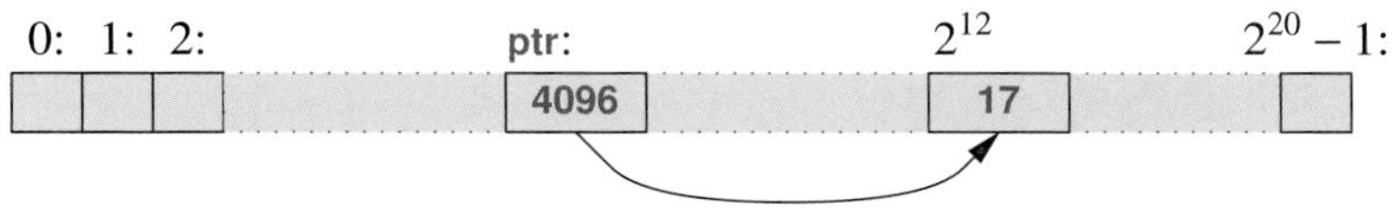

Basically, we view our computer's memory as a sequence of bytes numbered from 0 to the memory size minus 1. On some machines that's a simplification, but as an initial programming model of the memory, it will suffice.

Each type has a corresponding pointer type. For example:

```
int x = 17;
int* pi = &x;               // pointer to int

double e = 2.71828;
double* pd = &e;            // pointer to double
```

If we want to see the value of the object pointed to, we can do that using the "contents of" operator, unary *. For example:

```
cout << "pi == " << pi << "; contents of pi == " << *pi << "\n";
cout << "pd == " << pd << "; contents of pd == " << *pd << "\n";
```

The output for ***pi** will be the integer **17** and the output for ***pd** will be the double **2.71828**. The output for **pi** and **pd** will vary depending on where the compiler allocated our variables **x** and **e** in memory. The notation used for the pointer value (address) may also vary depending on which conventions your system uses.

The *contents of* operator (often called the *dereference* operator) can also be used on the left-hand side of an assignment:

```
*pi = 27;            // OK: you can assign 27 to the int pointed to by pi
*pd = 3.14159;       // OK: you can assign 3.14159 to the double pointed to by pd
*pd = *pi;           // OK: you can assign an int (*pi) to a double (*pd)
```

XX Note that even though a pointer value can be printed as an integer, a pointer is not an integer. "What does an **int** point to?" is not a well-formed question; **int**s do not point, pointers do. A pointer type provides the operations suitable for addresses, whereas **int** provides the arithmetic operations suitable for integers. So pointers and integers do not implicitly mix:

```
int i = pi;          // error: can't assign an int* to an int
pi = 7;              // error: can't assign an int to an int*
```

Similarly, a pointer to **char** (a **char***) is not a pointer to **int** (an **int***). For example:

```
char* pc = pi;       // error: can't assign an int* to a char*
pi = pc;             // error: can't assign a char* to an int*
```

Why is it an error to assign **pc** to **pi**? Consider one answer: a **char** is usually much smaller than an **int**, so consider this:

```
char ch1 = 'a';
char ch2 = 'b';
char ch3 = 'c';
char ch4 = 'd';
int* pi = &ch3;      // error: we cannot assign a char* to an int*, but let's pretend we could
*pi = 12345;         // write to an int-sized piece of memory
*pi = 67890;
```

Exactly how the compiler allocates variables in memory is implementation defined, but we might very well get something like this:

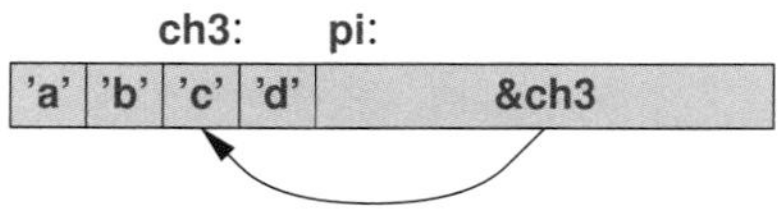

Now, had the compiler allowed the code, we would have been writing **12345** to the memory starting at **&ch3**. That would definitely have changed the value of some nearby memory, such as **ch2** or **ch4**. If we were really unlucky (which is likely), we would have overwritten part of **pi** itself! In that case, the next assignment (***pi=67890**) would place **67890** in some completely different part of memory. Be glad that such assignment is disallowed. It is called *memory corruption*. However, this is one of the very few protections offered by the compiler at this low level of programming.

We are really close to the hardware here. This is not a particularly comfortable place to be for a programmer. We have only a few primitive operations available and hardly any support from the language or the standard library. However, we had to get here to know how higher-level facilities, such as **vector**, are implemented. We need to understand how to write code at this level because not all code can be "high-level" (PPP2.Ch25). Also, we might better appreciate the convenience and relative safety of the higher levels of software once we have experienced their absence. Our aim is always to work at the highest level of abstraction that is possible given a problem and the constraints on its solution. In this chapter and in Chapter 16 to Chapter 18, we show how to get back to a more comfortable level of abstraction by implementing a **Vector**.

15.3.1 The sizeof operator

So how much memory does an **int** really take up? A pointer? The operator **sizeof** answers such questions: CC

```
void sizes(char ch, int i, int* p)
{
	cout << "the size of char is " << sizeof(char) << ' ' << sizeof(ch) << '\n';
	cout << "the size of int is " << sizeof(int) << ' ' << sizeof(i) << '\n';
	cout << "the size of int* is " << sizeof(int*) << ' ' << sizeof(p) << '\n';
}
```

As you can see, we can apply **sizeof** either to a type name or to an expression; for a type, **sizeof** gives the size of an object of that type, and for an expression, it gives the size of the type of the result. The result of **sizeof** is a positive integer and the unit is **sizeof(char)**, which is defined to be **1**. Typically, a **char** is stored in a byte, so **sizeof** reports the number of bytes.

> TRY THIS
>
> Execute the example above and see what you get. Then extend the example to determine the size of **bool**, **double**, and some other type.

The size of a type is *not* guaranteed to be the same on every implementation of C++. These days, **sizeof(int)** is typically 4 on a laptop or desktop machine. With an 8-bit byte, that means that an **int** is 32 bits. However, embedded systems processors with 16-bit **int**s and high-performance architectures with 64-bit **int**s are common.

How much memory is used by a **vector**? We can try

```
vector<int> v(1000);            // vector with 1000 elements of type int
cout << "the size of vector<int>(1000) is " << sizeof (v) << '\n';
```

The output will be something like

```
the size of vector<int>(1000) is 20
```

The explanation will become obvious over this chapter and the next (see also §16.1.1), but clearly, **sizeof** is not counting the **vector** elements.

15.4 Free store and pointers

CC Consider the implementation of **Vector** from the end of §15.2. From where does the **Vector** get the space for the elements? How do we get the pointer **elem** to point to them? When you start a C++ program, the compiler sets aside memory for your code (sometimes called *code storage* or *text storage*) and for the global variables you define (called *static storage*). It also sets aside some memory to be used when you call functions, and they need space for their arguments and local variables (§7.4.8) called *stack storage* or *automatic storage*. The rest of the computer's memory is potentially available for other uses; it is "free." We can illustrate that graphically:

Physical memory layout:

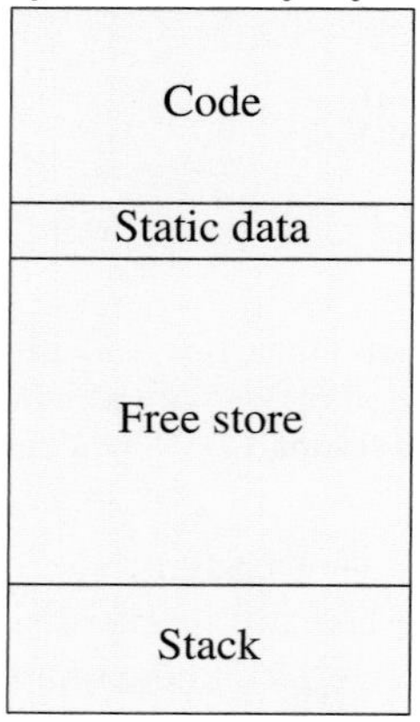

The C++ language makes this *free store* (also called the *heap* and *dynamic memory*) available through an operator called **new**. For example:

```
double* p = new double[4];          // allocate 4 doubles on the free store
```

This asks the C++ run-time system to allocate four **doubles** on the free store and return a pointer to the first **double** to us. We use that pointer to initialize our pointer variable **p**. We can represent this graphically:

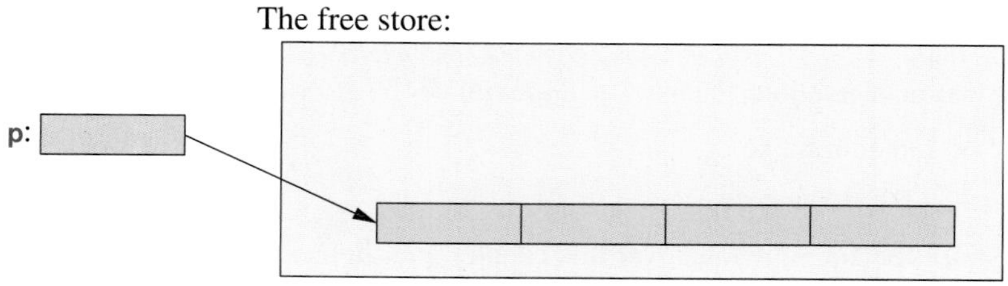

The **new** operator returns a pointer to the object it creates. If it created several objects (an array of objects), it returns a pointer to the first of those objects. If that object is of type **X**, the pointer returned by **new** is of type **X***. For example:

```
char* q = new double[4];        // error: a double* assigned to a char*
```

That **new** returns a pointer to a **double** and a **double** isn't a **char**, so we should not (and cannot) assign it to the pointer to **char** variable **q**.

We say that the pointer **q** points to an array of four elements of type **double**. An *array* is a contiguous sequence of elements of a given type.

15.4.1 Free-store allocation

CC

We request memory to be *allocated* on the *free store* by the **new** operator:

- The **new** operator returns a pointer to the allocated memory.
- A pointer value is the address of the first byte of the memory.
- A pointer points to an object of a specified type.
- A pointer does *not* know how many elements it points to (this is the root cause of many problems).

The **new** operator can allocate individual elements or sequences (arrays) of elements. For example:

```
int* pi = new int;              // allocate one int
int* qi = new int[4];           // allocate 4 ints (an array of 4 ints)

double* pd = new double;        // allocate one double
double* qd = new double[n];     // allocate n doubles (an array of n doubles)
```

Note that the number of objects allocated can be a variable. That's important because that allows us to select how many objects we allocate at run time. If **n** is **2**, we get

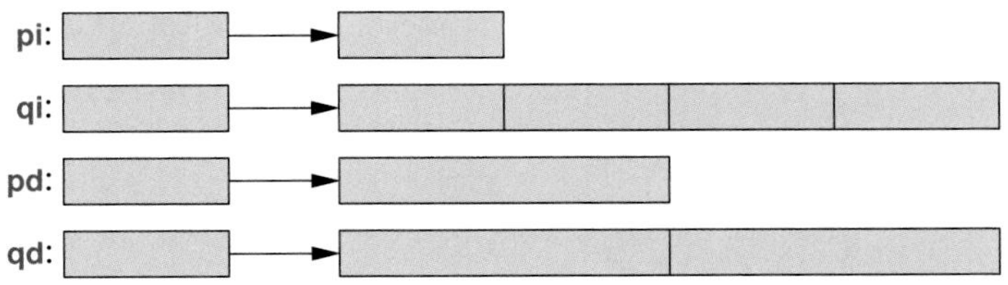

Pointers to objects of different types are different types. For example:

```
pi = pd;        // error: can't assign a double* to an int*
pd = pi;        // error: can't assign an int* to a double*
```

Why? After all, we can assign an **int** to a **double** and a **double** to an **int**. However, an **int** and a **double** may have different sizes. If so:

- Writes through a pointer to a larger element than was allocated can overwrite unrelated variables (§15.3).
- The **[ ]** operator relies on the size of the element type to figure out where to find an element. So if **sizeof(int)!=sizeof(double)** we could get some rather strange results if we allowed **qi** to point to the memory allocated for **qd**.

That's the "practical explanation." The theoretical explanation is simply "Allowing assignment of pointers to different types would allow type errors."

15.4.2 Access through pointers

In addition to using the dereference operator * on a pointer, we can use the subscript operator [ ]. For example:

```
double* p = new double[4];      // allocate 4 doubles on the free store
double x = *p;                  // read the (first) object pointed to by p
double y = p[0];                // read the 1st object pointed to by p
double z = p[2];                // read the 3rd object pointed to by p
```

Unsurprisingly, the subscript operator for a pointer counts from 0 just like **vector**'s subscript operator, so **p[2]** refers to the third element; **p[0]** is the first element so **p[0]** means exactly the same as ***p**. The **[ ]** and * operators can also be used for writing:

```
*p = 7.7;            // write to the (first) object pointed to by p
p[2] = 9.9;          // write to the 3rd object pointed to by p
```

A pointer points to an object in memory. The "contents of" operator (also called the *dereference* operator) allows us to read and write the object pointed to by a pointer **p**:

```
double x = *p;       // read the object pointed to by p
*p = 8.8;            // write to the object pointed to by p
```

When applied to a pointer, the **[ ]** operator treats memory as a sequence of objects (of the type specified by the pointer declaration) with the first one pointed to by a pointer **p**:

```
double x = p[3];     // read the 4th object pointed to by p
p[3] = 4.4;          // write to the 4th object pointed to by p
double y = p[0];     // p[0] is the same as *p
```

That's all. There is no checking, no implementation cleverness, just simple access to our computer's memory:

This is exactly the simple and optimally efficient mechanism for accessing memory that we need to implement a **vector**.

We can have pointers to any object in memory. That includes object of class types, such as **vectors**. For example:

```
vector<int>* p = new vector<int>{7,8,9};
cout << p->size();       // access using ->
cout << (*p).size();     // access using .
```

We access a class member through a pointer using the **->** operator. Alternatively, and equivalently, we can dereference the pointer (using operator *) and then use operator **.** (dot).

15.4.3 Initialization

As ever, we would like to ensure that an object has been given a value before we use it; that is, we want to be sure that our pointers are initialized and also that the objects they point to have been initialized. Consider:

```
double* p0;                    // uninitialized: likely trouble
double* p1 = new double;       // get (allocate) an uninitialized double
double* p2 = new double{5.5};  // get a double initialized to 5.5
double* p3 = new double[5];    // get (allocate) 5 uninitialized doubles
```

Obviously, declaring **p0** without initializing it is asking for trouble. Consider:

```
*p0 = 7.0;
```

This will assign **7.0** to some location in memory. We have no idea which part of memory that will be. It could be harmless, but never, never ever, rely on that. Sooner or later, we get the same result as for an out-of-range access: "My program crashed mysteriously" or "My program gives wrong output." A scary percentage of serious problems with old-style C++ programs ("C-style programs") is caused by access through uninitialized pointers and out-of-range access. We must do all we can to avoid such access, partly because we aim at professionalism, partly because we don't care to waste our time searching for that kind of error. There are few activities as frustrating and tedious as tracking down this kind of bug. It is much more pleasant and productive to prevent bugs than to hunt for them. Always initialize your variables. XX

Memory allocated by **new** is not initialized for built-in types. If you don't like that, you can specify values, as we did for **p2**: ***p2** is **5.5**. Note the use of **{ }** for initialization. This contrasts to the use of **[ ]** to indicate "array." XX

We can specify an initializer list for an array of objects allocated by **new**. For example:

```
double* p4 = new double[5] {0,1,2,3,4};
double* p5 = new double[] {0,1,2,3,4};
```

Now **p4** points to objects of type **double** containing the values **0.0**, **1.0**, **2.0**, **3.0**, and **4.0**. So does **p5**; the number of elements can be left out when a set of elements is provided.

As usual, we should worry about uninitialized objects and make sure we give them a value before we read them. Beware that compilers often have a "debug mode" where they by default initialize every variable to a predictable value (often 0). That implies that when turning off the debug features to ship a program, when running an optimizer, or simply when compiling on a different machine, a program with uninitialized variables may suddenly run differently. Don't get caught with an uninitialized variable. The standard-library **vector** helps avoid that by initializing its elements. XX

When we define our own types, we have better control of initialization. If a type **X** has a default constructor (§8.4.2), we get

```
X* px1 = new X;        // one default-initialized X
X* px2 = new X[17];    // 17 default-initialized Xs
```

If a type **Y** has a constructor, but not a default constructor, we have to explicitly initialize:

```
Y* py1 = new Y;            // error: no default constructor
Y* py2 = new Y{13};        // OK: initialized to Y{13}
Y* py3 = new Y[17];        // error: no default constructor
Y* py4 = new Y[17] {0,1,2,3,4,5,6,7,8,9,10,11,12,13,14,15,16};
```

Long initializer lists for **new** can be impractical, but they can come in very handy when we want just a few elements, and that is a common case.

15.4.4 The null pointer

If you have no other pointer to use for initializing a pointer, use the null pointer, **nullptr**:

```
double* p0 = nullptr;          // the null pointer
```

Often, we test whether a pointer is valid (i.e., whether it points to something) by checking whether it is **nullptr**. For example:

```
if (p0 != nullptr)          // consider p0 valid
```

This is not a perfect test, because **p0** may contain a "random" value that happens to be nonzero (e.g., if we forgot to initialize) or the address of an object that has been **deleted** (see §15.4.5). However, that's often the best we can do. We don't actually have to mention **nullptr** explicitly because an **if**-statement really checks whether its condition is **nullptr**:

```
if (p0)                    // consider p0 valid; equivalent to p0!=nullptr
```

AA We prefer this shorter form, considering it a more direct expression of the idea "**p0** is valid," but opinions vary.

We need to use the null pointer when we have a pointer that sometimes points to an object and sometimes not. That's rarer than many people think; consider: If you don't have an object for a pointer to point to, why did you define that pointer? Couldn't you wait until you have an object?

In older code, people often use **0** (zero) or **NULL** instead of **nullptr**. Both older alternatives can lead to confusion and/or errors, so prefer the more specific **nullptr**.

15.4.5 Free-store deallocation

The **new** operator allocates ("gets") memory from the free store. Since a computer's memory is limited, it is usually a good idea to return memory to the free store once we are finished using it. That way, the free store can reuse that memory for a new allocation. For large programs and for long-running programs such freeing of memory for reuse is essential. For example:

```
double* calc(int res_size, int max)
{
        double* p = new double[max];
        double* res = new double[res_size];
        // ... use p to calculate results to be put in res ...
        delete[] p;              // return the array pointed to by p to the free store
        return res;
}
```

```
double* r = calc(100,1000);
// ... use the result ...
delete[] r;              // return the array pointed to by r to the free store
```

The operator for returning memory to the free store is called delete. We apply delete to a pointer returned by new to make the memory available to the free store for future allocation. If the memory allocated by new is an array, we add [ ] to delete.

Forgetting to delete an object that was created by new is called a *memory leak* and is usually a bad mistake.

Deleting an object twice is also a bad mistake. For example: XX

```
int* p = new int{5};
delete p;                // fine: p points to an object created by new
// ...
delete p;                // error: p points to memory owned by the free-store manager
```

After the first delete, you don't own the object pointed to anymore so the free-store manager may have modified the memory pointed to or given that memory to some other part of the program that used new.

15.5 Destructors

Having to remember to call delete is an error-prone nuisance, so leave that to classes, such as vector that do so implicitly. For example:

```
vector<double> calc2(int res_size, int max)
{
     vector<double> p(max);
     vector<double> res(res_size);
     // ... use p to calculate results to be put in res ...
     return res;
}

void use()
{
     // ...
     vector<double> r = calc2(100,1000);
     // ... use the result ...
}
```

This is shorter and much cleaner code – no news and deletes to keep track of – and (surprisingly?) just as efficient as the original version.

The news and deletes disappeared into the vector. Let's see how that's done:

```
class Vector {          // a very simplified vector of doubles
public:
     Vector(int s);                  // constructor: allocate elements on the free store and initialize them
     ~Vector() { delete[] elem; }    // destructor: return elements to free store
     // ...
```

```
private:
      int sz;                      // the size
      double* elem;                // a pointer to the elements

};

Vector::Vector(int s)              // constructor
      :sz{s},                      // initialize sz
      elem{new double[s]}          // initialize elem to elements on the free store
{
      for (int i=0; i<s; ++i)      // initialize elements
            elem[i]=0;
}


Vector::~Vector()            // destructor
{
      delete[] elem;         // return elements to free store
}
```

So, **sz** is the number of elements. We initialize it in the constructor, and a user of **vector** can get the number of elements by calling **size()**. Space for the elements is allocated using **new** in the constructor, and the pointer returned from the free store is stored in the member pointer **elem**.

This **Vector** does not leak memory. The basic idea is to have the compiler know about a function that does the opposite of a constructor, just as it knows about the constructor. Inevitably, such a function is called a *destructor*, and its name is the name of the class preceded by the complement operator ~, here **~Vector**. In the same way that a constructor is implicitly called when an object of a class is created, a destructor is implicitly called when an object goes out of scope. A constructor makes sure that an object is properly created and initialized. Conversely, a destructor makes sure that an object is properly cleaned up before it is destroyed.

AA We are not going to go into great detail about the uses of destructors here, but they are great for handling resources that we need to first acquire (from somewhere) and later give back: files, threads, locks, etc. Remember how **iostreams** clean up after themselves? They flush buffers, close files, free buffer space, etc. That's done by their destructors. Every class that "owns" a resource needs a destructor.

The use of constructor/destructor pairs is the key to some of the most effective C++ programming techniques. Destructors make returning resources implicit. That's essential because we know from many fields of life and many programming problems that remembering to give something back when we are done using it is surprisingly hard.

15.5.1 Generated destructors

If a member of a class has a destructor, then that destructor will be called when the object containing the member is destroyed. For example:

```
struct Customer {
      string name;
      vector<string> addresses;
      // ...
};

void some_fct()
{
      Customer fred { "Fred", {"17 Oak St.", "232 Rock Ave."}};
      // ... use fred ...
}
```

When we exit **some_fct()**, so that **fred** goes out of scope, **fred** is destroyed; that is, the destructors for **name** and **addresses** are called. This is obviously necessary for destructors to be useful and is sometimes expressed as "The compiler generated a destructor for **Customer**, which calls the members' destructors." That is indeed often how the obvious and necessary guarantee that destructors are called is implemented. A generated destructor is often called the *default destructor*.

The destructors for members – and for bases (§12.3) – are implicitly called from a derived class destructor (whether user-defined or generated). Basically, all the rules add up to: "Destructors are called when the object is destroyed" (by going out of scope, by **delete**, etc.).

15.5.2 Virtual destructors

Destructors are conceptually simple but are the foundation for many of the most effective C++ programming techniques. The basic idea is simple: CC

- Whatever resources a class object needs to function, it acquires it in a constructor.
- During the object's lifetime it may release resources and acquire new ones.
- At the end of the object's lifetime, the destructor releases every resource still owned by the object.

The matched constructor/destructor pair handling free-store memory for **vector** is the archetypical example. We'll get back to that idea with more examples in §18.4. Here, we will examine an important application that comes from the use of free-store and class hierarchies in combination. Consider a use of **Shape** and **Text** from §12.2 and §11.8:

```
Shape* fct()
{
      Text tt {Point{200,200},"Anya"};                  // local Text variable
      // ...
      return new Text{Point{100,100},"Courtney"};       // Text object on the free store
}

void user()
{
      Shape* q = fct();
      // ... use the Shape without caring exactly which kind of shape it is ...
      delete q;
}
```

This looks fairly plausible – and it is. It all works, but let's see how, because that exposes an elegant, important, simple technique. The Text (§11.8) object tt is properly destroyed at the exit from fct(). Text has a string member, which obviously needs to have its destructor called – string handles its memory acquisition and release exactly like vector. For tt, that's easy; the compiler just calls Text's generated destructor as described in §15.5.1. But what about the Text object returned from fct()? The calling function user() has no idea that q points to a Text; all it knows is that it points to a Shape. Then how does delete q get to call Text's destructor?

In §12.2, we breezed past the fact that Shape has a destructor. In fact, Shape has a virtual destructor. That's the key. When we say delete q, delete looks at q's type to see if it needs to call a destructor, and if so it calls it. So, delete q calls Shape's destructor ~Shape(). But ~Shape() is virtual, so – using the virtual call mechanism (§12.3.2) – that call invokes the destructor of Shape's derived class, in this case ~Text(). Had Shape::~Shape() not been virtual, Text::~Text() would not have been called and Text's string member wouldn't have been properly destroyed.

AA As a rule of thumb: if you have a class with a virtual function, it needs a virtual destructor. The reason is that if a class has a virtual function, it is likely to be used as a base class and objects of its derived class are likely to be allocated using new and manipulated through pointers to their base. Thus, such derived class objects are likely to be deleted through pointers to their base.

CC Destructors are invoked implicitly for scoped objects or indirectly through delete. They are not called directly. That saves a lot of tricky work.

> TRY THIS
>
> Write a little program using base classes and members where you define the constructors and destructors to output a line of information when they are called. Then, create a few objects and see how their constructors and destructors are called.

But what about that delete q;? We just deemed having to remember to delete tedious and error-prone (§15.4.5). The standard library has a *smart pointer* (also called a *resource-management pointer)* to deal with that:

```
unique_ptr<Shape> fct()
{
    Text tt {Point{200,200},"Annemarie"};                  // local Text variable
    // ...
    return make_unique<Text>(Point{100,100},"Nicholas");   // Text object on the free store
}

void user()
{
    unique_ptr<Shape> q = fct();
    // ... use the Shape without caring exactly which kind of shape it is ...
}
```

A unique_ptr object holds a pointer (§18.5.2). When the unique_ptr goes out of scope, its destructor calls delete on that pointer. Again, we see the code become shorter and simpler by relying on a class with a destructor.

XX Also, please remember that a "naked" new outside a constructor is an opportunity to forget to delete the object that new created, thus creating a potentially serious resource leak. "Naked" news and "naked" deletes are sources of serious errors. Instead, use resource-management classes, such as vector, unique_ptr (§18.5.2), or Vector_ref (§11.7.3). Keep news in constructors and deletes in destructors (and in related resource-management functions (§17.4)).

15.6 Access to elements

For Vector to be usable, we need a way to read and write elements. For starters, we can provide simple get() and set() member functions:

```
class Vector {          // a very simplified vector of doubles
public:
        Vector(int s) :sz{s}, elem{new double[s]} { /* ... */ }         // constructor
        ~Vector() { delete[] elem; }                                    // destructor

        int size() const { return sz; }                                 // the current size

        double get(int n) const { return elem[n]; }                     // access: read
        void set(int n, double v) { elem[n]=v; }                        // access: write
private:
        int sz;                 // the size
        double* elem;           // a pointer to the elements
};
```

Both get() and set() access the elements using the [ ] operator on the elem pointer: elem[n].

Now we can make a Vector of doubles and use it:

```
Vector v(5);
for (int i=0; i<v.size(); ++i) {
        v.set(i,1.1*i);
        cout << "v[" << i << "]==" << v.get(i) << '\n';
}
```

This will output

```
v[0]==0
v[1]==1.1
v[2]==2.2
v[3]==3.3
v[4]==4.4
```

This is still an overly simple vector, and the code using get() and set() is rather ugly compared to the usual subscript notation. However, we start small and simple and then grow our programs step by step, testing along the way. This strategy of growth and repeated testing minimizes errors and debugging.

15.7 An example: lists

Lists are among the most common and useful data structures. Usually, a list is made out of "links" where each link holds some information and pointers to other links. This is one of the classical uses of pointers. For example, we could represent a short list of Norse gods like this:

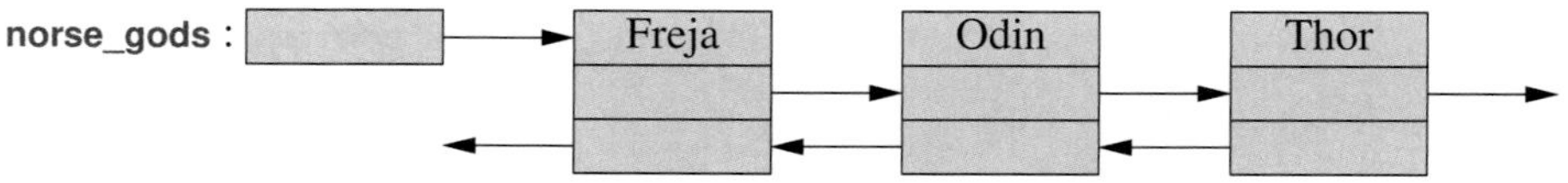

CC A list like this is called a *doubly-linked list* because given a link, we can find both the predecessor and the successor. A list where we can find only the successor is called a *singly-linked list*. We use doubly-linked lists when we want to make it easy to remove an element. We can define these links like this:

```
struct Link {
      Link(const string& v, Link* p = nullptr, Link* s = nullptr)
            : value{v}, prev{p}, succ{s} { }
      string value;
      Link* prev;
      Link* succ;
};
```

That is, given a **Link**, we can get to its successor using the **succ** pointer and to its predecessor using the **prev** pointer. We use **nullptr** to indicate that a **Link** doesn't have a successor or a predecessor. We can build our list of Norse gods like this:

```
Link* norse_gods = new Link{"Thor",nullptr,nullptr};
norse_gods = new Link{"Odin",nullptr,norse_gods};
norse_gods->succ->prev = norse_gods;
norse_gods = new Link{"Freja",nullptr,norse_gods};
norse_gods->succ->prev = norse_gods;
```

We built that list by creating the **Links** and tying them together as in the picture: first Thor, then Odin as the predecessor of Thor, and finally Freja as the predecessor of Odin. You can follow the pointer to see that we got it right, so that each **succ** and **prev** points to the right god. However, the code is obscure because we didn't explicitly define and name an insert operation:

```
Link* insert(Link* p, Link* n)        // insert n before p (incomplete)
{
      n->succ = p;                    // p comes after n
      p->prev->succ = n;              // n comes after what used to be p's predecessor
      n->prev = p->prev;              // p's predecessor becomes n's predecessor
      p->prev = n;                    // n becomes p's predecessor
      return n;
}
```

This works provided that **p** really points to a **Link** and that the **Link** pointed to by **p** really has a predecessor. Please convince yourself that this really is so. When thinking about pointers and linked structures, such as a list made out of **Links**, we invariably draw little box-and-arrow diagrams on paper to verify that our code works for small examples. Please don't be too proud to rely on this effective low-tech design technique.

That version of **insert()** is incomplete because it doesn't handle the cases where **n**, **p**, or **p–>prev** is **nullptr**. We add the appropriate tests for the null pointer and get the messier, but correct, version:

```
Link* insert(Link* p, Link* n)        // insert n before p; return n
{
      if (n==nullptr)
            return p;
      if (p==nullptr)
            return n;
      n–>succ = p;                    // p comes after n
      if (p–>prev)
            p–>prev–>succ = n;
      n–>prev = p–>prev;              // p's predecessor becomes n's predecessor
      p–>prev = n;                    // n becomes p's predecessor
      return n;
}
```

Given that, we could write

```
Link* norse_gods = new Link{"Thor"};
norse_gods = insert(norse_gods,new Link{"Odin"});
norse_gods = insert(norse_gods,new Link{"Freja"});
```

Now all the error-prone fiddling with the **prev** and **succ** pointers has disappeared from sight. Pointer fiddling is tedious and error-prone and *should* be hidden in well-written and well-tested functions. In particular, many errors in conventional code come from people forgetting to test pointers against **nullptr** – just as we (deliberately) did in the first version of **insert()**. **AA**

Note that we used default arguments (§13.3.1) to save users from mentioning predecessors and successors in every constructor use.

15.7.1 List operations

The standard library provides a **list** class, which we will describe in §19.3. It hides all link manipulation, but here we will elaborate on our notion of **list** based on the **Link** class to get a feel for what goes on "under the covers" of **list** classes and see more examples of pointer use.

What operations does our **Link** class need to allow its users to avoid "pointer fiddling"? That's to some extent a matter of taste, but here is a useful set:

- The constructor
- **insert**: insert before an element
- **add**: insert after an element
- **erase**: remove an element
- **find**: find a **Link** with a given value
- **advance**: get the *n* th successor

We could write these operations like this:

```
Link* add(Link* p, Link* n)          // insert n after p; return n
{
      // ... much like insert() ...
}

Link* erase(Link* p)        // remove *p from list; return p's successor
{
      if (p==nullptr)
            return nullptr;
      if (p->succ)
            p->succ->prev = p->prev;
      if (p->prev)
            p->prev->succ = p->succ;
      return p->succ;
}

Link* find(Link* p, const string& s)        // find s in list; return nullptr for "not found"
{
      while (p) {
            if (p->value == s)
                  return p;
            p = p->succ;
      }
      return nullptr;
}

Link* advance(Link* p, int n)          // move n positions in list; return nullptr for "not found"
      // positive n moves forward, negative backward
{
      if (p==nullptr)
            return nullptr;
      while (0<n) {
            --n;
            if (p->succ)
                  p = p->succ;
            return nullptr;
      }
      while (n<0) {
            ++n;
            if (p->prev)
                  p = p->prev;
            return nullptr;
      }
      return p;
}
```

We could have considered an attempt to **advance()** outside the list an error and thrown an exception, but we chose to return the **nullptr** thereby forcing the user to deal with that possibility. Why? Primarily because at this level of pointer use, the user has to be constantly aware of the possibility of nulltpr anyway. Yes, that's error prone, so we use higher-level constructs (such as the standard-library list; §20.6) whenever we can.

15.7.2 List use

As a little exercise, let's build two lists:

```
Link* norse_gods = new Link{"Thor"};
norse_gods = insert(norse_gods,new Link{"Odin"});
norse_gods = insert(norse_gods,new Link{"Zeus"});
norse_gods = insert(norse_gods,new Link{"Freja"});

Link* greek_gods = new Link{"Hera"};
greek_gods = insert(greek_gods,new Link{"Athena"});
greek_gods = insert(greek_gods,new Link{"Mars"});
greek_gods = insert(greek_gods,new Link{"Poseidon"});
```

"Unfortunately," we made a couple of mistakes: Zeus is a Greek god, rather than a Norse god, and the Greek god of war is Ares, not Mars (Mars is his Latin/Roman name). We can fix that:

```
Link* p = find(greek_gods, "Mars");
if (p)
      p->value = "Ares";
```

Note how we were cautious about find() returning a nullptr. We think that we know that it can't happen in this case (after all, we just inserted Mars into greek_gods), but in a real example someone might change that code.

Similarly, we can move Zeus into his correct Pantheon:

```
Link* p = find(norse_gods,"Zeus");
if (p) {
      erase(p);
      insert(greek_gods,p);
}
```

Did you notice the bug? It's quite subtle (unless you are used to working directly with links). What if the Link we erase() is the one pointed to by norse_gods? Again, that doesn't actually happen here, but to write good, maintainable code, we have to take that possibility into account:

```
Link* p = find(norse_gods, "Zeus");
if (p) {
      if (p==norse_gods)
            norse_gods = p->succ;
      erase(p);
      greek_gods = insert(greek_gods,p);
}
```

While we were at it, we also corrected the second bug: when we insert Zeus *before* the first Greek god, we need to make greek_gods point to Zeus's Link. Pointers are extremely useful and flexible, but subtle. They have to be handled with care and avoided in favor of less error-prone alternatives wherever possible.

Finally, let's print out those lists:

```
void print_all(Link* p)
{
      cout << "{ ";
      while (p) {
            cout << p->value;
            if (p=p->succ)
                  cout << ", ";
      }
      cout << " }";
}

print_all(norse_gods);
cout << '\n';

print_all(greek_gods);
cout << '\n';
```

This should give

```
{ Freja, Odin, Thor }
{ Zeus, Poseidon, Ares, Athena, Hera }
```

15.8 The this pointer

Note that each of our list functions takes a **Link*** as its first argument and accesses data in that object. That's the kind of function that we often make a member function. Could we simplify **Link** (or link use) by making the operations members? Could we maybe make the pointers private so that only the member functions have access to them? We could:

```
class Link {
public:
      string value;

      Link(const string& v, Link* p = nullptr, Link* s = nullptr)
            : value{v}, prev{p}, succ{s} { }

      Link* insert(Link* n);                       // insert n before this object
      Link* add(Link* n);                          // insert n after this object
      Link* erase();                               // remove this object from list

      Link* find(const string& s);                 // find s in list
      const Link* find(const string& s) const;     // find s in const list (see _oper.const_)

      Link* advance(int n) const;                  // move n positions in list
      Link* next() const { return succ; }
      Link* previous() const { return prev; }
```

```
private:
      Link* prev;
      Link* succ;
};
```

This looks promising. We defined the operations that don't change the state of a **Link** into **const** member functions. We added (nonmodifying) **next()** and **previous()** functions so that users could iterate over lists (of **Links**) – those are needed now that direct access to **succ** and **prev** is prohibited. We left **value** as a public member because (so far) we have no reason not to; it is "just data."

Now, let's try to implement **Link::insert()** by copying our global **insert()** and modifying it:

```
Link* Link::insert(Link* n)           // insert n before p; return n
{
      Link* p = this;                 // pointer to this object
      if (n==nullptr)                 // nothing to insert
            return p;
      if (p==nullptr)                 // nothing to insert into
            return n;
      n->succ = p;                    // p comes after n
      if (p->prev)
            p->prev->succ = n;
      n->prev = p->prev;              // p's predecessor becomes n's predecessor
      p->prev = n;                    // n becomes p's predecessor
      return n;
}
```

But how do we get a pointer to the object for which **Link::insert()** was called? Without help from the language we can't. However, in every member function, the identifier **this** is a pointer that points to the object for which the member function was called. Alternatively, we could simply use **this** instead of **p**: CC

```
Link* Link::insert(Link* n)           // insert n before this object; return n
{
      if (n==nullptr)
            return this;
      if (this==nullptr)
            return n;
      n->succ = this;                 // this object comes after n
      if (this->prev)
            this->prev->succ = n;
      n->prev = this->prev;           // this object's predecessor becomes n's predecessor
      this->prev = n;                 // n becomes this object's predecessor
      return n;
}
```

This is a bit verbose, but we don't need to mention **this** to access a member, so we can abbreviate:

```
Link* Link::insert(Link* n)      // insert n before this object; return n
{
      if (n==nullptr)
            return this;
      if (this==nullptr)
            return n;
      n->succ = this;             // this object comes after n
      if (prev)
            prev->succ = n;
      n->prev = prev;             // this object's predecessor becomes n's predecessor
      prev = n;                   // n becomes this object's predecessor
      return n;
}
```

In other words, we have been using the **this** pointer – the pointer to the current object – implicitly every time we accessed a member. It is only when we need to refer to the whole object that we need to mention it explicitly.

Note that **this** has a specific meaning: it points to the object for which a member function is called. It does not point to any old object. The compiler ensures that we do not change the value of **this** in a member function. For example:

```
struct S {
      // . . .
      void mutate(S* p)
      {
            this = p;         // error: this is immutable
            // ...
      }
};
```

15.8.1 More link use

Having dealt with the implementation issues, we can see how the use now looks:

```
Link* norse_gods = new Link{"Thor"};
norse_gods = norse_gods->insert(new Link{"Odin"});
norse_gods = norse_gods->insert(new Link{"Zeus"});
norse_gods = norse_gods->insert(new Link{"Freja"});

Link* greek_gods = new Link{"Hera"};
greek_gods = greek_gods->insert(new Link{"Athena"});
greek_gods = greek_gods->insert(new Link{"Mars"});
greek_gods = greek_gods->insert(new Link{"Poseidon"});
```

That's very much like before. As before, we correct our "mistakes." In this case, the name of the god of war is wrong, so we change it:

```
Link* p = greek_gods->find("Mars");
if (p)
      p->value = "Ares";
```

Move Zeus into his correct Pantheon:

```
Link* p2 = norse_gods->find("Zeus");
if (p2) {
      if (p2==norse_gods)
            norse_gods = p2->next();
      p2->erase();
      greek_gods = greek_god->insert(p2);
}
```

Finally, let's print out those lists:

```
void print_all(Link* p)
{
      cout << "{ ";
      while (p) {
            cout << p->value;
            if (p=p->next())
                  cout << ", ";
      }
      cout << " }";
}

print_all(norse_gods);
cout << '\n';

print_all(greek_gods);
cout << '\n';
```

This should again give

```
{ Freja, Odin, Thor }
{ Zeus, Poseidon, Ares, Athena, Hera }
```

So, which version do you like better: the one where **insert()**, etc. are member functions or the one where they are freestanding functions? In this case the differences don't matter much, but see §8.7.5.

One thing to observe here is that we still don't have a list class, only a link class. That forces us to keep worrying about which pointer is the pointer to the first element. This **Link** code is littered with naked **news** and there isn't a **delete** in sight. We hope you noticed and that it made you a bit queasy. We can do better – by defining a class **List** – but designs along the lines presented here are very common and the **Link** examples are meant to illustrate pointer manipulation, rather than resource management. The standard-library **list** is presented in §19.3. In general, subtle pointer manipulation is best encapsulated in a class (§12.3). **AA**

Drill

This drill has two parts. The first exercises/builds your understanding of free-store-allocated arrays and contrasts arrays with **vectors**:

[1] Allocate an array of ten **ints** on the free store using **new**.
[2] Print the values of the ten **ints** to **cout**.
[3] Deallocate the array (using **delete[]**).
[4] Write a function **print_array(ostream& os, int* a, int n)** that prints out the values of **a** (assumed to have **n** elements) to **os**.
[5] Allocate an array of ten **ints** on the free store; initialize it with the values 100, 101, 102, etc.; and print out its values.
[6] Allocate an array of 11 **ints** on the free store; initialize it with the values 100, 101, 102, etc.; and print out its values.
[7] Allocate an array of 20 **ints** on the free store; initialize it with the values 100, 101, 102, etc.; and print out its values.
[8] Did you remember to delete the arrays? (If not, do it.)
[9] Do 5, 6, and 7 using a **vector** instead of an array and a **print_vector()** instead of **print_array()**.

The second part focuses on pointers and their relation to arrays. Use **print_array()**:

[1] Allocate an **int**, initialize it to 7, and assign its address to a variable **p1**.
[2] Print out the value of **p1** and of the **int** it points to.
[3] Allocate an array of seven **ints**; initialize it to 1, 2, 4, 8, etc.; and assign its address to a variable **p2**.
[4] Print out the value of **p2** and of the array it points to.
[5] Declare an **int*** called **p3** and initialize it with **p2**.
[6] Assign **p1** to **p2**.
[7] Assign **p3** to **p2**.
[8] Print out the values of **p1** and **p2** and of what they point to.
[9] Deallocate all the memory you allocated from the free store.
[10] Allocate an array of ten **ints**; initialize it to 1, 2, 4, 8, etc.; and assign its address to **p1**.
[11] Allocate an array of ten **ints**, and assign its address to a variable **p2**.
[12] Copy the values from the array pointed to by **p1** into the array pointed to by **p2**.
[13] Repeat 10–12 using a **vector** rather than an array.

Review

[1] Why do we need data structures with varying numbers of elements?
[2] What four kinds of storage do we have for a typical program?
[3] What is the free store? What other name is commonly used for it? What operators support it?
[4] What is a pointer?
[5] What is a dereference operator and why do we need one?
[6] What is an address? How are memory addresses manipulated in C++?
[7] What information about a pointed-to object does a pointer have? What useful information does it lack?

[8] What can a pointer point to?
[9] What is a leak?
[10] What is a resource?
[11] What is another term for "free store"?
[12] How can we initialize a pointer?
[13] What is a null pointer? When do we need to use one?
[14] When do we need a pointer (instead of a reference or a named object)?
[15] What is a destructor? When do we want one?
[16] When do we want a **virtual** destructor?
[17] How are destructors for members called?
[18] How do we access a member of a class through a pointer?
[19] What is a doubly-linked list?
[20] What is **this** and when do we need to use it?

Terms

address	destructor	**nullptr**	address of: **&**
free store	pointer	allocation	**Link**
array	list	resource leak	dereference: *
vector	container	member access: **->**	subscript: **[ ]**
deallocation	memory	**this**	memory corruption
delete	memory leak	null pointer	**delete[]**
new	**virtual**		

Exercises

[1] What is the output format of pointer values on your implementation? Hint: Don't read the documentation.
[2] How many bytes are there in an **int**? In a **double**? In a **bool**? Do not use **sizeof** except to verify your answer.
[3] List two ways that a pointer can be misused in potentially disastrous ways. Give examples.
[4] Consider the memory layout in §15.4. Write a program that tells the order in which static storage, the stack, and the free store are laid out in memory. In which direction does the stack grow: upward toward higher addresses or downward toward lower addresses? In an array on the free store, are elements with higher indices allocated at higher or lower addresses?
[5] We have not said what happens when you run out of memory using **new**. That's called *memory exhaustion*. Find out what happens. You have two obvious alternatives: look for documentation, or write a program with an infinite loop that allocates but never deallocates. Try both. Approximately how much memory did you manage to allocate before failing?
[6] Write a program that reads characters from **cin** into an array that you allocate on the free store. Read individual characters until an exclamation mark (**!**) is entered. Do not use a **std::string**. Do not worry about memory exhaustion.

[7] Do the previous exercise again, but this time read into a **std::string** rather than to memory you put on the free store (**string** knows how to use the free store for you).

[8] Which way does the stack grow: up (toward higher addresses) or down (toward lower addresses)? Which way does the free store initially grow (that is, before you use **delete**)? Write a program to determine the answers.

[9] Look at your solution of exercise 6. Is there any way that input could get the array to overflow; that is, is there any way you could enter more characters than you allocated space for (a serious error)? Does anything reasonable happen if you try to enter more characters than you allocated?

[10] Complete the "list of gods" example from §15.7 and run it.

[11] Why did we define two versions of **find()** in §15.8?

[12] Modify the **Link** class from §15.7 to hold a value of a **struct God**. **struct God** should have members of type **string**: name, mythology, vehicle, and weapon. For example, **God{"Zeus", "Greek", "", "lightning"}** and **God{"Odin", "Norse", "Eight-legged flying horse called Sleipner", "Spear called Gungnir"}**. Write a **print_all()** function that lists gods with their attributes one per line. Add a member function **add_ordered()** that places its new element in its correct lexicographical position. Using the **Links** with the values of type **God**, make a list of gods from three mythologies; then move the elements (gods) from that list to three lexicographically ordered lists – one for each mythology.

[13] Modify the "list of gods" example from §15.7 not to leak memory.

[14] Could the "list of gods" example from §15.7 have been written using a singly-linked list; that is, could we have left the **prev** member out of **Link**? Why might we want to do that? For what kind of examples would it make sense to use a singly-linked list? Re-implement that example using only a singly-linked list.

[15] Look up (e.g., on the Web) *skip list* and implement that kind of list. This is not an easy exercise.

Postscript

Why bother with messy low-level stuff like pointers and free store when we can simply use **vector**? Well, one answer is that someone has to design and implement **vector** and similar abstractions, and it's generally useful to know how that's done. There are programming languages that dodge the problems with low-level programming. Basically, programmers of such languages delegate the tasks that involve direct access to hardware to C++ programmers (and programmers of other languages suitable for low-level programming). Our favorite reason, however, is simply that you can't really claim to understand computers and programming until you have seen how software meets hardware. People who don't know about pointers, memory addresses, and other basic low-level facilities often have the strangest ideas of how their programming language facilities work; such wrong ideas can lead to code that's "interestingly poor" (i.e., slow and/or unmaintainable).

16

Arrays, Pointers, and References

Caveat emptor!
– Good advice

This chapter describes the lower-level notions of arrays and pointers. We consider the uses of pointers, such as array traversal and address arithmetic, and the problems arising from such use. We also present the widely used C-style string; that is, a zero-terminated array of **chars**. Pointers and arrays are key to the implementation of types that save us from error-prone uses of pointers, such as **vector**, **string**, **span**, **not_null**, **unique_ptr**, and **shared_ptr**. As an example, we show a few ways we can implement a function that determines whether a sequence of characters represents a palindrome.

§16.1 Arrays
Pointer arithmetic
§16.2 Pointers and references
Pointer and reference parameters; Pointers as parameters
§16.3 C-style strings
§16.4 Alternatives to pointer use
span; **array**; **not_null**
§16.5 An example: palindromes
Palindromes using **string**; Palindromes using arrays; Palindromes using pointers; Palindromes using **span**

16.1 Arrays

So far, we have allocated all of our arrays on the free store; that's what we need to implement **vector**. However, we can also have arrays on the stack and in static memory (§15.4). For example:

```
int ai[4];                    // static array of 4 ints

void fct()
{
        char ac[8];           // on-stack array of 8 chars
}
```

C++ uses the conventional subscript notation **[ ]** to indicate "array." For most uses, **vector<T>** is a better choice than **T[]** for representing a contiguous sequence of elements of a type **T**. "Contiguous" means that there are no gaps between the elements.

AA You might have detected that we have a not-so-subtle bias in favor of **vectors** over arrays. Use **std::vector** where you have a choice – and you have a choice in most contexts. However, arrays existed long before **vectors** and are roughly equivalent to what is offered in other languages (notably C), so we must know arrays, and know them well, to be able to cope with older code and with code written by people who don't appreciate the advantages of **vector**.

XX The major problem with pointers to arrays is that a pointer doesn't "know" how many elements it points to. A pointer to an array is a pointer to the first element of the array, rather than to some "array object." Consider:

```
void use(double* pd)
{
        pd[2] = 2.2;
        pd[3] = 3.3;
        pd[−2] = −2.2;
}

void test()
{
        double a[3];
        use(a);           // a converts to a pointer to a[0] when used as an argument
}
```

What **use()** "sees" can be graphically represented:

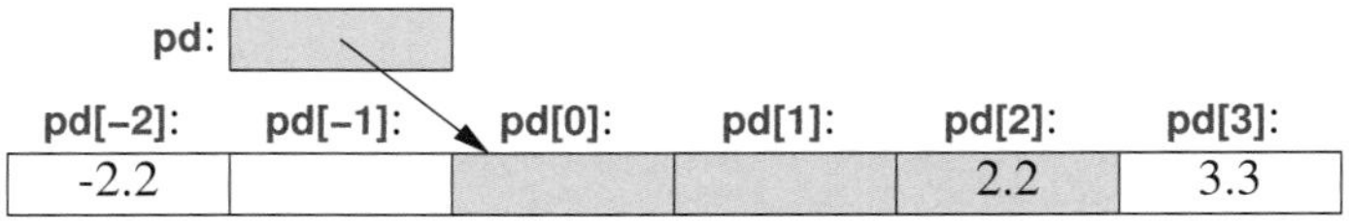

XX Does **pd** have a third element **pd[2]**? Does it have a fourth element **pd[3]**? If we look at **use(a)**, we find that the answers are yes and no, respectively. However, the compiler doesn't know that; it does not keep track of pointer values. Our code will simply access memory as if we had allocated enough memory. It will even access **pd[−2]** as if the location two **doubles** before what **pd** points to was part of our allocation.

We have no idea what the memory locations marked **pd[−2]** and **pd[3]** are used for. However, we do know that they weren't meant to be used as part of our array of three **doubles** pointed to by **pd**. Most likely, they are parts of other objects and we just scribbled all over those. That's not a good idea. In fact, it is typically a disastrously poor idea: "disastrous" as in "My program crashes mysteriously" or "My program gives wrong output." Try saying that aloud; it doesn't sound nice at all. We'll go a long way to avoid that. CC

Out-of-range access is often called *range error* or *buffer overflow*. Such errors are particularly nasty because apparently unrelated parts of a program are affected. An out-of-range read gives us a "random" value that may depend on some completely unrelated computation. An out-of-range write can put some object into an "impossible" state or simply give it a totally unexpected and wrong value. Such writes typically aren't noticed until long after they occurred, so they are particularly hard to find. Worse still: run a program with an out-of-range error twice with slightly different input and it may give different results. Bugs of this kind ("transient bugs") are some of the most difficult bugs to find. XX

We have to ensure that such out-of-range access doesn't happen. One of the reasons we use **vector** rather than directly using memory allocated by **new** is that a **vector** knows its size so that it (or we) can easily prevent out-of-range access. AA

One thing that can make it hard to prevent out-of-range access is that we can assign one **double∗** to another **double∗** independently of how many objects each points to. A pointer really doesn't know how many objects it points to. For example:

```
double* p = new double;           // allocate a double
double* q = new double[1000];     // allocate 1000 doubles

q[700] = 7.7;                     // fine: q points to 1000 doubles
q = p;                            // let q point to the same object as p does
double d = q[700];                // bad: q points to a single double: out-of-range access!
```

Here, in just three lines of code, **q[700]** refers to two different memory locations, and the last use is an out-of-range access and a likely disaster.

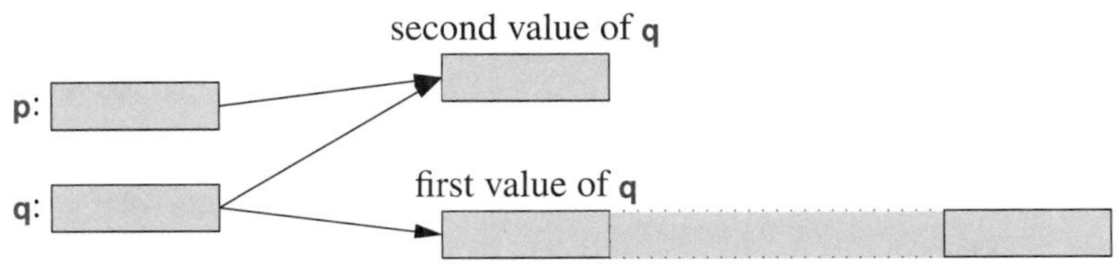

By now, we hope that you are asking, "But why can't pointers remember the size?" Obviously, we could design a "pointer" that did exactly that – a **vector** is almost that, and if you look through the C++ literature and libraries, you'll find many "smart pointers" that compensate for weaknesses of the low-level built-in pointers (e.g., see **span** in §16.4.1). However, somewhere we need to reach the hardware level and understand how objects are addressed – and a machine address does not "know" what it addresses. Also, understanding pointers is essential for understanding lots of real-world code.

16.1.1 Pointer arithmetic

A pointer can point to an element of an array. Consider:

```
double ad[8];
double* p = &ad[4];          // point to ad[4]; the 5th element of ad
```

We now have a pointer **p** to the **double** known as **ad[4]**:

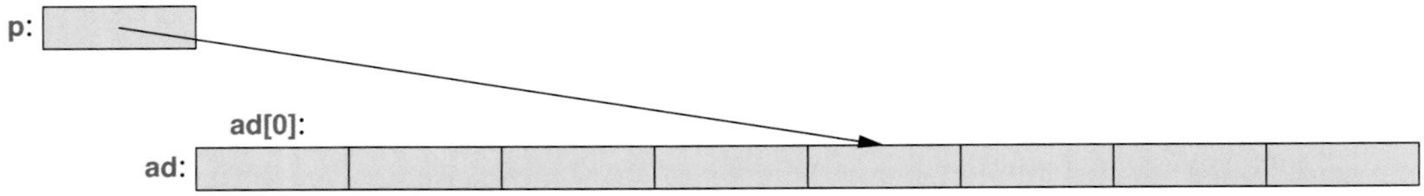

We can subscript and dereference that pointer:

```
*p =7;
p[2] = 6;
p[-2] = 9;
```

We get

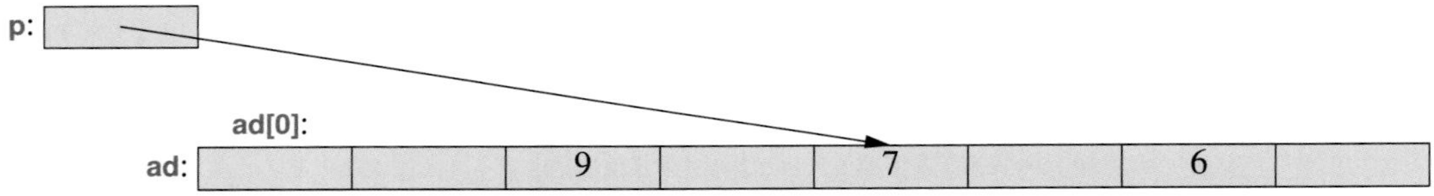

That is, we can subscript the pointer with both positive and negative numbers. As long as the resulting element is in range, all is well. However, access outside the range of the array pointed into is illegal (as with free-store-allocated arrays; see §16.1). Typically, access outside an array is not detected by the compiler and (sooner or later) is disastrous.

Once a pointer points into an array, addition and subscripting can be used to make it point to another element of the array. For example:

```
p += 2;          // move p 2 elements to the right
```

We get

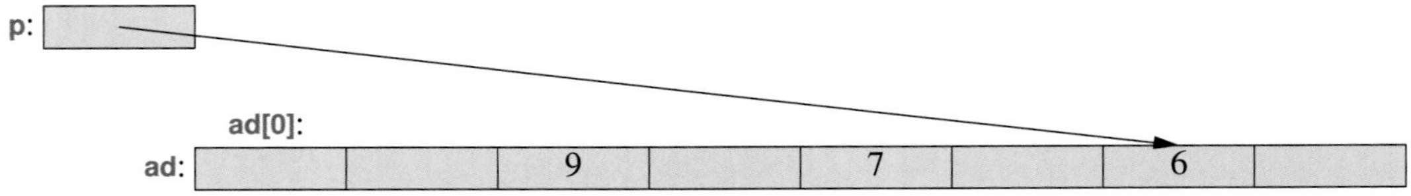

We can also move backwards:

```
p -= 4;          // move p 4 elements to the left
```

We get

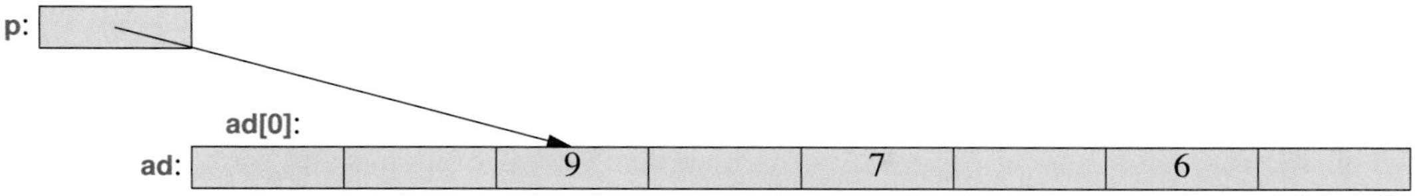

Using +, –, +=, and –= to move pointers around is called *pointer arithmetic*. Obviously, if we do that, we have to take great care to ensure that the result doesn't point to memory outside the array: CC

```
p += 1000;          // insane: p points into an array with just 8 elements
double d = *p;      // illegal: probably a bad value
*p = 12.34;         // illegal: probably scrambles some unknown data
```

Unfortunately, not all bad bugs involving pointer arithmetic are that easy to spot. The best policy is simply to avoid pointer arithmetic except when implementing facilities for which there is no reasonable alternative.

The most common use of pointer arithmetic is incrementing a pointer (using ++) to point to the next element and decrementing a pointer (using ––) to point to the previous element. For example, we could print the value of ad's elements like this:

```
const int max = sizeof(ad)/sizeof(*ad);          // one way to determine the number of elements of ad

for (double* p = &ad[0]; p<&ad[max]; ++p)
      cout << *p << '\n';
```

Or backward:

```
for (double* p = &ad[max–1]; p>=&ad[0]; ––p)
      cout << *p << '\n';
```

This use of pointer arithmetic is not uncommon. However, we find the last ("backward") example quite easy to get wrong. Why &ad[max–1] and not &ad[max]? Why >= and not >? These examples could equally well (and equally efficiently) be done using subscripting. Such examples could be done equally well using subscripting into a vector or a span (§16.4.1), which is more easily range checked. Also, many examples can be done using a range-for (§3.6.1) rather than by subscripting.

The way of finding the number of elements in an array (here, sizeof(ad)/sizeof(*ad)) may seem odd, but consider: sizeof reports sizes in the number of bytes used to store an object, so sizeof(ad) will be 8*sizeof(double) because we gave ad eight elements of type double. To get the number of elements (here 8) back, we must divide with the size of an element (here, *ad). When we lower the abstraction level, our code gets messier and more error-prone, and sizeof is about as low as we get.

Note that most real-world uses of pointer arithmetic involve a pointer passed as a function argument (like the use() example in §16.1). In that case, the compiler doesn't have a clue how many elements are in the array pointed into: you are on your own. That is a situation we prefer to stay away from whenever we can.

Why does C++ have (allow) pointer arithmetic at all? It can be such a bother and doesn't provide anything new once we have subscripting. For example:

```
double* pd = &ad[0];
double d1 = *(pd+7);
double d2 = &pd[7];
if (d2 != d3)
        cout << "impossible!\n";
```

CC Mainly, the reason is historical. These rules were crafted for C decades ago and can't be removed without breaking a massive amount of code. Partly, there can be some convenience gained by using pointer arithmetic in some important low-level applications, such as memory managers.

16.2 Pointers and references

CC You can think of a reference as an automatically dereferenced immutable pointer or as an alternative name for an object. Pointers and references differ in these ways:

- Assignment to a pointer changes the pointer's value (not the pointed-to value).
  - Assignment to a reference changes the value of the object referred to (not the reference).
- To initialize a pointer you use a pointer, a **new**, a **&**, or the name of an array.
  - To initialize a reference you use an object (maybe a pointer dereferenced by * or **[ ]**).
- To access an object pointed to by a pointer, we use * or **[ ]** (§16.1).
  - To access an object referred to by a reference, we just use the name of the reference.
- Beware of null pointers (§15.4.4).
  - A reference must be initialized to refer to an object, and cannot be made to refer to another object.

For example:

pointer	reference	comment
int x = 10;	int x = 10;	
int* p = &x;	int& r = x;	&x to get a pointer
p = x;	r = &x;	type errors
*p = 7;	r = 7;	write to the object pointed/referred to
p = 7;	*r = 7;	type errors
int x2 = *p;	int x2 = r;	read the value of the object pointed/referred to
int* p2 = p;	int& r2 = r;	make p2 point to the object pointed to by p
		make r2 refer to the object referred to by r
p = nullptr;	r = "nullref";	there is no nullref
p = &x2;		make p point to x2
	r = x2;	assign x2 to the object referred to by r

AA Note that **r=x2** will not make the reference refer to **x2**. There is no way to get a reference to refer to a different object after initialization, and that is a valuable guarantee. Instead, **r=x2** assigns the value of **x2** to the object referred to by **r**; that is, to **x**. If you need to point to something different at different times, use a pointer.

For ideas about when and how to use pointers, see §15.7 and §16.5.

A reference and a pointer are both implemented by using a memory address. They just use that address differently to provide you – the programmer – slightly different facilities.

16.2.1 Pointer and reference parameters

When you want to change the value of a variable to a value computed by a function, you have three choices. For example:

```
int incr_v(int x) { return x+1; }       // compute a new value and return it
void incr_p(int* p) { ++*p; }           // pass a pointer (dereference it and increment the result)
void incr_r(int& r) { ++r; }            // pass a reference
```

How do you choose? We think returning the value often leads to the most obvious (and therefore least error-prone) code; that is:

```
int x = 2;
x = incr_v(x);          // copy x to incr_v(); then copy the result out and assign it
```

We prefer that style for small objects, such as an **int**. In addition, if a "large object," such as **vector**, has a move constructor (§17.4.4) we can efficiently pass it back and forth.

How do we choose between using a reference argument and using a pointer argument? Unfortunately, either way has both attractions and problems, so again the answer is less than clear-cut. You have to make a decision based on the individual function and its likely uses.

If you use a pointer as a function argument, the function has to beware that someone might call it with a null pointer, that is, with a **nullptr**. For example: XX

```
incr_p(nullptr);        // crash: incr_p() will try to dereference the null pointer
int* p = nullptr;
incr_p(p);              // crash: incr_p() will try to dereference the null pointer
```

This is obviously nasty. The person who writes **incr_p()** can protect against this:

```
void incr_p(int* p)
{
        if (p==nullptr)
                error("null pointer argument to incr_p()");
        ++*p;           // dereference the pointer and increment the object pointed to
}
```

But now **incr_p()** suddenly doesn't look as simple and attractive as before. Chapter 4 discusses how to cope with bad arguments. In contrast, users of a reference (such as **incr_r()**) are entitled to assume that a reference refers to an object.

If "passing nothing" (passing no object) is acceptable from the point of view of the semantics of the function, we must use a pointer argument. However, "passing nothing" is not acceptable for our increment operation – hence the need for throwing an exception for **p==nullptr**.

So, the real answer is: "The choice depends on the nature of the function": AA

- For tiny objects prefer pass-by-value. By "tiny," we mean one or two values of built-in types (e.g., two **doubles**), or one or two class objects of equivalent size.

- For functions where "no object" (represented by **nullptr**) is a valid argument use a pointer parameter (and remember to test for **nullptr**).
- Otherwise, use a reference parameter.

See also §7.4.6, and don't forget pass-by-**const**-reference.

16.2.2 Pointers as parameters

XX Pointers are popular as parameters. For example:

```
void print_n(int* p, int n)
{
        if (p==nullptr)          // protect against nullptr
                return;

        for (int i = 0; i<n; ++i)
                cout << v[i] << ' ';
}

void user()
{
        int a[12];
        int* p = new int [10];
        // ... fill a and *p ...
        print_n(a,12);
        print_n(p,12);
}
```

There is much wrong with this code: verbosity, magic constants (§3.3.1), a memory leak (§15.4.5), and a range error (§4.6.2).

AA The root of the problem is that a pointer (by definition) doesn't "know" how many elements it points to is used as a parameter. We recommend that you don't pass a sequence of elements as a (pointer,count) pair. A pointer argument should be assumed to point to a single object or be the **nullptr**. Instead, pass an object that represents a range, e.g., a **span** (§16.4.1). For example:

```
void print_n(span<int> s)        // a span points to an array and "remembers" its number of elements (§16.4.1)
{
        for (int x : s)
                cout << x << ' ';
}

void user()
{
        int a[12];
        vector<int> v(10);
        // ... fill a and v ...
        print_n(a);              // prints 12 ints
        print_n(v);              // prints 10 ints
}
```

16.3 C-style strings

Since the earliest days of the C language, a character string has been represented in memory as a zero-terminated array of characters and accessed through pointers (PPP2.§27.5). For example:

```
const char* s = "Danger!";
```

We can represent s like this:

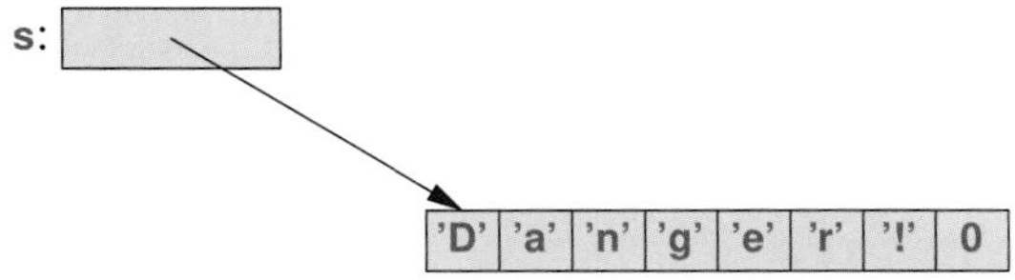

Our literal strings are C-style strings. Note that the characters of a literal string are const. If we want to change the characters, we need to use an array:

```
char s[] = "Modifiable";
cout << "modifiable: " << s;          // writes "Modifiable"

s[6] = 'e';
s[7] = 'd';
s[8] = 0;          // terminating zero

cout << "modifiable: " << s;          // writes "Modified"
```

To get the number of characters in a C-style string, we use strlen():

```
cout << strlen(s);   //      writes 8
```

Note that strlen() does not count the terminating 0; it gives the number of characters up to, and not including, that 0. That also means that if you place a 0 in the middle of a string, as we did for s, we can no longer determine how much memory was allocated for that string.

Our C-style "strings" are pointers and have pointer semantics. That implies that assignment, copy, and sizeof applies to the pointer, rather than what it points to. Consider:

```
string cat(const string& name, const string& addr)
{
     return id + '@' + addr;
}
```

Using C-style strings instead of std::string, this becomes:

```
char* cat2(const char* name, const char* addr)
{
     int nsz = strlen(name);
     int sz = nsz+strlen(addr)+2;                // +2 for '@' and the terminating zero
     char* res = (char*) malloc(sz);             // using the old allocation function
     strcpy(res,name);                           // copy from *name to *res until a zero is seen
     res[nsz+1] = '@';
```

```
        strcpy(res+2,addr);
        return res;
}
```

The C and C++ standard-library function **malloc()** allocates memory on the free store; the memory allocated by **malloc()** must be given back to the free-store manager using **free()**. You often see this instead of **new**/**delete** in C-style code – **string**, **new**, and **delete** are not part of C. The C and C++ standard-library function **strcpy()** copies the characters pointed to by its second argument into the location pointed to by its first argument until it encounters a terminating zero. The terminating zero is also copied.

XX Such code is verbose and error-prone. It uses the messy pointer arithmetic, and who will **free()** the memory returned by **cat2()**? We strongly recommend the use of **std::string** or similar high-level strings over C-style strings. As a reader or maintainer of code, would you rather see **cat()** or **cat2()**?

Why would anyone design something like C-string? When C-style strings were invented, a computer's memory was measured in dozens of kilobytes or – if you were lucky – hundreds of kilobytes. I remember being ecstatic when I got hold of a computer with a whole megabyte! C-style strings were close to optimal in time and space for the kinds of programs written then. The reason is that they don't compute or store any information that you might not need. Also, the initial users of C-style strings were far better programmers than today's average. They simply didn't make most of the obvious programming mistakes.

AA Why would anyone write such code today? Well, there are a lot of C programmers who don't have any alternatives and often bring their habits to C++. Also, many programmers believe that they can write optimal code without making errors. They are almost always wrong.

Really, a C-style string has many features that might come as a surprise to someone unacquainted with it. C-style strings really are pointers. For example, **=** assigns pointers, rather than the values they point to.

You have been warned! Prefer **std::string** when you have the option. Look up additional tutorial information and documentation (e.g., [cppref]) if you don't.

16.4 Alternatives to pointer use

AA Pointers can be used for essentially anything. That's why we try to avoid their use: looking at pointer-heavy code we cannot reliably determine the intent of the programmer. That makes many uses of pointers error prone. Consider alternatives:

- To hold a collection of values, use a standard-library container, such as **vector**, **set** (§20.5), **map** (§20.2), **unordered_map** (§20.3), or **array** (§16.4.2).
- To hold a string of characters, use the standard-library **string** (§2.4, §9.10.3 PPP2.§23.2).
- To point to an object, you own (i.e., must **delete**), use the standard-library **unique_ptr** (§18.5.2) or **shared_ptr** (§18.5.3).
- To point to a contiguous sequence of elements that you don't own, use the standard-library **span** (§16.4.1).
- To systematically avoid dereferencing a null pointer, use **not_null** (§16.4.3}

Often, there are alternatives to the standard-library components, but make the standard library as your default choice.

16.4.1 Span

Most of the uses of pointer involve keeping track of the number of elements that a pointer points to. Most of the problems that don't relate to ownership come from getting the number of elements wrong. So, we apply the obvious remedy: a "pointer" that keeps track of the number of its element. That type is called **span**. For example:

```
int arr[8];
span spn {arr};         // a span<int> that points to 8 ints
```

or graphically:

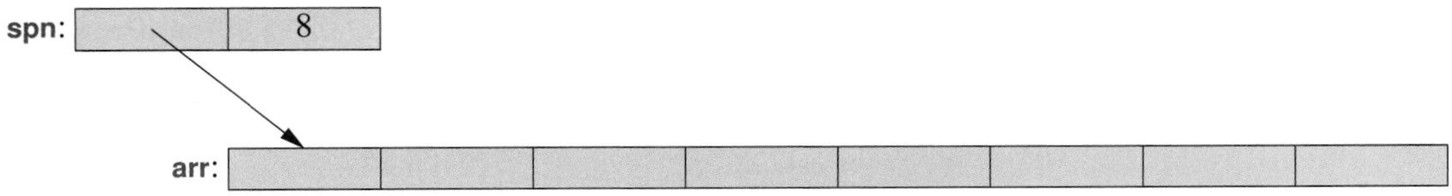

Here, **spn** was defined without mentioning the element type or the number of elements, those were deduced from the definition of **arr**. We don't always have that information available and we don't always want all of an array. Then, we must be explicit:

```
const int max = 1024;
int buf[max];
span<int>sp {buf,max/2};        // first half of buf
```

With **span**, we can get range checking and range-**for**:

```
void test(span<int> s)
{
    cout << "size: " << s.size() << '\n';
    for (int x : s)
        cout << x << '\n';
    try {
        int y = s[size()];
    }
    catch (...) {
        cout << "we have range checking\n";
        return;
    }
    cout << "no range checking! Boo Hoo!\n";
    terminate();            // exit the program
}
```

Unfortunately, **std::span** is not guaranteed to range check, though the version in **PPP_support** does.

16.4.2 array

The built-in array converts to a pointer at the slightest provocation. The resulting pointer lacks size information and can be confused with pointers that need to be **deleted**. However, the standard library provides an **array** type that doesn't implicitly produce a pointer. For example:

```
std::array<int,8> arr { 0,1,2,3,4,5,6,7 };
int* p = arr;                                // error (and that's good)
```

Unlike vector and string, array is not a handle to elements allocated elsewhere:

For good and bad, like the built-in array, array is a simpler and less flexible type than vector. Its size is not stored in memory, but remembered by the type system. An array doesn't use the free store unless you create it using new. Instead, an array uses only the kind of memory (e.g., stack or static) in which you create it, and that can be important.

Unfortunately, the number of elements of an array is never deduced, so it must be explicitly stated. On the other hand, if there are more elements than initializers, the remainder is default initialized. For example:

```
array<string,4> as { "Hello", " ", "World!" };        // as[3] is the empty string
```

16.4.3 not_null

Consider a possible implementation of strlen():

```
int strlen(const char* p)
{
        if (p==nullptr)
                return 0;
        int n = 0;
        while (*p++)
                ++n;
        return n;
}
```

Is the test for nullptr necessary? If we don't have it, strlen(p), where p is a null pointer, will most likely cause a crash; if not, it will give a wrong result. If we do have it, should it give a result? That is, should we pretend that the (imaginary) string pointed to by nullptr has zero elements? Or would it be better to give an error (e.g., throw an exception)?

> TRY THIS
>
> Look up the definition of std::strlen() to see what the standard requires. Then, try char* p = nullptr; size_t x = strlen(p); to see what your implementation does.

Whenever we use pointers, the question of what to do with the nullptr immediately surfaces. Does nullptr have a defined meaning? Is it a bug? If it is a bug, who is responsible for catching it? The caller or the callee? Documentation or comments may give the answers, but we don't always read the manuals. PPP_support provides a simple solution: a type that checks if its argument is the nullptr and throws not_null_error if it is. After that check, a not_null behaves just like a pointer.
If strlen() does not allow nullptr, we could have defined it like this:

```
int strlen(not_null<const char*> p)
{
	int n = 0;
	while (*p++)
		++n;
	return n;
}
```

If strlen() isn't defined like this – and being a C function from the 1970s it isn't – the implementer has to decide whether to trust the caller or defend against the possibility of a nullptr argument. In addition, every user would have to decide whether to make sure that no argument to strlen is nullptr. That's life at the lower levels of abstraction. Ideally, we stay out of such dilemmas by using higher-level types, such as vector and string. Where that's not possible, use not_null for pointer arguments that come from code you do not control.

16.5 An example: palindromes

Enough technical examples! Let's try a little puzzle. A *palindrome* is a word that is spelled the same from both ends. For example, *anna*, *petep*, and *malayalam* are palindromes, whereas *ida* and *homesick* are not. There are two basic ways of determining whether a word is a palindrome:

- Make a copy of the letters in reverse order and compare that copy to the original.
- See if the first letter is the same as the last, then see if the second letter is the same as the second to last, and keep going until you reach the middle.

Here, we'll take the second approach. There are many ways of expressing this idea in code depending on how we represent the word and how we keep track of how far we have come with comparing characters. We'll write a little program that tests whether words are palindromes in a few different ways just to see how different language features affect the way the code looks and works.

16.5.1 Palindromes using string

First, we try a version using the standard-library string with int indices to keep track of how far we have come with our comparison:

```
bool is_palindrome(const string& s)
{
	int first = 0;                 // index of first letter
	int last = s.length()–1;       // index of last letter
	while (first < last) {         // we haven't reached the middle
		if (s[first]!=s[last])
			return false;
		++first;                   // move forward
		––last;                    // move backward
	}
	return true;
}
```

We return **true** if we reach the middle without finding a difference. We suggest that you look at this code to convince yourself that it is correct when there are no letters in the string, just one letter in the string, an even number of letters in the string, and an odd number of letters in the string. Of course, we should not just rely on logic to see that our code is correct. We should also test. We can exercise **is_palindrome()** like this:

```
int main()
{
	for (string s; cin>>s; ) {
		cout << s << " is";
		if (!is_palindrome(s))
			cout << " not";
		cout << " a palindrome\n";
	}
}
```

Basically, the reason we are using a **string** is that "**string**s are good for dealing with words." It is simple to read a whitespace-separated word into a string, and a **string** knows its size. Had we wanted to test **is_palindrome()** with strings containing whitespace, we could have read using **getline()** (11.5). That would have shown *ah ha* and *as df fd sa* to be palindromes.

16.5.2 Palindromes using arrays

What if we didn't have **string**s (or **vector**s), so that we had to use an array to store the characters? Let's see:

```
bool is_palindrome(const char s[], int n)
	// s points to the first character of an array of n characters
{
	int first = 0;				// index of first letter
	int last = n–1;				// index of last letter
	while (first < last) {		// we haven't reached the middle
		if (s[first]!=s[last])
			return false;
		++first;				// move forward
		––last;					// move backward
	}
	return true;
}
```

To exercise **is_palindrome()**, we first have to get characters read into the array. One way to do that safely (i.e., without risk of overflowing the array) is like this:

```
istream& read_word(istream& is, char* buffer, int max)
	// read at most max-1 characters from is into buffer
{
	is.width(max);		// read at most max-1 characters in the next >>
	is >> buffer;		// read whitespace-terminated word and add zero after the last character read
	return is;
}
```

Setting the **istream**'s width appropriately prevents buffer overflow for the next **>>** operation. Unfortunately, it also means that we don't know if the read terminated by whitespace or by the buffer being full (so that we need to read more characters). Also, who remembers the details of the behavior of **width()** for input? The standard-library **string** and **vector** are really better as input buffers because they expand to fit the amount of input. That terminating **0** character is needed because many popular operations on arrays of characters (C-style strings) assume a terminating zero. Using **read_word()** we can write

```
int main()
{
    constexpr int max = 128;
    for (char s[max]; read_word(cin,s,max); ) {
        cout << s << " is";
        if (!is_palindrome(s,strlen(s)))
            cout << " not";
        cout << " a palindrome\n";
    }
}
```

The **strlen(s)** call returns the number of characters in the array after the call of **read_word()**, and **cout<<s** outputs the characters in the array up to the terminating **0**.

We consider this "array solution" significantly messier than the "**string** solution," and it gets much worse if we try to seriously deal with the possibility of long strings. See exercise 10. **AA**

16.5.3 Palindromes using pointers

Instead of using indices to identify characters, we could use pointers:

```
bool is_palindrome(const char* first, const char* last)
    // first points to the first letter, last to the last letter
{
    while (first < last) {          // we haven't reached the middle
        if (*first!=*last)
            return false;
        ++first;                    // move forward
        --last;                     // move backward
    }
    return true;
}
```

This is arguably the cleanest **is_palindrome()** so far, but its simplicity has been achieved by pushing the task of getting the range right onto its users:

```
int main()
{
    const int max = 128;
    for (char s[max]; read_word(cin,s,max); ) {
        cout << s << " is";
```

```
            if (!is_palindrome(&s[0],&s[strlen(s)-1]))
                  cout << " not";
            cout << " a palindrome\n";
      }
}
```

Just for fun, we rewrite is_palindrome() like this:

```
bool is_palindrome(const char* first, const char* last)
      // first points to the first letter, last to the last letter
{
      if (first<last)
            return (*first==*last) ? is_palindrome(first+1,last-1) : false;
      return true;
}
```

This code becomes obvious when we rephrase the definition of *palindrome*: a word is a palindrome if the first and the last characters are the same and if the substring you get by removing the first and last characters is a palindrome.

16.5.4 Palindromes using span

Basically, a span is simply a different, and usually better, alternative to using arrays or pointers. For example:

```
bool is_palindrome(span<char> s)
{
      return (s.size()) ? is_palindrome(s.data(),s.data()+s.size()) : true;    // implemented using pointers
}
```

Like all standard-library types, span has more useful member functions than fit into this book. Here, we used data() that returns a pointer to the first element of the span. An empty span doesn't have a first element, we first checked s's size.

This is_palindrome() is an example of how to map from one style to another, here from a modern style using span to an older one using pointers. In large, multi-year projects, it is not uncommon to have several styles present as facilities and fashions evolve. We can also map the other way:

```
bool is_palindrome(const char* first, const char* last)
{
      return is_palindrome(span<char>{first,last-first});                // implemented using span
}
```

Unfortunately, there is no simple and reliable run-time test that the pair of pointers first and last is plausible, so it is generally better to use span throughout:

```
bool is_palindrome(span<char> s)
{
      if (s.size()<2)
            return true;
      return (s.front()==s.back()) ? is_palindrome(span<int>{s.data()+1,s.size()-2}) : false;
}
```

Drill

In this chapter, we have two drills: one to exercise arrays and one to exercise vectors in roughly the same manner. Do both and compare the effort involved in each.

Array drill:

[1] Define a global int array ga of ten ints initialized to 1, 2, 4, 8, 16, etc.

[2] Define a function f() taking an int array argument and an int argument indicating the number of elements in the array.

[3] In f():
- Define a local int array la of ten ints.
- Copy the values from ga into la.
- Print out the elements of la.
- Define a pointer p to int and initialize it with an array allocated on the free store with the same number of elements as the argument array.
- Copy the values from the argument array into the free-store array.
- Print out the elements of the free-store array.
- Deallocate the free-store array.

[4] In main():
- Call f() with ga as its argument.
- Define an array aa with ten elements and initialize it with the first ten factorial values (1, 2*1, 3*2*1, 4*3*2*1, etc.).
- Call f() with aa as its argument.

Standard-library vector drill:

[1] Define a global vector<int> gv; initialize it with ten ints, 1, 2, 4, 8, 16, etc.

[2] Define a function f() taking a vector<int> argument.

[3] In f():
- Define a local vector<int> lv with the same number of elements as the argument vector.
- Copy the values from gv into lv.
- Print out the elements of lv.
- Define a local vector<int> lv2; initialize it to be a copy of the argument vector.
- Print out the elements of lv2.

[4] In main():
- Call f() with gv as its argument.
- Define a vector<int> vv and initialize it with the first ten factorial values (1, 2*1, 3*2*1, 4*3*2*1, etc.).
- Call f() with vv as its argument.

Review

[1] What does "Caveat emptor!" mean?

[2] What is an array?

[3] How do you copy an array?

[4] How do you initialize an array?

[5] When should you prefer a pointer argument over a reference argument? Why?

[6] When should you prefer a **span** over a pointer? Why?
[7] How does **std::array** differ from a built-in array?
[8] What good is range checking?
[9] What information do you need to do range checking?
[10] What good can a **not_null** do?
[11] What is a C-style string?
[12] What is a palindrome?

Terms

array	pointer	palindrome	pointer arithmetic
span	**array**	**not_null**	C-style string
*	**&**	**->**	subscripting
[ ]	**strlen()**	range error	**nullptr** dereference

Exercises

[1] Write a function, **void to_lower(char* s)**, that replaces all uppercase characters in the C-style string **s** with their lowercase equivalents. For example, **Hello, World!** becomes **hello, world!**. Do not use any standard-library function. A C-style string is a zero-terminated array of characters, so if you find a **char** with the value **0** you are at the end.

[2] Write a function, **char* str_dup(const char*)**, that copies a C-style string into memory it allocates on the free store. Do not use any standard-library function.

[3] Write a function, **char* find_x(const char* s, const char* x)**, that finds the first occurrence of the C-style string **x** in **s**.

[4] Write a function, **int str_cmp(const char* s1, const char* s2)**, that compares C-style strings. Let it return a negative number if **s1** is lexicographically before **s2**, zero if **s1** equals **s2**, and a positive number if **s1** is lexicographically after **s2**. Do not use any standard-library functions. Do not use subscripting; use the dereference operator * instead.

[5] Consider what happens if you give your **str_dup()**, **find_x()**, and **str_cmp()** a pointer argument that is not a C-style string. Try it! First figure out how to get a **char*** that doesn't point to a zero-terminated array of characters and then use it (never do this in real – non-experimental – code; it can create havoc). Try it with free-store-allocated and stack-allocated "fake C-style strings." If the results still look reasonable, turn off debug mode. Redesign and re-implement those three functions so that they take another argument giving the maximum number of elements allowed in argument strings. Then, test that with correct C-style strings and "bad" strings.

[6] See what happens if you give the standard-library function **strcmp()** a pointer argument that is not a C-style string.

[7] Write a function, **string cat_dot(const char* s1, const char* s2)**, that concatenates two strings with a dot in between. For example, **cat_dot("Niels", "Bohr")** will return a string containing **Niels.Bohr**.

[8] Write a version of **cat_dot()** that takes **const string&** arguments.

[9] Modify **cat_dot()** from the previous two exercises to take a string to be used as the separator (rather than dot) as its third argument.

[10] Write versions of the **cat_dot()**s from the previous exercises to take C-style strings as arguments and return a free-store-allocated C-style string as the result. Do not use standard-library functions or types in the implementation. Test these functions with several strings. Be sure to free (using **delete**) all the memory you allocated from free store (using **new**). Compare the effort involved in this exercise with the effort involved for exercises 5 and 6.

[11] Rewrite all the functions in §16.5 (palindromes) to use the approach of making a backward copy of the string and then comparing; for example, take **"home"**, generate **"emoh"**, and compare those two strings to see that they are different, so *home* isn't a palindrome.

[12] Look at the "array solution" to the palindrome problem in §16.5.2. Fix it to deal with long strings by (a) reporting if an input string was too long and (b) allowing an arbitrarily long string. Comment on the complexity of the two versions.

[13] Implement a version of the game "Hunt the Wumpus." "Hunt the Wumpus" (or just "Wump") is a simple (non-graphical) computer game originally invented by Gregory Yob. The basic premise is that a rather smelly monster lives in a dark cave consisting of connected rooms. Your job is to slay the wumpus using bow and arrow. In addition to the wumpus, the cave has two hazards: bottomless pits and giant bats. If you enter a room with a bottomless pit, it's the end of the game for you. If you enter a room with a bat, the bat picks you up and drops you into another room. If you enter the room with the wumpus or he enters yours, he eats you. When you enter a room, you will be told if a hazard is nearby:

- "I smell the wumpus": It's in an adjoining room.
- "I feel a breeze": One of the adjoining rooms is a bottomless pit.
- "I hear a bat": A giant bat is in an adjoining room.

For your convenience, rooms are numbered. Every room is connected by tunnels to three other rooms. When entering a room, you are told something like "You are in room 12; there are tunnels to rooms 1, 13, and 4; move or shoot?" Possible answers are **m13** ("Move to room 13") and **s13–4–3** ("Shoot an arrow through rooms 13, 4, and 3"). The range of an arrow is three rooms. At the start of the game, you have five arrows. The snag about shooting is that it wakes up the wumpus and he moves to a room adjoining the one he was in – that could be your room.

Probably the trickiest part of the exercise is to make the cave by selecting which rooms are connected with which other rooms. You'll probably want to use a random number generator (e.g., **randint()** from **PPP_support**) to make different runs of the program use different caves and to move around the bats and the wumpus. Hint: Be sure to have a way to produce a debug output of the state of the cave.

Postscript

Pointers and arrays are ubiquitous in C code and older C++ code. For example, string literals are C-style strings. Thus, we have to understand their use and learn how to avoid their misuses. The standard-library **span**, **array**, and **not_null** address many problems related to range errors and can be used where high-level types, such as **vector**, cannot be used consistently.

17

Essential Operations

When someone says
I want a programming language in which
I need only say what I wish done,
give him a lollipop.
– Alan Perlis

This chapter describes how vectors are copied and accessed through subscripting. To do that, we discuss copying in general and present the essential operations that must be considered for every type: construction, default construction, copy, move, and destruction. Like many types, vector offers comparisons, so we show how to provide operations such as == and <. Finally, we grapple with the problems of changing the size of a vector: why and how?

§17.1 Introduction
§17.2 Access to elements
§17.3 List initialization
§17.4 Copying and moving
Copy constructors; Copy assignments; Copy terminology; Moving
§17.5 Essential operations
Explicit constructors; Debugging constructors and destructors
§17.6 Other useful operations
Comparison operators; Related operators
§17.7 Remaining Vector problems
§17.8 Changing size
Representation; reserve() and capacity(); resize(); push_back(); Assignment
§17.9 Our Vector so far

17.1 Introduction

To get into the air, a plane has to accelerate along the runway until it moves fast enough to "jump" into the air. While the plane is lumbering along the runway, it is little more than a particularly heavy and awkward truck. Once in the air, it soars to become an altogether different, elegant, and efficient vehicle. It is in its true element.

CC In this chapter, we are in the middle of a "run" to gather enough programming language features and techniques to get away from the constraints and difficulties of plain computer memory. We want to get to the point where we can program using types that provide exactly the properties we want based on logical needs. To "get there" we have to overcome a number of fundamental constraints related to access to the bare machine, such as the following:

- An object in memory is of fixed size.
- An object in memory is in one specific place.
- The computer provides only a few fundamental operations on such objects (such as copying a word, adding the values from two words, etc.).

Basically, those are the constraints on the built-in types and operations of C++ (as inherited through C from hardware; see PPP2.§22.2.5 and PPP2.Ch27). In Chapter 15, we saw the beginnings of a **Vector** type that controls all access to its elements and provides us with operations that seem "natural" from the point of view of a user, rather than from the point of view of hardware.

This chapter focuses on the notion of copying. This is an important but rather technical point: What do we mean by copying a nontrivial object? To what extent are the copies independent after a copy operation? What copy operations are there? How do we specify them? And how do they relate to other fundamental operations, such as initialization and cleanup?

Please note that the details of **vector** are peculiar to **vector**s and the C++ ways of building new higher-level types from lower-level ones. However, every "higher-level" type (**string**, **vector**, **list**, **map**, etc.) in every language is somehow built from the same machine primitives and reflects a variety of resolutions to the fundamental problems described here.

17.2 Access to elements

The **Vector** as we left it at the end of Chapter 15 is still woefully incomplete compared to **std::vector**. In particular, it lacks an elegant way to access its elements. All it had was a pair of **get()** and **set()** functions. Code using **get()** and **set()** to access elements is rather ugly compared to the usual subscript notation:

```
Vector v(3);
v.set(0,1);
v.set(1,2);
v.set(2,3);
int x = v.get(2);
```

We can do better. The way to get the usual **v[i]** notation is to define a member function called **operator[]**. Here is our first (naive) try:

```
class Vector {
        int sz;                  // the size
        double* elem;            // a pointer to the elements
public:
        // ...
        double operator[](int n) { return elem[n]; }          // return element
};
```

That looks good, and especially it looks simple, but unfortunately it is too simple. Letting the subscript operator (operator[]()) return a value enables reading but not writing of elements:

```
Vector v(10);
double x = v[2];              // fine
v[3] = x;                     // error: v[3] is not an lvalue (§3.3)
```

Here, v[i] is interpreted as a call v.operator[](i), and that call returns the value of v's element number i. For this overly naive Vector, v[3] is a floating-point value, not a floating-point variable.

> TRY THIS
>
> Make a version of this Vector that is complete enough to compile and see what error message your compiler produces for v[3]=x;.

Our next try is to let operator[] return a pointer to the appropriate element:

```
class Vector {
        // ...
        double* operator[](int n) { return &elem[n]; }         // return pointer
};
```

Given that definition, we can write

```
Vector v(10);
for (int i=0; i<v.size(); ++i) {
        *v[i] = i;          // works, but still too ugly
        cout << *v[i];
}
```

Here, v[i] is interpreted as a call v.operator[](i), and that call returns a pointer to v's element number i. The problem is that we have to write * to dereference that pointer to get to the element. That's almost as bad as having to write set() and get(). Returning a reference from the subscript operator solves this problem:

```
class Vector {
        // ...
        double& operator[](int n) { return elem[n]; }                  // return a reference
        const double& operator[](int n) const { return elem[n]; }  // return a const& for a const (§8.7.4)
};
```

References are not just for function arguments.

Now we can write

```
Vector v(10);
for (int i=0; i<v.size(); ++i) {          // works!
        v[i] = i;           // v[i] returns a reference element i
        cout << v[i];
}
```

We have achieved the conventional notation: v[i] is interpreted as a call v.operator[](i), and that returns a reference to v's element number i.

Since vectors are often passed by const reference, the const version of operator[]() is an essential addition. That version could return a plain double, rather than a double&.

17.3 List initialization

Consider yet again our Vector:

```
class Vector {
        int sz;                 // the size
        double* elem;           // a pointer to the elements
public:
        Vector(int s) :sz{s}, elem{new double[s]} { /* ... */ }      // constructor: allocates memory
        ~Vector() { delete[] elem; }                                 // destructor: deallocates memory
        // ...
};
```

That's fine, but we would like to initialize a Vector with a list of values. For example:

```
Vector v1 = {1.2, 7.89, 12.34 };
```

Just setting the size and then assigning the values we want is tedious and error-prone:

```
Vector v2(2);           // tedious and error-prone
v2[0] = 1.2;
v2[1] = 7.89;
v2[2] = 12.34;          // Ouch! range error
```

So how do we write a constructor that accepts an initializer list as its argument? A { }-delimited list of elements of type T is presented to the programmer as an object of the standard-library type initializer_list<T>, a list of Ts. Its first element is identified by begin() and the end of the list by end(), so we can write:

```
class Vector {
        int sz;                 // the size
        double* elem;           // a pointer to the elements
public:
        Vector(int s)                           // constructor (s is the element count)
                :sz{s}, elem{new double[s]}     // uninitialized memory for elements
        {
                for (int i = 0; i<sz; ++i)
                        elem[i] = 0.0;          // initialize to a default value
        }
```

```
        Vector(initializer_list<double> lst)            // initializer-list constructor
              :sz{lst.end()-lst.begin()},
               elem{new double[sz]}                     // uninitialized memory for elements
        {
              copy(lst.begin(),lst.end(),elem);         // initialize using std::copy()
        }

        // ...
};
```

We used the standard-library copy algorithm. It copies a sequence of elements identified by its first two arguments (here, the initializer_list's begin() and end()) into the memory identified by its third argument (here, elem). This style of code is pervasive in the standard library, and is described briefly in §17.6 and in detail in Chapter 19 and Chapter 21.

Member initializers must appear in the order of the members themselves. This means that we can use a member as part of subsequent member initializers (here, as we did with sz).

Now we can write

```
Vector v1 = {1,2,3};        // three elements 1.0, 2.0, 3.0
Vector v2(3);               // three elements each with the (default) value 0.0
```

Note how we use ( ) for an element count and { } for element lists. We need a notation to distinguish them. For example:

```
Vector v1 {3};          // one element with the value 3.0
Vector v2(3);           // three elements each with the (default) value 0.0
```

This is not very elegant, but it is effective. If there is a choice, the compiler will interpret a value in a { } list as an element value and pass it to the initializer-list constructor as an element of an initializer_list. CC

In most cases – including all cases we will encounter in this book – the = before an { } initializer list is optional, so we can write

```
Vector v11 = {1,2,3};       // three elements 1.0, 2.0, 3.0
Vector v12 {1,2,3};         // three elements 1.0, 2.0, 3.0
```

The difference is purely one of style.

Note that we pass initializer_list<double> by value. That was deliberate and required by the language rules: an initializer_list is simply a handle to elements allocated "elsewhere."

Naturally, when we can initialize a Vector with a list, we expect to be able to assign a list to a Vector. For example:

```
v1 = {7,8,9,0};
```

For that, we define Vector::operator=(initializer_list<double>).

17.4 Copying and moving

Consider again our incomplete **Vector**:

```
class Vector {
	int sz;                   // the size
	double* elem;             // a pointer to the elements
public:
	Vector(int s) :sz{s}, elem{new double[s]} { /* ... */ }    // constructor: allocates memory
	~Vector() { delete[] elem; }                               // destructor: deallocates memory
	// ...
};
```

Let's try to copy one of these vectors:

```
void f(int n)
{
	Vector v(3);              // define a vector of 3 elements
	v[2] = 2.2;
	Vector v2 = v;            // what happens here?
	// ...
}
```

Ideally, **v2** becomes a copy of **v** (that is, **=** makes copies); that is, **v2.size()==v.size()** and **v2[i]==v[i]** for all **i**s in the range **[0:v.size())**. Furthermore, all memory is returned to the free store upon exit from **f()**. That's what the standard-library **vector** does (of course), but it's not what happens for our still-far-too-simple **Vector**. If you are lucky, your compiler will warn you.

Our task is to improve our **Vector** to get it to handle such examples correctly, but first let's figure out what our current version actually does. Exactly what does it do wrong? How? And why? Once we know that, we can probably fix the problems. More importantly, we have a chance to recognize and avoid similar problems when we see them in other contexts.

CC The default meaning of copying for a class is "Copy all the data members." That often makes perfect sense. For example, we copy a **Point** by copying its coordinates. But for a pointer member, just copying the members causes problems. In particular, for the **Vector**s in our example, it means that after the copy, we have **v.sz==v2.sz** and **v.elem==v2.elem** so that our **vector**s look like this:

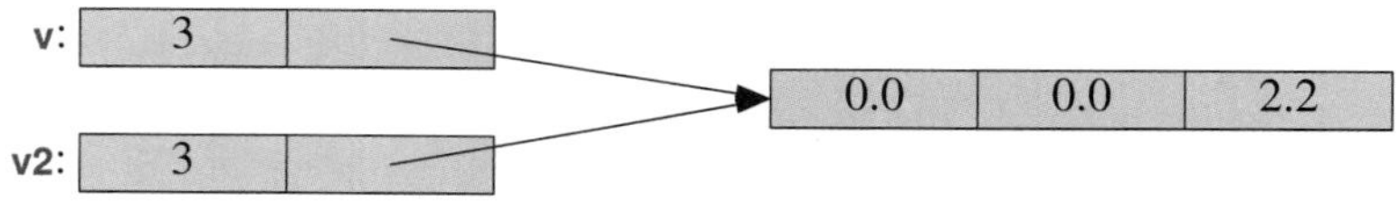

That is, **v2** doesn't have a copy of **v**'s elements; it shares **v**'s elements. We could write

```
v[1] = 99;                       // modify v
v2[0] = 88;                      // modify v2
cout << v[0] << ' ' << v2[1];
```

The result would be the output **88 99**. That wasn't what we wanted. Had there been no "hidden" connection between **v** and **v2**, we would have gotten the output **0 0**, because we never wrote to **v[0]** or to **v2[1]**. You could argue that the behavior we got is "interesting", "neat!", or "sometimes useful'', but that is not what we intended or what the standard-library **vector** provides. Also, what happens when we return from **f()** is an unmitigated disaster. Then, the destructors for **v** and **v2** are implicitly called; **v**'s destructor frees the storage used for the elements using

```
delete[] elem;
```

and so does **v2**'s destructor. Since **elem** points to the same memory location in both **v** and **v2**, that memory will be freed twice with likely disastrous results.

17.4.1 Copy constructors

So, what do we do? We do the obvious: provide a copy operation that copies the elements and make sure that this copy operation gets called when we initialize one **Vector** with another.

Initialization of objects of a class is done by a constructor. So, we need a constructor that copies. Unsurprisingly, such a constructor is called a *copy constructor*. It is defined to take as its argument a reference to the object from which to copy. So, for class **Vector** we need:

```
Vector(const Vector&);          // copy a Vector
```

This constructor will be called when we try to initialize one **Vector** with another. We pass by reference because we (obviously) don't want to copy the argument of the constructor that defines copying. We pass by **const** reference because we don't want to modify our argument (§7.4.4). So we refine **Vector** like this:

```
class Vector {
        int sz;
        double* elem;
public:
        Vector(const vector&);          // copy constructor: define copy
        // ...
};
```

The copy constructor sets the number of elements (**sz**) and allocates memory for the elements (initializing **elem**) before copying element values from the argument **Vector**:

```
Vector::Vector(const Vector& arg)       // allocate elements, then initialize them by copying
        :sz{arg.sz}, elem{new double[arg.sz]}
{
        copy(arg.elem,arg.elem+sz,elem);  // copy elements [0:sz) from elem.arg into elem
}
```

Given this copy constructor, consider again our example:

```
Vector v2 = v;
```

This definition will initialize **v2** by a call of **Vector**'s copy constructor with **v** as its argument. Again given a **Vector** with three elements, we now get

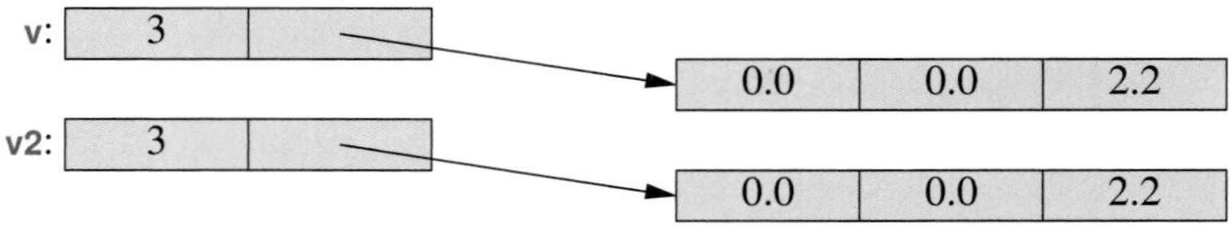

Given that, the destructor can do the right thing. Each set of elements is correctly freed. Obviously, the two **Vectors** are now independent so that we can change the value of elements in **v** without affecting **v2** and vice versa. For example:

```
v[1] = 99;                    // modify v
v2[0] = 88;                   // modify v2
cout << v[0] << ' ' << v2[1];
```

This will output **0 0**.

17.4.2 Copy assignments

CC We handle copy construction (initialization), but we can also copy **Vectors** by assignment. As with copy initialization, the default meaning of copy assignment is memberwise copy, so with **Vector** as defined so far, assignment will cause a double deletion (exactly as shown for copy constructors in §17.4) plus a memory leak. For example:

```
void f2(int n)
{
        Vector v(3);          // define a vector
        v[2] = 2.2;
        Vector v2(4);
        v2 = v;               // assignment: what happens here?
        // ...
}
```

We would like **v2** to be a copy of **v** (and that's what the standard-library **vector** does), but since we have said nothing about the meaning of assignment of our **Vector**, the default assignment is used; that is, the assignment is a memberwise copy so that **v2**'s **sz** and **elem** become identical to **v**'s **sz** and **elem**, respectively. We can illustrate that like this:

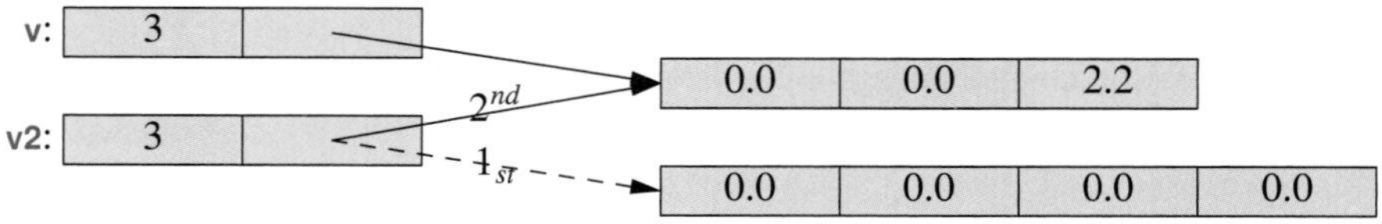

When we leave **f2()**, we have the same disaster as we had when leaving **f()** in §17.4 before we added the copy constructor: the elements pointed to by both **v** and **v2** are freed twice (implicitly using **delete[]**). In addition, we have leaked the memory initially allocated for **v2**'s four elements. We "forgot" to free those. If you ever make that mistake, hope for a compiler warning.

The remedy for this flawed copy assignment is fundamentally the same as for the flawed copy initialization: we define an assignment that copies properly:

```
class Vector {
        int sz;
        double* elem;
public:
        Vector& operator=(const Vector&);        // copy assignment
        // ...
};

Vector& Vector::operator=(const Vector& a)  // make this Vector a copy of a
{
        double* p = new double[a.sz];        // allocate new space
        copy(a.elem,a.elem+a.sz,p);          // copy elements [0:sz) from a.elem into p
        delete[] elem;                       // deallocate old space
        elem = p;                            // now we can reset elem
        sz = a.sz;
        return *this;                        // return a self-reference (§15.8)
}
```

Assignment is a bit more complicated than construction because we must deal with the old elements. Our basic strategy is to make a copy of the elements from the source Vector:

```
double* p = new double[a.sz];        // allocate new space
copy(a.elem,a.elem+a.sz,p);          // copy elements [0:sz) from a.elem into p
```

Then we free the old elements from the target Vector:

```
delete[] elem;                       // deallocate old space
```

Finally, we let elem point to the new elements:

```
elem = p;                            // now we can reset elem
sz = a.sz;
```

We can represent the result graphically like this:

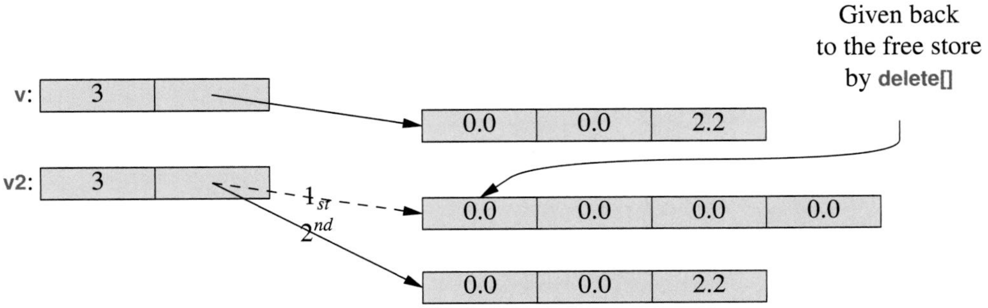

We now have a Vector that doesn't leak memory and doesn't free (delete[]) any memory twice.

When implementing the assignment, you could consider simplifying the code by freeing the memory for the old elements before creating the copy, but it is usually a very good idea not to **AA** throw away information before you know that you can replace it. Also, if you did that, strange things would happen if you assigned a **Vector** to itself:

```
Vector v(10);
v = v;              // self-assignment
```

Please check that our implementation handles that case correctly (if not optimally efficient).

17.4.3 Copy terminology

CC Copying is an issue in most programs and in most programming languages. The basic issue is whether you copy a pointer (or reference) or copy the information pointed to (referred to):

- *Shallow copy* copies only a pointer so that the two pointers now refer to the same object. That's what pointers and references do.
- *Deep copy* copies what a pointer points to so that the two pointers now refer to distinct objects. That's what **vector**s, **string**s, etc. do. We define copy constructors and copy assignments when we want deep copy for objects of our classes.

Here is an example of shallow copy:

```
int* p = new int{77};
int* q = p;              // copy the pointer p
*p = 88;                 // change the value of the int pointed to by p and q
```

We can illustrate that like this:

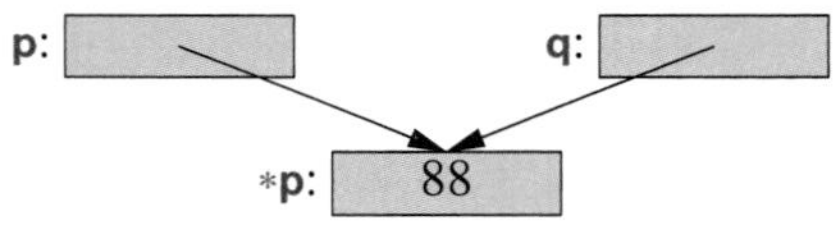

In contrast, we can do a deep copy:

```
int* p = new int{77};
int* q = new int{*p};        // allocate a new int, then copy the value pointed to by p
*p = 88;                     // change the value of the int pointed to by p
```

We can illustrate that like this:

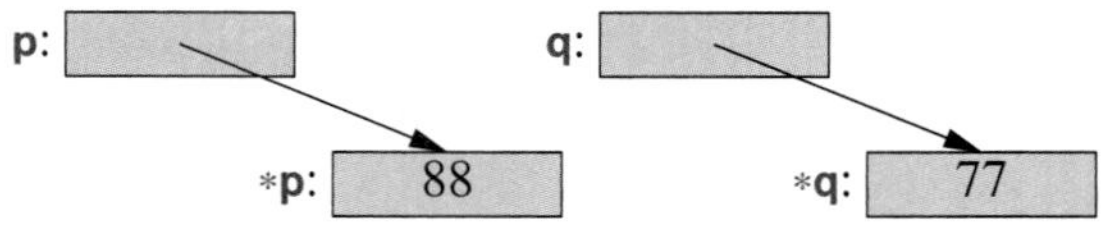

AA Using this terminology, we can say that the problem with our original **Vector** was that it did a shallow copy, rather than copying the elements pointed to by its **elem** pointer. Our improved **Vector**, like **std::vector**, does a deep copy by allocating new space for the elements and copying their values. Types that provide shallow copy (like pointers) are said to have *pointer semantics* or *reference semantics* (they copy addresses). Types that provide deep copy (like **string** and **vector**) are said to have *value semantics* (they copy the values pointed to). From a user perspective, types with value semantics behave as if no pointers were involved – just values that can be copied. One way of thinking of types with value semantics is that they “work just like integers” as far as copying is concerned.

17.4.4 Moving

If a vector has a lot of elements, it can be expensive to copy. So, we should copy **Vector**s only when we need to. Consider an example:

```
Vector fill(istream& is)
{
        Vector res;                        // assuming we have a default constructor (§17.5)
        for (double x; is>>x; )            // assuming support for range-for (§17.6)
                res.push_back(x);          // assuming we have a Vector::push_back (§17.8.4)
        return res;
}

void use()
{
        Vector vec = fill(cin);
        // ... use vec ...
}
```

Here, we fill the local **Vector**, **res**, from the input stream and return it to **use()**. Copying **res** out of **fill()** and into **vec** could be expensive. But why copy? We don't want a copy! We can never use the original (**res**) after the return. In fact, **res** is destroyed as part of the return from **fill()**. So how can we avoid the copy? Consider how **res** would be represented in memory if we had entered **0.0 1.1 2.2**:

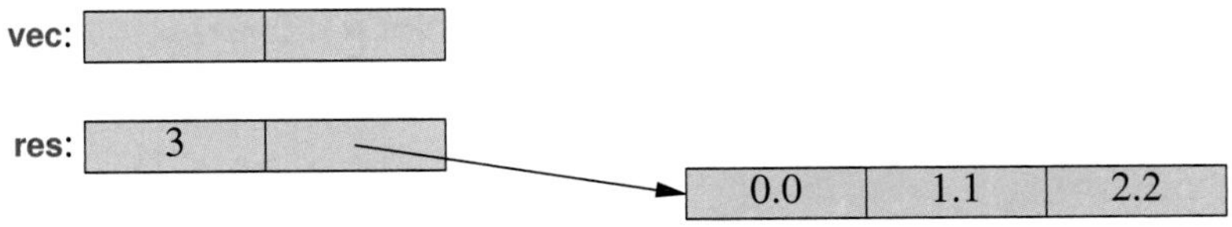

We would like to “steal” the representation of **res** to use for **vec**. In other words, we would like **vec** to refer to the elements of **res** without any copy. AA

After moving **res**'s element pointer and element count to **vec**, **res** holds no elements. We have successfully moved the value from **res** out of **fill()** to **vec**. Now, **res** can be destroyed (simply and efficiently) without any undesirable side effects:

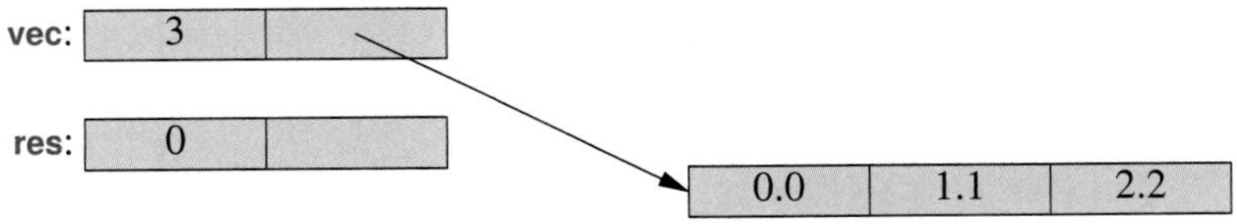

We have successfully moved 3 doubles out of fill() and into its caller at the cost of 4 single-word assignments. The cost would be the same had we moved 100,000 doubles out of fill().

In a simple case like this, a compiler can figure out how to do even better, and some have done so for decades. It simply constructs res in vec's location. That way, there never is a separate res to copy. This is called *copy elision*. However, to avoid copying in every case, we need to express such a move in C++ code. How? We define move operations to complement the copy operations:

```
class Vector {
      int sz;
      double* elem;
public:
      Vector(Vector&& arg);                       // move constructor
      Vector& operator=(Vector&& arg);            // move assignment
      // ...
};
```

AA The funny && notation is called an *rvalue reference*. We use it for defining move operations. Note that move operations do not take const arguments; that is, we write (Vector&&) and not (const Vector&&). Part of the purpose of a move operation is to modify the source, to make it "empty." The definitions of move operations tend to be simple. They tend to be simpler and more efficient than their copy equivalents. For Vector, we get

```
Vector::Vector(Vector&& arg)
       :sz{arg.sz}, elem{arg.elem}          // copy arg's elem and sz
{
      arg.sz = 0;                           // make arg the empty Vector
      arg.elem = nullptr;
}

Vector& Vector::operator=(Vector&& arg)           // move arg to this Vector
{
      if (this != &arg) {                   // protect against self-assignment (e.g., v=v)
            delete[] elem;                  // deallocate old space
            elem = arg.elem;                // copy arg's elem and sz
            sz = arg.sz;
            arg.elem = nullptr;             // make arg the empty Vector
            arg.sz = 0;
      }
      return *this;                         // return a self-reference (§15.8)
}
```

By defining a move constructor, we make it easy and cheap to move around large amounts of information, such as a vector with many elements. Consider again:

```
Vector fill(istream& is)
{
      Vector res;                           // assuming we have a default constructor (§17.5)
```

```
        for (double x; is>>x; )          // assuming support for range-for (§17.6)
                res.push_back(x);        // assuming we have a Vector::push_back (§17.8.4)
        return res;
}
```

The move constructor is implicitly used to implement the return. The compiler knows that the local value returned (res) is about to go out of scope, so it can move from it, rather than copy.

The importance of move constructors is that we do not have to deal with pointers or references to get large amounts of information out of a function. Consider this flawed (but conventional) alternative: XX

```
Vector* fill2(istream& is)
{
        Vector* res = new Vector;
        for (double x; is>>x; )
                res->push_back(x);
        return res;
}

void use2()
{
        Vector* vec = fill2(cin);
        // ... use vec ...
        delete vec;
}
```

Now we have to remember to delete the Vector. As described in §15.4.5, deleting objects placed on the free store is not as easy to do consistently and correctly as it might seem.

17.5 Essential operations

We have now reached the point where we can discuss how to decide which constructors a class should have, whether it should have a destructor, and whether you need to provide copy and move operations. There are seven essential operations to consider: CC

- Constructors from one or more arguments
- Default constructor (§17.5)
- Copy constructor (copy object of same type; §17.4.1)
- Copy assignment (copy object of same type; §17.4.2)
- Move constructor (move object of same type; §17.4.4)
- Move assignment (move object of same type; §17.4.4)
- Destructor (§15.5)

Usually, we need one or more constructors that take arguments needed to initialize an object. For example:

```
string s {"cat.jpg"};                    // initialize s to the character string "cat.jpg"
Image ii {Point{200,300},"cat.jpg"};     // initialize a Point with the coordinates{200,300},
                                         // then display the contents of file cat.jpg at that Point
```

The meaning/use of an initializer is completely up to the constructor. The standard **string**'s constructor uses a character string as an initial value, whereas **Image**'s constructor uses the string as the name of a file to open. Usually, we use a constructor to establish an invariant (§8.4.3). If we can't define a good invariant for a class that its constructors can establish, we probably have a poorly designed class or a plain data structure.

Constructors that take arguments are as varied as the classes they serve. The remaining operations have more regular patterns.

How do we know if a class needs a default constructor? We need a default constructor if we want to be able to make objects of the class without specifying an initializer. The most common example is when we want to put objects of a class into a standard-library **vector**. The following works only because we have default values for **int**, **string**, and **vector<int>**:

```
vector<double> vi(10);            // vector of 10 doubles, each initialized to 0.0
vector<string> vs(10);            // vector of 10 strings, each initialized to ""
vector<vector<int>> vvi(10);      // vector of 10 vectors, each initialized to vector{}
```

So, having a default constructor is often useful. The question then becomes: "When does it make sense to have a default constructor?" An answer is: "When we can establish the invariant for the class with a meaningful and obvious default value." For every type **T**, **T{}** is the default value, if a default exists. For example, **double{}** is **0.0**, **string{}** is **""**, **vector<int>{}** is the empty **vector** of **int**s, and in §8.4.2 we made our **Date{}** January 1, 2001. For our **Vector** that would be:

```
class Vector {
public:
        Vector() : sz{0}, elem{nullptr} {}
        // ...
};
```

AA A class needs a destructor if it acquires resources. A resource is something you "get from somewhere" and that you must give back once you have finished using it. The obvious example is memory that you get from the free store (using **new**) and have to give back to the free store (using **delete** or **delete[]**). Our **Vector** acquires memory to hold its elements, so it has to give that memory back; therefore, it needs a destructor. Other resources that you might encounter as your programs increase in ambition and sophistication are files (if you open one, you also have to close it), locks, thread handles, and sockets (for communication with processes and remote computers).

AA Another sign that a class needs a destructor is simply that it has members that are pointers or references. If a class has a pointer or a reference member, it often needs a destructor and copy operations.

AA A class that needs a destructor almost always also needs a copy and/or move operations (constructor and assignment). The reason is that if an object has acquired a resource (and has a pointer member pointing to it), the default meaning of copy (shallow, memberwise copy) is almost certainly wrong. Again, **vector** is the classic example.

AA In addition, a base class for which a derived class may have a destructor needs a **virtual** destructor (§15.5.2).

AA If a class needs any one of the essential operations, it probably needs all. This adds up to two popular rules of thumb:

- *Rule of zero*: If you don't need to, don't define any essential operation.
- *Rule of all*: if you need to define any essential operation, define them all.

That second rule is often called "the rule of three" or "the rule of five" because people don't agree on how to count operations (e.g., do you count assignment and construction as one or two? **const** and non-**const** versions?).

For example, a class like this doesn't need explicitly defined essential operations because the compiler correctly generates them from the ones provided by **string** and **vector**:

```
struct Club {
      string name;
      vector<Member> members;
};
```

17.5.1 Explicit constructors

A constructor that takes a single argument defines a conversion from its argument type to its class. This can be most useful. For example:

```
class complex {
public:
      complex(double);                    // defines double-to-complex conversion
      complex(double,double);
      // ...
};

complex z1 = 3.14;                        // OK: convert 3.14 to (3.14,0)
complex z2 = complex{1.2, 3.4};
```

However, implicit conversions should be used sparingly and with caution, because they can cause unexpected and undesirable effects. For example, our **Vector**, as defined so far, has a constructor that takes an **int**. This implies that it defines a conversion from **int** to **Vector**. For example: AA

```
class Vector {
      // ...
      Vector(int);
      // ...
};

Vector v = 10;                  // odd: makes a Vector of 10 doubles
v = 20;                         // eh? Assigns a new Vector of 20 doubles to v

void f(const Vector&);
f(10);                          // eh? Calls f with a new Vector of 10 doubles
```

It seems we are getting more than we have bargained for. Fortunately, it is simple to suppress this use of a constructor as an implicit conversion. A constructor-defined **explicit** provides only the usual construction semantics and not the implicit conversions. For example: CC

```
class Vector {
        // ...
        explicit Vector(int);
        // ...
};

Vector v = 10;                  // error: no implicit int-to-Vector conversion
v = 20;                         // error: no implicit int-to-Vector conversion
Vector v(10);                   // OK: considered explicit

void f(const Vector&);
f(10);                          // error: no implicit int-to-Vector conversion
f(Vector(10));                  // OK: considered explicit
```

To avoid surprising conversions, we – like the standard – define **Vector**'s single-argument constructors to be **explicit**. It's a pity that constructors are not **explicit** by default; if in doubt, make any constructor that can be invoked with a single argument **explicit**.

17.5.2 Debugging constructors and destructors

AA Constructors and destructors are invoked at well-defined and predictable points of a program's execution. However, we don't always write explicit calls, such as **vector<double>(2)**; rather we do something, such as returning a **vector** from a function, passing a **vector** as a by-value argument, or creating a **vector** on the free store using **new**. This can cause confusion for people who think in terms of syntax. There is not just a single syntax that triggers a constructor. It is simpler to think of constructors and destructors this way:

- Whenever an object of type **X** is created, one of **X**'s constructors is invoked.
- Whenever an object of type **X** is destroyed, **X**'s destructor is invoked.

A destructor is called whenever an object of its class is destroyed; that happens when names go out of scope, the program terminates, or **delete** is used on a pointer to an object. A constructor (some appropriate constructor) is invoked whenever an object of its class is created; that happens when a variable is initialized, when an object is created using **new** (except for built-in types), and whenever an object is copied.

But when does that happen? A good way to get a feel for that is to add print statements to constructors, assignment operations, and destructors and then just try. For example:

```
struct X {              // simple test class
        int val;

        void out(const string& s, int nv) { cout << this << "->" << s << ": " << val << " (" << nv << ")\n"; }

        X(){ out("X()",0); val=0; }                                     // default constructor
        X(int x) { out( "X(int)",x); val=x; }
        X(const X& x){out("X(X&) ",x.val); val=x.val; }                 // copy constructor
        X(X&& x){ out("X(X&&) ",x.val); val=x.val; x.val=0; }           // move constructor
```

```
        X& operator=(const X& x) { out("X copy assignment",x.val); val=x.val; return *this; }
        X& operator=(X&& x) { out("X move assignment",x.val); val=x.val; x.val=0; return *this; }
        ~X() { out("~X()",0); }                                    // destructor
};
```

Anything we do with this X will leave a trace that we can study. For example:

```
X glob {2};                         // a global variable

X copy(X a) { cout << "copy()\n"; return a; }
X copy2(X a) { cout << "copy2()\n"; X aa = a; return aa; }
X& ref_to(X & a) { cout << "ref_to()\n"; return a; }
X* make(int i) { cout << "make()\n";  X a(i); return new X(a); }

struct XX { X a; X b; };            // members

int main()
{
        X loc {4};                  // local variable
        X loc2 {loc};               // copy construction
        loc = X{5};                 // copy assignment
        loc2 = copy(loc);           // call by value and return
        loc2 = copy2(loc);
        X loc3 {6};
        X& r = ref_to(loc);         // call by reference and return
        delete make(7);
        delete make(8);
        vector<X> v(4);             // default values
        XX loc4;
        X* p = new X{9};            // an X on the free store
        delete p;
        X* pp = new X[5];           // an array of Xs on the free store
        delete[] pp;
}
```

> TRY THIS
>
> Try executing that. Then remove the move operations and run it again. The compilers can be very clever at avoiding unnecessary copies. We really mean it: do run this example and try to explain the result. If you do, you'll understand most of what there is to know about construction and destruction of objects.

Depending on the quality of your compiler, you may note some "missing copies" relating to our calls of copy() and copy2(). We (humans) can see that those functions do nothing: they just copy a value unmodified from input to output. A compiler is allowed to assume that a copy operation copies and does nothing else but copy. Based on that, it can eliminate redundant copies (copy elision; §17.4.4). Similarly, a compiler assumes that move operations do nothing but move. AA

Now consider: Why should we bother with this "silly class X"? It's a bit like the finger exercises that musicians have to do. After doing them, other things – things that matter – become easier. Also, if you have problems with constructors and destructors, you can insert such print statements in constructors for your real classes to see that they work as intended. For larger programs, this exact kind of tracing becomes tedious, but similar techniques apply. For example, you can determine whether you have a memory leak by seeing if the number of constructions minus the number of destructions equals zero. Forgetting to define copy constructors and copy assignments for classes that allocate memory or hold pointers to objects is a common – and easily avoidable – source of problems.

AA If your problems get too big to handle by such simple means, you will have learned enough to be able to start using the professional tools for finding such problems; they are often referred to as "leak detectors." The ideal, of course, is not to leak memory by using techniques that prevent such leaks.

17.6 Other useful operations

In addition to the essential operations, there are quite a few that are often important for common uses:

- Comparison operators, such as == and < (§17.6.1)
- **initializer_list** construction and assignment (§17.3)
- Iteration support functions, such as **begin()** and **end()**, as required for range-**for**
- **swap()** (§7.4.5, §18.4.3))

For **vectors**, **begin()** gives the position of the first element of a sequence and **end()** the one past the end location. For **Vector**, that becomes:

```
double* Vector::begin() const { return elem; }
double* Vector::end() const { return elem+sz; }
```

Or graphically:

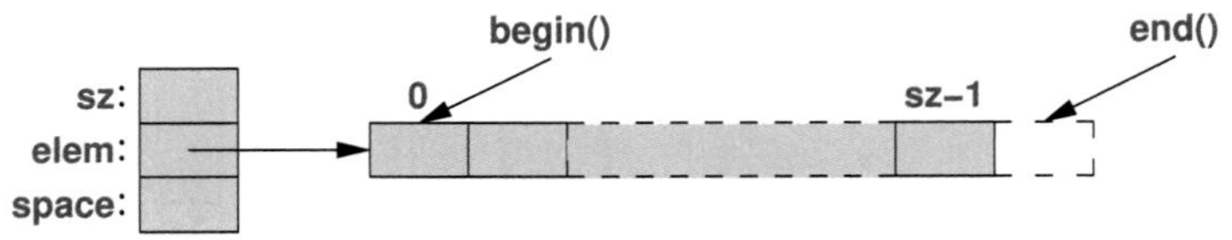

The **begin()/end()** pair is used to implement traversal of elements by many algorithms (Chapter 21) and by range-**for**.

17.6.1 Comparison operators

We can define operators for our types, not just **[ ]** and **=**, but essentially all operators. When we define assignment, **=**, we typically also need to define equality, **==**, so that we can say what it means for the target of an assignment to have the same value as its source. Usually, **a=b** implies that after the assignment we have **a==b**. For our **Vector**, that's easily done:

```
bool operator==(const Vector& v1, const Vector& v2)
{
        if (v1.size()!=v2.size())
                return false;
        for (int i = 0; i<v1.size(); ++i)
                if (v1[i]!=v2[i])
                        return false;
        return true;
}
```

Note the initial comparison of the number of elements. Without that, we could be wasting time comparing many elements before finding two that compared not equal. Also, having determined that the sizes are equal, we don't have to check both sizes as we loop through the elements. When dealing with containers, such simple optimizations can be most effective.

17.6.2 Related operators

Operators rarely stand by themselves, they come in "clusters" of related operators that jointly deliver a desired semantics:

- +, −, *, /, and sometimes % tend to go together.
- We saw that we needed *, −>, and [] for pointers.
- When we have == we usually also want !=.
- When we have = we usually also want == and !=.
- <, <=, >, and >= are comparisons. When we have those, we usually also want == and !=.

Operators have conventional meanings, and we should be careful to conform to those. A + that subtracted would seriously confuse readers.

Often the easiest and most efficient way to build one operator from a cluster of related operators is in terms of one of the others. Here is a != for our **Vector**:

```
bool operator!=(const Vector& v1, const Vector& v2)
{
        return !(v1==v2);
}
```

For historical reasons defining an operator is called *operator overloading* because doing so adds a meaning to that operator.

Naturally, the standard-library **std::vector** has comparison operators: ==, !=, <, <=, >, and >=. All we have been doing here is to continue our efforts to build our **Vector** in the image of the standard-library one.

Other operators that you can define for your own types include

- () application/call
- , comma
- << and >>
- & bitwise and, | bitwise or, ^ bitwise exclusive or, and ~ bitwise complement
- && logical and, and || logical or
- but unfortunately not . (dot)

No, you can't define your own operators (e.g., ** or =~=) or redefine the meaning of operators on the built-in types (e.g., + on integers always adds). We decided that the added confusion from allowing such flexibility outweighed the benefits gained in relatively few cases.

17.7 Remaining Vector problems

Our **Vector** class has reached the point where we can

- Create **Vectors** of double-precision floating-point elements (objects of class **Vector**) with whatever number of elements we want.
- Copy our **Vectors** using assignment and initialization.
- Move our **Vectors** cheaply from one scope to another using assignment and initialization.
- Use **initializer_lists** for assignment and initialization.
- Rely on **Vectors** to correctly release their memory when they go out of scope.
- Access **Vector** elements using the conventional subscript notation (on both the right-hand side and the left-hand side of an assignment).
- Compare **Vectors** using operators **==** and **!=**.
- Support range-**for** with **begin()** and **end()**.

That's all good and useful, but to reach the level of sophistication we expect (based on experience with **std::vector**), we need to address three more concerns:

- How do we change the size of a **Vector** (change the number of elements)?
- How do we catch and report out-of-range **Vector** element access?
- How do we specify the element type of a **Vector** as an argument?

For example, how do we define **Vector** so that this is legal, as it is for **std::vector**:

```
Vector<double> vd;              // elements of type double
for (double d; cin>>d; )
      vd.push_back(d);          // grow vd to hold all the elements

Vector<char> vc(100);           // elements of type char
int n = 0;
if (cin>>n && 0<n)
      vc.resize(n);             // make vc have n elements
```

CC Obviously, it is nice and useful to have **Vectors** that allow this, but why is it important from a programming point of view? What makes it interesting to someone collecting useful programming techniques for future use? We are using two kinds of flexibility. We have a single entity, the **Vector**, for which we can vary two things:

- The number of elements
- The type of elements

Those kinds of variability are useful in rather fundamental ways. We always collect data. Looking around my desk, I see piles of bank statements, credit card bills, and phone bills. Each of those is basically a list of lines of information of various types: strings of letters and numeric values. In front of me lies a phone; it keeps lists of phone numbers and names. In the bookcases across the room, there are shelf after shelf of books. Our programs tend to be similar: we have containers of elements of various types. We have many different kinds of containers (**vector** is just the most widely useful), and they contain information such as phone numbers, names, transaction amounts, and documents. Essentially all the examples from my desk and my room originated in some computer program or another. The obvious exception is the phone: it *is* a computer, and when I look at the numbers on it, I'm looking at the output of a program just like the ones we're writing. In fact, those numbers may very well be stored in a std::vector<Number>.

Not all vectors have the same type of elements. We need vectors of doubles, temperature readings, records (of various kinds), strings, operations, GUI buttons, Shapes, dates, pointers to Windows, etc. The possibilities are endless. We leave that problem to Chapter 18.

Not all containers have the same number of elements. Could we live with a vector that had its size fixed by its initial definition; that is, could we write our code without push_back(), resize(), and equivalent operations? Sure we could, and such vector-like containers can be most useful. However, that would put an unnecessary burden on the programmer: the basic trick for living with fixed-size containers is to move the elements to a bigger container when the number of elements grows too large for the initial size. For example, we could read into a vector without ever changing the size of a vector like this:

```
void grow(Vector& v)            // read elements into a vector without using push_back:
{
        int n = 0;                      // number of elements
        for (double d; cin>>d; ) {
                if (n==v.size()) {
                        Vector v2(v.size()+1);
                        for (int i; i<v.size(); ++i)
                                v2[i] = v[i];
                        v = v2;
                }
        }
        v[n] = d;                       // add the new element
}
```

That's not pretty. Are you convinced that we got it right? It's horrendously inefficient if we ever exceed the original size! One of the reasons to use containers, such as vector, is to do better; that is, we want our Vector to handle such size changes internally to save us – its users – the bother and the chance to make mistakes. In other words, we often prefer containers that can grow to hold the exact number of elements we happen to need. The standard-library equivalent to the code above is far simpler and also far more efficient:

```
void grow(vector<double>& v)    // use the standard library
{
        for (double d; cin>>d; )
                vd.push_back(d);
}
```

Are such changes of size common? If they are not, facilities for changing size are simply minor conveniences. However, such size changes are very common. The most obvious example is reading an unknown number of values from input. Other examples are collecting a set of results from a search (we don't in advance know how many results there will be) and removing elements from a collection one by one. Thus, the question is not whether we should handle size changes for CC containers, but how.

XX Why do we bother with changing sizes at all? Why not "just allocate enough space and be done with it"? That appears to be the simplest and most efficient strategy. However, it is that only if we can reliably allocate enough space without allocating grossly too much space – and we can't. When we can, we still have to keep track of how much of our pre-allocated space has been used so far. Experience shows that doing so is not trivial and a source of errors. Unless we carefully and systematically check for out-of-range access we suffer disasters. Thus, we prefer to let a properly designed and carefully implemented library take care of that.

There are many kinds of containers. This is an important point, and because it has important implications it should not be accepted without thought. Why can't all containers be **vector**s? If we could make do with a single kind of container (e.g., **vector**), we could dispense with all the concerns about how to program it and just make it part of the language. If we could make do with a single kind of container, we needn't bother learning about different kinds of containers; we'd just use **vector** all the time.

Well, data structures are the key to most significant applications. There are many thick and useful books about how to organize data, and much of that information could be described as answers to the question "How do I best store my data?" So, the answer is that we need many different kinds of containers, but it is too large a subject to adequately address here. However, we have already used **vector**s and **string**s (a **string** is a container of characters) extensively. In the next chapters, we will see **list**s, **map**s (a **map** is a tree of pairs of values), and matrices (PPP2.§24.5). Because we need many different containers, the language features and programming techniques needed to build and use containers are widely useful. In fact, the techniques we use to store and access data are among the most fundamental and most useful for all nontrivial forms of computing.

CC At the most basic memory level, all objects are of a fixed size and no types exist. What we do here is to introduce language facilities and programming techniques that allow us to provide containers of objects of various types for which we can vary the number of elements. This gives us a fundamentally useful degree of flexibility and convenience.

17.8 Changing size

What facilities for changing size does **std::vector** offer? It provides three simple operations. Given

```
vector<double> v;        // v.size()==0
```

we can change its size in three ways:

```
v.resize(10);            // v now has 10 elements

v.push_back(7);          // add an element with the value 7 to the end of v; v.size() increases by 1

v = v2;                  // assign another vector; v is now a copy of v2; v.size() now equals v2.size()
```

The standard-library **vector** offers more operations that can change a **vector**'s size, such as **erase()** and **insert()**, but here we will just see how we can implement **resize()**, **push_back()**, and **operator=()** for our **Vector**.

17.8.1 Representation

In §17.7, we show a simple, naive strategy for changing size: just allocate space for the new number of elements and copy the old elements into the new space. However, if you resize often, that's inefficient. In practice, if we change the size once, we usually do so many times. In particular, we rarely see just one **push_back()**. So, we can optimize our programs by anticipating such changes in size. In fact, all **vector** implementations keep track of both the number of elements and an amount of "free space" reserved for "future expansion." For example:

```
class Vector {
        // ...
private:
        int sz;                 // number of elements
        double* elem;           // address of first element
        int space;              // number of elements plus "free space"/"slots" for new elements
};
```

We can represent this graphically like this:

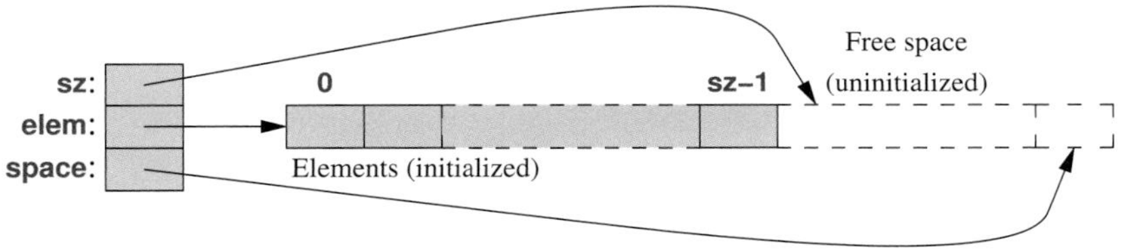

We number elements starting from **0**, so **sz** (the number of elements) refers to one beyond the last element and **space** refers to one beyond the last allocated slot. The pointers shown are really **elem+sz** and **elem+space**.

When a **Vector** is first constructed, **space==sz**; that is, there is no "free space":

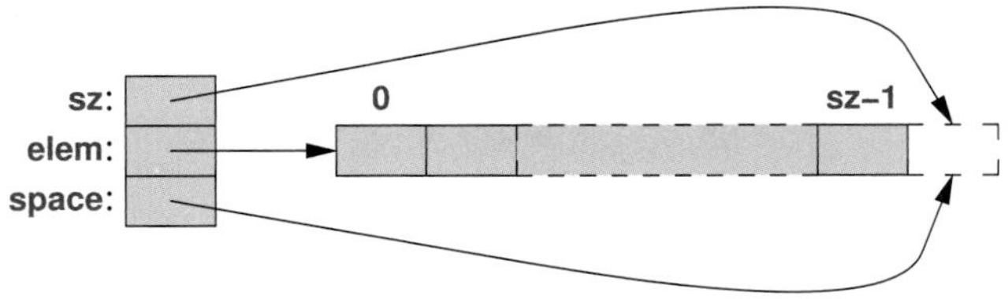

We don't start allocating extra slots until we begin changing the number of elements. Typically, **space==sz**, so there is no memory overhead unless we use **push_back()**.

The default constructor for **Vector** sets its integer members to **0** and its pointer member to **nullptr**:

```
Vector() :sz{0}, elem{nullptr}, space{0} {}
```

That gives

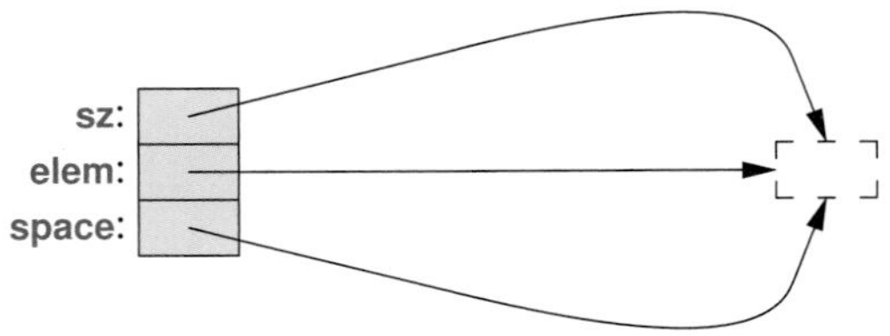

That one-beyond-the-end element is completely imaginary. The default constructor does no free-store allocation and occupies minimal storage (but see exercise 16).

Please note that our Vector illustrates techniques that can be used to implement a standard vector (and other data structures), but a fair amount of freedom is given to standard-library implementations so that std::vector on your system may use different techniques.

17.8.2 reserve() and capacity()

The most fundamental operation when we change sizes (that is, when we change the number of elements) is Vector::reserve(). That's the operation we use to add space for new elements:

```
void Vector::reserve(int newalloc)
{
        if (newalloc<=space)                    // never decrease allocation
                return;
        double* p = new double[newalloc];       // allocate new space
        for (int i=0; i<sz; ++i)                // copy old elements
                p[i] = elem[i];
        delete[] elem;                          // deallocate old space
        elem = p;
        space = newalloc;
}
```

Note that we don't initialize the elements of the reserved space. After all, we are just reserving space; using that space for elements is the job of push_back() and resize().

Obviously, the amount of free space available in a Vector can be of interest to a user, so we (like the standard) provide a member function for obtaining that information:

```
int Vector::capacity() const { return space; }
```

That is, for a Vector called v, v.capacity()−v.size() is the number of elements we could push_back() to v without causing reallocation.

The standard-library vector never implicitly decreases its allocation. It assumes that if we ever needed an amount of memory, we are likely to do so again. In case we don't, v.shrink_to_fit() will reduce capacity to size().

17.8.3 resize()

Given reserve(), implementing resize() for our Vector is fairly simple. We have to handle several cases:

- The new size is larger than the old allocation.
- The new size is larger than the old size, but smaller than or equal to the old allocation.
- The new size is equal to the old size.
- The new size is smaller than the old size.

Let's see what we get:

```
void Vector::resize(int newsize)
      // make the vector have newsize elements
      // initialize each new element with the default value 0.0
{
      reserve(newsize);
      for (int i=sz; i<newsize; ++i)          // initialize new elements
            elem[i] = 0;
      sz = newsize;
}
```

We let reserve() do the hard work of dealing with memory. The loop initializes new elements (if there are any).

We didn't explicitly deal with any cases here, but you can verify that all are handled correctly nevertheless.

> TRY THIS
>
> What cases do we need to consider (and test) if we want to convince ourselves that this resize() is correct? How about newsize == 0? How about newsize == –77?

17.8.4 push_back()

When we first think of it, push_back() may appear complicated to implement, but given reserve() it is quite simple:

```
void Vector::push_back(double d)
       // increase vector size by one; initialize the new element with d
{
      if (space==0)                 // start with space for 8 elements
            reserve(8);
      else if (sz==space)
            reserve(2*space);       // get more space
      elem[sz] = d;                 // add d at end
      ++sz;                         // increase the size (sz is the number of elements)
}
```

In other words, if we have no spare space, we double the size of the allocation. In practice that turns out to be a very good choice for the vast majority of uses of vector, and that's the strategy used by most implementations of std::vector.

17.8.5 Assignment

We can define vector assignment in several different ways. For example, we could have decided that assignment was legal only if the two vectors involved had the same number of elements.

However, in §17.4 we decided that vector assignment should have the general and arguably the most obvious meaning: after assignment **v1=v2**, the vector **v1** is a copy of **v2**. Consider:

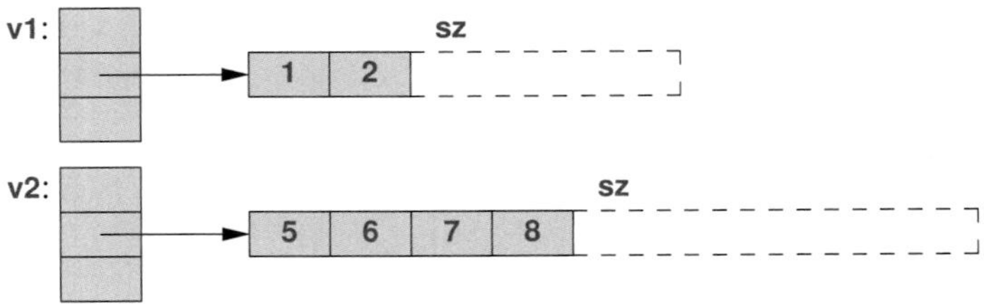

Obviously, we need to copy the elements as we did in §17.4.2, but what about the spare space? Do we "copy" the "free space" at the end? We don't: the new **Vector** will get a copy of the elements, but since we have no idea how that new **Vector** is going to be used, we don't bother with extra space at the end:

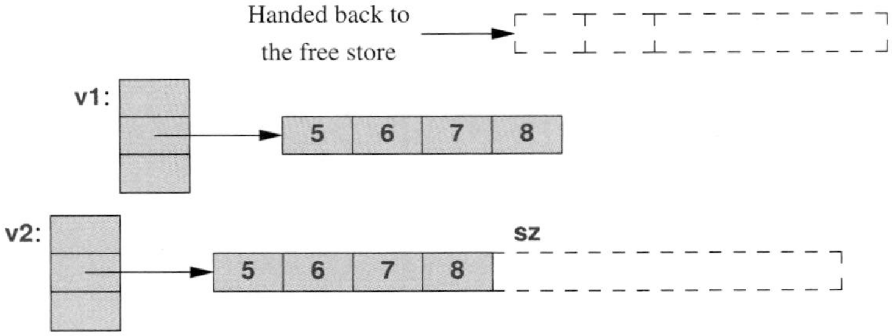

The simplest implementation of that is:

- Allocate memory for a copy.
- Copy the elements.
- Delete the old allocation.
- Set the **sz**, **elem**, and **space** to the new values.

Like this:

```
Vector& Vector::operator=(const Vector& a)
        // like copy constructor, but we must deal with old elements
{
        double* p = new double[a.sz];          // allocate new space
        for (int i = 0; i<a.sz; ++i)           // copy elements
                p[i] = a.elem[i];
        delete[] elem;                         // deallocate old space

        space = sz = a.sz;                     // set new size
        elem = p;                              // set new elements
        return *this;                          // return self-reference
}
```

By convention, an assignment operator returns a reference to the object assigned to. The notation for that is *this, which is explained in §15.8.

This implementation is correct, but when we look at it a bit, we realize that we do a lot of redundant allocation and deallocation. What if the Vector we assign to has more elements than the one we assign? What if the Vector we assign to has the same number of elements as the Vector we assign? In many applications, that last case is very common. In either case, we can just copy the elements into space already available in the target Vector:

```
Vector& Vector::operator=(const vector& a)
{
        if (this==&a)                           // self-assignment, no work needed
                return *this;

        if (a.sz<=space) {                      // enough space, no need for new allocation
                for (int i = 0; i<a.sz; ++i)    // copy elements
                        elem[i] = a.elem[i];
                sz = a.sz;
                return *this;
        }

        double* p = new double[a.sz];           // allocate new space
        for (int i = 0; i<a.sz; ++i)            // copy elements
                p[i] = a.elem[i];
        delete[] elem;                          // deallocate old space

        space = sz = a.sz;                      // set new size
        elem = p;                               // set new elements
        return *this;                           // return a self-reference
}
```

Here, we first test for self-assignment (e.g., v=v); in that case, we just do nothing. That test is logically redundant but sometimes a significant optimization. It does, however, show a common use of the this pointer: checking if the argument a is the same object as the object for which a member function (here, operator=()) was called.

Please convince yourself that this code actually works if we remove the this==&a case. The a.sz<=space is also just an optimization. Please convince yourself that this code actually works if we remove the a.sz<=space case.

17.9 Our Vector so far

Now we have an almost real Vctor of doubles:

```
class Vector {
/*
        invariant:
        if 0<=n<sz, elem[n] is element n
        sz<=space;
        if sz<space there is space for (space-sz) doubles after elem[sz-1]
*/
        int sz;                  // the size
        double* elem;            // pointer to the elements (or 0)
        int space;               // number of elements plus number of free slots
public:
        Vector() : sz{0}, elem{nullptr}, space{0} { }
        explicit Vector(int s) :sz{s}, elem{new double[s]}, space{s}
        {
                for (int i=0; i<sz; ++i)
                        elem[i]=0;       // elements are initialized
        }

        Vector(initializer_list<double> lst);                   // list initializer
        Vector& operator=(initializer_list<double> lst);        // list assignment

        Vector(const Vector&);                                  // copy constructor
        Vector& operator=(const vector&);                       // copy assignment

        Vector(vector&&);                                       // move constructor
        Vector& operator=(Vector&&);                            // move assignment

        ~Vector() { delete[] elem; }                            // destructor

        double& operator[ ](int n) { return elem[n]; }          // access: return reference
        const double& operator[](int n) const { return elem[n]; }

        int size() const { return sz; }
        int capacity() const { return space; }

        void resize(int newsize);                               // growth
        void push_back(double d);
        void reserve(int newalloc);

        double* begin() const { return elem; }                  // iteration support
        double* end() const { return elem+sz; }
};

bool operator==(Vector& v1, Vector &v2);
bool operator!=(Vector& v1, Vector &v2);
```

Note how it has the essential operations (§17.5): constructor, default constructor, copy operations, move operations, and destructor. It has an operation for accessing data (subscripting: [ ]) and for providing information about that data (size() and capacity()) and for controlling growth (resize(), push_back(), and reserve()).

Drill

Write a class Ptr that has as a double* private member called p. Give Ptr the essential operations as described in §17.5. A constructor should take a double argument, allocate a double on the free store, assign the pointer to it to p, and copy the argument into *p. Give Ptr an operator * that allows you to read and write *p. Test Ptr.

Review

[1] What is the default meaning of copying for class objects?
[2] When is the default meaning of copying of class objects appropriate? Inappropriate?
[3] What is a copy constructor?
[4] What is a copy assignment?
[5] What is a move constructor?
[6] What is a move assignment?
[7] What is a default constructor?
[8] What is the difference between a copy constructor and a move constructor?
[9] What is the difference between a copy constructor and a copy assignment?
[10] What is shallow copy? What is deep copy?
[11] How does the copy of a vector compare to its source?
[12] What is the point of copy elision?
[13] What are the essential operations for a class?
[14] What is an explicit constructor?
[15] When would you prefer a constructor not to be explicit?
[16] How do you define traversal for a container?
[17] What operations may be invoked implicitly for a class object?
[18] What operators are often user-defined?
[19] What is *the rule of zero*?
[20] What is *the rule of all*?
[21] Why don't we just always define a vector with a large enough size for all eventualities?
[22] Which vector operations can change the size of a vector after construction?
[23] What is the difference between reserve() and resize()?
[24] How much spare space do we allocate for a new vector?
[25] When must we copy vector elements to a new location?
[26] What is the value of a vector after a copy?

Terms

reserve()	deep copy	shallow copy	move assignment
capacity	default constructor	move construction	list initialization
copy assignment	essential operations	begin()	end()
copy constructor	explicit constructor	&&	push_back()
resize()	size	comparison	traversal
rule of zero	rule of all	== and !=	

Exercises

[1] Define class Matrix to represent a two-dimensional matrix of doubles. A constructor should take two integer arguments specifying the number of rows and columns, e.g.,Matrix{3,4} has 3 rows and 4 columns. Provide Matrix with operators = (assignment), == (equality), [ ] (subscript), and + (addition of corresponding elements). The subscript operator should take a pairs of indices, e.g., m[2,3] yields the element 3 of the 2nd row. Indexing should be zero-based. Range check your indices. Reject operations on two Matrixs with different dimensions. If your compiler doesn't allow multiple arguments for [ ], use ( ) instead. Store the elements of your Matrix in a single vector. Test Matrix.

[2] Provide << and >> for your Matrix.

[3] Make the representation of Matrix private. What would be a more complete set of members for Matrix? For example, would you like a += operator? What would be a good set of constructors? Make a list and give a brief argument for each operation. Implement and test your more complete Matrix.

[4] Implement a row(i) member function that returns a vector that is a copy of the ith row. Implement a column(i) member function that returns a vector that is a copy of the ith column.

Postscript

The standard-library vector is built from lower-level memory management facilities, such as pointers and arrays, and its primary role is to help us avoid the complexities of those facilities. Whenever we design a class, we must consider the essential operations: initialization, copying, moving, and destruction. In addition, we should consider what further operations are needed for that kind of type. For most types: == and !=. For containers: list initialization and assignment, begin(), end(), and swap(). The ultimate aim of such operations is to give the type a coherent and familiar semantics. Finally, we dramatically increase the flexibility of our Vector by adding operations that allow us to change a Vector's size: push_back(), resize(), and reserve().

The essential operations allow us to control the lifecycle of an object and to move objects between scopes. It is the foundation of reliable and efficient resource management. Other operators allow us to model concepts from application domains as types or sets of types. That's the basis for C++'s direct support for the kind of concepts we work with, the kind of entities that get drawn on our doodlepads and whiteboards.

18

Templates and Exceptions

Success is never final.
– Winston Churchill

This chapter completes the design and implementation of the most common and most useful STL container: **vector**. We show how to specify containers where the element type is a parameter and how to deal with range errors. As usual, the techniques used are generally applicable, rather than simply restricted to the implementation of **vector**, or even to the implementation of containers. The techniques rely on templates and exceptions, so we show how to define templates and give the basic techniques for resource management that are the keys to good use of exceptions. In this context, we discuss the general resource-management technique called "Resource Acquisition is Initialization" (RAII), resource-management guarantees, and the standard-library resource-management pointers **unique_ptr** and **shared_ptr**.

§18.1 Templates
Types as template parameters; Generic programming; Concepts; Containers and inheritance; Value template parameters

§18.2 Generalizing **Vector**
Allocators

§18.3 Range checking and exceptions
An aside: design considerations; Module **PPP_support**

§18.4 Resources and exceptions
Potential resource-management problems; Resource acquisition is initialization; Resource-management guarantees; RAII for **Vector**

§18.5 Resource-management pointers
Return by moving **unique_ptr**; **shared_ptr**

18.1 Templates

Obviously, not all **vectors** have the same type of elements. We need **vectors** of **doubles**, temperature readings, records (of various kinds), **strings**, operations, GUI buttons, shapes, dates, pointers to windows, etc. The possibilities are endless. We want to freely specify the element type for our **Vectors** like this:

```
Vector<double>
Vector<int>
Vector<Month>
Vector<Window*>              // Vector of pointers to Windows
Vector<Vector<Record>>       // Vector of Vectors of Records
Vector<char>
```

AA To do that, we must see how to define templates. We have used templates from day one, but until now we haven't had a need to define one. The standard library provides what we have needed so far, but we mustn't believe in magic, so we must examine how the designers and implementers of the standard library provide facilities such as the **vector** type and the **sort()** function (§21.5). This is not just of theoretical interest, because – as usual – the tools and techniques used for the standard library are among the most useful for our own code. For example, in Chapter 19 to Chapter 21, we show how templates can be used to implement the standard-library containers and algorithms.

CC Basically, a *template* is a mechanism that allows a programmer to use types as parameters for a class or a function. The compiler then generates a specific class or function when we later provide specific types as arguments.

18.1.1 Types as template parameters

CC We want to make the element type a parameter to our **Vector**. So we take **Vector** and replace **double** with **T** where **T** is a parameter that can be given "values" such as **double**, **int**, **string**, **Vector<Record>**, and **Window***. The C++ notation for introducing a type parameter **T** is the **template<typename T>** prefix, meaning "for all types **T**." For example:

```
template<typename T>          // for all types T (just like in math)
class Vector {
        int sz;               // the size
        T* elem;              // a pointer to the elements
        int space;            // size + free space
public:
        Vector() :sz{0}, elem{nullptr}, space{0} { }

        explicit Vector(int s) :sz{s}, elem{new T[s]}, space{s}
        {
                for (int i=0; i<sz; ++i)
                        elem[i]=0;            // elements are initialized
        }

        Vector(initializer_list<T>);                    // list constructor
        Vector& operator=(initializer_list<T>);         // list assignment
```

```
        Vector(const Vector&);                              // copy constructor
        Vector& operator=(const Vector&);                   // copy assignment

        Vector(vector&&);                                   // move constructor
        Vector& operator=(Vector&&);                        // move assignment

        ~Vector() { delete[] elem; }                        // destructor

        T& operator[](int n) { return elem[n]; }            // access: return reference
        const T& operator[](int n) const { return elem[n]; }

        int size() const { return sz; }                     // the current size
        int capacity() const { return space; }              // the current capacity

        void resize(int newsize);                           // growth
        void push_back(const T& d);
        void reserve(int newalloc);

        T* begin() const { return elem; }                   // iteration support
        T* end() const { return elem+sz; }
};

template<typename T>
bool operator==(const Vector<T>&, const Vector<T>&);

template<typename T>
bool operator!=(const Vector<T>&, const Vector<T>&);
```

That's just our Vector of doubles from §18.1 with double replaced by the template parameter T. We can use this class template Vector like this:

```
Vector<double> vd;           // T is double
Vector<int> vi;              // T is int
Vector<double*> vpd;         // T is double*
Vector<vector<int>> vvi;     // T is Vector<T>, in which T is int
```

One way of thinking about what a compiler does when we use a template is that it generates the class with the actual type (the template argument) in place of the template parameter. For example, when the compiler sees Vector<char> in the code, it (somewhere) generates something like this: **AA**

```
class Vector_char {
        int sz;             // the size
        char* elem;         // a pointer to the elements
        int space;          // size + free space
public:
        Vector_char() :sz{0}, elem{nullptr}, space{0} { }
```

```
        explicit Vector_char(int s) :sz{s}, elem{new char[s]}, space{s}
        {
                for (int i=0; i<sz; ++i)
                        elem[i]=0;              // elements are initialized
        }

        Vector(initializer_list<T>);                           // list constructor
        Vector& operator=(initializer_list<T>);                // list assignment

        Vector_char(const Vector_char&);                       // copy constructor
        Vector_char& operator=(const Vector_char&);            // copy assignment

        Vector_char(vector_char&&);                            // move constructor
        Vector_char& operator=(Vector_char&&);                 // move assignment

        ~Vector_char();                                        // destructor

        char& operator[] (int n) { return elem[n]; }           // access: return reference
        const char& operator[] (int n) const ) { return elem[n]; }

        int size() const;                                      // the current size
        int capacity() const;                                  // the current capacity

        void resize(int newsize);                              // growth
        void push_back(const char& d);
        void reserve(int newalloc);

        char* begin() const { return elem; }                   // iteration support
        char* end() const { return elem+sz; }
};

bool operator==(const Vector_char&, const Vector_char&);
bool operator!=(const Vector_char&, const Vector_char&);
```

Similarly, for **Vector<double>**, the compiler generates roughly the **Vector** (of **double**) from §17.9 (using a suitable internal name meaning **Vector<double>**).

CC Sometimes, we call a class template a *type generator*. The process of generating types (classes) from a class template given template arguments is called *specialization* or *template instantiation*. For example, **Vector<char>** and **Vector<Open_polyline*>** are said to be specializations of **Vector**. In simple cases, such as our **Vector**, instantiation is a pretty simple process. In the most general and advanced cases, template instantiation is horrendously complicated. Fortunately for the user of templates, that complexity is in the domain of the compiler writer, not the template user. Template instantiation (generation of template specializations) takes place at compile time or link time, not at run time.

Naturally, we can use member functions of such a class template. For example:

```
void fct(Vector<string>& v)
{
        int n = v.size();
        v.push_back("Ada");
        // ...
}
```

When such a member function of a class template is used, the compiler generates the appropriate function. For example, when the compiler sees **v.push_back("Ada")**, it generates a function

```
void Vector<string>::push_back(const string& d) { /* ... */ }
```

from the template definition

```
template<typename T>
void Vector<T>::push_back(const T& d) { /* ... */ };
```

That way, there is a function for **v.push_back("Ada")** to call. In other words, when you need a function for given object and argument types, the compiler will write it for you based on its template.

Instead of writing **template<typename T>**, you can write **template<class T>**. The two constructs mean exactly the same thing, but some prefer **typename** "because it is clearer" and "because nobody gets confused by **typename** thinking that you can't use a built-in type, such as **int**, as a template argument." We are of the opinion that **class** already means type, so it makes no difference. Also, **class** is shorter.

18.1.2 Generic programming

Templates are the basis for generic programming in C++. In fact, the simplest definition of "generic programming" in C++ is "using templates." That definition is a bit too simpleminded, though. We should not define fundamental programming concepts in terms of programming language features. Programming language features exist to support programming techniques – not the other way around. As with most popular notions, there are many definitions of "generic programming." We think that the most useful simple definition is CC

- *Generic programming*: Writing code that works with a variety of types presented as arguments, as long as those argument types meet specific syntactic and semantic requirements.

For example, the elements of a **vector** must be of a type that we can copy and move. In Chapter 19 to Chapter 21, we will see templates that require arithmetic operations on their arguments. When what we parameterize is a class, we get a *class template* (often called a *parameterized type* or a *parameterized class*). When what we parameterize is a function, we get a *function template*, (often called a *parameterized function* and sometimes also an *algorithm*). Thus, generic programming is sometimes referred to as "algorithm-oriented programming"; the focus of the design is more the algorithms than the data types they use. CC

Since the notion of parameterized types is so central to programming, let's explore the somewhat bewildering terminology a bit further. That way we have a chance of not getting too confused when we meet such notions in other contexts.

This form of generic programming relying on explicit template parameters is often called *parametric polymorphism*. In contrast, the polymorphism you get from using class hierarchies and virtual functions is called *ad hoc polymorphism* and that style of programming is called *object-* CC *oriented programming* (§12.3). The reason that both styles of programming are called *polymorphism* is that each style relies on the programmer to present many versions of a concept by a single interface. *Polymorphism* is Greek for "many shapes," referring to the many different types you can manipulate through a common interface. In the **Shape** examples from Chapter 10 to Chapter 13 we accessed many shapes (such as **Text**, **Circle**, and **Polygon**) through the interface defined by **Shape**. When we use **vectors**, we use many **vectors** (such as **vector<int>**, **vector<double>**, and **vector<Shape*>**) through the interface defined by the **vector** template.

There are several differences between object-oriented programming (using class hierarchies and virtual functions) and generic programming (using templates). The most obvious is that the choice of function invoked when you use generic programming is determined by the compiler at compile time, whereas for object-oriented programming, it is not determined until run time. For example:

```
v.push_back(x);          // put x into the vector v
s.draw();                // draw the shape s
```

For **v.push_back(x)** the compiler will determine the element type for **v** and use the appropriate **push_back()**, but for **s.draw()** the compiler will indirectly call some **draw()** function (using **s**'s **vtbl**; see §12.3.1). This gives object-oriented programming a degree of freedom that generic programming lacks, but leaves run-of-the-mill generic programming more regular, easier to understand, and better performing (hence the "ad hoc" and "parametric" labels).

CC To sum up:

- *Generic programming*: supported by templates, relying on compile-time resolution
- *Object-oriented programming*: supported by class hierarchies with virtual functions, allowing run-time resolution

Combinations of the two are possible and useful. For example:

```
void draw_all(vector<Shape*>& v)
{
        for (auto x : v)
                x->draw();
}
```

Here, we call a virtual function (**draw()**) on a base class (**Shape**) – that's certainly object-oriented programming. However, we also kept **Shape***s in a **vector**, which is a parameterized type, so we also used (simple) generic programming.

AA So – assuming you have had your fill of philosophy for now – what do people actually use templates for? For unsurpassed flexibility and performance:

- Use templates where performance is essential (e.g., numerics and hard real time; see PPP2.Ch24 and PPP2.Ch25).
- Use templates where flexibility in combining information from several types is essential (e.g., the C++ standard library; see Chapter 19 to Chapter 21).

18.1.3 Concepts

XX Templates with unconstrained parameters, **template<typename T>**, have many useful properties, such as great flexibility and near-optimal performance. In addition, we need a precise specification of what a template requires of its template arguments. For example, in much older C++ code, we find something like this:

```
template<typename T>        // for all types T
class Vector {
      // ...
};
```

This doesn't precisely state what is expected of an argument type T.

We call a set of requirements on a set of template arguments a *concept*. For example, a vector requires that its elements can be copied and moved, can have their address taken, and be default constructed (if needed). In other words, an element must meet a set of requirements, which we could call Element. We can make that explicit:

```
template<typename T>          // for all types T
      requires Element<T>()   // such that T is an Element
class Vector {
      // ...
};
```

This shows that a concept is really a type predicate, that is, a compile-time-evaluated (constexpr) function that returns true if the type argument (here, T) has the properties required by the concept (here, Element) and false if it does not. This notation is a bit long-winded, but a shorthand notation brings us to

```
template<Element T>      // for all types T, such that Element<T>() is true
class Vector {
      // ...
};
```

The mathematical vocabulary we use to describe concepts reflects the mathematical roots of concepts. Concepts represent a form of predicate logic.

The standard library provides many useful concepts, some of which we use in Chapter 19 to Chapter 21. Then, their meaning and utility will become clear.

- range<C>(): C can hold Elements and be accessed as a [begin():end()) sequence.
- input_iterator<In>(): In can be used to read a sequence [b:e) once only (like an input stream).
- output_iterator<Out>(): Out can be used to write to output (like an output stream). We cannot read using Out.
- forward_iterator<For>(): For can be used to traverse a sequence [b:e) (like a linked list, a vector, or an array). We can traverse [b:e) repeatedly using For.
- random_access_iterator<Ran>(): Ran can be used to read and write a sequence [b:e) repeatedly and supports subscripting using [ ].
- random_access_range<Ran>(): range with random_access_iterators.
- equality_comparable<T>(): We can compare two Ts for equality using == to get a Boolean result.
- equality_comparable_with<T,U>(): We can compare a T to a U for equality using == to get a Boolean result.
- predicate<P,T...>(): We can call P with a set of arguments of the N specified types T1, T2, ... to get a Boolean result.

- indirect_unary_predicate<P,I>(): We can call P with an iterator argument of type I to get a Boolean result.
- invocable<F,T...>(): We can call F with a set of arguments of the N specified types T1, T2, ...
- totally_ordered<T>(): We can compare two Ts with ==, !=, <, <=, >, and >= to get a Boolean result representing a total order.
- totally_ordered_with<T,U>(): We can compare a T and a U with ==, !=, <, <=, >, and >=, to get a Boolean result representing a total order.
- binary_operation<B,T,U>(): We can use B to do an operation on two Ts.
- binary_operation<B,T,U>(): We can use B to do an operation on a T and a U.
- derived_from<D,B>(): D is publicly derived from B.
- convertible_to<F,T>(): An F can be converted to a T.
- integral<T>(): A T is an integral type (like int).
- floating_point<T>(): A T is a floating point type (like double).
- copyable<T>(): A T can be copied.
- moveable<T>(): A T can be moved.
- semiregular<T>(): A T can be copied, moved, and swapped.
- regular<T>(): T is semiregular and equality_comparable.
- sortable<I>(): I is a random_access_iterator with value_type elements that can be compared using <.
- sortable<I,C>(): I is a random_access_iterator with value_type elements that can be compared using C.

There are many more to serve a variety of needs. In addition, we define a few that we need here:

- Element<E>(): E can be an element in a container. Roughly, that means that E is semiregular. Individual operations on a vector<E> can impose stricter requirements.
- Boolean<T>: T can be used as a Boolean (like bool).
- Number<N>(): N behaves like a number, supporting +, −, *, and /.
- Allocator<A>(): A can be used to acquire and release memory (like the free store).

For standard-library containers and algorithms, these concepts (and many more) are specified in excruciating detail. Here, especially in Chapter 19 to Chapter 21, we use them to specify our containers and algorithms.

The type of the elements of a container or iterator type, T, is called its *Value type* and is often defined as a member type T::value_type; see vector and list (§19.3).

18.1.4 Containers and inheritance

There is one kind of combination of object-oriented programming and generic programming that people always try, but it doesn't work: attempting to use a container of objects of a derived class as a container of objects of a base class. For example:

```
vector<Shape> vs;
vector<Circle> vc;
vs = vc;                    // error: vector<Shape> required
void f(vector<Shape>&);
f(vc);                      // error: vector<Shape> required
```

But why not? After all, you say, I can convert a **Circle** to a **Shape**! Actually, no, you can't (§12.4.1). You can convert a **Circle*** to a **Shape*** and a **Circle&** to a **Shape&**, but we deliberately disabled assignment of **Shapes**, so that you wouldn't have to wonder what would happen if you put a **Circle** with a radius into a **Shape** variable that doesn't have a radius (§12.3.1). What would have happened – had we allowed it – would have been what is called *slicing*; that is, only the **Shape** part of the **Circle** would have been copied and the result would have been an incomplete **Shape** that would have caused run-time errors if used. It is the class object equivalent of integer truncation (§2.9).

So we try again using pointers:

```
vector<Shape*> vps;
vector<Circle*> vpc;
vps = vpc;                          // error: vector<Shape*> required
void f(vector<Shape*>&);
f(vpc);                             // error: vector<Shape*> required
```

Again, the type system resists. Why? Consider what **f()** might do:

```
void f(vector<Shape*>& v)
{
        Shape s = new Rectangle{Point{0,0},Point{100,100}}
        v.push_back(s);             // put a Rectangle* into a vector<Shape*>
}
```

Obviously, we can put a **Rectangle*** into a **vector<Shape*>**, but not into a **Circle***. After all, the **Rectangle*** doesn't point to a **Circle**. However, had the type system allowed **f(vpc)** that would have been exactly what it did. Inheritance is a powerful and subtle mechanism and templates do not implicitly extend its reach. There are ways of using templates to express inheritance, but they are beyond the scope of this book. Just remember that "**D** is a **B**" does not imply "**C<D>** is a **C<B>**" for an arbitrary template **C** – and we should value that as a protection against accidental type violations. See also PPP2.§25.4.4.

18.1.5 Value template parameters

Obviously, it is useful to parameterize classes with types. How about parameterizing classes with "other things," such as integer values and string values? Basically, any kind of argument can be useful, but a detailed description of *value template parameters* is beyond the scope of this book, so we will show just one example. Consider a buffer type:

```
template<typename T, int sz>
class Buffer {
pblic:
        using value_type = T;
        const int size() { return sz; }
        // ... useful operations ...
private:
        T elem[sz];
};
```

We can use this to place fixed-sized buffers where they are needed. For example:

```
Buffer <int,1024> global;

void use()
{
      Buffer<Message,12> local;
      // ...
}
```

A type like **Buffer** is useful when we don't want to use the free store.

18.2 Generalizing Vector

When we generalized **Vector** from a class "**Vector** of **double**" to a template "**Vector** of **T**," we didn't review the definitions of **push_back()**, **resize()**, and **reserve()**. We must do that now because as they are defined in §17.8.2, §17.8.3, and §17.8.4 they make assumptions that are true for **doubles**, but not true for all types that we'd like to use as **Vector** element types, such as **strings** and **Dates**:

- How do we handle a **Vector<X>** where **X** doesn't have a default value?
- How do we cope with element types that have copy operators that may throw exceptions?
- How do we ensure that elements are destroyed when we are finished with them?

AA Must we solve those problems? We could say, "Don't try to make **Vectors** of types without default values" and "Don't use **Vectors** for types with destructors in ways that cause problems." For a facility that is aimed at "general use," such restrictions are annoying to users and give the impression that the designer hasn't thought the problem through or doesn't really care about users. Often, such suspicions are correct, but the designers of the standard library didn't leave these warts in place. To mirror the standard-library **vector**, we must solve these problems.

We can handle types without a default by giving the user the option to specify the value to be used when we need a "default value":

```
template<Element T>
void Vector<T>::resize(int newsize, T def = T{});
```

That is, use **T{}** as the default value unless the user says otherwise. For example:

```
Vector<double> v1;
v1.resize(100);            // add 100 copies of double{}, that is, 0.0
v1.resize(200, 0.0);       // add 100 copies of 0.0 – mentioning 0.0 is redundant
v1.resize(300, 1.0);       // add 100 copies of 1.0

class No_default {
      No_default(int);              // the only constructor
      // ...
};

Vector<No_default> v2(10);          // error: tries to make 10 No_default()s
Vector<No_default> v3;              // OK: makes no elements
```

```
v3.resize(100, No_default{2});        // add 100 copies of No_default(2)
v3.resize(200);                       // error: tries to add 100 No_default()s
```

The destructor problem is harder to address. Basically, we need to deal with something really awkward: a data structure consisting of some initialized data and some uninitialized data in the presence of destructors and exceptions. So far, we have gone out of our way to avoid uninitialized data and the programming errors that usually accompany it. Now – as implementers of **Vector** – we have to face that problem so that we – as users of **Vector** – don't have to in our applications.

18.2.1 Allocators

First, we need to find a way to get construction and destructions done correctly when manipulating uninitialized storage. Fortunately, the standard library provides a class **allocator**, which provides uninitialized memory. A slightly simplified version looks like this:

```
template<typename T>
class allocator {
public:
        // ...
        T* allocate(int n);                   // allocate space for n objects of type T
        void deallocate(T* p, int n);         // deallocate n objects of type T starting at p
};
```

Unsurprisingly, an **allocator** is exactly what we need for implementing **Vector<T>::reserve()**. We start by giving **Vector** an allocator parameter:

```
template<Element T, typename A = allocator<T>>
class Vector {
        A alloc;          // use allocate to handle memory for elements
        // ...
};
```

The standard-library allocator model is based on a type **pmr** (*polymorphic memory resource*) that is a generalization of our **allocator**. Look it up if you feel the need to use something more advanced than the default allocator used by operator **new**.

Except for providing an **allocator** – and using the standard one by default instead of using **new** – all is as before. As users of **Vector**, we can ignore allocators until we find ourselves needing a **Vector** that manages memory for its elements in some unusual way. As implementers of **Vector** and as students trying to understand fundamental problems and learn fundamental techniques, we must see how a **Vector** can deal with uninitialized memory and present properly constructed objects to its users. The only code affected is **Vector** member functions that directly deal with memory, such as **Vector<T>::reserve()**:

```
template<Element T, Allocator A>
void Vector<T,A>::reserve(int newalloc)
{
        if (newalloc<=space)                  // never decrease allocation
                return;
```

```
        T* p = alloc.allocate(newalloc);            // allocate new space
        uninitialized_move(elem,&elem[sz],p);       // move elements into uninitialized space
        destroy(elem,space);                        // destroy old elements
        alloc.deallocate(elem,capacity());          // deallocate old space
        elem = p;
        space = newalloc;
}
```

We move an element to the new space by constructing a copy in uninitialized space and then destroying the original. We can't use assignment because for types such as **string**, assignment assumes that the target area has been initialized. We use the standard-library function **uninitialized_move()** to move the elements into the newly allocated space; **uninitialized_move(b,e,p)** moves from the range [**b**:**e**) into the range [**p**:**p+(e−b)**). We use the standard-library function **destroy()** to call the destructors for the old copies; **destroy(b,e)** invokes the destructors for elements in the range [**b**:**e**). In Chapter 21, we show many more algorithms operating on half-open ranges, such as [**b**:**e**).

Given **reserve()**, **Vector<T,A>::push_back()** is simple:

```
template<Element T, Allocator A>
void Vector<T,A>::push_back(const T& val)
{
        reserve((space==0) ? 8 : 2*space);          // get more space
        construct_at(&elem[sz],val);                // add val at end
        ++sz;                                       // increase the size
}
```

This uses the standard-library function **construct_at()** to construct the new element in its correct position in the uninitialized space.

Similarly, **Vector<T,A>::resize()** is not too difficult:

```
template<Element T, Allocator A>
void Vector<T,A>::resize(int newsize, T val = T())
{
        reserve(newsize);
        if (sz<newsize)
                uninitialized_fill(&elem[sz],&elem[newsize],val);   // initialize added elements to val
        if (newsize<sz)
                destroy(&elem[newsize],&elem[sz]);                  // destroy surplus original elements
        sz = newsize;
}
```

Note that because some types do not have a default constructor, we again provide the option to supply a value to be used as an initial value for new elements. The **uninitialized_fill()** is a cousin of **uninitialized_move()** that repeatedly assigns a single value, rather than moving from a sequence of elements.

CC The other new thing here is the destruction of "surplus elements" in the case where we are resizing to a smaller **Vector**. Think of the destructor as turning a typed object back into "raw memory." Conversely, a constructor turns "raw memory" into a typed object.

XX "Messing with allocators" is pretty advanced stuff, and tricky. Leave it alone until you are ready to become an expert.

18.3 Range checking and exceptions

We look at our **Vector** so far and find (with horror?) that access isn't range checked. The implementation of **operator[]** is simply

```
template<Element T,Allocator A>
T& Vector<T,A>::operator[](int n)
{
	return elem[n];
}
```

So, consider:

```
Vector<int> v(100);
v[-200] = v[200];			// oops!
for (int i; cin>>i; )
	v[i] = 999;			// maul an arbitrary memory location
```

This code compiles and runs, accessing memory not owned by our **Vector**. This could mean big trouble! In a real program, such code is unacceptable. Let's try to improve our **Vector** to deal with this problem. The simplest approach would be to add a checked access operation, called **at()**:

```
struct out_of_range { /* ... */ };		// class used to report range access errors

template<Element T, Allocator A = allocator<T>>
class Vector {
	// ...
	T& at(int n);				// checked access
	const T& at(int n) const;		// checked access

	T& operator[](int n);			// unchecked access
	const T& operator[](int n) const;	// unchecked access
	// ...
};

template<Element T, Allocator A>
T& Vector<T,A>::at(int n)
{
	if (n<0 || sz<=n)
		throw out_of_range();
	return elem[n];
}

template<Element T, Allocator A>
T& Vector<T,A>::operator[](int n)		// as before
{
	return elem[n];
}
```

Given that, we could write

```
void print_some(Vector<int>& v)
{
	int i = -1;
	while(cin>>i && i!=-1)
		try {
			cout << "v[" << i << "]==" << v.at(i) << "\n";
		}
		catch(out_of_range) {
			cout << "bad index: " << i << "\n";
		}
}
```

Here, we use at() to get range-checked access, and we catch out_of_range in case of an illegal access.

The general idea is to use subscripting with [ ] when we know that we have a valid index and at() when we might have an out-of-range index.

Obviously, these range checks make sense only if the size() of a Vector is reasonable. What about Vector(-100)? That doesn't make sense and we "forgot" to check the size argument to the constructor. However, our constructor used new T[s] and new tests its size argument, and -100 would make it throw a bad_array_new_length exception. The standard-library vector has its own opinion about what's reasonable and would throw a length_error. We can do the same for Vector:

```
int reasonable_size = std::numeric_limit<int>::max;     // largest int (possibly 2'147'483'647).

template<Element T>
explicit Vector(int s) :sz{s}, elem{new T[s]}, space{s}
{
	if (!0<s && s<reasonable_size))
		throw std::length_error{"size too large for Vector"};
	for (int i=0; i<sz; ++i)
		elem[i]=T{};                  // elements are initialized
}
```

18.3.1 An aside: design considerations

CC So far, so good, but why didn't we just add the range check to operator[]()? Well, std::vector provides checked at() and potentially unchecked operator[]() as shown here. Let's try to explain how that makes some sense. There are basically four arguments:

[1] *Compatibility*: People have been using unchecked subscripting since long before C++ had exceptions.

[2] *Efficiency*: You can build a checked-access operator on top of an optimally fast unchecked-access operator, but you cannot build an optimally fast access operator on top of a checked-access operator.

[3] *Constraints*: In some environments, exceptions are unacceptable.

[4] *Optional checking*: The standard doesn't actually say that you can't range check vector, so if you want checking, use an implementation that checks, such as the one from PPP_support but preferably one supported by your standard-library provider.

18.3.1.1 Compatibility

People really, really don't like to have their old code break. For example, if you have a million lines of code, it could be a very costly affair to rework it all to use exceptions correctly. We can argue that the code would be better for the extra work, but then we are not the ones who have to pay (in time or money). Furthermore, maintainers of existing code usually argue that unchecked code may be unsafe in principle, but their particular code has been tested and used for years and all the bugs have already been found. We are skeptical about that argument, but again nobody who hasn't had to make such decisions about real code should not be too judgmental. Naturally, there was no code using the standard-library **vector** before it was introduced into the C++ standard, but there were many millions of lines of code that used very similar **vector**s that (being pre-standard) didn't use exceptions. Much of that code was later modified to use the standard.

18.3.1.2 Efficiency

Yes, range checking can be a burden in extreme cases, such as buffers for network interfaces and matrices in high-performance scientific computations. However, the cost of range checking is rarely a concern in the kind of "ordinary computing" that most of us spend most of our time on. Thus, we recommend and use a range-checked implementation of **vector** whenever we can. In general, it is a mistake to try to optimize every detail of a program. That leads to brittle code and distracts from optimizing the program as a whole. **AA**

18.3.1.3 Constraints

The arguments against using exceptions hold for some programmers and some applications. In fact, it holds for a whole lot of programmers and shouldn't be lightly ignored. However, if you are starting a new program in an environment that doesn't involve hard real time (PPP2.Ch25.2.1), prefer exception-based error handling and range-checked **vector**s.

18.3.1.4 Optional checking

The ISO C++ standard simply states that out-of-range **vector** access is not guaranteed to have any specific semantics, and that such access should be avoided. It is perfectly standards-conforming to throw an exception when a program tries an out-of-range access. So, if you like **vector** to throw and don't need to be concerned by the first three reasons for a particular application, use a range-checked implementation of **vector**. That's what we are doing for this book. The long and the short of this is that real-world design can be messier than we would prefer, but there are ways of coping. **AA**

18.3.2 Module PPP_support

Like our **Vector**, most implementations of **std::vector** don't guarantee to range check the subscript operator (**[ ]**) but provide **at()** that checks. So where did those **std::out_of_range** exceptions in our programs come from? Basically, we chose "option 4" from §18.3.1: a **vector** implementation is not obliged to range check **[ ]**, but it is not prohibited from doing so either, so we arranged for checking to be done. What you might have been using is our version from **PPP_support**. It cuts down on errors and debug time at little cost to performance.

Module **PPP_support** has the following outline:

```
export module PPP_support;

export import std;

export namespace PPP {
	using namespace std;                       // make all of std available

	// except for what we want to provide ourselves for PPP:

	template <Element T>
	class Checked_vector : std::vector<T> { /* ... */ };  // range-checked vector

	class Checked_string : std::string { /* ... */ };       // range-checked string

	template<Element T>
	class Checked_span : std::span { /* ... */ };              // range-checked span

	// added features:

	// ...

} // namespace PPP
```

This demonstrates the power of modules, namespaces, and inheritance.

PPP_support::Checked_vector is defined like this:

```
namespace PPP {
	template<Element T>                        // constrain element types
	struct Checked_vector : public std::vector<T> {
		using size_type = typename std::vector<T>::size_type;
		using value_type = T;
		using vector<T>::vector;               // use vector<T>'s constructors

		T& operator[](size_type i)             // rather than return at(i);
		{
			return std::vector<T>::at(i);
		}

		const T& operator[](size_type i) const
		{
			return std::vector<T>::at(i);
		}
	}; // Checked_vector
} // namespace PPP
```

Deriving from **std::vector** gives us all of **vector**'s member functions for **PPP_support::Checked_vector**. The first **using** introduces a convenient synonym for **std::vector**'s **size_type**. The second **using** gives a name to the element type. The third **using** gives us all of **std::vector**'s constructors for **PPP_support::Checked_vector**.

This **PPP_support::Checked_vector** has been useful in debugging nontrivial programs. The alternative is to use a systematically checked implementation of the complete standard-library **vector**. Unfortunately, there is no standard, portable, complete, and clean way of getting range checking from an implementation of **std::vector**'s **[ ]**. All major implementations of the standard library have one, but at the time of writing there is no standard way of installing them. We find module **PPP_support** a significant help, especially when we use a C++ Core Guidelines rules checker to keep us out of nasty "dark corners" of the language. In general, avoid data structures that don't have sufficient information to do range checks. **AA**

18.4 Resources and exceptions

So, **vector** can throw exceptions, and we recommend that when a function cannot perform its required action, it throws an exception to tell that to its callers (Chapter 4). Now is the time to consider what to do when we write code that must deal with exceptions thrown by **vector** operations and other functions that we call. The naive answer – "Use a **try**-block to catch the exception, write an error message, and then terminate the program" – is too crude for many systems. For example, many embedded systems cannot just stop and a financial system cannot just abort in the middle of a transaction. Often, we need to do a bit of clean-up before terminating or to re-start the system in a known good state. For some kinds of errors, we know enough about the state of the program to be able to recover. For example, failing to compute an answer, we might try again using a different algorithm or a different set of resources. For some kinds of errors, we might even decide not to recover but to produce an answer that's not the desired one but considered harmless. For example, failing to correctly display an image, we might decide to display an image signifying "we couldn't produce the image you asked for."

One of the fundamental principles of programming is that if we acquire a resource, we must – somehow, directly or indirectly – return it to whatever part of the system manages that resource. Examples of resources are **CC**

- Memory
- Locks
- File handles
- Thread handles
- Sockets
- Windows

Basically, we define a resource as something that is acquired and must be given back (released) or reclaimed by some "resource manager." The simplest example is free-store memory that we acquire using **new** and return to the free store using **delete**. For example: **CC**

```
void suspicious(int s, int x)
{
        int* p = new int[s];          // acquire memory
        // ...
        delete[] p;                   // release memory
}
```

As we saw in §15.4.5, it's not always easy to remember to release memory. When we add exceptions to the picture, resource leaks can become common; all it takes is ignorance or some lack of care. In particular, we view code, such as **suspicious()**, that explicitly uses **new** and assigns the resulting pointer to a local variable with great suspicion. To write reliable software, we must make the release of resources, such as memory, implicit. Doing so also makes writing the code easier.

CC We call an object, such as a **vector**, that is responsible for releasing a resource the *owner* or a *handle* of the resource for which it is responsible.

18.4.1 Potential resource-management problems

XX One reason for suspicion of apparently innocuous pointer assignments such as

```
int* p = new int[s];          // acquire memory
```

is that it can be hard to verify that the **new** has a corresponding **delete**. At least **suspicious()** has a **delete[] p;** statement that might release the memory, but let's imagine a few things that might cause that release not to happen. What could we put in the ... part of **suspicious()** to cause a memory leak? The problematic examples we find should give you cause for thought and make you suspicious of such code. They should also make you appreciate the simple and powerful alternative to such code.

Consider:

```
void suspicious(int s, int x)
{
        int* p = new int[s];                // acquire memory
        // ...
        if (x<0)
                p = q;                      // make p point to another object
        if (x==0)
                return;                     // we may return
        if (0<x)
                p[x] = v.at(x);             // subscripting may throw
        // ...
        delete[] p;                         // release memory
}
```

This code will never delete **p**; it leaks memory. The reason for that varies depending on the value of **x**. Obviously, we'd never deliberately write such messy code, but the three ways of messing up illustrated do turn up in real-world code where functions are longer and the control structures more complicated. Often, the problem wasn't in the original code, but was inserted by mistake years later by someone maintaining the code.

When people first encounter the exception throw version of this problem, they tend to consider it a problem with exceptions rather than a general resource-management problem. Having misclassified the root cause, they come up with a solution that involves catching the exception:

```
void suspicious(int s, int x)               // messy code
{
        int* p = new int[s];            // acquire memory
        vector<int> v;
        // ...
```

```
        try {
            if (x)
                p[x] = v.at(x);     // subscripting may throw
            // ...
        }
        catch (...) {               // catch every exception
            delete[] p;             // release memory
            throw;                  // re-throw the exception
        }
        // ...
        delete[] p;                 // release memory
    }
```

This solves the problem at the cost of some added code. In other words, this solution is ugly; worse, it doesn't generalize well. Consider acquiring more resources:

```
    void suspicious(int s)
    {
        int* p = new T[s];
        // ...
        int* q = new T[s];
        // ...
        delete[] p;
        // ...
        delete[] q;
    }
```

The **try-catch** technique works for this example also, but we will need several **try**-blocks, and the code is repetitive and ugly. We don't like repetitive and ugly code because "repetitive" translates into code that is a maintenance hazard, and "ugly" translates into code that is hard to get right, hard to read, and a maintenance hazard. In particular, if we try to handle resource leaks with **try-catch**, we have to remember to use **try-catch** consistently. That's not a good idea. Experience shows that we sometimes forget. It is easy to forget to release a resource; just ask any librarian! Release must be implicit and guaranteed. XX

Having a lot of **try**-blocks is a sign of poor design and an indicator of likely problems with error handling. We must – and can – do better.

> TRY THIS
>
> Add **try**-blocks to this last example to ensure that all resources are properly released in all cases where an exception might be thrown.

We use the **new/delete** example just because it's easy to understand and experiment with. However, most examples of resource leaks are less easy to spot. Consider an old-style example that can still be found in many programs:

```
void old_style()
{
        FILE* output = fopen("myfile","r");           // acquire
        fprintf(output,"Hello, old world!\n");        // print to file
        // ...
        fclose(output);
}
```

Here use the (C and C++) standard-library functions **fopen()** and **fclose()** to open and close a file. Again, it is easy for code in the ... part to exit the function without closing the file. If so, the output buffer may never be flushed, leaving us without a hint of why no output was produced.

18.4.2 Resource acquisition is initialization

Fortunately, we don't need to plaster our code with complicated **try ... catch** statements to deal with potential resource leaks. Consider a combination of **suspicious()** and **old_style()**:

```
void user(int s)
{
        vector<T> p(s);
        vector<T> q(s);
        ifstream in {"myfile"};
        // ...
}
```

CC This is better. More importantly, it is *obviously* better. The resources (here, free-store memory and a file handle) are acquired by constructors and released by the matching destructors. We actually solved this particular "exception problem" when we solved the memory leak problems for vectors. The solution is general; it applies to all kinds of resources: acquire a resource in the constructor for some object that manages it and releases it again in the matching destructor. Examples of resources that are usually best dealt with in this way include character strings, database transactions, locks, sockets, and I/O buffers (**iostreams** do it for you). This technique is usually referred to by the awkward phrase "Resource Acquisition Is Initialization," abbreviated to RAII.

Consider the example above. Whichever way we leave **user()**, the destructors for **p**, **q**, and **in** are invoked appropriately. This general rule holds: when the thread of execution leaves a scope, the destructors for every fully constructed object and sub-object are invoked. An object is considered constructed when its constructor completes. Exploring the detailed implications of those two statements might cause a headache, but they simply mean that constructors and destructors are invoked as needed.

AA In particular, use **vector** rather than explicit **new** and **delete** when you need a nonconstant amount of storage within a scope.

Finally, consider an artificial example concocted to test error handling:

```
void test()
{
        string name;
        cin>>name;
```

```
        ifstream in {name};                                // §9.3
        if (!in)
              error("couldn't open ",name);

        vector<string> v {"hello"};
        for (string s; in>>s; )
              v.push_back(s);
        v[3] += "odd";

        Simple_window win;                                 // Chapter 10
        auto ps = make_unique<Shape>(read_shape(cin));    // §18.5.2, §12.2
        Smiley_face face {Point{0,0},20};
        win.attach(face);
        // ...
}
```

Real-world code can be far more complex than that:

- Imagine what it would take to re-write this **test()** with types that did not have destructor.
- Imagine what it would take to re-write this **test()** and catch and correctly report all possible errors without using exceptions.

Note that we didn't rely on exceptions when opening the file. We could have done so, but there is nothing exceptional about not being able to open a file, so we dealt with that possibility locally.

18.4.3 Resource-management guarantees

When we leave a function – or just a scope – what kinds of guarantees can we offer to make resource management comprehensible? To be able to think rationally about such problems, consider these basic concepts: **CC**

- *The basic guarantee*: A function either succeeds or throws an exception without having leaked any resources. All code that is part of a program that we expect to recover from an exception **throw** (or any other form of error affecting resources) should provide the basic guarantee. All standard-library code provides the basic guarantee.
- *The strong guarantee*: A function provides the basic guarantee and also ensures that all observable values (all values not local to the function) are the same after failure as they were when we called the function. The strong guarantee is the ideal when we write a function: either the function succeeded at doing everything it was asked to do or else nothing happened except that an exception was thrown to indicate failure.
- *The no-throw guarantee*: Unless we could do simple operations without any risk of failing or throwing an exception, we would not be able to write code to meet the basic guarantee or the strong guarantee. Fortunately, essentially all built-in facilities in the C++ language provide the no-throw guarantee: they simply can't throw. To avoid throwing, simply avoid **throw** itself, **new**, and **dynamic_cast** of reference types. The main danger is a simple return that leaves a required resource unreleased.

The basic guarantee and the strong guarantee are most useful for thinking about correctness of programs. RAII is essential for implementing code written according to those ideals simply and with high performance.

18.4.4 RAII for Vector

As an example of resource management, let's look at how we can provide guarantees for Vector assignment. As we saw in §17.8, the key to memory management and element initialization for Vector is the reserve() operation, so we must start there. That reserve() was written without thought about exceptions. However, the call to allocate more memory may fail (throwing an exception) and so might the move of the elements into the newly allocated space. Ouch! We could try adding a try-block, but in that direction lies complexity (§18.4.1). A better solution is to step back and realize that "memory for a Vector" is a resource; that is, we can define a class Vector_rep to represent the fundamental concept we have been using all the time, the picture with the three elements defining a Vector's memory use:

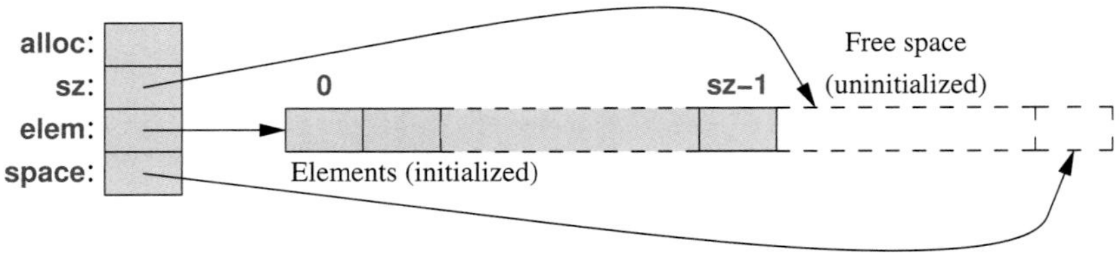

In code, that is (after adding the allocator for completeness):

```
template<typename T, typename A = allocator<T>>
struct Vector_rep {
      A alloc;              // allocator
      int sz;               // number of elements
      T* elem;              // start of allocation
      int space;            // amount of allocated space

      Vector_rep(const A& a, int n)
            : alloc{ a }, sz{ n }, elem{ alloc.allocate(n) }, space{ n } { }
      ~Vector_rep() { alloc.deallocate(elem, space); }
};
```

That Vector_rep deals with memory rather than (typed) objects. Our Vector implementation can use that to hold objects of the desired element type. Basically, Vector (dealing with typed elements) is simply a convenient interface to Vector_rep (dealing with "raw" memory):

```
template<typename T, typename A = allocator<T>>
class Vector {
      Vector_rep<T,A> r;
public:
      Vector() : r{A{},0} { }
```

```
        explicit Vector(int s) :r{A{},s}
        {
                for (int i = 0; i < r.sz; ++i)
                        r.elem[i] = 0;          // elements are initialized
        }
        // ...
}
```

We must revise all member functions to use the Vector_rep. In particular, we can rewrite reserve() from §18.2.1 to something simpler and more correct:

```
template<typename T, typename A>
void Vector<T, A>::reserve(int newalloc)
{
        if (newalloc <= r.space)                                // never decrease allocation
                return;
        Vector_rep<T, A> b{ r.alloc,newalloc };                 // allocate new space
        uninitialized_move(r.elem, r.elem+r.sz, b.elem);        // move
        destroy(r.elem, r.elem + r.sz);                         // destroy the old elements
        swap(r, b);                                             // swap representations
}
```

We use the standard-library functions uninitialized_move() and destroy() to do most of the work.

When we exit reserve(), the old allocation is automatically freed by Vector_rep's destructor if the copy operation succeeded. If instead that exit is caused by a move operation throwing an exception, the new allocation is freed. The swap() function is a standard-library algorithm that exchanges the value of two objects.

Wait! "A move operation throwing an exception!" Is that possible? Is that allowed? Move operations are simple and have no reason to throw. They don't acquire new resources. Make sure that that no move you write ever throws. That's not hard. However, it turns out that there are quite a few types from before the introduction of move operations for which the move is synthesized by copying into the target followed by destructing the source. **AA**

So how does uninitialized_move() cope with throwing move operations? To offer the basic guarantee, it mustn't leak any resource. In my experience, throwing move operations are very rare, but uninitialized_move() must still handle the cases like the one where three objects are successfully moved and then the fourth move throws. It does so by keeping track of which objects have been constructed and then destroying those (and only those) before re-throwing the exception to signal that the uninitialized_move() failed. Yes, writing serious foundational software is challenging, but also important and at times exciting!

With reserve() coping with exceptions, push_back() and resize() work as written in §18.2.1, so we can look at assignments again:

```
template<typename T, typename A>
Vector<T>& Vector::operator=(const Vector<T>& arg)
{
        auto tmp = arg;                 // copy all elements
        swap(*this,arg);                // then swap (Vector handles): strong guarantee
        return *this;
}
```

We first copy and then swap. That means that for **v1=v2**, **v1** gets **v2**'s elements and the old elements from **v1** (now in **tmp**) are destroyed upon exit from **operator=()**. We never get to the **swap**, if the copy throws. So an exception thrown from the copy operation will have no effect on either **v1** or **v2**. That is, our **operator=()** offers the strong guarantee.

Vector's **swap()** just moves the pointers in the **Vector** objects (§7.4.5), so it provides the no-throw guarantee. If it wasn't for pointers and moves, we wouldn't be able to provide any useful guarantees.

We can even write that **operator=()** even simpler:

```
template<typename T, typename A>
Vector<T>& Vector::operator=(const Vector<T> arg)
{
	swap(*this,arg);		// then swap (Vector handles): strong guarantee
	return *this;
}
```

The pass-by value (§7.4.3) makes the copy for us.

But what about the optimized version of **Vector::operator=()** that copies elements straight into its target if there is sufficient room (§17.8.5):

```
template<typename T, typename A>
Vector<T>& Vector::operator=(const Vector<T>& arg)
{
	if (arg.size()<=size()) {					// enough space; copy directly
		move(arg.r.elem,arg.r.elem+arg.size(),r.elem);
		destroy(r.elem+arg.size(),r.elem+size());	// destroy surplus elements
	}

	auto tmp = arg;		// copy all elements
	swap(*this,arg);		// then swap (Vector handles): strong guarantee
	return *this;
}
```

We move, so we can only offer the basic guarantee: elements may have been overwritten before an exception was thrown. Also this optimized **operator=()** is twice the size of the elegant, "pure **swap()**" version. Is the optimization worth the effort and the loss of the strong guarantee? In the case of **vector**, the answer is yes: the difference in performance can be very significant and there are many important performance-sensitive applications where **vectors** of the same or smaller size are assigned from. For example, think of matrix computations where matrix elements are stored in **vectors**. So, **std::vector**'s **=** is optimized. If you need the strong guarantee, you can easily write a function to give that:

```
template<typename T>
strong_assign(Vector<T>& target, const Vector<T> arg)
{
	swap(target,arg);		// then swap (vector handles): strong guarantee
}
```

Don't optimize without reason, without being reasonably sure that an optimization is worthwhile in important code.

18.5 Resource-management pointers

There are many common uses of pointers, such as:

- Returning large objects from functions
- Passing interfaces to polynomic objects as arguments (OOP)
- Passing the position of elements of a container to an algorithm (Chapter 21)
- Implementing high-level (easy to use, efficient, RAII, etc.) types, such as **vector**

To cope, we need to distinguish different possible uses of pointers.

- Where are pointers necessary? Often we have superior alternatives (§16.4, §18.5.1)
- Where does a pointer just identify an object?
- Where does a pointer identify a sequence of objects? Don't use built-in pointers to identify sequences of elements; they don't know how many elements they point to (§16.1). Use a container (Chapter 19) or a **span** (§16.4.1) instead.
- Where does a pointer represent ownership (i.e. needs to be deleted)? (§18.5.2, §18.5.3)

Here, we will consider the first and the last of these cases.

18.5.1 Return by moving

The technique of returning a lot of information by placing it on the free store and returning a pointer to it is very common. It is also a source of a lot of complexity and one of the major sources of memory management errors: Who **delete**s a pointer to the free store returned from a function? Are we sure that a pointer to an object on the free store is properly **delete**d in case of an exception? Unless we are systematic about the management of pointers the answer will be something like "Well, we think so," and that's not good enough:

```
Vector<int>* make_vec()     // make a filled vector
{
        auto res = new Vector<int> res;
        // ... fill the Vector with data; this may throw an exception ...
        return res;      // return a pointer
}

auto p = make_vec();
// ...
delete p;
```

Someone, some day, will forget to **delete** some result returned by this **make_vec()**.

Fortunately, when we added move operations to **Vector**, we solved that problem for **Vector**s: just use a move constructor to get the ownership of the elements out of the function. For example:

```
Vector<int> make_vec()     // make a filled Vector
{
        Vector<int> res;
        // ... fill the vector with data; this may throw an exception ...
        return res;      // the move constructor efficiently transfers ownership
}

auto v = make_vec();
```

This version of make_vec() is far simpler and the one we recommend. The move solution generalizes to all containers and further still to all resource handles. For example, fstream uses this technique to keep track of file handles (we can move an fstream but not copy it). The move solution is simple and general. Using resource handles simplifies code and eliminates a major source of errors. Compared to the direct use of pointers, the run-time overhead of using such handles is nothing, or very minor and predictable.

18.5.2 unique_ptr

The technique of returning an object is ideal in many cases, but what if we really need a pointer? Consider:

```
Shape* read_shape(istream& is)
{
    // ... read a variety of shapes ...
}
```

This is OK if "someone" keeps track of the returned pointer and deletes the object pointed to when it is no longer needed. However, that's not common. We need to indicate that the returned pointer represents ownership; that is, it must be deleted. Here is a way:

```
unique_ptr<Shape> read_shape(istream& is)        // pseudo code
{
    // ... read a variety of shapes ...
    // ... if we read a Circle ...
        return make_unique<Circle>(center,radius);
}
```

A unique_ptr is an object that holds a pointer and represents ownership of what that pointer points to. We create one using std::make_unique(). Because unique_ptr is a kind of pointer, inheritance works correctly: we can return a unique_ptr<Circle> as a unique_ptr<Shape> and our OOP techniques are still useful.

You can use -> and * on a unique_ptr exactly like a built-in pointer. However, the unique_ptr owns the object pointed to: when the unique_ptr is destroyed, it deletes the object it points to.

A unique_ptr is very much like an ordinary pointer, but it has one significant restriction: you cannot assign one unique_ptr to another to get two unique_ptrs to the same object. That has to be so, or confusion could arise about which unique_ptr owned the pointed-to object and had to delete it. For example:

```
void no_good()
{
    unique_ptr<X> p = make_unique<X>();
    unique_ptr<X> q = p;                // error: fortunately
    // ...
} // here p and q both delete the X
```

If you want to have a "smart" pointer that both guarantees deletion and can be copied, use a shared_ptr (§18.5.3). However, that is a more heavyweight solution that involves a use count to ensure that the last copy destroyed destroys the object referred to.

In contrast, unique_ptr has no overhead compared to an ordinary pointer.

In addition to being used as a way of transferring ownership, a unique_ptr can be used to guarantee deletion in case of an exception being thrown:

```
void trouble(int n)
{
      int* naked = new int[n];
      auto covered = make_unique<int[]>(n);
      // ... a return or a throw somewhere here ...
      delete[] naked;
}
```

The make_unique protects against the likely leak but the "naked new" does not.

Finally, a unique_ptr can be used instead of a "naked" pointer to represent ownership. Consider §15.5. There, we use a destructor to handle the deletion of the elements and the memory holding them. With a unique_ptr we can make that implicit and thus eliminate the possibility of getting the destructor wrong: CC

```
template<Elem T>
class Vector {
public:
      Vector(int s) :sz{s}, elem{std::make_unique<T[]>(s)} { }      // construct a Vector
      T& operator[](int i) { return elem[i]; }                      // element access: subscripting
      int size() { return sz; }
      // ...
private:
      int sz;                        // the number of elements
      std::unique_ptr<T[]> elem;     // pointer to the elements
      int alloc;
};
```

The generated destructor for Vector (§15.5.1) will call elem's destructor.

Why didn't we use that simplification from the very beginning? We wanted to show how resource-management classes were constructed, and (of course?) unique_ptr is constructed with exactly the same techniques and basic language features as we showed for Vector.

18.5.3 Shared_ptr

What if you need many pointers to an object and it is not clear which pointer should be deleted? We can try to avoid this by having an object allocated in such a way that it "outlives" all pointers to it. That's often ideal and can be achieved by having the object in an outer scope to all pointers to it. However, there are significant uses where that's hard to achieve simply and reliably. In that case, we can use the standard-library shared_ptr. It is used much like unique_ptr:

```
shared_ptr<Shape> read_shape(istream& is)      // pseudo code
{
      // ... read a variety of shapes ...
      // ... if we read a Circle ...
            return make_shared<Circle>(center,radius);
}
```

However, **shared_ptr** differs from **unique_ptr** by allowing many copies. It keeps a use count, that is a count of **shared_ptr**s to a given object and when that use count goes to zero, the **shared_ptr**'s destructor deletes the object pointed to. That's sometimes colloquially referred to as "last person out switch off the lights."

Please note that **shared_ptr** is still a pointer: you need to use * or **->** to access its object and you can create circular references:

```
struct Slink {
      string name;
      shared_ptr<Slink> next;
};

auto p = make_shared<Slink>("Friday",nullptr);
auto q =make_shared<Slink>("viernes",p);
p->next = q;
```

Those two **Slink**s will live "forever." To break such loops, you need a standard-library **weak_ptr**, but if you can, it is best simply not to create such loops.

Drill

[1] Define **template<typename T> struct S { T val; };**.
[2] Add a constructor, so that you can initialize with a **T**.
[3] Define variables of types **S<int>**, **S<char>**, **S<double>**, **S<string>**, and **S<vector<int>>**; initialize them with values of your choice.
[4] Read those values and print them.
[5] Make **val** private.
[6] Add a member function **access()** that returns a reference to **val**.
[7] Put the definition of **access()** outside the class.
[8] Do 4 again using **access()**.
[9] Add a **S<T>::operator=(const T&)**. Hint: Much simpler than §17.8.5.
[10] Provide **const** and non-**const** versions of **access()**.
[11] Define a function **template<typename T> read_val(T& v)** that reads from **cin** into **v**.
[12] Use **read_val()** to read into each of the variables from exercise 3 except the **S<vector<int>>** variable.
[13] Bonus: Define input and output operators (**>>** and **<<**) for **vector<T>**s. For both input and output use a **{ val, val, val }** format. That will allow **read_val()** to also handle the **S<vector<int>>** variable.

Remember to test after each step.

Review

[1] Why would we want to have different element types for different **vector**s?
[2] What is a template?
[3] What is generic programming?

[4] How does generic programming differ from object-oriented programming?
[5] What is a concept?
[6] What benefits do we get from the use of concepts?
[7] Name four standard-library concepts.
[8] How does **resize()** differ from **reserve()**?
[9] What is a resource? Define and give examples.
[10] What is a resource leak?
[11] List the three resource-management guarantees.
[12] How can the use of a built-in pointer lead to a resource leak? Give examples.
[13] What is RAII? What problem does it address?
[14] What is **unique_ptr** good for?
[15] What is **shared_ptr** good for?

Terms

constraint	owner	specialization	**at()**
push_back()	strong guarantee	basic guarantee	RAII
template	exception	**resize()**	template parameter
guarantees	resource	handle	re-throw
throw;	instantiation	**unique_ptr**	**concept**
range checking	**shared_ptr**	**regular**	**equality_comparable**
sortable	**requires**	**throw;**	

Exercises

For each exercise, create and test (with output) a couple of objects of the defined classes to demonstrate that your design and implementation actually do what you think they do. Where exceptions are involved, this can require careful thought about where errors can occur.

[1] Write a template function **add()** that adds the elements of one **vector<T>** to the elements of another; for example, **add(v1,v2)** should do **v1[i]+=v2[i]** for each element of **v1**.
[2] Write a template function that takes a **vector<T> vt** and a **vector<U> vu** as arguments and returns the sum of all **vt[i]*vu[i]**s.
[3] Write a template class **Pair** that can hold a pair of values of any type. Use this to implement a simple symbol table like the one we used in the calculator (§6.8).
[4] Modify class **Link** from §15.7 to be a template with the type of value as the template argument. Then redo exercise 13 from Chapter 16 with **Link<God>**.
[5] Define a class **Int** having a single member of class **int**. Define constructors, assignment, and operators **+**, **–**, *****, **/** for it. Test it, and improve its design as needed (e.g., define operators **<<** and **>>** for convenient I/O).
[6] Repeat the previous exercise, but with a class **Number<T>** where **T** can be any numeric type. Try adding **%** to **Number** and see what happens when you try to use **%** for **Number<double>** and **Number<int>**.

[7] Try your solution to exercise 2 with some **Numbers**.

[8] Implement an allocator (§18.2) using the most basic standard-library allocation functions **malloc()** and **free()**. Get **Vector** as defined by the end of §18.3 to work for a few simple test cases.

[9] Re-implement **Vector::operator=()** (§17.8.5) using an allocator (§18.2) for memory management.

[10] Implement a simple **unique_ptr** supporting only a constructor, destructor, **->**, *****, and **release()**. Delete the assignment and copy constructors.

[11] Design and implement a **Counted_ptr<T>** that is a type that holds a pointer to an object of type **T** and a pointer to a "use count" (an **int**) shared by all counted pointers to the same object of type **T**. The use count should hold the number of counted pointers pointing to a given **T**. Let the **Counted_ptr**'s constructor allocate a **T** object and a use count on the free store. Let **Counted_ptr**'s constructor take an argument to be used as the initial value of the **T** elements. When the last **Counted_ptr** for a **T** is destroyed, **Counted_ptr**'s destructor should **delete** the **T**. Give the **Counted_ptr** operations that allow us to use it as a pointer. This is an example of a "smart pointer" used to ensure that an object doesn't get destroyed until after its last user has stopped using it. Write a set of test cases for **Counted_ptr** using it as an argument in calls, container elements, etc.

[12] Define a **File_handle** class with a constructor that takes a **string** argument (the file name), opens the file in the constructor and closes it in the destructor.

[13] Write a **Tracer** class where its constructor prints a string and its destructor prints a string. Give the strings as constructor arguments. Use it to see where RAII management objects will do their job (i.e., experiment with **Tracers** as local objects, member objects, global objects, objects allocated by **new**, etc.). Then add a copy constructor and a copy assignment so that you can use **Tracer** objects to see when copying is done.

[14] Provide a GUI interface and a bit of graphical output to the "Hunt the Wumpus" game from the exercises in Chapter 16. Take the input in an input box and display a map of the part of the cave currently known to the player in a window.

[15] Modify the program from the previous exercise to allow the user to mark rooms based on knowledge and guesses, such as "maybe bats" and "bottomless pit."

[16] Sometimes, it is desirable that an empty **vector** be as small as possible. For example, someone might use **vector<vector<vector<int>>>** a lot but have most element vectors empty. Define a **Vector** so that **sizeof(Vector<int>)==sizeof(int*)**, that is, so that the **Vector** itself consists only of a pointer to a representation consisting of the elements, the number of elements, and the **space** pointer.

[17] Define a function **finally()** that takes a function object as its arguments and returns an object with a destructor that invokes that function object. Thus

```
auto x = finally([](){ cout<< "Bye!\n"; });
```

will "say" **Buy!** whenever we exit the scope of **x**. For what might **finally()** be useful?

Postscript

Templates and exceptions are immensely powerful language features. They support programming techniques of great flexibility – mostly by allowing people to separate concerns, that is, to deal with one problem at a time. For example, using templates, we can define a container, such as vector, separately from the definition of an element type. Similarly, using exceptions, we can write the code that detects and signals an error separately from the code that handles that error. Given templates and exceptions, we completed our Vector by considering how to improve push_back(), resize(), and reserve() so that they handle construction and destruction in the presence of errors. Concepts allow us to provide well-defined interfaces for templates.

19

Containers and Iterators

Any problem in computer science can be solved
with another layer of indirection.
Except, of course,
the problem of too many indirections.
– David J. Wheeler

This chapter and the next two present the STL, the containers and algorithms part of the C++ standard library. The STL is an extensible framework for dealing with data in a C++ program. After a first simple example, we present the general ideals and the fundamental concepts. We discuss iteration, linked-list manipulation, and STL containers. The key notions of sequence and iterator are used to tie containers (data) together with algorithms (processing). This chapter lays the groundwork for the general, efficient, and useful algorithms presented in Chapter 21. As an example, we present a framework for text editing as a sample application.

§19.1 Storing and processing data
Working with data; Generalizing code; STL ideals
§19.2 Sequences and iterators
Back to the Jack-and-Jill example
§19.3 Linked lists
List operations; Iteration
§19.4 Generalizing **Vector** yet again
Container traversal; **insert()** and **erase()**; Adapting our **Vector** to the STL
§19.5 An example: a simple text editor
Lines; Iteration
§19.6 **vector**, **list**, and **string**

19.1 Storing and processing data

Before looking into dealing with larger collections of data items, let's consider a simple example that points to ways of handling a large class of data-processing problems. Jack and Jill are each measuring vehicle speeds, which they record as floating-point values. Jack was brought up as a C programmer and stores his values in an array and uses pointers, whereas Jill stores hers in a vector and relies on move semantics (§17.4.4). Now we'd like to use their data in our program. How might we do this?

We could have Jack's and Jill's programs write out the values to a file and then read them back into our program. That way, we are completely insulated from their choices of data structures and interfaces. Often, such isolation is a good idea, and if that's what we decide to do we can use the techniques from Chapter 9 for input and a vector<double> for our calculations.

But what if using files isn't a good option for the task we want to do? Let's say that the data-gathering code is designed to be invoked as a function call to deliver a new set of data every second. Once a second, we call Jack's and Jill's functions to deliver data for us to process:

```
double* get_from_jack(int* count);        // Jack fills an array and puts the number of elements in *count
vector<double> get_from_jill();           // Jill fills a vector

void fct()
{
      int jack_count = 0;
      double* jack_data = get_from_jack(&jack_count);
      vector<double> jill_data = get_from_jill();
      // ... process ...
      delete[] jack_data;
}
```

Assume that we can't rewrite Jack's and Jill's code or wouldn't want to.

19.1.1 Working with data

Clearly, this is a somewhat simplified example, but it is not dissimilar to a vast number of real-world problems. If we can handle this example elegantly, we can handle a huge number of common programming problems. The fundamental problem here is that we don't control the way in which our "data suppliers" store the data they give us. It's our job to either work with the data in the form in which we get it or to read it and store it the way we like better.

What do we want to do with that data? Sort it? Find the highest value? Find the average value? Find every value over 65? Compare Jill's data with Jack's? See how many readings there were? The possibilities are endless, and when writing a real program, we simply do the computation required. Here, we just want to do something to learn how to handle data and do computations involving lots of data. Let's first do something really simple: find the element with the highest value in each data set. We can do that by inserting this code in place of the "... process ..." comment in fct():

```
double h = -1;
double* jack_high;        // jack_high will point to the element with the highest value
double* jill_high;        // jill_high will point to the element with the highest value
```

```
for (int i=0; i<jack_count; ++i)
      if (h<jack_data[i]) {
            jack_high = &jack_data[i];              // save address of largest element
            h = jack_data[i];                        // update "largest element"
      }

h = -1;
for (double& x : jill_data)
      if (h<x) {
            jill_high = &x;          // save address of largest element
            h = x;                   // update "largest element"
      }

cout << "Jill's max: " << *jill_high
      << "; Jack's max: " << *jack_high;
```

19.1.2 Generalizing code

What we would like is a uniform way of accessing and manipulating data so that we don't have to write our code differently each time we get data presented to us in a slightly different way. Let's look at Jack's and Jill's code as examples of how we can make our code more abstract and uniform. CC

Obviously, what we do for Jack's data strongly resembles what we do for Jill's. However, there are annoying differences: Jack's traditional **for**-loop and subscripting vs. Jill's range-**for**. We could eliminate the latter difference by using a traditional **for**-loop for Jill's data:

```
vector<double>& v = jill_data;

for (int i=0; i<v.size(); ++i)
      if (h<v[i]) {
            jill_high = &v[i];
            h = v[i];
      }
```

This is tantalizingly close to the code for Jack's data. What would it take to write a function that could do the calculation for Jill's data as well as for Jack's? We can think of several ways (see exercise 3), but for reasons of generality which will become clear over the next two chapters, we chose a solution based on pointers:

```
double* high(double* first, double* last)
      // return a pointer to the element in [first:last) that has the highest value
{
      double h = -1;
      double* high;
```

```
        for (double* p = first; p!=last; ++p)
                if (h<*p) {
                        high = p;
                        h = *p;
                }
        return high;
}
```

Given that, we can write

```
double* jack_high = high(jack_data,jack_data+jack_count);
double* jill_high = high(&jill_data[0],&jill_data[0]+jill_data.size());
```

This looks better. We don't introduce so many variables and we write the loop and the loop body only once (in **high()**). If we want to know the highest values, we can look at ***jack_high** and ***jill_high**. For example:

```
cout << "Jill's max: " << *jill_high
        << "; Jack's max: " << *jack_high;
```

Note that **high()** relies on a vector storing its elements in an array, so that we can express our "find highest element" algorithm in terms of pointers into an array.

> TRY THIS
>
> We left two potentially serious errors in this little program. One can cause a crash, and the other will give wrong answers if **high()** is used in many other programs where it might have been useful. The general techniques that we describe below will make them obvious and show how to systematically avoid them. For now, just find them and suggest remedies.

This **high()** function is limited in that it is a solution to a single specific problem:

- It works for arrays only. We rely on the elements of a **vector** being stored in an array, but there are many more ways of storing data, such as **lists** (§19.3) and **maps** (§20.2).
- It can be used for **vectors** and arrays of **doubles**, but not for arrays or **vectors** with other element types, such as **vector<double*>** and **char[10]**.
- It finds the element with the highest value, but there are many more calculations that we want to do on such data.

Let's explore how we can support this kind of calculation on sets of data in far greater generality.

Please note that by deciding to express our "find highest element" algorithm in terms of pointers, we "accidentally" generalized it to do more than we required: we can – as desired – find the highest element of an array or a **vector**, but we can also find the highest element in part of an array or in part of a **vector**. For example:

```
// ...
vector<double>& v = *jill_data;
double* middle = &v[0]+v.size()/2;
double* high1 = high(&v[0], middle);               // max of first half
double* high2 = high(middle, &v[0]+v.size());      // max of second half
// ...
```

Here **high1** will point to the element with the largest value in the first half of the **vector** and **high2** will point to the element with the largest value in the second half. Graphically, it will look something like this:

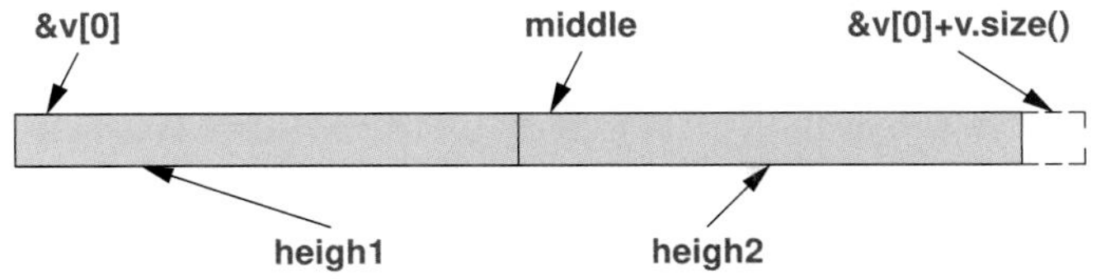

We used pointer arguments for **high()**. That's a bit low-level and can be error-prone. We suspect that for many programmers, the obvious function for finding the element with the largest value in a **vector** would look like this:

```
double* find_highest(vector<double>& v)
{
	double h = -1;
	double* high = nullptr;
	for (int& x : v)
		if (h<x) {
			high = &x;
			h = x;
		}
	return high;
}
```

However, that wouldn't give us the flexibility we "accidentally" obtained from **high()** – we can't use **find_highest()** to find the element with the highest value in part of a **vector**. We actually achieved a practical benefit from writing a function that could be used for both arrays and **vector**s by "messing with pointers." We will remember that: generalization can lead to functions that are useful for more problems.

19.1.3 STL ideals

The C++ standard library provides a framework for dealing with data as sequences of elements, called the STL. STL is usually said to be an acronym for "standard template library." The STL is the part of the ISO C++ standard library that provides containers (such as **vector**, **list**, and **map**) and generic algorithms (such as **sort**, **find**, and **accumulate**). Thus we can – and do – refer to facilities, such as **vector**, as being part of both "the STL" and "the standard library." Other standard-library features, such as **ostream** (Chapter 9) and C-style string functions (PPP2.Ch23), are not part of the STL. To better appreciate and understand the STL, we will first consider the problems we must address when dealing with data and the ideals we have for a solution.

There are two major aspects of computing: the computation and the data. Sometimes we focus on the computation and talk about **if**-statements, loops, functions, error handling, etc. At other times, we focus on the data and talk about arrays, vectors, strings, files, etc. However, to get useful work done we need both. A large amount of data is incomprehensible without analysis, **CC** visualization, and searching for "the interesting bits." Conversely, we can compute as much as we like, but it's going to be tedious and sterile unless we have some data to tie our computation to something real. Furthermore, the "computation part" of our program ideally has to elegantly interact with the "data part."

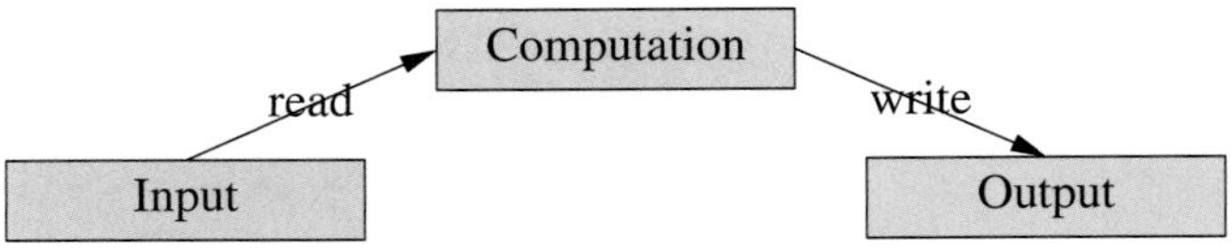

AA When we talk about data in this way, we think of lots of data: dozens of **Shapes**, hundreds of temperature readings, thousands of log records, millions of points, billions of Web pages, etc.; that is, we talk about processing containers of data, streams of data, etc. In particular, this is not a discussion of how best to choose a couple of values to represent a small object, such as a complex number, a temperature reading, or a circle. For such types, see Chapter 8, §9.3.2, and §11.7.4.

Consider some simple examples of something we'd like to do with "a lot of data":

- Sort the words in dictionary order.
- Find a number in a phone book, given a name.
- Find the highest temperature.
- Find all values larger than 8800.
- Find the first occurrence of the value 17.
- Sort the telemetry records by unit number.
- Sort the telemetry records by time stamp.
- Find the first value lexicographically larger than "Petersen."
- Find the largest amount.
- Find the first difference between two sequences.
- Compute the pair-wise product of the elements of two sequences.
- Find the highest temperature for each day in a month.
- Find the top ten best sellers in the sales records.
- Count the number of occurrences of "Stroustrup" on the Web.
- Compute the sum of the elements.

Note that we can describe each of these tasks without actually mentioning how the data is stored. Clearly, we must be dealing with something like lists, vectors, files, input streams, etc. for these tasks to make sense, but we don't have to know the details about how the data is stored (or gathered) to talk about what to do with it. What is important is the type of the values or objects (the element type), how we access those values or objects, and what we want to do with them.

These kinds of tasks are very common. Naturally, we want to write code performing such tasks simply and efficiently. Conversely, the problems for us as programmers are:

- There is an infinite variation of data types ("kinds of data").
- There is a bewildering number of ways to store collections of data elements.
- There is a huge variety of tasks we'd like to do with collections of data.

To minimize the effect of these problems, we'd like our code to take advantage of commonalities among types, among the ways of storing data, and among our processing tasks. In other words, we want to generalize our code to cope with these kinds of variations. We really don't want to handcraft each solution from scratch; that would be a tedious waste of time.

To get an idea of what support we would like for writing our code, consider a more abstract view of what we do with data:

- Collect data into containers
  - Such as vector, list, and array
- Organize data
  - For printing
  - For fast access
- Retrieve data items
  - By index (e.g., the 42nd element)
  - By value (e.g., the first record with the "age field" 7)
  - By properties (e.g., all records with the "temperature field" >32 and <100)
- Modify a container
  - Add data
  - Remove data
  - Sort (according to some criteria)
- Perform simple numeric operations (e.g., multiply all elements by 1.7)

We'd like to do these things without getting sucked into a swamp of details about differences among containers, differences in ways of accessing elements, and differences among element types. If we can do that, we'll have come a long way toward our goal of simple and efficient use of large amounts of data.

Looking back at the programming tools and techniques from the previous chapters, we note that we can (already) write programs that are similar independently of the data type used:

- Using an int isn't all that different from using a double.
- Using a vector<int> isn't all that different from using a vector<string>.
- Using an array of double isn't all that different from using a vector<double>.

We'd like to organize our code so that we have to write new code only when we want to do something really new and different. In particular, we'd like to provide code for common programming tasks so that we don't have to rewrite our solution each time we find a new way of storing the data or find a slightly different way of interpreting the data. **AA**

- Finding a value in a vector isn't all that different from finding a value in an array.
- Looking for a string ignoring case isn't all that different from looking at a string considering uppercase letters different from lowercase ones.
- Graphing experimental data with exact values isn't all that different from graphing data with rounded values.
- Copying a file isn't all that different from copying a vector.

We want to build on these observations to write code that's

- Easy to read
- Easy to modify
- Regular
- Short
- Fast

CC To minimize our programming work, we would like

- Uniform access to data
  - Independently of how it is stored
  - Independently of its type
- Type-safe access to data
- Easy traversal of data
- Compact storage of data
- Fast
  - Retrieval of data
  - Addition of data
  - Deletion of data
- Standard versions of the most common algorithms
  - Such as copy, find, search, sort, sum, ...

The STL provides that, and more. We will look at it not just as a very useful set of facilities, but also as an example of a library designed for maximal flexibility and performance. The STL was designed by Alex Stepanov to provide a framework for general, correct, and efficient algorithms operating on data structures. The ideal was the simplicity, generality, and elegance of mathematics.

XX The alternative to dealing with data using a framework with clearly articulated ideals and principles is for each programmer to craft each program out of the basic language facilities using whatever ideas seem good at the time. That's a lot of extra work. Furthermore, the result is often an unprincipled mess; rarely is the result a program that is easily understood by people other than its original designers, and only by chance is the result code that we can use in other contexts.

Having considered the motivation and the ideals, let's look at the basic definitions of the STL, and then finally get to the examples that'll show us how to approximate those ideals – to write better code for dealing with data and to do so with greater ease.

19.2 Sequences and iterators

CC The central concept of the STL is the *sequence*, also called a *range*. From the STL point of view, a collection of data is a sequence. A sequence has a beginning and an end. We can traverse a sequence from its beginning to its end, optionally reading or writing the value of each element. We identify the beginning and the end of a sequence by a pair of iterators. An *iterator* is an object that identifies an element of a sequence. We can think of a sequence like this:

Here, **begin** and **end** are iterators; they identify the beginning and the end of the sequence. An STL sequence is what is usually called "half-open"; that is, the element identified by **begin** is part of the sequence, but the **end** iterator points one beyond the end of the sequence. The usual mathematical notation for such sequences (ranges) is [**begin**:**end**). The arrows from one element to the next indicate that if we have an iterator to one element we can get an iterator to the next.

What is an iterator? An iterator is a rather abstract notion. For example, if **p** and **q** are iterators to elements of the same sequence: CC

Basic standard iterator operations	
p==q	true if and only if **p** and **q** point to the same element or both point to one beyond the last element
p!=q	**!(p==q)**
***p**	refers to the element pointed to by **p**
***p=val**	writes to the element pointed to by **p**
val=*p	reads from the element pointed to by **p**
++p	makes **p** refer to the next element in the sequence or to one beyond the last element

Clearly, the idea of an iterator is related to the idea of a pointer (§15.4). In fact, a pointer to an element of an array is an iterator. However, many iterators are not just pointers; for example, we can define a range-checked iterator that throws an exception (§20.7.2) if you try to make it point outside its **[begin:end)** sequence or dereference **end**. It turns out that we get enormous flexibility and generality from having iterator as an abstract notion rather than as a specific type. This chapter and the next will give several examples.

> TRY THIS
>
> Write a function **void copy(int* f1, int* e1, int* f2)** that copies the elements of an array of **int**s defined by **[f1:e1)** into another **[f2:f2+(e1−f1))**. Use only the iterator operations mentioned above (not subscripting).

Iterators are used to connect our code (algorithms) to our data. The writer of the code knows about the iterators (and not about the details of how the iterators actually get to the data), and the data provider supplies iterators rather than exposing details about how the data is stored to all users. The result is pleasingly simple and offers an important degree of independence between algorithms and containers. To quote Alex Stepanov: "The reason STL algorithms and containers work so well together is that they don't know anything about each other." Instead, both understand about sequences defined by pairs of iterators.

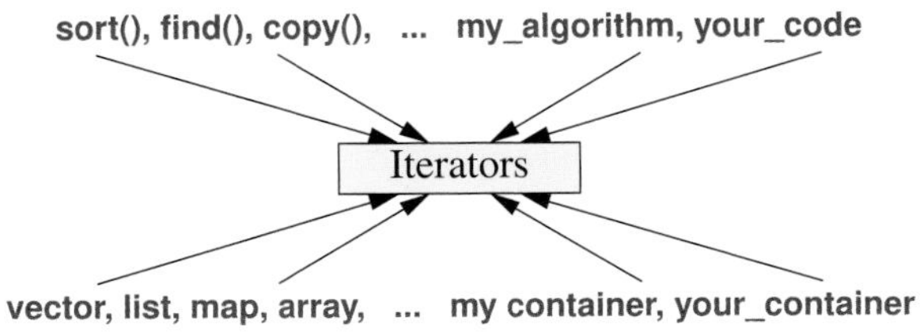

In other words, algorithms no longer have to know about the bewildering variety of ways of storing and accessing data; they just have to know about iterators. Conversely, data providers no longer have to write code to serve a bewildering variety of users; they just have to implement an iterator for their kind of data. At the most basic level, an iterator is defined by just the *, ++, ==, and != operators. That makes them simple and fast. To further increase flexibility and their range of uses, all STL containers are parameterized with their element type (§18.1.1) and an allocator (§18.2.1).

The STL framework consists of about a dozen containers and about 125 algorithms connected by iterators (Chapter 21). That's about 1,500 combinations represented by about 150 pieces of code. In addition, many organizations and individuals provide containers and algorithms in the style of the STL. The STL is probably the best-known and most widely used example of generic programming (§18.1.2, §21.1.2). If you know the basic concepts and a few examples, you can use the rest.

19.2.1 Back to the Jack-and-Jill example

Let's see how we can express the "find the element with the largest value" problem using the STL notion of a sequence:

```
template<forward_iterator Iter>
Iter high(Iter first, Iter last)
          // return an iterator to the element in [first:last) that has the highest value
{
          Iter high = first;
          for (Iter p = first; p!=last; ++p)
                    if (*high<*p)
                              high = p;
          return high;
}
```

Note that we eliminated the local variable h that we had used to hold the highest value seen so far. When we don't know the name of the actual type of the elements of the sequence, the initialization by -1 seems completely arbitrary and odd. That's because it is arbitrary and odd! It was also an error waiting to happen: in our example -1 worked only because we happened not to have any negative velocities. We knew that "magic constants," such as -1, are bad for code maintenance (§3.3.1, §6.6.1, §9.9.1, etc.). Here, we see that they can also limit the utility of a function and can be a sign of incomplete thought about the solution; that is, "magic constants" can be – and often are – a sign of sloppy thinking.

Note that this "generic" high() can be used for any element type that can be compared using <. For example, we could use high() to find the lexicographically last string in a vector<string> (see exercise 7).

The high() template function can be used for any sequence defined by a pair of iterators. For example, we can exactly replicate our example program:

```
double* get_from_jack(int* count);          // Jack fills an array and puts the number of elements in *count
vector<double> get_from_jill();             // Jill fills the vector

void fct()
{
          int jack_count = 0;
          double* jack_data = get_from_jack(&jack_count);
          vector<double> jill_data = get_from_jill();
```

```
        double* jack_high = high(jack_data,jack_data+jack_count);
        double* jill_high = high(jill_data.begin(),jill_data.end());

        cout << "Jill's high " << *jill_high << "; Jack's high " << *jack_high;
        delete[] jack_data;
}
```

For the two calls here, the **Iterator** template argument type for **high()** is **double***. Apart from (finally) getting the code for **high()** correct, there is apparently no difference from our previous solution. To be precise, there is no difference in the code that is executed, but there is a most important difference in the generality of our code. The templated version of **high()** can be used for every kind of sequence that can be described by a pair of iterators. Before looking at the detailed conventions of the STL and the useful standard algorithms that it provides to save us from writing common tricky code, let's consider a couple of more ways of storing collections of data elements.

> TRY THIS
>
> We again left a serious error in that program. Find it, fix it, and suggest a general remedy for that kind of problem.

The process of analyzing pieces of code for similarities and generalizing them into a single piece of code is often called *lifting*. We can lift the Jack-and-Jill example further using ideas from the STL and the STL itself; see the exercises.

19.3 Linked lists

Consider again the graphical representation of the notion of a sequence: CC

Compare it to the way we visualize a **vector** in memory:

Basically, the subscript **0** identifies the same element as does the iterator **v.begin()**, and the subscript **v.size()** identifies the one-beyond-the-last element also identified by the iterator **v.end()**.

The elements of the **vector** are consecutive in memory. That's not required by STL's notion of a sequence, and it so happens that there are many algorithms where we would like to insert an element in between two existing elements without moving those existing elements. The graphical representation of the abstract notion suggests the possibility of inserting elements (and of deleting elements) without moving other elements. The STL notion of iterators supports that.

The data structure most directly suggested by the STL sequence diagram is called a *linked list*. The arrows in the abstract model are usually implemented as pointers. An element of a linked list is part of a "link" consisting of the element and one or more pointers. A linked list where a link has just one pointer (to the next link) is called a *singly-linked list* and a list where a link has pointers to both the previous and the next link is called a *doubly-linked list*. We will sketch the implementation of a doubly-linked list, which is what the C++ standard library provides under the name of **list**. Graphically, it can be represented like this:

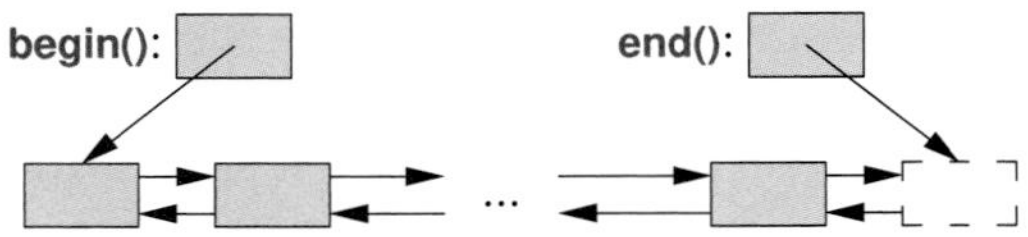

This can be represented in code as

```
template<Element T>
struct Link {
      Link* prev;          // previous link
      Link* succ;          // successor (next) link
      T val;               // the value
};

template<Element T> struct List {
      Link<T>* first;
      Link<T>* last;       // one beyond the last link
};
```

We can present the layout of a **Link** like this

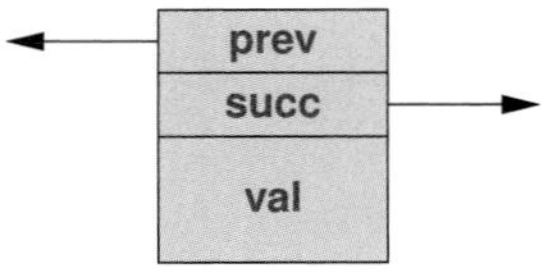

There are many ways of implementing linked lists and presenting them to users. Here, we'll just outline the key properties of a list (you can insert and delete elements without disturbing existing elements), show how we can iterate over a list, and give an example of list use.

When you try to think about lists, we strongly encourage you to draw little diagrams to visualize the operations you are considering. Linked-list manipulation really is a topic where a picture is worth 1K words. See also the list example in §15.7.

19.3.1 List operations

What operations do we need for a list? CC

- The operations we have for **vector** (constructors, size, etc.) (§18.1.1), except subscripting.
- Operations **insert()** (add an element) and **erase()** (remove an element); **vector** also has those (see §19.4.2).
- Something that can be used to refer to elements and to traverse the list: an iterator.

In the STL, that iterator type is a member of its class, so we'll do the same:

```
template<Element T>
class List {
    // ... representation and implementation details ...
public:
    // ... constructors, destructor, etc. ...

    class iterator;                 // member type: iterator

    iterator begin();               // iterator to first element
    iterator end( );                // iterator to one beyond last element

    iterator insert(iterator p, const T& v);    // insert v into list after p
    iterator erase(iterator p);                 // remove p from the list

    void push_back(const T& v);                 // insert v at end
    void push_front(const T& v);                // insert v at front
    void pop_front();                           // remove the first element
    void pop_back();                            // remove the last element

    T& front();     // the first element
    T& back();      // the last element
};
```

Just as our **Vector** is not the complete standard-library **vector**, this **List** is not the complete definition of the standard-library **list**. There is nothing wrong with this **List**; it simply isn't complete. The purpose of our **List** is to convey an understanding of what linked lists are, how a **list** might be implemented, and how to use the key features. For more information see an expert-level C++ book.

The iterator is central to the definition of an STL **list**. Iterators are used to identify places for insertion and elements for removal (erasure). They are also used for "navigating" through a list rather than using subscripting. This use of iterators is very similar to the way we used pointers to traverse arrays and vectors in §16.1.1 and §17.6. This style of iterators is the key to the standard-library algorithms (§21.1).

Why not subscripting for **List**? We could subscript a list, but it would be a surprisingly slow operation: **lst[1000]** would involve starting from the first element and then visiting each link along the way until we reached element number **1000**. If we want to do that, we can do it ourselves (or use **advance()**; see §19.5.2). Consequently, **std::list** doesn't provide the innocuous-looking subscript operator, **[ ]**. XX

We made List's iterator type a member (a nested class) because there was no reason for it to be global. Also, this allows us to name every container's iterator type iterator. In the standard library, we have list<T>::iterator, vector<T>::iterator, map<K,V>::iterator, and so on.

19.3.2 Iteration

The List iterator must provide *, ++, ==, and !=. Since std::list is a doubly-linked list, it also provides -- for iterating "backward" toward the front of the list:

```
template<Element T>
class List<Elem>::iterator {
      LinkT>* curr;                    // current link
public:
      iterator(Link<T>* p) :curr{p} { }

      iterator& operator++() {curr = curr->succ; return *this; }          // forward
      iterator& operator--() { curr = curr->prev; return *this; }         // backward
      T& operator*() { return curr->val; }                                 // get value (dereference)

      bool operator==(const iterator& b) const { return curr==b.curr; }
      bool operator!= (const iterator& b) const { return curr!=b.curr; }
};
```

These functions are short and simple, and obviously efficient: there are no loops, no complicated expressions, and no "suspicious" function calls. If the implementation isn't clear to you, just have a quick look at the diagrams above. This List iterator is just a pointer to a link with the required operations. Note that even though the implementation (the code) for a list<T>::iterator is very different from the simple pointer we have used as an iterator for vectors and arrays, the meaning (the semantics) of the operations is identical. Basically, the List iterator provides suitable ++, --, *, ==, and != for a Link pointer.

Now look at high() again:

```
template<input_iterator Iter>
Iter high(Iter first, Iter last)
      // return an iterator to the element in [first,last) that has the highest value
{
      Iter high = first;
      for (Iter p = first; p!=last; ++p)
            if (*high<*p)
                  high = p;
      return high;
}
```

We can use it for a list or a List:

```
void f()
{
        list<int> lst;
        for (int x; cin >> x; )
                lst.push_front(x);

        list<int>::iterator p = high(lst.begin(), lst.end());
        cout << "the highest value was " << *p << '\n';
}
```

Here, the "value" of high()'s Iter argument is list<int>::Iterator, and the implementation of ++, *, and != has changed dramatically from the array case, but the meaning is still the same. The template function high() still traverses the data (here a list) and finds the highest value. We can insert an element anywhere in a list, so we used push_front() to add elements at the front just to show that we could. We could equally well have used push_back() as we do for vectors.

> TRY THIS
>
> The standard-library vector doesn't provide push_front(). Why not? Implement push_front() for vector and compare it to push_back().

Now, finally, is the time to ask, "But what if the list is empty?" In other words, "What if lst.begin()==lst.end()?" In that case, *p will be an attempt to dereference the one-beyond-the-last element, lst.end(): disaster! Or – potentially worse – the result could be a random value that might be mistaken for a correct answer.

The last formulation of the question strongly hints at the solution: we can test whether a list is empty by comparing begin() and end() – in fact, we can test whether any STL sequence is empty by comparing its beginning and end: CC

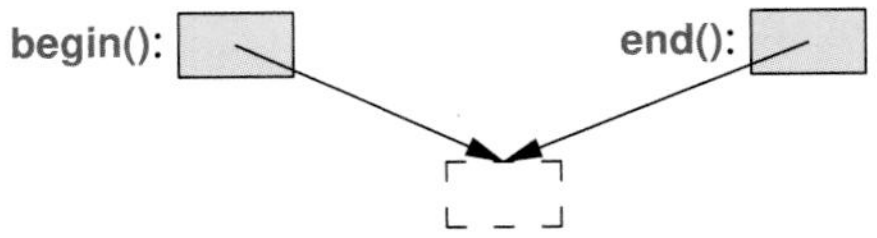

That's the deeper reason for having end point one beyond the last element rather than at the last element: the empty sequence is not a special case. We dislike special cases because – by definition – we have to remember to write special-case code for them.

In our example, we could use that like this:

```
list<int>::iterator p = high(lst.begin(), lst.end());
if (p==lst.end())                       // did we reach the end?
        cout << "The list is empty";
else
        cout << "the highest value is " << *p << '\n';
```

We use testing against end() – indicating "not found" – systematically with STL algorithms.

Because the standard library provides a list, we won't go further into the implementation here. Instead, we'll have a brief look at what lists are good for (see exercises 12–14 if you are interested in list implementation details).

19.4 Generalizing Vector yet again

The standard-library **vector** has an **iterator** member type and **begin()** and **end()** member functions (just like **std::list**). However, those we provided for our **Vector** in §18.1.1 just returned pointers. What does it really take for different containers to be used more or less interchangeably in the STL generic programming style? First, we'll outline the solution and then explain it:

```
template<Element T, Allocator A = allocator<T>>
class Vector {
public:
        using size_type = int;
        using value_type = T;
        using iterator = T*;
        using const_iterator = const T*;

        // ...

        iterator begin();
        const_iterator begin() const;
        iterator end();
        const_iterator end() const;

        size_type size();

        // ...
};
```

CC A **using** declaration creates an alias for a type; that is, for our **Vector**, **iterator** is a synonym, another name, for the type we chose to use as our iterator: **T***. Now, for a **Vector** called **v**, we can write

```
vector<int>::iterator p = find(v.begin(), v.end(),32);
```

and

```
for (vector<int>::size_type i = 0; i<v.size(); ++i)
        cout << v[i] << '\n';
```

To write that, we don't actually have to know what types are named by **iterator** and **size_type**. In particular, because the code above is expressed in terms of **iterator** and **size_type**, it will work with a variety of standard library containers and on a variety of systems with different representations of container types and iterator types. For example, we can provide a range-checked iterator type (§20.7.2). The **size_type** is usually an unsigned integer type (PPP2.§25.5.3) but here we have used **int** for simplicity. To safely convert between signed and unsigned types, we use **narrow** (§7.4.7).

The standard defines **list** and the other standard containers similarly. For example:

```
template<Element T, Allocator A = allocator<T>>
class List {
public:
        using size_type = int;
        using value_type = T;
```

```
        class Link;
        class iterator;                  // see §19.3
        class const_iterator;            // like iterator, but not allowing writes to elements
        // ...

        iterator begin();
        const_iterator begin() const;
        iterator end();
        const_iterator end() const;

        size_type size();
        // ...
};
```

19.4.1 Container traversal

Using size(), we can traverse one of our vectors from its first element to its last. For example:

```
void print1(const vector<double>& v)
{
        for (int i = 0; i<v.size(); ++i)
                cout << v[i] << '\n';
}
```

However, this doesn't work for lists because list does not provide subscripting. However, we can traverse a standard-library vector and list using iterators. For example: CC

```
void print2(const vector<double>& v, const list<double>& lst)
{
        for (vector<T>::iterator p = v.begin(); p!=v.end(); ++p)
                cout << *p << '\n';

        for (list<T>::iterator p = v.begin(); p!=v.end(); ++p)
                cout << *p << '\n';
}
```

This works for both the standard-library containers and for our Vector and List. CC

In generic code, type names can get unpleasantly long. We don't really like to type names like vector<T>::iterator repeatedly and we know that the value returned by begin() is an iterator of the appropriate type. So we typically use auto to simplify such code:

```
void print2(const vector<double>& v, const list<double>& lst)
{
        for (auto p = v.begin(); p!=v.end(); ++p)
                cout << *p << '\n';

        for (auto p = v.begin(); p!=v.end(); ++p)
                cout << *p << '\n';
}
```

When we don't need the position of an element, we can do better still. The range-for-loop is simply "syntactic sugar" for a loop over a sequence using iterators, so we get:

```
void print3(const vector<double>& v, const list<double>& lst)
{
        for (double x : v)
                cout << x << '\n';

        for (double x : lst)
                cout << x << '\n';
}
```

The techniques used for print2() and print3() can be used for all standard-library containers (§20.6).

19.4.2 insert() and erase()

AA The standard-library vector is our default choice for a container. It has most of the desired features, so we use alternatives only if we have to. Its main problem is its habit of moving elements when we do list operations (insert() and erase()); that can be costly when we deal with vectors with many elements or vectors of large elements. Don't be too worried about that, though. We have been quite happy reading half a million floating-point values into a vector using push_back() – measurements confirmed that pre-allocation didn't make a noticeable difference. Always measure before making significant changes in the interest of performance. Even for experts, guessing about performance is very hard.

XX Moving elements also implies a logical constraint: don't hold iterators or pointers to elements of a vector when you do list operations (such as insert(), erase(), and push_back()): if an element moves, your iterator or pointer will point to the wrong element or to no element at all. This is the principal advantage of lists (and maps (§19.4.2) over vectors. If you need a collection of large objects or of objects that you point to from many places in a program, consider using a list.

Let's compare insert() and erase() for a vector and a list. First we take an example designed only to illustrate the key points:

```
vector<int>::iterator p = v.begin();        // take a vector
++p; ++p; ++p;                              // point to its 4th element
vector<int>::iterator q = p;
++q;                                        // point to its 5th element
```

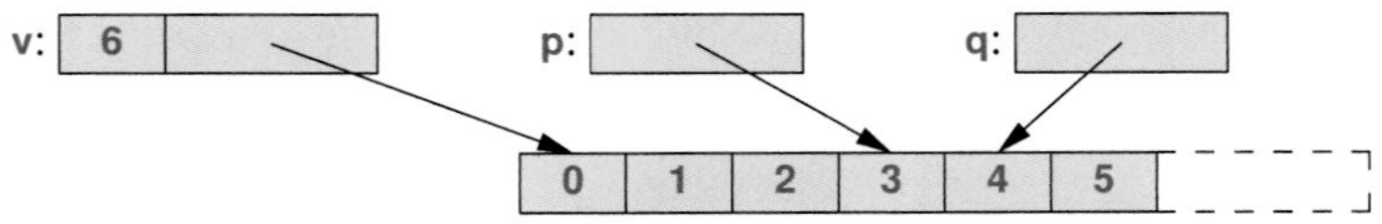

```
p = v.insert(p,99);                  // p points to the inserted element
```

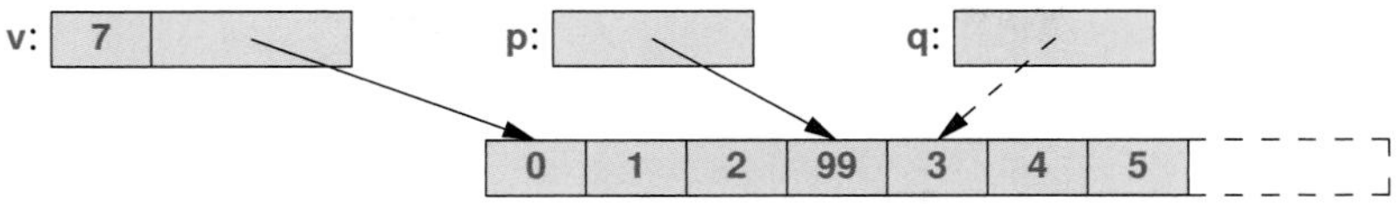

Note that **q** is now invalid. The elements may have been reallocated as the size of the vector grew. If **v** had spare capacity, so that it grew in place, **q** most likely points to the element with the value **3** rather than the element with the value **4**, but don't try to take advantage of that.

```
p = v.erase(p);                      // p points to the element after the erased one
```

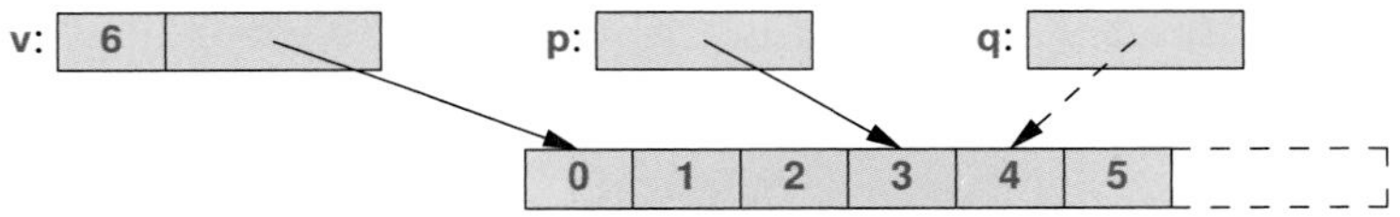

That is, an **insert()** followed by an **erase()** of the inserted element leaves us back where we started, but with **q** invalidated. However, in between, we moved all the elements after the insertion point, and maybe all elements were relocated as **v** grew.

To compare, we'll do exactly the same with a **list**:

```
list<int>::iterator p = lst.begin();   // take a list
++p; ++p; ++p;                         // point to its 4th element
list<int>::iterator q = p;
++q;                                   // point to its 5th element
```

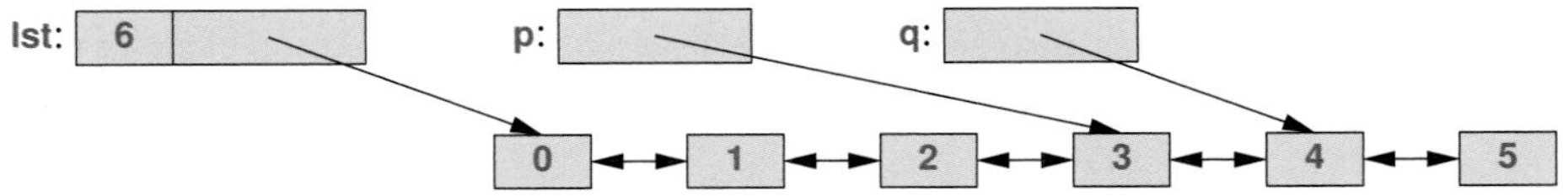


```
p = v.insert(p,99);                  // p points to the inserted element
```

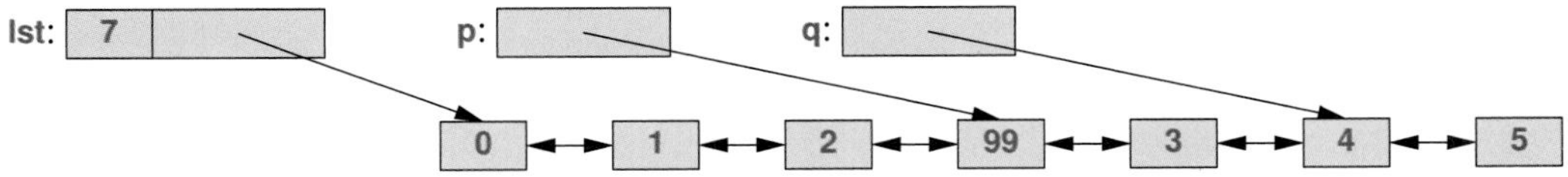

Note that **q** still points to the element with the value **4**.

```
p = v.erase(p);                    // p points to the element after the erased one
```

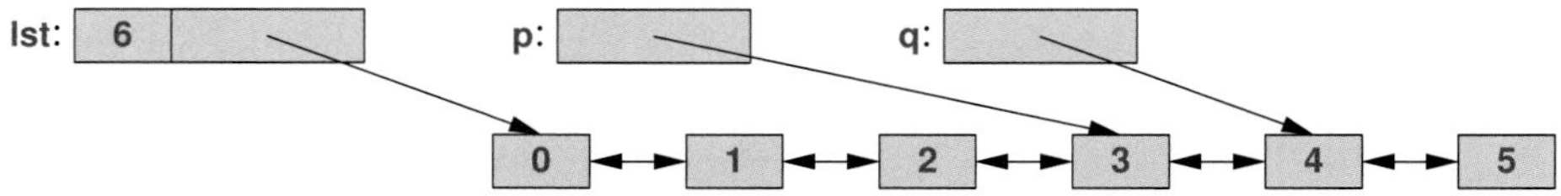

Again, we find ourselves back where we started. However, for **list** as opposed to for **vector**, we didn't move any elements and **q** was valid at all times.

19.4.3 Adapting our vector to the STL

After adding **begin()**, **end()**, and the type aliases in §19.4, our **Vector** now just lacks **insert()** and **erase()** to be as close an approximation of **std::vector** as we need it to be:

```
template<Element T, Allocator A = allocator<T>>          // §18.4.4
class Vector {
      Vector_rep<A> r;
public:
      // ...
      iterator insert(iterator p, const T& val);
      iterator erase(iterator p);
};
```

We again used a pointer to the element type, **T***, as the iterator type. That's the simplest possible solution. We left providing a range-checked iterator as an exercise (exercise 18).

AA Typically, people don't provide list operations, such as **insert()** and **erase()**, for data types that keep their elements in contiguous storage, such as **vector**. However, list operations, such as **insert()** and **erase()**, are immensely useful and surprisingly efficient for **vector**s with small elements or small numbers of elements. We have repeatedly seen the usefulness of **push_back()**, which is another operation traditionally associated with lists.

Basically, we implement **Vector<T,A>::erase()** by copying all elements after the element we erase (remove, delete). Using the definition of **Vector** from §18.1.1 with the additions from §18.4.4 and §19.4, we get

```
template<Element T, Allocator A>
Vector<T,A>::iterator Vector<T,A>::erase(iterator p)
{
      if (p==end())
            return p;
      move(p+1,r.sz,p);                   // move each element one position to the left
      destroy_at(r.elem()+r.sz-1));       // destroy surplus last element
      --r.sz;
      return p;
}
```

We use standard-library functions **move()** and **destroy_at** to avoid messier lower-level facilities.

It is easier to understand such code if you look at a graphical representation:

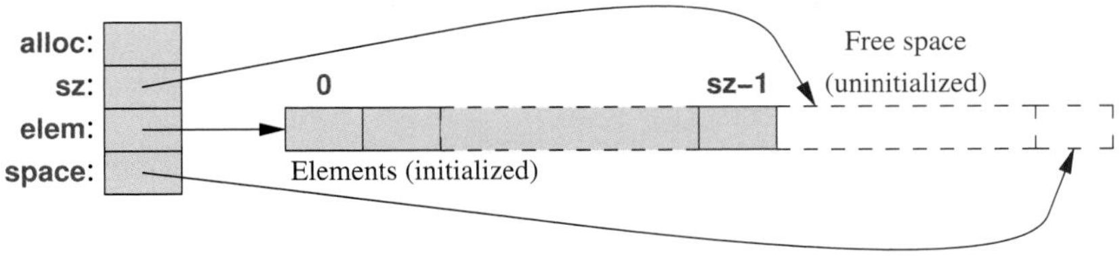

The code for **erase()** is quite simple, but it may be a good idea to try out a couple of examples by drawing them on paper. Is the empty **Vector** correctly handled? Why do we need the **p==end()** test? What if we erased the last element of a **Vector**? Would this code have been easier to read if we had used the subscript notation?

Implementing **Vector<T,A>::insert()** is a bit more complicated:

```
template<Element T, Allocator A>
Vector<T,A>::iterator Vector<T,A>::insert(iterator p, const T& val)
{
        int index = p–begin();                          // save index in case of relocation
        if (size()==capacity())
                reserve(size()==0?8:2*size());          // make sure we have space
        p = begin()+i;                                  // p now points into the current allocation
        move_backward(p,r.sz–1,p+1);                    // move each element one position to the right
        *(begin()+index) = val;                         // "insert" val
        ++r.sz;
        return pp;
}
```

Please note:

- An iterator may not point outside its sequence, so we use pointers, such as **elem+sz**, for that. That's one reason that allocators are defined in terms of pointers and not iterators.
- When we use **reserve()**, the elements may be moved to a new area of memory. Therefore, we must remember the index at which the element is to be inserted, rather than the iterator to it. When **Vector** reallocates its elements, iterators into that **Vector** become invalid – you can think of them as pointing to the old memory.
- We use the standard-library function **move_backward()** instead of **std::move()** to make sure that the last element is the first to be moved. Plain **move()** would move the first element first, thus overwriting the second before that was moved.
- It is subtleties like these that make us avoid dealing with low-level memory issues whenever we can. Naturally, **std::vector** – and all other standard-library containers – get that kind of important semantic detail right. That's one reason to prefer the standard library over "home brew."

For performance reasons, you wouldn't usually use **insert()** and **erase()** in the middle of a 100,000-element **vector**; **lists** and **maps** are designed for that (§19.4.2). However, the **insert()** and **erase()** operations are available for all **vectors**, and their performance is unbeatable when you are just moving a few words of data – or even a few dozen words – because modern computers are really good at this kind of copying; see exercise 20. Avoid (linked) lists for representing a list of a few small elements.

19.5 An example: a simple text editor

CC The essential feature of a list is that you can add and remove elements without moving other elements of the list. Let's try a simple example that illustrates that. Consider how to represent the characters of a text document in a simple text editor. The representation should make operations on the document simple and reasonably efficient.

Which operations? Let's assume that a document will fit in your computer's main memory. That way, we can choose any representation that suits us and simply convert it to a stream of bytes when we want to store it in a file. Similarly, we can read a stream of bytes from a file and convert those to our in-memory representation. That decided, we can concentrate on choosing a convenient in-memory representation. Basically, there are five things that our representation must support well:

- Constructing it from a stream of bytes from input
- Inserting one or more characters
- Deleting one or more characters
- Searching for a string
- Generating a stream of bytes for output to a file or a screen

The simplest representation would be a vector<char>. However, to add or delete a character we would have to move every following character in the document. Consider:

```
This is he start of a very long document.
There are lots of ...
```

We could add the t needed to get

```
This is the start of a very long document.
There are lots of ...
```

However, if those characters were stored in a single vector<char>, we'd have to move every character from h onward one position to the right. That could be a lot of copying. In fact for a 70,000-character-long document (such as this chapter, counting spaces), we would, on average, have to move 35,000 characters to insert or delete a character. The resulting real-time delay is likely to be noticeable and annoying to users. Consequently, we "break down" our representation into "chunks" so that we can change part of the document without moving a lot of characters around. We represent a document as a list of "lines," list<Line>, where a Line is a vector<char>. For example:

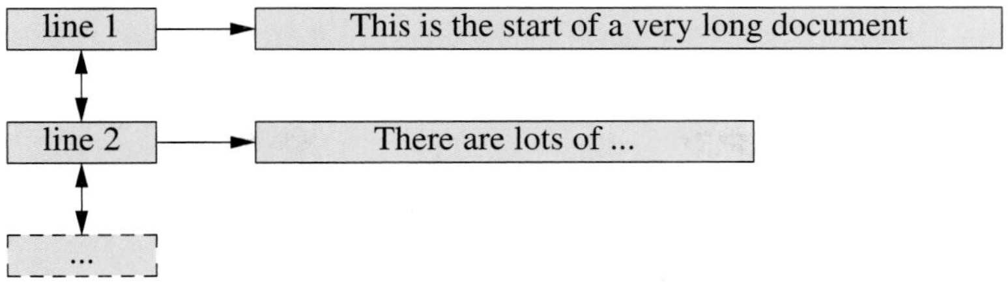

Now, when we inserted that t, we only had to move the rest of the characters on that line. Furthermore, when we need to, we can add a new line without moving any characters. For example, we could insert **This is a new line.** after **document.** to get

```
This is the start of a very long document.
This is a new line.
There are lots of ...
```

All we needed to do was to insert a new "line" in the middle:

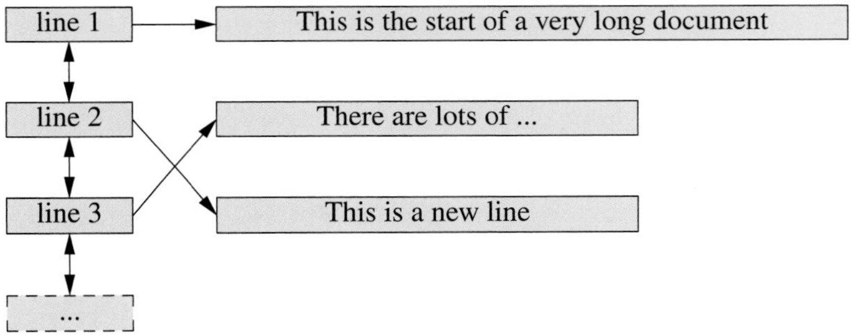

The logical reason that it is important to be able to insert new links in a list without moving existing links is that we might have iterators pointing to those links or pointers (and references) pointing to the objects in those links. Such iterators and pointers are unaffected by insertions or deletions of lines. For example, a word processor may keep a vector<list<Line>::iterator> holding iterators to the beginning of every title and subtitle in the current Document:

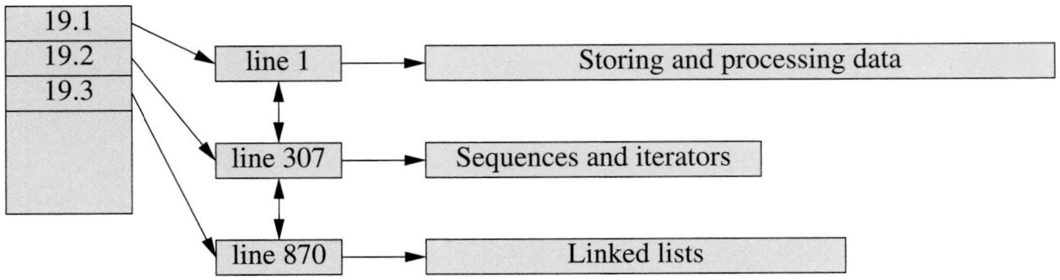

We can add lines to "paragraph 19.2" without invalidating the iterator to "paragraph 19.3."

AA In conclusion, we use a **list** of lines rather than a **vector** of lines or a **vector** of all the characters for both logical and performance reasons. Please note that situations where these reasons apply are rather rare so that the "by default, use **vector**" rule of thumb still holds. You need a specific reason to prefer a **list** over a **vector** – even if you think of your data as a list of elements! See §19.6. A list is a logical concept that you can represent in your program as a (linked) **list** or as a **vector**. The closest STL analog to our everyday concept of a list (e.g., a to-do list, a list of groceries, or a schedule) is a sequence, and most sequences are best represented as **vectors**.

19.5.1 Lines

How do we decide what's a "line" in our document? There are three obvious choices:

[1] Rely on newline indicators (e.g., '\n') in user input.
[2] Somehow parse the document and use some "natural" punctuation (e.g., **. (dot)**).
[3] Split any line that grows beyond a given length (e.g., 50 characters) into two.

There are undoubtedly also some less obvious choices. For simplicity, we use alternative 1 here.

We will represent a document in our editor as an object of class **Document**. Stripped of all refinements, our document type looks like this:

```
using Line = vector<char>;          // a line is a vector of characters

struct Document {
      list<Line> line;              // a document is a list of lines
      Document() { line.push_back(Line{}); }
};
```

Every **Document** starts out with a single empty line: **Document**'s constructor makes an empty line and pushes it into the list of lines.

Reading and splitting into lines can be done like this:

```
istream& operator>>(istream& is, Document& d)
{
      for (char ch; is.get(ch); ) {
            d.line.back().push_back(ch);   // add the character
            if (ch=='\n')
                  d.line.push_back(Line{});// add another line
      }
      if (d.line.back().size())
            d.line.push_back(Line{});      // add final empty line
      return is;
}
```

Both **vector** and **list** have a member function **back()** that returns a reference to the last element. To use it, you have to be sure that there really is a last element for **back()** to refer to – don't use it on an empty container. That's why we defined a **Document** to end with an empty **Line**. Note that we store every character from input, even the newline characters ('\n'). Storing those newline characters greatly simplifies output, but you have to be careful how you define a character count (just counting characters will give a number that includes space and newline characters).

19.5.2 Iteration

If the document was just a vector<char> it would be simple to iterate over it. How do we iterate over a list of lines? Obviously, we can iterate over the list using list<Line>::iterator. However, what if we wanted to visit the characters one after another without any fuss about line breaks? We could provide an iterator specifically designed for our Document:

```
class Text_iterator {            // keep track of line and character position within a line
    list<Line>::iterator ln;
    Line::iterator pos;
public:
    Text_iterator(list<Line>::iterator ll, Line::iterator pp)
        // line ll's character position pp
        :ln{ll}, pos{pp} { }

    char& operator*() { return *pos; }
    Text_iterator& operator++();
    bool operator==(const Text_iterator& other) const
        { return ln==other.ln && pos==other.pos; }
    bool operator!=(const Text_iterator& other) const
        { return !(*this==other); }
};

Text_iterator& Text_iterator::operator++()
{
    ++pos;                       // proceed to next character
    if (pos==ln->end()) {
        ++ln;                    // proceed to next line
        pos = ln->begin();       // bad if ln==line.end(); so make sure it isn't
    }
    return *this;
}
```

To make Text_iterator useful, we need to equip class Document with conventional begin() and end() functions:

```
struct Document {
    list<Line> line;

    Text_iterator begin()              // first character of first line
        { return Text_iterator{line.begin(), line.begin()->begin()}; }

    Text_iterator end()                // one beyond the last character of the last line
    {
        auto last = line.end();
        --last;                        // we know that the document is not empty
        return Text_iterator{last, (*last).end()};
    }
};
```

We can now iterate over the characters of a document like this:

```
void print(Document& d)
{
        for (auto p : d)
                cout << p;
}
```

Presenting the document as a sequence of characters is useful for many things, but usually we traverse a document looking for something more specific than a character. For example, here is a piece of code to delete line n:

```
void erase_line(Document& d, int n)
{
        if (!(0<=n && n<d.line.size()))
                return;
        auto p = d.line.begin();
        advance(p,n);
        d.line.erase(p);
}
```

A call advance(p,n) moves an iterator p n elements forward; advance() is a standard-library function, but we could have implemented it ourselves like this:

```
template<forward_iterator Iter>
void advance(Iter& p, int n)
{
        while (0<n) {
                ++p;
                --n;
        }
}
```

Note that advance() can be used to simulate subscripting. In fact, for a vector called v, p=v.begin(); advance(p,n); *p=x is roughly equivalent to v[n]=x. Note that "roughly" means that advance() laboriously moves past the first n–1 elements one by one, whereas the subscript goes straight to the nth element. For a list, we have to use the laborious method. It's a price we have to pay for the more flexible layout of the elements of a list.

AA For an iterator that can move both forward and backward, such as the iterator for list, a negative argument to the standard-library advance() will move the iterator backward. For an iterator that can handle subscripting, such as the iterator for a vector, std::advance() will go directly to the right element rather than slowly moving along using ++. Clearly, the standard-library advance() is a bit smarter than ours. That's worth noticing: typically, the standard-library facilities have had more care and time spent on them than we could afford, so prefer the standard facilities to "home brew."

> TRY THIS
>
> Rewrite advance() so that it will "go backward" when you give it a negative argument.

Probably, a search is the kind of iteration that is most obvious to a user. We search for

- individual words (e.g., milkshake and Gavin)
- for sequences of letters that can't easily be considered words. (e.g., secret\nhomestead – i.e., a line ending with secret followed by a line starting with homestead)
- for regular expressions (e.g., [bB]\w*ne – i.e., an upper- or lowercase B followed by zero or more letters followed by ne). See PPP2.§23.5-9.
- and more.

Let's see how to handle the second case, finding a string, using our Document layout. We use a simple – non-optimal – algorithm:

- Find the first character of our search string in the document.
- See if that character and the following characters match our search string.
- If so, we are finished; if not, we look for the next occurrence of that first character.

For generality, we adopt the STL convention of defining the text in which to search as a sequence defined by a pair of iterators. That way we can use our search function for any part of a document as well as a complete document. If we find an occurrence of our string in the document, we return an iterator to its first character; if we don't find an occurrence, we return an iterator to the end of the sequence:

```
Text_iterator find_txt(Text_iterator first, Text_iterator last, const string& s)
     // find s in [first:last)
{
     if (s.size()==0)               // can't find an empty string
          return last;
     char first_char = s[0];

     auto p = last;
     for (p = find(first,last,first_char); !(p==last || match(p,last,s)), ++p)
          // do nothing
          ;
     return p;
}
```

Returning the end of the sequence to indicate "not found" is an important STL convention. The match() function is trivial; it just compares two sequences of characters. Try writing it yourself. The find() used to look for a character in the sequence of characters is arguably the simplest standard-library algorithm (§21.1.1). We can use our find_txt() like this:

```
auto p = find_txt(my_doc.begin(), my_doc.end(), "secret\nhomestead");
if (p==my_doc.end())
     cout << "not found";
else {
     // do something
}
```

Our "text processor" and its operations are very simple. Obviously, we are aiming for simplicity and reasonable efficiency, rather than at providing a "feature-rich" editor. Don't be fooled into thinking that providing *efficient* insertion, deletion, and search for arbitrary character sequences is trivial, though. We chose this example to illustrate the power and generality of the STL concepts sequence, iterator, and container (such as **list** and **vector**) together with some STL programming conventions (techniques), such as returning the end of a sequence to indicate failure. Note that if we wanted to, we could develop **Document** into an STL container – by providing **Text_iterator** we have done the key part of representing a **Document** as a sequence of values.

19.6 vector, list, and string

Why did we use a **list** for the lines and a **vector** for the characters? More precisely, why did we use a **list** for the sequence of lines and a **vector** for the sequence of characters? Furthermore, why didn't we use a **string** to hold a line?

We can ask a slightly more general variant of this question. We have now seen five ways to store a sequence of characters:

- **char[N]** (array of **N** characters)
- **array<char,N>** (**std::array** of **N** characters; §20.6.2)
- **vector<char>**
- **string**
- **list<char>**

CC How do we choose among them for a given problem? For really simple tasks, they are interchangeable; that is, they have very similar interfaces. For example, given an iterator, we can walk through each using **++** and use ***** to access the characters. If we look at the code examples related to **Document**, we can actually replace our **vector<char>** with **list<char>** or **string** without any logical problems. Such interchangeability is fundamentally good because it allows us to choose based on performance. However, before we consider performance, we should look at logical properties of these types: what can each do that the others can't?

- **T[N]**: Doesn't know its own size. Doesn't have **begin()**, **end()**, or any of the other useful container member functions. Instead, we can use **begin(a)** and **end(a)** for an array, though (obviously) not for a pointer. Can't be systematically range checked. Can be passed to functions written in C and C-style functions. The elements are allocated contiguously in memory. The size of the array is fixed at compile time. Comparison (**==** and **!=**) and output (**<<**) use the pointer to the first element of the array, not the elements.
- **array<T,N>**: Like **T[N]**, but with no implicit conversion to a pointer (§20.6.2). Has the usual value semantics for copying and comparison.
- **vector<T>**: Can do just about everything, including **insert()** and **erase()**. Provides subscripting. List operations, such as **insert()** and **erase()**, typically involve moving elements (that can be inefficient for large elements and large numbers of elements). Can be range checked. The elements are allocated contiguously in memory. A **vector** is expandable (e.g., use **push_back()**). Elements of a vector are stored (contiguously) in an array. Comparison operators (**==**, **!=**, **<**, **<=**, **>**, and **>=**) compare elements.
- **string**: Elements are characters. Provides all the common and useful operations plus specific text manipulation operations, such as concatenation (**+** and **+=**). The elements are guaranteed to be contiguous in memory. A **string** is expandable. Comparison operators (**==**, **!=**, **<**, **<=**, **>**, and **>=**) compare elements.

- list<T>: Provides all the common and usual operations, except subscripting. We can **insert()** and **erase()** without moving other elements. Needs two words extra (for link pointers) for each element. It can be expensive to iterate over the elements. A **list** is expandable. Comparison operators (==, !=, <, <=, >, and >=) compare elements.

AA

As we have seen (§16.1), arrays are useful and necessary for dealing with memory at the lowest level and for interfacing with code written in C (PPP2.§27.1.2, PPP2.§27.5). Apart from that, **vector** is preferred because it is easier to use, more flexible, and safer.

A **list<char>** takes up at least three times as much memory as the other three alternatives – on a PC a **list<char>** uses 12 bytes per element; a **vector<char>** uses 1 byte per element. For large numbers of characters, that can be significant.

AA

In what way is a **vector** superior to a **string**? Looking at the lists of their properties, it seems that a **string** can do all that a **vector** can, and more. That's part of the problem: since **string** has to do more things, it is harder to optimize. In fact, **vector** tends to be optimized for "memory operations" such as **push_back()**, whereas **string** tends to be optimized for copying, for dealing with short strings, and for interaction with C-style strings. In the text editor example, we chose **vector** because we were using **insert()** and **erase()**. That is a performance reason, though. The major logical difference is that you can have a **vector** of just about any element type. We have a choice only when we are thinking about characters. In conclusion, prefer **vector** to **string** unless you need string operations, such as concatenation or reading whitespace-separated words.

> TRY THIS
>
> What does that list of differences mean in real code? For each of **char[]**, **vector<char>**, **list<char>**, and **string**, define one with the value **"Hello"**, pass it to a function as an argument, write out the number of characters in the string passed, try to compare it to **"Hello"** in that function (to see if you really did pass **"Hello"**), and compare the argument to **"Howdy"** to see which would come first in a dictionary. Copy the argument into another variable of the same type.

> TRY THIS
>
> Do the previous **TRY THIS** for an array of **int**, **vector<int>**, and **list<int>** each with the value **{ 1, 2, 3, 4, 5 }**.

Drill

[1] Define an array of **int**s with the ten elements { 0, 1, 2, 3, 4, 5, 6, 7, 8, 9 }.

[2] Define a **vector<int>** with those ten elements.

[3] Define a **list<int>** with those ten elements.

[4] Define a second array, vector, and list, each initialized as a copy of the first array, vector, and list, respectively.

[5] Increase the value of each element in the array by 2; increase the value of each element in the vector by 3; increase the value of each element in the list by 5.

[6] Write a simple **copy()** operation,

```
template<input_iterator Iter1, output_iterator Iter2>
Iter2 copy(Iter1 f1, Iter1 e1, Iter2 f2);
```

that copies [f1,e1) to [f2,f2+(e1−f1)) and returns f2+(e1−f1) just like std::copy(). Note that if f1==e1 the sequence is empty, so that there is nothing to copy.

[7] Use your copy() to copy the array into the vector and to copy the list into the array.

[8] Use std::find() to see if the vector contains the value 3 and print out its position if it does; use find() to see if the list contains the value 27 and print out its position if it does. The "position" of the first element is 0, the position of the second element is 1, etc. Note that if find() returns the end of the sequence, the value wasn't found.

Remember to test after each step.

Review

[1] Why does code written by different people look different? Give examples.
[2] What are simple questions we ask of data?
[3] What are a few different ways of storing data?
[4] What basic operations can we do to a collection of data items?
[5] What are some ideals for the way we store our data?
[6] What is an STL sequence?
[7] What is an STL iterator? What operations does it support?
[8] How do you move an iterator to the next element?
[9] How do you move an iterator to the previous element?
[10] What happens if you try to move an iterator past the end of a sequence?
[11] What kinds of iterators can you move to the previous element?
[12] Why is it useful to separate data from algorithms?
[13] What is the STL?
[14] What is a linked list? How does it fundamentally differ from a vector?
[15] What is a link (in a linked list)?
[16] What does insert() do? What does erase() do?
[17] How do you know if a sequence is empty?
[18] What operations does an iterator for a list provide?
[19] How do you iterate over a container using the STL?
[20] When would you use a string rather than a vector?
[21] When would you use a list rather than a vector?
[22] What is a container?
[23] What should begin() and end() do for a container?

Terms

algorithm	empty sequence	singly-linked list	list
array container	end()	size_type	auto
erase()	STL	begin()	insert()
traversal	container	iteration	using
contiguous	iterator	type alias	doubly-linked list
range	linked list	value_type	element
sequence	lifting	generalize	

Exercises

[1] If you haven't already, do all **TRY THIS** exercises in the chapter.

[2] Get the Jack-and-Jill example from §19.2.1 to work. Use input from a couple of small files to test it.

[3] Look at the palindrome examples (§16.5); redo the Jack-and-Jill example from §19.2.1 using that variety of techniques.

[4] Find and fix the errors in the Jack-and-Jill example from §19.2.1 by using STL techniques throughout.

[5] Define an input and an output operator (>> and <<) for vector.

[6] Write a find-and-replace operation for Documents based on §19.5.

[7] Find the lexicographical last string in an unsorted vector<string>.

[8] Define a function that counts the number of characters in a Document.

[9] Define a program that counts the number of words in a Document. Provide two versions: one that defines *word* as "a whitespace-separated sequence of characters" and one that defines *word* as "a sequence of consecutive alphabetic characters." For example, with the former definition, alpha.numeric and as12b are both single words, whereas with the second definition they are both two words.

[10] Define a version of the word-counting program where the user can specify the set of white-space characters.

[11] Given a list<int> as a (by-reference) parameter, make a vector<double> and copy the elements of the list into it. Verify that the copy was complete and correct. Then print the elements sorted in order of increasing value.

[12] Complete the definition of list from §19.3 and get the high() example to run. Allocate a Link to represent one past the end.

[13] We don't really need a "real" one-past-the-end Link for a list. Modify your solution to the previous exercise to use nullptr to represent a pointer to the (nonexistent) one-past-the-end Link (list<Elem>::end()); that way, the size of an empty list can be equal to the size of a single pointer.

[14] Define a singly-linked list, Slist, in the style of std::list. Which operations from list could you reasonably eliminate from Slist because it doesn't have back pointers?

[15] Define a Pvector to be like a vector of pointers except that it contains pointers to objects and its destructor deletes each object.

[16] Define an **Ovector** that is like **Pvector** except that the **[ ]** and $*$ operators return a reference to the object pointed to by an element rather than the pointer.

[17] Define an **Ownership_vector** that holds pointers to objects like **Pvector** but provides a mechanism for the user to decide which objects are owned by the vector (i.e., which objects are **delete**d by the destructor). Hint: This exercise is simple if you were awake for Chapter 11.

[18] Define a range-checked iterator for **vector** (a random-access iterator).

[19] Define a range-checked iterator for **list** (a bidirectional iterator).

[20] Run a small timing experiment to compare the cost of using **vector** and **list**. You can find an explanation of how to time a program in §20.4. Generate *N* random **int** values in the range [0: *N*). As each **int** is generated, insert it into a **vector<int>** (which grows by one element each time). Keep the **vector** sorted; that is, a value is inserted after every previous value that is less than or equal to the new value and before every previous value that is larger than the new value. Now do the same experiment using a **list<int>** to hold the **int**s. For which *N* is the **list** faster than the **vector**? Try to explain your result. This experiment was first suggested by John Bentley.

[21] Define and test a **Checked_iterator**; that is, an iterator that "knows" the size of its range and throws an exception if we try to access outside that. Hint: §20.7.2.

Postscript

CC If we have *N* kinds of containers of data and *M* things we'd like to do with them, we can easily end up writing $N*M$ pieces of code. If the data is of *K* different types, we could even end up with $N*M*K$ pieces of code. The STL addresses this proliferation by having the element type as a parameter (taking care of the *K* factor) and by separating access to data from algorithms. By using iterators to access data in any kind of container from any algorithm, we can make do with $N+M$ algorithms. This is a huge simplification. For example, if we have about 12 containers and about 125 algorithms (not even counting the range algorithms), the brute-force approach would require 1,500 functions, whereas the STL strategy requires only 125 functions and 12 definitions of iterators: we just saved ourselves 90% of the work. In fact, this underestimates the saved effort because many algorithms take two pairs of iterators and the pairs need not be of the same type (e.g. **copy()**). In addition, the STL provides conventions for defining algorithms that simplify writing correct code and composable code, so the saving is greater still.

20

Maps and Sets

Write programs that do one thing
and do it well.
Write programs to work together.
– Doug McIlroy

The C++ standard library offers more containers than **vector** and **list**. In this chapter, we introduce the associative containers **map** and **unordered_map** in which we can look up a value by giving a "key." For example, looking for a record by quoting a name. Such types are pervasive in applications because they simplify and speed up common tasks. Some types are not standard-library containers, but can be seen as a sequence of elements. Examples are built-in arrays and I/O streams. The notion of iterators is so flexible that such types can be fitted into the framework. To benefit from that flexibility, we generalize ranges.

§20.1 Associative containers
§20.2 **map**
Structured binding; **map** overview; Another **map** example
§20.3 **unordered_map**
§20.4 Timing
Dates
§20.5 **set**
§20.6 Container overview
Almost containers; **array**; Adapting built-in arrays to the STL; Adapting I/O streams to the STL; Using a **set** to keep order
§20.7 Ranges and iterators
Iterator categories; Output ranges

20.1 Associative containers

CC After vector, the most useful standard-library container is probably the map. A map (§20.2) is an ordered sequence of (key,value) pairs in which you can look up a value based on a key; for example, my_phone_book["Nicholas"] could be Nicholas' phone number. The only potential competitor to map in a popularity contest is unordered_map (§20.3), and that's a map optimized for keys that are strings. Data structures similar to map and unordered_map are known under many names, such as *associative arrays*, *hash tables*, and *red-black trees*. In the standard library, we collectively call such data structures *associative containers*. Popular and useful concepts always seem to have many names.

The standard library provides eight associative containers:

Associative containers	
map	an ordered container of (key,value) pairs
set	an ordered container of keys
unordered_map	an unordered container of (key,value) pairs
unordered_set	an unordered container of keys
multimap	a map where a key can occur multiple times
multiset	a set where a key can occur multiple times
unordered_multimap	an unordered_map where a key can occur multiple times
unordered_multiset	an unordered_set where a key can occur multiple times

20.2 Map

Consider a conceptually simple task: make a list of the number of occurrences of words in a text. The obvious way of doing this is to keep a list of words we have seen together with the number of times we have seen each. When we read a new word, we see if we have already seen it; if we have, we increase its count by one; if not, we insert it in our list and give it the value 1. We could do that using a list or a vector, but then we would have to do a search for each word we read. That could be slow. A map stores its keys in a way that makes it easy to see if a key is present, thus making the searching part of our task trivial:

```
int main()
{
        map<string,int> words;                          // keep (word,frequency) pairs
        for (string s; cin>>s; )
                ++words[s];                             // note: words is subscripted by a string
        for (const pair<string,int>& p : words)
                cout << p.first << ": " << p.second << '\n';
}
```

The really interesting part of the program is ++words[s]. As we can see from the first line of main(), words is a map of (string,int) pairs; that is, words maps strings to ints. In other words, given a string, words can give us access to its corresponding int. So, when we subscript words with a string (holding a word read from our input), words[s] is a reference to the int corresponding to s.

Let's look at a concrete example: words["sultan"]. If we have not seen the string "sultan" before, "sultan" will be entered into words with the default value for an int, which is 0. Now, words has an entry ("sultan",0). It follows that if we haven't seen "sultan" before, ++words["sultan"] will associate the value 1 with the string "sultan". CC

Now look again at the program: ++words[s] takes every "word" we get from input and increases its value by one. The first time a new word is seen, it gets the value 1. Now the meaning of the loop is clear:

```
for (string s; cin>>s; )
      ++words[s];                    // note: words is subscripted by a string
```

This reads every (whitespace-separated) word on input and computes the number of occurrences for each. Now all we have to do is to produce the output. We can iterate through a map, just like any other STL container. The elements of a map<string,int> are of type pair<string,int>. The first member of a pair is called first and the second member second (§20.2.2):

```
for (const pair<string,int>& p : words)
      cout << p.first << ": " << p.second << '\n';
```

As a test, we can feed the opening statements of the first edition of *The C++ Programming Language* [TC++PL] to our program:

> "*C++ is a general purpose programming language designed to make programming more enjoyable for the serious programmer. Except for minor details, C++ is a superset of the C programming language. In addition to the facilities provided by C, C++ provides flexible and efficient facilities for defining new types.*"

We get the output

```
C: 1
C++: 3
C,: 1
Except: 1
In: 1
a: 2
addition: 1
and: 1
by: 1
defining: 1
designed: 1
details,: 1
efficient: 1
enjoyable: 1
facilities: 2
flexible: 1
for: 3
general: 1
is: 2
language: 1
language.: 1
make: 1
```

```
minor: 1
more: 1
new: 1
of: 1
programmer.: 1
programming: 3
provided: 1
provides: 1
purpose: 1
serious: 1
superset: 1
the: 3
to: 2
types.: 1
```

If we don't like to distinguish between upper- and lowercase letters or would like to eliminate punctuation, we can do so: see exercise 1.

20.2.1 Structured binding

Looking at **map** nodes is an example of using functions returning more than one value. In fact, dereferencing a **map** iterator gives us a **pair** with members **first** and **second**. Why **first** and **second**? Well, why not? The implementer of **pair** had to call them something. On the other hand, as users of this particular **pair<string,int>**, we think of those values as **key** and **value**. A mechanism called *structured binding* lets us name members of structures returned from functions. For example:

```
for (const auto& [key,value] : words)
    cout << key << ": " << value << '\n';
```

The iteration over **words** returns references to **pair<key,value>** objects. The structured binding simply allows us to use our preferred names **key** and **value** for those **pair's first** and **second**. No additional copying is done.

Like all powerful mechanisms, structured binding can be overused and lead to obscure code, but in this case, as in many others, we think it makes the code more readable.

20.2.2 map overview

CC So what is a **map**? There are a variety of ways of implementing maps, but the STL **map** implementations tend to be balanced binary search trees; more specifically, they are red-black trees. We will not go into the details, but now you know the technical terms, so you can look them up in the literature or on the Web, should you want to know more. A tree is made out of nodes:

map node :
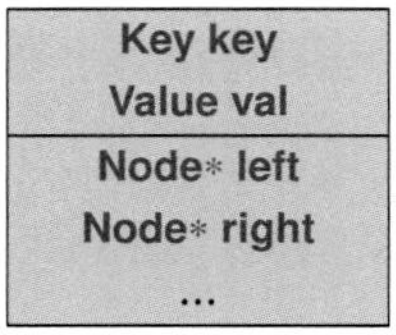

A **Node** holds a key, its corresponding value, and pointers to two descendant **Node**s.

Assuming a type **Fruit** with a suitable constructor, we can write

```
map<Fruit,int> fruits = { {Kiwi,100}, {Quince,0}, {Plum,8}, {Apple,7}, {Grape,2345}, {Orange,99} };
```

This generates a data structure like this:

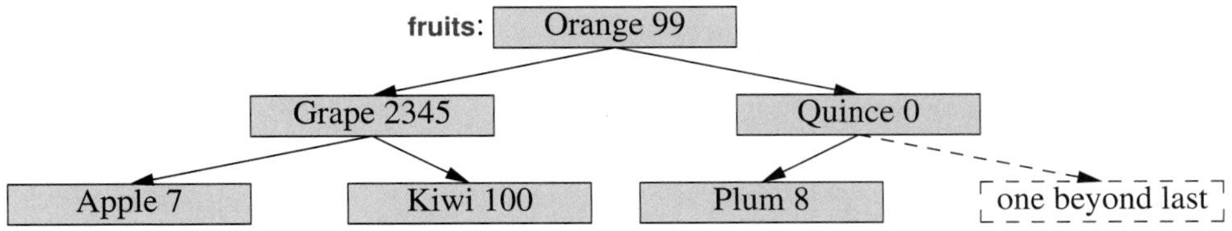

Calling the key member of a **map<Fruit,int>** node **key**, the basic rule of a binary search tree is

```
left−>key<key && key<right−>key
```

That is, for every node,

- Its left sub-node's key is less than the node's key, and
- The node's key is less than its right sub-node's key

You can verify that this holds for each node in the tree. That allows us to search "down the tree from its root." Curiously enough, in computer science literature, trees grow downward from their roots. In the example, the root node is **{Orange,99}**. We just compare our way down the tree until we find what we are looking for or the place where it should have been. A tree is called *balanced* when (as in the example above) each sub-tree has approximately as many nodes as every other sub-tree that's equally far from the root. Being balanced minimizes the average number of nodes we have to visit to reach a node. **AA**

A balanced-tree **Node** typically also holds some data which the map will use to keep its tree of nodes balanced. If a tree with *N* nodes is balanced, we have to at most look at *log2(N)* nodes to find a node. That's much better than the average of *N/2* nodes we would have to examine if we had the keys in a list and searched from the beginning (the worst case for such a linear search is *N*). (See also §20.3.) For example, have a look at an unbalanced tree:

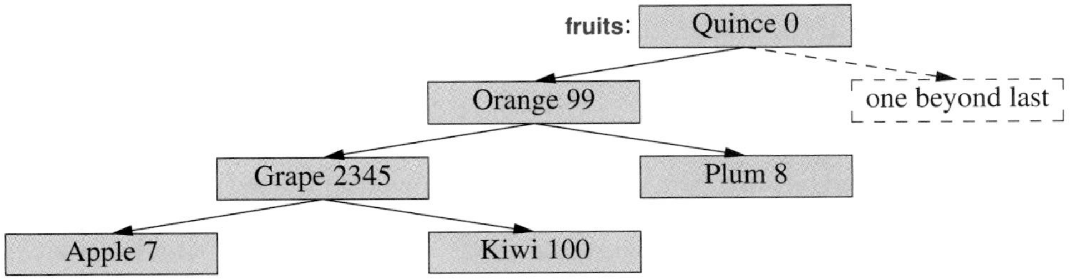

This tree still meets the criteria that the key of every node is greater than that of its left sub-node and less than that of its right sub-node:

```
left−>key<key && key<right−>key
```

However, this version of the tree is unbalanced, so we now have three "hops" to reach Apple and Kiwi, rather than the two we had in the balanced tree. For trees of many nodes the difference can be very significant, so the trees used to implement maps are balanced.

We don't have to understand about trees to use map. It is just reasonable to assume that professionals understand at least the fundamentals of their tools. What we do have to understand is the interface to map provided by the standard library. Here is a slightly simplified version:

```
template<typename Key, typename Value, binary_operation<Value> Cmp = less<Key>>
class map {
        // ...
        using value_type = pair<Key,Value>;                    // a map deals in (Key,Value) pairs

        using iterator = sometype1;                            // similar to a pointer to a tree node
        using const_iterator = sometype2;

        iterator begin();                                      // points to first element
        iterator end();                                        // points one beyond the last element

        Value& operator[](const Key& k);                       // subscript with k

        iterator find(const Key& k);                           // is there an entry for k?

        iterator erase(iterator p);                            // remove element pointed to by p
        pair<iterator, bool> insert(const value_type&);        // insert a (key,value) pair
        // ...
};
```

CC You can imagine the iterator to be similar to a Node*, but you cannot rely on your implementation using that specific type to implement iterator.

The similarity to the interfaces for vector and list (§19.4) is obvious. The main difference is that when you iterate over a map, the elements pointed to by the iterators are pairs – of type pair<Key,Value>. That type is another useful STL type:

```
template<typename T1, typename T2>
struct pair {                                  // simplified version of std::pair
        T1 first;
        T2 second;
        // ...
};
```

CC Note that when you iterate over a map, the elements will come in the order defined by the key. For example, using structured binding (§20.2.1) to get nicer names than first and second:

```
for (const auto& [key,value] : fruits)
        cout << '(' << key << ',' << value << ") ";
```

gives:

```
(Apple,7) (Grape,2345) (Kiwi,100) (Orange,99) (Plum,8) (Quince,0)
```

The order in which we inserted those fruits doesn't matter.

The **insert()** operation has an odd return value, which we most often ignore in simple programs. It is a pair of an iterator to the (key,value) element and a **bool** which is **true** if the (key,value) pair was inserted by this call of **insert()**. If the key was already in the map, the insertion fails and the **bool** is **false**.

Note that you can define the meaning of the order used by a map by supplying a third argument (**Cmp** in the map declaration). For example: CC

```
map<string, double, No_case> m;
```

No_case defines case-insensitive compare; see §21.5. By default the order is defined by **less<Key>**, meaning "less than."

20.2.3 Another map example

To better appreciate the utility of **map**, consider a stock market index. The way that works is to take a set of companies and assign each a "weight." For example, when last we looked in the Dow Jones Industrial Index, Alcoa had the weight of 2.4808. To get the current value of the index, we multiply each company's share price with its weight and add all the resulting weighted prices together. For example:

```
// calculate the Dow Jones Industrial index:
vector<double> dow_price = {        // share price for each company
        81.86, 34.69, 54.45,
        // ...
};

list<double> dow_weight = {        // weight in index for each company
        5.8549, 2.4808, 3.8940,
        // ...
};

double dji_index = 0;
for (size_t i = 0; i<dow_price.size(); ++i)
      dji_index += dow_price[i]*dow_weight[i];

cout << "DJI value " << dji_index << '\n';
```

The code there was correct if and only if all weights appear in the same position in their **vector** as their corresponding name. That's implicit and could easily be the source of an obscure bug. There are many ways of attacking that problem, but an attractive one is to keep each weight together with its company's ticker symbol, e.g., ("AA",2.4808). A "ticker symbol" is an abbreviation of a company name used where a terse representation is needed. Similarly, we can keep the company's ticker symbol together with its share price, e.g., ("AA",34.69). Finally, for those of us who don't regularly deal with the U.S. stock market, we can keep the company's ticker symbol together with the company name, e.g., ("AA","Alcoa Inc."); that is, we could keep three maps of corresponding values.

First we make the (symbol,price) map:

```
map<string,double> dow_price = { // Dow Jones Industrial index (symbol,price);
                                  // for up-to-date quotes see www.djindexes.com
        {"MMM",104.48},
        {"AAPL",165.02},
        {"MSFT",285.76},
        // ...
};
```

The (symbol,weight) map:

```
map<string,double> dow_weight = {        // Dow (symbol,weight)
        {"MMM", 2.41},
        {"AAPL",2.84},
        {"MSFT",4.88},
        // ...
};
```

The (symbol,name) map:

```
map<string,string> dow_name = {   // Dow (symbol,name)
        {"MMM","3M"},
        {"AAPL","Apple"},
        {"MSFT","Microsoft"},
        // ...
};
```

Given those maps, we can conveniently extract all kinds of information. For example:

```
double caterpillar = dow_price ["CAT"];           // read values from a map
double boeing_price = dow_price ["BA"];

if (dow_price.find("INTC") != dow_price.end())          // find an entry in a map
        cout << "Intel is in the Dow\n";
```

Iterating through a map is easy:

```
for (const auto& [symbol,price] : dow_price)
        cout << symbol << '\t' << price << '\t' << dow_name[symbol] << '\n';
```

AA Why might someone keep such data in **maps** rather than **vectors**? We used a **map** to make the association between the different values explicit. That's one common reason. Another is that a **map** keeps its elements in the order defined by its key. When we iterated through **dow** above, we output the symbols in alphabetical order; had we used a **vector** we would have had to sort. The most common reason to use a **map** is simply that we want to look up values based on the key. For large sequences, finding something using **find()** is far slower than looking it up in a sorted structure, such as a **map**.

> TRY THIS
>
> Get this little example to work. Then add a few companies of your own choice, with weights of your choice.

20.3 unordered_map

To find an element in a **vector**, **find()** needs to examine all the elements from the beginning to the element with the right value or to the end. On average, the cost is proportional to the length of the **vector** (*N*); we call that cost *O(N)*.

To find an element in a **map**, the subscript operator needs to examine all the elements of the tree from the root to the element with the right value or to a leaf. On average, the cost is proportional to the depth of the tree. A balanced binary tree holding *N* elements has a maximum depth of *log2(N)*, so the lookup cost is *O(log2(N))*; that is, cost proportional to *log2(N)*, and that is actually pretty good compared to *O(N)*:

N	16	128	1024	16∗1024	1024∗1024	1024∗1024∗1024
log2(N)	4	7	10	14	20	30

The actual cost will depend on how soon in our search we find our values and how expensive comparisons and iterations are. It is usually somewhat more expensive to chase pointers (as the **map** lookup does) than to increment a pointer (as **find()** does in a **vector**).

For some types, notably integers and character strings, we can do even better than a **map**'s tree search. We will not go into details, but the idea is that given a key, we compute an index into a **vector**. That index is called a *hash value*, the function that computes it is called a *hash function*, and a container that uses this technique is typically called a *hash table*. The number of possible keys is far larger than the number of slots in the hash table. For example, we often use a hash function to map from the billions of possible strings into an index for a **vector** with 1000 elements. This can be tricky, but it can be handled well and is especially useful for implementing large maps. The main virtue of a hash table is that on average the cost of a lookup is (near) constant and independent of the number of elements in the table, that is, *O(1)*. Obviously, that can be a significant advantage for large maps, say a map of 500,000 URLs. For more information about hash lookup, you can look at the documentation for **unordered_map** (available on the Web) or just about any basic text on data structures (look for "hash table" and "hashing"). The standard library provides reasonable hash functions for the built-in types and strings. Graphically:

- Lookup in unsorted **vector**:

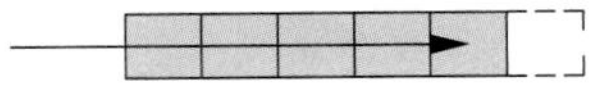

- Lookup in **map** (balanced binary tree):

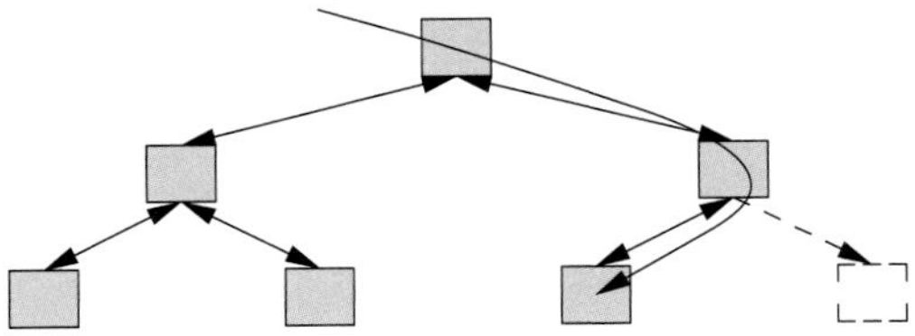

• Lookup in unordered_map (hash table):

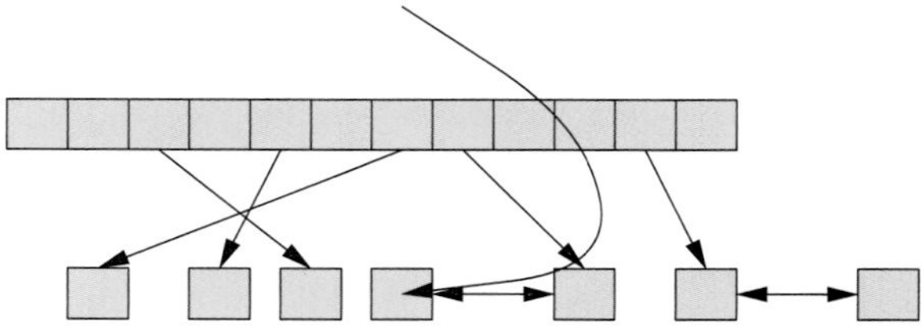

AA The STL unordered_map is implemented using a hash table, just as the STL map is implemented using a balanced binary tree, and an STL vector is implemented using an array. Part of the utility of the STL is to fit all of these ways of storing and accessing data into a common framework together with algorithms. The rule of thumb is:

- Use vector unless you have a good reason not to.
- Use map if you need to look up based on a value (and if your key type has a reasonable and efficient less-than operation).
- Use unordered_map if you need to do a lot of lookup in a large map and you don't need an ordered traversal (and if you can find a good hash function for your key type).

Here, we will not describe unordered_map in any detail. You can use an unordered_map with a key of type string or int exactly like a map, except that when you iterate over the elements, the elements will not be ordered. For example, we could rewrite part of the Dow Jones example from §20.2.3 like this:

```
unordered_map<string,double> dow_price;

for (const auto& [symbol,price] : dow_price)
      cout << symbol << '\t' << price << '\t' << dow_name[symbol] << '\n';
```

Lookup in dow might now be faster. However, that would not be significant because there are only 30 companies in that index. Had we been keeping the prices of all the companies on the New York Stock Exchange, we might have noticed a performance difference. We will, however, notice a logical difference: the output from the iteration will now not be in alphabetical order.

20.4 Timing

We have mentioned efficiency and the speed of operations. But how fast do these containers really operate? We consider talking about "efficiency" without concrete measurement suspect: Don't make claims about efficiency without backing up those claims with measurements. The big-O complexity measures (§20.3) are all very good and one – often excellent – thing to consider, but if performance might matter, we would like to measure how much time a piece of code really takes to run. Consider:

```
using namespace chrono;                // that's where the timing support is

auto t0 = system_clock::now();         // the point of time of the call
auto x = do_something();
auto t1 = system_clock::now();
cout << "res: " << x <<'\n';
cout << t1-t0 << '\n';                 // that's how long it took
```

The basic technique is that simple, but modern computers are fast, so this style of measurements requires a fair amount of computation to get meaningful results. It also requires that we run our tests repeatedly, say 3 or 5 times, to make it likely that our result isn't corrupted by something else going on on the computer.

A clock's **now()** function returns a point in time, a **time point**, so subtracting two **time_points** gives a period of time, a **duration**.

Why did we write **res** to output? Well, if we didn't use a result from **do_something()**, the optimizer would decide that we didn't need to run the code and eliminate it. That is, the time measured would be **0**.

That said, let's try to measure the cost of lookup in a **vector** and a **map** using the random number generators from §4.7.5:

```
using namespace chrono;                                  // that's where the timing support is

vector<pair<string,int>> v = generate(1'000'000);        // generate some data (§4.7.5):
string x = v[v.size()/2].first;                          // pick a string to search for (§20.2.2)

auto t0 = system_clock::now();                           // the point of time of the call
auto pv = ranges::find_if(v, [&x](const auto& s) { return s.first == x; });          // linear search
auto t1 = system_clock::now();
cout << "vector: " << pv->second << '\n';
cout <<  duration_cast<microseconds>(t1-t0).count() << "us\n\n";         // count() is a number of "clock ticks"

map<string, int> m {v.begin(), v.end()}; ;
auto t2 = system_clock::now();
auto vm = m[x];                                          // tree search; may add an element
auto t3 = system_clock::now();
cout << "map[]: " << vm << '\n';
cout << duration_cast<microseconds>(t3-t2).count() << "us\n\n";

auto t22 = system_clock::now();
auto pm = ranges::find_if(m, [&x](const auto& s) { return s.first == x; });          // linear search
auto t32 = system_clock::now();
cout << "map find_if: " << pm->second << '\n';
cout << duration_cast<microseconds>(t32-t22).count() << "us\n";
```

We got:

```
vector: 665618
3085us

map[]: 665618
2us

map find_if: 665618
81749us
```

The exact results will be different on your machine.

We could have output the results with the simpler statement:

```
cout << t1−t0 << "\n";
```

However, we preferred to be explicit about the unit of measurement and **duration_cast** does that; **us** is a common abbreviation for microsecond because it looks a bit like the Greek letter μ.

We find simple timing measurements immensely useful for getting a feel for run-time costs. They are not perfect, but far better than guessing. It is seriously hard to guess about the performance of real-world code on modern computers.

> TRY THIS
>
> Run your own version of that timing experiment. Run it at least three times and with at least three different numbers of elements. Explain your results.

In §4.7.5, we promised to give some details about how our **random_int()** functions worked. Here is the implementation:

```
namespace Random {
        using engine = default_random_engine;
        using distribution = uniform_int_distribution;

        engine ran;

        int random_int(int min, int max) { return distribution {min, max } (ran); }
        int random_int(int max) { return random_int(0, max); }
        void seed(int s) { Random::ran.seed(s); }
        void seed() { Random::ran.seed(random_device{}()); }
}
```

The **PPP::random_int()** and other functions are redundant; they just call their **Random** equivalents. In professional code, we'd use **Random::random_int()**.

The reason for the namespace **Random** is to have a common engine for all uses, rather than a bunch of different ones, while still avoiding polluting the global namespace. Having a single engine improves randomness. The definition of **seed()** is a bit of black magic. It digs deep into the guts of the operating environment to gain almost perfect randomness, but it is still part of the ISO C++ standard library. The **using**-declarations allow us to quickly change our engine and distribution. We could have parameterized these functions with an integer type but decided to keep it all simple by sticking to **int**.

20.4.1 Dates

Dates has nothing to do with **unordered_maps** or containers in general, but after talking about timing and the notions of **time_point** and **duration**, we inevitably think about days, weeks, and dates.

Here is a simple example:

```
using namespace chrono;

auto now = system_clock::now();                // clock's precision, probably microseconds or less
auto today = floor<days>(now);                 // round the time to days
cout << weekday(today) << '\n';                // Tue
cout << format("{:%A}\n", weekday(today));     // Tuesday
```

First we get the time, then we round it down to the precision of days (rather than some much smaller unit of time), and then we write out the weekday. The default output was **Tue**, but if we don't like the abbreviation, we can get **Tuesday** by using **format()** (§9.10.6).

We can use the facilities in **chrono** to make calendars and operations on those. For example:

```
sys_days xmas = December/24/2023;
cout << "New Year " << xmas + days{7} << '\n';
```

In the likely event that you have to write code that deals with time on a human scale, read up on the standard-library **chrono** facilities for dates and time zones. This library component is far more likely to give correct results than someone's "homebrew" code. A standard-library component is tested and documented. Also, its designers are likely to have thought of many more real-world needs and constraints than we are likely to while working on a problem we need to solve in a reasonable time. For example, **chrono** handles time zones and leap seconds correctly. If your reaction to that nugget of information is "but time zones change in irrational ways every year!" and "what is a leap second?" you have made our point.

On top of that, the **chrono** library is blindingly fast.

20.5 Set

We can think of a **set** as a **map** where we are not interested in the values, or rather as a **map** without separate values. We can visualize a **set** node like this: CC

set node :

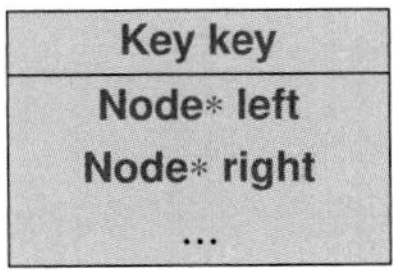

We can represent the **set** of fruits used in the **map** example (§20.2.2) like this:

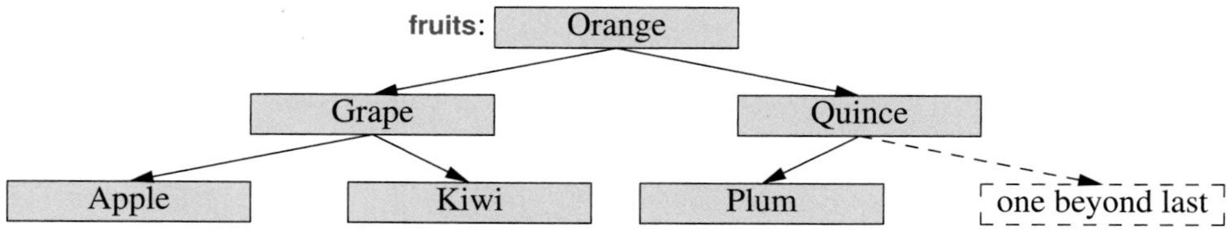

What are sets useful for? As it happens, there are lots of problems that require us to remember if we have seen a value. Keeping track of which fruits are available (independently of price) is one example; building a dictionary is another. A slightly different style of usage is having a set of "records"; that is, the elements are objects that potentially contain "lots of" information – we simply use a member as the key. For example:

```
struct Fruit {
        string name;
        int count;
        double unit_price;
        Date last_sale_date;
};

struct Fruit_order {
        bool operator()(const Fruit& a, const Fruit& b) const
        {
                return a.name<b.name;
        }
};

set<Fruit, Fruit_order> inventory;            // use Fruit_order(x,y) to compare Fruits
```

Here again, we see how using a function object (§21.2) can significantly increase the range of problems for which an STL component is useful.

CC Since **set** doesn't have a value type, it doesn't support subscripting (**operator[]()**) either. We must use "list operations," such as **insert()** and **erase()**, instead. Unfortunately, **map** and **set** don't support **push_back()** either – the reason is obvious: the **set** and not the programmer determines where the new value is inserted. Instead use **insert()**. For example:

```
inventory.insert(Fruit{"quince",5});
inventory.insert(Fruit{"apple",200,0.37});
```

One advantage of **set** over **map** is that you can use the value obtained from an iterator directly: the dereference operator gives a value of the element type:

```
for (auto p = inventory.begin(); p!=inventory.end(); ++p)
        cout << *p << '\n';
```

Assuming, of course, that you have defined << for **Fruit**. Or we could equivalently write

```
for (const auto& x : inventory)
        cout << x << '\n';
```

20.6 Container overview

The STL provides quite a few containers:

Standard containers	
vector	a contiguously allocated sequence of elements; use it as the default container
list	a doubly-linked list; use when you need to insert and delete elements without moving existing elements
forward_list	a singly-linked list; use for lists that are mostly empty
deque	a cross between a list and a vector; don't use until you have expert-level knowledge of algorithms and machine architecture
map	a balanced ordered tree; use it when you need to access elements by value (§20.2)
multimap	a balanced ordered tree where there can be multiple copies of a key; use it when you need to access elements by value
unordered_map	a hash table; an optimized version of map; use for large maps when you need high performance and can devise a good hash function (§20.3)
unordered_multimap	a hash table where there can be multiple copies of a key; an optimized version of multimap; use for large maps when you need high performance and can devise a good hash function
set	a balanced ordered tree; use it when you need to keep track of individual values (§20.5)
multiset	a balanced ordered tree where there can be multiple copies of a key; use it when you need to keep track of individual values
unordered_set	like unordered_map, but just with values, not (key,value) pairs
unordered_multiset	like unordered_multimap, but just with values, not (key,value) pairs

You can look up incredible amounts of additional information on these containers and their use in books and online documentation.

AA

Do you feel cheated? Do you think we should explain all about containers and their use to you? That's just not possible. There are too many standard facilities, too many useful techniques, and too many useful libraries for you to absorb them all at once. Programming is too rich a field for anyone to know all facilities and techniques – it can also be a noble art. As a programmer, you must acquire the habit of seeking out new information about language facilities, libraries, and techniques when you need it. Programming is a dynamic and rapidly developing field, so just being content with what you know and are comfortable with is a recipe for being left behind. "Look it up" is a perfectly reasonable answer to many problems, and as your skills grow and mature, it will more and more often be the answer.

On the other hand, you will find that once you understand vector, list, and map and the standard algorithms presented in Chapter 21, you'll find other STL and STL-style containers easy to use. You'll also find that you have the basic knowledge to understand non-STL containers and code using them.

CC What is a container? You can find the definition of an STL container in all of the sources above. Here we will just give an informal definition. An STL container

- Has a sequence of elements [**begin():end()**).
- Provides copy operations that copy all elements.
- Provides move operations that move all elements.
- Names its element type **value_type**.
- Has iterator types called **iterator** and **const_iterator**. Iterators provide *, **++** (both prefix and postfix), **==**, and **!=** with the appropriate semantics. The iterators for **list** also provide **--** for moving backward in the sequence; that's called a *bidirectional iterator*. The iterators for **vector** also provide **--**, **[ ]**, **+**, and **-** and are called *random-access iterators* (§20.7.1).
- Provides **insert()** and **erase()**, **front()** and **back()**, **push_back()** and **pop_back()**, **size()**, **swap()**, etc.; **vector** and **map** also provide subscripting (e.g., operator **[ ]**).
- Provides comparison operators (**==**, **!=**, **<**, **<=**, **>**, and **>=**) that compare the elements. Containers use lexicographical ordering for **<**, **<=**, **>**, and **>=**; that is, they compare their elements in order starting with the first.

The **forward_list** is an example of a container that offers a forward iterator, but no more. That is, we can traverse a **forward_list** from its beginning to its end, but not the other way.

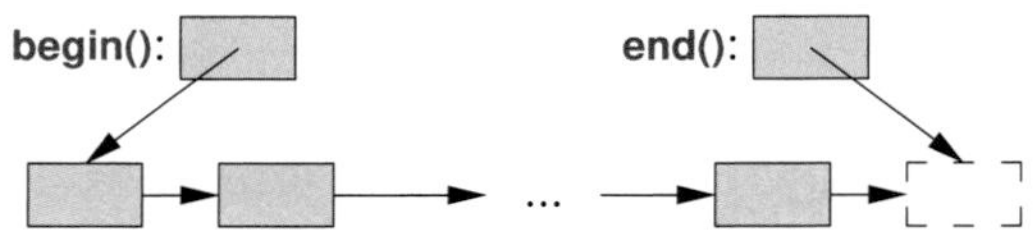

For example:

```
forward_list<double> lst = {0.0,1.1,2.2,3.3};
for (auto p = lst.begin(); p!=lst::end(); ++p)          // OK (but verbose)
      cout << *p << '\n';
for (auto p = lst.end(); p!=lst::begin(); --p)          // error: can't go backwards (no --)
      cout << *p << '\n';
for (const int x : lst)                                 // OK
      cout << *p << '\n';
size_t sz = lst.size();                                 // error: a forward_list doesn't have size()
size_t sz2 = 0;
for (auto p = lst.begin(); p!=lst::end(); ++p)          // OK
      ++sz2;
```

Why no **size()**? By *not* storing the size, a **forward_list** can be represented as a single pointer to its first node, if any. That minimal size is important because a common use of **forward_list**s is where many thousands of usually empty containers are needed. If you want to know the number of elements of a **forward_list**, just count them.

Note that in the example we traversed **lst** three times. The difference between an input iterator and a forward iterator is that you can traverse a sequence repeatedly using a forward iterator.

20.6.1 Almost containers

Some data types provide much of what is required from a standard container, but not all. We sometimes refer to those as "almost containers." The most interesting of those are:

"Almost containers"	
T[n]	a built-in array; no size() or other member functions; prefer a container, such as vector, string, or array, over a built-in array when you have a choice.
array	a fixed-size array that doesn't suffer most of the problems related to the built-in arrays (§20.6.2).
string	holds only characters but provides operations useful for text manipulation, such as concatenation (+ and +=); prefer the standard string to other strings.
valarray	a numerical vector with mathematical vector operations, but with many restrictions to encourage high-performance implementations; use only if you do a lot of vector arithmetic.

In addition, many people and many organizations have produced containers that meet the standard container requirements, or almost do so.

If in doubt, use **vector**. Unless you have a solid reason not to, use **vector**. **AA**

20.6.2 array

We have repeatedly pointed out the weaknesses of the built-in arrays: they implicitly convert to pointers at the slightest provocation, they can't be copied using assignment, they don't know their own size, etc. (§16.1). We have also pointed out their main strength: they model physical memory almost perfectly. To get the best of both worlds, the standard library offers **array<T,N>** that "knows" that its size is **N** (§16.4.2). As an example, we can write an **array** version of the **high()** example from §19.3.2:

```
void f()
{
        array<double,6> arr = { 0.0, 1.1, 3.3, 5.5, 2.2, 4.4 };
        auto p = high(arr.begin(), arr.end());
        cout << "the highest value was " << *p << '\n';
}
```

Note that we did not think of **array** when we wrote **high()**. Being able to use **high()** for an **array** is a simple consequence of following standard conventions for both.

Needing to find the largest element in a sequence is common, so the standard library has a version. We could even have said:

```
auto p = ranges::max_element(arr);        // p is an iterator to the highest value element in arr
```

Given that **array<T,N>** knows its number of elements, we can (and do) provide assignment, **==**, **!=**, etc. just as for **vector**.

20.6.3 Adapting built-in arrays to the STL

When we have the definition of a built-in array in scope, we can actually see how many elements it has. For example:

```
void f(int[] a1)        // int[] looks like an array, but really is just a pointer: int*
{
        int a2[10];     // obviously 10 elements
        // ...
}
```

We have all the information needed to refer to **a2** as a [begin:end) sequence, we just need a convenient way of referring to that. The standard library provides that **begin()** and **end()**:

```
void f(int[] a1)  // int[] looks like an array argument, but really is just a pointer: int*
{
        int a2[10];                     // obviously 10 elements
        // ...
        sort(begin(a2),end(a2));        // OK
        sort(begin(a1),end(a1));        // error: we don't know where the end of a1 is
        // ...
}
```

The definitions of **begin()** and **end()** use a general mechanism called *traits*. Look it up if you really need to, but most programmers don't need to. It also allows us to say **begin(v)** for a **vector** instead of **v.begin()**.

20.6.4 Adapting I/O streams to the STL

CC You will have heard the phrases "copy to output" and "copy from input." That's a nice and useful way of thinking of some forms of I/O, and we can actually use the standard-library **copy()** to do exactly that.

Remember that a sequence is something

- With a beginning and an end
- Where we can get to the next element using **++**
- Where we can get the value of the current element using *

Now sequence is a very general concept, so we can fit input and output streams into that model. The standard library provides **ostream_iterator**, an iterator that you can use to write values of type **T**. For example:

```
ostream_iterator<string> oo {cout};             // assigning to *oo is to write to cout

*oo = "Hello, ";                                // meaning cout << "Hello, "
++oo;                                           // "get ready for next output operation"
*oo = "World!\n";                               // meaning cout << "World!\n"
```

You can imagine how this could be implemented.

Similarly, the standard library provides **istream_iterator<T>** for reading values of type **T**:

```
istream_iterator<string> ii {cin};      // reading *ii is to read a string from cin
```

```
string s1 = *ii;                // meaning cin>>s1
++ii;                           // "get ready for the next input operation"
string s2 = *ii;                // meaning cin>>s2
```

Using ostream_iterator and istream_iterator, we can use copy() for our I/O. For example, we can make a "quick and dirty" dictionary like this:

```
int main()
{
        string from, to;
        cin >> from >> to;                          // get source and target file names

        ifstream is {from};                         // open input stream
        ofstream os {to};                           // open output stream

        istream_iterator<string> ii {is};           // make input iterator for stream
        istream_iterator<string> eos;               // input sentinel
        ostream_iterator<string> oo {os,"\n"};      // make output iterator for stream

        vector<string> b {ii,eos};                  // b is a vector initialized from input
        sort(b.begin() ,b.end());                   // sort the buffer
        copy(b.begin() ,b.end() ,oo);               // copy buffer to output
}
```

The iterator eos is the stream iterator's representation of "end of input." When an istream reaches end of input (often referred to as eof), its istream_iterator will equal the default istream_iterator (here called eos).

Note that we initialized the vector by a pair of iterators. As the initializers for a container, a pair of iterators (a,b) means "Read the sequence [a:b) into the container." Naturally, the pair of iterators that we used was (ii,eos) – the beginning and end of input. That saves us from explicitly using >> and push_back(). We strongly advise against the alternative XX

```
vector<string> b {max_size};       // don't guess about the amount of input!
copy(ii,eos,b.begin());
```

People who try to guess the maximum size of input often find that they have underestimated, and serious problems emerge – for them or for their users – from the resulting buffer overflows. Such overflows are also a source of security problems.

> TRY THIS
>
> First get the program as written to work and test it with a small file of, say, a few hundred words. Then try the *emphatically not recommended* version that guesses about the size of input and see what happens when the input buffer b overflows. Note that the worst-case scenario is that the overflow led to nothing bad in your particular example, so that you would be tempted to ship it to users.

In our little program, we read in the words and then sorted them. That seemed an obvious way of doing things at the time, but why should we put words in "the wrong place" so that we later have to sort? Worse yet, we find that we store a word and print it as many times as it appears in the input.

We can solve the latter problem by using **unique_copy()** instead of **copy()**. A **unique_copy()** simply doesn't copy repeated identical values. For example, using plain **copy()** the program will take

the man bit the dog

and produce

```
bit
dog
man
the
the
```

If we used **unique_copy()**, the program would write

```
bit
dog
man
the
```

AA Where did those newlines come from? Outputting with separators is so common that the **ostream_iterator**'s constructor allows you to (optionally) specify a string to be printed after each value:

```
ostream_iterator<string> oo {os,"\n"};     // make output iterator for stream
```

Obviously, a newline is a popular choice for output meant for humans to read, but maybe we prefer spaces as separators? We could write

```
ostream_iterator<string> oo {os," "};     // make output iterator for stream
```

This would give us the output

```
bit dog man the
```

20.6.5 Using a set to keep order

There is an even easier way of getting that output; use a **set** rather than a **vector**:

```
int main()
{
        string from, to;
        cin >> from >> to;              // get source and target file names

        ifstream is {from};             // make input stream
        ofstream os {to};               // make output stream

        set<string> b {istream_iterator<string>{is}, istream_iterator<string>{}};
        copy(b.begin() ,b.end() , ostream_iterator<string>{os," "});          // copy buffer to output
}
```

CC When we insert values into a **set**, duplicates are ignored. Furthermore, the elements of a **set** are kept in order so no sorting is needed. With the right tools, most tasks are easy.

Naturally, we could even have used **ranges::copy()**:

```
ranges::copy(b, ostream_iterator<string>{os," "});        // copy buffer to output
```

20.7 Ranges and iterators

We have now used ranges for a long while. They are our preferred way of using sequences and algorithms over sequences because they are easier to write and don't offer opportunities for mistakes that direct use of iterators does. Consider:

```
sort(v.end(),v.start());          // Oops!
sort(v1.start(),v2.end());        // Oops!
```

Ranges are less flexible than explicit use of iterators and that implies less opportunities for errors:

```
ranges::sort(v);                  // if this doesn't make sense the compiler will tell us
```

So far, we have considered a range to be defined by a pair of iterators referring to the first element (if any) and one-beyond-the-last element. However, the stream iterators show that this view is a simplification. In fact, we can define a range in three ways:

- **{begin,end}**: a pair of iterators
- **{begin,length}**: an iterator and a number of elements
- **{begin,predicate}**: an iterator and predicate to determine if the end has been reached

20.7.1 Iterator categories

We have mostly talked about iterators as if all iterators are interchangeable. They are interchangeable if you do only the simplest operations, such as traversing a sequence once reading each value once. If you want to do more, such as iterating backward or subscripting, you need one of the more advanced iterators.

Iterator categories	
input iterator	Can iterate forward using **++** and read element values using *. This is the kind of iterator that **istream** offers; see §20.6.4. If **(*p).m** is valid, **p->m** can be used as a shorthand.
output iterator	Can iterate forward using **++** and write element values using *. This is the kind of iterator that **ostream** offers; see §20.6.4.
forward iterator	An input iterator that can iterate repeatedly over a sequence and repeatedly read from or write to an element. This is the kind of iterator that **forward_list** offers §20.6.
bidirectional iterator	A forward iterator that can move backward (using **--**). This is the kind of iterator that **list**, **map**, and **set** offer.
random-access iterator	A bidirectional iterator that can move forward and backwards **n** positions using **+=n**, **+**, **-=n**, and **-**.
contiguous iterator	A random-access iterator where the elements are allocated contiguously. This is the kind of iterator that **vector** offers.

From the operations offered, we can see that wherever we can use an output iterator or an input iterator, we can use a forward iterator. A bidirectional iterator is also a forward iterator, and a random-access iterator is also a bidirectional iterator. Graphically, we can represent the iterator categories like this:

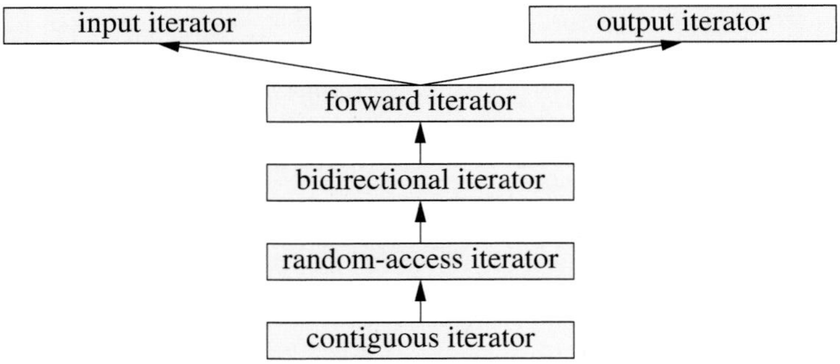

Note that since the iterator categories are not classes, this hierarchy is not a class hierarchy implemented using derivation. There are concepts (§18.1.3) representing these iterator categories.

For each iterator category, there is a corresponding range category. For example:

```
template<input_iterator In>          // simplified
In find(In b, In e);

template<ranges::input_range R>
ranges::iterator_t<R> find(R r);
```

Naturally, since **R** is an **input_range**, its iterator, referred to as **iterator_t<R>**, is an **input_iterator**. You may wonder how we can have an input range when we can't have a pointer to the end of input, but the notion of iterators is sufficiently flexible to cope with the idea of "from the start of input to the end of input" (§20.6.4).

20.7.2 Output ranges

The standard library offers output iterators, but unfortunately not output ranges. That's a pity because an output range can be used to catch range errors. An output range is like an output iterator that kept track of which element in the range we are writing to. Consider a simple implementation of this idea:

```
template<ranges::range R>
class Output_range {
public:
     using value_type = ranges::range_value_t<R>;
     using difference_type = int;

     Output_range(R r) : b{ r.begin() }, e{ r.end() }, p{ b } {}
```

```
        Output_range& operator++() { check_end(); ++p; return *this; }
        Output_range operator++(int) { check_end(); auto t{ *this }; ++p; return t; }

        value_type& operator*() const { check_end();  return *p; }
private:
        void check_end() const { if (p == e) throw Overflow{}; }

        ranges::iterator_t<R> b;
        ranges::iterator_t<R> e;
        ranges::iterator_t<R> p;
};
```

Obviously, there is a cost compared to using an ordinary iterator, but then there is often a cost imposed by range errors.

This is not "industrial strength" or "ISO C++ standard-library quality", but it actually works for a range of uses:

```
vector<int> v = {0,1,2,3,4,5};
vector<int> v1(10);
vector<int> v2(5);

ranges::copy(v,Output_range{v1});        // copies v into v1
ranges::copy(v,Output_range{v2});        // throws Range_error
```

The STL is an extensive framework. Sometimes we must extend it to get what we want. However, that is rarely a task for beginners.

Output_range is really an iterator that keeps track of the range it is iterating over, so we could have called it Checked_iterator.

Drill

After each operation (as defined by a line of this drill) print the vector.

[1] Define a struct Item { string name; int iid; double value; /* ... */ };, make a vector<Item>, vi, and fill it with ten items from a file.

[2] Sort vi by name.

[3] Sort vi by iid.

[4] Sort vi by value; print it in order of decreasing value (i.e., largest value first).

[5] Insert Item{"horse shoe",99,12.34} and Item{"Canon S400", 9988,499.95}.

[6] Remove (erase) two Items identified by name from vi.

[7] Remove (erase) two Items identified by iid from vi.

[8] Repeat the exercise with a list<Item> rather than a vector<Item>.

Now try a map:

[1] Define a map<string,int> called msi.

[2] Insert ten (name,value) pairs into it, e.g., msi["lecture"]=21.

[3] Output the (name,value) pairs to cout in some format of your choice.

[4] Erase the (name,value) pairs from msi.

[5] Write a function that reads value pairs from **cin** and places them in **msi**.
[6] Read ten pairs from input and enter them into **msi**.
[7] Write the elements of **msi** to **cout**.
[8] Output the sum of the (integer) values in **msi**.
[9] Define a **map<int,string>** called **mis**.
[10] Enter the values from **msi** into **mis**; that is, if **msi** has an element (**"lecture",21**), **mis** should have an element (**21,"lecture"**).
[11] Output the elements of **mis** to **cout**.

Review

[1] What is a container?
[2] What containers does the STL provide?
[3] What is an associative container? Give at least three examples.
[4] Is **list** an associative container? Why not?
[5] What is a hash function?
[6] What is the basic ordering property of binary tree?
[7] What (roughly) does it mean for a tree to be balanced?
[8] How much space per element does a **map** take up?
[9] How much space per element does a **vector** take up?
[10] Why would anyone use an **unordered_map** when an (ordered) **map** is available?
[11] What is a big-O measure?
[12] How does a **set** differ from a **map**?
[13] How does a **multimap** differ from a **map**?
[14] How does an associative container differ from other containers?
[15] Why is an array not a container?
[16] Why bother to time code?
[17] How do you time a piece of code?
[18] When does structured binding clarify code? When does it obscure it?
[19] What containers does the STL offer?
[20] What is an iterator category?
[21] What kinds of iterators does the STL offer? Mention at least eight.
[22] What operations are provided by a random-access iterator, but not a bidirectional iterator?

Terms

associative container	**map**	associative array	structured binding
balanced tree	**unordered_map**	big-O	**duration**
now()	**time_point**	clock	date
set	container	almost container	**array**
istream_iterator	**ostream_iterator**	range	iterator category
random-access iterator	output range	hash function	**ranges::**

Exercises

[1] Rewrite the word-counting program from §20.2 to not distinguish between uppercase and lowercase letters and to treat punctuation characters as whitespace.

[2] In the Fruit example (§20.5), we copy Fruits into the set. What if we didn't want to copy the Fruits? We could have a set<Fruit*> instead. However, to do that, we'd have to define a comparison operation for that set. Implement the Fruit example using a set<Fruit*, Fruit_comparison>. Discuss the differences between the two implementations.

[3] Take the word-frequency example from §20.2 and modify it to output its lines in order of frequency (rather than in lexicographical order). An example line would be 3: C++ rather than C++: 3.

[4] Read a file of integers into a vector. Measure how long the reading took. Use chrono (§20.4). Sort the vector, and measure how long the sorting took. You will need a large file to get any useful data. Generate the file of at least a million integers using random (§20.4).

[5] Read the file of integers from the previous exercise into a set. Measure how long the reading and creation of the set took.

[6] Do the previous exercise with an unsorted_set. Did the timings from this and the previous two exercises match your expectations?

[7] Repeat the previous three exercises with a file of random character strings. Each string should contain only letters and digits. Each string should have between 4 and 24 characters.

[8] Read a sequence of (name,height) pairs into a map. Names should be represented as strings and heights by ints. Output the pairs lexicographically sorted by name. Print a name : height per line.

[9] Output the pairs from the previous exercise sorted by height in decreasing order (tallest first).

[10] Read the lines from a file of text and output the unique lines (once only). Hint: read the lines into a map and output a line only if it hasn't been seen before. This is the AWK program (!a[$0]++).

[11] Build a map of (English word, Spanish word) pairs of words with equivalent meaning. Each word is a string. Read the pairs from a file, and display them on the screen. A couple of dozen pairs will do. Give a user the choice of displaying the words in English lexicographical order or Spanish lexicographical order.

[12] Repeat the previous exercise, but handle cases where a word has more than one meaning. For example, (sheet,hoja) and (leaf,hoja). Hint: multimap.

Postscript

Choosing an appropriate data structure to hold an application's data is key to simplifying the code CC
and to maximizing performance. Thick books have been written about this. Here, we focus on a few container types that are often good choices: map, unordered_map, set, array, string, and of course vector. These are, in fact, relatively simple and therefore compact and fast. The extensive parameterization makes them extremely flexible. Their design and implementation techniques provide a useful pattern for the development of more specific containers.

21

Algorithms

In theory, practice is simple.
– Trygve Reenskaug

This chapter completes our presentation of the fundamental ideas of the STL and our survey of the facilities it offers. Here, we focus on algorithms. Our primary aim is to introduce about a dozen of the most useful ones, which will save you days, if not months, of work. Each is presented with examples of its uses and of programming techniques that it supports. Our second aim here is to give you sufficient tools to write your own – elegant and efficient – algorithms if and when you need more than what the standard library and other available libraries have to offer.

§21.1 Standard-library algorithms
The simplest algorithm: find(); Some generic uses; Generalizing search: find_if()
§21.2 Function objects
An abstract view of function objects; Predicates on class members; Lambda expressions
§21.3 Numerical algorithms
Accumulate; Generalizing accumulate(); Inner product; Generalizing inner_product()
§21.4 Copying
The simplest copy: copy(); Generalizing copy: copy_if()
§21.5 Sorting and searching

21.1 Standard-library algorithms

The standard library offers about 125 algorithms. All are useful for someone sometimes; we focus on some that are often useful for many and on some that are occasionally very useful for someone:

Selected standard algorithms	
p=find(b,e,v)	**p** points to the first occurrence of **v** in [**b**:**e**).
p=find_if(b,e,p)	**p** points to the first element **x** in [**b**:**e**) so that **p(x)** is **true**.
x=count(b,e,v)	**x** is the number of occurrences of **v** in [**b**:**e**).
x=count_if(b,e,p)	**x** is the number of elements in [**b**:**e**) so that **p(x)** is **true**.
sort(b,e)	Sort [**b**:**e**) using **<**.
sort(b,e,p)	Sort [**b**:**e**) using **p**.
x=is_sorted(b,e)	If [**b**:**e**) is sorted **x** is **true**.
b2=copy(b,e,b2)	Copy [**b**:**e**) to [**b2**:**b2+(e−b)**); there had better be enough elements after **b2** to hold [**b**:**e**).
b2=move(b,e,b2)	move [**b**:**e**) to [**b2**:**b2+(e−b)**); there had better be enough elements after **b2** to hold [**b**:**e**).
b2=uninitialized_copy(b,e,b2)	Copy [**b**:**e**) to an uninitialized [**b2**:**b2+(e−b)**); there had better be enough elements after **b2** to hold [**b**:**e**).
b2=unique_copy(b,e,b2)	Copy [**b**:**e**) to [**b2**:**b2+(e−b)**); don’t copy adjacent duplicates.
e2=merge(b,e,b2,e2,r)	Merge two sorted sequences [**b**:**e**) and [**b2**:**e2**) into [**r**:**r+(e−b)+(e2−b2)**).
[p,q]=equal_range(b,e,v)	[**p**:**q**) is the subsequence of the sorted range [**b**:**e**) with the value **v**, basically, a binary search for **v**.
equal(b,e,b2)	Do all elements of [**b**:**e**) and [**b2**:**b2+(e−b)**) compare equal? The sequences must be sorted.
x=accumulate(b,e,i)	**x** is the sum of **i** and the elements of [**b**:**e**).
r=max(x,y)	**r** is a reference to the larger of **x** and **y**.
p=max_element(b,e)	**p** points to the largest element in [**b**:**e**).
iota(b,e,i)	[**b**:**e**) becomes the sequence **i**, **i+i**, **i+2**, ...

CC By default, comparison for equality is done using **==** and ordering is done based on **<** (less than). These algorithms take one or more sequences. An input sequence is defined by a pair of iterators; an output sequence is defined by an iterator to its first element. Typically, an algorithm is parameterized by one or more operations that can be defined as function objects or as functions. The algorithms usually report “failure” by returning the end of an input sequence. For example, **find(b,e,v)** returns **e** if it doesn’t find **v**.

A sequence can also be represented as a *range* (§20.7), so instead of **find(b,e,v)** we can write **ranges::find(r,v)**. This is the case for most algorithms.

Also, the standard library provides parallel and vectorized versions of key algorithms to allow people to take better advantage of hardware facilities. Look them up if you need more performance than is provided by the default implementations of the algorithms.

The STL algorithms, containers, and iterators offer a model that we can use to write our own versions for needs beyond what the standard directly addresses.

21.1.1 The simplest algorithm: find()

Arguably, the simplest useful algorithm is **find()**. It finds an element with a given value in a sequence:

```
template<input_iterator In, equality_comparable<In::value_type> T>     // §18.1.3
In find(In first, In last, const T& val)        // find the first element in [first,last) that equals val
{
        while (first!=last && *first!=val)
                ++first;
        return first;
}
```

Let's have a look at this definition of **find()**. It is slightly simplified compared to what you can find looking at a **std::find()** implementation, e.g., it doesn't handle plain pointers such as **int*** because those don't have a **value_type** member. The technique for that is beyond this book (if you are seriously curious, look up *iterator traits*). Naturally, you can use **find()** without knowing exactly how it is implemented – in fact, we have used it already (e.g., §19.5.2). However, the definition of **find()** illustrates many useful design ideas, so it is worth looking at.

CC

First of all, **find()** operates on a sequence defined by a pair of iterators. We are looking for the value **val** in the half-open sequence [**first:last**). The result returned by **find()** is an iterator. That result points either to the first element of the sequence with the value **val** or to **last**. Returning an iterator to the one-beyond-the-last element of a sequence is the most common STL way of reporting "not found." So we can use **find()** like this:

```
void f(vector<int>& v, int x)
{
        auto p = find(v.begin(),v.end(),x);
        if (p!=v.end()) {
                // ... we found x in v; we can use *p ...
        }
        else {
                // ... no x in v; don't dereference p ...
        }
        // ...
}
```

Here, as is common, the sequence consists of all the elements of a container (an STL **vector**). We check the returned iterator against the end of our sequence to see if we found our value. The type of the value returned is the iterator passed as an argument.

To avoid naming the type returned by **find()**, we used **auto** (§2.10). The **auto** type specifier is particularly useful in generic code, such as **find()** where it can be tedious to name the actual type (here, **vector<int>::iterator**).

We now know how to use **find()** and therefore also how to use a bunch of other algorithms that follow the same conventions as **find()**. Before proceeding with more uses and more algorithms, let's just have a closer look at that definition:

```
template<input_iterator In, equality_comparable<In::value_type> T>
In find(In first, In last, const T& val)        // find the first element in [first,last) that equals val
{
        while (first!=last && *first!=val)
                ++first;
        return first;
}
```

Did you find that loop obvious at first glance? We didn't. It is actually minimal, efficient, and a direct representation of the fundamental algorithm. However, until you have seen a few examples, it is not obvious. Let's write it "the pedestrian way" and see how that version compares:

```
template<input_iterator In, equality_comparable<In::value_type> T>
In find(In first, In last, const T& val)        // find the first element in [first,last) that equals val
{
        for (In p = first; p!=last; ++p)
                if (*p==val)
                        return p;
        return last;
}
```

These two definitions are logically equivalent, and a really good compiler will generate the same code for both. However, in reality many compilers are not good enough to eliminate that extra variable (p) and to rearrange the code so that all the testing is done in one place. Why worry and explain? Partly, because the style of the first (and preferred) version of find() has become very popular, and you must understand it to read other people's code; partly, because performance matters exactly for small, frequently used functions that deal with lots of data.

> TRY THIS
>
> Are you sure those two definitions are logically equivalent? How would you be sure? Try constructing an argument for their being equivalent. That done, try both on some data. A famous computer scientist (Don Knuth) once said, "I have only proven the algorithm correct, not tested it." Even mathematical proofs can contain errors. To be confident, you need to both reason and test.

21.1.2 Some generic uses

CC The find() algorithm is generic. That means that it can be used for different data types. In fact, it is generic in two ways; it can be used for

- Any STL-style sequence (that can be read from)
- Any element type (that can be compared to the iterator's value type)

Here are some examples (consult the diagrams in §19.3 if you get confused):

```
void f(vector<int>& v, int x)        // works for vector of int
{
        vector<int>::iterator p = find(v.begin(),v.end(),x);
```

```
        if (p!=v.end()) {
                // ...we found x ...
        }
        // ...
}
```

Here, the iteration operations used by find() are those of a vector<int>::iterator; that is, ++ (in ++first) simply moves a pointer to the next location in memory (where the next element of the vector is stored) and * (in *first) dereferences such a pointer. The iterator comparison (in first!=last) is a pointer comparison, and the value comparison (in *first!=val) simply compares two integers. CC

Let's try with a list:

```
void f(list<string>& v, string x)        // works for list of string
{
        list<string>::iterator p = find(v.begin(),v.end(),x);
        if (p!=v.end()) {
                // ... we found x ...
        }
        // ...
}
```

Here, the iteration operations used by find() are those of a list<string>::iterator. The operators have the required meaning, so that the logic is the same as for the vector<int> above. The implementation is very different, though; that is, ++ (in ++first) simply follows a pointer in the Link part of the element to where the next element of the list is stored, and * (in *first) finds the value part of a Link. The iterator comparison (in first!=last) is a pointer comparison of Link*s and the value comparison (in *first!=val) compares strings using string's != operator. CC

So, find() is extremely flexible: as long as we obey the simple rules for iterators, we can use find() to find elements for any sequence we can think of and for any container we care to define. For example, we can use find() to look for a character in a Document as defined in §19.5:

```
void f(Document& v, char x)        // works for Document of char
{
        Text_iterator p = find(v.begin(),v.end(),x);
        if (p!=v.end()) {
                // ... we found x ...
        }
        // ...
}
```

This kind of flexibility is the hallmark of the STL algorithms and makes them more useful than most people imagine when they first encounter them.

The most common use of an algorithm like find() is to look at a complete container. In such case, the compiler can find the relevant begin() and end() for us and we can write

```
template<class T>
void use(vector<T>& v, T& x)
{
        auto p = ranges::find(v,x);
```

```
        if (p!=v.end()) {
                // ... we found x ...
        }
        // ...
}
```

Having to write that **ranges::** is most unfortunate. The reason has to do with problems related to having both old-style unconstrained versions of algorithms (for compatibility reasons) and properly constrained (type checked) versions.

21.1.3 Generalizing search: find_if()

We don't actually look for a specific value all that often. More often, we are interested in finding a value that meets some criteria. Then, we can get a much more useful **find** operation when we can define our search criteria ourselves. Maybe we want to find a value larger than 42. Maybe we want to compare strings without taking case (uppercase vs. lowercase) into account. Maybe we want to find the first odd value. Maybe we want to find a record where the address field is **"17 Cherry Tree Lane"**.

The standard algorithm that searches based on a user-supplied criterion is **find_if()**:

```
template<input_iterator In, predicate<In::value_type> Pred>
In find_if(In first, In last, Pred pred)
{
        while (first!=last && !pred(*first))
                ++first;
        return first;
}
```

Obviously (when you compare the source code), it is just like **find()** except that it uses **!pred(*first)** rather than ***first!=val**; that is, it stops searching once the predicate **pred()** succeeds rather than when an element equals a value.

CC A predicate is a function that returns **true** or **false**. Clearly, **find_if()** requires a predicate that takes one argument so that it can say **pred(*first)**. We can easily write a predicate that checks some property of a value, such as "Does the string contain the letter **x**?" "Is the value larger than 42?" "Is the number odd?" For example, we can find the first odd value in a vector of **int**s like this:

```
bool odd(int x) { return x%2; }        // % is the modulo operator

void f(vector<int>& v)
{
        auto p = find_if(v.begin(), v.end(), odd);
        if (p!=v.end()) {
                // ... we found an odd number ...
        }
        // ...
}
```

For that call of **find_if()**, **find_if()** calls **odd()** for each element until it finds the first odd value. Note that when you pass a function as an argument, you don't add **()** to its name because doing so would call it.

Similarly, we can find the first element of a list with a value larger than 42 like this:

```
bool larger_than_42(double x) { return x>42; }

void f(list<double>& v)
{
        auto p = find_if(v.begin(), v.end(), larger_than_42);
        if (p!=v.end()) {
                // ... we found a value > 42 ...
        }
        // ...
}
```

This last example is not very satisfying, though. What if we next wanted to find an element larger than 41? We would have to write a new function. Find an element larger than 19? Write yet another function. There has to be a better way!

If we want to compare to an arbitrary value **v**, we need somehow to make **v** an implicit argument to **find_if()**'s predicate. We could try (choosing **v_val** as a name that is less likely to clash with other names)

```
double v_val;          // the value to which larger_than_v() compares its argument
bool larger_than_v(double x) { return x>v_val; }

void f(list<double>& v, int x)
{
        v_val = 31;             // set v_val to 31 for the next call of larger_than_v
        auto p = find_if(v.begin(), v.end(), larger_than_v);
        if (p!=v.end()) {
                // ... we found a value > 31 ...
        }

        v_val = x;        // set v_val to x for the next call of larger_than_v
        auto q = find_if(v.begin(), v.end(), larger_than_v);
        if (q!=v.end()) {
                // ... we found a value > x ...
        }
        // ...
}
```

Yuck! We are convinced that people who write such code will eventually get what they deserve, but we pity their users and anyone who gets to maintain their code. Again: there has to be a better way! And, of course, there is. XX

> TRY THIS
>
> Why are we so disgusted with that use of **v**? Give at least three ways this could lead to obscure errors. List three applications in which you'd particularly hate to find such code.

21.2 Function objects

So, we want to pass a predicate to find_if(), and we want that predicate to compare elements to a value we specify as some kind of argument. In particular, we want to write something like this:

```
void f(list<double>& v, int x)
{
        auto p = find_if(v.begin(), v.end(), Larger_than{31});
        if (p!=v.end()) {
                // ... we found a value > 31 ..
        }

        auto q = find_if(v.begin(), v.end(), Larger_than{x});
        if (q!=v.end()) {
                // ... we found a value > x ...
        }
        // ...
}
```

Obviously, Larger_than must be something that

- can be called as a predicate, e.g., pred(*first)
- can hold a value, such as 31 or x, for use when called

CC For that we need a "function object"; that is, an object that can behave like a function. We need an object because objects can store data, such as the value with which to compare. For example:

```
class Larger_than {
        int v;
public:
        Larger_than(int vv) : v{vv} { }                    // store the argument
        bool operator()(int x) const { return x>v; }       // compare
};
```

Interestingly, this definition makes the example above work as specified. Now we just have to figure out why it works. When we say Larger_than{31} we (obviously) make an object of class Larger_than holding 31 in its data member v. For example:

```
find_if(v.begin(),v.end(),Larger_than{31})
```

Here, we pass that object to find_if() as its parameter called pred. For each element of v, find_if() makes a call

```
pred(*first)
```

This invokes the call operator, called operator(), for our function object using the argument *first. The result is a comparison of the element's value, *first, with 31.

CC What we see here is that a function call can be seen as an operator, the "( ) operator," just like any other operator. The "( ) operator" is also called the *function call operator* and the *application operator*. So ( ) in pred(*first) is given a meaning by Larger_than::operator(), just as subscripting in v[i] is given a meaning by vector::operator[ ].

21.2.1 An abstract view of function objects

We have here a mechanism that allows for a "function" to "carry around" data that it needs. Clearly, function objects provide us with a very general, powerful, and convenient mechanism. Consider a more general notion of a function object: CC

```
class F {              // abstract example of a function object
      S s;             // state
public:
      F(const S& ss) :s(ss) { /* establish initial state*/ }
      T operator() (const S& ss) const
      {
            // do something with ss to s
            // return a value of type T (T is often void, bool, or S)
      }

      const S& state() const { return s; }        // reveal state
      void reset(const S& ss) { s = ss; }         // reset state
};
```

An object of class **F** holds data in its member **s**. If needed, a function object can have many data members. Another way of saying that something holds data is that it "has state." When we create an **F**, we can initialize that state. Whenever we want to, we can read that state. For **F**, we provided an operation, **state()**, to read that state and another, **reset()**, to write it. However, when we design a function object, we are free to provide any way of accessing its state that we consider appropriate. And, of course, we can directly or indirectly call the function object using the normal function call notation. We defined **F** to take a single argument when it is called, but we can define function objects with as many parameters as we need.

Use of function objects is the main method of parameterization in the STL. We use function objects to specify what we are looking for in searches (§21.2), for defining sorting criteria (§21.2.2), for specifying arithmetic operations in numerical algorithms (§21.3), for defining what it means for values to be equal (§21.1.3), and for much more. The use of function objects is a major source of flexibility and generality. CC

Function objects are usually very efficient. In particular, passing a small function object by value to a template function typically leads to optimal performance. The reason is simple, but surprising to people more familiar with passing functions as arguments: typically, passing a function object leads to significantly smaller and faster code than passing a function! This is true only if the object is small (something like zero, one, or two words of data) or passed by reference and if the function call operator is small (e.g., a simple comparison using **<**) and defined to be inline (e.g., has its definition within its class itself). Most of the examples in this chapter follow this pattern. The basic reason for the high performance of small and simple function objects is that they preserve sufficient type information for compilers to generate optimal code. Even older compilers with unsophisticated optimizers can generate a simple "greater-than" machine instruction for the comparison in **Larger_than** rather than calling a function. Calling a function typically takes 10 to 50 times longer than executing a simple comparison operation. In addition, the code for a function call is several times larger than the code for a simple comparison. AA

21.2.2 Predicates on class members

As we have seen, standard algorithms work well with sequences of elements of basic types, such as **int** and **double**. However, in many areas, containers of class values are far more common. Consider an example that is key to applications in many areas, sorting a record by several criteria:

```
struct Record {
      string name;            // standard string for ease of use
      char addr[24];          // old style to match database layout
      // ...
};

vector<Record> vr;
```

Sometimes we want to sort **vr** by name, and sometimes we want to sort it by address. Unless we can do both elegantly and efficiently, our techniques are of limited practical interest. Fortunately, doing so is easy. We can write

```
// ...
ranges::sort(vr, Cmp_by_name{});          // sort by name
// ...
ranges::sort(vr, Cmp_by_addr{});          // sort by addr
// ...
```

CC **Cmp_by_name** is a function object that compares two **Record**s by comparing their **name** members. **Cmp_by_addr** is a function object that compares two **Record**s by comparing their **addr** members. To allow the user to specify such comparison criteria, the standard-library **sort** algorithm takes an optional third argument specifying the sorting criteria. **Cmp_by_name{}** creates a **Cmp_by_name** for **sort()** to use to compare **Record**s. That looks OK – meaning that we wouldn't mind maintaining code that looked like that. Now all we have to do is to define **Cmp_by_name** and **Cmp_by_addr**:

```
// different comparisons for Record objects:

struct Cmp_by_name {
      bool operator()(const Record& a, const Record& b) const
            { return a.name < b.name; }
};

struct Cmp_by_addr {
      bool operator()(const Record& a, const Record& b) const
            { return strncmp(a.addr, b.addr, 24) < 0; }          // Huh?
};
```

The **Cmp_by_name** class is pretty obvious. The function call operator, **operator()()**, simply compares the **name** strings using the standard **string**'s **<** operator. However, the comparison in **Cmp_by_addr** is ugly. That is because we chose an ugly representation of the address: an array of 24 characters (not zero terminated). We chose that partly to show how a function object can be used to hide ugly and error-prone code and partly because this particular representation was once presented to me as a challenge: "an ugly and important real-world problem that the STL can't handle." Well, the STL could. The comparison function uses the C (and C++) standard-library function **strncmp()** that compares fixed-length character arrays, returning a negative number if the second "string" comes lexicographically after the first. Look it up if you ever need such an obscure comparison.

21.2.3 Lambda expressions

Defining a function object (or a function) in one place in a program and then using it in another can be tedious. In particular, it is a nuisance if the action we want to perform is very easy to specify, easy to understand, and will never again be needed. In that case, we can use a lambda expression (§13.3.3). Probably the best way of thinking about a lambda expression is as a shorthand notation for defining a function object (a class with an operator ( )) and then immediately creating an object of it. For example, we could have written

```
// ...
ranges::sort(vr, [](const Record& a, const Record& b) { return a.name < b.name; });
// ...
ranges::sort(vr, [](const Record& a, const Record& b) { return strncmp(a.addr, b.addr, 24) < 0; });
// ...
```

In this case, we wonder if a named function object wouldn't give more maintainable code. Maybe `Cmp_by_name` and `Cmp_by_addr` have other uses.

However, consider the `find_if()` example from §21.1.3. There, we needed to pass an operation as an argument and that operation needed to carry data with it:

```
void f(list<double>& v, int x)
{
	auto p = ranges::find_if(v, [](double a) { return a>31; });
	if (p!=v.end()) {
		// ... we found a value > 31 ...
	}

	auto q = ranges::find_if(v, [&](double a) { return a>x; });
	if (q!=v.end()) {
		// ... we found a value > x ...
	}

	// ...
}
```

The comparison to the local variable `x` makes the lambda version attractive. In particular, it can be a great help that you don't have to look in two places to understand what's going on. This can be significant when the unique operation doesn't have an obvious simple name.

The `[&]` and `[]` are called *lambda captures*:

- `[]`: If there is nothing between `[` and `]`, the lambda is just like an ordinary function: it can access its arguments, its own local variables, and names in the global (namespace) scope (§7.3).
- `[&]`: If we use `[&]`, the lambda can also use names from the scope in which it is defined, its enclosing scope. Now it acts like a local function.
- `[=]`: You can even ask to access copies of variables in the enclosing scope: `[=]`.

There are more subtle ways of capturing, but those are beyond the scope of this book.

21.3 Numerical algorithms

Most of the standard-library algorithms deal with data management issues: they copy, sort, search, etc. data. However, a few help with numerical computations. These numerical algorithms can be important when you compute, and they serve as examples of how you can express numerical algorithms within the STL framework.

There are a few STL-style standard-library numerical algorithms:

Numerical algorithms	
x=accumulate(b,e,i)	Add a sequence of values; e.g., for {a,b,c,d} produce i+a+b+c+d. The type of the result x is the type of the initial value i.
x=inner_product(b,e,b2,i)	Multiply pairs of values from two sequences and sum the results; e.g., for {a,b,c,d} and {e,f,g,h} produce i+a*e+b*f+c*g+d*h. The type of the result x is the type of the initial value i.
r=partial_sum(b,e,r)	Produce the sequence of sums of the first n elements of [b:e); e.g., for {a,b,c,d} produce {a, a+b, a+b+c, a+b+c+d}.
r=adjacent_difference(b,e,b2,r)	Produce the sequence of differences between elements of [b:e); e.g., for {a,b,c,d} produce {a,b-a,c-b,d-c}.
iota(b,e,v)	Fill the range [b:e) with the values v, v+1, v+2, ...; The values are computers using prefix ++.
x=midpoint(a,b)	Compute the midpoint between a and b; roughly (a+b)/2 without overflow
x=gcd(a,b)	x is the greatest common divisor of a and b
x=lcm(a,b)	x is the least common multiple of a and b

We'll describe the first two here and leave it for you to explore the rest if you feel the need. There are also inclusive_scan(), exclusive_scan(), transform_inclusive_scan(), and transform_exclusive_scan() that are beyond the scope of this book.

21.3.1 Accumulate

The simplest and most useful numerical algorithm is accumulate(). In its simplest form, it adds a sequence of values:

```
template<input_iterator In, Number T>
T accumulate(In first, In last, T init)
{
	while (first!=last) {
		init = init + *first;
		++first;
	}
	return init;
}
```

Given an initial value, init, it simply adds every value in the [first:last) sequence to it and returns the sum. The variable in which the sum is computed, init, is often referred to as the *accumulator*. For example:

```
int a[] = { 1, 2, 3, 4, 5 };
cout << accumulate(a, a+sizeof(a)/sizeof(int), 0);
```

This will print 15, that is, 0+1+2+3+4+5 (0 is the initial value). Obviously, accumulate() can be used for all kinds of sequences:

```
void f(vector<double>& v, int* p, int n)
{
      double sum = accumulate(v.begin(), v.end(), 0.0);
      int sum2 = accumulate(p,p+n,0);
}
```

For mysterious reasons, the ranges versions of the numerical algorithms didn't make it into C++20, but they are not hard to define. For example:

```
template<input_range R, output_iterator Out, typename T>
T accumulate(R r, Out oo, T init)
{
      return accumulate(begin(r),end(r),oo,init);
}
```

The type of the result (the sum) is the type of the variable that accumulate() uses to hold the accumulator. This gives a degree of flexibility that can be important. For example:

```
void g(vector<int>& v)
{
      int s1 = accumulate(v, 0);                  // sum into an int
      long sl = accumulate(v, long{0});           // sum the ints into a long
      double s2 = accumulate(v, 0.0);             // sum the ints into a double
}
```

A long has more significant digits than an int on some computers. A double can represent larger (and smaller) numbers than an int, but possibly with less precision.

Using the variable in which you want the result as the initializer is a popular idiom for specifying the type of the accumulator: **AA**

```
void f(vector<double>& v)
{
      double s1 = 0;
      s1 = accumulate(v, s1);
      int s2 = accumulate(v, s2);          // oops
      float s3 = 0;
      accumulate(v, s3);                   // oops
}
```

Do remember to initialize the accumulator and to assign the result of accumulate() to the variable. In this example, s2 was used as an initializer before it was itself initialized; the result is therefore undefined. We passed s3 to accumulate() (pass-by-value; see §7.4.3), but the result is never assigned anywhere; that compilation is just a waste of time. **XX**

21.3.2 Generalizing accumulate()

So, the basic three-argument **accumulate()** adds. However, there are many other useful operations, such as multiply and subtract, that we might like to do on a sequence, so the STL offers a second four-argument version of **accumulate()** where we can specify the operation to be used:

```
template<input_iterator In, typename T, invocable<T,In::value_type> BinOp>
[[nodiscard]]   // warn if the return value isn't used by a caller
T accumulate(In first, In last, T init, BinOp op)
{
        while (first!=last) {
                init = op(init, *first);
                ++first;
        }
        return init;
}
```

The **invocable** concept is from the standard library (§18.1.3). Any binary operation that accepts two arguments of the accumulator's type and the iterator's **value_type** can be used here. For example:

```
vector<double> a = { 1.1, 2.2, 3.3, 4.4 };
cout << accumulate(a.begin(),a.end(), 1.0, multiplies<double>());
```

This will print **35.1384**, that is, 1.0*1.1*2.2*3.3*4.4 (**1.0** is the initial value). The binary operator supplied here, **multiplies<double>()**, is a standard-library function object that multiplies; **multiplies<double>** multiplies **doubles**, **multiplies<int>** multiplies **ints**, etc. There are other binary function objects: **plus** (it adds), **minus** (it subtracts), **divides**, and **modulus** (it takes the remainder).

Note that for products of floating-point numbers, the obvious initial value is **1.0**.

CC As in the **sort()** example (§21.2.2), we are often interested in data within class objects, rather than just plain built-in types. For example, we might want to calculate the total cost of items given the unit prices and number of units:

```
struct Record {
        double unit_price;
        int units;        // number of units sold
        // ...
};
```

We can let **accumulate**'s operator extract the **units** from a **Record** element as well as multiplying it to the accumulator value:

```
double price(double v, const Record& r)
{
        return v + r.unit_price * r.units;            // calculate price and accumulate
}

void f(const vector<Record>& vr)
{
        double total = accumulate(vr.begin(), vr.end(), 0.0, price);
        // ...
}
```

We were "lazy" and used a function, rather than a function object, to calculate the price – just to show that we could do that also. We tend to prefer function objects (including lambdas):

- If they need to store a value between calls, or
- If they are so short that inlining can make a difference (at most a handful of primitive operations)

In this example, we might have chosen a function object for the second reason.

> TRY THIS
>
> Define a **vector<Record>**, initialize it with four records of your choice, and compute their total price using the functions above.

21.3.3 Inner product

Take two vectors, multiply each pair of elements with the same subscript, and add all of those products. That's called the *inner product* of the two vectors and is a most useful operation in many areas (e.g., physics and linear algebra). If you prefer code to words, here is the STL version:

```
template<input_iterator In, input_iterator In2, typename T>
T inner_product(In first, In last, In2 first2, T init)
     // note: this is the way we multiply two vectors (yielding a scalar)
{
     while(first!=last) {
          init = init + (*first) * (*first2);   // multiply pairs of elements
          ++first;
          ++first2;
     }
     return init;
}
```

This generalizes the notion of inner product to any kind of sequence of any type of element. As an example, consider the stock market index example from §20.2.3. The way that works is to take a set of companies and assign each a "weight." We could replace the loop calculating the DJII from the **vector** version of **dow_price** and **dow_weight**with a single call of **inner_product**:

```
double dji_index = inner_product(  // multiply (weight,value) pairs and add
                         dow_price.begin(), dow_price.end(),
                         dow_weight.begin(),
                         0.0
                    );

cout << "DJI value " << dji_index << '\n';
```

Note that **inner_product()** takes two sequences. However, it takes only three arguments: only the beginning of the second sequence is mentioned. The second sequence is supposed to have at least as many elements as the first. If not, we have a run-time error. As far as **inner_product()** is concerned, it is OK for the second sequence to have more elements than the first; those "surplus elements" will simply not be used. XX

> TRY THIS
>
> Define an inner_product() that takes two input ranges. Then try the examples above with your version.

21.3.4 Generalizing inner_product()

The inner_product() can be generalized just as accumulate() was. For inner_product() we need two extra arguments, though: one to combine the accumulator with the new value, exactly as for accumulate(), and one for combining the element value pairs:

```
template<input_iterator In, input_iterator In2, typename T, typename BinOp, typename BinOp2>
     requires invocable<BinOp,T,In::value_type>
          && invocable<BinOp2,T,In2::value_type>
T inner_product(In first, In last, In2 first2, T init, BinOp op, BinOp2 op2)
{
     while(first!=last) {
          init = op(init, op2(*first, *first2));
          ++first;
          ++first2;
     }
     return init;
}
```

We can even do some computation directly using map version of dow_price and dow_weight. In particular, we can calculate the index, using the standard-library algorithm inner_product() (§21.3.3). We have to extract share values and weights from their respective maps and multiply them. We can easily write a function for doing that for any two map<string,double>s:

```
double weighted_value(const pair<string,double>& a, const pair<string,double>& b)
     // extract values and multiply
{
      return a.second * b.second;   // using the pairs' second member
}
```

Now we just plug that function into the generalized version of inner_product() and we have the value of our index:

```
double dji_index = inner_product(
                    dow_price.begin(), dow_price.end(),     // all companies
                    dow_weight.begin(),                     // their weights
                    0.0,                                    // initial value
                    plus<double>(),                         // add (as usual)
                    weighted_value                          // extract values and weights, then multiply
                         );
```

A ranges version of inner_product() would make that code even nicer.

21.4 Copying

In §21.1.1, we deemed find() "the simplest useful algorithm." Naturally, that point can be argued. Many simple algorithms are useful – even some that are trivial to write. But why bother to write new code when you can use what others have written and debugged for you, however simple? When it comes to simplicity and utility, copy() gives find() a run for its money. The STL provides three versions of copy:

Copy operations	
b2=copy(b,e,b2)	Copy [b:e) to [b2:b2+(e–b)).
b2=unique_copy(b,e,b2)	Copy [b:e) to [b2:b2+(e–b)); suppress adjacent copies.
b2=copy_if(b,e,b2,p)	Copy [b:e) to [b2:b2+(e–b)), but only elements that meet the predicate p.

21.4.1 The simplest copy: copy()

The basic copy algorithm is defined like this:

```
template<input_iterator In, output_iterator Out>
Out copy(In first, In last, Out res)
{
        while (first!=last) {
                *res = *first;          // copy element
                ++res;
                ++first;
        }
        return res;
}
```

Given a pair of iterators, copy() copies a sequence into another sequence specified by an iterator to its first element. For example:

```
void f(vector<double>& vd, list<int>& li)
        // copy the elements of a list of ints into a vector of doubles
{
        if (vd.size() < li.size())
                error("target container too small");
        copy(li.begin(), li.end(), vd.begin());
        // ...
}
```

Note that the type of the input sequence of copy() can be different from the type of the output sequence. That's a useful generality of STL algorithms: they work for all kinds of sequences without making unnecessary assumptions about their implementation. We remembered to check that there was enough space in the output sequence to hold the elements we put there. It's the programmer's job to check such sizes. STL algorithms are programmed for maximal generality and optimal performance; they do not (by default) do range checking or other potentially expensive tests to protect their users. At times, you'll wish they did, but when you want checking, you can add it as we did above.

21.4.2 Generalizing copy: copy_if()

The copy() algorithm copies unconditionally. The unique_copy() algorithm suppresses adjacent elements with the same value. The third copy algorithm copies only elements for which a predicate is true:

```
template<input_iterator In, output_operator Out, predicate<In::value_type> Pred>
Out copy_if(In first, In last, Out res, Pred p)
     // copy elements that fulfill the predicate p into res
{
     while (first!=last) {
          if (p(*first)) {
               *res = *first;
               ++res;
          }
          ++first;
     }
     return res;
}
```

For example, using the ranges version of copy_if(), we can copy all elements of a sequence larger than 6 like this:

```
void f(const vector<int>& v)          // copy all elements with a value larger than 6 into v2
{
     vector<int> v2(v.size());
     ranges::copy_if(v, v2.begin(), [](int x){ return x>6;});
     // ...
}
```

21.5 Sorting and searching

CC Often, we want our data ordered. We can achieve that either by using a data structure that maintains order, such as map and set, or by sorting. The most common and useful sort operation in the STL is the sort() that we have already used several times. By default, sort() uses < as the sorting criterion, but we can also supply our own criteria:

```
template<random_access_iterator Ran>
void sort(Ran first, Ran last);

template<random_access_iterator Ran, less_than_comparable<Ran::value_type> Cmp>
void sort(Ran first, Ran last, Cmp cmp);
```

As an example of sorting based on a user-specified criterion, we'll show how to sort strings without taking case into account:

```
struct No_case {
	bool operator()(const string& x, const string& y) const		// is lowercase(x) < lowercase(y)?
	{
		for (int i = 0; i<x.length(); ++i) {
			if (i == y.length())		// y<x
				return false;
			char xx = tolower(x[i]);
			char yy = tolower(y[i]);
			if (xx<yy)		// x<y
				return true;
			if (yy<xx)		// y<x
				return false;
		}
		if (x.length()==y.length())		// x==y
			return false;
		return true;		// x<y (fewer characters in x)
	}
};

void sort_and_print(vector<string>& vc)
{
	ranges::sort(vc,No_case{});
	for (const auto& s : vc)
		cout << s << '\n';
}
```

Once a sequence is sorted, we no longer need to search from the beginning using **find()**; we can use the order to do a binary search. Basically, a binary search works like this: **CC**

Assume that we are looking for the value *x*; look at the middle element:

- If the element's value equals *x*, we found it!
- If the element's value is less than *x*, any element with value *x* must be to the right, so we look at the right half (doing a binary search on that half).
- If the value of *x* is less than the element's value, any element with value *x* must be to the left, so we look at the left half (doing a binary search on that half).
- If we have reached the last element (going left or right) without finding *x*, then there is no element with that value.

For longer sequences, a binary search is much faster than **find()** (which is a linear search). The standard-library algorithms for binary search are **binary_search()** and **equal_range()**. What do we mean by "longer"? It depends, but ten elements are usually sufficient to give **binary_search()** an advantage over **find()**. For a sequence of 1000 elements, **binary_search()** will be something like 200 times faster than **find()** because its cost is *O(log2(N));* see §20.3. **AA**

The **binary_search** algorithm comes in two variants:

```
template<random_access_range Ran, typename T>
bool binary_search(Ran r, const T& val);

template<random_access_range Ran, typename T, predicate<Ran::value_type,Ran::value_type> Cmp>
bool binary_search(Ran r, const T& val, Cmp cmp);
```

XX Obviously, there are also versions that take a pair of iterators. These algorithms require and assume that their input sequence is sorted. If it isn't, "interesting things", such as infinite loops, might happen. A binary_search() simply tells us whether a value is present:

```
void f(vector<string>& vs)          // vs is sorted
{
        if (binary_search(vs.begin(),vs.end(),"starfruit")) {
                // we have a starfruit
        }
        // ...
}
```

AA So, binary_search() is ideal when all we care about is whether a value is in a sequence or not. If we care about the element we find, we can use lower_bound(), upper_bound(), or equal_range() (PPP2.§23.4). In the cases where we care which element is found, the reason is usually that it is an object containing more information than just the key, that there can be many elements with the same key, or that we want to know which element met a search criterion. For example:

```
template<class T>
void print same(const vector<T>& v, const T& x)
{
        for (const auto& x : ranges::equal_range(v,x))        // equal_range() returns a sub-range
                cout << x << '\n';
}
```

Drill

[1] Read some floating-point values (at least 16 values) from a file into a vector<double> called vd.
[2] Output vd to cout.
[3] Make a vector vi of type vector<int> with the same number of elements as vd; copy the elements from vd into vi.
[4] Output the pairs of (vd[i],vi[i]) to cout, one pair per line.
[5] Output the sum of the elements of vd.
[6] Output the difference between the sum of the elements of vd and the sum of the elements of vi.
[7] There is a standard-library algorithm called reverse that takes a sequence (pair of iterators) as arguments; reverse vd, and output vd to cout.
[8] Compute the mean value of the elements in vd; output it.
[9] Make a new vector<double> called vd2 and copy all elements of vd with values lower than (less than) the mean into vd2.
[10] Sort vd; output it again.

Review

[1] What are examples of useful STL algorithms?
[2] What does find() do? Give at least five examples.
[3] What does count_if() do?
[4] What does sort(b,e) use as its sorting criterion?
[5] How does an STL algorithm take a container as an input argument?
[6] How does an STL algorithm take a container as an output argument?
[7] How does an STL algorithm usually indicate "not found" or "failure"?
[8] What is a function object?
[9] In which ways does a function object differ from a function?
[10] What is a predicate?
[11] Why would you use a function or function object rather than a lambda as an argument?
[12] What does accumulate() do?
[13] What does inner_product() do?
[14] Why use a copy() algorithm when we could "just write a simple loop"?
[15] What is a binary search?

Terms

accumulate()	find_if()	searching	algorithm
function object	sequence	application: ()	generic
set	sort()	iota()	find()
inner_product()	sorting	binary_search()	upper_bound()
lambda	copy()	lower_bound()	predicate
unique_copy()	copy_if()	equal_range()	invocable

Exercises

[1] Go through the chapter and do all **Try this** exercises that you haven't already done.
[2] Find a reliable source of STL documentation and list every standard-library algorithm.
[3] Implement count() yourself. Test it.
[4] Implement count_if() yourself. Test it.
[5] What would we have to do if we couldn't return end() to indicate "not found"? Redesign and re-implement find() and count() to take iterators to the first and last elements. Compare the results to the standard versions.
[6] Write a binary search function for a vector<int> (without using the standard one). You can choose any interface you like. Test it. How confident are you that your binary search function is correct? Now write a binary search function for a list<string>. Test it. How much do the two binary search functions resemble each other? How much do you think they would have resembled each other if you had not known about the STL?
[7] Define an Order class with (customer) name, address, data, and vector<Purchase> members. Purchase is a class with a (product) name, unit_price, and count members. Define a mechanism for reading and writing Orders to and from a file. Define a mechanism for printing

`Orders`. Create a file of at least ten `Orders`, read it into a `vector<Order>`, sort it by name (of customer), and write it back out to a file. Create another file of at least ten `Orders` of which about a third are the same as in the first file, read it into a `list<Order>`, sort it by address (of customer), and write it back out to a file. Merge the two files into a third using `std::merge()`.

[8] Compute the total value of the orders in the two files from the previous exercise. The value of an individual `Purchase` is (of course) its `unit_price*count`.

[9] Provide a GUI interface for entering `Orders` into files.

[10] Provide a GUI interface for querying a file of `Orders`; e.g., "Find all orders from `Joe`," "Find the total value of orders in file `Hardware`," and "List all orders in file `Clothing`." Hint: First design a non-GUI interface; then, build the GUI on top of that.

[11] Write a program to "clean up" a text file for use in a word query program; that is, replace punctuation with whitespace, put words into lowercase, replace *don't* with *do not* (etc.), and remove plurals (e.g., *ships* becomes *ship*). Don't be too ambitious. For example, it is hard to determine plurals in general, so just remove an *s* if you find both *ship* and *ships*. Use that program on a real-world text file with at least 5000 words (e.g., a research paper).

[12] Write a program (using the output from the previous exercise) to answer questions such as: "How many occurrences of *ship* are there in a file?" "Which word occurs most frequently?" "Which is the longest word in the file?" "Which is the shortest?" "List all words starting with *s*." "List all four-letter words."

[13] Provide a GUI for the program from the previous exercise.

Postscript

AA The STL is the part of the ISO C++ standard library concerned with containers and algorithms. As such, it provides very general, flexible, and useful basic tools. It can save us a lot of work: reinventing the wheel can be fun, but it is rarely productive. Unless there are strong reasons not to, use the STL containers and basic algorithms. What is more, the STL is an example of generic programming, showing how concrete problems and concrete solutions can give rise to a collection of powerful and general tools. If you need to manipulate data – and most programmers do – the STL provides an example, a set of ideas, and an approach that often can help.

I

Index

Knowledge is of two kinds.
We know a subject ourselves,
or we know where
we can find information on it.
– Samuel Johnson

Token

!= not equal 500
&
  address of 439
  reference to 194, 196
&&
  move 494
  rvalue reference 494
()
  application, operator 610
  call, operator 610
  initializer 46
  vector initializer 72
*
  contents of 439
  dereference 440, 444
  iterator 553
*= scaling 40
+
  addition 34
  concatenation 36
++
  increment 39, 58
  iterator 553
+= 39
->
  auto 205
  dereference 444
  member access 444
.
  member 73, 223
  member access 444
/* comment 163
// comment 19
:: 144
  member 229
  namespace 209
; semicolon 59
<<
  output operator 19
  user-defined 266
<
  less than 500
  less-than operator 58
  order 604
= 494
  == and 35
  assignment 36
  assignment operator 57, 490
  delete 375
  initializer 32, 46
  Vector assignment 507

==
    and = 35
    equal 34, 500, 604
    equality operator 57
    iterator 553
={} initializer 46
=0 pure virtual 374
>>
    input operator 31, 33
    string 33
    user-defined 267
[]
    {} lambda 412
    map 578
    subscript 444, 464, 466
    subscript, operator 484
{}
    block 66
    format() argument 281
    initializer 36, 46
    lambda, [] 412
~ destructor name 448

A

AA 2
abstract class 361
abstraction 54
access 373
    . member 444
    -> member 444
    control 362
accumulate() 614
activation record, function 201
ad hoc polymorphism 517
Ada 516
addition, + 34
address 439
    of, & 439
adjacent_difference() 614
age group example 397
Alan Perlis 483
Albert Einstein 151
Alex Stepanov 435, 553
algorithm 517
    and container 553
    fail 604
    numerical 614
    parallel 604
    ranges 604
    standard-library 604
    STL 604
    vector 604
all, rule of 496
allocation, new 443
allocator 523
almost container 593
alternatives
    I/O error handling 261
    to pointer 472
analysis 117
animation 426
Annemarie 32
Anya 449
application
    domain 356
    operator () 610
Application gui_main() 421
approximation 392
argument 69
    {}, format() 281
    checking, function 199
    conversion, function 199
    declaration 190
    default 387
    error 94
    formal 190
    name 191
    pointer 470
    value template 521
arithmetic, pointer 466
array 443
    associative 578
    built-in 594
array 473, 593
assertion 104
assignment
    = 36
    =, Vector 507
    and initialization 38
    copy 490
    move 494
    operator, = 57, 490
    self 491
associative
    array 578
    container 578
attach() 291
attribute
    [[fallthrough]] 64
    [[nodiscard]] 616
auto 561
    -> 205
    return type 205
    variable type 46
automatic store 442
avoiding error 99
Axis 297, 385, 390

B

:b, format() 282
bad() 258
balanced tree 580
base class 318, 367
basic guarantee 533
begin() 594
  end() 500
benefits of OOP 376
bibliography 13
big-O 585, 621
binary tree 580
binary_operation, concept 520
binary_search() 621
binding, structured 580
Bjarne Stroustrup 10, 13
block, {} 66
body, function 69
bool 32
bottom-up, top-down 128
box, dialog 417
Brian Kernighan 17
browser I/O 410
buffer 143
  I/O 253
  overflow 465
builder, GUI 431
built-in
  array 594
  type 222
Button 415
byte 439

C

C
  C++ and 10
  with classes 10
C++
  and C 10
  and Simula 10
  compiler 12
  Core Guidelines 10, 12
  design 11
  evolution 11
  Foundation 12
  history 10
  ISO 8
  stability 11
C++11 10
C++14 11
C++17 11
C++20 11
C++98 10
calculator example 119
call
  cost of virtual 370
  implementation, function 200
  operator () 610
  recursive function 203
  stack, function 203
callee error handling 91
caller error handling 90
capacity(), Vector 506
capture, lambda 613
case 62
cat() 471
catch
  exception 95
  try 530
category, iterator 597
CC 2
CG 12
char 32
character literal 32
Checked_iterator 599
checking
  function argument 199
  optional 527
  range 525
chrono 245, 586
Churchill, Winston 513
cin input stream 31
Circle 342
  and Ellipse 345
class 123, 222
  abstract 361
  base 318, 367
  constructor 227
  derived 367, 370
  graphics interface 316
  GUI interface 316
  hierarchy 368
  implementation 223
  interface 223, 237
  member 123, 223
  member function 226
  parameterized 517
  private 142
  public 142
  scope 186
  template 517
classification, I/O 252
cleaning code 158
clipping 339
Closed_polyline 329
  Polygon and 334
  Rectangle and 302
code
  cleaning 158
  file, object 21

file, source 21
generalize 547
pseudo 119
ugly 56, 190
Color 323
invisible 339
RGB 325
comment 102, 162
// 19
/* 163
comparison operator 500
compatibility 527
compilation 21
compiler
C++ 12
explorer 12
compile-time
computation 204
error 24, 84, 86
completing a program 152
computation 52
compile-time 204
concatenation, + 36
concept, predicate 620
concept 518
binary_operation 520
convertible_to 520
copyable 520
derived_from 520
equality_comparable 519
equality_comparable_with 519
floating_point 520
forward_iterator 519
indirect_unary_predicate 520
input_iterator 519
integral 520
invocable 616, 618
invocable 520
moveable 520
output_iterator 519
predicate 519
random_access_iterator 519
random_access_range 519
range 519
regular 520
semiregular 520
sortable 520
totally_ordered 520
totally_ordered_with 520
console I/O 410
const 57
declaration 184
member function 242
reference, pass-by 194
constant
expression 56
magic 159
symbolic 159
consteval 205
constexpr 56, 204
constraint on solution 527
construct_at() 524
constructor
class 227
copy 239, 489
default 240, 496
explicit 497
move 494
container
algorithm and 553
almost 593
and inheritance 520
associative 578
list 591
map 578
multimap 591
multiset 591
overview 591
set 589
STL 592
unordered_map 585
vector 591
contents of, * 439
contract 104
control 414
access 362
inversion 411, 422
conversion 44
function argument 199
narrowing 45
to enum 234
widening 45
convertible_to, concept 520
coordinate 296
copy 488
assignment 490
constructor 239, 489
deep 492
default 488
elision 494
I/O example 594
shallow 492
copy() 487, 619
copyable, concept 520
copy_if() 620
Core Guidelines, C++ 10, 12
correctness 53
corruption, memory 440
cost
of virtual call 370
of virtual, memory 370
Courtney 449

cout output stream 19
.cpp 21
cppreference 12
C-style string 471

D

:d, format() 282
data 546
    graphing 397
date 589
Date example 266, 270
David Wheeler 65, 545
deallocation
    delete 446
    delete[] 446
debugging 101, 498
    GUI 427
declaration 42, 181
    argument 190
    const 184
    function 71
    return type 190
    using 210
    variable 184
deep copy 492
default
    argument 387
    constructor 240, 496
    copy 488
    destructor 448
    initialization 34, 185
    member initializer 242
default 62
default_random_engine 108
definition 42, 182
    function 69
    in-class 144
    member function 229
    operator 236, 501
delete
    = 375
    deallocation 446
    naked 450
    new and 446
delete[] deallocation 446
dereference
    -> 444
    * 440, 444
    nullptr 469
derived 366
    class 367, 370
derived_from, concept 520
design 117
    C++ 11
    strategy 117
destroy() 523
destroy_at() 564
destructor 447–448
    default 448
    generated 448
    name, ~ 448
    pointer 496
    resource 496
    virtual 449, 496
development strategy 117
device
    input 252
    output 252
dialog box 417
directive, using 210
dispatch 367
display model 290
distribution, random number 108
divide-and-conquer 54
domain, application 356
Donald Knuth 606
double 32
    int to 89
doubly-linked list 556, 591
Doug McIlroy 577
Dow Jones example 583
draw() 291
draw_all() example 518
Drill 3, 24
duration 587
duration_cast 588
dynamic memory 442

E

editor example 566
efficiency 53, 527
Einstein, Albert 151
elision, copy 494
Ellipse 344
    Circle and 345
else 60
empty
    statement 59
    string 34
    string 72
encapsulation private 368
end() 594
    begin() 500
    fail 604
engine, random number 108, 588
entity 184
enum
    class 233
    conversion to 234
    enumeration 233

plain 235
scoped 233
underlying type 234
enumeration, enum 233
enumerator 233
environment, programming 24
eof() 258
equal, == 34, 500, 604
equality operator, == 57
equality_comparable, concept 519
equality_comparable_with, concept 519
equal_range() 622
erase()
list 562
Vector 564
vector 562
error
argument 94
avoiding 99
compile-time 24, 84, 86
finding 99
handling 154
handling alternatives, I/O 261
handling, callee 91
handling, caller 90
input 97
I/O 258
link-time 24, 84, 88
logic 24, 84, 89
range 95, 465
reporting 93
run-time 24, 84, 89
sources of 85
syntax 84, 86
throw on I/O 260
transient 465
type 84, 87
error() 90
essential operation 495
estimation 100
Euler, Leonhard 1
evaluation
order of 206–207
short-circuit 207
evolution, C++ 11
example
age group 397
calculator 119
copy I/O 594
Date 266, 270
Dow Jones 583
draw_all() 518
editor 566
exponentiation 392
Expression 128
Fruit 589
get10() 261
get_int() 264
gods 452
grid 321
grow() 503
int_to_month() 234
Jack-and-Jill 546, 554
Larger_than 610
Lines_window 419
Link 452
Menu 418
No_case 620
Output_range 598
palindrome() 76, 475
Random 588
Reading 257
read-one-value 261
Record 612
skip_to_int() 263
suspicious() 530
TC++PL 579
temperature 74, 256
Text_iterator 569
to_int() 234
Token 121
Token_stream 142
traffic-light 426
Vector 437, 451, 502, 514, 522, 534, 560, 564
word counting 578
exception 525
catch 95
exception 98
out_of_range 96
resource and 529
runtime_error 98
throw 94
exception exception 98
executable file 23
Exercise 3
expect() 105
explicit constructor 497
explorer, compiler 12
exponential_distribution 108
exponentiation example 392
export 211
expression 55
constant 56
lambda 106, 389, 613
Expression example 128
extern 182

F

fail
algorithm 604
end() 604

fail() 258
fall through 192
[[fallthrough]] attribute 64
false 32
feature creep 127, 135
Feynman, Richard 251
file 254
  executable 23
  header 25, 213
  object code 21
  read 256, 269
  source code 21
  stream, fstream 255
  stream, ifstream 255
  stream, ofstream 255
  write 256
fill 304
finally() 542
find() 605
find_if() 608
finding error 99
first, pair 580
five, rule of 496
floating-point literal 32
floating_point, concept 520
Font 347
for
  range 73, 562
  statement 67
formal argument 190
format, output 281
format()
  argument {} 281
  :b 282
  :d 282
  :o 282
  :x 282
forward_iterator, concept 519
forward_list 592
Foundation, C++ 12
framework, test 108
free store 442
free() 472
Fruit example 589
fstream file stream 255
function 68
  activation record 201
  argument checking 199
  argument conversion 199
  body 69
  call implementation 200
  call, recursive 203
  call stack 203
  class member 226
  const member 242
  declaration 71
  definition 69
  definition, member 229
  graphing 382
  hash 585
  local 613
  member 73
  modifying 243
  object 610–611
  parameterized 517
  pure virtual 374
  purpose of 69
  table, virtual 369
  template 517
  utility 265
  virtual 367, 370
Function 299, 386

G

Gavin 571
generalize code 547
generated destructor 448
generator
  random number 109
  type 516
generic programming 517–518
Gerald Weinberg 51
get10() example 261
get_int() example 264
gif 351
global
  initialization of 208
  scope 186
gods example 452
good() 258
grammar 127
  notation 129
granularity 357
graphical layout 400
graphics 290, 356
  interface class 316
  model 295
graphing
  data 397
  function 382
Graph_lib namespace 292
grid example 321
grow, vector 73
grow() example 503
guarantee
  basic 533
  no-throw 533
  resource 533
  strong 533
GUI
  builder 431

debugging 427
interface class 316
I/O 410
starting with 311
Guidelines, C++ Core 10, 12
gui_main() 367
Application 421

H

handling, error 154
hash
function 585
table 578
header
file 25, 213
PPP.h 11
PPPheaders.h 11
heap 442
Hein, Piet 221
Hello, World! 18
hiding, implementation 453
hierarchy, class 368
high-level programming 7
history, C++ 10

I

ideal 380
ideals, STL 549
if statement 60
ifstream file stream 255
Image 306, 350
implementation 117
class 223
function call 200
hiding 453
inheritance 376
implicit
release 530
release of resource 448
import 20, 211
In_box 416
in-class
definition 144
initializer 242
#include 25, 213
increment, ++ 39, 58
indentation 190
indirect_unary_predicate, concept 520
inheritance 367
container and 520
implementation 376
interface 376
initialization
assignment and 38
default 34, 185
of global 208
with list 486
initializer
{} 36, 46
() 46
={} 46
= 32, 46
() vector 72
default member 242
in-class 242
new 445
order, member 420, 487
initializer_list 486
inline 231
in-memory representation 42, 270
inner_product() 617
input 52
device 252
error 97
operator, >> 31, 33
stream, cin 31
input_iterator, concept 519
insert()
list 562
Vector 565
vector 562
installation instructions 311
installing Qt 311
instantiation, template 516
instructions, installation 311
int 32
to double 89
integer literal 32
integral, concept 520
interface
class 223, 237
class, graphics 316
class, GUI 316
inheritance 376
minimal 357
int_to_month() example 234
invariant 229, 335
inversion, control 411, 422
invisible, Color 339
invocable
concept 616, 618
concept 520
I/O 53
browser 410
buffer 253
classification 252
console 410
error 258
error handling alternatives 261

error, throw on 260
GUI 410
stream 253
iota() 614
is kind of 318, 367
ISO
C++ 8
standard 245
istream 253
width() 477
istream_iterator 594
istringstream 283
iterate 65, 558
iteration statement 65
iterator
++ 553
* 553
== 553
category 597
range 597
sequence and 552

J

Jack-and-Jill example 546, 554
Johnson, Samuel 627
jpg 306, 351

K

Kernighan, Brian 17
keyword 41
Knuth, Donald 606
Kristen Nygaard 115

L

lambda
[] {} 412
capture 613
expression 106, 389, 613
Larger_than example 610
layout
graphical 400
object 368
lcd() 614
lcm() 614
leak
memory 447
resource 530, 539
Leonhard Euler 1
less than, < 500
less-than operator, < 58
library 118
standard 20
lifting 555
Line 318
Lines 320
Line_style 325
Lines_window example 419
Link example 452
linked list 452
linking 23
link-time error 24, 84, 88
list
doubly-linked 556, 591
initialization with 486
linked 452
operation 453
singly-linked 556, 591
List 555
list
container 591
erase() 562
insert() 562
string, vector 572
literal
character 32
floating-point 32
integer 32
string 19, 32
local
function 613
scope 186
static variable 208
logic error 24, 84, 89
look-ahead 121
loop
variable 66–67
wait 413
Louis Pasteur 29
lowercase 620
low-level programming 7
lvalue 55, 58

M

magic constant 159
main() 20, 192
make_shared() 539
make_unique() 450, 538
malloc() 472
management, resource 530
map 580
[] 578
container 578
Mark 348
Marked_polyline 330
Marks 332
Maurice Wilkes 83
McIlroy, Doug 577

measuring time 586
member
. 73, 223
:: 229
access, . 444
access, -> 444
class 123, 223
function 73
function, class 226
function, const 242
function definition 229
initializer, default 242
initializer order 420, 487
memory 439
corruption 440
cost of virtual 370
dynamic 442
leak 447
raw 524
Menu example 418
midpoint() 614
minimal interface 357
model 356
graphics 295
modifying function 243
module 23, 211
PPP_graphics 292, 317
PPP_support 11, 527
scope 186
std 20
move 493
&& 494
assignment 494
constructor 494
return 537
moveable, concept 520
multimap container 591
multiset container 591
mutability 359

N

\n 19
naked
delete 450
new 450
new 539
name 40
~ destructor 448
argument 191
namespace 209
:: 209
Graph_lib 292
scope 186
std 19
naming style 358
narrow() 200
narrowing conversion 45
Negroponte, Nicholas 409
nested scope 188
new 442
allocation 443
and delete 446
initializer 445
naked 450
naked 539
Nicholas 31
Negroponte 409
no op 365
No_case example 620
[[nodiscard]] attribute 616
Norah 55
not equal, != 500
notation
grammar 129
shorthand 519
no-throw guarantee 533
not_null 474
now() 586
null
pointer 468
reference 468
nullptr 446
dereference 469
test 469
numerical algorithm 614
Nygaard, Kristen 115

O

:o, format() 282
object 30, 42
code file 21
function 610–611
layout 368
object-oriented programming 368, 518
of course 126
ofstream file stream 255
OOP 368
benefits of 376
Open_polyline 328
operation
essential 495
list 453
style 357
operator 34, 57
() application 610
= assignment 57, 490
() call 610
== equality 57
>> input 31, 33
< less-than 58

  - << output 19
  - [] subscript 484
  - comparison 500
  - definition 236, 501
  - overloading 236, 501
  - relational 500
- optional checking 527
- order
  - < 604
  - member initializer 420, 487
  - of evaluation 206–207
- ostream 253
- ostream_iterator 594
- ostringstream 283
- out of range 465
- Out_box 417
- out_of_range exception 96
- output 52
  - device 252
  - format 281
  - operator, << 19
  - range 598
  - stream, cout 19
- output_iterator, concept 519
- Output_range example 598
- overflow 396
  - buffer 465
- overloading, operator 236, 501
- override 366, 370–371
- overview, container 591

P

- Painter, Qt 329
- pair 582
  - first 580
  - second 580
- palindrome() example 76, 475
- parallel algorithm 604
- parameter 69, 190
  - type template 514
- parameterized
  - class 517
  - function 517
- parametric polymorphism 517
- parser 128, 130
  - recursive descent 140
- partial_sum() 614
- pass-by
  - const reference 194
  - reference 196
  - value 193
  - value or const-reference 197
- Pasteur, Louis 29
- perfection 239
- Perlis, Alan 483
- philosophy, teaching 5
- Piet Hein 221
- Point 317
- pointer 439
  - alternatives to 472
  - and reference 468–469
  - argument 470
  - arithmetic 466
  - destructor 496
  - null 468
  - problem 443, 464–465
  - semantics 492
  - this 456
  - use 537
- Polygon 300
  - and Closed_polyline 334
- polyline 328
- polymorphism
  - ad hoc 517
  - parametric 517
  - run-time 367
- portability 9
- postcondition 106
- Postscript 4
- PPP support 11
- PPP_graphics module 292, 317
- PPP.h, header 11
- PPPheaders.h, header 11
- PPP_support, module 11, 527
- precondition 104
- predicate 612
- predicate
  - concept 519
  - concept 620
- preprocessor 215
- printf() 281
- private 223, 362
  - class 142
  - encapsulation 368
- problem, pointer 443, 464–465
- problems, startup 12
- program 18
  - completing a 152
  - structure 146
- programming
  - environment 24
  - generic 517–518
  - high-level 7
  - low-level 7
  - object-oriented 368, 518
- promotion 44
- protected 368
- prototype 119
- pseudo code 119
- public 223
  - class 142

pure
  virtual, =0 374
  virtual function 374
purpose of function 69
push_back()
  Vector 507
  vector 73

Q

Qt 12, 295
  installing 311
  Painter 329

R

RAII 532
random
  number 108
  number distribution 108
  number engine 108, 588
  number generator 109
  number seed() ,
Random example 588
random_access_iterator, concept 519
random_access_range, concept 519
random_int() 109, 588
range
  checking 525
  error 95, 465
  for 73, 562
  iterator 597
  output 598
  sequence and 552
range, concept 519
ranges algorithm 604
raw memory 524
read file 256, 269
Reading example 257
read-one-value example 261
Record example 612
Rectangle 301, 336
  and Closed_polyline 302
recursive
  descent parser 140
  function call 203
red-black tree 578
redraw() 366
Reenskaug, Trygve 603
reference
  && rvalue 494
  material 13
  null 468
  pass-by 196
  pass-by const 194
  pointer and 468–469
  semantics 492
  to, & 194, 196
regular, concept 520
relational operator 500
release 531
  1.0 156
  implicit 530
  of resource, implicit 448
repeat 65
reporting, error 93
representation
  in-memory 42, 270
  Vector 505
requirement 117
requires 519
reserve(), Vector 506
resize(), Vector 506
resource 448
  and exception 529
  destructor 496
  guarantee 533
  implicit release of 448
  leak 530, 539
  management 530
resources, Web 12
return
  type, auto 205
  type, suffix 205
return
  move 537
  type declaration 190
  value 192
Review 4, 26
RGB Color 325
Richard Feynman 251
round_to() 200
rule
  of all 496
  of five 496
  of zero 496
run-time
  error 24, 84, 89
  polymorphism 367
runtime_error exception 98
rvalue 55
  reference, && 494

S

safety, type 43
Samuel Johnson 627
scaling 401
  *= 40
scope 186
  class 186

global 186
local 186
module 186
namespace 186
nested 188
statement 186
search
sort 620
tree 580
second, pair 580
seed(), random number ,
selection statement 60
self assignment 491
semantics
pointer 492
reference 492
value 492
semicolon, ; 59
semiregular, concept 520
sequence
and iterator 552
and range 552
vector 71
set container 589
setfill() 284
shallow copy 492
Shape 297, 360
shared_ptr 539
short-circuit evaluation 207
shorthand notation 519
Simple_window 293, 412
simplicity 53
Simula, C++ and 10
singly-linked list 556, 591
size(), vector 72
sizeof 441
skip_to_int() example 263
slice 521
solution, constraint on 527
sort search 620
sort() 76, 620
sortable, concept 520
source code file 21
sources of error 85
span 473
specification 117
stability, C++ 11
stack
function call 203
store 442
standard
ISO 245
library 20
standard-library algorithm 604
starting with GUI 311
startup problems 12
state 52, 222
stream 258
valid 229
statement 58
empty 59
for 67
if 60
iteration 65
scope 186
selection 60
switch 62
while 65
static store 442
static variable, local 208
std
module 20
namespace 19
Stepanov, Alex 435, 553
STL
algorithm 604
container 592
ideals 549
store
automatic 442
free 442
stack 442
static 442
strategy
design 117
development 117
strcpy() 472
stream
cin input 31
cout output 19
fstream file 255
ifstream file 255
I/O 253
ofstream file 255
state 258
string 283
string
C-style 471
empty 72
literal 19, 32
string 30, 32, 593
>> 33
empty 34
stream 283
vector list 572
strlen() 472
strong guarantee 533
Stroustrup, Bjarne 10, 13
structure, program 146
structured binding 580
style
naming 358

operation 357
subclass 367
subscript
[] 444, 464, 466
operator [] 484
suffix return type 205
superclass 367
support, PPP 11
Sure! 135
suspicious() example 530
switch statement 62
symbolic constant 159
syntax error 84, 86
sys_days 589
system_clock 586

T

table
hash 578
virtual function 369
TC++PL example 579
teaching philosophy 5
technicalities 180
temperature example 74, 256
template 514
argument, value 521
class 517
function 517
instantiation 516
parameter, type 514
Terms 4
test 107, 117, 162
framework 108
nullptr 469
testing 154
Text 305, 346
Text_iterator example 569
thinking 116
this pointer 456
throw
exception 94
on I/O error 260
time, measuring 586
time_point 587
timer_wait() 426
to_int() example 234
Token example 121
Token_stream example 142
top-down bottom-up 128
totally_ordered, concept 520
totally_ordered_with, concept 520
traffic-light example 426
transient error 465
translation unit 23
transparency 325
traverse, vector 72
tree
balanced 580
binary 580
red-black 578
search 580
true 32
truncate 45
Try this 4
try catch 530
Trygve Reenskaug 603
type 30, 42
auto return 205
auto variable 46
built-in 222
enum underlying 234
error 84, 87
generator 516
safety 43
suffix return 205
template parameter 514
user-defined 222

U

ugly code 56, 190
underlying type, enum 234
uniform_int_distribution 108
uninitialized variable 44
uninitialized_fill() 524
uninitialized_move() 523
unique_copy() 619
unique_ptr 450, 538
Vector 539
unit 588
translation 23
unordered_map container 585
use
case 119
pointer 537
user-defined
>> 267
<< 266
type 222
using
declaration 210
directive 210
utility function 265

V

valarray 593
valid state 229
value 42
or const-reference, pass-by 197

pass-by 193
return 192
semantics 492
template argument 521
variable 30, 32, 42
declaration 184
local static 208
loop 66–67
type, auto 46
uninitialized 44
vector algorithm 604
Vector
assignment = 507
capacity() 506
erase() 564
example 437, 451, 502, 514, 522, 534, 560, 564
insert() 565
push_back() 507
representation 505
reserve() 506
resize() 506
unique_ptr 539
vector 436
container 591
erase() 562
grow 73
initializer, () 72
insert() 562
list string 572
push_back() 73
sequence 71
size() 72
traverse 72
vector<int> 72
vector<string> 72
virtual 365
=0 pure 374
call, cost of 370
destructor 449, 496
function 367, 370
function, pure 374
function table 369
memory cost of 370
Vitruvius 355
void 191
Voltaire 381
vtbl 369

W

wait loop 413
wait_for_button() 359, 367, 411, 413
Web resources 12
weekday() 589
Weinberg, Gerald 51
Wheeler, David 65, 545
while statement 65
whitespace 33
widening conversion 45
Widget 414
and Window 415
width(), istream 477
Wilkes, Maurice 83
Window, Widget and 415
Winston Churchill 513
word counting example 578
write file 256

X

:x, format() 282
XX 2

Y

year_month_date 245

Z

zero, rule of 496

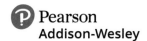